MW01098801

The Adam Smith Review
Volume 9

Adam Smith's contribution to economics is well recognised, but in recent years scholars have been exploring anew the multidisciplinary nature of his works. *The Adam Smith Review* is a rigorously refereed annual review that provides a unique forum for interdisciplinary debate on all aspects of Adam Smith's works, his place in history, and the significance of his writings to the modern world. It is aimed at facilitating debate between scholars working across the humanities and social sciences, thus emulating the reach of the Enlightenment world which Smith helped to shape.

This ninth volume brings together leading scholars from across several disciplines to consider topics as diverse as Smith's work in the context of scholars such as Immanuel Kant, Yan Fu and David Hume, Smith as the father of modern economics, and Smith's views on education and trade. This volume also has a particular focus on Asia, and includes a section that presents articles from leading scholars from the region.

Fonna Forman is Associate Professor of Political Science and Founding Co-Director of the Center on Global Justice and the Blum Cross-Border Initiative at the University of California, San Diego, USA. She is Editor of *The Adam Smith Review* on behalf of the Adam Smith Society.

The Adam Smith Review

Published in association with the International Adam Smith Society

Editor: Fonna Forman (Department of Political Science, University of California, San Diego)
Book Review Editor: Craig Smith (School of Social and Political Sciences, University of Glasgow)
Editorial Assistant: Aaron Cotkin (Department of Political Science, University of California, San Diego)

The Adam Smith Review is a multidisciplinary annual review sponsored by the International Adam Smith Society. It aims to provide a unique forum for vigorous debate and the highest standards of scholarship on all aspects of Adam Smith's works, his place in history, and the significance of his writings for the modern world. *The Adam Smith Review* aims to facilitate interchange between scholars working within different disciplinary and theoretical perspectives, and to this end it is open to all areas of research relating to Adam Smith. The *Review* also hopes to broaden the field of English-language debate on Smith by occasionally including translations of scholarly works at present available only in languages other than English.

The Adam Smith Review is intended as a resource for Adam Smith scholarship in the widest sense. The Editor welcomes comments and suggestions, including proposals for symposia or themed sections in the *Review*. Future issues are open to comments and debate relating to previously published papers.

The website of *The Adam Smith Review* is: http://www.adamsmithreview.org/

For details of membership of the International Adam Smith Society and reduced rates for purchasing the *Review*, please visit the website at https://smithsociety.org./

For a full list of titles in this series, please visit www.routledge.com/series/ASR

The Adam Smith Review (Volume 8)	**The Adam Smith Review (Volume 9)**
Edited by Fonna Forman	*Edited by Fonna Forman*
Published 2014	*Published 2017*

The Adam Smith Review

Volume 9

Edited by
Fonna Forman

Routledge
Taylor & Francis Group

LONDON AND NEW YORK

IASS

First published 2017
by Routledge
2 Park Square, Milton Park, Abingdon, Oxon OX14 4RN

and by Routledge
711 Third Avenue, New York, NY 10017

Routledge is an imprint of the Taylor & Francis Group, an informa business

British Library Cataloguing in Publication Data
A catalogue record for this book is available from the British Library

Library of Congress Cataloging in Publication Data
A catalog record for this book has been requested

ISBN: 978-1-138-65256-9 (hbk)
ISBN: 978-1-315-62416-7 (ebk)

Typeset in Times New Roman
by Keystroke, Neville Lodge, Tettenhall, Wolverhampton

Contents

Contributors

Olivia Bailey is a Ph.D. candidate in philosophy at Harvard University. She is interested in historical and contemporary accounts of the relations between epistemic and ethical goods. Her dissertation is concerned with empathy's contributions to understanding and the ethical significance of making sense of others.

Christopher J. Berry is Professor (Emeritus) of Political Theory and Honorary Professorial Research Fellow at the University of Glasgow. In addition to seminal articles, he co-edited *The Oxford Handbook of Adam Smith* (Oxford 2013) and is the author of seven books, including *The Idea of Commercial Society in the Scottish Enlightenment* (Edinburgh University Press 2013; Japanese translation forthcoming), *Social Theory of the Scottish Enlightenment* (Edinburgh University Press 1997; Chinese translation 2013), *The Idea of Luxury* (Cambridge University Press 1994; Chinese translation 2005) and *David Hume* (Continuum 2009). He has given invited series of lectures in Japan and China on several occasions as well as in Chile, Europe and the US. He is an elected Fellow of the Royal Society of Edinburgh (Scotland's 'National Academy'), of which Adam Smith was a founder member.

Toni Vogel Carey, Ph.D., Columbia University, is an independent scholar who writes about philosophy and the history of ideas. She has been published in scholarly journals since 1976, on topics ranging from moral philosophy to the history of scientific method. She is also a regular contributor to the British magazine *Philosophy Now*, and serves on its board of US advisors.

Maria A. Carrasco is Professor of Philosophy at the Pontificia Universidad Católica de Chile, Santiago. She is the author of several articles on Adam Smith, in both English and Spanish. Her papers on the topic include: 'Adam Smith's Reconstruction of Practical Reason', *Review of Metaphysics* (2004); 'Adam Smith: Liberalismo y Razón Práctica', *Revista Pensamiento* (2006); 'Adam Smith y el Relativismo', *Anuario Filosófico* (2009); 'From Psychology to Moral Normativity', *Adam Smith Review* (2011); 'Reinterpretación del Espectador Imparcial: Impersonalidad Utilitarista o Respeto a la Dignidad', *Crítica* (2014); and 'Adam Smith: Virtues and Universal Principles', *Revue*

Internationale de Philosophie (2014). She is also co-editor of the monographic issue on Adam Smith of the Spanish journal *Empresa y Humanismo* (2009), and author of the book *Consecuencialismo. Por qué no* (Eunsa 1999).

David Casassas holds a Ph.D. in sociology from the University of Barcelona, where he did a thesis on the republican roots of Adam Smith and classical political economy. He has conducted postdoctoral research on social and political theory and social policy at the Hoover Chair of Economic and Social Ethics (Université Catholique de Louvain, Belgium), the Centre for the Study of Social Justice (University of Oxford) and the Group in Analytical Sociology and Institutional Design (Universitat Autònoma de Barcelona). He has been the Secretary of the Basic Income Earth Network (BIEN) and is now a member of its International Advisory Board. He has published on republicanism in history of thought and in contemporary political theory and has explored the link between republican theory and basic income. His book on Adam Smith's commercial republicanism was published by Montesinos in 2010.

Jeng-Guo S. Chen is currently an Associate Research Fellow at the Institute of History and Philology and the Centre for Political Thought at Academia Sinica in Taipei. His interest lies in the Scottish Enlightenment, the interplay between British ideas and other worlds, and the Asian reception of the European Enlightenment. He has published articles on cultural and intellectual history in eighteenth-century Britain in both Chinese and English in *Eighteenth Century: Theory and Interpretation*, *British Journal for Eighteenth-Century Studies*, *EurAmerica* and others. He is currently preparing a book in Chinese to be titled *Adam Smith and his Worlds*.

Sam Fleischacker is Professor of Philosophy at the University of Illinois-Chicago. He is the author, most recently, of *The Good and the Good Book* (Oxford University Press 2015) and *What Is Enlightenment?* (Routledge 2013). Prior publications include *On Adam Smith's Wealth of Nations: A Philosophical Companion* (Princeton University Press 2003) and *A Third Concept of Liberty: Judgment and Freedom in Kant and Adam Smith* (Princeton University Press 1999), in addition to articles on Smith and cultural relativism, Smith and self-deception, and Smith's reception in Germany and the United States. Together with Vivienne Brown, he edited the collection *The Philosophy of Adam Smith* (Routledge 2010). From 2006 to 2010, he was President of the International Adam Smith Society.

Ryan Patrick Hanley holds the Mellon Distinguished Professorship in Political Science at Marquette University. He is the author of *Adam Smith and the Character of Virtue* (Cambridge University Press 2009), editor of the Penguin Classics edition of *The Theory of Moral Sentiments* (Penguin 2010), editor of *Adam Smith: A Princeton Guide* (Princeton University Press forthcoming), and past President of the International Adam Smith Society. His most recent book is *Love's Enlightenment: Rethinking Charity in Modernity* (Cambridge University Press forthcoming).

Bradley K. Hobbs is the BB&T Distinguished Professor of Free Enterprise at Florida Gulf Coast University. He earned his undergraduate degree in history and his Ph.D. in economics from Florida State University (1991). His interests are wide in range, encompassing property rights, economic freedom, economic growth, financial markets, economic and intellectual history, the philosophical foundations of markets, and teaching. He has published in *Entrepreneurship Theory and Practice*, *Journal of Accounting and Finance Research*, *Journal of Real Estate Research*, *Laissez-Faire*, *Journal of Executive Education*, *Journal of Private Enterprise*, *Financial Practice and Education*, and *Research in Finance*, among others. Current research projects include a stream of literature on the relationships between economic freedom, economic growth, entrepreneurial behaviour and cognitive abilities; changes in historical living standards; and classical liberal themes in novels. He spent 2012–2013 at Clemson University, serving one year as the F. A. Hayek Visiting Scholar in the Institute for the Study of Capitalism. He serves as a Research Fellow at the James Madison Institute in Tallahassee, Florida. He is a past President of the Association of Private Enterprise Education and a member of the Mont Pelerin Society.

Neven Leddy studies the migration of people and ideas in the Atlantic world with a focus on Scotland, Geneva and the early American Republic. He teaches history and the humanities at Concordia University in Montreal. He is the co-editor of *On Civic Republicanism*: *Ancient Lessons for Global Politics* (University of Toronto Press forthcoming).

Luo Weidong is Professor of Economics and Vice-President of Zhejiang University. He trained as an economist and has been teaching economics for many years. He was also a pupil of Hiroshi Mizuta on a sabbatical year in Japan. Thereafter, he committed himself to the study of Adam Smith. The result was the publication of a book that evolved from his Ph.D. thesis: *Ethics of Adam Smith: Sentiment, Order, and Virtue*. He has also published extensively on analytical and comparative economics, including *Theoretical Analysis of the Transition of China: A Perspective from Austria School*, *Selected Fundamental Readings for Economics* (ed.), *Toward a Unified Social Science: Ideas from Santa Fe Institute* (ed. with Dingding Wang and Hang Ye), and *Analysis of Comparative Economic Systems* (with Xianguo Yao), among others.

Eun Kyung Min is Professor of English at Seoul National University. She received her Ph.D. in Comparative Literature from Princeton University. A specialist in eighteenth-century British literature and culture, she is currently completing a book entitled *China and the Making of English Literary Modernity, 1660–1770*. Her published work has appeared in such journals as *The Eighteenth Century: Theory and Interpretation*, *Eighteenth-Century Studies*, *Studies on Voltaire and the Eighteenth Century*, *Social Text*, and *English Literary History*. She has received fellowships and travel grants from the International Society for Eighteenth-Century Studies, Lewis Walpole

Library, Clark Library, Radcliffe Institute for Advanced Study, and the Korea Research Foundation.

Thomas Nenon is Professor of Philosophy and interim Dean of the College of Arts and Sciences at the University of Memphis. He has a Ph.D. from the University of Freiberg and was an editor at the Husserl Archives. He has served as Review Editor for *Husserl Studies*, as a member of the Executive Committee of the Society for Phenomenology and Existential Philosophy, and as Director of the Center for the Humanities. His current research interests include Husserl's theories of personhood and subjectivity, and Kant and Hegel's practical philosophy.

Evan Osborne is the Brage Golding Distinguished Professor of Research at Wright State University. He most enjoys teaching basic economic principles and the economics of state and society. Much of his recent research in English and Chinese focuses on economic liberalism in Chinese society since the late Qing period. He has also done work on ethnic conflict and socioeconomic diversity more generally, anti-corporate thought and activism, the relationship between political theory and virtual worlds, the economics of art, sports economics, and the philosophy of market competition. In addition, he has investigated market reform and economic growth and the economics of litigation.

Fania Oz-Salzberger is Professor of History at the Faculty of Law and the Center for German and European Studies, University of Haifa. Her books include *Translating the Enlightenment: Scottish Civic Discourse in Eighteenth-Century Germany* (Oxford University Press 1995) and the Cambridge University Press edition of *Adam Ferguson's Essay on the History of Civil Society* (1767/1995). She has published numerous articles on the Enlightenment, the history of translation, and the history of political thought. Her most recent book is *Jews and Words* (Yale University Press 2012), co-authored with Amos Oz.

Maria Pia Paganelli is an Associate Professor of Economics at Trinity University. She works on Adam Smith, David Hume, eighteenth-century monetary theories, and the links between the Scottish Enlightenment and behavioural economics. She is the Book Review Editor for the *Journal of the History of Economic Thought* and co-edited the *Oxford Handbook on Adam Smith*.

Thierry C. Pauchant is Professor of Management and Evolutionary Ethics at HEC Montréal, the University of Montréal's business school, where he holds the Chair in Ethical Management. He is the author or co-author of 120 articles that have appeared in the *Academy of Management Review*, *Business and Society*, *Éthique Publique*, *Gestion*, *Journal of Business Ethics*, *Journal of Humanistic Psychology*, *Organizational Studies*, and *Strategic Management Journal*, among others, as well as ten books, including *In Search of Meaning* (Jossey-Bass 1995), *Ethics and Spirituality at Work* (Quorum Books 2002), and *36 façons d'être éthique au travail* (Fides 2009). He is currently working on a book about Condorcet and his commentaries on Adam Smith's *Wealth of Nations*.

Paul Raekstad is a Ph.D. candidate in Philosophy at the University of Cambridge, working on realist and comparative approaches to political theory, conceptions of human development and flourishing, and Marxist and anarchist critiques of capitalism and the state. More of his work can be found at: http://cambridge.academia.edu/PaulRaekstad, and he can be contacted at paul. raekstad@cantab.net.

Dennis C. Rasmussen is Associate Professor of Political Science at Tufts University. He is the author of *The Problems and Promise of Commercial Society: Adam Smith's Response to Rousseau* (Penn State University Press, 2008) and *The Pragmatic Enlightenment: Recovering the Liberalism of Hume, Smith, Montesquieu, and Voltaire* (Cambridge University Press, 2014). He is currently writing a book on Smith's friendship with David Hume.

Tatsuya Sakamoto is Professor of History of Social and Economic Thought in the Faculty of Economics at Keio University. He has published widely on Hume, Smith, other European thinkers, and modern Japanese intellectuals, including Yukichi Fukuzawa. He has held visiting research fellowships in the universities of Glasgow, Boston and Cambridge. His major publications in Japanese are *Hume's Civilized Society* (1995), *Hume's Skeptical Optimism* (2011), and *A History of Social Thought from Machiavelli to Rawls* (2014). He edited (in English with Hideo Tanaka) *The Rise of Political Economy in the Scottish Enlightenment* (2003). His contributions on Hume's economic thought are included in *A Companion to Hume*, edited by Elizabeth S. Radcliffe (2008 and 2011) and *The Oxford Handbook of David Hume*, edited by Paul Russell (2015). He is currently working on the genealogy of modern European morals surrounding the issues deriving from Hume's and Smith's theories of sympathy and justice.

Roberto Resende Simiqueli holds a Master's degree in Political Science and a Ph.D. in Economic Development, both from the Universidade Estadual de Campinas (Unicamp), in Campinas, Brazil. He has done research on Adam Smith's comments on the British Empire, defending that the author's emphasis on strategic gains to be secured from a shift to free trade reveals that his proposals do not rely solely on the moral virtues of liberalism. His interests stretch from classical liberalism, intellectual and economic history and imperialism to radical institutionalism and critical theory. He is currently studying the exchanges between Thorstein Veblen and John A. Hobson, and the possibilities presented by Veblen's analysis of the leisure class in explaining cooperation and cooptation of regional élites in the nineteenth and twentieth centuries.

Craig Smith is Adam Smith Lecturer in the Scottish Enlightenment in the School of Social and Political Sciences at the University of Glasgow. He is the author of *Adam Smith's Political Philosophy: The Invisible Hand and*

Spontaneous Order and with Christopher J. Berry and Maria Pia Paganelli edited *The Oxford Handbook of Adam Smith*.

Barry Stocker teaches philosophy and political theory at Istanbul Technical University. He holds a doctorate from the University of Sussex and previous degrees from the University of Warwick. He specialises in Continental approaches to political thought, including work on earlier history in the field informed by that approach. Within Enlightenment thought he has particular interest in the philosophy of history, ethics, law, republicanism, liberty and the thought of Vico. Other areas of philosophical work include aesthetics and philosophy and literature. His books include the monograph *Kierkegaard on Politics* (Palgrave 2014) and *Nietzsche as Political Philosopher* (De Gruyter 2014), which he co-edited. Current political thought research is focused on liberty in Foucault. Other current research topics include law and legislation, philosophy of Europe, and republican libertarianism. A paper on 'Statism and Distributive Injustice in Adam Smith' is scheduled for publication in an edited volume from De Gruyter on *Pluralism and Conflict*.

Fotini Vaki is a Senior Lecturer in History of Philosophy in the Department of History at Ionian University, Corfu. She is the author of *Progress in the Enlightenment: Faces and Facets* (in Greek). She has also written many papers centred on critical theory as well as the political philosophy and the philosophy of history of the Enlightenment published in Greek and English. In January and September 2015 she was elected a member of the Hellenic Parliament for SYRIZA. She is the parliamentary representative of SYRIZA and a member of the parliament's Committee on Educational Affairs.

Benoît Walraevens is Assistant Professor in Economics at the University of Caen Lower Normandy in France. He received his Ph.D. in Economics from the University of Paris 1 Panthéon Sorbonne for a thesis titled 'Growth and Progress in Adam Smith's Thought'. Since then he has published several papers on Smith in the *European Journal of the History of Economic Thought*, *History of Economic Ideas*, *Cahiers d'Economie Politique* and *Revue Economique*, along with book reviews of the *Oxford Handbook of Adam Smith* and Nicholas Phillipson's intellectual biography of Smith. He is currently working on papers on Hume, Smith and Rousseau.

Nathaniel Wolloch is an independent Israeli scholar. He is a historian of the long eighteenth century, specialising in European intellectual and cultural history, with an emphasis on the history of attitudes toward nature and animals, the history of historiography, and the history of economic thought. He is the author of numerous articles, as well as of two books: *Subjugated Animals: Animals and Anthropocentrism in Early Modern European Culture* (2006); and *History and Nature in the Enlightenment: Praise of the Mastery of Nature in Eighteenth-Century Historical Literature* (2011). Recently he has been studying the conceptualisation of natural resources in the history of economic thought.

From the editor

Volume 9 presents a rich, far-ranging collection of essays by an international mixture of authors, both new and more established, exemplifying the diversity and interdisciplinarity that the *Adam Smith Review* was meant to achieve. I am delighted to see Volume 9 appear, and I would like to thank the many authors, guest editors, referees, and editorial staff who contributed to it. I would especially like to thank our editor at Routledge, Emily Kindleysides, for her commitment to the journal; and my editorial assistant, Aaron Cotkin, for his editorial skill and impeccable scholarly judgement.

I first read David Raphael's *The Impartial Spectator* in college. It was the first book about Adam Smith that I ever read, and it sparked my lifelong interest in Smith's ethics. It is a great honour to dedicate this issue to his memory.

Fonna Forman
Editor

David Raphael (1916–2015)

A personal appreciation

Christopher J. Berry

I first met David Raphael in the autumn of 1969 when, at the ridiculous age of twenty-three, I went to Glasgow for a job interview. He was the chief inquisitor. I still remember his 'killer question': who was my favourite philosopher? I was coy, saying I found Nietzsche stimulating but Hume was the one I agreed with. It must have been the right answer because to my surprise I was on the day offered the job of Assistant Lecturer in Social and Political Philosophy. I started as a Glasgow academic in January 1970 but in the meantime David left Glasgow briefly (and not altogether happily) for Reading before Imperial College, London. Imperial, which vies with Cambridge as the premier UK institution for the study of science and engineering, proved more congenial. He once said he much enjoyed teaching philosophy to bright physicists.

Although I thus never had the privilege of working with him as a (very junior) colleague, I do, of course, remain ever grateful that he saw enough potential to appoint me. Our paths continued to cross over the years, the last time in 2009 when I invited him as a special guest at a conference in Glasgow to mark 250 years since the first edition of *The Theory of Moral Sentiments*. Although by then frail, in key respects he never changed. Sharp in body but especially in mind, he was an embodiment of analytical acuity and clear thinking. Despite his work on Smith (and other eighteenth-century thinkers) there were several books that dealt with concepts and issues in moral and political thinking, some of which, such as *Problems of Political Philosophy* (Macmillan 1970), were based on his Glasgow lecture course (he was a proud upholder of the Glasgow tradition where 'the' professor lectured to first-year undergraduates). For all his admiration for Smith he declared in a public, subsequently published, lecture that he judged David Hume's *Treatise of Human Nature* to be 'the greatest work of philosophy written in the English language'. In part this was an act of contrition for criticisms of Hume made in his first book, *The Moral Sense* (Oxford 1947), which was based on his Oxford D.Phil (he had a stellar, prize-winning career at both undergraduate and postgraduate level).

David Raphael always maintained high intellectual standards and, whatever the audience or the setting, as an exemplar of lucidity he was a ferocious and daunting critic of anyone (no matter their academic status) whom he judged to be vague or sloppy. As his last book on the *Impartial Spectator* (Oxford 2007) testifies, all his writings were to the point. Not for him lengthy tomes: brevity was the soul of clarity, prolixity typically the symptom of fuzziness. With his death the great editorial team of the Glasgow edition of Smith's works is no more but their work will live on and his (with 'Alec' MacFie) edition of *The Theory of Moral Sentiments* will remain a key memorial to a remarkable scholar.

Sorbonne symposium

Adam Smith on empire, the invisible hand and the progress of society

Guest editor: Benoît Walraevens

Introduction

Benoît Walraevens

From the 3 to 6 July 2013, Jean-François Dunyach from the Centre Roland Mousnier of the University of Paris IV Sorbonne organized, at the Sorbonne in Paris, the 26th annual international conference of the Eighteenth Century Scottish Studies Society which was, for the first time, organized in partnership with the International Adam Smith Society. Keynote speakers included Amartya Sen, Emma Rothschild, and Michael Biziou. The general topic of the conference was "Scotland, Europe and Empire in the Age of Adam Smith and Beyond." This section of the book comprises a selection of papers on Smith, drafts of which were presented to the conference and then prepared and submitted to *The Adam Smith Review*, which followed its usual review process. Of the six selected papers, three deal with the main topic of the conference: Smith's analysis of colonialism and the British Empire. They offer new insights on Smith's rather neglected political thinking and on how his vision of the ancient colonies nurtures his reflections on the fate of the British Empire. History is also at the heart of his theory of the progress of society, the famous "four-stage theory," which is the main issue of two papers here. The first of these proposes to end the controversy over the paternity of that theory. Based on a new reading of the "Anderson notes," it claims that Smith gives the first formulation of the four-stage theory in 1749 in a public lecture. The second shows how the importance of material progress in the four-stage theory went from a historiographical outlook to a political economy outlook in Smith. The last paper is about the idea of the invisible hand and its intellectual legacy, especially in natural sciences.

Paper 1: "Adam Smith and Immanuel Kant as critics of empire: international trade companies and global commerce versus *jus commercii*" by Fotini Vaki

Smith's ambiguous assessment of commercial society has always been a source of conjecture (for recent treatments see Rasmussen 2008 and Hanley 2009). Vaki here starts by identifying two seemingly contradictory narratives in the *WN*: one in which commercial society is presented as the happy and natural end of history, guaranteed by an unchanging human nature, and another darker and much more pessimistic vision of that type of society, so much so that Smith seems sometimes closer to Ferguson's civic humanism (and even Marx) than to Turgot or Condorcet. The paper aims to show that Smith does not contradict himself about commercial society because this twofold narrative, according to the author, represents two epistemological standpoints, a normative and a descriptive. The former, which is incarnated by the system of natural liberty and the natural right of commerce (or *jus commercii*), serves as an ideal to judge and criticize past and present historical systems and institutions. To highlight that point, Vaki focuses on Smith's severe critique of the corruption of international trade companies which, against the ideal vision of *doux commerce*, make commerce a source of endless conflict and war. Colonialism in general is, for Smith, undoubtedly unjust because it violates the "most sacred right of mankind," the right of natural liberty. Joint stock companies are granted political power, acting as substitutes of the sovereign. They violate man's sacred and natural right of commerce. From Smith's defence of *jus commercii* to Kant's *jus cosmopoliticum*, the author claims, there is only one step because commerce in the eighteenth century had a broad meaning, encompassing every kind of communication or exchange, be that of words, ideas or opinions. So Vaki finds in Smith and Kant a commonality of views in their moral and humanistic critique and condemnation of colonial practices.

Paper 2: "*Apoikia* and *colonia*: Smith's comments on the 'recent disturbances' in the colonies" by Roberto Resende Simiqueli

It is well known now that Smith had a long-lasting (he had advised the British government on colonial tax policy in the 1760s) and deep interest in colonial policy and the empire and probably delayed the publication of the *WN* to learn more about the situation in the colonies of North America and think about the fate of the British Empire (see Winch 2013; Ortmann and Walraevens 2016). In this paper, Simiqueli analyses the legacy and influence of Smith's thinking on colonialism and the British Empire on the foreign and economic policies of the British crown. Benians (1925) had written about these topics, trying to understand why some of Smith's advice had been followed, in particular the liberalization of commerce with the colonies, while other aspects were rejected, like colonial representativeness in the (British) Parliament. Benians argued that Smith's project for a new empire was mainly founded on a moral critique of British colonial practices and crucially appeared "ahead of his time." Against this, Simiqueli argues, first, that moral arguments are only part of the story and that one should rather see in Smith's critique of colonialism and his proposal for a new empire a mix of economic, political and strategic arguments, aiming at a reasonable compromise. The author underlines a peculiar methodological approach by Smith in Book IV, and particularly in chapter 7, where he contrasts classical, Greco-Roman colonialism with its modern form. For Smith, history can shed light on the present. Indeed, the author claims, the Greek *apoikia* and the Roman *colonia* serve as two ideal types from which the political and economic realities of mercantilist Europe are judged. Smith seems to favour the Greek model where colonies are independent from the mother city and he details the peculiarities of the colonies of North America that make them close to the ideal expressed in Greek colonialism. Modern colonies provide the mother country with neither military force nor increased revenues. Examples taken from the ancient world offer a "welcome contribution to Smith's theses" by clearly demonstrating that excessive regulations from the empire are economically inefficient (because they hinder the colony's development) and politically harmful for the metropolis. Therefore, Smith's plea for colonies' representativeness to the Parliament "arises not entirely of moral inspirations, but, in a way, as a compromise solution between metropolitan aristocracy and colonial elites." Smith was not, according to Simiqueli, "ahead of his time"; rather, he "foresees the foreseeable" and offers "a pragmatic response to an objective demand."

Paper 3: "Smith on the colonialism and republicanism of the moderns compared with that of the ancients" by Barry Stocker

In this paper, Smith's analysis of colonialism and empire is seen as a major indication of his importance as a political thinker. His comparison of the different forms of colonialism, ancient and modern, is studied here from another perspective, that of the political form of government, with special emphasis placed on republicanism – for which, Stocker claims, Smith had a preference. Stocker argues that this preference appears most clearly in Smith's account of modern colonialism in which the destructive effects of monarchy and their collusion with economic elites are most visible. In other words, as he rightly notices, "the account of colonialism in *WN* is itself a part of an account of mercantilism" which leads to injustice and self-defeating economic practices. Stocker focuses on the best case of modern colonialism, the British colonization of North America, with respect to which Smith lauds the republicanism, the abundance of free land and the lack of hereditary aristocracy as primary causes of prosperity. There is a contrast between the absolutist, negative models of colonialism (as in the Spanish and Portuguese colonies of South America) and the republican, positive models exemplified by ancient Greek colonies and the British colonies of North America. Interestingly, the paper focuses on the possibility of men enjoying a specific, radical kind of liberty, autonomy and independence in the latter, not unlike that of the savage or barbarian in pre-commercial societies, but supposedly unknown to civilized societies. The American colonies are, in Smith's mind, a model for the future "as a repetition of the Greek colonial system," if they are granted independence, as he desperately wishes them to be. Yet, they include slavery, which Smith finds more persistent under republican regimes. Stocker also notices how Smith sees in the lack of knowledge of the representative principle one of the reasons for the moral and political decline of the Roman republic and suggests that it was probably in his mind when he thought about his project for a new British Empire. All in all, the paper presents Smith as a sophisticated, though usually neglected, political thinker.

Paper 4: "Adam Smith's four-stages theory of socio-cultural evolution: new insights from his 1749 lecture" by Thierry Pauchant

This paper is about the genesis of Smith's theory of the progress of society. Pauchant tries to put an end to the controversy over the paternity of the four-stage theory. The origin of this controversy lies in the fact that the only published version of Smith's four-stage theory is found in the *WN* of 1776, which is much later than other Scottish (and French) versions of that theory (from Robertson, Ferguson and so on). Even the version of the first set of *Lectures on Jurisprudence* dates back only to 1762, which is not old enough to prove that Smith was the initiator of the four-stage theory. That notwithstanding, Meek (1976) studied the history and genealogy of that theory and concluded that Smith and Turgot were the first to develop it, independently, at the beginning of the 1750s. Some people argue that the four-stage theory was just inherited from the natural law tradition but Smith, Pauchant recalls, has been rightly credited for adding essential features to that tradition. First, there is a consensus in considering Smith as the one who conceived of the three "states" discussed in the natural law tradition (hunting and fishing, herding and farming) as three "stages" of evolution with specific manners, institutions, property relations and so on. Smith is also credited, Pauchant adds, with suggesting that humans really started their long social evolution as soon as they domesticated animals and then adding to his evolutionary view of history a fourth stage, the age of commerce, positing that it was qualitatively different from the others. Last but not least, Smith added to the natural law tradition "a developmental theory of mind and language, triggering different manners, customs and institutions." Nonetheless, scholars were reluctant to assign him paternity of the theory. Stewart, Smith's first biographer, claimed that the latter used conjectural history in his lectures prior to 1750. From a new reading of the "Anderson notes" (Anderson, later a colleague of Smith at Glasgow University, captured a synthesis of Smith's public lectures), discovered in 1970 but studied only by Meek until now, Pauchant aims to end that controversy. Where Meek dated the lecture to 1753 or later, our author claims that Smith was the first to introduce the theory in a public lecture in 1749. This then influenced other members of the Scottish Enlightenment, and other thinkers beyond that circle. He also characterizes Smith's theory as a socio-cultural theory of evolution mixing different biological, instinctual, psychosocial and cultural processes, and proposes avenues for further research on the topic, in particular advocating for more integration between the natural, social and human sciences.

Paper 5: "The idea of historical progress in the transition from Enlightenment historiography to classical political economy" by Nathaniel Wolloch

While this paper also studies Smith's theory of the progress of society, it adopts a different perspective. Here, Wolloch illuminates how, in Smith, stadial notions moved from mere historiographical inquiries to political-economic ones. It focuses on two related points: Smith's original though neglected view and use of history as a guide for future conduct; and the seminal importance of material progress in the progress of society. As to the first point, Wolloch makes several interesting claims. He underlines how Smith tried to define the (causal) laws of history, as he tried to with the laws of nature, as a need for explanation and, most importantly here, in order to predict future events. Historical writing for Smith aims at instructing people about proper behaviour. Smith is convinced that we can learn valuable, prescriptive lessons from the past to prepare a better future. Understanding the laws of historical progress was, for Smith, the key to further-ing the progress of society. Wolloch convincingly claims that Smith "evinced the typical Enlightenment attitude toward historiography, combining erudition, narrative style and a philosophical approach," as represented by the figure of the *historien philosophe*, which Smith quite favoured. As to the second point, Wolloch extends Meek's well-known "materialist" interpretation of Smith's four-stage theory, representing the latter as a history of the progress of man's mastery over nature – that is, as "a conjectural history of human material culture underlining higher forms of cultural phenomena." With this emphasis on material progress in general (rather than only on the means of procuring subsistence), Smith's stadial theory becomes "an early form of economic history." It was thus in this field "in which historiographical insights were transformed into prescriptive socio-economic recommendations for future conduct," as is the case in the *WN* with public expenditures for the judicial system or national defence. Wolloch shows us how Smith endorsed the Enlightenment view of history as a means toward enhancing human material, social and moral progress.

Paper 6: "Adam Smith's invisible hand: a brief history" by Toni Vogel Carey

The final paper in this section offers a (necessarily) selective analysis of the history and legacy of the idea(s) of the "invisible hand," especially in the natural sciences. While the words appear only three times in Smith's entire corpus, the idea pervades all of his work, which is probably why, as Carey claims, it is what Smith is best known for today, so much so that Smith scholars have identified up to a dozen invisible hands in his works. Here, Carey chooses to focus on two ideas of the invisible hand. One is the invisible hand of the *WN* which is about the unknown and unforeseen consequences, for the individual and for society as a whole, for better or for worse, of individual actions. The other is that of spon-taneous order, or order without design, an idea which, as our author remarks, "does not appear in any of the three invisible hand statements, but of which Smith is considered a major contributor," among other Scottish philosophers. Carey proposes an interesting and novel comparison between these two ideas of the invisible hand and the distinction between mixtures and compounds in chemistry. In other words, "the idea of societal betterment is additive or conjunctive, and like a mixture, entails changes only in *degree*," whereas "spontaneous order is transformative; like a compound, it involves differences in *kind* that are difficult or impossible to reverse." Part 2 prepares the ground for the rest of Carey's paper, highlighting that Smith used many mechanistic analogies in his work, but also redundant biological images. Part 3 studies the idea of evolutionism, which was developed in the eighteenth century by Diderot and Maupertuis, and then suggests that this idea could have gone from Smith to Darwin through Hutton and Playfair. Going further, our author identifies significant parallels between Darwin and Smith, along the lines of Haakonssen, including the notions that Darwin's *On the Origin of Species* is a book in conjectural history, that natural selection is unobservable, like Smith's famous invisible hand, and most importantly that natural selection looks like the invisible hand of spontaneous order. Part 4 extends the Smith–Darwin relationship around the nineteenth-century epistemological concept of "consilience." And Part 5 deals with a modern synonym of spontaneous order, the idea of "self-organization," which today pervades many sciences, from cosmology (Smolin and the idea that the universe made itself) to economics (Krugman on "emergence"). Like Pauchant, Carey shows us how Smith's ideas create bridges between the social and natural sciences. To conclude on the invisible hand, maybe we should follow our author in seeing "the term 'invisible hand' as a placeholder for an explanation that Smith knew he was not yet able to furnish."

Bibliography

Benians, E. A. (1925). "Adam Smith's project of an empire." *Cambridge Historical Journal*, 3: 249–283.

Hanley, Ryan (2009). *Adam Smith and the Character of Virtue.* Cambridge: Cambridge University Press.

Ortmann, Andreas and Walraevens, Benoît (2016). "The rhetorical structure of Adam Smith's *Wealth of Nations*." Working paper.

Rasmussen, Dennis (2008). *The Problems and Promise of Commercial Society: Adam Smith's Response to Rousseau.* University Park: Pennsylvania State University Press.

Winch, Donald (2013). "The political economy of empire." Unpublished manuscript.

Adam Smith and Immanuel Kant as critics of empire

International trade companies and global commerce versus *jus commercii*

Fotini Vaki

1. The two narratives in *The Wealth of Nations*

There are two narratives running through *The Wealth of Nations.* On the one hand, dominant is the normative assessment of the commercial society as the happy end of history and humanity, the imminent advent of which is guaranteed by the main features of a uniform human nature. The *primum mobile* of the historical teleology implicit in the four-stages theory of Smith and the Scottish conjectural history[1] are the main features of human nature such as, first, its "propensity to track, barter and exchange one thing for another"[2] and, second,

> the uniform, constant, and uninterrupted [desire] for bettering our condition, a desire which, though generally calm and dispassionate, comes with us from the womb, and never leaves us till we go into the grave. In the whole interval which separates those two moments, there is scarce perhaps a single instant in which any man is so perfectly and completely satisfied with his situation as to be without any wish of alteration or improvement of any kind.[3]

And since, for Smith, an "augmentation of fortune is the means by which the greater part of men propose and wish to better their condition," that propensity of human nature becomes the motor force of economic affluence and prosperity. Apparently, the uniform human nature, when left unimpeded, inevitably brings about the commercial society. And, conversely, it is only within the context of the latter that the former can flourish and realize itself. In the opening pages of *The Wealth of Nations*, commercial society is depicted as the paradise on earth which not only augments the "skill, dexterity and judgment"[4] of its subjects but also makes their lives superior to that of an African king.[5]

On the other hand, the encomium of commercial society seems to recede and give way to a gloomy picture which, strangely enough, brings Smith closer to Ferguson and anticipates Marx's theory of alienation. In the progress of the division of labour, Smith claims, the confinement of the "far greater part of those who live by labor" to "a few very simple operations"[6] and their exclusion from the public deliberations, in which their voices are "little heard and less regarded,"[7] numb their ability to judge and make them "stupid and ignorant" to such an extent that they are "not only incapable of relishing or bearing a part in any rational conversation but of conceiving any generous, noble or tender sentiment and consequently of forming any just judgment concerning many even of the ordinary duties of private life."[8] Smith does not even hesitate to take sides with Ferguson in reproaching commercial society for eliminating the courage of its subjects rendering them equally incapable of defending their country in war.[9] The historical teleology implicit in Smith's four-stages model seems to collapse as soon as he praises the disdained "rude stage of humanity" in which every man is a warrior and exerts his judgment to confront problems and remove difficulties. How far is that insight from Ferguson's praising of the barbarian's robustness evinced in wars in which they "preferred death to captivity."[10] And how far is the above gloomy illustration of commercial society from Ferguson's bitter remark that behind the so-called "skill, dexterity and judgment" brought about by the distribution of labour lies hidden a "nation of helots" rather than free citizens?[11] Is there finally, as Donald Winch maintains, a civic republican strain in Smith?[12] And most importantly, how can one view the tension inherent in *The Wealth of Nations* apparent by the coexistence of the two narratives?

In what follows I will try to show that Smith neither lapses into a civil republican tradition nor contradicts himself by presenting commercial society as a eulogy and a hell at the same time. What appears as a twofold contradictory narrative is, in fact, two epistemological standpoints: a normative and a descriptive. The general view developed on the system of natural liberty translatable in the right of commerce – *jus commercii* – becomes the normative standpoint of the critique of historical systems and institutions that were unjust. The elaboration of the concept of natural liberty imprinted in the famous metaphor of the invisible hand is a sought-after ideal and the normative yardstick for denouncing the gap between the "ought" and the "is," the ideal and its distorted realization in the domain of history. That intertwining of a descriptive narrative with a fair number of strong normative comments not only refutes the famous "Adam Smith problem" according to which *The Wealth of Nations*, unlike *The Theory of Moral Sentiments*, is the amoral discourse par excellence restricted to value-free judgments concerning the possibilities of economic affluence; it mainly makes claims of social justice, albeit implicitly, by underlining what is unjust. I intend to illuminate that point by focusing on Smith's severe critique of the exclusive companies of the merchants from the standpoint of *jus commercii*. Paradoxically, his criticism brings him closer (though from a radically different methodological route) to Kant's *jus cosmopoliticum.*

2. Smith's criticism of the international trade companies

The discourse on commerce as the substitute for war and the guarantee of social stability and economic affluence crosses the boundaries of local/national Enlightenments and becomes the dominant eighteenth-century discourse. Unlike the contemporary use of the term which identifies it exclusively with the market-oriented trade of goods, in the eighteenth-century context commerce has broader connotations and signifies interaction and communication. *Jus commercii* could be argued to encompass *jus cosmopoliticum*.[13] For a considerable portion of the Scottish Enlightenment, commerce goes hand in hand with "civility" – that is, the refinement of morals and "good manners."[14] The so-called *doux commerce* referring to the gradual finesse of the senses and aesthetic pleasures are seen as the almost natural outcomes of the commercial society.[15] At the other end of the spectrum, Kant argues in his *Perpetual Peace* that "the spirit of commerce takes hold of every people and cannot exist side by side with war."[16] Commerce for Kant, together with the republican state and the principle of publicity, is becoming the means to realize the cosmopolitan order in history.

In the fourth Book of *The Wealth of Nations* Smith bitterly claims that "commerce which ought naturally to be, among nations as among individuals, a bond of union and friendship has become the most fertile source of discord and animosity,"[17] while he remarks that "to expect . . . that the freedom of trade should ever be entirely restored in Great Britain, is as absurd as to expect that an Oceana or Utopia should ever be established in it."[18] Smith's pessimistic comments are most probably dictated by his active involvement in the pamphlet wars about the East India Company's illegal, unjust and imperial conduct as well as by his assessment of the Seven Years War, which, for him, "was altogether a colony quarrel" among the leading European states,[19] fuelled by the interests of international trade companies and their merchants. The Enlightenment's pious wish of commerce as the substitute for war was so contradicted by the existing commercial practices that Smith closes *The Wealth of Nations* by urging Britain to stop building imaginary great empires and instead "endeavour to accommodate her future views and designs to the real mediocrity of her circumstances."[20]

Smith's distrust and condemnation of the merchants is very well known. Acting exclusively in the name of monopoly, which, for Smith, is the "sole engine of the mercantile system,"[21] the merchants keep the market constantly understocked, sell their commodities much above the natural price,[22] impose "high duties and prohibitions upon all those foreign manufactures which can come into competition with their own"[23] and always remain "silent with regard to the pernicious effects of their own gains. They complain only of those of other people."[24] For Smith, however, the most tangible proofs of the corruption of commerce are the practices of the international trade companies and, in particular, of the so-called joint-stock companies such as the South Sea Company, the Royal African Company, the Hudson's Bay Company and the famous East India Company. Those companies are managed by a court of directors subject to the control of a general court of proprietors which, by frequently being appointed by the directors themselves, is more concerned with earning its yearly dividend than watching over the company's activities.[25] Furthermore, insofar as the directors are "managers of other people's money" who share "in the common profit or loss in proportion to their share in this stock,"[26] "it cannot be well expected that they should watch over it with the same anxious vigilance with which the partners in a private compartnery frequently watch over their own."[27] Smith's criticism of the joint-stock companies is deeply humanistic and egalitarian. First of all, he decries them as "burdensome or useless" enterprises that have "either mismanaged or confined the trade"[28] since they are exclusively oriented to extracting profit by all means: by keeping the market understocked, restraining competition, discouraging new ventures from entering into the trade and, last but not least, buying and supplying slaves and plundering defenceless natives. Smith unveils the immense hypocrisy behind "the pious purpose of converting them to Christianity"[29] which sanctifies every impunity and injustice Europeans committed by means of the superiority of force.[30] He condemns colonialism as a sheer folly and injustice[31] from the standpoint of common humanity[32] as well as from that of the "most sacred right of mankind" – natural liberty. In Smith's words: "To prohibit a great people . . . from making all that they can of every part of their own produce, or from employing their stock and industry in the way that they judge most advantageous to themselves is a manifest violation of the most sacred right of mankind."[33] The idea of "natural liberty" as the standpoint of criticism of obsolete and corrupt practices impeding it, such as mercantilism, apprenticeships, guilds, bounties, monopolies and so forth, is assigned with instrumental, cognitive/epistemological and moral/political dimensions.

First, in relation to its instrumental role, natural liberty is a synonym of the famous invisible hand, according to which whenever people are left free to pursue their own self-interest they unwillingly promote the public good. The mechanism of the commercial society is such that private self-interest is transmuted into public benefit. Conversely, our self-interest can be realized only when we collaborate with our fellows, regardless of our intentions.

Second, in relation to its cognitive/epistemological dimension, for Smith, our knowledge is inductively inferred by experience. What we know most firmly are our immediate circumstances and "we often err when we try to extrapolate general principles of human behavior from those circumstances and project them into the future."[34]

Third, the empiricist epistemological premises governing Smith's account of natural liberty render the latter not merely a methodological tool or a descriptive approach to social theory,[35] but first and foremost a value judgment with moral and political connotations characteristic of Smith's aversion to the architects of Utopia who view history as a guinea pig in the lab of theory and design their grandiose plans by being indifferent to the particularities of historical circumstances and the facts of human nature. "I have never known," Smith writes, "much good done by those who affected to trade for the public good."[36] Considering progress as the gradual process of accumulating experience rather than the pompous plan of an intellectual and political avant-garde, Smith claims that the individual agent "can in his local situation judge much better than any statesman or lawgiver can do for him."[37] In the end, "in the great chess board of human society, every single piece has a principle of motion of its own, altogether different from that which the legislature might chuse to impress upon it."[38] But the whole story has not yet been told.

For Smith, the most worrying symptom of the corruption effects of the joint-stock companies is their function as the substitutes for the sovereign. The merchants are taking on the political mantle but they can never act as a sovereign ought to act precisely because their sole aim is the extortion of profit by every possible means: by committing atrocities and injustices, and causing much suffering to the subjects they rule. The political rule of the international companies that prioritize absolutely profits over the well-being of their subjects can only assume the form of a bloodthirsty, tyrannical, militaristic regime. The only political rule is the rule of violence since a merchants' government lacks legitimacy and promotes interests that are diametrically opposite to those of the country.[39] The subjection of the political will to the ruthless and dictatorial imperatives of the companies not only infringes upon the sacred and natural right of commerce,[40] the hallmarks of which are the justice and equality guaranteed by, in Smith's words, "the mutual communication of knowledge and of all sorts of improvements,"[41] but also encroaches on "the right one has to the free use of his person and in a word to do what he has in mind when it does not prove detrimental to any other person."[42] Smith's condemnation of the exclusive companies as "nuisances in every respect, always more or less inconvenient to the countries in which they are established and destructive to those which have the misfortune to fall under their government"[43] makes him – if we are allowed an anachronism – a tragically relevant critic of capitalist globalization from the standpoint of cosmopolitanism. But it also brings him close to Kant's criticism of colonialism.

3. Kant's *jus cosmopoliticum*

While the cradle of the Smithian ideas is the historical context and the field of experience, Kant deduces his juridical or even deontological-ethical postulates in fashioning a cosmopolitan order from the a priori principles of reason. While, for Smith, the precondition of autonomy is free commerce inasmuch as it takes place among equal and autonomous agents each exercising his judgment and pursuing his interest not "by every servile and fawning attention to obtain"[44] the others' goodwill but through mutually advantageous, respectful free exchange, for Kant the institutional locus of autonomy and cosmopolitanism is the republican state.

Yet the Kantian *jus cosmopoliticum*, referring to a principle of right rather than a philanthropic (ethical) idea,[45] is almost identical to the Smithian right of commerce to the extent that it is identified with "a community of possible physical interaction" and the right to "engage in commerce with any other."[46] Furthermore, just as Smith grounds the natural right of commerce upon natural liberty, Kant resorts to the "right of humanity in one's own person" and the innate right of freedom denoting the coexistence of the freedom of each with "the freedom of any other in accordance with a universal law"[47] to decry colonialism. This is reinforced by his thesis on the right to property I intend to explicate in what follows.

In *The Metaphysics of Morals* the transition from the natural to the political or lawful condition, which, for Kant, is set as a duty, is becoming the context within which the right to property is grounded. In his treatment of private right pertaining to the natural state Kant already mentions sensible or physical and intelligible or rightful possession.[48] The fact that I hold an object or my body dwells on a piece of land is not necessarily a condition of property. Property, for Kant, refers instead to intelligible possession, which, in his own words, consists in "a merely rightful connection of the subject's will with that object . . . independently of any relation to it in space and time."[49] In other words, something is mine even if it is not in the same place with me.

Yet possession in the state of nature is only natural or sensible possession and, therefore, provisionally rightful possession.[50] Conclusive possession is possible instead only in a lawful condition, namely one governed by public law.[51] That is because, for Kant, the right to property is not only conceived of as a right to a thing but as a right to the private use of a thing. By the latter is meant the right versus any other person who possesses that thing with others in common. The idea of the common possession becomes the condition of the possibility of the exclusion of every other possessor from the private property of an object.[52]

Nevertheless, several questions arise with relation to Kant. What happens with the land property? When is a land mine? And if the *sine qua non* of property is the political condition, what happens with those who do not wish to constitute civil society? Can anyone usurp their land? And, finally, does the Kantian theory of property, on the one hand, and the Kantian thesis that the constitution of a republican state as a duty, on the other, legitimate unwillingly colonial practices or "humanitarian" interventions in the name of the "noble" mission of civilizing "savages"? The answer to that presupposes, on the one hand, Kant's theory of land property and, on the other, his definition and elucidation of the cosmopolitan right.

Starting from the idea of the original possession in common, Kant maintains, first, that all human beings, before proceeding to any act of instituting rights, "have a right to be wherever nature or chance (apart from their will) has placed them. This kind of possession (*possession*) – which is to be distinguished from residence (*sedes*), a chosen and therefore an acquired *lasting* possession – is a possession *in common*,"[53] and that possession is common because

> the spherical surface of the earth unites all the places on its surface; for if its surface were an unbounded plane, people could be so dispersed on it that they would not come into any community with one another, and community would not then be a necessary result of their existence on the earth.[54]

Second, the right to the land property is established by the temporal priority of its possession.[55] In other words, the first possessor of a piece of land is entitled to resist anyone who tries to usurp it.

It is precisely at this point that Kant formulates a theory of property in stark opposition to John Locke's. For if, according to Locke, labour and use in general are becoming the conditions of property, the opposite holds for Kant: property is the condition of use. Kant's argumentation at this point is inspired by the Aristotelian pair of substance and accident. The cultivation, the enclosure, the transformation by and large of a piece of land through labour are all considered accidents – *symvevikota* – which cannot establish the right to the possession of the substance. Thus, the labour expenditure on land which is not already considered property is merely a waste of time and effort.[56]

The Kantian interpretation of the land property on the basis of the temporal priority of its possession rather than its use and appropriation condemns unequivocally the foundation of colonies under the pretext of the vast, unexploited-by-the-natives pieces of land the use and development of which would be a significant step to material progress. But "it is easy to see through this veil of injustice [Jesuitism], which would sanction any means to good ends. Such a way of acquiring land is therefore to be repudiated."[57] Nevertheless, there seems to be a contradiction at this point. According to Kant, in the state of nature – that is, in the absence of public law – the property of land is regarded as provisional. And if the foundation of a political state is a duty, just as the incessant struggle for perfection of the human being is a moral duty, would that not legitimize the foreign occupation of land with the intent to integrate – even by violence – the "savages" into a lawful, political condition?

Kant claims that European colonial practices are to be condemned for two reasons, despite their supposedly good intentions. First, they are morally unacceptable. As Kant writes in "Perpetual Peace":

> America, the Negro countries, the Spice Islands, the Cape, etc. were looked upon at the time of their discovery as ownerless territories; for the native inhabitants were counted as nothing. In East India (Hindustan), foreign troops were brought in under the pretext of merely setting up trading posts. This led to oppression of the natives, incitement of the various Indian states to widespread wars, famine, insurrection, treachery and the whole litany of evils which can afflict the human race . . . and all this is the work of powers who make endless ado about their piety, and who wish to be considered as chosen believers while they live on the fruits of iniquity.[58]

Second, the colonial practices infringe upon the idea of the cosmopolitan right. By encouraging a sense of co-belonging the latter confines itself in a right of hospitality. For Kant,

> the stranger cannot claim the right of a guest to be entertained, for this would require a special friendly agreement whereby he might become a member of the native household for a certain time. He may only claim a right of resort, for all men are entitled to present themselves in the society of others by virtue of their right to communal possession of the earth's surface. Since the earth is a globe, they cannot disperse over an infinite area, but must necessarily tolerate one another's company.[59]

However, the contradiction remains. For, on the one hand, Kant regards it as the moral duty of every single human being to develop his capacities while, on the other, he grounds as a kind of a categorical imperative man's exit from the state of nature. But is it also a duty of a whole people to perfect themselves? Moreover, is it a duty of a human being to improve his fellow human beings? And, accordingly, is it a duty of a people to civilize another people?

Kant's answer is "no," because in *The Metaphysics of Morals* he maintains that it is at people's own discretion to choose how they want to live upon the earth. At this point, Kant resorts to the sole, innate right every human being bears in virtue of his "humanness," which is that of freedom conceived of as emancipation from the constraints brought about by others' choices and as the possibility of our freedom to coexist with another's freedom according to a universal law.

4. Conclusion

In this paper I have tried to underline the normative aspects permeating Smith's *Wealth of Nations*, in particular the idea of natural liberty translatable, on the one hand, into the famous metaphor of the invisible hand, and, on the other, into the idea of *jus commercii* implying not merely the trade of goods but actual communication and interaction among different cultures and states. The emphasis upon the "normative" Smith of *The Wealth of Nations* serves a twofold purpose. First, it refutes the "Adam Smith problem" according to which *The Wealth of Nations*, unlike *The Theory of Moral Sentiments*, is an amoral, "value-free" discourse. The system of natural liberty becomes on the contrary the standpoint of a forceful criticism of the injustice and enormity of existing trading practices that are mainly exercised by the international trade companies. *Jus commercii* as the concrete embodiment of the ideal of natural liberty is therefore becoming the severe indictment of the corrupting practices and mismanagement of joint-stock companies exclusively oriented to extracting profit, of colonialism and of the merchants' substitution for the sovereign of the state.

Admittedly, there seem to be very deep differences between Kant and Smith. For Smith, autonomy is confined to the domain of the market implying exchanges in equal terms, whereas, for Kant, the loci of autonomy are the a priori principles of reason. While Smith resorts to the idea of fair trade sustained by acts the state undertakes to legislate as the institutional form of "natural liberty," Kant considers the republican state as the *sine qua non* condition of autonomy.

Notwithstanding these differences, however, Smith's idea of natural liberty as the critical weapon against obsolete and unjust practices, such as mercantilism, monopolies, bounties and colonialism, can be read along the lines of Kant's *jus cosmopoliticum*. Sustained by the "right of humanity in one's own person" and the idea of freedom – that is, the possibility of our freedom coexisting with another's freedom according to a universal law – Kant's idea of the cosmopolitan right serves as the standpoint of the criticism and denunciation of colonial practices.

Notes

1   Smith was the first to proceed to the elaboration and formulation of the four-stages theory, the forerunners of which, according to Meek, are Grotius and the Physiocrats. Yet the innovation of the Scots consists in bringing forth the four-stages theory as

the explanatory model of a theory or philosophy of history rather than as a moral theory within the context of the natural law. See Ronald Meek, "Smith, Turgot and the 'four stages' theory," *History of Political Economy*, 3(1) (1971): 9–27 and Ronald Meek, *Social Science and the Ignoble Savage*, Cambridge: Cambridge University Press, 1976, p. 14. Smith divides the social formations into four stages on the basis of the mode of producing the material means of subsistence, developing thereby an evolutionary model that is applicable to any type of society. The first stage is that of hunters, the second that of shepherds, the third that of agriculture, and the fourth the much-desired commercial society. See Adam Smith, *Lectures on Jurisprudence*, ed. R.L. Meek, D.D. Raphael and P.G. Stein, Oxford: Oxford University Press, p. 14. For Smith, each stage does not annul but assimilate the preceding one. To give one example, in commercial society, hunting and fishing do not vanish but remain as leisure activities rather than determining modes of production.

2 Adam Smith, *An Inquiry into the Nature and Causes of the Wealth of Nations*, ed. R.H. Campbell and A. S. Skinner, Oxford: Clarendon Press, 1976, p. 117.
3 Ibid., II.iii.28, p. 341.
4 Ibid., I.i.1, p. 13.
5 Ibid., I.i.11, p. 24.
6 Ibid., V.i.f.50, p. 781.
7 Ibid., I.xi.p, p. 266.
8 Ibid., V.i.f.50, p. 782.
9 Ibid., V.i.f.50, p. 782.
10 Adam Ferguson, *An Essay on the History of Civil Society* [1767], ed. Fania Oz-Salzberger, Cambridge: Cambridge University Press, 1995, p. 105.
11 Ibid., p. 177.
12 Winch grounds his claim on Smith's calling upon the intervention of persons of "real political wisdom" and patriotism to appease social conflicts (Adam Smith, *The Theory of Moral Sentiments* [1759], ed. D. D. Raphael and A. L. Macfie, Oxford: Clarendon Press, 1976, VI.ii.2.13, p. 232). See Donald Winch, *Adam Smith's Politics*, Cambridge: Cambridge University Press, 1978, pp. 159–160. For a different line of interpretation, see Vivienne Brown's *Adam Smith's Discourse*, London: Routledge, 1994, pp. 210–211, 120–140. Brown has shown that politicians, although necessary, do not play a regular role in promoting the good of society. For an interpretation closer to Brown's, see Samuel Fleischacker, *On Adam Smith's Wealth of Nations*, Princeton, NJ: Princeton University Press, p. 232.
13 As Sankar Muthu pointedly claims, the institutions, practice and sense of flux the Enlightenment thinkers had in mind when using the term "commerce" could be depicted in the concept of globalization, although that might sound like an anachronism. See Sankar Muthu, "Adam Smith's critique of international trading companies: Theorizing 'globalization' in the Age of Enlightenment," *Political Theory*, 36 (2008): 185–212, p. 188. On the use of the concept of globalization in that context, see also: Giovanni Arrighi, *Adam Smith in Beijing: Lineages of the 21st Century*, London: Verso, 2007; and Emma Rothschild, "Globalization and the return of history," *Foreign Policy*, 115 (1999): 106–116.
14 David Hume, "Of refinement in the arts" [1777], in *Essays, Moral, Political and Literary*, ed. E. F. Miller, Indianapolis, IN: Liberty Fund, 1985, p. 268.
15 See the brilliant studies of J. G. A. Pocock, *Virtue, Commerce and History*, Cambridge: Cambridge University Press, 1985, pp. 49–50, 114–115, and Albert Hirschmann, *The Passions and the Interests*, Princeton, NJ: Princeton University Press, 1977, p. 56.
16 I. Kant, "Perpetual peace: A philosophical sketch," in *Kant's Political Writings*, ed. Hans Reiss, Cambridge: Cambridge University Press, 1992, p. 114.
17 *Wealth of Nations*, IV.iii.c.9, p. 493.
18 Ibid., IV.ii.43, p. 471.
19 Ibid., IV.vii.c.64, p. 615.

20   Ibid., V.iii.92, p. 947.
21   Ibid., IV.vii.c.89, p. 630.
22   Ibid., I.vii.26, p. 78.
23   Ibid., IV.iii.c.10, p. 494.
24   Ibid., I.ix.24, p. 115.
25   Ibid., V.I.e.18, p. 741.
26   Ibid., V.i.e.6, p. 733.
27   Ibid., V.i.e.18, p. 741.
28   Ibid., V.I.e.5, p. 733
29   Ibid., IV.vii.a, p. 561.
30   Ibid., IV.vii.c.80, p. 626.
31   Ibid., IV.vii.b.59, p. 588.
32   Ibid., IV.vii.b.54, p. 587.
33   Ibid., IV.vii.b.44, p. 582. And in IV.ix.51, p. 687: "Every man as long as he does not violate the laws of justice is left perfectly free to pursue his own interest his own way and to bring both his industry and capital into competition with those of any other man or order of men."
34   Fleischacker, *On Adam Smith's Wealth of Nations*, p. 34.
35   I depart at this point from interpretations such as those propounded by Craig Smith, according to which the "spontaneous order argument" is viewed as a descriptive method of social theory deprived of its political, moral or ideological role. See Craig Smith, *Adam Smith's Political Philosophy: The Invisible Hand and Spontaneous Order*, London: Routledge, 2006, p. 1.
36   *Wealth of Nations*, IV.ii.9, p. 456.
37   Ibid., IV.ii.10, p. 456.
38   *The Theory of Moral Sentiments*, VI.ii.2.13, p. 232.
39   *Wealth of Nations*, IV.vii.c.103, p. 638.
40   In his *Lectures on Jurisprudence* in 1762, Smith includes the right of commerce – i.e., "the right of trafficking with those who are willing to deal with him" – among the "natural rights of humanity." See Adam Smith, *Lectures on Jurisprudence*, ed. R. L. Meek, D. D. Raphael and P. G. Stein, Indianapolis: Liberty Fund, 1982; Oxford: Clarendon, 1978, A.i.11, p. 8.
41   *Wealth of Nations*, IV.VII.c.80, p. 627.
42   *Lectures on Jurisprudence*, A.i.13.8.
43   *Wealth of Nations*, IV.vii.c.108, p. 641.
44   Ibid., I.ii.2.
45   Immanuel Kant, *The Metaphysics of Morals* [1797], ed. Mary Gregor, Cambridge: Cambridge University Press, 1996, par. 62, p. 121.
46   Ibid.
47   Ibid., p. 30.
48   Ibid., p. 37.
49   Ibid., p. 43.
50   Ibid., p. 45.
51   Ibid., p. 45.
52   As the title of par. 8 in ibid., p. 44, suggests.
53   Ibid., par. 13, p. 50.
54   Ibid.
55   Ibid., p. 51.
56   "Moreover, in order to acquire land, is it necessary to develop it (build on it, cultivate it and so on)? No. For since these forms [of specification] are only accidents, they make no object of direct possession and can belong to what the subject possesses only insofar as the substance is already recognized as his" (ibid., p. 52; see also p. 55).
57   Ibid., p. 53.
58   "Perpetual peace," pp. 106–107.
59   Ibid., p. 106.

Apoikia and *colonia*

Smith's comments on the 'recent disturbances' in the colonies

Roberto Resende Simiqueli

The theoretical works of Adam Smith are inscribed in a far-reaching debate about human nature, representing the attempt at dialogue between a long tradition of British/Scottish moral philosophy, guided by the constitution of a particular model of economic subject, and the echoes of the reflection on social and political issues undertaken in the continent at his time. Challenging the mercantilist legacy, clearly perceptible in eighteenth-century England, Smith presents arguments that play a decisive role in the change of course on foreign and economic policies then applied by the British crown.

However, there are a number of discrepancies between the original formulation of these arguments and their incorporation into the political liberal lexicon in the mid-nineteenth century. Much of the theoretical work done by the author about the motives of the colonial system and its fundamental logic of action is lost amid the lobbying for the repeal of the Corn Laws and further liberalization of the Empire. We believe, in this sense, that revisiting some of the positions entertained by Smith on the history and situation of modern colonies would help us reconstitute some of the peculiarities of this specific moment in the history of liberal thought, especially if we take into account the gap formed between the *philosophe*'s treatment of the issue at hand and its incorporation into liberal political praxis.

The independence of the American colonies figures as one of the main topics of discussion among the enlightened Scots. Hume, even when gravely debilitated, a mere few months before his death, does not shy away from discussing the subject extensively. His references to the 'problems in America' in the letters he exchanged with William Strahan[1] and Baron Mure of Caldwell give several examples of the philosopher's position on the direction being taken by the Empire. As he writes to Strahan in October 1775:

> I must, before we part, have a little Stroke of Politics with you, notwithstanding my Resolution to the contrary. We hear that some of the Ministers have propos'd in Council, that both Fleet and Army be withdrawn from America, and these Colonists be left entirely to themselves. I wish I had been a Member of His Majesty's Cabinet Council, that, I might have seconded this Opinion. I should have said, that this Measure only anticipates the necessary Course of

Events a few Years; that a forced and every day more precarious Monopoly of about 6 or 700,000 Pounds a year of Manufactures, was not worth contending for; that we should preserve the greater part of this Trade even if the Ports of America were open to all Nations; that it was very likely, in our method of proceeding, that we should be disappointed in our Scheme of conquering the Colonies and that we ought to think beforehand how we were to govern them, after they were conquer'd . . . Let us, therefore, lay aside all Anger; shake hands, and part Friends. Or if we retain any anger, let it only be against ourselves for our past Folly; and against that wicked Madman, Pitt; who has reduced us to our present Condition.

(Hume 1888: 288–289)

The cautious tone that introduces Hume's inflamed critique of the hostilities can be explained by two factors. He and Strahan had stopped exchanging letters after a disagreement, resuming their friendship only after the latter made some timid advances. However, one other possible (and far more feasible) reason for the caution expressed here is the publisher's drastic change of political alignment at the end of his political career, when he replaced the Whig sympathies common to most of the illustrious Scottish gentlemen of the period with a solid defence of the Tories' treatment of colonial insubordination. The provocation at the end of the previous letter is not left unanswered in Strahan's reply:

But I differ from you, toto caelo, with regard to America. I am entirely for coercive methods with those obstinate madmen: And why should we despair of success? – Why should we suffer the Empire to be so dismembered, without the utmost exertions on our part? I see nothing so very formidable in this business, if we become a little more unanimous, and could stop the mouths of domestic traitors, from whence the evil originated. – Not that I wish to enslave the Colonists, or to make them one jot less happy than ourselves; but I am for keeping them subordinate to the British Legislature, and their trade in a reasonable degree subservient to the interest of the Mother Country; an advantage she well deserves, but which she must inevitably lose, if they are emancipated as you propose. I am really surprised you are of a different opinion.

(Hume 1888: 289)

Two elements are of particular interest in this response. First, the mention (albeit brief and possibly hasty) of the association between colonial domination and slavery gives us some idea of the echoes of the long debate on Scottish sovereignty throughout the eighteenth century. More important, however, is Strahan's recognition of the fundamental issues present in this dispute with America – colonial trade and the gains achieved through its customary means, primarily via taxation. A few days after this missive, Hume explains to Strahan what he considers to be the real losses incurred should the Empire lose control of the North American territories: 'but the worst effect of the loss of America, will not be the Detriment of our Manufactures, Which will be a mere trifle, or to our Navigation, Which will not be Considerable, but to the Credit and Reputation of Government, Which has already but too little Authority' (Hume 1888: 308). On another occasion, while defending the idea of granting independence to the American colonists to Baron Mure of Caldwell, Hume evokes once again the little difference that the loss of the colonies would make to English trade: 'I am American in my Principles, and wish we would let Them alone to govern or misgovern Themselves As They think proper: The Affair is of no Consequence, or of little Consequence to us' (Hume 2011: 303).[2]

Unable to discuss the issue in public, the philosopher is reduced to exchanging views on the War of Independence in the private sphere. Many of his contemporaries, however, did not hesitate to make use of the opportunity to launch pamphlets in defence of the Americans. Burke, defending ideas close to those of Hume, wrote in March 1775 that trade with the Americas amounted to one-third of the total maintained with the rest of the globe, so the hostilities were doing great damage to the British coffers (Burke 1999: 231).[3] Moreover, he would develop his reasoning on the political values common to Englishmen and Americans, seeking to attract the sympathy of his compatriots to the cause of independence. In his 'Speech on Conciliation with the Colonies', Burke states:

> In this character of the Americans, a love of freedom is the predominating feature which marks and distinguishes the whole: and as an ardent is always a jealous affection, your colonies become suspicious, restive, and untractable, whenever they see the least attempt to wrest from them by force, or shuffle from them by chicane, what they think the only advantage worth living for. This fierce spirit of liberty is stronger in the English colonies probably than in any other people of the earth; and this from a great variety of powerful causes; which, to understand the true temper of their minds, and the direction which this spirit takes, it will not be amiss to lay open somewhat more largely.
>
> (Burke 1999: 236)

Several pages later he adds:

> How long it will continue in this state, or what may arise out of this unheard-of situation, how can the wisest of us conjecture? Our late experience has taught us that many of those fundamental principles, formerly believed infallible, are either not of the importance they were imagined to be; or that we have not at all adverted to some other far more important and far more powerful principles, which entirely overrule those we had considered as omnipotent. I am much against any further experiments, which tend to put to the proof any more of these allowed opinions, which contribute so much to the public tranquillity. In effect, we suffer as much at home by this loosening of all ties, and this concussion of all established opinions, as we do abroad. For, in order to prove that the Americans have no right to their liberties, we are every day endeavouring to subvert the maxims which preserve the whole

spirit of our own. To prove that the Americans ought not to be free, we are obliged to depreciate the value of freedom itself; and we never seem to gain a paltry advantage over them in debate, without attacking some of those principles, or deriding some of those feelings, for which our ancestors have shed their blood.

(Burke 1999: 245)[4]

Smith, who did not share the habit of publishing political pamphlets common to most of the philosophers of this period, also studied the topic extensively. According to Donald Winch (1978: 146), in a thorough study of the political issues present in the work of the Scottish thinker, despite constant and dismissive references to the American Revolution as 'recent disturbances', there is sufficient reason to believe that the issue mattered much more to Smith than this offhand description implies. Over the years in London shortly before the publication of *The Wealth of Nations*, Smith would have devoted much of his time to discussion of the topic, deepening his knowledge of the War of Independence. The confirmation of that interest comes in a letter from Hume, sent on 8 February 1776:

The Duke of Bucleugh tells me, that you are very zealous in American Affairs. My Notion is, that the Matter is not so important as is commonly imagind. If I be mistaken, I shall probably correct my Error, when I see you or read you. Our Navigation and general Commerce may suffer more than our Manufactures. Shoud London fall as much in its Size, as I have done, it will be the better. It is nothing but a Hulk of bad and unclean Humours.

(Hume to Smith, in Smith 1987: 186)

Unlike Hume, Smith saw a central point of interest in the recent complications in America. To some extent, this interest could be explained by the advice given to Townshend on the taxation of the colonies in the 1760s (which would lead the author to see the revolution and the repression partially as consequences of his inability to foresee the results of the measures proposed), as advocated by Winch. Andrew Skinner (1976), on the other hand, reads Adam Smith's interpretation of the American colonies as an illustration of his theoretical precepts. This thesis is also supported by Pocock's (2006) view of the specific usefulness of history in the work of the Scottish philosopher – not as a field of autonomous interest or investigation, but as an explanatory device.

Both texts point, ultimately, to the treatment given by Ernest H. Benians to the Smithian project for the Empire, published in the first quarter of the twentieth century. Reassessing the trajectory of the British Empire in the decades following the publication of *The Wealth of Nations*, Benians problematizes the incorporation of some elements of Smithian analysis to the motivations of foreign and economic policy-makers, noting the strong adherence to the idea of liberalizing relationships with the colonial possessions without establishing lasting political links between the various "branches" of the Empire in the form of the system of colonial representatives advocated by Smith.

In the following pages, we try to shed some light not only on the peculiar reading of the Smithian critique of colonialism envisioned by Benians, but also on some of its structural problems. Although very thorough and well thought out, Benians' analysis leaves aside a few important components of Smithian thought and culminates in a series of conjectures that contribute little to the further development of the assertions raised.

1. Smith's critique of colonialism in historical perspective

Starting from the simultaneity between the publication of *The Wealth of Nations* and the Declaration of American Independence, E. H. Benians, a direct disciple of Alfred Marshall and Chair of Political Economy at Cambridge University in the 1920s, proposes to investigate the presence, in Smith's magnum opus, of a draft for a revision of the British Empire. Author of a paradigmatic critique of the colonial system, the Scottish thinker would have been responsible for making objective proposals to reformulate the mercantilist institutional framework towards a progressive "liberalization" of the Empire.

According to Benians, the proposal could be summarized in the moral opposition to colonial oppression and to the corporate privileges preserved in the overseas arms of the Empire. In his words,

> In place of this fictitious empire, with its lack of cohesion, its 'impertinent badges of slavery' on the colonies and its burdensome futility for the mother country, he proposed a close and equal union of Great Britain and her colonies – a united Parliament, a common system of taxation and complete freedom of trade within the empire – equality, in fact, of status, burden and opportunity between mother country and colony. The proposal entailed a complete departure from the old colonial system in certain fundamental matters to which either British or colonial opinion was firmly wedded – the abolition of the monopoly of colonial trade, a proportionate distribution of the burden of imperial defense and a proper representation of the colonies in the Parliament.
>
> (Benians 1925: 251)

From this passage, we can draw both the motivations for the revision of this 'fictitious Empire' and what Benians understands as the normative proposal developed by Smith. The critique of the colonial system would remain centred on three distinct problems – lack of political cohesion, unequal relations between the colonies and the Empire and the excessive expenditure involved in its maintenance – issues that were representative of the political and economic dilemmas faced by the metropolitan administration. The trajectory of this endeavour is briefly outlined by the Scottish *philosophe* as following from its origin in the overseas initiatives of the Iberian powers. Highlighting the foundations of the Spanish colonial enterprise, Smith observes the ends presented by Columbus to the Council of Castile as justification for their activities in the New World: the acquisition of bullion, mineral wealth manifest in gold and silver, directly from its source. In the author's words,

> a project of conquest gave occasion to all the establishments of the Spaniards in those newly discovered countries. The motive which excited Them to this conquest was a project of gold and silver mines; and a course of accidents, the human wisdom which could foresee, rendered this project much more successful than the undertakers had any reasonable grounds for expecting.
>
> (Smith 1976: IV.vii.21)

Based on the problems involved in the establishment of the first colonies on American soil, Smith examines the paths leading to the diverging situation of the territories occupied by the following migratory waves. The abundant land available in the North American colonies as well as little-to-no government interference in their internal regulations are seen as elements that contributed to their fortune, independent of (and, to some extent, contrary to) the designs of modern states toward the New World:

> In the plenty of good land, the European colonies established in America and the West Indies resemble, and even greatly surpass, those of ancient Greece. In their dependency upon the mother state, they resemble those of ancient Rome; but their great distance from Europe has in all of them alleviated more or less the effects of this dependency. Their situation has placed them less in the view and less in the power of their mother country. In pursuing their interest their own way, their conduct has, upon many occasions, been over-looked, either because not known or not understood in Europe; and upon some occasions it has been fairly suffered and submitted to, because their distance rendered it difficult to restrain it . . . The progress of all the European colonies in wealth, population, and improvement, has accordingly been very great.
>
> (Smith 1976: IV.vii.6)

In this passage, it is clear how the continuity given to the *proposed* intervention of European mercantile powers in the colonial territories associated with the *impossibility* of maintaining this same course of action allowed settlers to pursue their own interests. If these territories thrived, they thrived *in spite of*, not *because of*, the efforts of the mercantilist powers to strengthen their control over the colonies. And it is on the charges arising from the successive attempts of interference that lies the harshest criticism put forth by Smith to the trade monopolies to which the North American territories were victim. Discussing the possibilities of taxation of occupied territories, they demonstrate, based on the costs involved in colonial business, how a significant portion of these was primarily destined to defend the conquered overseas territories and preserve their political subordination, while a relatively small amount was channelled into establishing a structure devoted to the administration of local affairs. According to Smith,

> The English colonists have never yet contributed any thing towards the defence of the mother country, or towards the support of its civil government. They themselves, on the contrary, have hitherto been defended almost entirely at the expence of the mother country. But the expence of fleets and armies is out of all proportion greater than the necessary expence of civil government. The expence of their own civil government has always been very moderate ... The most important part of the expence of government, indeed, that of defence and protection, has constantly fallen upon the mother country.
>
> (Smith 1976: IV.vii.20)

With the expenses involved in maintaining the English navy, the colonies represented to Smith a system that was not only inefficient but also directly opposed to the mercantile logic that motivated government actions in this field. It is proven, in his reasoning, without the need to discuss the economic validity of the goal of accumulating mineral wealth, that the colonial system appears more as a source of political instability and expense than income for the state.

Benians reflects upon these criticisms in his analysis, focusing on the perspective of the autonomy of the locals against the inability of the British colonial administration to maintain the cohesion of the whole and its fragility, in the great game of international politics:

> There was the effective collaboration of its different parts for purposes of defense. Local liberty had far outrun imperial organization. There was no adequate central control. An antiquated and ill-adapted machinery, the confusion of Authorities, the number of rights Exercised and resented, with the vague and disputed power of Parliament in the background – such were the means of colonial government.
>
> (Benians 1925: 254)

Given the reasons for the crisis of this system, Benians makes clear those he considers to be the referrals suggested by Smith for its reformulation; these depended on the abolition of colonial monopolies, and the opening of channels of representation in Parliament (Benians 1925: 270). The link between these two proposals and the rest of the work is evident. The colonial monopolies are understood, economically, as one of the central causes of the structural inefficiency of relations maintained by the British Empire with its possessions under the colonial system, unable to compensate for the expense that is necessary to defend the territories or contribute to the enrichment of the nation. Nothing could be more reasonable, in this logic, than proposing its dissolution. However, the second measure deserves special attention. In it resides the main intellectual innovation of this so-called project of an Empire, which would represent, to the author, the theoretical singularity of the review undertaken throughout Book IV. To what extent can we imagine the continued link between metropolis and colony subtracted from its central determinant, the colonial monopolies? And how ensuring political representation to the colonists might contain the impending crisis?

To Benians, the Smithian proposal could be understood as a pioneering way of rethinking the Empire's budget. If the American colonies had potential for economic development, rather than focusing on the gains of the traditional commercial companies, it would be wise to invest in creating an institutional framework that favoured direct taxation of colonial products. And the first step on this path would involve granting parliamentary seats to the colonists' representatives – an idea advocated not only by Smith but also by Benjamin Franklin, Thomas Pownall and James Otis, among others. For the Americans to accept the heavy tariffs, it would be necessary for them to join the Empire not as the submissive population of a distant land, the result of territorial conquest and expropriation subject to political/economic terms in its most barbaric form. The expectations gravitated toward full citizenship, sharing the rights – and responsibilities – of their 'compatriots' in the British Isles. The abolition of monopolies can be reinterpreted, then, not as the means to eliminate one of the reasons for the Empire's economic inefficiency, but as one of the steps of the solution proposed by Smith to the dilemmas faced by the old colonial system in its final phase, based on establishing political equality between colony and metropolis.

In the final pages of the chapter that is devoted to these issues, Smith presents his ideas about the representation of the colonies in Parliament in clear terms:

> The parliament of Great Britain insists upon taxing the colonies; and they refuse to be taxed by a parliament in which they are not represented. If to each colony, which should detach itself from the general confederacy, Great Britain should allow such a number of representatives as suited the proportion of what it contributed to the publick revenue of the empire, in consequence of its being subjected to the same taxes, and in compensation admitted to the same freedom of trade with its fellow-subjects at home . . . Unless this or some other method is fallen upon, and there seems to be none more obvious than this, of preserving the importance and of gratifying the ambition of the leading men of America, it is not very probable that they will ever voluntarily submit to us; and we ought to consider that the blood which must be shed in forcing them to do so, is, every drop of it, the blood either of those who are, or of those whom we wish to have for our fellow-citizens.
>
> (Smith 1976: IV.vii.75)

The impact of this proposal on the debates on British colonial policy is carefully monitored by Benians, with the conclusion (with some regret) that of the two propositions, only the prognostic concerning abandoning the colonial trade monopolies has been followed in accordance with its original proposal. The author lists many reasons why this first prospect for a 'brotherhood of nations' in the terms of what was supposedly devised by Smith, with equal representation of the settlers in the British Parliament, ends up falling into oblivion. The central justification, however, refers once again to the discussion of colonialism in moral terms. Benians sees the vested interests and the attachment of the people on both sides of the Atlantic to their own political institutions as the main obstacle to integration between Britain and its American colonies:

> The adaptation and attachment of people on both sides of the Atlantic to the political life and institutions they had shaped for themselves could not be lightly dismissed as prejudice. Reason and logic and the necessity of the hour might be on the side of a bold reconstruction of the empire, but history could furnish no appropriate parallel or encouraging precedent, and the stream of English tradition had run for long in another channel.
>
> (Benians 1925: 264)

Benians sees in Smith's draft for the restructuring of the English colonies a model of politically progressive representation and international integration, claiming it was at several times a proposal 'way ahead of his time'. When this programme approaches its completion, in the 1850s, it has already taken an altogether different form. By this time, 'the Empire had become a league of nations, comprising vast dependencies in varying stages of political development, and his unit could only be conceived in other terms and maintained properly its new form and spirit' (Benians 1925: 270) The proposed integration policy through a central representative structure was no longer on the horizon of British MPs, and the alternative to the 'Old Empire' could not go much beyond a chaotic whole composed of separate political possessions, with little in common beyond the demarcation by the 'red lines'.

Focusing on the presentation of an alternative to modern colonialism in Smith's interpretation, Benians has the merit to tread an unusual path amongst the hundreds of readers of one of the theoretical pillars of classical political economy. His analysis, gifted with a large degree of originality, distances itself from conventional interpretations of the Scottish thinker and the attachment to Books I and II of his great work, the core of his theory of value and home to a large extent of the 'clichés' and recurrent commonplace quotes that are representative of the myth built around the historical figure of the author.[5]

However, we believe the analytical perspective advocated by Ernest Benians to be marred by a few shortcomings. By focusing on the arguments presented in the last pages of chapter VII, the author misses the broader picture of the critique proposed by Smith to modern colonialism, and leaves out the specific form of its presentation, endowed with its own peculiarities. We believe that the structure of the chapter in question would have precious indications of the meaning intended by Smith to his propositions (and his draft on the revision of the Empire), beyond the formal representation proposal outlined by Benians. Additionally, the Cambridge economist loses sight of some of the specific objectives of this project, to stick mainly to the *moral* dimension of the Smithian arguments, which are also developed in *political*, *economic* and *strategic* terms.

2. *Apoikia* and *colonia:* the role of colonialism in the writing of Book IV

There appears to be a stark methodological contrast between the first books of *The Wealth of Nations* and the statements developed by the author with respect to the colonial system. If, during his musings on the social division of labour, the role of individual liberties in the wealth of a nation and his theory of value, Smith focuses on the *moral* conditions of the propensity of individuals to work and exchange – the search for personal gain and satisfaction as the driving force of economic behaviour – in Books III and IV the central issue seems to be presented in *historical* and *political* terms. The transition from the analysis of the performance of *individuals* to *nations* requires more than a change of scope, impacting upon the text's structure, its presentation and especially the position of many analytical variables that are present in the Smithian theoretical system. There is some consensus among analysts on crediting this change to the time the author spent in France and to the influence of a circle of London intellectuals who were present as he wrote and revised the last chapters. Salim Rashid locates in the period between 1774 and the actual publication of the book Smith's review of the passages on the colonies. Throughout this period, the Scottish thinker would have deepened his contact with the writings of the Reverend Josiah Tucker, who also dealt with the issue of the then 'comprehensible' separation between America and Britain. In the author's words,

> If we remember that Smith left for London in 1774 planning to get the *Wealth of Nations* published but revised it over three years paying special attention to the colonial question (according to his biographer), there seems good circumstantial evidence to suggest that Tucker influenced Smith. The greater political prescience of Tucker is clearly seen by the fact that in the first edition of the *Wealth of Nations*, Smith refers to the colonial conflicts as the 'late disturbances' in the colonies. Smith clearly expected the disturbances to be over by the time his book was published in the spring of 1776.
>
> (Rashid 1982: 456–457)

Dalphy Fagerstrom, in turn, contextualizes the interest in political dilemmas relevant to the binomial colony–Empire as a consequence of some peculiar passages from the biography of Smith – his association with the merchants of Glasgow during his stay in that city, from 1751 to 1764, the questions posed to Scotland as part of the Union and the relationship with Benjamin Franklin play an essential role in changing Smith's disposition. In any case, the adoption of a peculiar methodological approach is clearly noticeable throughout Book IV but especially in chapter VII: the contrast between classical, Greco-Roman colonialism and the course taken by modern colonial enterprises.

The most significant demonstrations of the uses of this peculiar view of history are, not coincidentally, in the sections where Benians focuses his analysis. Divided into three parts – 'Of the Motives for establishing new Colonies', 'Causes of Prosperity of new Colonies' and 'Of the Advantages which Europe has derived from the Discovery of America, and from that of a Passage to the East Indies by the Cape of Good Hope' – chapter VII starts with a digression about the nature of Greek and Roman colonies. According to the *philosophe*, the manifestations of colonialism in these two empires were profoundly different. As for the Greeks, he argues that:

> The mother city, though she considered the colony as a child, at all times entitled to great favour and assistance, and owing in return much gratitude and respect, yet considered it as an emancipated child, over whom she pretended to claim no direct authority or jurisdiction. The colony settled its own form of government, enacted its own laws, elected its own magistrates, and made peace or war with its neighbours as an independent state, which had no occasion to wait for the approbation or consent of the mother city. Nothing can be more plain and distinct than the interest which directed every such establishment.
>
> (Smith 1976: IV.vii.2)

As for the Romans, Smith saw at the origins of the republic the reasons for the establishment of a colonial system that was very different from that applied by the Greek city-states. Being that Rome, 'like most of the other ancient republics, was originally founded upon an Agrarian law which divided the public territory in a certain proportion among the different citizens who composed the state' (Smith 1976: IV.vii.3), incurred in the need of constant acquisition of new territories to maintain the strata of wealthy landowners on favourable economic and political terms, given the gradual fragmentation of private property by marriage, inheritance and succession. Following the same logic, the Roman Empire was governed through explicitly interventionist practices, derived from a model defined by centralization of political and economic power between colonies and the sprawling metropolis, the imperial core of public life. Regarding the establishment of Roman populations into new territories following this model, Smith would claim that

> [Rome] assigned them lands generally in the conquered provinces of Italy, where, being within the dominions of the republick, they could never form any independent state; but were at best but a sort of corporation, which, though it had the power of enacting bye-laws for its own government, was at all times subject to the correction, jurisdiction, and legislative authority of the mother city. The sending out a colony of this kind, not only gave some satisfaction to the people, but often established a sort of garrison too in a newly conquered province, of which the obedience might otherwise have been doubtful. A Roman colony, therefore, whether we consider the nature of the establishment itself, or the motives for making it, was altogether different from a Greek one.
>
> (Smith 1976: IV.vii.3)

Such is, for Smith, the difference between the two 'ideal types' of old colonialism that he dedicates a central part of the chapter to discussing the two words used by

Greeks and Romans to denominate their 'colonies': *apoikia* (αποιχια) 'signifies a separation of dwelling, a departure from home, a going out of the house', while the Roman *colonia* 'is simply a *plantation*' (Smith 1976: IV.vii.3). The distinction, elementary as it may seem, is evoked (albeit subtly) on several pages that are devoted to dealing with the evils of market exclusivity and the formation of colonies by modern nations, providing the *ideal* plan for the analysis of the political and economic *realities* of mercantilist Europe.

Still in Book IV, Smith details some of the peculiarities of the Northern colonies that would confer on them the status of 'positive' colonies, thus closer to the ideal expressed in Greek colonialism. Among these, worth mentioning is the 'absence' of an exclusive trade relationship between the territories and a specific trading company, considered deeply harmful to the possessions of other empires. 'Under so liberal a policy the colonies are enabled both to sell their own produce and to buy the goods of Europe at a reasonable price', states Smith, adding that 'this has always been the policy of England' (Smith 1976: IV.vii.24). The twist comes in one of the subsequent passages dealing with genres and capabilities arising from the American trade, since the main commodities traded by these territories would be 'grain of all sorts, lumber, salt provisions, fish, sugar and rum' (Smith 1976: IV.vii.26), all of which are necessary for the promotion and maintenance of British naval activities. The fishing activities undertaken by the settlers, for example, are extremely well regarded by the author:

> To increase the shipping and naval power of Great Britain, by the extension of the fisheries of our colonies, is an object which the legislature seems to have had almost constantly in view. Those fisheries, upon this account, have had all the encouragement which freedom can give them, and they have flourished accordingly. The New England fishery in particular was, before the late disturbances, one of the most important, perhaps, in the world. The whale-fishery which, notwithstanding an extravagant bounty, is in Great Britain carried on to so little purpose, that in the opinion of many people (which I do not, however, pretend to warrant) the whole produce does not much exceed the value of the bounties which are annually paid for it, is in New England carried on without any bounty to a very great extent. Fish is one of the principal articles with which the North Americans trade to Spain, Portugal, and the Mediterranean.
>
> (Smith 1976: IV.vii.30)

This passage provides a clear example of what we seek with a review of the position taken by Smith on the colonial system. Referring to the development of fisheries in the American colonies, he states an important principle of his system of free trade, often overlooked by interpreters focused on principles governing the behaviour and motivations of rational agents or the debate on trade liberalization: the role that *military or naval strategy* played in the adoption of liberal policies in *The Wealth of Nations*. The liberties given to settlers and colonists to pursue the activities for which the recently occupied territories demonstrated natural predispositions that are meritorious not only when judged by the principles of the moral defence of self-interests as an ideal but also when Smith considers the professional capabilities of the colonial workforce, trained in a vast assortment of skills related to building and manning ships. These individuals could be relied upon by the British navy in times of need. A similar situation is observed with respect to the timber trade between the New World and the British Isles, although in this case the interest in commercialization is due mainly to a grant maintained by the crown. The British dependency on raw materials for its shipbuilding industry is notorious, and has always represented one of the strategic reasons present in the occupation of the American territories. Interestingly, Smith sees in this case of intervention very positive results for the development of the colonies as autonomous economies,

> the tendency of some of these regulations to raise the value of timber in America, and thereby to facilitate the clearing of the land, was neither, perhaps, intended nor understood by the legislature. Though their beneficial effects, however, have been in this respect accidental, they have not upon that account been less real.
>
> (Smith 1976: IV.vii.38)

In this sense, the Greek *apoikia* is once again preferable to the Roman *colonia*, if we follow the opposition proposed by Smith at the beginning of the chapter. By promoting the autonomy of local populations, government authorities would ensure their involvement in activities that would eventually give the metropolis the necessary resources to maintain British power on the international stage – able crews and raw materials for shipbuilding, for example – by easing the monopolies and regulations adopted by the mother country. The Latin *colonia*, on the other hand, represents a demeaning structure, for which exorbitant expenses simply could not be compensated, since the strategic advantages of colonial possession would be spent on the maintenance of an organized, repressive force to keep colonists in line, should the need arise. In Smith's view, this not only acts against the colonies, but against Great Britain itself, existing only to tend to the interests of a specific 'conspiracy against the public', to quote a memorable phrase from the first books. In this sense, rather than a condemnation of colonialism per se, Smith's attack on the colonial monopolies is a critique of a *specific form of colonialism*; concomitantly, alternatives to this peculiar (and inefficient) structure are presented through the several proposals grouped under his liberal review of the Empire.

More than moral constraints, Smith focuses on the political and economic developments of colonial domination to justify its abandonment – and the justification for the contraposition to the classical case arises specifically from the emphasis given to these conditions. Understanding his defence of liberalism as analogous to the autonomy enjoyed by the Greek *apoikia* in face of its mother city, Smith proceeds by demonstrating how the freedom of the 'small nations' of ancient Greece would be worthwhile not only morally but (especially) in pragmatic terms. The defence of free trade is developed here somewhat beyond the self-centred, tautological, categorically positive ideal of *laissez-faire*: the abandonment of the archaic set of mercantilist economic policies could be understood as choosing a more appropriate system to consolidate British international primacy.

The part of the chapter in question that is devoted to the benefits reaped by Europe through colonial trade is emblematic in this sense. Smith initially considers that colonization undertaken by the European powers would have provided a general increase in its inhabitants' satisfaction, given the huge variety of goods placed in their consumption patterns, adding this factor to a significant increase in economic activity, given the intensity of the commercial traffic between the newly occupied territories and the production centres of the Old World. However, considering that the exclusive trade maintained by the colonizers would eventually decrease the satisfaction and the activity of the whole, but especially the colonies, its effects would be detrimental to the collectivity, albeit amid specific and considerable gains for a few parties involved in the colonial trade.

Interestingly, the first of these items discussed by the author are the *military reinforcement* and *revenue increase* provided by the colonies. Revisiting the differences between the Greek and Roman models of colonialism, he states that 'the Roman colonies furnished occasionally both the one and the other', while 'the Greek colonies, sometimes, furnished a military force, but seldom any revenue' (Smith 1976: IV.vii.11), to then strengthen the parallels between the ideal of the Roman *colonia* and modern European colonies, which 'have never yet furnished any military force for the defense of the mother country', since 'their military force has never yet been sufficient for their own defense' (Smith 1976: IV.vii.12). Moreover, the defence of those territories represented a permanent distraction for the military forces of each nation involved, which would constitute yet another burden to the empire in question.

On the revenues resulting from colonial trade, Smith is careful to distinguish between the positive and negative aspects of the relationship between the colonies and the metropolis. In his words,

> We must carefully distinguish between the effects of the colony trade and those of the monopoly of that trade. The former are always and necessarily beneficial; the latter always and necessarily hurtful. But the former are so beneficial, that the colony trade, though subject to a monopoly, and notwithstanding the hurtful effects of that monopoly, is still upon the whole beneficial, and greatly beneficial; though a good deal less so than it otherwise would be.
>
> (Smith 1976: IV.vii.47)

According to this reasoning, as long as the Northern colonies remained under the Greek model, a significant portion of the disadvantages could be avoided while the positive aspects remained present.

We believe that much of the argument developed by Smith not only in this chapter but throughout Book IV as a whole moves in this direction. The definitions and examples extracted from the ancient world are not employed merely to provide a classic tone to these passages. Instead, they provide a welcome contribution to Smith's thesis: a clear demonstration of how excessive regulations from the Empire not only harm and hinder the colony's development but also contribute to compromising the metropolis politically. It is in this spirit that the effective review of the terms of representation of the colonies is presented. This, however, comes with more than a little scepticism:

> To propose that Great Britain should voluntarily give up all authority over her colonies, and leave them to elect their own magistrates, to enact their own laws, and to make peace and war as they might think proper, would be to propose such a measure as never was, and never will be adopted, by any nation in the world.
>
> (Smith 1976: IV.vii.66)

As many reasons as there might be for maintaining colonial dominion over overseas territories (most of them private, in the views entertained by Smith), there are several crucial reasons for abandoning it:

> If it was adopted, however, Great Britain would not only be immediately freed from the whole annual expence of the peace establishment of the colonies, but might settle with them such a treaty of commerce as would effectually secure to her a free trade, more advantageous to the great body of the people, though less so to the merchants, than the monopoly which she at present enjoys. By thus parting good friends, the natural affection of the colonies to the mother country, which, perhaps, our late dissentions have well nigh extinguished, would quickly revive. It might dispose them not only to respect, for whole centuries together, that treaty of commerce which they had concluded with us at parting, but to favour us in war as well as in trade, and, instead of turbulent and factious subjects, to become our most faithful, affectionate, and generous allies; and the same sort of parental affection on the one side, and filial respect on the other, might revive between Great Britain and her colonies, which used to subsist between those of ancient Greece and the mother city from which they descended.
>
> (Smith 1976: IV.vii.66)

This remains the clearest indication of the relationship between political autonomy and military support of the liberated colonies. Instead of the bonds of slavery that would only aggravate potential hostilities with other countries (since the colonists would always be willing to tip the scales in favour of an eventual aggressor in the hope of thus acquiring freedom from the metropolis), Smith sees the very likely chance of liberated colonies joining the mother nation out of 'filial respect' and the bonds cemented by a common cultural background. At a different level, this takes us again to Benians' position. It can be seen, by now, that the project for adding colonial representatives to the British Parliament arises not entirely from moral inspiration, but, in a way, as a compromise solution between metropolitan aristocracy and colonial elites. The distinction is crucial – here, we see how a *strategic imperative* could be considered the paramount guide behind the establishment of morally sound political practices.

In light of this reassessment of the arguments discussed by Benians and some neglected points of the chapter in question, a few of the terms in which we disagree become clearer. First, having set aside the terminology used in the *presentation* of the critique of modern colonialism, Benians loses sight of the conciliatory nature of the Smithian proposal for colonial representation – fruit of the virtual impossibility of proposing abolition of colonial ties when he is writing. More than a thinker 'ahead of his time', we can say that Smith foresees the foreseeable, or imagines the imaginable – his reflection on the colonies belongs to the context in which he writes, and it attempts to address the specific problems within this scenario. More than formulating 'principles of imperial government regarded as applicable in all circumstances' (Benians 1925: 268), what we have here is a pragmatic response to an objective demand, then open to the pantheon of political, economic and moral thinkers of England and Scotland.

Thinking about the historical context in which *The Wealth of Nations* is published gives us another measure of circumstances in which the ambience of the Scottish Enlightenment and the debacle of the rule over the Northern colonies influence the author. Writing at the very moment of crisis and collapse of the structural foundations of the ancient colonial system, the work can be seen as an analysis born of the spirit of its time, and the transition from the decaying mercantilist conception of economics and politics to the liberal order in consolidation. It is interesting to think how, in this context, the effort Smith puts into describing the political and economic issues involved in preserving the control exercised over the colonies (the impossibility of maintaining the original project of making use of the colonies as a source of metallic wealth, the complications inherent in maintaining military control over overseas populations, the huge degree of political instability present in metropolitan–colonial relations) can be read as one of the certificates of the collapse of mercantilism as a theoretical perspective and its institutional apparatus as a system. If the writings of Smith bequeath to the next century something like a 'project of empire', it is important to understand that this is not manifest in objective terms. More than the paragraphs in which the idea of colonial representation is developed, the main theoretical legacy left by the Scottish thinker for proponents of British foreign policy is the understanding of a *strategic*[6] dimension of free trade, and how the adoption and promotion of this could benefit Britain internationally.[7]

Acknowledgements

This paper expands on some of the themes discussed in my Master's thesis, defended in 2012 at the *Universidade Estadual de Campinas – Unicamp*, under the title *Entre as nações e o império – Smith, Cobden e os rumos do liberalismo britânico* (*Between the Nations and the Empire – Smith, Cobden and the development of British liberalism*), made possible by a Capes scholarship. Preliminary drafts have been presented (in Portuguese) at meetings of the *Associação Brasileira de Pesquisadores em História Econômica*, in 2009 and 2012, and at the *Revista de Economia Política e História Econômica*, in 2014. I would like to thank Lígia Maria Osório Silva, Eduardo Barros Mariutti, Paulo Sérgio Fracalanza and Reginaldo Carmello Corrêa de Moraes, from Unicamp, for the continual support and high-level contributions, and Mark Spencer, from Brock University, for his warm welcome at the ECSSS meeting.

Notes

1   A close friend of several of the Scottish *philosophes*, Member of Parliament and the editor responsible for publishing not only Hume's works, but those of Smith and Gibbon. Although the publisher established bonds of friendship with some of the leaders of the independence movement – such as Benjamin Franklin, whose acquaintance he made on the basis of common editorial interests – Strahan demonstrates a clear antipathy towards the insurrection.

2   Hume's treatment of the question arises, in great measure, from his previous writings on British commerce (and the need to avoid state intervention in commercial life). On this topic, Livingston (2009 and 2010), Gallegos (1998) and Danford (2006) provide interesting perspectives.

3   The risk of inflicting damage to human and natural resources is also mentioned: 'A further objection to force is, that you impair the object by your very endeavours to preserve it. The thing you fought for is not the thing which you recover; but depreciated, sunk, wasted, and consumed in the contest. Nothing less will content me, than whole America. I do not choose to consume its strength along with our own; because in all parts it is the British strength that I consume. I do not choose to be caught by a foreign enemy at the end of this exhausting conflict; and still less in the midst of it. I may escape; but I can make no insurance against such an event. Let me add, that I do not choose wholly to break the American spirit; because it is the spirit that has made the country' (Hume 1888: 236).

4   Besides Hume and Burke, Ferguson also comments on the War of Independence. However, his positions are in the vein of a defence of British intervention within and control over the rebellious territories. For an appraisal of his debate with Price, after the armistice is signed, see Hamowy (2006).

5   Warren S. Gramm develops upon the concentration of interpretations of *The Wealth of Nations* on its first two books, debating its reasons and consequences. According to Gramm: 'Of the 1.438 pages written by Adam Smith in his two major published works, only a few lines from several pages of the *Wealth of Nations* are regularly mentioned in orthodox economics texts. These are the statements on division of labor, paradox of value, the invisible hand, and the functions of government. On these grounds, he is known primarily for rationalizing individual self-interest as the necessary, strategic medium for promoting economic welfare. Yet it may be argued that a correct understanding of Smith's perspective leads to the opposite conclusion. That is, when his life's work is considered as a unit, his political-economic perspective is seen to be social, not primarily individualistic, and his major contributions to economic analysis involve elucidation of economic growth' (Gramm 1980: 120).

6   The conception of mercantilism as a power system, found in the seminal analysis of Eli Heckscher, leads us to think about how the liberal order filled the spaces left by the

absolutist states. As Gustav Schmoller writes, 'in its innermost kernel, it is nothing but state making' (Schmoller 1989: 50). Although Smithian economic liberalism did not present the military strengthening of a given nation as a primary objective, this stands out as one of its indirect results, which is nevertheless taken into account by the author.

7   The direction taken by the Empire as well as the relationship between free trade and the maintenance of British hegemony throughout the nineteenth century are masterfully discussed by Gallagher and Robinson (1953). The theoretical developments of the authors engaged in the Gallagher and Cain–Hopkins debates, dealing with the consequences of this thesis in its original formulation, help us to understand the reason for the non-completion of the project initiated by Benians – the possibility of maintaining British rule overseas without the need for political representation in return. For a thorough discussion of the debate on free trade and empire, see Gallagher and Robinson (1953), Cain and Hopkins (1980), Semmel (1970) and Simiqueli (2011).

Bibliography

Benians, E. A. (1925) 'Adam Smith's Project of an Empire', *Cambridge Historical Journal*, 3:249–283.

Broadie, A. (2007) *The Scottish Enlightenment: The Historical Age of the Historical Nation.* Edinburgh: Birlinn.

Broadie, A. (ed.) (2003) *The Cambridge Companion to the Scottish Enlightenment.* Cambridge: Cambridge University Press.

Burke, E. (1999) 'Speech of Edmund Burke, Esq., on Moving His Resolutions for Conciliation with the Colonies', in *Select Works of Edmund Burke: A New Imprint of the Payne Edition.* Indianapolis: Liberty Fund.

Cain, P. J. and Hopkins, A. G. (1980) 'The Political Economy of British Expansion Overseas, 1750–1914', *Economic History Review* (New Series), 33(4):463–490.

Danford, J. W. (2006) 'Getting our bearings: Machiavelli and Hume', in Paul Anthony Rahe (ed.), *Machiavelli's Liberal Republican Legacy.* Cambridge: Cambridge University Press.

Fletcher, A. (2011) *A Discourse of Government with Relation to Militias.* Charleston, SC: Nabu Press.

Gallagher, J. and Robinson, R. (1953) 'The Imperialism of Free Trade', *Economic History Review* (New Series), 1:1–15.

Gallegos, J. (1998) *Hume and Revolution: Twenty-fifth Conference of the Hume Society. University of Stirling – Stirling, Scotland, July 20–24, 1998.* Available online at: www.bu.edu/wcp/Papers/Poli/PoliGall.htm, accessed 25 May 2016.

Gramm, W. (1980) 'The Selective Interpretation of Adam Smith', *Journal of Economics Issues*, 1:119–142.

Haakonsen, K. (ed.) (2006) *The Cambridge Companion to Adam Smith.* Cambridge: Cambridge University Press.

Hamowy, R. (2006) 'Scottish Thought and the American Revolution: Adam Ferguson's Response to Richard Price', in David Womersely (ed.), *Liberty and American Experience in the Eighteenth Century.* Indianapolis: Liberty Fund.

Hecksher, E. F. (1994) *Mercantilism.* London: Routledge.

Hume, D. (1888) *Letters of David Hume to William Strahan.* Oxford: Clarendon Press.

Hume, D. (2011) *The Letters of David Hume*, Volume II: *1766–1776*, ed. J. Y. T. Greig. Oxford: Oxford University Press.

Livingston, D. (2009) 'David Hume and the Conservative Tradition', *Intercollegiate Review*, 44(2):30–41.

Livingston, D. (2010) 'David Hume and the Republican Tradition of Human Scale', *Arator: A Journal of Southern History, Thought, and Culture*, 1(1). Available at: www. theimaginativeconservative.org/2011/03/david-hume-and-republican-tradition-of.html, accessed 26 April 2016.

Long, D. (2006) 'Adam Smith's Politics', in K. Haakonsen (ed.), *The Cambridge Companion to Adam Smith*. Cambridge: Cambridge University Press.

Olz-Salzberger, F. (2003) 'The Political Theory of the Scottish Enlightenment', in A. Broadie (ed.), *The Cambridge Companion to the Scottish Enlightenment*. Cambridge: Cambridge University Press.

Pocock, J. G. A. (2006) 'Adam Smith and History', in K. Haakonsen (ed.), *The Cambridge Companion to Adam Smith*. Cambridge: Cambridge University Press.

Rashid, S. (1982) '"He Startled . . . as if He Saw a Spectre": Tucker's Proposal for American Independence', *Journal of the History of Ideas*, 3:439–460.

Schmoller, G. (1989) *The Mercantile System and Its Historical Significance*. Fairfield, NJ: Augustus M. Kelley.

Semmel, B. (1970) *The Rise of Free Trade Imperialism: Classical Political Economy, the Empire of Free Trade and Imperialism 1750–1850*. Cambridge: Cambridge University Press.

Simiqueli, R. (2011) 'Imperialismo do Livre-Comércio: elites, capitalismo financeiro e hegemonia internacional das teses Gallagher–Robinson e Cain–Hopkins', *Revista de Geopolítica*, 2(2). Available at: www.revistageopolitica.com.br/index.php/revistageo politica/article/view/35/34, accessed 26 April 2016.

Skinner, A. S. (1976) 'Adam Smith and the American Economic Community: An Essay in Applied Economics', *Journal of the History of Ideas*, 1:59–78.

Smith, A. (1976) *An Inquiry into the Nature and Causes of the Wealth of Nations*, ed. R. H. Campbell and A. S. Skinner. Oxford: Oxford University Press; Glasgow edition.

Smith, A. (1987) *Correspondence of Adam Smith*, ed. E. C. Mossner and I. S. Ross. Oxford: Oxford University Press; 2nd Glasgow edition.

Winch, D. (1978) *Adam Smith's Politics: An Essay in Historiographic Revision*. Cambridge: Cambridge University Press.

Smith on the colonialism and republicanism of the moderns compared with that of the ancients

Barry Stocker

Smith's account of colonialism is in some dimensions an account of republic-anism, differentiating between Greek, Roman, and modern models. The Greek model is one of overseas colonies that are independent of the original republic though tied to it by family type relations (*WN* IV.vii.a.2 and IV.vii.c.66). The Roman model is one of the extension of the territory of the original republic, so that it is a case of that republic expanding in size rather than founding new republics in a loose family (*WN* IV.vii.a.iii). In both cases, colonialism is a way of dealing with a population that appears excessive in relation to the resources of the home republic. The modern model (*WN* IV.vii), or that aspect which Smith draws attention to, is the overseas commercial empire where colonies are largely founded to further mercantilist schemes which aim, if misguidedly, to secure economic benefits for the home state. Modern colonialism is often undertaken by states of a monarchical character rather than a republican character, but the issues of a republic, and associated concerns with liberty and government by consent of the people, arise, even in the most monarchical colonising powers, in the negative sense of what reinforces anti-republican government. Smith does not present a clear commitment to republicanism as a principle of government, and certainly does not deny the legitimacy of monarchical governments, or deny the possibility of progress in liberty and prosperity under a monarchy. Nevertheless, there is a preference for republicanism, if more as an underlying assumption than an explicitly argued claim. This preference for republicanism emerges most clearly in his account of modern colonialism, since it is here that the destructive effects of monarchy and of the political power of economic elites, what was classically known as oligarchy, are most clear to the people so governed.

The account of colonialism in *An Inquiry into the Nature and Causes of the Wealth of Nations* is itself part of an account of mercantilism (*WN* IV), the product of monarchical and oligarchic distortions of government, which try to reserve economic benefits for the politically privileged sectors of the community. Mercantilism in international commerce and colonialism itself has levels of injustice combined with economically self-destructive action. The worst is the Spanish (and Portuguese) colonisation of South and Central America, a form of direct grasping of economic resources by the crown in the colonising country, with economically destructive effects all round, except for the crown and those closest to it (*WN* IV.vii.a and IV.vii.b) – that is, the monarchical colonisation of what is now known as Latin America.

The best is the British colonisation of North America (*WN* I.viii.26, III.i.5 and IV.vii.b.15–21), which has allowed the formation of self-governing republics with no hereditary aristocracy, as Smith emphasises with considerable republican enthusiasm, which is one reason to be cautious (Rasmussen 2008) with regard to claims that modern liberalism in Smith and others emerges through denial of the classical republican tradition (Thom 1995: 53–57). Though there are certainly criticisms of republics in Smith as well. The account of model republics in North America that received a relatively good trade deal from Britain is compared with the situation of the inhabitants of India under the domination of the East India Company (*WN* I.viii.26 and IV.vii.b.22). Smith certainly deplores the restrictions on trade that Britain imposed on its American colonies, but notes that the terms were more favourable to the colonies, exempting them from tariffs imposed on goods imported into Britain from outside the Empire (*WN* IV.vii.b.20–53). Danish colonial activities in the Americas are held up as a counter-example of the bad that results from restricting the imports and exports of colonies (*WN* IV.vii.b.11). Smith does not say so, but he was presumably aware that Denmark was an absolutist monarchy at the time, so he has a point to make in comparing a republican-leaning monarchy, as in Britain, with a more pure example of monarchy.

Somewhere between the absolutist and republican models of colonialism, there are the regulated companies and the joint-stock companies. Regulated companies (*WN* V.i.e.1–14), like the one for trade with 'Turkey' (*WN* V.i.e.2), as Smith terms the Ottoman lands, are recognised by the state, have monopolistic power and are dominated by the self-interest of individual traders in the company who are rarely concerned with the good of the company as a whole, which is essentially an aggregate of individual interests licensed by the state. Joint-stock companies (not really understood as what we largely think of as joint-stock companies today) pool the risks and benefits for individual traders and so are dominated by the common economic good of the enterprise (*WN* V.i.e.15–40). These work more like states than the regulated companies, and in Smith's time the East India Company was administering a large part of India, as a kind of junior partner state, or sub-state, of the British state, a situation which prevailed until the mid-nineteenth century. The joint-stock company is a more effective economic unit than the regulated company, but is in that case all the more complicit with the injustices and economic disadvantages of mercantilist colonialism. The joint-stock companies subject colonised peoples to an alien government which is not concerned with their interests, but with the interests of investors in the home country.

The completely anti-republican nature of the negative models of colonialism is matched by the purity of the positive forms of republicanism, comprising the ancient Greek colonies and the British colonies in North America. The British in North America model even presents a kind of liberty beyond republican liberty.

> When an artificer has acquired a little more stock than is necessary for carrying on his own business in supplying the neighbouring country, he does not, in North America, attempt to establish with it a manufacture for more distant sale, but employs it in the purchase and improvement of uncultivated land. From artificer he becomes planter, and neither the large wages nor the empty subsistence which that country affords to artificers, can bribe him to rather to work for other people than for himself. He feels that an artificer is the servant of his customers, from whom he derives his subsistence; but that a planter who cultivates his own land, and derives his necessary subsistence from the labour of his own family, is really a master, and independent of all the world.
>
> (*WN* III.i.5)

Smith refers to the solitary freedom of the settler in the vast open spaces of North America. This is a liberty unconstrained by government and laws, republican or otherwise. There are two aspects to this: first, an interest in a liberty beyond political liberty, or civil liberty of any kind; second, an interest in the liberty of 'barbarians' and 'savages', as will be explained below, after some thoughts about radical individual liberty. This isolated, free individual living a life of self-sufficiency mostly distant from other humans, apart from his family, cannot be defined and supported by laws or political institutions. It is a kind of liberty that is difficult to contain within even the most liberty-oriented political thought. Smith is here partly moving towards the sphere of the sublime, as discussed by Kant – the sense of inner freedom and transcendence which can come from experiencing the great spaces of nature. That is the mathematical sublime in Kant's *Critique of the Power of Judgement* (2000). There is a strong hint in Smith of the aspect of individuality which always feels at odds with any form of community, all laws and institutions, and which has been a cultural concern since Smith's time. That kind of asocial radical individual liberty provides a melancholic context for Smith's progressivist tendencies, which refer to ever-increasing sympathy and commercial union between humans. Colonialism provides the disruptive experience of radical liberty, because it is a place where people are isolated on a new frontier, so questioning the community and its ethics in the home country.

In the second aspect, that liberty in North America is something other than republicanism as understood by the ancient Greeks and Romans. The type of liberty in North America is something to be understood, in Greek and Roman republican thought, as something that applies to barbarians. It may even belong to philosophical limit situations, like the god or animal that Aristotle thinks of in the *Politics* (1932) as living outside the human *politea* or republic. Smith and other Scottish Enlightenment thinkers themselves had ways of thinking about this with reference to the savage and barbarian stages of human history, stages that contain a kind of liberty of natural force not found in civilisation which can be admired in some respects, but still threatens civilisation. We can find this discussion in Hume as well as in Smith, and most richly in Ferguson's (1995)

History of Civil Society. The association of the peoples of relatively simple societies, labelled as barbarians or savages, possessing a natural liberty of great force,
unconstrained by morality, both fearful and admirable, goes back to Tacitus. It
may go even further back, but Tacitus' discussion of the many nations of Britain
and Germany in *Agricola* and *Germania* (both Tacitus 1989), respectively, is a
canonical starting point for republican and liberty-oriented discussions of the
relation between two concepts of liberty. That is, the contrast between: liberty
constrained by morality and law, in which the early force of humans declines
in civilised comforts; and the unconstrained natural liberty of peoples living in
technologically and socially simple conditions, limited by the authority of chiefs
and unwritten customs rather than general systems of morality and law. This contrast was explored a little earlier in the eighteenth century than when Smith was
writing, first in Italy by Vico (1984), then in France by Rousseau (1984, 2008) and
Montesquieu (1999), and later in Scotland by Ferguson (1995) and Hume (2000:
III.ii). Smith himself addressed the contrasting forms of liberty not only in *The
Wealth of Nations* (Smith 1976a) but also in his *Lectures on Jurisprudence* (Smith
1978) and *The Theory of Moral Sentiments* (Smith 1976b). An illuminating
discussion, which itself contributes to political thought, can be found in Foucault
(2003).

We can see these analyses continuing into the nineteenth century as part
of the structuring assumptions of Tocqueville's (1988) understanding of the
United States in *Democracy in America*, where the liberty of the 'Indians' is an
important counterpoint to the growth of commercial and political liberty amongst
whites, particularly in the non-slave states. The bondage of African-Americans
in the slave states provided another counterpoint to despotic social relations, and
the possibility of unlimited force erupting between whites and blacks in a
race war.

In Smith, in an area of tension he shares with other Enlightenment thinkers, the
isolated liberty of an individual in the wilderness has an intensity of natural
liberty lacking in the natural liberty he discerns in civilised commercial states
and which he wishes to improve. The idea of natural liberty itself leads Smith
into concerns about what can go wrong with trying to make natural liberty
too systematic and perfect. The idea of the isolated settler in the wilderness of
North America presents another extreme aspect of liberty, where it disappears
in the sense that Smith and others generally use it – of the liberty obtaining in a
community under law.

The way that Tocqueville used the Enlightenment historical stages to
analyse the America of the 1830s should itself remind us of the way that Smith,
Hume and Ferguson referred to distinctions within Britain and Ireland. The period
of the formation of their thought covers the Jacobite Rebellion of 1745, which
largely ended with the victory of Hanoverian forces at the Battle of Culloden the
following year. Charles Edward Stuart drew on support from clans in the Gaelic-
speaking islands and mountains of Scotland, where different laws, customs and
authority structures prevailed from those in the Scots- and standard English-
speaking Lowlands. The Hanoverian victory in defence of the settlement of 1688

did not end all of those differences, since traditional landowners in the Highlands had a feudal style of authority over peasants well into the nineteenth century, but a major state offensive took place against the self-governing Gaelic communities to the north and west of the Highland line. Crown authority became complete beyond the line, with suppression of distinctive language, dress and custom, forcibly integrating the Highlanders into Hanoverian Great Britain.

Before and after the crushing of the 1745 uprising, social conditions in the Scottish islands and mountains, while not strictly barbaric or savage in the definitions of the time, could seem so in relation to the Enlightenment centres of Aberdeen, Glasgow and Edinburgh, or Smith's home town, the commercial centre of Kirkcaldy. Smith's account of historical stages in *Lectures on Jurisprudence*, for example, refers to an age of hunters corresponding to savagery, an age of shepherds corresponding to barbarism, an age of agriculture, and an age of commerce (*LJA* i.26–27). The Scottish Highlands had reached the age of agriculture, but the dispersed nature of the society, a conglomeration of warring clans, in which the chieftain was a figure of absolute patriarchal authority, meant that the Highlanders seemed barbarian or even savage to Lowlanders. A similar way of thinking could be applied to the Gaelic-speaking rural parts of Ireland in relation to Dublin, the English-speaking aristocracy, and the Presbyterians of Ulster, who made their own contribution to the Scottish Enlightenment through Francis Hutcheson. These are crude distinctions, and Edmund Burke for one would not fit neatly into the category of Protestant upper-class cosmopolitan remote from Catholic peasant culture. Many other qualifications can and should be made to distinctions between civilised English-speaking moderate Protestant Enlightenment Britain and Ireland and their 'barbarian' or 'savage' opposites. Nevertheless, there is some reality to them, enough to push Smith and others in the direction of a savage/barbarian–civil and commercial society understanding of history, where the civil and commercial communities are perpetually at risk from being overwhelmed by the natural strength of the less civil and commercial communities. This is not an explicit part of Smith's writing, but the application of his own terms, the general Enlightenment understanding of historical stages and Lowland reactions to Highlanders is very suggestive.

We should think of Smith's work on colonialism and empire as including relations between England, Scotland and Ireland, and relations between the Anglo parts of Ireland and Scotland and the rest. This is largely an implicit issue, though he does have a lot to say about the injustice of not allowing equal trade terms to Ireland with Great Britain (*WN* I.xi.m.9 and I.xi.m.11). Smith says little on what he thinks about the Jacobite Uprising and the means used to put it down, but he expresses disapproval in the 1766 *Lectures on Jurisprudence*:

> In the year 1745 four or five thousand naked unarmed Highlanders took possession of the improved parts of this country without any opposition from the unwarlike inhabitants. They penetrated into England and alarmed the whole nation, and had they not been opposed by a standing army they would have seized the throne with little difficulty. 200 years ago such an attempt

would have rouzed the spirit of the nation. Our ancestors were brave and warlike, their minds were not enervated by cultivating arts and commerce, and they were already with spirit and vigour to resist the most formidable foe.

(LJB 331–332)

From this, it seems reasonable to assume that Smith preferred the Hanoverian cause to the Jacobite cause, linking the latter at least symbolically to a return to the more absolutist model of monarchy preceding the Glorious Revolution of 1688, and that he regarded the Highlanders as, to some degree, savage. Did he approve of the harsh measures used to crush the social basis of Jacobitism after Culloden? That seems at odds with his general emphasis on justice in the state and sympathy in ethics, but maybe he did see some violence against savages and barbarian tendencies in a remote agricultural part of Britain as necessary to the emergence and preservation of morally advanced and commercial society. He was deeply aware of the fate of ancient states based on some measure of liberty and commercial life, and their defeat by more barbaric peoples, as in the domination of the Greece of free republics by the Macedonian monarchy or the defeat of the Roman Empire in the West by barbarians (*WN* III.ii.1–2 and V.i.a). He sometimes seems deeply pessimistic about the survival chances of liberty and commercial society in the modern world. For example, he has a rather exaggerated view of the triumphs of Louis XIV, the model of absolutist monarchy, over the republican and commercial Dutch Republic (*LJB* 332). He also displays great pessimism about the prospect of republics progressing in liberty for all, suggesting that it is a republic of the greatest liberty for its citizens that is least likely to extend rights to non-citizens. He fears that slavery will never be abolished, partly because the most free republics, like the American colonies, will be unwilling to emancipate their slaves. Their system of liberty is embedded in the political economy of slavery, so how is it possible to hope the citizens benefiting from that system will dismantle it? He looks at the Roman Republic in the same light, noting the amelioration in the conditions of slaves during the Empire (*WN* IV.vii.b.55). Sometimes Smith seems caught up in a pessimistic acceptance of a Ferguson (1995) or Vico (1984) style of cyclical history in which savagery or barbarism – that is, the divine and heroic ages in Vico's *New Science* – will keep returning, which may also reflect a fear that ethical and civil progress means a loss of natural strength.

That Ferguson and Vico style fear of the loss of primitive strength and passion – the kind of liberty which exists in the unity of physical force and immediacy of imagination – is present in Smith as it is in many Enlightenment thinkers. In this respect we can see a positive attitude to barbaric, or even savage, republicanism in his work. The wish to restore the strength of civic republicanism by reabsorbing some element of barbaric community and politics goes back at least to the accounts of the ancient Britons and Germans in Tacitus, so it is itself part of antique republicanism.

Among civilized nations, the virtues which are founded upon humanity, are more cultivated than those which are founded upon self-denial and the

command of the passions. Among rude and barbarous nations, it is quite otherwise, the virtues of self-denial are more cultivated than those of humanity.
The general security and happiness which prevail in ages of civility and
politeness, afford little exercise to the contempt of danger, to patience in
enduring labour, hunger, and pain. Poverty may easily be avoided, and the
contempt of it therefore almost ceases to be a virtue. The abstinence from
pleasure becomes less necessary, and the mind is more at liberty to unbend
itself, and to indulge its natural inclinations in all those particular respects.

(*TMS* V.2.8)

The element of admiration above for the cultivation of self-denial in what we can
call barbaric republics suggests some wish to reabsorb, at least in part, virtues of
contempt for pain, danger, poverty and hard labour. Of course, there were people
in the Scotland, and Europe, of Smith's time with such lives, and he was very
aware of them. The point here is that his hope that commercial society will elevate
their condition is mingled with anxieties about lingering barbarism and that the
strengths of lingering barbarism will vanish as trade, commerce and growing
moral sympathy do their work, and society will purely comprise those who know
no barrier to pleasure and therefore may become slaves to such pleasure.

The subdued theme of wishing to reabsorb some parts of barbaric republics can
also be found in passages from the *Lectures on Jurisprudence* (*LJA* ii.152–153,
iii.6–7, iv.1–5 and iv.38–49), where barbaric communities are discussed with
regard to the executive power of governments, law and criminal justice. There
is a very limited amount of government, law and criminal justice in barbarian
communities, as kings have limited power and cannot intervene much in society.
Smith presumes that this limitation also applies to any democratic assemblies in
such communities that act to make laws, preserve existing customs, and monitor
kings. Criminal justice largely consists of recompense to the victims of crime
from the perpetrator, with no further punishment for the guilty. In this circumstance,
we might think the concept of guilt hardly exists anyway. Smith presumes that
with strengthening of the powers of barbarian kings, some violent punishments
are introduced for the most extreme crimes, particularly those of treason towards
the king himself. As civil government is fully developed, harsh legal codes are
imposed as part of the evolution from barbarian customs. Smith deplores the
cruelty of such laws, presuming that further development of civility leads to their
moderation. At least in this sense he regrets the movement from barbarian republics, at the edge of any concept of republicanism because of the weakness of
political institutions, to antique urban republics, and regards recent commercial
society as to some degree a return to barbarism in criminal justice. The return is
one of moderation in punishment rather than a return to compensatory justice, but
the latter might be one way of developing Smith's preference for moderation in
punishment. So there is no straightforward way in which Smith favours the
vanquishing of all barbarian republicanism in all aspects, which may explain his
general silence on the 'barbarians' within the British state, which subordinated
and then 'civilised' them.

When Smith looks for a more contemporary and commercial version of a republic, the American colonies seem to be a model for the future, as a repetition of the Greek colonial system, if Britain grants them independence, as Smith hopes. However, that proposed birth of perfected liberty in American republics incorporates both the slavery which Smith fears persists more wherever greater republican liberty is found, and the liberty in the American wilderness which cannot be incorporated into a republican – or other 'natural' – system of liberty (*WN* IV.vii.b.55). Colonisation of the New World produces a model of pure political absolutism and economic robbery in the Spanish Americas, and a model of liberty so pure it collapses in the British Americas. The fear that American liberty could be torn between despotism over slaves and extreme disaggregation of individuals in the wilderness might explain some of Smith's silence about the dark side of monarchical–republican liberty in Britain, as if that may be the best that could be hoped for, rather than the experiment in pure liberty that Smith hopes for and fears in the Americas. The barbarian republic is present in the possible disintegration of the American republic (or republics) in the wilderness, which also hints in a very subdued way at the American 'barbarian' republics of the Native Americans, a theme which again Smith does not wish to discuss more explicitly.

Smith hopes for an end to colonialism, though, as with other hopes, in a manner tinged with pessimism. He argues that Britain would benefit from relinquishing the colonies, so saving itself the expense of providing external security and the broader economic costs of distorted trade. Despite the historical precedents he identifies in the ancient Greek model of the relationship between parental republic and descendent republics, he seems to despair of the possibility of a voluntary termination of colonialism. The advantages of free trade and friendship, based on voluntary association between states, may never outweigh the narrow self-interests behind mercantilism.

> To propose that Great Britain should voluntarily give up all authority over her colonies, and leave them to elect their own magistrates, to enact their own laws, and to make peace and war as they might think proper, would be to propose such a measure as never was, and never will be adopted, by any nation in the world. No nation ever voluntarily gave up the domination of any province, how troublesome soever it might be to govern it, and how small the revenue which it afforded might be in proportion to the expence which it occasioned . . . It might dispose them not only to respect, for whole centuries together, that treaty of commerce which they had concluded with us at parting, but to favour us in war as well as in trade, and instead of turbulent and factious subjects, to become our most faithful, affectionate, and generous allies; and the same sort of parental affection on the one side, and filial respect on the other, might revive between Great Britain and her colonies, which used to subsist between those of ancient Greece and the mother city from which they descended.
>
> (*WN* IV.vii.66)

The unspoken issue is: should the crown and the real source of power in the semi-republican oligarchy give up not only overseas colonies but also Ireland and Scotland, or maybe just the Scottish Highlands and Western Isles and the Gaelic parts of Ireland along with the Welsh-speaking parts of Wales?

We can infer from Smith the desirability of a European 'empire', in the sense of a continent unified by free trade and good communications, to avoid hunger (*WN* IV.v.b.39), in which he thinks of colonies leaving the 'confederacy', something he understands as an asymmetrical political union with the colonial centre (*WN* IV.vii.c.75). The trade element would bring great economic benefits, and some kind of shared representative government is Smith's ideal model for overseas colonies. The lack of the representative principle in antiquity made republican government impossible in the imperial stage of the Roman Republic and the fully imperial stage of the Roman state. The political and moral decline of the Roman Republic, after the imperial expansion associated with victory over the Carthaginian Republic, was an issue in the late Republic, in Renaissance republicanism and in the European Enlightenment thought of Montesquieu (1989, 1999) and Rousseau (2008). Smith continues this analysis, as in his discussion of the weakening of the enlarged Roman Republic caused by the lack of a representative principle:

> The idea of representation was unknown in ancient times. When the people of one state were admitted to the right of citizenship in another, they had no other means of exercising that right but by coming in a body to vote and deliberate with the people of that other state. The admission of the greater part of the inhabitants of Italy to the privileges of Roman citizens, completely ruined the Roman republick. It was no longer possible to distinguish between who was and was not a Roman citizen. No tribe could know its own members. A rabble of any could be introduced into the assemblies of the people, could drive out the real citizens, and decide upon the affairs of the republick as if they themselves had been such.
>
> (*WN* IV.vii.c.77)

This is presumably in the background of Smith's thoughts about modern empire. The two approaches to modern empire – dissolving it or establishing a free political association through representative government – are never properly presented as alternatives. The second option is referred to as something the Romans should have established but did not. The implications for the three core kingdoms of the British monarchy (England, Scotland and Ireland) are not fully explored, or at least the issue of coercion in the interests of crown and mercantilist oligarchy is not addressed, perhaps because in some respects Smith believed in the justice of a coercive civilising state, an impression confirmed by his doubts about pure republicanism.

Careful reading of Smith suggests that his remarks on empires and colonies are embedded in his thoughts about politics, and about his own nation or nation within a nation – that is, Scotland within Great Britain. The ways that empires and colonies appear in *The Wealth of Nations* and elsewhere are very suggestive with regard to ancient and modern states, stages of history, political liberty, political authority and the promotion of commercial life. These ways in which empire and colonies appear in Smith's work are a major indication of his importance as a political thinker, who is no less important because his ideas about political thought are dispersed throughout his texts and not unified in an explicit theory. It might have been difficult for benevolent, moderate Adam Smith, as he appears in most of his moral, economic and political thought, to produce a theory in which his unsympathetic hostility to the less commercial people of his own nation, Scotland, and high level of toleration for intense state coercion of such people becomes apparent. The Scottish Highlands themselves were a kind of nation within the Scottish nation, itself a nation within the nation Great Britain, itself embedded in an imperial statehood with global reach. Smith's mostly latent and sometimes manifest thoughts about how a nation can exist in an imperial relationship with its inner barbarians or savages reveals itself through the intersection of his stages of history with the nature of the states and colonies. Commercial peoples are threatened internally by those at a lower stage, and in Smith's remarks on the Scottish Highlanders we see a tendency to hyperbole about the savagery of people who have certainly reached the stage of settled agriculture above savagery and barbarism.

The ways in which ancient commercial states were overthrown by barbarians is displaced into a more general anxiety about historically backward peoples, who are nevertheless above the savage and barbarian stages, while still threatening commercial states. The Kingdom of Macedonia was not savage or even barbarian by any proper definition, such as those used by Smith himself, though it could be seen as backward compared with the ancient Greek republics. Eighteenth-century France was very far from barbarism on any account of historical stages, but still seems so when compared with commercial, republican Holland and commercial, semi-republican Britain. We can see the more melancholic side of Smith's thought when we consider these themes. He is less the optimistic analyst of the compatibility of commercial society with progress and natural liberty, more the pessimistic analyst of the difficulty of joining all forms of liberty, civility and historical progress in a harmonious whole.

The tensions in the attempted integration include the distinction between ancients and moderns, and that distinction itself is very suggestive of the impossibility of integration across time of political forms, including types of colonialism. Though Smith brings Greek colonialism into his suggestions regarding the best form of modern colonialism, the integration is limited by the lack of representative institutions he acknowledges for the ancients. The Roman model is not mentioned directly in relation to modern colonialism, but is present in the nation within a nation within the British Empire. The underlying reality is that Great Britain itself, including Ireland, which at that time was under the British crown but not integrated into the state, was something like the Roman model of colonialism. In pre-Norman medieval history, the Kingdom of Wessex expanded to absorb all of England (except Cornwall); then, in the post-Conquest medieval period, Wales and Cornwall were absorbed, followed by the fusion of the English and Scottish crowns in 1603, which itself was followed by the 1707 Act of Union, joining the two states. The Roman model becomes even more relevant when we consider that the colonisation of Ireland, particularly in Ulster, rested on giving land to British Protestant settlers. The Roman model of military expansion and land grabs in neighbouring territories is darker than the Greek model of overseas colonies that are largely independent of the home city state, which is probably why Smith does not mention it directly in relation to Britain – another evasion, similar to those discussed above. The Roman model undermines its own democratic republican institutions through over-expansion, and though Smith suggests the solution of representative institutions, it is an account built on loss of popular sovereignty and political participation pervading modern politics, operating in lands built out of imperial expansion.

Bibliography

Aristotle (1932) *Politics*, trans. H. Rackham, Cambridge, MA: Loeb Books.
Ferguson, A. (1995) *History of Civil Society*, ed. F. Oz-Salzberger, Cambridge: Cambridge University Press.
Foucault, M. (2003) *Society Must Be Defended*, trans. D. Macey, New York: Picador/St Martin's Press.
Hume, D. (2000) *A Treatise of Human Nature*, ed. D. F. Norton and M. J. Norton, Oxford: Oxford University Press.
Kant, I. (2000) *Critique of the Power of Judgment*, trans. P. Guyer and E. Matthews, Cambridge: Cambridge University Press.
Montesquieu, C. (1989) *The Spirit of the Laws*, trans. A. Cohler, B. Miller and H. Stone, Cambridge: Cambridge University Press.
Montesquieu, C. (1999) *Consideration on the Cause of the Greatness of the Romans and their Decline*, trans. D. Lowenthal, Indianapolis, IN: Hackett.
Rasmussen, D. (2008) *The Problems and Promises of Commercial Society*, University Park: Pennsylvania State University Press.
Rousseau, J.-J. (1984) *A Discourse on Inequality*, trans. M. Cranston, London: Penguin.
Rousseau, J.-J. (2008) *The Social Contract*, trans. C. Betts, Oxford: Oxford University Press.
Smith, A. (1976a) *An Inquiry into the Nature and Causes of the Wealth of Nations*, ed. R. H. Campbell and A. S. Skinner, Oxford: Oxford University Press; Glasgow edition.
Smith, A. (1976b) *The Theory of Moral Sentiments*, ed. D. D. Raphael and A. L. MacFie, Oxford: Oxford University Press; Glasgow edition.
Smith, A. (1978) *Lectures on Jurisprudence*, ed. R. L. Meek, D. D. Raphael and P. G. Stein, Oxford: Oxford University Press; Glasgow edition.
Tactitus (1989) *Agricola, Germania, Dialogus*, trans. M. Hutton and W. Peterson, Cambridge, MA: Loeb Books.
Thom, M. (1995) *Republics, Nations and Tribes*, London: Verso Books.
Tocqueville, A. de (1988) *Democracy in America*, trans. G. Lawrence, New York: HarperPerennial.
Vico, G. (1984) *The New Science of Giambattista Vico*, trans. T. G. Bergin and M. H. Fisch, Ithaca, NY: Cornell University Press.

Adam Smith's four-stages theory of socio-cultural evolution

New insights from his 1749 lecture[1]

Thierry C. Pauchant

Introduction

Some notions are so often taken for granted that we sometimes forget their origin. For example, it seems obvious today that human evolution has proceeded from the age of hunting and fishing to the pastoral age, the agricultural age and the present age of commerce and industry. This grand narrative of historical evolution, with some variants, has structured the foundations of different scientific fields, including anthropology, economics, historiography, law, moral philosophy, political sciences and sociology.

We also often forget that narratives are not neutral. The way a story is structured is both an affirmation of how we see the world and how we ought to act in it (Foucault, 2004; Ricoeur, 2004). For example, a narrative drawn from Christian theology affirms the existence of an eternal after-world and the necessity to prepare for it during one's presence on earth. Differently, a Marxist lens suggests that the motor of history is class struggle, prompting the need for political reform in the modes of ownership and production. Then again, authors who draw from the utilitarian tradition insist on the supremacy of reason for realizing the greatest good for the greatest number of people. Or, as a last example, the still dominant theory in economics, wrongly associated with Adam Smith, suggests that the order of the world is engendered by the invisible hand of the market and the price mechanism.

Globally, many commentators also fail to realize that the first theories of socio-cultural evolution were introduced by a specific group of people at a specific period in time: the Scottish Enlightenment (Berry, 2001, 2015; Broadie, 2003; Bryson, 1968; Griswold, 1999; Meek, 1976b; Pocock, 1999; Rasmussen, 2014; Sher, 2006; Weinstein, 2013). Often when we evoke the "Enlightenment," we tend to think about the French Revolution, perhaps drawn by its drama. As a whole, the Scottish Enlightenment was much less bloody and even less rationalistic than its French counterpart (Rasmussen, 2014).[2] The Scots "had little use for Cartesian rationalism [but] . . . placed their trust in the 'wisdom of nature'" (Carey, 2011, p. 226). These scientists introduced a "social theory" (Berry, 2001, p. vii), grounded in the bourgeoning science of human nature. While adopting a very long time-frame and a cautious belief in progress, they were "less confident than the French, or Englishmen like Priestley, that this [progress] is automatic and necessarily always an improvement" (Berry, 2001, p. 7).

The three main disciplines of the Scottish Enlightenment were "moral philosophy, historiography and political economy" (Broadie, 2003, p. 4). However, they also attempted to integrate the new discoveries introduced in many other disciplines, including, for example, neuroscience, medicine, chemistry, geology, botany, agriculture and engineering (Bonnyman, 2014; Whitaker *et al.*, 2007; Wilson, 2009; Wolloch, 2011). As such, if Francis Hutcheson, David Hume, Lord Kames, Adam Smith, Adam Ferguson, John Millar or William Robertson represented more the social sciences, they extended their friendship, as well as their lively discussions, to many others grounded in the "hard" sciences. These included Joseph Black (chemistry), William Cullen (medicine and neuroscience), James Hutton (geology), John Robison (physics), Robert Bakewell (agriculture), James Watt and John Anderson (both engineering). In addition, there were interactions with Erasmus Darwin (Charles's grandfather) and the Lunar Society (Uglow, 2002), Benjamin Franklin, John Adams and Thomas Jefferson in the US, and the *"encyclopédistes"* in France, such as D'Alembert, Diderot, Condorcet and Turgot. Some of them, and Adam Smith in particular, studied the work of entomologists, botanists, zoologists and other naturalists, such as Daubenton, de Réaumur, Von Linné and de Buffon (Wolloch, 2011). Smith insisted on their importance in an article published in the *Edinburgh Review* (*EPS*, pp. 242–254)[3] and he spent time with them when he lived in Paris (Massot-Bordenave, 2013).

Gladys Bryson, the author of the first general book on the Scottish Enlightenment in 1945, was puzzled by the relative lack of acknowledgement of this multidisciplinary movement. Her commentaries are still valid today. Currently, one can be trained in anthropology, philosophy, sociology or political science, studying the works of Durkheim, Engels, Hegel, Marx, Morgan, Saint-Simon, Spencer, Tylor or Weber, without being much exposed to the multi- or trans-disciplinary enquiry of the Scottish Enlightenment. As Bryson (1968, p. 4) wrote:

> It is strange that historians of social theory have so long neglected a detailed analysis of [the Scottish Enlightenment movement], when the opening of any book of the general title of "moral philosophy" reveals discussions of human nature, social forces, progress, marriage and family relationships, economic processes, maintenance of government, religion, international relations, elementary jurisprudence, primitive customs, history of institutions, ethics, aesthetics.

One of the most famous contributions of this movement was its introduction of a four-stages theory, encompassing all the subjects mentioned above by Bryson and more. This theory, in relation to the Scots, is also called "conjectural history," "natural history," "natural philosophy" or "stadial theory." (For summaries of the theory, its origins and influences, see, in particular: Berry, 2001, pp. 91–119, and 2015, pp. 32–65; Harris, 2001, pp. 25–52; Hont, 1987; Höpfl, 1978; Marouby, 2004, pp. 17–55; Meek, 1976b; Pittock, in Broadie, 2003, pp. 258–279; Pocock,

1999; Spector, 2005; Weinstein, 2013, pp. 219–238; Wilson, 2009; and Wolloch, 2011, pp. 73–135).

In this paper, I suggest that it was Adam Smith who first introduced this theory in 1749, influencing the other members of the Scottish Enlightenment and other authors around the world. As explained below, the subject of the paternity of this theory has been controversial since its introduction. It is also a delicate issue as paternities are never neutral. While all the Scots have been said to belong to the same "family" (Berry, 2001, p. 1), sharing both a social and a political vision, as well as a large publication project (Sher, 2006, p. 44), there are differences of tone and nuance, and even some disagreements, among them.

Thus, the focus here is on historical evidence. In the next section, I present some of the controversies surrounding Smith's paternity of the theory. In the two following sections, I critically assess Ronald Meek's analysis of the so-called "Anderson notes," challenging first his interpretation and, second, his dating of this document. In conclusion, I propose avenues for further research.

The controversy over the paternity of the four-stages theory

The controversy revolves around the fact that Adam Smith's only book which featured a full-blown four-stages theory was published in 1776: *The Wealth of Nations* (Pocock, 1999, pp. 311–329). This publication appeared after other members of the Scottish Enlightenment – such as Lord Kames, David Hume, William Robertson, Adam Ferguson, John Millar, James Steuart, Gilbert Stuart, Lord Monboddo and a few others – had published their versions of the theory. (For a full list of these publications and their dates, see Sher, 2006, pp. 620–687.)

Marvin Harris, in anthropology, and Ronald Meek, in the history of economics, were two key authors in the 1960s and 1970s who attempted to trace this paternity. They reviewed the work of many authors in antiquity and during the Enlightenment, including Charlevoix, Lafitau, Vico, Voltaire, Montesquieu, Rousseau, Herder and many others. Harris, in 1968, acknowledged the foundational contributions of the Scottish Enlightenment. However, he reduced Smith's theory to a "capitalist ideology" (Harris, 2001, p. 106). Differently, Meek concluded that both Turgot in France and Smith in Scotland fathered similar theories of evolution in the 1750s (Meek, 1976b). It appears that Meek was misguided in the case of Turgot. More recent research suggests that the latter's texts were rewritten at a much later date (Larrere, in Binoche, 2005, p. 99). By contrast, as discussed below, this present study confirms Meek's assessment of Smith's paternity, but with different meanings and with an earlier date.

Several authors have suggested that searching for such a paternity could be a waste of time. The argument is that various versions of a stage theory were proposed by different authors, so it became a "common property" (Hont, 1987; Pocock, 1999, p. 315). For example, Hont (1987) suggested that Scottish authors followed and expanded the tradition espoused by the natural law theorists, such as Grotius and Pufendorf, who themselves were influenced by Christian teaching, the Stoics and Aristotle. For example, as Pufendorf wrote in his classic _On the Duty of Man and Citizen_, published in 1673 (Pufendorf, 1991, pp. 84–85):

> It is the condition of the human body that it needs to take in its sustenance from without and to protect itself from anything that would destroy its integrity . . . We may therefore safely infer that it is clearly the will of the supreme governor of the world that man may use other creatures for his own benefit . . . In the beginning all these things are thought to have been made available by God to all men indifferently . . . In the course of time, however, men multiplied and began to cultivate things which produce food and clothing. To avoid conflict . . . they took the step of dividing the actual body of things amongst themselves, and each was assigned his own proper portion.

It is important to note that Pufendorf suggested two natural conditions for human life – the necessity to sustain life for oneself and to assure the multiplication of the species. Both of these necessities were seen as dictated by divine will after the fall of Babel. It was also understood that human beings have to revere the will of God and labour only for the duty of sustaining life, avoiding all excesses and the sin of vanity, securing for themselves a place in heaven or, in a different version, having been "elected" (Moore and Silverthorne, in Hont and Ignatieff, 1985, p. 83). In addition, several researchers have suggested that Smith was greatly influenced by the notion of _socialitas_, emphasized by classical authors and the natural law tradition. This notion suggests that humans have the cognitive capacity to realize that they need to cooperate with one another if they wish to survive (Forman-Barzilai, 2010, p. 44).

Increasingly, the Scots proposed that this sustaining of life and evolution could be more precisely explained though scientific inquiry. Their theories were based on the unfolding of natural and human propensities, affecting and being affected by many variables located at different levels. Adam Smith, for example, used in part a biological framework to explain some of the conditions of human nature (Carey, 1998). For instance, he stated in his _Theory of Moral Sentiments_ that "the two great purposes of nature [are] the support of the individual and the propagation of the species" (_TMS_, II.ii.3.5, p. 87). This view seems surprising from an author who is supposed to have fathered the _Homo economicus_ paradigm and not a Darwinian _Homo sapiens_ theory. This first paradigm, often wrongly attributed to Smith, emphasizes rationality, with the purpose of maximizing one's economic utility (Griswold, 1999, p. 9; Sen, 2011). Differently, Smith did add to the natural law foundation a more biological and naturalistic understanding of human life without, however, implying any determinism (Evensky, 2007; Fleischacker, 2004). His view on this subject was similar to the one espoused by many of the other members of the Scottish Enlightenment. As recent research has suggested, the relationship with nature, ecology and agriculture has been central to the overall idea of the "Enlightenment" (Bonnyman, 2014; Wolloch, 2011). But when these authors invoked, for example, the notion of "moral instinct, [it] was not, as it often is today, as an attempt to reduce morality to biology" (Carey, 2011, p. 227).

Smith also proposed in his theory of moral sentiments that the process of *sympathy* explained better the emergence of both law and ethics in society rather than the explanations given in the natural law tradition. Again, this notion challenges the traditional view of Smith as a hardcore Chicago School economist: the process of sympathy requires a theory of mind aware of self, of others and of contexts, encompassing the interplay of instinctual, intuitional, emotional and cognitive processes (Bessone and Biziou, 2009; Weinstein, 2013), or what contemporary authors have called a "sub-rationality" (Carey, 2011). We will see that Smith held some of these views as early as 1749.

John Pocock has argued subtly, and I believe rightly, that many of the Scots rejected religious dogmatism, but did not directly challenge the views of the Church or the natural law tradition, except perhaps David Hume. As Pocock (1999, pp. 313–314) proposed:

> The strategy of the Enlightenment in Scotland was the development of a science of morality, which on the assumption that humans were intrinsically social beings became a science of society in all its ramifications. [It] . . . took the form of jurisprudence, which was then organized into history and next [was applied] . . . into political economy. Smith at Glasgow lectured on jurisprudence as a professor of moral philosophy, Millar as professor of civil law. Both proceeded from the assumption that since humans were moral and social beings, the pursuit of justice in society . . . was capable of supplying a complete lexicon and map of moral life. Here of course was a fundamental departure from the Calvinist position that human morality entailed a relationship with God and, since the Fall, could not be conducted without the operation of divine grace . . . [They, however, did not] deny the efficacy of grace.

In the mid-eighteenth century, the Scots' distance from religion allowed them to develop an innovative scientific model. Adopting a comparative method, they did not draw their data primarily from the Bible. They also used textual evidence provided in classical history, accounts of travellers exploring newly discovered territories such as America and Asia, and direct observations and comparisons of different populations (Marouby, 2004; Meek, 1976b). Authors who grounded themselves in natural law, such as Grotius, Pufendorf, Bossuet and even, to some extent, Locke and Montesquieu, were still much influenced by the biblical views of authors who were (Meek, 1976b, p. 22; Hont, 1987, p. 254). Thus, as Genesis indicated that "Abel was a shepherd and Cain a tiller of the soil" (Meek, 1976b, p. 25), these authors postulated that the states of hunting, shepherding and farming all existed concurrently in a first age of the world (Pocock, 1999).

Many commentators have mentioned the developments brought to the natural law tradition by authors such as Carmichael and Hutchinson at the very beginning of the Scottish Enlightenment (Hont and Ignatieff, 1985, chapter 3). However, it is Adam Smith who is credited with adding several definite new features to this tradition. For example, it is widely accepted that he conceived that the three *states* of the natural law tradition – hunting and fishing, herding, and farming – were in fact three *stages* of evolution (Hont, 1987; Pocock, 1999, p. 315). Smith realized that each stage, while they could coexist for a while together and did not necessarily proceed in a linear fashion, was associated with different conditions in societies which formed a pattern, in terms of property, institutions, government relations or even manners, customs, legal and ethical practices.

Smith is also credited with the notion that humans started their long social and cultural evolution as soon as they domesticated animals, rather than merely hunted, fished or gathered fruit. As Pocock (1999, pp. 315–316) explained:

> Smith's remarkable contribution to the natural history of society was his insistence that the shepherd stage was dynamic, a decisive break with the hunting and food-gathering . . . In most previous systems of this kind, the shepherd was little distinguished from the hunter, and the origins of civilization were located in the change from a nomadic to a sedentary way of life.

Smith is also credited with adding a fourth stage to this evolutionary view of history – the age of commerce (Hont and Ignatieff, 1985, p. 33). He postulated that this stage was qualitatively different from the other three, as the earlier ones were all connected to a direct exploitation of land (Hont, 1987, p. 254). Of course, Smith was not the only author to write about commercial activities and he realized that commerce and banking had existed for a very long time. But – and this was his original contribution – he proposed that when the majority of the people in a nation (that is, more than 50 per cent) no longer worked on the land and exchanged their products, society had reached a different stage. For Smith, this new stage triggered a host of differences, some positive, others negative. As he proposed in *The Wealth of Nations* (*WN*, I.xi.c, p. 180, and I.iv, p. 37; emphasis added):

> When . . . the labour of half the society becomes sufficient to provide food for the whole . . . the other half . . . or at least the greater part of them, can be employed in providing other things, or in satisfying the other wants and fancies of mankind . . . [Also] when the division of labour has been once thoroughly established . . . [Man] supplies the far greater part [of his wants] by exchanging [the] surplus part of the produce of his own labour, which is over and above his own consumption . . . Every man thus lives by exchanging, or becomes in some measure a merchant, and the society itself grows to be what is properly [called] a *commercial society*.

Finally, Smith added to the natural law tradition a developmental theory of mind and language, triggering through the sympathetic process different manners, customs and institutions. Thus, for Smith, and for many other members of the Scottish Enlightenment, abstract notions such as "property," "contract" and "labour" emerged slowly in the human race. As emphasized by Christopher Berry (2001, p. 95), the "Scots have added a cognitive development perspective [to the natural law tradition], so that although Pufendorf allows for a 'history' of property he does not plot the history as a 'natural history of mankind.'" Smith has been particularly sensitive to this view at least since 1749, as suggested below. For example, while he proposed in *The Wealth of Nations* that the notion of the division of labour was central to the development of institutions and societies, he also reminded his readers that this activity itself emerged from the developmental "consequence of the faculties of reason and speech" (*WN*, I.ii.1, p. 25). This subtle point is often overlooked (Rothschild, 2001, p. 150; Weinstein, 2013, p. 140).

Given the innovations that Smith introduced, many authors have proposed that his ideas were seminal in the emergence of the four-stages theory. However, all of them have been reluctant to attribute the *paternity* of this theory to Smith because of a lack of objective proof. As suggested above, *The Wealth of Nations* was published *after* the publication of other books which presented various stadial theories. Of course, Smith's *Lectures on Jurisprudence*, consisting of notes taken by students, contain many in-depth descriptions of these different stages and their diverse relations in different countries with manners, customs, law, ethics and institutions (Haakonssen, 1981; Winch, 1978). However, these lectures were dated at the earliest from 1762 and they were never published as a book, formally endorsed by the author.

Many scholars have thus been careful with the language they used about Smith's contribution in this domain. They have proposed, for example, that Smith could not be called an "historian," as Gibbon, Hume or Robertson could. Instead, they have suggested that Smith "played a major part in transforming the discipline [of history]" (Pocock, 1999, p. 329) or that he was "a philosopher of history and ought to be read as such" (Weinstein, 2013, p. 220). Some have suggested that Smith provided "one of the earliest models" in social evolution (Pittock, in Broadie, 2003, p. 262). Some have written that he gave "the most concise and lucid outline of the four stages theory" (Wolloch, 2011, p. 93) or that this was "one of the very first explicit and achieved" models (Marouby, 2004, p. 29). Still others have suggested that Smith's contribution in this domain was "crucial" (Berry, 2001, p. 93) or that he has been "a particularly influential figure" (Skinner, 1996, p. 98). In the words of John Pocock (1999, p. 159), as a way of summary:

> After Montesquieu were to come the Glasgow and Edinburgh professors who, with the aid of a Pufendorfian natural jurisprudence were to set about organizing the whole field of moral behavior into systems some of which might be arranged in a historical order; a new science, [John Millar] was to claim, of which "Montesquieu was the Bacon and Adam Smith was the Newton."

This claim (Ross, 2010, p. 118), made by one of the most celebrated exponents of the four-stages theory, John Millar, has achieved some public impact. The testimony offered by Dugald Stewart, Smith's first biographer, also made a strong impression. Stewart suggested that Smith used a new method of his own invention (theoretical history) in all his publications and lectures, some of them dating to before 1750. I return to these issues below. Further, the testimony of John Callander of Craigforth raised doubts. He declared that Smith taught "civil law to students in jurisprudence" in 1749–1750 and observed that "Dr Robertson had borrowed the first volume of his history of Charles V from them, as every student could testify" (Scott, 1965, pp. 54–55). Finally, a manuscript on Smith's early views, related to his use of the four-stages theory, was discovered in 1970. Known as the "Anderson notes," this document reignited the search for the paternity of the Scottish four-stages theory. What follows is a new analysis of these notes.

Revisiting the "Anderson notes" and Meek's interpretation

The textual evidence on which I base my hypothesis came to us courtesy of a colleague of Adam Smith, the celebrated John Anderson. Like Smith (1723–1790), Anderson (1723–1796) studied at the University of Glasgow with the "never to be forgotten Francis Hutcheson" (*Corr.*, p. 309). Anderson graduated from Glasgow in 1745, when Smith was finishing his studies at Oxford (Butt, 1996, p. 1). He shared many of Smith's interests, including "natural philosophy and natural history" (Wilson, 2009, p. 172). Specializing in engineering and working as a professor at the University of Glasgow, he became one of Smith's colleagues for many years. Considering his interests and activities, "more than anyone else, [he] represented natural philosophy for the students and citizens of Glasgow and the West of Scotland for four decades" (Wilson, 2009, p. 173). As a very innovative engineer, he, for example, installed the first lighting conductors in Glasgow. He also worked with several celebrated inventors, such as Benjamin Franklin and James Watt. Very concerned about developing "places of useful learning" that would be open to men and women alike, he founded a college in Glasgow which is now the University of Strathclyde. This university houses a special collection on Anderson, including his notes on a lecture authored by Smith.

Anderson did not capture Smith's lecture verbatim but rather noted down a synthesis of his views, presented in short sentences or even bullet points. Only one scholar, Ronald L. Meek, has so far analysed these notes in detail (Meek, 1976a). Researchers who have studied Smith's life and work are of little help on the subject. They usually comment that Anderson was "quarrelsome and litigious" (Butt, 1996, p. 12) and had disputes with several people (see, for example, Phillipson, 2010, p. 301; Ross, 2010, pp. 134, 155–154; and Wilson, 2009, p. 171). Ian Simpson Ross did offer a short summary of the notes, but without conducting an original analysis. Instead, he relied on Meek's views (Ross, 2010, pp. 119–120).

We are thus very much indebted to the scholarship of Ronald Meek for confirming that the notes are indeed a summary of an Adam Smith lecture. He wrote several key books and scholarly articles on Smith, the Physiocrats and Karl Marx (Meek, 1971, 1976a, 1976b, 1977), and edited (with D. D. Raphael and P. G. Stein) the invaluable *Lectures on Jurisprudence*, published by Glasgow and Oxford Universities in 1978, the year of Meek's death. In this article, I refer to Meek's seminal 1976 article when quoting from the Anderson notes as it is the only place where one can access the text in full (Meek, 1976a, pp. 467–477), without making a trip to the University of Strathclyde.[4]

As Meek (1976a, pp. 440–441) explained, the notes on Smith's lecture appear on pages 292–368 in the first of three brown leather-covered notebooks – also called "commonplace books" – and total about 4400 words. A page from the notebook is shown at the end of this chapter as Figure 1. A. H. Brown, of St Antony's College, Oxford, discovered the notes in July 1970, and they were later sent to Meek, at the University of Leicester, who was asked to verify that the lecture was the work of Smith. He did this via three different methods of comparison (Meek, 1976a, pp. 453–454).

Besides confirming the notes' authenticity, Meek's overall conclusion was that they proved that Smith used a four-stages theory early in his career. Meek proposed that, when structuring his lecture, Smith used a first stage "characterized by hunting and fishing"; a second stage "characterized by the acquisition of property in common by a clan or a nation"; and a third stage "characterized by the emergence of agriculture, permanent settlements, and private property in land" (Meek, 1976a, pp. 465–466). He was able to infer these conclusions after studying Smith's words, as they were recorded in Anderson's notes (Meek, 1976a, p. 467):

> Hunting and fishing are all the arts that prevail in the first state of society. To deprive a man of the beast or fish he has caught or of the fruit he has gathered, is depriving him of what cost him labor and so giving him pain and is contrary to the laws of the rudest society . . . When a clan or nation hunt and fish long (i.e. have lived long) in one tract of country, they acquire an exclusive property and it is considered as theirs, i.e., they acquire property in common . . . which is the second state of perfection in society. When confined to one country their arable ground and crops are in common. When their numbers increase, when instruments of husbandry are invented . . . and when they have built huts and towns . . . will arise private property in lands, . . . which is the third state of society advancing towards perfection.

As suggested previously, Smith's language here clearly indicates that he viewed these "stages" in an evolutionary way. Smith also mentions the so-called "fourth stage" six times in this document – that is, the "commercial stage" (Meek, 1976a, pp. 470 and 472). However, contrary to Meek's view, Smith did not invoke the sole issue of property and ownership to characterize this stage. Nor did he paint a rosy picture of the commercial stage. As mentioned previously, the Scots held a mixed view of "progress." They allowed many exemptions or even regressions in their historical model (Berry, 2001; Marouby, 2004).

Accordingly, Smith did not idealize the commercial stage in the Anderson notes. For example, he did suggest that the invention of "bills of exchange" and "credit upon government security" were good innovations, but he also argued, based on previous experience of large financial crises, that these innovations were potentially dangerous and needed to be strongly regulated by law in order to avoid "great frauds" (Meek, 1976a, p. 470). He even recommended that "the government of any country may reduce [i.e. regulate] the legal interest" (Meek, 1976a, p. 470). He maintained this position, many years later, in *The Wealth of Nations* (*WN*, II.iv.15, p. 357). The issue about the regulation of the financial and banking industry and the role of government in this domain is an issue we are still struggling with today at the international level. As noted by many, Smith insisted that society needed to prevent such crises by strong regulation and enhanced education, yet he is still presented by some as the champion of *laissez-faire* (Charolles, 2006; Griswold, 1999; Pauchant and Franco, 2014; Rockoff, 2011; Sen, 2011; Walraevens, 2014; Wight, 2011).

The Scottish Enlightenment, as a movement, also did not discredit previous civilizations. They did not view them as "inferior" (Berry, 2001; Harris, 2001; Höpfl, 1978; Meek, 1976b). As seen in the previous quotation from the Anderson notes, Smith proposed that each stage was "perfect" – that is, well adapted to its circumstances – until its potential transformation. He was also against slavery and colonization. In 1776, he even called the wish for a British Empire a "golden dream" and advised Great Britain to "accommodate her future views and designs to the real mediocrity of her circumstances" (*WN*, V.iii.92, p. 947). Grounded in empirical evidence – that is, a detailed analysis of the historical data – the Scots considered "their conceptual explanations as contributions to knowledge rather than supports for a particular political agenda" (Smith, 2009, p. 24). Accordingly, Smith denounced the colonial crimes of Europeans in America, China and India. His remarks perhaps anticipate our current situation, considering the recent development in both China and India and their increased power bases (*WN*, IV.vii.c.80, p. 626):

> The discovery of America, and that of a passage to the East Indies by the Cape of Good Hope, are the two greatest and most important events recorded in the history of mankind . . . To the natives, however, . . . all the commercial benefits which can have resulted from those events have been sunk and lost . . . At the particular time when these discoveries were made, the superiority of force happened to be so great on the side of the Europeans, that they were enabled to commit with impunity every sort of injustice in those remote countries. Hereafter, perhaps, the natives of those countries may grow stronger, or those of Europe may grow weaker, and the inhabitants of all the different quarters of the world may arrive at that equality of courage and force which, by inspiring mutual fear, can alone overawe the injustice of independent nations into some sort of respect for the rights of one another.

Again, we are very much indebted to the scholarship of Ronald Meek for confirming the authenticity of the Anderson notes and for testifying that Smith presented in them a four-stages theory (Meek, 1976a, p. 465). However, Meek suggested that Smith grounded his views in the notion of "ownership" (common versus private) and "in terms of different modes of subsistence" (Meek, 1976a, p. 466). This way of framing the issue respects Smith's emphasis on the biological requirements of life – that is, assuring subsistence of self and procreation. As suggested above, these pressures were seen by Smith and other Scots as central. But these pressures were not the *sole* explanation for the evolution of stages (Berry, 2001, p. 96). Furthermore, Meek's insistence on the centrality of ownership and the modes of production derives from a particular grand narrative: the Marxist narrative (Levine, 1987). Meek excused himself jokingly on this issue, stating "in the good old days . . . I was a fierce young Marxist instead of a benign middle-age Meekist" (Meek, 1971, p. 9). However, several of his contemporaries, such as Donald Winch (1978) and Andrew Skinner (1975), warned that Meek emphasized the Marxist importance of materialism and ownership too exclusively. By contrast, Adam Smith viewed these two notions as essential but not exclusive.

The imposition of this grand narrative on Smith's views was unfortunate as it masked the fact that Smith introduced a very rich socio-cultural theory of evolution, encompassing many variables and considerations. As the Anderson notes were presented through this grand narrative, or for other reasons, the notes were not included in the official work and correspondence corpus of Adam Smith, even though they seem essential for a better understanding of his views at the very start of his career. Furthermore, Anderson captured many designations used by Smith for distinguishing each stage, going far beyond the issues of subsistence, ownership and modes of production. While this is not emphasized by Meek, Anderson noted that Smith spoke of the "first state," "the second state," the "third state" (Meek, 1976a, p. 467); "rude government," "rude countries" and "rude societies" (pp. 471, 472, 474); "the ancients" (p. 472); the "first age" and the "heroic age" (pp. 473, 475); "polished ages" and "polished nations" (pp. 473, 476).

Beyond the sole issue of subsistence or ownership, Smith also described these stages in terms of different thought patterns and customs. As suggested previously, he also insisted on the emergence of different systems of laws and ethics, different degrees of complexity in the arts, science and technology, and different degrees of sophistication in democracy and institutional, constitutional and international arrangements. In turn, all these elements had some effect on the maintenance and/ or transformation of each stage. As an evolutionist adopting a multi-dimensional perspective, Smith refrained from attributing to one consideration a causal role for all of the others. In our current language, he did not posit that one independent variable, such as ownership, drove all of the dependent ones.

This key difference is currently emphasized in systems and complexity theory through the notion of "co-evolution" (Jantsch, 1979; Mitroff *et al.*, 2013). To come back to the four grand narratives I mentioned in the introduction of this article, Smith did not affirm, in the Anderson notes, that the will of God determined all aspects of life; he did not state that the modes of subsistence were the sole engine of evolution; he did not presuppose that the rise of reason causes constant progress; and he certainly did not propose that neither the market nor the price mechanism causes eternal prosperity and happiness. This being said, while Smith avoided all of these grand narratives, he *did* discuss how the existence or belief in the divine or in reason, as well as the need for subsistence and the effects of markets, interacted with each other. He emphasized that all of these considerations, and many more, co-evolved together, leading to intended as well as unintended consequences (Rothschild, 2011, p. 155).

Further, and as a whole, the Scots rejected a determinist view, where a few strict causes lead with certainty to a precise outcome. As emphasized by Christopher Berry, in a recent book on the commercial stage, "there was nothing inevitable about the commercial society. History for the Scots . . . was at once ineliminably open to contingency while also being properly susceptible to causal explanation" (Berry, 2015, p. 51). The stages theory introduced by Smith could perhaps be compared to an "ideal type" theory (Weinstein, 2013, p. 220), akin to the one used by Weber. In this way, each stage can preserve its flexibility, its contingency, as "historical laws are fuzzier than the laws of physics" (Weinstein, 2013, p. 228).

Interestingly, in the Anderson notes, Smith postulated two general principles. He used these two principles to structure his theory on the evolution of different modes of subsistence, propriety, production, arts, sciences, customs, laws, ethics and institutions. As suggested below, he mixed in these principles the influence of biological instincts, the process of sympathy as well as the emergence of social conventions and institutions. Unfortunately, Meek, by focusing on "mode-of-subsistence," concluded that these two principles were not the key for under-standing Smith's views and that he later "emancipated" his theory from them (Meek, 1976a, p. 466). Smith stated these principles at the very beginning of the notes as follows (Haakonssen, in Hanley, 2016, p. 53; Meek, 1976a, p. 467):

> 1st Principle: To deprive a man of life or limbs or to give him pain is shocking to the rudest of our species when no enmity or grudge subsists, i.e., where no punishment is due or danger apprehended.

> 2nd Principle: We acquire a liking for those creatures or things which we are much conversant with and thus to deprive us of them must give us pain.

The first notion implied in these principles is the instinct of *self-preservation* and the survival of the species, expressed by the words "To deprive a man of life" and "species" itself. As suggested above, Smith derived this understanding from Stoicism and from the natural law tradition, consolidated with the naturalist notions emerging in his times. Charles Darwin would confirm them more than a century later from a wealth of empirical evidence. The second notion implied by Smith in these principles is the one of *sympathy*, which is used several times and explicitly in the Anderson notes (Meek, 1976a, pp. 468, 475), ten years before the publication of *The Theory of Moral Sentiments*. Of course, sympathy is key in Smith's system (Bessone and Biziou, 2009; Forman-Barzilai, 2010; Frazer, 2010; Weinstein, 2013). Thus, in his first principle, Smith proposed that even the "rudest of our species" (in the above quotation) will feel a sympathetic pain and will find cognitively shocking that another person is hurt without good reason – that is, a crisis ("enmity" and "grudge" in the text) – "danger" (perhaps triggering self-defence), or "punishment due" – that is, a collective decision made. This collective decision, implying a "social convention," perhaps crystallized in institutions, is the third notion introduced by Smith in his first principle.

The same three notions of instinct, sympathy and convention are also implied in Smith's second principle: the language used emphasizes a positive sentiment and the importance of the passage of time for a convention or a norm to become established and shared in a collectivity ("we acquire a liking" in the text), as well as the sympathetic pain felt as we lose either a person we like and have known for a long time ("much conversant with"), or an animal ("those creatures"), or possibly some property ("or things").

Globally, Smith explained in the Anderson notes how the first, second, third and fourth stages of human evolution (to call them in that fashion) emerged in many ways unintentionally as answers, in part, to scarce resources, endangering the lives of individuals and even the species, but also through intentional actions (Berry, 2001, pp. 61–71). These answers triggered, through the sympathetic process, the crystallization of different social conventions, such as manners, customs, laws, ethical preferences and types of institutions, influencing in turn the characteristics of each stage. As suggested previously, Smith did not imply that this process was either linear or invariant across cultures (Frazer, 2010; Weinstein, 2013). For example, when reflecting on the specific development of Europe, which was different from that in China, for instance, Smith explained the rise of feudalism as follows in the Anderson notes (Meek, 1976a, p. 468; for a longer explanation of the same subject, see *LJ*, i.116–132, pp. 49–55):

> Where there are no manufactures and where agriculture is little minded, the country must soon be overstocked with inhabitants. Hence the Teutons made their invasions [of richer countries in Europe]. "Feu," the German word, signifies pay, as "fee" in English. As the conquests were made by armies and by generals who were not able to maintain them, [the conquerors] were put in possession of the lands [and the period of feudalism emerged].

To give another example at a more micro-level, Smith explained, in the Anderson notes, the custom for criminals and smugglers to pay their debts scrupulously. In so doing, he invoked a sympathetic process, based on felt sentiment, for explaining why legal penalties, an institutionalized norm, are heavier in the case of killing than in the case of white-collar crime (Meek, 1976a, p. 471; for a similar discussion, using another example, see *TMS*, II.ii.3.3–12, pp. 87–91):

> In order to judge of the reasonableness and origin of different punishments we must call to mind what a private person feels when injured. Our aversion to a murderer is principally fear and terror, our aversion to a thief, contempt and disregard. Hence murderers have always suffered the last punishment, and thieves have been fined, ducked or punished with infamy. In general, where there are penal laws against any action that very circumstance [enforces the respect of] contracts . . . Hence, debts of honor are religiously kept by cheating gamesters. And the smugglers in England, when a boat

comes . . . sell their goods and receive payment by the buyers throwing the
money put up in bag into the smugglers ship. They have not time to count this
money and can have no redress in case of a fraud.

This last example, which invites the reader to enter through sympathy into the
sentiments of others, describing in a vignette a concrete scene of day-to-day life
which, through time, could crystallize into an institutionalized norm, is a typical
example of how Smith composed his texts. Emma Rothschild (2011, p. 7) has
suggested that Smith introduced a "new kind of micro-history."

Revisiting the dating of the Anderson notes

In the previous section I argued that Smith proposed, in the Anderson notes, a
subtle and non-linear socio-cultural theory of evolution, mixing different biological, instinctual, psycho-social, cultural and institutional processes. As I
explained above, this interpretation is different from the one presented by Meek.
In this section, I review the evidence for dating the Anderson notes. The conclusion reached by Meek was that the notes were probably composed between 1755
and 1762 (Meek, 1976a, p. 461). By contrast, I have concluded that Anderson
wrote them in 1749 or 1750, from a lecture drafted by Smith in 1749, for delivery
in the fall session.

Reviewing the internal evidence of the notes, Meek rightly concluded that they
could not have been composed prior to 1748. In the notes, Smith mentions several
times a book which influenced him greatly (Ross, 2010, p. 119): Montesquieu's
De l'esprit des lois, which was published in late 1748. However, Meek strangely
concludes that the notes could not have been written prior to 1753, as Smith
appears to mention three texts (by David Hume, Robert Wallace and Jean Jacob
Vernet) which were published in that year. I say "strangely" as one cannot identify
the exact title of Hume's essay in the Anderson notes. Smith could have been
referring to any one of many earlier essays by Hume. Also, as he met Hume
probably during or just after the summer of 1749 (Ross, 2010, p. 103), Smith
could have had access to a new manuscript, not yet published. In addition, Meek
admitted that it was probably Anderson himself who added the reference to
Wallace, and that Vernet's text was available in French (a language that Smith had
mastered) as early as 1745 (Meek, 1976a, pp. 456–457).

Having formulated these hypotheses, Meek attempted to trace a student (a
"Mr Campbell"), who could have transcribed one of Smith's lectures between
1753 and 1762, and from whom Anderson may have copied the notes. However,
Meek failed to prove that possibility and failed to identify the person (Meek,
1976a, p. 460).

Unfortunately, all of these suppositions led Meek to suggest that the notes could
have been produced as late as 1762 – that is, as part of Smith's *Lectures on
Jurisprudence* – but after several books that used a historical or stages model had
already been published, such as the first volume of Hume's *History of Great
Britain* (1754) or Lord Kames's *Historical Law-Tracts* (1758).

When I studied the notes in their original manuscript form at the University of Strathclyde, I realized that Meek did not have to make any of these assumptions. It is probable that, while he certainly saw the commonplace books, he primarily worked from a typed transcription of the notes. He thus distanced himself from the actual manuscript. The insight I got, looking at the handwriting, was that Anderson did not meticulously copy someone else's notes from an Adam Smith lecture. Rather, he took the notes himself *while listening to Smith*, who was speaking right in front of him. The physical structure of Anderson's handwriting is consistent with this hypothesis. As shown in Figure 2 (at the end of this article), when Anderson transcribed notes from an existing document, his handwriting was neat, straight and well ordered with relatively small letters. He would also indicate the page numbers from which he was copying. However, in the transcription of Smith's lecture (Figure 1), his handwriting is much less neat, less straight, more disordered, and there are a lot of corrections. Moreover, the letters are relatively large, which probably signifies that he was writing hurriedly, as one would during a lecture.

Having concluded that these notes were taken "live," I embarked on a bit of detective work. I needed to discover when both Adam Smith and John Anderson could have been present at the same time in a lecture hall. On Anderson's side, we know:

1. That he was present in Glasgow, as a tutor, between 1749 and August 1750 (Butt, 1996, p. 2).
2. This is confirmed by a letter he wrote when attending his sister's wedding in the city on 14 February 1750 (Strathclyde University MS GB 249 OA/2/1).
3. He left Glasgow in the fall of 1750 for London to serve as a tutor to Lord Doune, and remained there until August 1753 (Butt, 1996, p. 2).
4. There is evidence that Anderson knew Smith prior to December 1750, as he stated in a letter posted that month that he was glad to hear that Smith was being considered for a chair at Glasgow, as he was an "able candidate" (Strathclyde University MS GB 249 OA/2/2).
5. After London, Anderson resided in France in 1754, returned to Glasgow for a short visit in June 1755, and then took up his university position, and so became one of Smith's colleagues, in October 1756 (Butt, 1996, p. 3).
6. However, these dates are of little interest for our investigation as the lecture notes we are interested in appear in the first volume of Anderson's commonplace books, which covers roughly the period 1748–1751 (Meek, 1976a, p. 457). The other commonplace books cover later years.

All of this evidence leads me to conclude that Anderson must have transcribed Smith's lecture between 1749 and the fall of 1750.

On Smith's side, we know:

1. That he taught his first Edinburgh lectures from October 1748 to June 1749 on the subject of rhetoric and belles lettres (Ross, 2010, pp. 82–83; *LR&BL*, preface), which is not the subject that is covered in the Anderson notes.

2. He started a second round of Edinburgh lectures from October 1749 to June 1750, expanding on his "philosophical history" and adding material on civil law and jurisprudence (Ross, 2010, pp. 102–103). This corresponds to the material covered in the Anderson notes.
3. He repeated these lectures from October 1750 to June 1751, and took up his chair position at the University of Glasgow in October 1751 (Ross, 2010, p. 108).
4. These dates are, however, too late for our purposes, as Anderson had already left Glasgow in the fall of 1750.

I have thus concluded that Anderson must have transcribed Smith's lecture between October 1749 and the fall of 1750, either during the general lectures Smith gave at Edinburgh or during the private lectures he gave in the same city on civil law (Ross, 2010, p. 103).

While we cannot be sure of the precise date of the lecture during which Anderson took his notes, we can be relatively certain that the material he transcribed was imagined, composed and delivered by Adam Smith in 1749, as explained below. We can thus safely refer to these notes as "Adam Smith's 1749 lecture." The notes constitute the first recorded Adam Smith lecture we currently have. Furthermore, they were composed years before any other Scot, or indeed anyone else, proposed a version of the four-stages theory.

Smith confirmed this 1749 date to Dugald Stewart. This was affirmed in a paper and a conference speech he gave in 1755 on "certain leading principles both political and literary" for which he considered himself to be the originator (*EPS*, IV.23, p. 321). Smith's remark, included in a paper that seems to have been lost, has generated considerable debate (e.g., Kennedy, 2005, pp. 241–248; Ross, 2010, pp. 105–107). It could be that Smith realized that his innovative and evolutionary theories were being used by others without proper credit and/or that they were being developed in a manner of which he disapproved. As Smith, quoted by Stewart, explained (*EPS*, IV.26, p. 322):

> A great part of the opinions enumerated in this [1755] paper is treated of at length in some lectures which I have still by me, and which were written in the hand of a clerk who left my service six years ago [i.e., 1749]. They have all of them been the constant subjects of my lectures since I first taught Mr Craigie's class, the first winter I spent in Glasgow, down to this day, without any considerable variation. They had all of them been the subjects of lectures which I read at Edinburgh the winter before I left it [i.e., 1749–1750], and I can adduce innumerable witnesses both from that place and from this, who will ascertain them sufficiently to be mine.

The evidence I have presented above, both on content and dating, sustains the hypothesis that Adam Smith introduced the first socio-cultural theory of evolution in 1749, in which he proposed a general pattern structured by a model with four general but flexible stages, proposed as "ideal types," called by different names and allowing many variations across cultures. While more research on this question could confirm this hypothesis, the evidence presented here is consistent with the remarks made by Smith's heir, John Millar. As suggested above, Smith took on board the views expressed by Hume and Montesquieu, and many other authors, but he then went beyond them. These attestations are also consistent with John Callander of Craigforth's testimony that he heard Smith lecture on this subject in 1749–1750, as well as Dugald Stewart's comments. Stewart affirmed that Smith introduced a new methodology, a new type of inquiry called a "Theoretical or Conjectural History," a "Natural History," or, in French, "[une] Histoire raisonnée" (*EPS*, II.48, p. 293). Smith himself referred to his methodology as a "philosophical history" (Ross, 2010, p. 85). In addition, in 1793, after Smith's death, Stewart proposed that this new type of inquiry was visible in all of Smith's works, both lectures and books, some of them composed in the late 1740s – that is, literature, rhetoric, law, ethics, political economy and philosophy of science. As Stewart stated (*EPS*, II.44–45, p. 292):

> [Smith was fond of] a particular sort of inquiry, which, so far as I know, is entirely of modern origin . . . Something very similar to it may be traced in all his different works, whether moral, political, or literary; and on all these subjects he has exemplified it with the happiest success. When, in such a period of society as that in which we live, we compare our intellectual acquirements, our opinions, manners, and institutions, with those which prevail among rude tribes, it cannot fail to occur to us as an interesting question, by what gradual steps the transition has been made from the first simple efforts of uncultivated nature, to a state of things so wonderfully artificial and complicated.

But Stewart was fully aware that Smith's innovation triggered a larger movement. His public lectures did not go unnoticed. They influenced many people both in Scotland and elsewhere. These lectures were indeed successful and important events, attracting "innumerable" attendants, as Smith himself stated (*EPS*, IV. 26, p. 322). They influenced a good number of people who spoke and wrote to others afterwards, in Scotland and abroad, or published and lectured on similar subjects. A list of attendees may include Hugh Blair, John Callander of Craigforth, George Home Drummond, William Johnstone, Lord Kames, James Oswald, John Millar, William Robertson, Alexander Wedderburn, James Wodrow, perhaps even David Hume, and, obviously, John Anderson (Rae, 2002, pp. 30–41; Ross, 2010, pp. 82–83). The introduction of Smith's four-stages model, proposed as "ideal types," allowed for the first time a more rigorous comparison among different time periods and civilizations, proposing a co-evolutionary theory grounded in the natural sciences, the social sciences and the humanities. Smith himself felt compelled to write a paper and deliver another public lecture on the subject in 1755, in which he took care to restate his original 1749 views.

Conclusion

My purpose in this paper has been to propose that in 1749 Adam Smith introduced a socio-cultural theory of evolution that had a significant influence on later authors. In this conclusion, I suggest several lines of new research that this hypothesis could trigger. Space constraints mean that I can mention only a few of these avenues.

This new hypothesis could prompt a renewed effort in the history of ideas on the emergence of the four-stages theory in the world at large. This research would continue and deepen the works of, for example, Meek (1976b), Harris (2001) and Rasmussen (2014). For example, and considering the emphasis placed on Turgot in this history of ideas (Meek, 1971; Binoche, 2005), an in-depth comparison between his views and the new ones revealed in this article on Smith would be particularly welcome.

This hypothesis could also trigger new research on the Scottish Enlightenment itself. This would build on the works of, for example, Berry (2001), Broadie (2003) Whitaker *et al.* (2007) and Wilson (2009). This new research could compare Smith's foundational views with the works that his colleagues published later, uncovering their similarities and differences. For example, recent scholarship has suggested that "unequivocal expressions of four stages [are present only] in Smith, Millar, Kames and Blair" (Berry, 2015, p. 39). While Berry has recently compared these different versions, relative to the commercial stage, his analysis could be enriched by the new evidence uncovered in this article.[5]

In addition, parallels with Smith's theory could be drawn with authors from around the world who have recently proposed diverse evolutionary analyses of the earth's beginnings and the unfolding of civilizations. These works, in the fields of "world history," "big history" and "world mythology," attempt to reactualize the past into our present by integrating different biological, sociological and cultural changes in an evolutionary fashion (Christian, 2004; Diamond, 2003; Fukuyama, 2011; Stokes Brown, 2012; Witzel, 2013). While these works echo the spirit of Smith's "philosophical history," they also integrate different methodologies which were non-existent or only emerging in Smith's time, such as archaeology, comparative linguistics, geological history, molecular biology, paleoanthropology and populations genetics.

This comparative type of research, comparing the views of different authors with Smith's own perspectives, could be facilitated by the suggestions made in this article. As I have proposed, in 1749 he embraced a cautious view of progress. Recent scholarship agrees that Smith, during his lifetime, remained "committed to the tradition of grand narrative" (Weinstein, 2013, p. 221), but that he evaluated the nature of this "progress" retrospectively, from a very long time perspective, using a pluralistic lens (Weinstein, 2013, p. 230). However, I have also suggested that Smith's views differ with the grand narratives used by many authors during his time and later, such as the natural law perspective, the Marxist view, the utilitarian and positivist philosophy and the spontaneous order of the market paradigm. Comparative research will gain, I suggest, from taking these differences into consideration. It is also likely that this type of research will be fruitful for the ongoing debate on the nature–culture divide (Boyd and Richerson, 2005) as well as on the legitimacy of grand narratives (Foucault, 2004).

But this focus on grand theories runs the risk of not addressing all the subjective subtleties introduced by Smith. As suggested in this article, he did not use his 1749 theory only as a grand narrative to survey human evolution across the centuries. He also introduced a great number of well-crafted vignettes and short stories, while avoiding mere anecdotes. Smith understood that the purpose of history is not only to explain great trends but also to express how these events "[affect] the minds of the actors or spectators" (*LR&BL*, ii.63, p. 60), immersing readers into these experiences. Thus, he used many such vignettes in his 1749 lecture in an attempt to trigger the sympathetic or empathic processes of his listeners or readers. In parallel with rational explanations, he hoped that his audience might encounter people of other times, countries or occupations, put themselves into their shoes and expand their imagination. Jonathan Wight (2006), or Michael Amrozowick (in Berry et al., 2013, pp. 143–174), have insisted that Smith's compositions aimed also at character education, stimulating an internal dialogue with one's "impartial spectator." Emma Rothschild (2010, p. 32) has also recently suggested that Smith increasingly introduced in his works or re-editions of his works different historical illustrations. For her, these micro-histories allowed Smith to engage in "a sort of virtual conversation" with his readers, inviting them to go beyond their parochial views. In a similar vein, Martha Nussbaum (2001) has called for an "upheaval of thought," praising Smith for his understanding of the delicate process of empathic sentiments and internal dialogue, as well as his use of narrative ethics in an attempt to elicit them. It is unsurprising that Smith, after lecturing extensively on rhetoric and belles lettres in 1748 (Ross, 2010, p. 80), used this literary pedagogy the following year. This characteristic of his work should also be considered in any comparative research.

Finally, I feel that we need to improve our understanding of the similarities and differences between the socio-cultural theory of evolution introduced (potentially) by Adam Smith in 1749 and the natural evolution theory introduced by Charles Darwin in 1859. As we have seen, Smith integrated in his inquiry many biological, instinctual and natural elements. In the 1970s, Edward Wilson attempted to rediscover a "consilience" between the natural and the social sciences by advocating the development of the field of *sociobiology*. His call, to put it mildly, has not been well received. In part, he has been mainly perceived as Charles Darwin's heir. However, he also grounded his proposal in the Scottish social sciences, mentioning explicitly Francis Hutcheson, David Hume and Adam Smith (Wilson, 1999, p. 275). Most of the commentators who have attacked the field of sociobiology have denounced the abuses of social Darwinism, its perceived deterministic and selfish ethos, the exaggerated claims of evolutionary psychologists, or even the dark spectres of eugenics and Nazism (Boyd and Richerson, 2005; Carey, 2011; Clark, 2009; Pava, 2008).

I suggest that basing this greater consilience in the socio-cultural theory of evolution introduced by Adam Smith could be less controversial and more encompassing than attempting to ground it in the natural theory of evolution introduced by Charles Darwin. To put it simply, in 1749 Smith (potentially) introduced an outline for a "system of social science" (Skinner, 1996), integrating many natural processes. As this article has explained, he mixed the influence of instincts, sympathy and conventions. By contrast, Darwin focused exclusively on these natural processes in *On the Origin of Species by Means of Natural Selection*. It was only later that he included the human reality and its socio-cultural developments, in *The Descent of Man* (1871) and *The Expression of the Emotions in Man* (1872). However, standard biology has only partly integrated these later views (Wilson, 2006). Several researchers have already started to explore the similarities and differences between Smith and Darwin, not focusing on mere analogies but comparing textual evidence (Carey, 1998, 2011; van der Weele, 2011; Wight, 2009; Wilson, 2015). It seems that this line of research could lead to some important breakthroughs.

We are living in an exciting time during which an increasing number of authors in the social sciences, the natural sciences and the humanities are trying to build a more consilient science. A similar aim was pursued by Hume, Smith and the Scottish Enlightenment in general. In that search, it seems that, once more, Adam Smith's insights could prove invaluable. Rediscovering and deepening his theory of socio-cultural co-evolution is important not only from a historical perspective. As Smith is often touted as the founding father of an economic theory that is detrimental to our present world, countering this "kidnapping" (Moene, 2011, p. 191) is an urgent task. We need to rebuild an evolutionary theory that is convivial for the economic, social, moral and ecological wealth of our nations, an aim that Smith, it seems, pursued as early as 1749, at the age of twenty-six. As Amartya Sen (2011, p. 270) suggests:

> Along with appropriate uses of Smith [in economics] there is also a great many abuses . . . This does need serious rectification . . . [but] there are additional uses to which Smith's ideas can be put that have been unduly neglected in the world of knowledge and understanding, particularly in moral, political, and legal philosophy . . . There is a great deal of life left in the thought of that remarkable thinker.

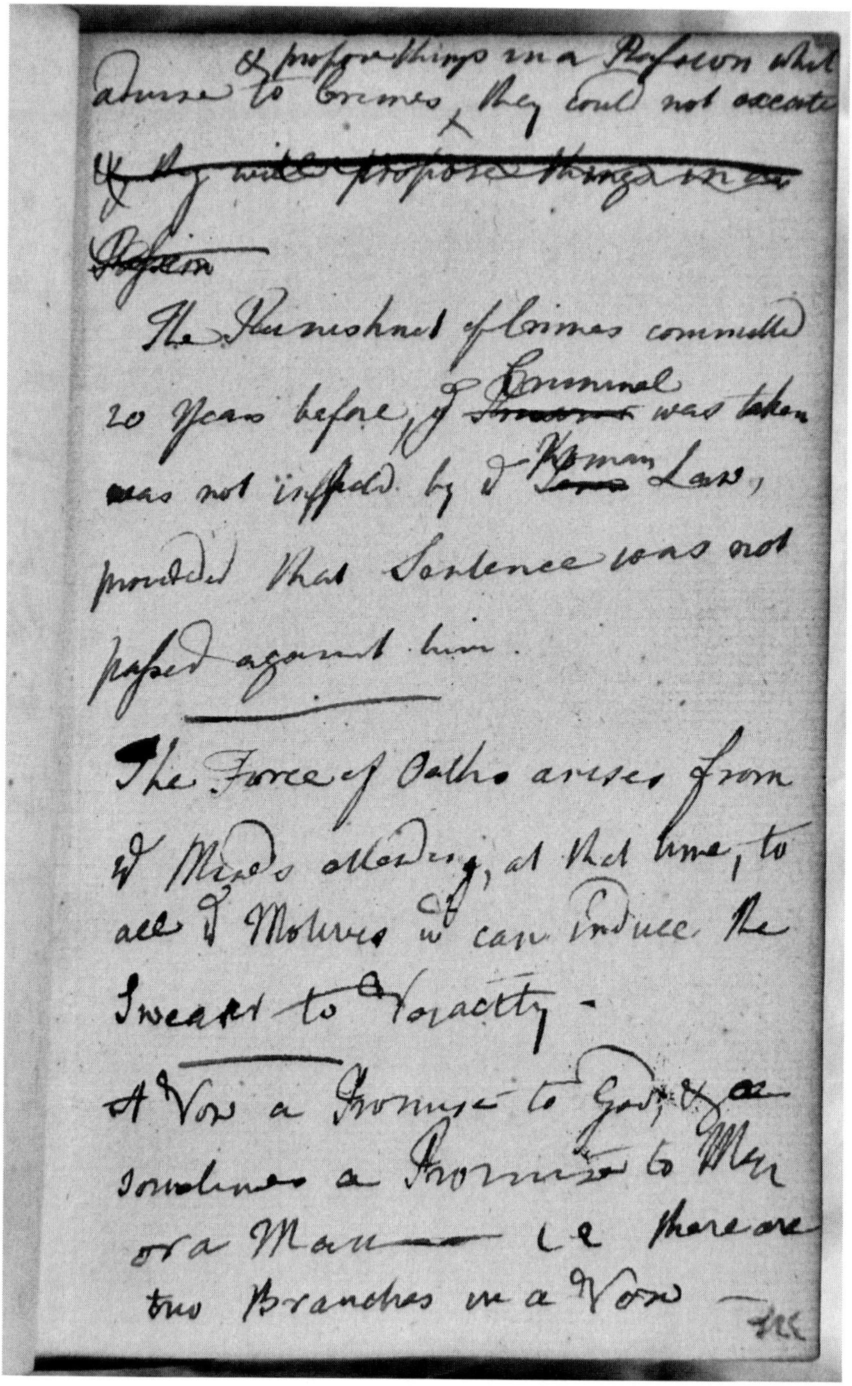

Figure 1 A typical page where John Anderson took notes during Adam Smith's lecture
(Special Collections Department, University of Strathclyde, Glasgow, GB 249,
OA/7/1, p. 326)

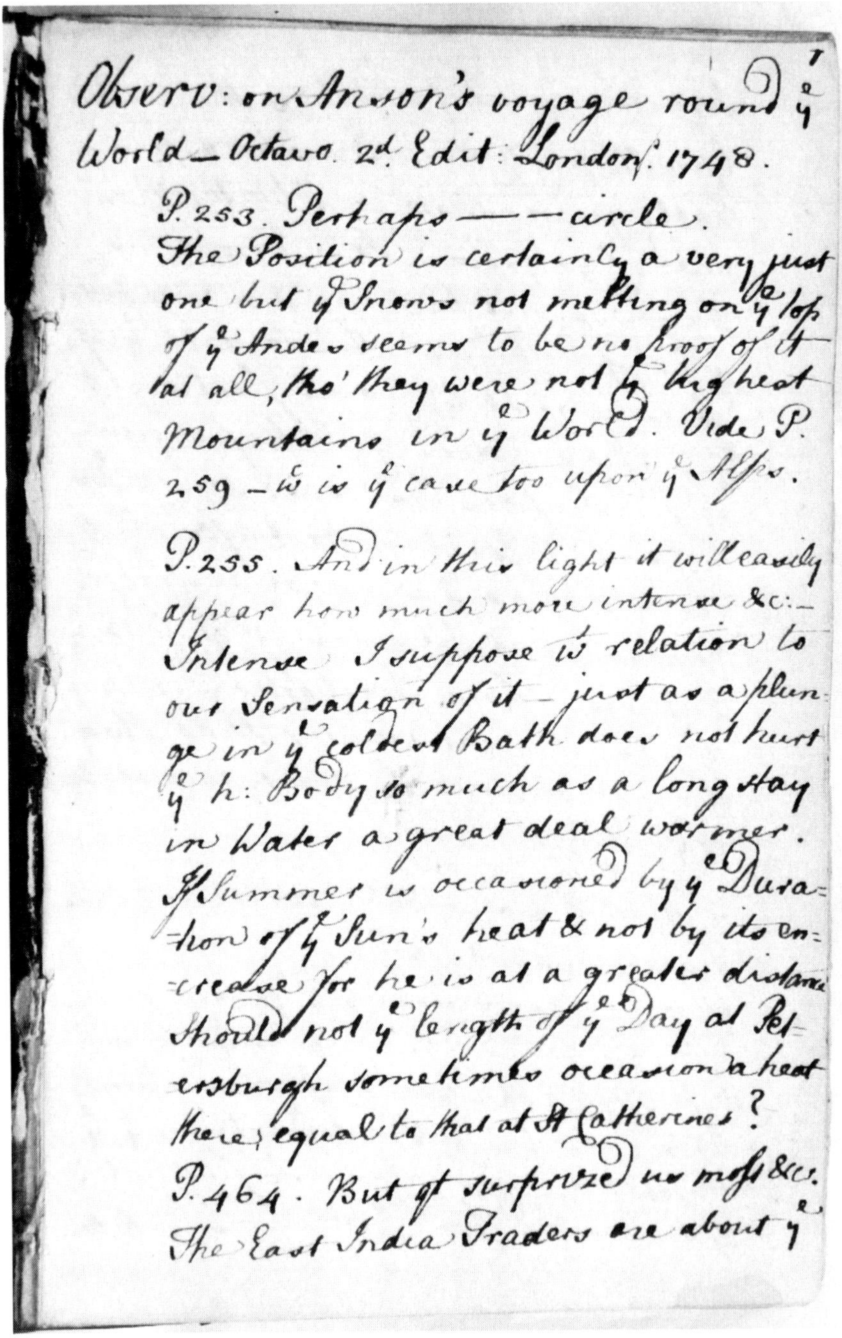

Observ: on Anson's voyage round $\frac{2}{4}$
World — Octavo. 2d Edit: London. 1748.

P. 253. Perhaps — — — circle.
The Position is certainly a very just
one but y Snows not melting on y top
of y Andes seems to be no proof of it
at all, tho' they were not y highest
Mountains in y World. Vide P.
259 — w is y case too upon y Alps.

P. 255. And in this light it will easily
appear how much more intense &c:—
Intense I suppose is relation to
our Sensation of it — just as a plun-
ge in y coldest Bath does not hurt
y h: Body so much as a long stay
in Water a great deal warmer.
If Summer is occasioned by y Duration of y Sun's heat & not by its en-
crease for he is at a greater distance
should not y length of y Day at Pet-
ersburgh sometimes occasion a heat
there, equal to that at St Catherines?
P. 464. But yt surprized us most &c.
The East India Traders are about y

Figure 2 A typical page where John Anderson took notes from an existing book (Special
Collections Department, University of Strathclyde, Glasgow, GB 249, OA/7/1,
p. 1)

Notes

1   This paper was presented at Sorbonne University, Paris, on 6 July 2013, during the conference "Scotland, Europe and Empire in the Age of Adam Smith and Beyond." I would like to thank Toni Vogel Carey, Eugene Heath, Jerome Lange, Philippe Massot, John R. Young, Nathaniel Wolloch and others for their commentaries as well as those from this anthology's two anonymous reviewers. I also wish to thank the AMF (FESG programme) for its financial assistance in this research. Of course, all errors remain my own.

2   Dennis Rasmussen has recently argued that, contrary to popular belief, many Scottish and French authors during the Enlightenment did not promote a hegemonic stance on reason. Drawing in particular from Hume, Smith, Montesquieu and Voltaire, he proposed that they "all held that it is the sentiments or passions, rather than reason, that serve as both the chief motivating force of human action and the ultimate basis from which moral standards are derived" (Rasmussen, 2014, p. 139).

3   In this article, I use the standard Adam Smith references, abbreviating each of his publications, which are listed in full in the bibliography, such as *EPS* (*Essays on Philosophical Subjects*), *TMS* (*The Theory of Moral Sentiments*), *WN* (*Wealth of Nations*), and so on.

4   I did make that trip, and sincerely wish to thank Victoria Peters, University Archivist, and Anne Cameron, from the University of Strathclyde's Special Collections Department, for their very professional and generous assistance while I analysed the manuscript in 2011, during a sabbatical year.

5   David Hume's comments, in a letter sent to Adam Smith from 12 April 1759, are interesting on this subject. In this letter, Hume comments on Lord Kames's two-volume *Historical Law-Tracts*, published in 1758 and considered to be one of the first declarations of a four-stages model (Berry, 2015, p. 39). While Hume did not himself propose a four-stages theory, it is clear that he compares Kames's views with his ideal of a stadial theory. As Hume wrote: "I am afraid of Lord Kaims's Law Tracts. A man might as well think of making a fine sauce by a mixture of wormwood and aloes as an agreeable composition by joining metaphysics and Scot law. However, the book has merit" (*Corr.*, p. 34).

Bibliography

Berry, C. J. (2001). *Social Theory of the Scottish Enlightenment* (reprint). Edinburgh: Edinburgh University Press.

Berry, C. J., M. P. Paganelli and C. Smith (eds.) (2013). *The Oxford Handbook of Adam Smith*. Oxford: Oxford University Press.

Berry, C. J. (2015). *The Idea of Commercial Society in the Scottish Enlightenment* (paperback edition). Edinburgh: Edinburgh University Press.

Bessone, M. and M. Biziou (eds) (2009). *Adam Smith philosophe. De la morale à l'économie ou philosophie du libéralisme*. Rennes: Presses Universitaires de Rennes.

Binoche, B. (ed.) (2005). *Les équivoques de la civilisation*. Paris: Champ Vallon.

Bonnyman, B. (2014). *The Third Duke of Buccleuch and Adam Smith: Estate Management and Improvement in Enlightenment Scotland*. Edinburgh: Edinburgh University Press.

Boyd, R. and P. J. Richerson (2005). *The Origin and Evolution of Cultures*. New York: Oxford University Press.

Broadie, A. (ed.) (2003). *The Cambridge Companion to the Scottish Enlightenment*. Cambridge: Cambridge University Press.

Bryson, G. (1968). *Man and Society. The Scottish Enquiry and the Eighteenth Century*. New York: August M. Kelley (originally published 1945).

Butt, J. (1996). *John Anderson's Legacy: The University of Strathclyde and its Antecedents, 1796–1996*. Glasgow: Tuckwell Press/University of Strathclyde.

Carey, T. V. (1998). The Invisible Hand of Natural Selection, and Vice Versa. *Biology and Philosophy*, 13, 427–442.

Carey, T. V. (2011). The "Sub-Rational" in Scottish Moral Science. *Journal of Scottish Philosophy*, 9, 2, 225–238.

Charolles, V. (2006). *Le Libéralisme contre le capitalisme*. Paris: Fayard.

Christian, D. (2004). *Maps of Time: An Introduction to Big History*. Berkeley: University of California Press.

Clark, H. C. (2009). Adam Smith and Neo-Darwinian Debate over Sympathy, Strong Reciprocity, and the Reputation Effects. *Journal of Scottish Philosophy*, 7, 1, 47–64.

Diamond, J. (2003). *Guns, Germs, and Steel: The Fates of Human Societies* (2nd edition). New York: W. W. Norton.

Evensky, J. (2007). *Adam Smith's Moral Philosophy: A Historical and Contemporary Perspective on Markets, Law, Ethics and Culture*. Cambridge: Cambridge University Press.

Fleischacker, S. (2004). *On Adam Smith's Wealth of Nations: A Philosophical Companion*. Princeton, NJ: Princeton University Press.

Forman-Barzilai, F. (2010). *Adam Smith and the Circles of Sympathy: Cosmopolitanism and Moral Theory*. Cambridge: Cambridge University Press.

Foucault, M. (2004). *Naissance de la biopolitique. Cours au Collège de France*. Paris: Gallimard Seuil.

Frazer, M. L. (2010). *The Enlightenment of Sympathy: Justice and the Moral Sentiments in the Eighteenth Century and Today*. New York: Oxford University Press.

Fukuyama, F. (2011). *The Origins of Political Order. From Pre-human Times to the French Revolution*. New York: Farrar, Straus and Giroux.

Griswold, C. L. Jr. (1999). *Adam Smith and the Virtues of Enlightenment*. Cambridge: Cambridge University Press.

Haakonssen, K. (ed.) (1981). *The Science of a Legislator: The Natural Jurisprudence of David Hume and Adam Smith*. Cambridge: Cambridge University Press.

Hanley, R. P. (ed.) (2016). *Adam Smith: His Life, Thought and Legacy*. Princeton, NJ: Princeton University Press.

Harris, M. (2001). *The Rise of Anthropological Theory: A History of Theories of Culture* (updated edn). Walnut Creek, NY: Atamira Press.

Hont, I. (1987). The Language of Sociability and Commerce: Samuel Pufendorf and the Theoretical Foundations of the Four Stages. In A. Pagden (ed.), *The Language of Political Theory in Early Modern Europe*. Cambridge: Cambridge University, 227–299.

Hont, I. and M. Ignatieff (eds) (1985). *Wealth and Virtue: The Shaping of Political Economy in the Scottish Enlightenment*. Cambridge: Cambridge University Press.

Höpfl, H. M. (1978). From Savage to Scotsman: Conjectural History in the Scottish Enlightenment. *Journal of British Studies*, 2, 19–40.

Jantsch, E. (1979). *The Self-organizing Universe: Scientific and Human Implications of the Emerging Paradigm of Evolution*. Oxford: Pergamon Press.

Kennedy, G. (2005). *Adam Smith's Lost Legacy*. London: Palgrave Macmillan.

Levine, N. (1987). The German Historical School of Law and the Origins of Historical Materialism. *Journal of the History of Ideas*, 48, 3, 431–451.

Marouby, C. (2004). *L'Économie de la nature. Essai sur Adam Smith et l'anthropologie de la croissance*. Paris: Édition du Seuil.

Massot-Bordenave, P. (2013). Adam Smith: Voyages en France, voyageur impartial, spectateur invisible. Doctoral thesis, Toulouse II Le Mirail.

Meek, R. L. (1971). Smith, Turgot, and the Four Stages Theory. *History of Political Economy*, 3, 1, 9–27.

Meek, R. L. (1976a). New Light on Adam Smith's Glasgow Lectures on Jurisprudence. *History of Political Economy*, 8, 4, 439–477.

Meek, R. L. (1976b). *Social Science and the Ignoble Savage*. Cambridge: Cambridge University Press.

Meek, R. L. (1977). *Smith, Marx and After: Ten Essays in the Development of Economic Thought*. London: Chapman and Hall.

Mitroff, I. I., L. B. Hill and C. M. Alpaslan (2013). *Rethinking the Education Mess: A Systems Approach to Education Reform*. New York: Palgrave Macmillan.

Moene, K. O. (2011). The Moral Sentiments of *Wealth of Nations*. *Adam Smith Review*, 6, 190–206.

Nussbaum, M. (2001). *Upheavals of Thought: The Intelligence of Emotions*. Cambridge: Cambridge University Press.

Pauchant, T. and E. Franco (2014). Adam Smith au-delà de sa caricature néo-libérale. Suggestions réglementaires et éthiques pour la banque, la finance et l'économie. *Éthique Publique*, 1, 4, 378–401.

Pava, M. L. (2008). The Exaggerated Moral Claims of Evolutionary Psychologists. *Journal of Business Ethics*, 85, 391–401.

Phillipson, N. (2010) *Adam Smith: An Enlightened Life*. London: Allen Lane.

Pocock, J. G. A. (1999). *Barbarism and Religion*. Volume Two: *Narratives of Civil Government*. Cambridge: Cambridge University Press.

Pufendorf, S. (1991). *On the Duty of Man and Citizen* (ed. J. Tully). Cambridge: Cambridge University Press.

Rae, J. (2002). *Life of Adam Smith*. Honolulu, HA: University Press of the Pacific (originally published 1895).

Rasmussen, D. C. (2014). *The Pragmatic Enlightenment. Recovering the Liberalism of Hume, Smith, Montesquieu, and Voltaire*. London: Cambridge University Press.

Ricoeur, P. (2004). *Parcours de la reconnaissance*. Paris: Stock.

Rockoff, H. (2011). Upon Daedalian Wings of Paper Money. Adam Smith and the Crisis of 1772. *Adam Smith Review*, 6, 237–268.

Ross, I. S. (2010). *The Life of Adam Smith* (2nd edition). Oxford: Oxford University Press.

Rothschild, E. (2001). *Economic Sentiments: Adam Smith, Condorcet, and the Enlightenment*. Cambridge, MA: Harvard University Press.

Rothschild, E. (2010). *The Theory of Moral Sentiments* and the Inner Life. *Adam Smith Review*, 5, 25–36.

Rothschild, E. (2011). *Inner Life of Empires: An Eighteenth Century History*. Princeton, NJ: Princeton University Press.

Scott, W. R. (1965). *Adam Smith as Student and Professor*. New York: Augustus M. Kelley.

Sen, A. (2009). *The Idea of Justice*. Cambridge, MA: Harvard University Press.

Sen, A. (2011). Uses and Abuses of Adam Smith. *History of Political Economy*, 43, 2, 257–271.

Sher, R. B. (2006). *The Enlightenment and the Book: Scottish Authors and their Publishers in Eighteenth Century Britain, Ireland and America*. Chicago, IL: University of Chicago Press.

Skinner, A. S. (1975). Adam Smith: An Economic Interpretation of History. In S. Skinner and T. Wilson (eds), *Essays on Adam Smith*. Oxford: Clarendon Press, 154–178.

Skinner, A. S. (1996). *A System of Social Science: Papers Relating to Adam Smith* (2nd edition). Oxford: Clarendon Press.

Smith, A. (1979). *Lectures on Jurisprudence* (ed. R. L. Meek, D. D. Raphael and P. G. Stein). Indianapolis, IN: Liberty Fund; and Oxford: Oxford University Press.

Smith, A. (1981). *An Inquiry into the Nature and Causes of the Wealth of Nations* (Vols. I and II) (ed. R. H. Campbell and A. S. Skinner). Indianapolis, IN: Liberty Fund; and Oxford: Oxford University Press.

Smith, A. (1982). *Essays on Philosophical Subjects* (ed. W. P. D. Wichtman, J. C. Bryce and I. S. Ross). Indianapolis, IN: Liberty Fund; and Oxford: Oxford University Press.

Smith, A. (1982). *The Theory of Moral Sentiments* (ed. D. D. Raphael and A. L. Macfie). Indianapolis, IN: Liberty Fund; and Oxford: Oxford University Press.

Smith, A. (1985). *Lectures on Rhetoric and Belles Lettres* (ed. J. C. Bryce). Indianapolis, IN: Liberty Fund; and Oxford: Oxford University Press.

Smith, A. (1987). *The Correspondence of Adam Smith* (ed. E. C. Mossner and I. S. Ross). Indianapolis, IN: Liberty Fund; and Oxford: Oxford University Press.

Smith, C. (2009). The Scottish Enlightenment, Unintended Consequences and the Science of Man. *Journal of Scottish Philosophy*, 7, 1, 9–27.

Stokes Brown, C. (2012). *Big History: From the Big Bang to the Present*. New York: The New Press.

Spector, C. (2005). Sciences des moeurs et théorie de la civilisation. De l'esprit des lois de Montesquieu à l'École historique Écossaise. In B. Binoche (ed.), *Les Équivoques de la civilisation*. Paris: Champ Vallon, 136–160.

Uglow, J. (2002). *The Lunar Men: The Friends who Made the Future, 1730–1810*. London: Faber and Faber.

Walraevens, B. (2014). Vertus et justice du marché chez Adam Smith. *Revue Économique*, 2, 65, 419–438.

van der Weele, C. (2011). Empathy's Purity, Sympathy's Complexities: De Waal, Darwin and Adam Smith. *Biological Philosophy*, 26, 583–593.

Weinstein, J. R. (2013). *Adam Smith's Pluralism. Rationality, Education, and the Moral Sentiments*. New Haven, CT: Yale University Press.

Whitaker, H., C. U. M. Smith and S. Finger (eds) (2007). *Brain, Mind and Medicine: Essays in Eighteenth-Century Neuroscience*. New York: Springer.

Wight, J. B. (2006). Adam Smith's Ethics and the "Noble Arts." *Review of Social Economy*, 64, 2, 155–180.

Wight, J. B. (2009). Adam Smith on Instincts, Affections, and Informal Learning: Proximate Mechanisms in Multilevel Selection. *Review of Social Economy*, 68, 1, 95–113.

Wight, J. B. (2011). Institutional Divergence in Economic Development. *Adam Smith Review*, 6, 309–326.

Wilson, D. B. (2009). *Seeking Nature's Logic. Natural Philosophy in the Scottish Enlightenment*. University Park: Pennsylvania State University Press.

Wilson, D. S. (2015). *Does Altruism Exist? Culture, Genes, and the Welfare of Others*. New Haven, CT: Yale University Press.

Wilson, E. O. (1999). *Consilience: The Unity of Knowledge*. New York: Vintage.

Wilson, E. O. (ed.) (2006). *From so Simple a Beginning: The Four Great Books of Charles Darwin*. New York: W. W. Norton.

Winch, D. (1978). *Adam Smith's Politics: An Essay in Historiographic Revision*. Cambridge: Cambridge University Press.

Witzel, M. (2013). *The Origins of the World's Mythologies*. New York: Oxford University Press.

Wolloch, N. (2011). *History and Nature in the Enlightenment: Praise of the Mastery of Nature in Eighteenth-Century History Literature*. Burlington, VT: Ashgate.

The idea of historical progress in the transition from Enlightenment historiography to classical political economy

Nathaniel Wolloch

In *The Wealth of Nations* Adam Smith claimed that it was 'not the actual greatness of national wealth, but its continual increase, which occasions a rise in the wages of labour. It is not, accordingly, in the richest countries, but in the most thriving, or in those which are growing rich the fastest, that the wages of labour are highest' (*WN* I.viii.22). What mattered more than material affluence was whether a country was in the process of acquiring that affluence, not whether it already possessed it, let alone was in the process of losing it. 'The progressive state is in reality the chearful and the hearty state to all the different orders of the society. The stationary is dull; the declining, melancholy' (*WN* I.viii.43). These well-known observations catered to the common eighteenth-century praise of progress. Yet it should be emphasized that for eighteenth-century intellectuals progress was not in itself a stationary concept, but rather a civilizing process, to use Norbert Elias's later phrase (Elias 1994). It was thus in essence a histori-cized term. It referred principally to the historical changes which all societies inevitably underwent in historical time. In the eighteenth century the seeds were sown for the subsequent Hegelian emphasis on the dynamic nature of meaningful history.

Since Smith obviously regarded progressive change as a key prism through which to consider in detail many topics of social and economic processes, the question should be asked: was he, in addition to his other intellectual and scholarly pursuits, also a historian? In a recent study, Jack Weinstein has claimed that Smith's writing has a unified character which also includes a role for historical writing. Furthermore, Smith believed that history and progress were both natural. "[W]hether or not Smith was a historian, he is most certainly a *philosopher of history*" (Weinstein 2013: 219–28; quotation at 220). Comparing Smith's and Foucault's historiographies, Weinstein uses the former to criticize postmodern-ism (ibid.: 239–63). J. G. A. Pocock has asserted that while traditional narrative historiography was not a significant part of Smith's concerns, a historical perspec-tive was essential to many of his analyses of juridical, economic and social issues (see Pocock 2006; see also Pocock 1999: 309–29). Eric Schliesser has criticized this approach, while discerning a more sophisticated approach to historiography in Smith's works (Schliesser 2008). It seems, however, that most scholars agree that Smith was, on the one hand, not a historian in the full sense of the word, yet, on the other, that he was significantly influenced by a historiographical approach to various topics.

In this light, the purpose of the present discussion is to emphasize one specific and crucial manner in which a historiographical outlook impacted some of Smith's key intellectual pursuits (see also Allan 2013: 325–7). In particular, it will be claimed that the Enlightenment emphasis on material progress, most conspicuously evident in the four-stages theory, metamorphosed in Smith's work from a historiographical outlook into a distinctly political-economic one. Given Smith's unparalleled impact on the rise of modern economic theory, this was to have key implications for the shaping of our contemporary economic notions of growth and progress. Yet, like so much else regarding Smith, his own original outlook on this issue was subsequently distorted. We should note here that while stadial theory had an immediate impact on eighteenth-century historical literature, not least on Smith's friend Edward Gibbon (see Pocock 1981), our concern here will be rather with the opposite direction of influence – in other words, with how stadial notions migrated from more historiographical contexts and inquiries to distinctly political-economic ones. History offered the analytics, the key to understanding what propelled social progress; political economy then offered the blueprint for how best to impel such progress into the future.

Underlying any attempt to perceive how human phenomena behaved was the Humean realization that causation, its ontological veracity incomprehensible though it was, remained an epistemological *sine qua non*. If one could not perceive certain causes and effects related to human behaviour and culture, then no significant insights could be offered into the 'science of man'. Following Hume and Montesquieu in this respect, Smith was to emphasize other specific aspects of human cultural causation, although, like them, history for him served as a prime context for perceiving and analysing such causation.

Smith's historical perspective bridged the natural history of humanity, on the one hand, and civil and social history, on the other (for a recent assessment see Sebastiani 2013: 45–71). Consequently, how the natural-historical perspective on causation was influential regarding a 'scientific', causal conception of history can also be illuminated by Smith's discussion of natural causation. In *The History of Astronomy* Smith claimed that human beings reacted with wonder when confronted with a succession of natural phenomena, the connection between which they could not explain. However, once this causal connection was perceived and comprehended, wonder, and perhaps apprehension, disappeared. In this manner natural philosophy allayed the tumults of the imagination when confronted with unexplained irregularities, thus helping the human mind to return to tranquillity and composure, which Smith, in typical stoic vein, regarded as the best state of mind (Astronomy II.4–12). He then proceeded to claim that his intention, in discussing the history of astronomy, was to describe precisely the history of the natural-philosophical investigation of natural phenomena, and how they developed in relation to their ability to elucidate the causal connections in nature. 'Philosophy', he wrote, 'therefore, may be regarded as one of those arts which address themselves to the imagination; and whose theory and history, upon that account, fall properly within the circumference of our subject ... Its history, therefore, must, upon all accounts, be the most entertaining and the most instructive' (Astronomy II.12; compare also the survey of moral systems in *TMS* VII.i.1–iv.37). Systems of nature were to be discussed in accordance with the extent to which they had been

> fitted to sooth the imagination, and to render the theatre of nature a more coherent, and therefore a more magnificent spectacle, than otherwise it would have appeared to be. According as they have failed or succeeded in this, they have constantly failed or succeeded in gaining reputation and renown to their authors; and this will be found to be the clew that is most capable of conducting us through all the labyrinths of philosophical history: for, in the mean time, it will serve to confirm what has gone before, and to throw light upon what is to come after, that we observe, in general, that no system, how well soever in other respects supported, has ever been able to gain any general credit in the world, whose connecting principles were not such as were familiar to all mankind.
>
> (Astronomy II.12)

In other words, the more conspicuous unexplained natural phenomena seemed, the more they required explanation in the eyes of the greater number of people, and the greater the renown of those naturalists who were finally able to provide such explanations. More important, however, is the fact that Smith seemed, at least implicitly, to project this same logic onto the need for historical comprehension in general. This is warranted by his claim that familiarity in one field of knowledge often helped understanding of the occurrences in another field, in the course of which philosophers 'explained to themselves the phaenomena, in that which was strange to them, by those in that which was familiar' (Astronomy II.12).

This in turn illuminates the meaning of the phrase 'to confirm what has gone before, and to throw light upon what is to come after'. Human beings were in need of a reassuring comprehension not only of the causally unexplained phenomena of nature, but of the unexplained events of human history. Smith's history of astronomy catered to both needs. It was a history of science, of the study of the natural world, which projected the scientific causal viewpoint onto the historiographical one. 'To confirm what has gone before' was not arbitrarily followed by 'throw[ing] light upon what is to come after'; the latter was a causal result of the former. In other words, historical comprehension enabled an understanding of the laws of history, and thus a prediction of how human events might, at least on a general level, develop in the future. As we will see, this viewpoint was an underlying motive in the transference of historiographical analyses into the field of political-economic prescriptions. If one could elucidate the laws of historical progress, one could institute future political, social and economic policies which would propel such progress. The fact that Smith evinced this outlook in his history of astronomy was significant, furthermore, also because a history of science was a history of the growth of human command of nature. This would come into play even more forcefully in Smith's stadial theory, which was also a causal historiographical model for understanding the historical progress of human mastery of nature, and consequently material progress in general.

In the *Lectures on Rhetoric and Belles Lettres* Smith addressed historical writing directly. Human beings, he claimed, were chiefly interested in the history of human events rather than natural history, because their ability to feel sympathy for non-human creatures, let alone inanimate objects, was much more limited. Moreover:

> The design of historicall writing is not merely to entertain; (this perhaps is the intention of an epic poem) besides that it has in view the instruction of the reader. It sets before us the more interesting and important events of human life, points out the causes by which these events were brought about and by this means points out to us by what manner and method we may produce similar good effects or avoid Similar bad ones.
>
> (*LRBL* ii.16–17; see also Pocock 2006: 272)

What was unique to historical literature was its ability to instruct, and specifically its ability to provide a guide for proper behaviour. The study of history 'points out the causes' and 'by this means points out' how human beings should behave to avoid past errors and augment proper conduct. Smith made perfectly clear that it was the object of historical study to ascertain the causation behind historical phenomena chiefly in order to provide a guide to ameliorating human conduct. He thus evinced the typical Enlightenment attitude toward historiography, combining erudition, narrative style and a philosophical approach (see Pocock 1999, *passim*; Momigliano, 1966, 1980; Levine 1999: 123–5, 157–82). The latter was particularly significant in the late Enlightenment, manifested in the ideal of *l'historien philosophe*, which Smith seemed to share enthusiastically. He evidently shared the sentiment of his contemporary William Robertson, who wrote of 'that indignation which became an historian' (Robertson 1759/1794: I, 377–8). For Smith, as for his contemporaries more directly concerned with historical writing, such as Voltaire, Hume, Gibbon and Robertson, there seemed no serious purpose to study history if its prime objective was not to apply moral standards in judging past events, and thus to learn valuable lessons which would help make the world a better place in the future. In contrast with them, however, Smith concentrated on the prescriptive lessons history was able to teach, more than on the detailed study of history per se.

Nevertheless, this still made factual historical veracity absolutely vital. In contrast with fiction, Smith claimed, historical writing had to be based on verified facts. 'The facts must be real, otherwise they will not assist us in our future conduct, by pointing out the means to avoid or produce any event' (*LRBL* ii.18). Yet facts in themselves could not offer a proper prescription for conduct unless the causes which brought them about were also known. 'If the events are very interesting they will so far attract our attention that we can not be satisfied unless we know something of the causes which brought them about' (*LRBL* ii.19).

If sufficiently intriguing, the need would arise to understand the chain of causation leading to events, even though the direct causes remained of prime importance (*LRBL* ii.19). Once again, it was the causation behind events, not their actual occurrence, which offered the true key to learning valuable lessons from history. 'There is no connection with which we are so much interested as this of cause and effect; we are not satisfied when we have a fact told us which we are at a loss to conceive what it was that brought it about' (*LRBL* ii.32).

Smith was somewhat inconsistent when he claimed that more ostensibly impressive occurrences, usually external rather than internal to the human mind, were often less important than seemingly less impressive, often internal, events. Nevertheless, he regarded it as the task of historians to describe first and foremost the causes of impressive external occurrences. However, there was something quite methodologically modern, almost Rankean, in Smith's claim that a resort to psychological explanations of the motives of historical protagonists was something reserved for those historical narrators who did not have enough knowledge of the historical facts themselves. Thucydides was particularly commended by Smith in this respect, because he explained the causes of events while completely avoiding accounts of the characters of historical figures (*LRBL* ii.22–7, ii.v.18–20). It was not that studying 'inner' human characters was unimportant. On the contrary, it was even more so than external events. Yet, in Smith's estimation, it was not the province of historical study. It was on this point that he diverged from those more directly concerned with historical study. For Smith, the study of history was indispensable, yet mainly as a key to unearthing certain universal laws of human development. The social and psychological factors which underlay human behaviour were reserved for other types of study, which, of course, occupied him much more.

Smith's divergence from typical contemporaneous historiography was also evident in his rather conservative approach to the narrative style of historical literature. He regarded historical writing as concerned with factual accuracy. Therefore, historians, in contrast with rhetoricians or orators, were obliged to arouse the feelings of readers only by narrating the historical facts in the most accurate and proper manner. Neither should historians engage in laboured didactic demonstrations, which Smith claimed had become too common in the historical works of his time, mainly due to religious and political contentions. The same also held for various reflections, observations and inserted dissertations which disrupted the flow of the factual narration (*LRBL* ii.37–42, ii.v.39–40). This was probably another reason why Smith did not write historical works in the strict sense. Here he was being inconsistent. On the one hand, as we have already noted, his search for historical causation put him in line with the philosophical approach to historiography. On the other, however, he regarded the direct and seemingly objective narration of the great classical historians as an ideal which regrettably had not been sufficiently followed by his contemporaries. It is however significant that for someone who regarded historical composition as chiefly concerned with what would today be termed 'grand narrative', Smith was quite modern and interdisciplinary in the attention he gave to writing histories of such topics as philosophy, jurisprudence and education, not to mention a history of historical writing (for the latter, see *LRBL* ii.44–73). These and other historical discussions occur in various places throughout his writings. Yet, while from our perspective they qualify as aspects of historiography, for him they were primarily quests for factual buttressing of his claims about universal human phenomena. His approach to historical writing was thus ambiguous: on the one hand, its main arena was grand narrative in the classical mould; on the other, it was indispensable to apply a historiographical approach to studying much more mundane aspects of human phenomena. In this sense Smith was a reluctant historian. Or perhaps one might see him as a link in the chain of historical sociologists running from Montesquieu, through Tocqueville, and on to Norbert Elias (see Wolloch 2011).

In any event, studying the past could not be avoided. This was most conspicuous in Smith's consistent utilization of the four-stages theory of human progress (hunting, shepherding, agriculture, commerce). Much has been written in recent years about the preoccupation of many key figures of the Scottish Enlightenment with this conjectural-history model of human social development (see Meek 1976; Pocock 2005; Hont 2005; Höpfl 1978; Berry 2001; Whelan 2009; Garrett 2003; Emerson 1984; Withers 2007: 136–63; Palmeri 2008; Sebastiani 2013). For Smith, in particular it provided a significant prism through which to discuss various topics (see Pocock 1999: 309–29; Pitts 2005: 25–58; Marouby 2007). In what follows it is therefore unnecessary to provide a general discussion of his use of stadial theory. Instead, I shall focus, first, on Smith's emphasis, specifically in stadial-history discussions, on historical causation, and on the ability of historical comprehension to guide future conduct; and, second, on the sustained emphasis of stadial theory on the material, economic basis for human development. The latter point is, of course, common knowledge ever since Ronald Meek emphasized that stadial theory was concerned primarily with advancing forms of acquiring sustenance (Meek 1976). It is possible, however, to broaden Meek's approach to all aspects of utilizing natural resources for human material advancement. Stadial theory should thus be considered as a conjectural history of human material culture underlining higher forms of cultural phenomena; hence Smith's application of stadial theory to the study of such seemingly contrasting topics as militarism and jurisprudence. In modern terms stadial theory was an early form of economic history. It was therefore, unsurprisingly, the field in which historiographical insights were transformed into prescriptive socio-economic recommendations for future conduct, specifically in relation to governmental policies.

A prime example of Smith's utilization of stadialism was his discussion of public expenditure on the military in *The Wealth of Nations*. This included a history of military culture heavily imbued with stadial observations, and meant to prove the necessity of a standing army for defending civilized nations (*WN* V.i.a). The economic material basis for the development of military culture was evident, for example, when Smith wrote: '[A]mong those nations of husbandmen who have little foreign commerce and no other manufactures, but those coarse and houshold ones which almost every private family prepares for its own use; every man, in the same manner, either is a warrior, or easily becomes such' (*WN* V.i.a.6).

The material condition of various segments of society, what today we would term their 'socio-economic situation', predetermined their susceptibility to sharing in various military duties varying at different stages of social and political development. It was specifically material causation which provided the basis for cultural development.

Smith's emphasis on such material, socio-economic, historical causation was also evident in his discussion of public expenditure on the judicial system, which included a history of the development of jurisprudence, underlined by various stadial observations (*WN* V.i.b). In almost Lockean terms, it was first and foremost the possession of property which became the object of judicial development. For Smith, it was this, not physical injury at the early stage of human social development, which prompted the initial rise of detailed forms of legal justice. He accepted that the rise of property prompted the rise of inequality, particularly from the shepherding stage, yet in contrast to Rousseau he did not regard this as a negative development. However, in this situation those with property needed the law to protect them from the envy and harm of those without property. 'The acquisition of valuable and extensive property, therefore, necessarily requires the establishment of civil government. Where there is no property, or at least none that exceeds the value of two or three days labour, civil government is not so necessary' (*WN* V.i.b.2, V.i.b.12). Economic progress thus propelled social and legal progress. This seemed to be a causal law of historical development.

This approach was even more pronounced in the opening pages of the first set of *Lectures on Jurisprudence*, where Smith gave his most detailed theoretical observations on the four-stages theory. These made clear that, for Smith, stadial progress was indeed concerned not only with advancing forms of procuring sustenance, but with material progress in general. The preoccupation with mastering natural resources for purposes other than direct procuring of food became more evident as stadial progress itself was attained. Thus, at the hunting stage, human beings gathered wild fruit and hunted animals. 'The only thing amongst them which deserved the appellation of a business would be the chase' (*LJA* i.27–8). As their numbers rose, and this type of existence became tenuous, the best solution they came up with was 'to tame some of those wild animalls they caught, and by affording them better food than what they could get elsewhere they would enduce them to continue about their land themselves and multiply their kind. Hence would arise the age of shepherds' (*LJA* i.28). As the domestication of animals usually preceded that of plants, in most societies shepherding preceded agriculture. With rising population, however, this type of existence also became insufficient. 'Then they would naturally turn themselves to the cultivation of land and the raising of such plants and trees as produced nourishment fit for them' (*LJA* i.30). Agricultural existence would eventually, in its turn, lead to further progress. 'As society was farther improved, the severall arts, which at first would be exercised by each individual as far as was necessary for his welfare, would be separated; some persons would cultivate one and others others, as they severally inclined' (*LJA* i.31). This increasing division of labour at the agricultural stage would ultimately lead to that surplus of commodities, varying in nature from place to place based on climatic and cultural circumstances, which would lead to the sophisticated internal and international trade of the fourth – commercial – stage. A society which attained this stage, the final one of the natural scheme of human progress, 'has done all in its power towards its ease and convenience' (*LJA* i.32). Historical progress in material culture meant ever more acquisition of property by all members of society, hence increasing progress in higher culture, not least jurisprudence. 'The more improved any society is and the greater length the severall means of supporting the inhabitants are carried, the greater will be the number of their laws and regulations necessary to maintain justice, and prevent infringements of the right of property' (*LJA* i.35).

It should be kept in mind that this detailed consideration of the four stages of progress came at the beginning of lectures on jurisprudence. Preceding these stadial observations, almost at the outset of these lectures, Smith had written:

> In treating of that branch of jurisprudence which relates to government, we shall consider the different methods which have been taken to raise the sum necessary for the expense of the state in different countries, and how far they are adapted to do this with the least loss or hindrance to the industry of the people, which ought to be the chief thing in view. For it will also be shewn that the same summ may be raised in some ways which would mightily discourage the industry and improvement of the country and in others which would have those bad effects in a much less proportion.
>
> (*LJA* i.6)

The phrase 'the different methods *which have been taken*' emphasizes how, for Smith, the consideration of the past, of history, served as a guide to enlighten how consideration of the future, specifically the tasks of government, should be undertaken in order to offer 'the least loss or hindrance to the industry of the people, which ought to be the chief thing in view'. This outlook was repeated a little later when Smith claimed that 'The first thing that comes to be considered in treating of rights is the originall or foundation from whence they arise.' In itself, such a statement need not necessarily imply a historiographical perspective, simply a conception of the emergence of various types of judicial rights in society. Yet it is no accident that Smith proceeded almost immediately to the discussion of stadial progress noted above. Before considering the various judicial consider-ations of property, it was, in his view, necessary to realize that these varied in the different contexts of these four historical stages (*LJA* i.24).

For Smith, the stadial pattern of progress was universal, a law of history, yet it was not teleological. The fourth stage of commerce was the acme of historical progress, but it was also both precarious and open-ended. As we have already seen, for Smith, what mattered more than a nation's level of wealth was whether it was in the process of acquiring such wealth; otherwise, it was either stationary or declining. In modern terms this meant that maintaining growth was more significant than wealth per se. The level to which commercial civilization might progress was left unresolved by Smith, but he seems not to have contemplated a *fifth* stage of history. Hence, any future progress would be achieved by commercial societies.

This, however, leaves a crucial problem. If European civilization exemplified the clearest case of stadial historical progress in the best conditions, why had European history not been a tale of linear development, and why had it included such clear examples of injustice? As an Enlightenment philosopher, Smith was obliged to consider this problem. One place where he did so was in the third book of *The Wealth of Nations*, which centred on the history of medieval feudalism, which Smith considered both socially unjust and economically inefficient. He noted that primogeniture resulted from a universal principle – the preference of the male over the female. Yet, while the development of primogeniture might have been understandable in the conditions of early medieval society, it eventually led to the rise of entails, and to the nobles engrossing the land. This was not merely unjust; it also retarded the proper cultivation of the land (*WN* III.ii.3–6). The reason for this seemingly illogical diversion from the proper development of social progress was, according to Smith, that in the Middle Ages the normal stages of historical change were inverted. The natural course of social development was always from agriculture, through manufactures, and then to commerce. Yet historical contingencies, what Smith termed 'human institutions', had thwarted and inverted this natural course. Consequently, in Europe, foreign commerce had preceded, and in fact introduced, the finer types of manufactures, which *then* led to agricultural improvements (*WN* III.i.1–9). Yet, for Smith, this did not invalidate the laws of history. On the contrary, it confirmed them. The unsettled conditions following the fall of the Roman Empire had created a set of circumstances which made this seemingly unnatural historical development perfectly logical. 'The manners and customs which the nature of their original government introduced, and which remained after that government was greatly altered, necessarily forced them into this unnatural and retrograde order' (*WN* III.i.9). 'Laws frequently continue in force long after the circumstances, which first gave occasion to them, and which could alone render them reasonable, are no more' (*WN* III.ii.4).

This helped explain the development of feudal society and its imperfection. The inverted order of historical development also shed light on why agricultural and social improvements were not advanced by either the large landowners or their tenants. Yet, as Smith noted, this inverted order could not remain in force for ever. He described the rise of medieval towns, and how ultimately the normal interdependence between town and country developed (*WN* III.iii.1–20, III.iv.4). Moreover, it was the inverted historical development which ultimately corrected itself and returned the direction of history to its proper course. The influence of foreign commerce initially augmented feudal injustice by affording the lords a market for their produce which they did not share with their poor tenants. Yet, they were forced to grant long-term leases on their lands in order to maintain their wasteful lifestyles. Eventually this made the tenants more independent, stabilized country governance, and relegated the landlords to the status of burghers or urban traders (*WN* III.iv.10–15). Smith's penchant for the law of unintended consequences helped explain how the laws of history made the demise of the feudal order a foregone conclusion, even if its realization was a slow process. In America, where land was more bountiful and the hindrances of historical contingencies less in force, historical development was more normal and un-hindered. In Europe, however, the inverted order of development made progress 'necessarily both slow and uncertain', but ultimately there too it became evident (*WN* III.iv.17–19).

Smith's history of feudalism therefore described both the inconsistencies which could occur in historical development and the self-correcting mecha-nisms which ensured that if progress were maintained in the long run, the normal course of development had to be retrieved in one way or another. It was the contin-gencies of history, such as the fall of the Roman Empire, and 'human institutions', political decisions, which might avert normal progress. But they could not do so indefinitely and evade the basic laws of history. In this, as in many other respects, Smith's outlook influenced those of subsequent political economists, not least John Stuart Mill. In his *Principles of Political Economy* Mill made the famous distinction between production and distribution. The former was subjected to strict scientific causation, while the latter was amenable to human decisions and preferences:

> Human beings can control their own acts, but not the consequences of their acts either to themselves or to others. Society can subject the distribution of wealth to whatever rules it thinks best: but what practical results will flow from the operation of those rules, must be discovered, like any other physical or mental truths, by observation and reasoning.
>
> (Mill 1965: I, 199–200)

Like Smith, Mill believed that social development was based on historical and economic causation, akin to the scientific laws of physical nature, combined with the historical contingencies resulting from human decisions. The latter could either facilitate or obstruct the normal positive development toward prosperity which the former made possible, given an adequate natural environment. Mill, however, gave Smith's outlook a utilitarian perspective which the Scotsman's original analysis did not necessarily imply.

A historical perspective, either stadial or more traditional, was in any event an essential part of Smith's intellectual project. His consideration of historical litera-ture was rather conservative, viewing it primarily as centring on the classical model of grand narratives. Nevertheless, he recognized that serious consideration of political-economic, social, judicial and ethical topics was impossible without a serious consideration of the histories of these various aspects of human culture. These histories were often, if not exclusively, stadial in nature, though when suf-ficient sources existed Smith described them in more traditional historical style, particularly regarding European history. In any event, what interested him was utilizing the historical prism to decipher the laws of human cultural development, or, in other words, the causal links which emerged from history. These causal links were in essence laws, which meant that they remained invariable throughout history, even though they unfolded differently in the context of varying contingent historical circumstances. This enabled Smith to use historical observations to elucidate human social phenomena in his own time. History offered the analytical laboratory for theoretical models of human development. These, in their turn, served to formulate prescriptions, not least economic, for enhancing progress into the future (see Skinner 1975). For Smith, the latter was more important. Dealing with history was a necessity, but his main aim was to influence the policy of his own time. As attentive readers of Smith's works, particularly *The Wealth of Nations*, are no doubt aware, his historical discussions are almost always directly connected with prescriptive recommendations regarding contemporaneous governmental policies.

Smith, of course, was the pivotal figure in the emergence of the modern discipline of economics. It is therefore vital to recognize that the Enlightenment view of history was incorporated into the emerging science of political economy. Like contemporary historians such as his friend Gibbon, Smith was actuated by a desire to criticize the injustices of the past, as well as to attempt to ameliorate present and future realities. The Enlightenment view of history was oriented toward enhancing human progress, material, social and moral. Yet, like so much regarding the Enlightenment in general, and Smith in particular, this vision has been distorted in more recent times. As Smith scholars are well aware, his sophisticated thought in no way fitted the one-dimensional neo-liberal image that is regrettably often invoked in his name. This pertains to his interest in history as to other aspects of his work. The Enlightenment view of history did indeed emphasize the need for material growth as a key to prosperity, but it was much more cognizant of the inherent ethical complications than modern economists tend to be. This intricate topic lies outside the scope of this discussion, but it should be emphasized that as nascent political economy imbibed Enlightenment notions of historical progress, it also accepted the accompanying notion of historical causation as a guide to political and social action.

Bibliography

Allan, D. (2013) 'Identity and Innovation: Historiography in the Scottish Enlightenment', in S. Bourgault and R. Sparling (eds) *A Companion to Enlightenment Historiography*, Leiden and Boston, MA: Brill.

Berry, C. J. (2001) *Social Theory of the Scottish Enlightenment*, Edinburgh: Edinburgh University Press.

Elias, N. (1994) *The Civilizing Process*, trans. Edmund Jephcott, Oxford and Cambridge, MA: Blackwell.

Emerson, R. L. (1984) 'Conjectural History and Scottish Philosophers', *Historical Papers/Communications Historiques*, 19: 63–90.

Garrett, A. (2003) 'Anthropology: The "Original" of Human Nature', in A. Broadie (ed.) *The Cambridge Companion to the Scottish Enlightenment*, Cambridge: Cambridge University Press.

Hont, I. (2005) *Jealousy of Trade: International Competition and the Nation-State in Historical Perspective*, Cambridge, MA, and London: Harvard University Press.

Höpfl, H. M. (1978) 'From Savage to Scotsman: Conjectural History in the Scottish Enlightenment', *Journal of British Studies*, 17: 19–40.

Levine, J. M. (1999) *The Autonomy of History: Truth and Method from Erasmus to Gibbon*, Chicago and London: University of Chicago Press.

Marouby, C. (2007) 'Adam Smith and the Anthropology of the Enlightenment: The "Ethnographic" Sources of Economic Progress', in L. Wolff and M. Cipolloni (eds) *The Anthropology of the Enlightenment*, Stanford, CA: Stanford University Press.

Meek, R. L. (1976) *Social Science and the Ignoble Savage*, Cambridge: Cambridge University Press.

Mill, J. S. (1965) *Principles of Political Economy, with Some of Their Applications to Social Philosophy*, ed. J. M. Robson, Toronto and London: University of Toronto Press.

Momigliano, A. (1966) 'Gibbon's Contribution to Historical Method', in idem, *Studies in Historiography*, London: Weidenfeld and Nicolson.

Momigliano, A. (1980) 'Eighteenth-Century Prelude to Mr Gibbon', in idem, *Sesto Contributo alla Storia degli Studi Classici e del Mondo Antico*, Rome: Edizioni di Storia e Letteratura.

Palmeri, F. (2008) 'Conjectural History and the Origins of Sociology', *Studies in Eighteenth-Century Culture*, 37: 1–21.

Pitts, J. (2005) *A Turn to Empire: The Rise of Imperial Liberalism in Britain and France*, Princeton, NJ: Princeton University Press.

Pocock, J. G. A. (1981) 'Gibbon and the Shepherds: The Stages of Society in the *Decline and Fall*', *History of European Ideas*, 2: 193–202.

Pocock, J. G. A. (1999) *Barbarism and Religion*, Vol. 2: *Narratives of Civil Government*, Cambridge: Cambridge University Press.

Pocock, J. G. A. (2005) *Barbarism and Religion*, Vol. 4: *Barbarians, Savages and Empires*, Cambridge: Cambridge University Press.

Pocock, J. G. A. (2006) 'Adam Smith and History', in K. Haakonssen (ed.) *The Cambridge Companion to Adam Smith*, Cambridge: Cambridge University Press.

Robertson, W. (1759/1794) *The History of Scotland during the Reigns of Queen Mary and of King James VI* (14th edn), London: T. Cadell.

Schliesser, E. (2008) 'The Philosophical Subtlety of Smith', *Adam Smith Review*, 4: 231–7.

Sebastiani, S. (2013) *The Scottish Enlightenment: Race, Gender, and the Limits of Progress*, trans. Jeremy Carden, New York: Palgrave Macmillan.

Skinner, A. S. (1975) 'Adam Smith: An Economic Interpretation of History', in A. S. Skinner and T. Wilson (eds) *Essays on Adam Smith*, Oxford: Clarendon Press.

Smith, A. (1976a) *An Inquiry into the Nature and Causes of the Wealth of Nations*, ed. R. H. Campbell and A. S. Skinner, Oxford: Oxford University Press; Glasgow edition.

Smith, A. (1976b) *The Theory of Moral Sentiments*, ed. D. D. Raphael and A. L. Macfie, Oxford: Oxford University Press; Glasgow edition.

Smith, A. (1978) *Lectures on Jurisprudence*, ed. R. L. Meek, D. D. Raphael and P. G. Stein, Oxford: Oxford University Press; Glasgow edition.

Smith, A. (1980) *Essays on Philosophical Subjects*, ed. W. P. D. Wightman, Oxford: Oxford University Press; Glasgow edition.

Smith, A. (1983) *Lectures on Rhetoric and Belles Lettres*, ed. J. C. Bryce, Oxford: Oxford University Press; Glasgow edition.

Weinstein, J. R. (2013) *Adam Smith's Pluralism: Rationality, Education, and the Moral Sentiments*, New Haven, CT, and London: Yale University Press.

Whelan, F. G. (2009) *Enlightenment Political Thought and Non-Western Societies: Sultans and Savages*, New York and London: Routledge.

Withers, C. W. J. (2007) *Placing the Enlightenment: Thinking Geographically about the Age of Reason*, Chicago and London: University of Chicago Press.

Wolloch, N. (2011) 'The Civilizing Process, Nature, and Stadial Theory', *Eighteenth-Century Studies*, 44: 245–59.

Adam Smith's invisible hand

A brief history

Toni Vogel Carey

Few terms in the lexicon are less explanatory than Adam Smith's 'invisible hand'. So we should not really be surprised that it appears only three times in the Smith corpus, and in places so hidden that they too are almost invisible: 'The Principles which Lead and Direct Philosophical Enquiries; Illustrated by the History of Astronomy' (*AST* III.2; 1980: 49); *The Theory of Moral Sentiments* (*TMS* IV.i.10; 1976a: 184); and *The Wealth of Nations* (*WN* IV.ii; 1976b: 456).[1] Why, then, is it for *this* that he is best known?

Oddly, that question is seldom asked, although the answer lies close to hand. For while the *term* does not amount to much, the *idea* – that much in human life is the product of human action but not of human design – 'permeates all his social and moral theories', as Karen Vaughn notes (1987: 998). I have counted at least nine appearances of this idea in *WN* (II.iii: 343; II.v.37: 374; III.iv.17: 422; IV.ii.4: 454; IV.ii.9: 456; IV.v.b.3: 525; IV.vii.c.88: 630; IV.ix.28: 674; V.i.g.25: 803–4) and two in *TMS* (II.i.v.10: 77–8; IV.i.10: 83–5). It lies at the foundation of 'Considerations Concerning the First Formation of Languages' in Smith's *Lectures on Rhetoric and Belles Lettres* (*LRBL*; 1983: 201–26), his four-stages theory of socio-economic development (hunting, shepherding, agriculture, commerce) presented in the *Lectures on Jurisprudence* (*LJA* i.27–35; 1978: 14–16), and the four-stage development of science in the 'Astronomy' essay.[2]

We now have good historical research on the term (Rothschild 2001: 118–21; Samuels 2011: 21–9), but far less toward a history of the idea, which is the subject of this paper. What I can offer here is only a brief overview of this very large topic. I will say something about its roots in the concept of *laissez-faire*, both ancient and in early modern medicine and the law; its transitional place within Scottish 'sociological evolutionism' (Forbes 1954: 645–6) between seventeenth-century physics and nineteenth-century biology; its kinship with the nineteenth-century concept of 'consilience'; and its recent rebirth in the contemporary science of 'self-organization'. My purpose is to bring out important developments in the history of the invisible hand concept, both before and particularly since Smith's time, which have received little notice to date in the scholarly Smith literature.

1. Two invisible hands

First, though, I need to provide some clarification of the concept, because com-mentators have claimed to see four (Ahmad 1990), ten (Grampp 2000), even forty-eight invisible hands in Smith's writings.[3] I think two will suffice: the one that gets the lion's share of attention; and the one that quietly does more of the real work.[4]

Most of the attention, of course, has gone to the idea presented in the invisible hand statement in *WN* (IV.ii.9: 456): that individuals, in pursuing solely their own private gain, are led by an invisible hand to promote the interests of society, some-times more effectively than when they *try* to promote it. This idea poses the kind of paradox dear to Smith's heart, for it goes against the well-entrenched assumption that commerce is a zero-sum (win–lose) game, and presents the free market as basically a win–win phenomenon (Vivenza 2001: 63; Fleischacker 2004: 91). People usually associate unintended consequences with surprises to the downside, and Smith certainly recognizes that there can be invisible 'backhands' as well as 'forehands'.[5] He does not mince words, for example, that the monotony caused by the division of labour can render factory workers 'as stupid and ignorant as it is possible for a human creature to become' (*WN* V.i.f.50: 782). Still, Smith's theory turns on the premise that invisible hand surprises are predominantly to the upside.

That is one invisible hand principle, which I will call IH-1. The *other*, IH-2, concerns what is known as 'spontaneous order'.[6] IH-2 is also paradoxical, for it goes against the well-entrenched assumption that social order must be the product of deliberate design. It does not appear in any of the three invisible hand state-ments,[7] yet it is 'perhaps the single most significant sociological contribution' of the Scottish Enlightenment (Hamowy 1987: 3). Consider David Hume's remark, for example, in the *Dialogues of Natural Religion* ([1779] VII; 1935: 221):[8]

> A tree bestows order and organization on that tree which springs from it, without knowing the order: an animal, in the same manner, on its offspring: a bird, on its nest. And instances of this kind are even more frequent in the world, than those of order which arise from reason and contrivance.

In the *Treatise of Human Nature* Hume combines both invisible hands in a single sentence ([1739–40] III.ii.6; 1978: 529), asserting that 'self-love' is 'the real origin' of moral rules (IH-2), a system that is 'advantageous to the public, tho' it be not intended for that purpose by the inventors' (IH-1).[9]

The *locus classicus* of the idea of spontaneous order, though, is arguably Adam Ferguson's *Essay on the History of Civil Society*. 'Nations stumble upon establishments', he wrote in 1767 (1819: 222), as 'the result of human action, but not the execution of any human design'.

> The artifices of the beaver, the ant, and the bee are ascribed to the wisdom of nature. Those of polished nations are ascribed to themselves, and are supposed to indicate a capacity superior to that of rude minds. But the establishments

of men, like those of every animal, are suggested by nature, and are the result of instinct. [They] arose from successive improvements ... made without any sense of their general effect.

(Ibid.: 327–8)

These 'establishments' include the very foundations of human society: language and law, money and morality. 'No single genius, however vast,' Ferguson says in the *Principles of Moral and Political Science* ([1792] I.i.4; 1973: 42), 'is equal to the invention of a language such as even the vulgar speak.' Ferguson's social science rests on IH-2, and it is doubtless for this reason that Gibbon and others have identified him as the father of the field (Trevor-Roper 1967: 1657; Lehmann 1930: 238–40).

Craig Smith (2006: 7) identifies the invisible hand of societal betterment (IH-1) with the American libertarian tradition, and the hand of spontaneous order (IH-2) with British classical liberalism. I do not disagree at all with this distinction, but I want to suggest a comparison that is particularly useful for our purposes: that between mixtures and compounds in chemistry. IH-1 is like a mixture; it is additive, involving merely changes in *degree*. IH-2 is like a compound; it is transformative, involving differences in *kind* that are difficult, if not impossible, to reverse.

Emma Rothschild (2001: 116, 153 and *passim*) has dismissed Smith's invisible hand as little more than 'a mildly ironic joke'. But her acknowledgement that her evidence for this reading is only indirect (ibid.: 117) goes largely unnoticed, as does her suggestion that the *term* describes an *idea* 'of profound importance to his theoretical system' (ibid.: 121). Twice on one page (ibid.: 135) she calls 'the metaphor of the invisible hand ... serious, and unironic in its intimation that there can be order without design'. I do not consider one meaning silly and the other serious; but I do consider one more serious than the other; and we agree which one this is.

2. *Laissez-faire la nature*

Laissez-faire encompasses both IH-1 and IH-2. It goes back to the ancient premise of Taoism, that the *Tao* does nothing, yet it is the Way by which all things are done.[10] Calling on a distinction going back to Aristotle's *Physics* (254b12–255a7) that Smith mentions in *AST* (IV.38: 78), Dugald Stewart glosses Hume's position that 'the policy of ancient times was VIOLENT, and contrary to the NATURAL course of things':

I presume he means that it aimed too much at modifying, by the force of positive institutions, the order of society ... without trusting sufficiently to those principles of the human constitution, which, wherever they are allowed free scope, not only conduct mankind to happiness, but lay the foundation of a progressive improvement in their condition and in their character. The advantages which modern policy possesses over the ancient arose principally from its conformity, in some of the most important articles of political economy, to an order of things recommended by nature.

([1795] IV.11; 1980: 314)

Stewart also quotes from a Smith manuscript of 1755 (ibid. IV.26: 322) that directly addresses the superiority of nature to the designs of 'projectors' in bringing the wealth of nations:

> [Rather than] disturb nature in the course of her operations in human affairs ... it requires no more than to let her alone, and give her fair play in the pursuit of her ends, that she may establish her own designs ... Little else is requisite to carry a state to the highest degree of opulence from the lowest barbarism, but peace, easy taxes, and a tolerable administration of justice; all the rest being brought about by the natural course of things.

In later antiquity the *laissez-faire* basis of the invisible hand goes back to Stoic ideas prominently used in *TMS*: that everyone is 'first and principally recommended to his own care' (VI.ii.1.1: 219),[11] the 'eternal art which educes good from ill' (I.ii.3.4: 36), and the like.

Political economics has roots in both law and medicine (the two professional degrees other than theology awarded in medieval European universities). In early modern history its dominant philosophy was mercantilism, based on economic regulation in order to protect a state's markets and power. The 'cameralist' school in Germany (from the medieval Latin *camera*, meaning 'treasury') similarly promoted central planning and regulation of socio-economic affairs. *Laissez-faire* economics developed largely in reaction to mercantilism, and by the mid-eighteenth century it largely prevailed. The phrase '*laissez-faire, laissez-passer*' is associated with the Physiocrat Quesnay, whose position, according to the Original Index for *WN* (1976b: 1064), Smith 'generally subscribed to', but whom he also criticized (see below).

Similar to the split in political economics is that between *statute* law, which is a product of conscious human design, and *natural* law, which harks back to the Stoic trust in nature (Wollheim 1967: 451). Smith says explicitly in the last sentence of *LJA* that he has covered 'both the laws of nature and the laws of nations'. Common law is a cross between the two. Like statute law, it is man-made; like natural law, it lacks any deliberate plan or end-in-view. Thus it is a product of human action but not of human design. And its proponents hold that its invisible hand character makes common law more stable than statute law, because it is less easily subverted by special interest groups and the shenanigans of individual legislators (Barry 1988: 52).

Medicine shows a parallel bifurcation between a *laissez-faire* and a cameralist school, the latter, again, centred in Germany. Cameralists followed Paracelsus (1493–1541) in holding that physicians should 'improve on Nature by proactively intervening in the life of a patient', overseeing such things as diet, sanitation and working conditions (Olson 2003: 452). By contrast, men like John Locke (who served as Lord Shaftesbury's physician and also wrote treatises on economics) followed Galen and Hippocrates in considering illness a pathological interference with otherwise self-regulating natural processes. According to this *laissez-faire* school of medicine, the job of a physician is simply to remove the impediment, and then let nature takes its course. Think of Smith's 'unknown principle of animal life', which 'frequently restores health and vigour to the constitution, in spite, not only of the disease, but of the absurd prescriptions of the doctor' (*WN* II.iii.31: 343).

In his *Elements of Commerce* of 1755 Josiah Tucker connected the dots between the physical and political bodies:

> The physician to the body politic may learn to imitate the conduct of the physician to the body natural, in removing those disorders which a bad habit, or a wrong treatment hath brought upon the constitution; and then to leave the rest to nature, who best can do her own work. For after the constitution is restored to the use and exercise of its proper faculties and natural powers, it would be wrong to multiply laws relating to commerce as it would be to be forever prescribing physic.
>
> (Quoted in Olson 2003: 452–3)

Smith also connects these dots, in the process chiding Quesnay ('who was himself a physician') for thinking the political body 'would thrive only under . . . the exact regimen of perfect liberty and perfect justice'. If a nation could not prosper except under these ideal conditions,

> there is not in the world a nation which could ever have prospered. In the political body, however, the wisdom of nature has fortunately made ample provision for remedying many of the bad effects of the folly and injustice of man; in the same manner as it has done in the natural body for remedying those of his sloth and intemperance.
>
> (*WN* IV.ix.28: 674)

3. Sociological evolutionism

Well before 1700, Samuel Pufendorf was grounding moral tenets not in biblical texts, but in 'the nature of things and the circumstances of human life' (Moore and Silverthorne 1983: 76). The final Query 31 of Newton's *Opticks* contains the pregnant suggestion, 'If Natural Philosophy, in all its Parts, by pursuing this Method, shall at length be perfected, the Bounds of Moral Philosophy will also be enlarged.'[12] The title page of George Turnbull's *Principles of Moral Philosophy* of 1740 quotes both Newton's Query 31 and Alexander Pope's *mot* in the *Essay on Man*: 'account for moral, as for nat'ral things'. David Fordyce (2003: 24) asks in his *Elements of Moral Philosophy* of 1748, 'To what Conduct are we obliged?' and answers: 'Attend to Nature, and Nature will tell with a Voice irresistibly audible and commanding.'

But what did the Scottish philosophers mean by 'Nature'? One thing they did not mean was mere mechanical matter-in-motion. We hear a lot about Smith's allusions to mechanics – society as 'an immense machine' (*TMS* VII.iii.1.2: 316), a philosophical system as 'an imaginary machine invented to connect together in the fancy those different movements and effects which are already in reality performed' (*AST* IV.19: 66), and so on. We hear a good deal less about his biological images, although they are at least as significant. It can hardly be a coincidence, for example, that at least four times in *TMS* (II.i.5.10: 77; II.ii.3.5: 87; III.iii.13: 142; IV.i.10: 185) – including the only appearance of the term 'invisible hand' in this work – Smith refers to the 'propagation' or 'multiplication of the species'. In contrast to the Cartesian split between humans as *res cogitans* and everything else, including animals, as merely *res extensa*, the Scottish thinkers considered humans more like than unlike (other) animals. 'Every animal', Smith declares, citing 'the founder of the Stoical doctrine', is 'endowed with the principle of self-love' (*TMS* VII.ii.1.15: 272).

Boerhaave's mechanistic physiology in Leiden had dominated medicine for more than a century. But at the Edinburgh medical school (the first in Britain, founded in 1726), Robert Whytt and others 'reintroduced the soul into the body' with the idea of *sympathy*, a mutuality of feeling among different bodily parts transmitted through the nervous system. That put 'sensibility and its special case "sympathy"' at the basis of morality and physiology alike, which puts a 'new' cast on sympathy as the central sentiment in *TMS* that commentaries need to take into account (Lawrence 1979: 20–8; Carey 2011: 227–8).

In light of these developments it is not enough merely to note Smith's outsized admiration for Newton's principle of gravity as 'the greatest discovery that ever was made by man' (*AST* IV.76: 105). Nor is it enough to note Dugald Stewart's comment (1829: 240) that the Scottish philosophers did not preclude a 'still happier system in time to come' in natural philosophy, or Ferguson's (1973: 194) that 'as Newton did not acquiesce in what was observed by Kepler and Galileo, no more have successive astronomers restricted their view to what Newton has demonstrated'. These remarks show the Scots' admirable openness to new ideas, and their enlightened view of science as an inherently open-ended process (Montes 2006; Schliesser 2005a). But in light of scientific developments well under way in Scotland by mid-century, we need to understand 'the science of the connecting principles of nature' (*AST* II.11: 45) as embracing an increasingly broad range of connections. In the *Lectures on Jurisprudence* (*LJB* 114: 443), for example, Smith declares that 'the laws of nature are the same everywhere, the laws of gravity and attraction the same, and why not the laws of generation[?]' Even as the Scots extolled the scientific achievements of the seventeenth century, they were making advances toward developments to come in the nineteenth.

This Janus-like position is particularly striking because seventeenth-century mechanics and nineteenth-century biology do not go together like love and marriage. I mentioned the difference between mixtures and compounds in chemistry. In classical economics, society is like a mixture, merely the sum of its individual parts. But organisms, as Stephen Jay Gould (2003b: 227) points out, must be explained 'as organisms, and not as a summation of genes', even if all we have to work with are the genes and their interactions. There is a difference in *type*, that is, between the antecedent or cause (the dispersed activity of individuals/genes) and the consequent or effect (the origin of language/species). And if you're looking for a path from one to the other, sorry, 'you can't get there from here' (Hands 1997: S112–13).[13]

4. Smith and Darwin

Yet Scottish physiologists were well on their way 'there', having crossed over from a mechanistic to an organic view of animal life, and unified humans and other living creatures through sub-rational functions like sentiment and instinct, which they considered more foundational even in human affairs than full-blown reason (Bryson 1945: 56; Carey 2011).

In this light it is noteworthy that the historian of biology Sylvan Schweber (1977: 277–80) points to 'the Scottish view of trying to understand the whole in terms of the individual parts and their interactions'. And he goes on to suggest that Darwin's reading of Smith and Dugald Stewart in the summer of 1838 – just before he read Thomas Malthus and hit upon the idea of natural selection – led him to dispense with the idea that the struggle for survival occurs between *species*, as he had formerly assumed, and accept that it occurs between *individuals* within the same species.

We know from his journals that Darwin at least 'skimmed' parts of *TMS*, and noted that it 'ought to be studied for comparison of man & animals' (Vorzimmer 1977: 129). In *The Descent of Man* he mentions Smith by name, referring specifically to the notion of sympathy in 'the first and striking chapter' of *TMS* (Darwin 1981: 81 and n.17). Later in this work he expressly says that sympathy 'was originally acquired, like all the other social instincts, through natural selection' (ibid.: 164).

IH-2 gives rise to new social institutions; natural selection to new species. Both posit the emergence of complex structures that we would normally attribute to conscious design, human or divine. Both explain these developments as unplanned and unintended products of dispersed individual activity. And both suppose that the tendency over time will be 'the multiplication of the species' – to quote not Darwin but Smith.

TMS was published in 1759, *On the Origin of Species* in 1859. I do not mean to imply, though, that Scottish sociological evolutionists were the only 'Darwinians before Darwin' (Hayek 1973: 23 and n.33), or that they believed they were. Smith's library contained sophisticated biological evolutionary theories advanced in France by Diderot (1754), Buffon (1750) and Maupertuis (1756).[14] There was also an idea, mentioned in passing by Rousseau, that *Homo sapiens* and the 'orang-outang' belong to the same species. Lord Monboddo made much of this, leading one nineteenth-century Scot to wax poetic (Lovejoy 1948: 41, 45, 61):

> Though Darwin now proclaims the law . . .
> The man that first the secret saw
> Was honest old Monboddo.

The 'origin of new species' goes to the idea of spontaneous order (IH-2). But what about the idea of overall progress or improvement (IH-1)? Biologists typically refuse to countenance anything beyond 'local progress' – that is, superior adaptation of an organism to its immediate ecological environment. The philosopher and historian of biology Michael Ruse once described Darwin's view of evolution as 'a directionless process, going nowhere rather slowly'. However, even the most die-hard opponents of 'global progress' have a hard time denying that 'by almost any standard man represents a higher level than primeval mud' (Dobzhansky 1974: 310). And Ruse has changed his mind, for a reason worth quoting: 'People who deny that Darwin was a progressionist – and I was one of them – are just plain wrong,' he says. 'After all, he was the heir of the eighteenth-century British Enlightenment – David Hume, Adam Smith, and . . . Erasmus Darwin and his circle' (Ruse 1988: 97, 104; 1996: 169).[15]

Darwin himself was very reluctant to talk about one organism being 'higher' than another in the scale of being, and 'global' progress was hardly an important theme in *On the Origin of Species* (Bowler 1975: 101). But it is there, and note the language of economics in which it is couched:

> [Through] Natural Selection . . . each creature tends to become more and more improved in relation to its conditions. This [local] improvement inevitably leads to the gradual advancement of the organisation of the greater number of living beings throughout the world. But here we enter on a very intricate subject, for naturalists have not defined to each other's satisfaction what is meant by an advance in organisation . . . Von Baer's standard seems the most widely applicable and the best, namely, the amount of differentiation of the parts of the same organic being . . . and their specialisation for different functions; or, as Milne Edwards would express it, the completeness of the division of physiological labour.[16]
>
> (Darwin 1991: 92–3)

Finally, Darwin was of one mind with the Scottish thinkers about the *laissez-faire* idea that nature's handiwork is far superior to that of conscious human design:

> How fleeting are the wishes and efforts of man! how short his time! and consequently how poor will be his results, compared with those accumulated by Nature during whole geological periods! Can we wonder, then, that Nature's productions should . . . bear the stamp of far higher workmanship?
>
> (Ibid.: 62)

5. Consilience

Smith extolled Newton's principle of gravity for at least two reasons: that the parts of his system were 'more strictly connected together than those of any other philosophical hypothesis', but also that these connections emerged out of what had formerly seemed just 'disjointed appearances' (*AST* IV.76: 104). That order emerges out of apparent chaos in this way is surprising, which means that for Smith surprise triggers not only the *beginning* of the scientific process, but sometimes also the *end* (*AST* 4.33: 75).[17]

In 1830 the astronomer John Herschel legitimized surprise as a mainstream scientific criterion of confirmation in his *Preliminary Discourse on the Study of Natural Philosophy*:

> The surest and best characteristic of a well-founded and extensive induction
> . . . is when verifications of it spring up, as it were, spontaneously, into notice,
> from quarters where they might be least expected, or even among instances
> of that very kind which were at first considered hostile to them. Evidence of
> this kind is irresistible, and compels assent with a weight which scarcely any
> other possesses.
>
> (Herschel 1830: sec.180)[18]

Herschel developed this idea concurrently, if not collaboratively, with a lifelong friend from his Cambridge undergraduate days, William Whewell, who sketched it out in an unpublished manuscript in the late 1820s, even listing it among his 'Rules of Philosophizing' (Laudan 1971: 381). In 1840 Whewell coined the term 'consilience of inductions', from the Latin *salire* (to jump) and *con* (together). His favourite example of consilience was universal gravitation, for Newton had found that different kinds of phenomena all 'leapt to' the inverse-square law of attraction (Snyder 2011: 333).

By 1843, J. S. Mill was using the term in his *System of Logic*. This work is also of interest to us for its early use of the term 'spontaneous order'. Scottish Enlightenment scholars seldom trace this term back further than Michael Polanyi in 1941 or 1951; and these may be the first uses of it in the sense we have in mind (Smith 2006: 10). But consilience is a close conceptual relative of spontaneous order, so it is worth noting that both terms go back to the 1840s.[19]

Whewell believed consilience would lead to 'a constant Convergence . . . towards Simplicity and Unity' (1967 [1840]: 2: 74). Neither he nor Smith put much stock in the mere accumulation of data; and these two stand out in the history of philosophy of science for putting connectivity and simplicity above even conformity to fact.[20] What interested them was what Whewell called a 'colligation', an act of imagination uniting disparate-seeming facts in 'a new point of view' (ibid.: 2: 469). Thus both men emphasized the elements of imagination and surprise.[21]

We begin to wonder, given the distinctive similarities in their thinking, if Smith may have influenced Whewell. And it turns out that the question is not so much *whether* as *how much*, for in 1822 Whewell wrote to a friend: 'I still meditate doing something about the History of the Metaphysics of Mechanics though as yet it is only intention. Something like Smith's History of Astronomy but with more historical facts.'[22]

The idea of consilience, as a criterion of both discovery and confirmation, has continued to be embraced by important philosophers of science, although it has never quite become commonplace. Polanyi (1946: 34) describes scientific discovery as 'a process of spontaneous mental reorganization uncontrolled by conscious effort'. Karl Popper (1962: 342; original italics) singles out as '*the main task of the theoretical social sciences . . . to trace the unintended social repercussions of intentional human actions*'. Popper 'required a "good" hypothesis to do precisely what Whewell expected it to do' (Laudan 1981: 196), which, of course, was also what Smith wanted it to do. And Gould (2003a: 257) sounds for all the world like Smith in describing consilience as a 'highly salutary simplicity of explanation [for] a previously chaotic system of unconnected facts'.

Of those who have made central use of the criterion of consilience, few have done so because of its association with Herschel and Whewell; but Darwin did. Reading the *Preliminary Discourse* as a Cambridge undergraduate gave him 'a burning zeal to add even the most humble contribution to . . . Natural Science' (Darwin 1958: 67–8), and there was no one whose good opinion he craved more for his theory of descent than Herschel's. Unfortunately, he did not receive it, or Whewell's either,[23] even though he rested his case for natural selection heavily on consilience.[24] He wrote to Asa Gray in 1859, as *On the Origin of Species* was just coming out: 'I cannot possibly believe that a false theory would explain so many classes of facts; [and] on these grounds I drop my anchor, and believe that the difficulties will slowly disappear' (Darwin 1994, 7: 369). He wrote something similar in a letter to Herschel in 1861 (ibid., 9: 135–6), and in 1860 he incorporated the point in *On the Origin* itself (1991: 401).

Gould (2003a: 211) asserts that 'Darwin constructed the *Origin of Species* as a brief for evolution by consilience', indeed 'the most instructive case for consilience in all of science'. So it is understandable that scholars in a number of different domains have recognized a close conceptual connection between natural selection and the invisible hand,[25] although once again probably none go as far as Gould (1990: 14), who calls the two concepts 'isomorphic – that is, structurally similar point for point, even though the subject matter differs'.

6. Self-Organization

During the last century the invisible hand became the central idea in *WN* for economists, who also increasingly analysed this work in terms of equilibrium theory, Pareto optimality and perfectly rational agents acting on purely self-interested motives. Leonidas Montes (2006: 255–8) is surely right that none of this is what Smith had in mind.[26] These ideas seem off the mark with regard to IH-1, and irrelevant with regard to IH-2.

That is particularly unfortunate since there are other contemporary concepts that closely resemble spontaneous order (IH-2). Consider 'self-organization' and 'emergence', terms now used in all the sciences, physical, biological and social. 'Self-organization' entered the lexicon in the mid-twentieth century in cybernetics, then became identified with Ilya Prigogine (Prigogene and Stengers 1984), 1977 Nobel laureate in chemistry, and later gravitated to Stuart Kauffman and the Santa Fe Institute.[27] Its association with Smith and the Scottish Enlightenment is clear from a book just published as I write, *Invisible Hands: Self-Organization and the Eighteenth Century* (Sheehan and Wahrman 2015), and another recent title, *Sync*:

The Emerging Science of Spontaneous Order (Strogtz 2003). Unfortunately, the Scottish thinkers do not figure prominently in these books; nor either in a 1996 publication, *The Self-Organizing Economy* by Paul Krugman, who won the Nobel prize for economics in 1998 for his elegant, highly mathematical theoretical work (work that bears little resemblance to the op-ed pieces and television commentaries for which he is known today). Krugman cites Smith only once, briefly (1996: 3), but what little he says is worth noting: 'When Adam Smith wrote of the way that markets lead their participants "as if by an invisible hand" to outcomes that nobody intended, what was he describing but an emergent property? And examples of emergence abound in economic theory'. Krugman talks about emergent self-organizing systems like embryos and hurricanes, and describes a growing city as 'a lot like a developing embryo' (ibid.: 1).

Which brings me to the physicist Lee Smolin's 1997 book *The Life of the Cosmos*. Smolin's cosmological theory is based on the combined processes of natural selection and self-organization (Smolin 1997: 138), and his conclusion is that the whole universe has simply *made itself*. He cites William Paley's argument from design – that just as a clock must have a clock-maker, so the world must have had a world-maker, and this is God. Smolin argues differently. 'There is a clock-maker', he says, but there is 'no city-maker'; and 'if a city can make itself, without a maker, why can the same not be true of the universe?' (ibid.: 299).

Rothschild does not discuss natural selection or self-organization in *Economic Sentiments*,[28] but she grazes Smolin's point in discussing what she calls 'the modern version' of the 'argument about design': 'If the world, or the economy, is [naturally] so orderly that it *could* have been designed by a sovereign (or a planning commission)', she says, 'then there is no need for *actual* designs (or commissions) . . . Why therefore should we have a planner?' (Rothschild 2001: 139; emphasis added). Robert Nozick (1974: 19) makes a similar point in saying simply that invisible hand explanations are 'more satisfying' than those in terms of conscious human design. He does think there may be times when 'something that can arise by an invisible-hand process might better arise or be maintained through conscious intervention' (Nozick 1994: 314). So there may be no need to posit an either/or dichotomy between the two; perhaps, as Lee Cronk (1988: 302, n.5) suggests, both spontaneous and planned orders fall along a 'continuum'.

Not having access to natural selection or self-organization, Smith could only point to some 'unknown principle', as he does at least twice in *WN* (II.iii.31: 343, IV.ix.28: 674). He seems to have sensed that a real explanation would have to await later developments, and that his term 'invisible hand' was merely a place-holder for such an explanation (Carey 2011: 231). That said, his work on the invisible hand *idea* helped pave the way for later developments of the first importance, and Whewell, Darwin and recent self-organization theorists have acknowledged his contribution to their own thinking. This recognition may be scantier than we would like, but scientists do not often give much credit, understandably, to non-scientists.

The editors of *TMS* say, 'commentators have laid too much stress on the term "invisible hand"' (Introduction: 7), and they have a point, considering how little it tells us. But when you think about it, how informative is 'natural selection' or 'spontaneous order' or 'self-organization'? As I said at the outset, it is not the terms but the ideas they represent that are important.

One thing I have tried to show here is that Smith's most celebrated idea – whether we label it 'invisible hand' or 'spontaneous order' or 'self-organization' – has a bona fide place in the history of science and scientific method. And, given the importance he placed on 'the connecting principles of nature' (*AST* II.12: 45), and what A. L. Macfie (1971: 598–9) identifies as his overarching goal, a 'comprehensive, interrelated system of thought – his interpretation of the "great system of nature"', I can hardly think of anything that would have pleased Adam Smith more.

Notes

1 As Emma Rothschild (2001: 118) points out, Dugald Stewart and others gave its treatment by Smith little notice – although as she also notes (ibid.: 122), Stewart did use the term in his own work.

2 That is, from a primitive pre-scientific appeal to 'the invisible hand of Jupiter' (III.2: 49) to Aristotelian essentialist explanation of each species separately (*LRBL* ii.133: 145), to Descartes, the first to posit an 'invisible chain' of conceptual connections (IV.61: 92), to Newtonian gravity, the 'most admirable improvement that was ever made in philosophy' (IV.67: 98).

3 Warren Samuels, according to Montes (2004: 152, n.42). Grampp may not subscribe to all ten.

4 On two invisible hands, see Forget (2001: 193). Rosenberg's 1988 title is a bit misleading, since one of the two hands is Darwin's. Ullmann-Margalit's (1978) treatment is also misleading, because while she delineates two invisible hands, both Smith's, she then effectively discredits one of them; on this, see Carey (1998: 432–4).

5 I take these terms from Pettit (1993: 270 and *passim*). The invisible hand sometimes produces mixed results, advantaging those who could be expected to lose and disadvantaging (or doing nothing for) those we would expect to win. In *WN* (V.i.g.25: 803–4) 'the inferior ranks of people' are advantaged at the expense of their overlords. In *TMS* (IV.i.10: 184–5) the invisible hand does nothing for the landlord who orders his table set with far more food than he can eat (after all, his stomach is no bigger than anyone else's), but it enables his servants to dine almost as well as he does on the left-overs. Also see Nozick (1994: 314).

6 On the history of 'spontaneous order', see Hamowy (1987: 6–10) and Smith (2006: 4–7).

7 It does precede the invisible hand statement in *TMS* (IV.i.10: 183), where nature's 'deception' is said to have led people, from a misguided desire for 'wealth and greatness', to 'cultivate the ground . . . found cities . . . to invent and improve all the sciences and arts . . . [things] which have entirely changed the whole face of the globe'.

8 This work was begun and largely completed in the 1750s (Ross 1995: 338).

9 Hume does say these rules are not of 'a natural origin, but . . . of artifice and contrivance'. But by 'contrivance' here I take him to mean merely that individuals act for what they perceive is their own advantage, not that anything like central planning is involved.

10 I have seen this idea traced to the sixth century BC; Hamowy (1987: 6) traces it to the fourth.

11 Smith has no use for Stoic doctrine where it goes *against* this idea and requires individuals to subordinate their own interests and concerns to the good of the universe

as a whole; that is 'altogether different', he says, from what 'Nature has sketched out for our conduct' (*TMS* VII.ii.1.43: 292).

12   The first edition of the *Opticks* appeared in 1704, but the final Query 31 did not appear until the second edition of 1718.

13   Also see Olson (2003: 439).

14   Bonar (1932: 37, 56); Mizuta (1967: 39); and see Zirkle (1941: 89–91, 93); Bryson (1945: 53).

15   None of this, I should make clear, has to do with social Darwinism, the position that biological 'survival of the fittest' explains and justifies dog-eat-dog economic competition. This idea comes neither from Smith nor from Darwin, but from Herbert Spencer, and even he did not coin the term. Its notoriety is quite recent, dating mostly from Richard Hofstadter's book *Social Darwinism in American Thought* (1944).

16   As Schweber (1980: 256) explains, Milne-Edwards was a highly respected name in biology, and therefore better situated than Smith to 'license' Darwin's use of the 'metaphor of the industrial economy and its driving force – competition and division of labor – in a biological context'.

17   According to Schliesser (2005b: 710), 'Smith is claiming that it is a mark of a successful theory that it is unexpected, even surprising'.

18   Note the term 'spontaneous' here. And note Herschel's ultimate appeal to an inner psychological criterion, much like Smith's belief that discovering 'the invisible chains which bind together all these disjointed objects' brings 'repose and tranquility to the imagination', which for Smith is 'the ultimate end of philosophy' (*AST* IV.13: 61). According to Richard Olson (1975: 253), 'Herschel's ideas were so similar to those of the Scottish school that there is little doubt of a direct relation.' Unfortunately, Olson gives scant direct evidence for this claim.

19   'It would evidently be a great assistance if . . . one element in the complex existence of social man is preeminent over all others . . . For we could then take the progress of that one element as the central chain . . . each successive link of which . . . would by this alone be presented in a kind of spontaneous order, far more nearly approaching to the real order of their filiation than could be obtained by any other merely empirical process' (Mill 1974: 8: 925). This passage wins no prizes for lucidity, but it is interesting in calling to mind the conceptual chains emphasized in Smith's 'Astronomy' essay. Mill used the term again in 1873 in *Three Essays on Religion* (Forget 2001: 194).

20   Dugald Stewart also declared that 'the probability of a hypothesis increases in proportion to the number of phenomena for which it accounts, *and to the simplicity of the theory by which it explains them*; and . . . this probability may amount to a moral certainty' (Stewart 1829: 299–300; original emphasis). Unlike Smith, though, Stewart was not of one mind about this, since he was strongly drawn to his mentor Thomas Reid's Baconian inductivism.

21   It is unfortunate that in his 1998 book *Consilience*, as Gould (2003a) points out in a long critique, E. O. Wilson makes 'consilience' the name for 'a program that directly contradicts' Whewell's (ibid.: 203). Wilson (1998: 27) advocates a 'deliberate, systematic linkage . . . across the disciplines', whereas what Herschel and Whewell – and Smith – had in mind was the serendipitous discovery of interconnections. So it may create more confusion than clarity to call Whewell's concept and Wilson's by the same name.

22   My source for the Whewell letter is Schliesser (2005a: 70, n.131). Jonathan Smith, archivist at the Trinity College Library, Cambridge, tells me that the library did not acquire a copy of the *Essays on Philosophical Subjects* until 1969; so Whewell, who spent his life at Trinity, as student, professor and then master, evidently found *AST* on his own.

23   On Herschel, see Darwin to Lyell (Darwin 1994, 7: 392, 423); on Whewell, see Carey (2009).

24 On this, see Ruse (1989: 9–17).
25 In addition to all those mentioned elsewhere in this paper, others would include Thomson (1965); Ylikoski (1995); Hull (1988); Marciano and Pelissier (2000).
26 Montes (2004; 2006) traces the association of Smith with equilibrium theory to Joseph Schumpeter, who credited Leon Walras (1834–1910) with the discovery.
27 Darwin (1991: 4) expressly left room for other evolutionary processes, saying at the conclusion of the Introduction to *On the Origin*, 'I am convinced that Natural Selection has been the most important but not the exclusive means of modification.'
28 Rothschild (2001: 146–53) discusses 'evolved orders' in terms of 'the equilibrium version of the modern invisible hand'; her only mention of Darwin (ibid.: 248) concerns Engels's evolutionary view of class struggle. And with regard to Hayek as representing 'the evolutionary version of the invisible hand', she dismisses his view of the emergence of 'rules and conventions whose significance and importance we largely do not understand' as somehow 'very far, here, from Adam Smith' (ibid.: 147).

Bibliography

Ahmad, Syed (1990) 'Adam Smith's four invisible hands', *History of Political Economy* 22: 137–44.

Barry, Norman P. (1988) *The Invisible Hand in Economics and Politics*, London: Institute of Economic Affairs.

Bonar, James (1932) *A Catalogue of the Library of Adam Smith*, London: Macmillan.

Bowler, Peter J. (1975) 'The Changing Meaning of "Evolution"', *Journal of the History of Ideas* 36: 95–114.

Bryson, Gladys (1945) *Man and Society: The Scottish Inquiry of the Eighteenth Century*, Princeton, NJ: Princeton University Press.

Carey, Toni V. (1998) 'The Invisible Hand of Natural Selection, and Vice Versa', *Biology and Philosophy* 13: 427–42.

Carey, Toni V. (2009) Letter to the Editor, *Isis* 100: 861–2.

Carey, Toni V. (2011) 'The "Sub-Rational" in Scottish Moral Science', *Journal of Scottish Philosophy* 9.2: 225–38.

Cronk, Lee (1988) 'Spontaneous Order Analysis and Anthropology', *Cultural Dynamics* 1: 282–308.

Darwin, Charles (1958) *The Autobiography of Charles Darwin, 1809–1882*, ed. N. Barlow, New York: W. W. Norton.

Darwin, Charles (1981) [1871] *The Descent of Man, and Selection in Relation to Sex*, Princeton, NJ: Princeton University Press.

Darwin, Charles (1991) [1859] *The Origin of Species by Means of Natural Selection*, Buffalo, NY: Prometheus.

Darwin, Charles (1994) *The Correspondence of Charles Darwin*, vols. 7 and 9, ed. F. Burkhardt *et al.*, Cambridge: Cambridge University Press.

Dobzhansky, Theodosius (1974) 'Chance and Creativity in Evolution', in *Studies in the Philosophy of Biology*, ed. F. Ayala and T. Dobzhansky, Berkeley: University of California Press, pp. 307–54.

Ferguson, Adam (1819) [1767] *An Essay on the History of Civil Society*, 8th edn, Philadelphia, PA: A. Finley.

Ferguson, Adam (1973) [1792] *Principles of Moral and Political Science*, vol. 1, New York: AMS Press.

Fleischacker, Samuel (2004) *On Adam Smith's 'Wealth of Nations'*, Princeton, NJ: Princeton University Press.

Forbes, Duncan (1954) '"Scientific" Whiggism: Adam Smith and John Millar', *Cambridge Journal* 7: 643–70.

Fordyce, David (2003) [1748, 1754] *The Elements of Moral Philosophy*, ed. T. Kennedy, Indianapolis, IN: Liberty Fund.

Forget, Evelyn L. (2001) 'Jean-Baptiste Say and Spontaneous Order', *History of Political Economy* 33: 193–217.

Gould, Stephen Jay (1990) 'Darwin and Paley Meet the Invisible Hand', *Natural History* 99: 8–16.

Gould, Stephen Jay (2003a) *The Hedgehog, the Fox, and the Magister's Pox*, New York: Three Rivers Press.

Gould, Stephen Jay (2003b) *I Have Landed*, New York: Three Rivers Press.

Grampp, William D. (2000) 'What Did Smith Mean by the Invisible Hand?', *Journal of Political Economy* 108: 441–65.

Hamowy, Ronald (1987) *The Scottish Enlightenment and the Theory of Spontaneous Order*, Carbondale: Southern Illinois University Press.

Hands, D. Wade (1997) 'Caveat Emptor: Economics and Contemporary Philosophy of Science', *Philosophy of Science* 64 (Proceedings): S107–S116.

Hayek, Friedrich (1973) *Law, Legislation and Liberty*, vol. 1, Chicago: University of Chicago Press.

Herschel, John F. W. (1830) *A Preliminary Discourse on the Study of Natural Philosophy*, London: Longman, Rees, Orme, Brown, and Green.

Hull, David (1988) *Science as a Process: An Evolutionary Account of the Social and Conceptual Development of Science*, Chicago: University of Chicago Press, ch. 10.

Hume, David (1935) [1779] *Hume's Dialogues Concerning Natural Religion*, ed. N. K. Smith, Oxford: Clarendon Press.

Hume, David (1978) [1739–40] *A Treatise of Human Nature*, 2nd edn, ed. L. A. Selby-Bigge and P. H. Nidditch, Oxford: Clarendon Press.

Krugman, Paul (1996) *The Self-Organizing Economy*, Cambridge, MA: Blackwell.

Laudan, Laurans (1971) 'William Whewell on the Consilience of Inductions', *Monist* 55: 368–91.

Laudan, Laurans (1981) *Science and Hypothesis*, Dordrecht: D. Reidel.

Lawrence, Christopher (1979) 'The Nervous System and Society in the Scottish Enlightenment', in *Natural Order: Historical Studies of Scientific Culture*, ed. B. Barnes and S. Shapin, Beverly Hills, CA: Sage Publications, pp. 19–40.

Lehmann, W. O. (1930) Adam Ferguson and the Beginnings of Modern Sociology, Ph.D. dissertation, Columbia University, New York.

Lovejoy, A. O. (1948) 'Monboddo and Rousseau', in idem, *Essays in the History of Ideas*, Baltimore, MD: Johns Hopkins Press, pp. 38–61.

Macfie, A. L. (1971) 'The Invisible Hand of Jupiter', *Journal of the History of Ideas* 32: 595–9.

Marciano, Alain and Maud Pelissier (2000) 'The Influence of Scottish Enlightenment on Darwin's Theory of Cultural Evolution', *Journal of the History of Economic Thought* 22: 239–49.

Mill, John Stuart (1973–4) [1843] *A System of Logic Ratiocinative and Inductive*, ed. J. M. Robson, vols. 7–8 of *Collected Works of John Stuart Mill*, Toronto: University of Toronto and Routledge and Kegan Paul.

Mizuta, Hiroshi (1967) *Adam Smith's Library: A Supplement to Bonar's Catalogue*, Cambridge: Cambridge University Press.

Montes, Leonidas (2004) 'Smith and Newton: Some Methodological Issues Concerning General Economic Equilibrium Theory', in *Adam Smith in Context*, ed. L. Montes, Houndsmills: Palgrave Macmillan, pp. 130–64.

Montes, Leonidas (2006) 'On Adam Smith's Newtonianism and General Economic Equilibrium Theory', in *New Voices on Adam Smith*, ed. L. Montes and E. Schliesser, London: Routledge, pp. 247–70.

Moore, James and Michael Silverthorne (1983) 'Gershom Carmichael and the Natural Jurisprudence Tradition in Eighteenth-Century Scotland', in *Wealth and Virtue*, ed. I. Hont and M. Ignatieff, Cambridge: Cambridge University Press, pp. 73–87.

Nozick, Robert (1974) *Anarchy, State, and Utopia*, New York: Basic Books.

Nozick, Robert (1994) 'Invisible-Hand Explanations', *American Economic Review* 84.2: 314–18.

Olson, Richard (1975) *Scottish Philosophy and British Physics, 1750–1880*, Princeton, NJ: Princeton University Press.

Olson, Richard (2003) 'The Human Sciences', in *Cambridge History of Science*, vol. 4, ed. R. Porter, Cambridge: Cambridge University Press, pp. 436–62.

Pettit, Philip (1993) *The Common Mind*, New York: Oxford University Press.

Polanyi, Michael (1946) *Science, Faith and Society*, Chicago: University of Chicago Press.

Polanyi, Michael (1969) [1962] 'The Republic of Science: Its Political and Economic Theory', in *Knowing and Being: Essays by Michael Polanyi*, ed. M. Grene, Chicago: University of Chicago Press, pp. 49–72.

Popper, Karl (1962) *Conjectures and Refutations: The Growth of Scientific Knowledge*, New York: Basic Books.

Prigogine, Ilya and Stengers, Isabelle (1984) *Order out of Chaos: Man's New Dialogue with Nature*, New York: Bantam.

Rosenberg, Alexander (1988) 'Two Kinds of Invisible Hands', in idem, *Philosophy of Social Science*, Boulder, CO: Westview Press.

Ross, Ian S. (1995) *The Life of Adam Smith*, Oxford: Oxford University Press.

Rothschild, E. (2001) *Economic Sentiments: Adam Smith, Condorcet, and the Enlightenment*, Cambridge, MA: Harvard University Press.

Ruse, Michael (1988) 'Molecules to Men: Evolutionary Biology and Thoughts of Progress', in *Evolutionary Progress*, ed. M. H. Nitecki, Chicago: University of Chicago Press, pp. 97–126.

Ruse, Michael (1989) *The Darwinian Paradigm*, London: Routledge.

Ruse, Michael (1996) *Monad to Man: The Concept of Progress in Evolutionary Biology*, Cambridge, MA: Harvard University Press.

Samuels, Warren J. (2011) *Erasing the Invisible Hand*, Cambridge: Cambridge University Press.

Schliesser, Eric (2005a) 'Some Principles of Adam Smith's Newtonian Methods in the *Wealth of Nations*', in *Research in the History of Economic Thought and Methodology*, ed. W. J. Samuels *et al.*, Amsterdam: Elsevier, pp. 33–74.

Schliesser, Eric (2005b) 'Wonder in the Face of Scientific Revolutions: Adam Smith on Newton's "Proof" of Copernicanism', *British Journal for the History of Philosophy* 13: 697–732.

Schweber, Sylvan S. (1977) 'The Origin of the *Origin* Revisited', *Journal of the History of Biology* 10: 229–316.

Schweber, Sylvan S. (1980) 'Darwin and the Political Economists: Divergence of Character', *Journal of the History of Biology* 13: 195–289.

Sheehan, Jonathan and Dror Wahrman (2015) *Invisible Hands: Self-Organization and the Eighteenth Century*, Chicago: University of Chicago Press.

Smith, Adam (1976a) [1759–90]: *The Theory of Moral Sentiments*, ed. D. D. Raphael and A. L. Macfie, Oxford: Oxford University Press.

Smith, Adam (1976b) [1776] *An Inquiry into the Nature and Causes of the Wealth of Nations*, ed. R. H. Campbell and A. S. Skinner, Oxford: Oxford University Press.

Smith, Adam (1978) *Lectures on Jurisprudence*, ed. R. L. Meek *et al.*, Oxford: Oxford University Press.

Smith, Adam (1980) 'The Principles Which Lead and Direct Philosophical Enquiries; Illustrated by the History of Astronomy', in idem, *Essays on Philosophical Subjects*, ed. W. P. D. Wightman and J. C. Bryce, Oxford: Oxford University Press, pp. 31–105.

Smith, Adam (1983) 'Considerations Concerning the First Formation of Languages', in idem, *Lectures on Rhetoric and Belles Lettres*, ed. J. C. Bryce, Oxford: Oxford University Press, pp. 201–26.

Smith, Craig (2006) *Adam Smith's Political Philosophy: The Invisible Hand and Spontaneous Order*, London: Routledge.

Smolin, Lee (1997) *The Life of the Cosmos*, New York: Oxford University Press.

Snyder, Laura J. (2011) *The Philosophical Breakfast Club*, New York: Broadway Books.

Stewart, Dugald (1980) [1795] 'Account of the Life and Writings of Adam Smith, LL.D.', ed. I. S. Ross, in Adam Smith, *Essays on Philosophical Subjects*, ed. W. P. D. Wightman and J. C. Bryce, Oxford: Oxford University Press, pp. 263–351.

Stewart, Dugald (1829) *Elements of the Philosophy of the Human Mind*, vol. 2 of *The Works of Dugald Stewart*, Cambridge: Hilliard and Brown.

Strogtz, Steven (2003) *Sync: The Emerging Science of Spontaneous Order*, New York: Hyperion.

Thomson, Herbert (1965) 'Adam Smith's Philosophy of Science', *Quarterly Journal of Economics* 79: 212–33.

Trevor-Roper, Hugh (1967) 'The Scottish Enlightenment', *Studies in Voltaire and the Eighteenth Century* 58: 1635–58.

Turnbull, George (2005) [1740] *The Principles of Moral and Christian Philosophy*, vol. 1, ed. A. Broadie, Indianapolis, IN: Liberty Fund.

Ullmann-Margalit, Edna (1978) 'Invisible-Hand Explanations', *Synthese* 39: 263–91.

Vaughn, Karen I. (1987) 'Invisible Hand', in *The New Palgrave: A Dictionary of Economics*, vol. 2, ed. J. Eatwell *et al.*, London: Macmillan, pp. 997–9.

Vivenza, Gloria (2001) *Adam Smith and the Classics*, Oxford: Oxford University Press.

Vorzimmer, Peter J. (1977) 'The Darwin Reading Notebooks (1838–1860)', *Journal of the History of Biology* 10: 107–53.

Whewell, William (1967) [1840] *Philosophy of the Inductive Sciences, Founded upon Their History*, vol. 2, New York: Johnson Reprint Corp.

Wilson, E. O. (1998) *Consilience*, New York: Vintage, Knopf.

Wollheim, Richard (1967) 'Natural Law', in *The Encyclopedia of Philosophy*, vol. 5, ed. P. Edwards, New York: Macmillan, pp. 450–4.

Ylikoski, Petri (1995) 'The Invisible Hand and Science', *Science Studies* 8.2: 32–43.

Zirkle, Conrad (1941) 'Natural Selection before the "Origin of Species"', *Proceedings of the American Philosophical Society* 84: 71–123.

Adam Smith in international contexts

Guest editor: Jeng-Guo S. Chen

Introduction

Jeng-Guo S. Chen

The articles in this section have evolved from papers presented at a workshop, 'Adam Smith in International Contexts', which took place at the Centre for Political Thought of Academia Sinica in Taipei in December 2012. I am greatly indebted to this institution for its support for this project. As the organizer of the workshop, what I had in mind when planning such a colloquium for Smith students – in William Pitt the Younger's sense of the word – was how to think about Smith internationally, and how Smithian studies in Asia in both the past and the present could be meaningful in relation to European and American models of Smithian scholarship.

In studying Smith in Asia, particularly in the Far East, today, one is inevitably thinking about three issues simultaneously. First, one has to ask oneself what Smith actually meant to say to his contemporary readers or to the immediately succeeding generations. Second, one needs to investigate how Smith has been understood differently in various societies in the past. Finally, one may read and reread Smith to understand contemporary world concerns. The reason one has to tackle these three different textual, contextual and international issues at the same time is simply because Smith is such a towering figure in our conceptualization and understanding of the modern world, even though we might not completely agree with one another about the exact constituents and meanings of modernity. Studying Smith is itself, in one way or another, an expression of what we think, or make, of modernity; understanding what modernity we have inherited and what next we might envisage.

Modernity is taking different trajectories in the West and East, however. Not until the last few decades of last century did *TMS* start to gain close attention from students of Smith in different disciplines. This paradigmatic focus on *TMS* in Smithian scholarship is due to various reasons, from the most superficial ones, such as academic craving to advance different viewpoints, to the acute concern for the human condition in post-capitalist societies. Capitalism has brought tremendous affluence to some areas of the world. At the same time, it has created unprecedented ecological problems, gross disparities of income, new forms of forced labour, and many other social difficulties. In addition, many regions of the world remain in great poverty even though trade and capital flows connect them to the global politico-economic order. History has not come to an end as some modern, complacent Hegelians have presumed. Instead, social, religious and political ideological strife, soft or capitalist imperialism, and terrorism frequently disturb internal politics and sometimes cause bloodshed not only in the military conflicts of the Middle East and Eastern Europe, but also in the cities of Africa, Europe, Asia and the Americas. September 11 is but an exemplary and controversial tragedy of the post-capitalist-cum-post-nationalist world order. In this best and worst of all possible worlds, how should civilians respond and react? Is Smith, with his sentimentalist moral principles and sympathy theory of society, re-emerging as a plausible and promising source of inspiration?

He certainly is. Nowhere in Smith can one find the panacea for all contemporary discontents in the world. Nor should we put our own suggestions and ideals into Smith's mouth. But in post-capitalist and post-Marxist societies, Smith's soul-searching (re)consideration of the intriguing relationship between wealth and virtue, interest and justice, providence and human actions, parochial identity and international commerce, private welfare and public good, sympathy and self-love, among others, deserves re-evaluation, re-engagement and ongoing debate. What 'on earth' does happiness consist of for us and for Smith, the economist and moral philosopher? Is Smith the patron saint of Wall Street, as an allegory for capitalist imperialism, on which the ruins of the World Trade Center in the self-same city symbolizes the scar of his sainthood? Is civil society, to Smith, a precondition for or a consequence of a well-ordered government or responsible state? And, above all, to what extent are Smith's moral and political ideas relevant in the context of the nationalist and ultranationalist striving for state self-empowerment in the materialist and capitalist patterns currently prevailing in China, Singapore, Japan, Korea, India, Taiwan, Malaysia and other Asian countries? Beyond any doubt, Smithian studies are of great relevance to the changing modern world, as the essays in this section clearly illustrate.

The topics of these essays can be placed in three categories. The first presents a rethinking of Smith within the European Enlightenments; the second places him in intercultural and international contexts; and the third seeks to fit him into thinking about the modern world. Oz-Salzberger's essay borders on the first and second categories. It accounts for the slow penetration of Smith's liberalism into the German soil guarded by Frederick the Great and Cameralism, from the 1770s to the early Napoleonic Wars. According to Oz-Salzberger, Smith's call for free trade, his concern with individual property rights and prosperity, and his emphasis on the primacy of civil society were not appreciated by either German writers or officials during this early reception period. On the other hand, while, around 1806, some German writers began to champion individual liberty according to Smithian economic doctrines, they generally neglected his concern for the problem of poverty and the need for public spending to create a non-discriminating society. Oz-Salzberger further examines Smith's reception in Germany within the broader context of the late German Enlightenment's reading of the Scottish Enlightenment. To Oz-Salzberger, the most serious weakness in the German reception of the Scottish Enlightenment was, probably, a misreading of the Scots type of republicanism to which Smith and, particularly, Adam Ferguson were responding. Although it promoted civic virtue and personal independence, like many other forms of republicanism, this Scots republicanism was built on the science of political economy and relied on a mixed monarchy constitution. Oz-Salzberger describes this as 'residual republicanism', as distinguished from earlier forms.

The reception of Smith in Germany betrays, by default, the national-specific attributes of the German and Scottish Enlightenments. But are some predominant attributes cross-national? Modern historians are now more inclined to study the more specific 'Enlightenment in national context' than a wider European Enlightenment. Samuel Fleischacker's essay further complicates the historiography, because he forcefully engages and questions Jonathan Israel's presentation of Smith as a 'moderate' kind of luminary. Israel deals with Smith in his formidable trilogy of Enlightenment studies, which presents a schematic distinction of radical and moderate Enlightenments in Europe. For many historians, including Gertrude Himmelfarb, Nicholas Phillipson, John Pocock, John Robertson, Richard Sher and many others, the Scottish Enlightenment has intellectual characteristics of moderatism or scepticism, clericalism and conservatism, in comparison to the Enlightenment in France as embodied in Rousseau's radical egalitarianism, the *Encyclopédie*'s materialism and Voltaire's secularism. This interpretive tradition which serves as the baseline for Israel's distinction has been strengthened by his own powerful intervention, bringing Spinoza's rationalism into play. Fleischacker aptly problematizes the distinction by drawing our attention to Smith's ideas of progress, antipathy to clerical control, sympathetic attitude to the poor, and other sentimental or intellectual attributes. He argues by implication that Smith might support the 'egalitarian reform' of society. Fleischacker's critique of Israel's work raises some issues with regard to the study of the Enlightenment in general and of Smith in particular. First, the distinction or dichotomy between radical and moderate Enlightenments in Europe is, perhaps, a welcome method of conceptualizing historical time. Moreover, it differentiates the Enlightenment not in its national but in its international setting. Finally, it reflects enduring debates on rationalism versus experientialism, universalism versus particularism, historical inevitability and open-ended presumption of human evolution, among others. The problem, as far as Smith is concerned, is how can we use such broad concepts to scrutinize any individual member of the Enlightenment? Can we describe Smith, to borrow Duncan Forbes's term, as a 'scientific whig' sympathetic to egalitarian values, while holding an evolutionary or moderate approach to reform? Or, to put it more bluntly, can we describe Smith as a 'methodological moderate' in comparison with other egalitarians or utilitarians? Besides the historiographical or heuristic delicacy in characterizing how physical time becomes human history, more significant is Fleischacker's philosophical critique prompting modern historians to rethink Smith's position in the Scottish Enlightenment seriously. On the one hand, Smith is a convinced disbeliever in political invention, moral perfection, and any form of all-curing agenda. He believed, instead, in social improvement led by a well-informed class of people in accordance with human principles of justice, sympathy and socialized self-love. This long-term, open-ended evolutionary view of progress is commonly shared by the Scottish luminaries. Unlike his sceptical fellow-luminaries, such as Hume, however, Smith is also a confessed believer in the view that every individual is an independent moral agent capable of moral improvement and of contributing to the public welfare in one way or another, despite opting out of any collective mobilization or action. This Hutchesonian precept of the moral individual inspired the anti-slavery movement in North America and may inform the universal and egalitarian reforms which Fleischacker addresses.

With many meticulous exegeses, Ryan Hanley's essay investigates Smith's intellectual debt to Diderot and D'Alambert's *Encyclopédie*, particularly the entries on '*economie*', '*eclectisime*', '*grammaire*' and '*epingle*'. Smith was certainly one of the most perceptive of the Scots luminaries who made use of the *Encyclopédie*. This essay is most interesting methodologically because it mines Smith's intellectual sources not in persons, but in materialized repertoires of knowledge. Besides the most studied French source of the Physiocrats and Rousseau, Hanley brings us a Smith who confronts not a specified ideology as represented by a Rousseau or a Quesnay, but the new cultural and intellectual climate embodied in the *Encyclopédie*. A characteristic bridge between Smithian studies and the history of the book and of reading, the essay may be regarded as a 'cultural turn' in Smithian studies. The *Encyclopédie* is, of course, a repertoire of up-to-date knowledge, but, as the predominant embodiment of the French Enlightenment and an unprecedented product of printing, it also demonstrates refreshing ways of representing, observing, delineating and illustrating secular and quotidian lives, industries and sciences. It is in Scotland that one finds the first edition of the *Encyclopaedia Britannica*. Via Smith, the rapport between the *Encyclopédie* and the Scottish Enlightenment certainly deserves further investigation, because it reveals the differences and similarities of these two Enlightenments in a nutshell.

As has been stated above, Smith regarded each individual as a moral agent who has the potential to do good to himself and society. But this possibility is qualified by his other claim that any publicly concerned decision we come to make has to be based not on sheer reason per se but on almost perfect knowledge of society and particular circumstances. The notion of each individual as a moral agent underlies Eun Kyung Min's essay. An unlikely contribution at first sight, Min's article turns out to be a sophisticated and valuable addition to this collection. A philosophical and universalist reading of Smith, concerned with how 'Smith's ideas of sympathy and spectatorship may be related to, and updated for our technological, global age', it brings Smith into an intimate interlocution with Roland Barthes, Jacques Rancière and, above all, Susan Sontag. It concludes that Smith's introspective view of sympathy and spectatorship leads to a more positive attitude to the visual technology of the modern world in cultivating moral sentiments than Sontag's. The Straussian reading of Smith has been commonplace in the works of Charles Griswold, Michael Frazer and many other modern critics. Min aptly adds an acute dimension of 'global' and technological context to this reading. In the technologically global world in which distance, identity circle, the sense of time and even history are drastically different from those of Smith's own age, how can we make sense of his moral philosophy, which was primarily concerned with a communal situation? With the global context in mind, I believe that future Smithian studies in Asia must look more closely at studies in the rest of the world, and vice versa.

Oz-Salzberger, Fleischacker and Hanley address issues with regard to Smith in the context of European Enlightenments, in close temporal proximity with Smith's own age. The remaining three essays – by Tatsuya Sakamoto, Jeng-Guo S. Chen and Luo Weidong – deal with Smith's legacy for non-European nations in much later times. Though not completely escaping the attention of modern historians, Smith's legacy for the culture of modern Asia is certainly understudied. To note but the simplest indicator: we are short of a treatise about the 'Smithian moment' in liberal thinking in Asia. This shortage is not due to the underdevelopment of liberal thinking in the region, though there may be a grain of truth in this. One of the difficulties in exploring the relationship between Smith and liberalism in Asia is that one cannot possibly fulfil the task unless one delves deep into the historical studies of Smith and, at the same time, keeps a close eye on contemporary Asia. None of these three essays claims complete fulfilment of this task, but each serves as a good source for a process of advancement in this regard.

Sakamoto eloquently explains how Uchida understood Smith and justified his importance and relevance to post-war Japanese society. As Hiroshi Mizuta and some others have shown, Japan has its own national heritage of Smithian studies, conducted since the Meiji era of the 1870s. Yoshihiko Uchida (1913–89), the subject of Sakamoto's essay, represents the first generation of Smith scholars who approached him with academic seriousness in Japan. Sakamoto seeks to interpret Uchida's contribution to Smithian scholarship on the international level, by default. Because of the governmental suppression of Marxism before the Second World War, Smith's writings became an intellectual asylum for those sympathetic to Marxism. Accordingly, Japanese intellectuals, including Uchida, read Smith with Marxist concerns for justice, equality and moral justification of civil society in mind. Uchida, according to Sakamoto, concentrates his attention on the problem of mercantilism. Uchida's interpretation of the Smithian rejection of mercantilism reveals his originality. First, Uchida argues that Smith reaches his conclusion to reject mercantilism because he considers economics to be based on a theory of justice in opposition to the Humean justice derived from the idea of public utility but in line with natural jurisprudence, which has been famously propagated recently by Istvan Hont, Knud Haakonssen and others. Second, Uchida deliberately brings Rousseau into play because they were both faced with the status quo problem of civilization. Unlike Rousseau, who proposes a revolutionary reform of the legislative system centred on the idea of the general will, Smith criticized the ancien régime and proposed a legislative demolition of mercantilism in order to reinstate social liberty. Uchida's sophisticated reading of Smith represented, as Sakamoto judiciously remarks, an academic advancement of Japanese thinking about liberalism since the Meiji era, on the one hand, and a valuable contribution to international Smithian scholarship, on the other.

Chen's essay is devoted to the first major attempt to introduce Western liberal thinking into China with Smith's writings and legacy, via Yan Fu's translation and interpretation of *WN*. This essay argues that Smith's liberalism in China is a historical creation of both structural and convergent factors, and is constructed in line with Cobdenite free-trade doctrine, Darwin–Huxley's idea of evolution, and the social Darwinist notion of the struggle for survival. Yan Fu adopts the ideas of evolution and social Darwinism in order to explain the advancement of the social sciences and, accordingly, the national strength of European states, and, by contrast, the wretched condition of China and the dire predicament it faced with respect to the imperialist powers after the first Opium War. Having conflated the ideas of competition (of the price) with struggle (for survival among individuals and nations), Yan Fu argues in his lengthy commentaries that individual liberty, not only in property but in thought, and liberal policy are the inevitable ways to embark on the natural evolution of advancement for a nation. His radical *laissez-faire* and free-trade interpretation of Smith is not his own innovation but informed by the Gladstonian policy that was forcefully promulgated by Edwin Rogers, whose edition of *WN* Yan consulted in preparation for his translation. Indeed, many Victorian moralists tended to read Smith as a precursor of Darwin, or to criticize him for inspiring social Darwinism, as Leslie Stephen did. The *laissez-faire* and free-trade mode of interpreting Smith saw its acknowledged revival in Taiwan after the 1950s via Hayek. By introducing a Victorian Smith, Yan Fu propagates a type of individualistic liberalism that overlooks the requisite tension and negotiation between the individual and society that Smith's oeuvre duly illustrates.

Luo's essay is a succinct historical account of the Smithian studies in China from the foundation of the People's Republic in 1949 to the present. Divided into three stages, the essay relates how Smithian studies in China are closely related to the country's macro-socio-economic conditions and top-down reforms. In the first stage, from 1949 to 1978, Smith is visible to the Chinese public only in the shadow of or appendix to Marxist doctrines, or as a historical redundancy of capitalism, or as the predecessor of the theory of the value of labour. This suggests that Yan Fu's legacy was considerably weakened during the Communist regime after 1949. In the second phase of the history, from the first open policy in 1979 to 1994, Smith's economic liberty, in the vein of the Austrian and Chicago schools of economics, is heavily utilized to explain the function and nature of the free market. In the meantime, Zhu Shaowen, a pupil of the Japanese economist Okochi Tazuo, stands out as a representative of Smithian studies with regard to the idea of *Homo economicus*. In the third and final stage, from the first Chinese translation of *TMS* in 1995 to the present, Smithian studies have turned their attention to his moral philosophy, with growing momentum after 2000 in response to the statesman Wen Jiabao's apologist remark about the importance of *TMS*.

The burgeoning interest in Smith's moral philosophy in China has two local consequences. First, the class of merchants, as Luo rightly remarks, is considered far less productive, meritorious and virtuous than those of manufacturers, farmers and literati. Many Chinese economists, inspired and empowered by institutional economics, have proclaimed that economics is essentially amoral. Smith's discussions of virtue are, under these circumstances, introduced to explain how morality and rocketing economic development, particularly in the sectors of ecology and consumption, can coexist. Second, informed by the revival of Confucianism, Smith's idea of sympathy is frequently compared with the key notion of Confucian morality – *ren* – the capacity to understand other people's situations and needs. Yan Fu famously read Smith's and the French Physiocrats' economic liberalism into the Chinese Daoist notion of *wuwei* (doing nothing). This Confucianized image of Smith is a far cry from the Victorian Smith, who was created to represent the *laissez-faire* doctrine and the zeitgeist of unleashed competition. More importantly, it indicates that the gravity of Smithian studies in China has been moving from the natural or physical order of the economy to the ethical order of society. But, as Chen remarks in his essay, it remains open how far Smith's theory of sentimentalism will inform and influence those Chinese critics who are reassessing liberty in civil society in the context of the top-down reform of the economy.

These papers relating to Smithian studies in Asia merely scratch the surface of a much deeper and richer mine of history. We want more studies of Smith to emerge in South Asia, South East Asia and the Muslim world. As far as the 'international contexts' are concerned, Africa, Latin America and some other regions are very thinly touched by Smithian studies. Two general lessons are yielded by the collective efforts of the authors who have contributed to this section. First, it is always fruitful to bring Smithian studies into multivocal dialogues and comparative perspectives. Second, the studies of Smithian ideas in international arenas in the past and the present already go beyond the parameters of studies of Smith in translation. As this section amply demonstrates, if one is to understand Smith properly in international contexts, one has to study German, Japanese, Chinese, Taiwanese and many other societies as closely as Smith's own Scotland. Not many people can ignite intellectual passion for traversing this far afield. Adam Smith is one of them, however.

Adam Smith and the radical Enlightenment

A response to Jonathan Israel

Sam Fleischacker

I

In a mammoth, much-discussed trilogy of books, Jonathan Israel has argued for a sharp distinction between "radical" and "moderate" strands in the Enlightenment. The radicals, he says, opposed colonialism, slavery, and an array of other social ills, grounding their egalitarian ideals in the monism, rationalism, and rejection of traditional religion that they learned from Spinoza.[1] The moderates were, by contrast, either not as egalitarian or less willing to push for the implementation of their ideals in practice. They held back from a thorough-going egalitarianism out of an attachment to sentiment or tradition, a residual faith in a providential God who would improve the world irrespective of whether we acted, and a residual idealism that led them to hope for an afterlife, and hence to care less than the radicals did about human happiness in this world.[2]

In part, this is an explanatory thesis, meant to shift our conception of the main players in and location of the Enlightenment's signature achievements. Since I am about to criticize a number of Israel's claims, perhaps I should say first that I think much of what he has to say in the explanatory mode is helpful and plausible. In particular, he has restored the importance of Spinoza, and of Spinoza's followers in Holland and France, to the Enlightenment's critique of religion and social hierarchy. He has also made it easier once again to talk of "*the* Enlightenment" – a somewhat unified set of cultural practices and attitudes – as opposed to those who would have us speak only of this or that *local* Enlightenment. And he has brought back into view the ideological sources of the French Revolution, in opposition to decades of historiography that traced that revolution to material causes alone.[3] On all of these counts, it seems to me that he has made a major contribution to how we think about the period.

But Israel also has a strong normative agenda, which I believe is much more problematic. It leads him to misread his sources in many ways, and to impose a grid on the Enlightenment's rich array of intellectual positions that does them deep disservice. That Israel has this agenda is clear. He wants to tell us what we *should* most value in the Enlightenment, and how we should understand our own debt to the Enlightenment when we pursue progressive, humanitarian ideals today; he is concerned with the moral reception of the Enlightenment. "Radical

Enlightenment," he says, "is the system of ideas that . . . has principally shaped the Western World's most basic social and cultural values in the post-Christian age" (*RM* xi). It is the source of our commitments to "racial and sexual equality; individual liberty of lifestyle; full freedom of thought, expression, and the press; eradication of religious authority from the legislative process and education; and full separation of church and state" (*RM* vii–viii). It is "the chief hope and inspiration of numerous besieged and harassed humanists, egalitarians, and defenders of human rights, who, often against great odds, heroically champion [the] . . . freedom and dignity . . . of women, minorities, homosexuals, and religious apostates" (*RM* xi). This colorful language is meant to encourage in us a ringing *endorsement* of the radicals in the Enlightenment, as opposed to the moderates and their heirs.[4] Israel implies strongly that everyone should be a philosophical monist; everyone should see morality as grounded in reason alone; and everyone should reject belief in a providential God. Otherwise, we will be too ready to compromise with the forces that maintain inegalitarian social structures, or that interfere with human liberty in the name of taboo or tradition. Dualism and sentimentalism and traditional religion lead us to leave great sources of oppression and human misery unchallenged, to be moderates – which is to say, obstructionists – where radical reform is necessary.

Unsurprisingly, perhaps, Israel insists that Adam Smith belongs among the moderates. For Israel, Smith is not the beacon of progressivism that many of us have seen in him, but an obstacle in the way of true progress. This is a mistake, I think, but the problem does not lie simply in Israel's readings of Smith. I will try to show that Israel gets Smith badly wrong, but I am really after larger game: I have my sights on the very distinction between radical and moderate Enlightenments on which Israel so fervently insists, and the implications he draws from that distinction for the Enlightenment's impact on later progressivism. Like the other pieces in this collection, therefore, my topic is one of reception, although not Smith's reception in a particular country. Rather, I am concerned with Smith's influence on the wide swathe of European and American political thinkers and activists, from his day to our own, who identify themselves with progressive causes. Israel unquestionably identifies one *strand* of "the system of ideas that . . . has . . . shaped" the humanistic values that he describes, but he wrongly identifies that strand with the whole. A better appreciation of Smith can help clarify what he misses.

II

Two preliminary remarks, before turning to Israel's readings of Smith. First, as I have already indicated, Israel's explanatory schema has trouble with a number of figures, not just Smith. Israel insists that radicals had to be rationalists rather than sentimentalists in morals, yet he includes John Millar, Benjamin Rush, and Thomas Jefferson as radicals, all of whom were in fact sentimentalists.[5] He also insists that radicalism had to reject traditional religion: he writes, for instance, it "had to be anchored in forms of philosophy built on blanket denial of a prior transcendental order" (*EC* 591). Rush was quite religious, however,[6] and Richard Price, one of Israel's main heroes, can hardly be described as denying "a prior transcendental order to the world."[7] On the other hand, Israel struggles mightily to attribute to Hume – one of his "moderates" – much greater respect for religion than he actually had.[8] A classificatory system that counts Rush and Price as radical challengers of traditional Christianity, and Hume as one of its defenders, has gone badly wrong somewhere.

Second, it is worth recalling the multitude of ways in which Smith has been seen as a source for progressive thinkers and movements. Emma Rothschild has brought out Smith's influence on the Marquis de Condorcet, an advocate of public education and of racial and gender equality; she also notes that "there is something of Smith" on the left as well as the right side of the parliamentary debate over a minimum wage at the end of the eighteenth century.[9] I would add that there is also something of Smith on the left as well as the right side of the debate over Britain's 1799 Combination Acts. William Pitt, who had admired Smith since his college days,[10] got the Combination Acts passed, but Sir Francis Burdett and Benjamin Hobhouse, who opposed them, quoted Smith in support of their opposition.[11] And two devoted Smithians – Joseph Hume and Francis Place – were crucial, twenty-four years later, to the movement that repealed the Combination Acts and made trade unions legal.[12]

Less ambiguously, Smith was a major source for the abolitionist movement in Britain and America,[13] and greatly influenced John Millar, one of Israel's favored "radicals." Several of his other radicals – Mary Wollstonecraft, William Godwin, Jeremy Bentham, Richard Price, and Tom Paine, for instance – also admired Smith.[14] In America, Smith influenced Thomas Jefferson as well as the fervent abolitionist Noah Webster, and perhaps also Rush;[15] in Prussia, he was a major inspiration for the 1807 Stein–Hardenberg reforms, which included the abolition of serfdom, the expansion of the vote, and the granting of citizenship to Jews.[16] And today there are ardent admirers of Smith among supporters of the welfare state: Gordon Brown and Amartya Sen are prominent examples. So the idea that Smith is properly understood as a "conservative," favoring hierarchy and blocking rather than inspiring reforms in favor of the oppressed, should be seen from the outset as a surprising one that requires the historian to bring new evidence to bear, or to engage in a deep rereading of Smith writings.

III

Israel does neither. Instead, he gives us a caricature of Smith, filled with distortions or even outright errors. To begin with, Israel reads Smith as having a complacent religious faith that kept him from true radicalism. According to Israel, Smith assumed that a benevolent Providence always guides human affairs for the best, and was therefore far less concerned than the radicals with human efforts to bring about progress.[17] But while there are many references to a providential Nature in *TMS*, no such idea appears in *WN*;[18] and even in *TMS*, Smith explicitly insists that it is a grave moral wrong to "neglect . . . the smallest active duty" in favor of the contemplation of the greatness of God, or the performance of religious rituals unconnected to human welfare (*TMS* 237, 132–4, 170). By promoting "the happiness of mankind," Smith says, we "co-operate with the Deity, and advance as far as in our power the plan of Providence" (*TMS* 166).[19] A belief in Providence is thus morally and politically pleonastic for him, in no way altering, much less substituting for, our duty to do the best we can for our fellow human beings. Indeed, most scholars of Smith today dismiss his references to Providence and regard him as an agnostic, or even an atheist, by the end of his life. I believe, to the contrary, that throughout his life he held a proto-Kantian moral faith according to which belief in God can encourage us in our duties.[20] But even on this view, Smith's religious beliefs would do nothing to distract us from progressivist action.

On religion, Israel at least has some textual evidence to support his claims. On other issues, however, he simply gets Smith wholly – jaw-droppingly – wrong. Start with Smith's views on slavery. Israel says that "emancipating enslaved blacks is simply not an issue that figures at all substantially in [Smith's] perspective" (*DE* 240). He suggests that Smith's "argument against slavery, such as it is, . . . pivots on the economic inefficiency of the institution" and that he "offers no real moral objection to the continued use of slavery" where it seems economically necessary, as it did in sugar and tobacco colonies. In support of these claims, he quotes Smith's remark that the Quakers in Pennsylvania would never have agreed to free their slaves if slaves "made any considerable part of their property" (*WN* 388). Smith, he implies, thinks that slaves should not be freed if they contribute significantly to a person's wealth.

To explain just how misleading this characterization is, we might begin with a crucial text that Israel ignores:

> There is not a negro from the coast of Africa who does not . . . possess a degree of magnanimity which the soul of his sordid master is . . . scarce capable of conceiving. Fortune never exerted more cruelly her empire over mankind than when she subjected those nations of heroes to the refuse of the jails of Europe, to wretches . . . whose levity, brutality and baseness, so justly expose them to the contempt of the vanquished.
>
> (*TMS* 206–7)[21]

It's hard to imagine this remark being made by someone with "no real moral objection to . . . slavery"; Israel saves himself the trouble of having to explain that paradox by ignoring the passage.

And he distorts Smith badly in the texts that he does cite. Consider the beginning of the paragraph in *WN* that includes the remark about the Quakers: "The pride of man makes him love to domineer," says Smith, "and nothing mortifies him so much as to be obliged to condescend to persuade his inferiors." This is Smith's explanation of why people hold slaves – they maintain slavery out of pride even though, in his view, it is economically counter-productive. Accordingly, far from endorsing the idea that slavery is necessary to the profitability of sugar and tobacco plantations, Smith declares that the profitability of sugar and tobacco is so great that those plantations *"can afford the expence* of slave cultivation" (my emphasis). In this context, the remark on the Quakers that follows, two sentences later, clearly means that even Quakers are so filled with pride that they would refuse to give up their slaves – for all the economic cost of that refusal – if they held many of them. Smith is expressing pessimism about whether slavery *will* ever be abolished, not reservations about whether it *should* be abolished. A parallel passage in his lectures on jurisprudence makes this clear:

> It is . . . almost impossible that [slavery] should ever be totally or generally abolished. In a republican government it will scarcely ever happen that it should be abolished. The persons who make all the laws in that country are persons who have slaves themselves. These will never make any laws miti-gating their usage; whatever laws are made with regard to slaves are intended to strengthen the authority of the masters and reduce the slaves to a more absolute subjection.
>
> (*LJA* 181; compare *WN* 587–8)

For this reason, Smith wonders whether it would not be better to retain monarchies rather than move toward greater democracy:

> Opulence and freedom, the two greatest blessings men can possess, tend greatly to the misery of [the enslaved population], which in most countries where slavery is allowed makes by far the greatest part. A humane man would wish therefore if slavery has to be generally established that these greatest blessings . . . were never to take place.
>
> (*LJA* 185)

"The greatest blessings [that] men can possess" should be passed up, Smith says, if they come at the cost of slavery. It is nonsense, then, to say that he had "no real moral objection" to slavery. His moral objection to it was thorough-going, bitter, and expressed in some of the rare outbursts of explicit moral passion that he allowed himself. That Israel missed this suggests that he has not bothered to read much Smith.

Israel's interpretation of Smith is similarly unreliable on almost every other point. He presents Smith as a friend of aristocracy, but in fact Smith regularly characterizes aristocrats as vain fools who have "usurped . . . unjust advantage[s] over . . . their fellow-citizens."[22] He presents Smith as a friend of empire, but a vehement critique of empire runs through *WN*, which ends, famously, with a recommendation that Britain should give up its fantasies of world dominion.[23] And what Israel has to say about Smith on poverty is utterly irresponsible. Unwilling to accept the general view among scholars that Smith was a "friend of the poor," Israel insists that Smith's "occasional remarks expressing indignation at how law and institutions are manipulated by the rich at the expense of the poor mostly occur in unpublished papers and remained marginal to his thought" (*DE* 238). It's hard to know where to start in listing the errors and distortions in this claim. First, Israel backs it up by citing Emma Rothschild's *Economic Sentiments*, but in the pages he cites Rothschild largely discusses *WN*, not "unpublished papers."[24] Second, Smith does not just make "occasional remarks" about the well-being of the poor. A polemic on their behalf runs through *WN*, and shows up in much of *TMS* as well.[25] Nor is this a personal commitment independent of Smith's main lines of thought. *TMS* contains a careful analysis of just why our moral sentiments tend, balefully but inevitably, to overlook the poor (*TMS* 50–1, 61–2), and one of *WN*'s central themes is that economies should serve the bulk of the population – overwhelmingly poor, in Smith's time – rather than national glory, or the interests of merchants or aristocrats.[26] It was for good reason that Smith was regarded in his time by friend and foe alike as championing the dignity of working people. As we saw earlier, his admirers on this score included such heroes of Israel's radical Enlightenment as Millar, Paine, Bentham, Jefferson, Condorcet, Wollstonecraft, and Godwin.

I have argued elsewhere that what Smith bequeathed to these other progressives was above all a sea-change in attitudes towards the poor: an undermining of the hitherto reigning views according to which poor people should be kept in their place.[27] Very few people before Smith thought that the world either could or should do without a class of poor people. Until the late eighteenth century, most Christians believed that God had ordained a hierarchical organization for society, with the truly virtuous occupying positions of wealth and power at the top, and "the poor and inferior sort" at the bottom.[28] Of course, the people at the top were supposed to *help* those at the bottom, but not enough to raise them above their "proper" place. Others, like Bernard Mandeville,[29] offered secular reasons for keeping poor people poor: their innate laziness, lack of self-control, and addiction to various vices would lead them to destroy themselves if they lacked a constant incentive to work. Smith was a virulent opponent of the notion that the poor are morally or intellectually inferior in any way to the rich. Over and over again, he pricked the vanity upholding contemptuous pictures of the poor. He presented them as having the same native abilities as everyone else. "The difference in natural talents in different men is, in reality, much less than we are aware of," he says (*WN* 29); habit and education account for most of that supposedly great gap between the philosopher and the common street porter.[30] To those who complain that the poor are naturally indolent,[31] Smith declares that, on the contrary, they are "very apt to over-work themselves" (*WN* 100). To those who saw indulgence in drink as a characteristic vice of poor people – and these were legion, even among defenders of the poor[32] – Smith replies that "Man is an anxious animal and must have his care swept off by something that can exhilarate the spirits" (*LJ* 497).[33] To those who complained that the poor were affecting the manners of their betters, and should be prevented from buying luxury goods in the name of social hierarchy,[34] Smith says that it is "but equity" for the lower ranks of society to have a fair share of the food, clothes, and housing they themselves produce (*WN* 96). And to those who claimed to be protecting the poor from their own prodigality, he says it is "the highest impertinence and presumption, . . . in kings and ministers, to pretend to watch over the economy of private people" (*WN* 346).

Any one of these points would have shown an extraordinary respect, in the eighteenth century, for the judgment and virtues of poor people; *together*, they add up to a portrayal of the poor that is utterly unprecedented. And there are yet more aspects of that portrayal. Smith defends the religious choices of poor people against the contempt and fear of his Enlightenment colleagues, pointing out that the religious sects that they tend to join, while sometimes "disagreeably rigorous and unsocial," provide them with community and moral guidance (*WN* 794–6). He praises the virtues and accomplishments of independent laborers, making clear that in his view it is unnecessary as well as inappropriate to monitor and control their lives (*WN* 101–2, 335–6, 412–20). He even tries to excuse, if not quite justify, the mob violence characteristic of workers in their struggles with their employers (*WN* 84).

In sum, Smith presents a remarkably dignified picture of the poor, on which they make choices every bit as respectable as those of their social superiors – a picture, therefore, in which there are no true "inferiors" and "superiors" at all. Individual people may be good or bad, but Smith urges his well-off readers to see the average poor person as just like themselves: equal in intelligence, virtue, ambition, and interests with every other human being, hence equal in rights and deserts, in dignity. This picture of the poor person set up the possibility of seeing poverty itself as a harm, something that no one should have to endure. The possibility that people might have a right not to *be* poor was one that could open up only once Smith's dignified portrayal of the poor replaced the view that had reigned unquestioned for centuries, by which poverty went with a difference in kinds of people, not merely a difference in luck. Smith seems to have achieved this change in the image of the poor by employing his own theory of sympathy in *TMS*, and "thinking himself into their situation." It is, in any case, among the signal achievements of *WN*. In missing it, Israel virtually inverts Smith's role in the history of thinking about poverty.

IV

One moral to take away from all this is that political positions tend to come in untidier packages than Israel presumes. Smith was a moral sentimentalist, but nonetheless a deep believer in human equality; he was anticlerical, and heterodox in his religious beliefs, but inclined to limit rather than end the power of state churches; and he favored republicanism and disliked aristocracy, yet supported a slow, incremental reform of monarchy and social hierarchy rather than revolution. In part this reflects a different reading of the political situation around him from that of Israel's French radicals (the British situation was also in fact different from the one in France), and of how politics works in general. As we have seen, for instance, he thought that republics were less likely to end slavery than monarchies, and he also thought that an abrupt end to church establishments could breed unnecessary turbulence among those who work for or look up to that church (*WN* 798–9). Accordingly, he favored different tactics from many of the people Israel designates as "radical." That does not mean he had different goals.

Of course, a difference over tactics can reflect deeper differences. For instance, Smith's moral psychology led him to be more committed than most of his contemporaries to types of political change that ordinary people can easily accept, and to be suspicious of activists and political leaders with schemes for transforming society from the top down.[35] He also believed emphatically that moral convictions work through our sentiments, and he had great respect for the importance of tradition in human life. But, once again, these commitments do not show that he believed any less strongly than Israel's radicals in egalitarian social change.[36] They suggest instead a belief that egalitarian reform must work by *way* of a change in people's sentiments and traditions. Indeed, Smith's respect for sentiment and tradition – for the way ordinary people, and not just philosophical reasoners, live their lives – may reflect a more thorough-going egalitarianism than that of people who think they know better than anyone else how to remake society.

I think Israel fundamentally goes wrong in his insistence that those who stand for truly radical change cannot respect the attitudes, practices and beliefs upheld by ordinary people in common life: that radical change cannot work *through* common-life beliefs and attitudes but must instead call for their abandonment. Of course, it may be that the very word "radical" connotes such a stance, that it is synonymous with "revolutionary." But that would earn Israel too easy a victory: his point is not supposed to be a purely verbal one. It would also short-circuit debate over whether the ideals that political progressives have adopted since the Enlightenment – equality among the races and sexes, the elimination of poverty, war, capital punishment, and religious discrimination – require revolution. Can one stand for such ideals, sincerely and effectively, while still being a gradualist or a reformer, rather than a revolutionary? If the answer to that question is "yes," then the door is open for a thorough-going progressive to be a moral sentimentalist rather than a rationalist, and an agnostic on the existence of God – or even a believer – rather than a militant materialist and opponent of religion.

Smith provides a good case study for exploring this possibility because he was precisely, in my view, a phenomenologist of common life, trying to change it here and there from within rather than standing outside it and reworking it from the ground up. He was indeed, I think, one of the first philosophical anti-foundationalists, and accordingly held a brief for neither materialism nor idealism, neither theism nor atheism.[37] He was also, of course, a moral sentimentalist rather than a rationalist. I think this commitment was itself dictated largely by a belief that sentimentalism explains the phenomenology of common morality better than rationalism. In all these ways, then, Smith is very far from the Spinozism Israel identifies with his Enlightenment radicals, yet he shares many of those radicals' ideals and aims. This suggests that Israel is drawing his lines in the wrong place.

How useful is Israel's dichotomy between "radicals" and "moderates" more generally? I am inclined to say that we should be suspicious of all such dichotomies. General schemata in which to slot the people and ideas in a period as rich and diverse as the Enlightenment are always likely to be problematic. They involve what Smith describes as the mistake of the "man of system": forgetting that one is dealing with human beings, with complex characteristics that cannot be reduced to simple categories and a "principle of motion" which impels them to put their own stamp on the movements and dogmas that come their way. I do not wish to deny that, within a limited framework and with due qualification, we can sometimes usefully say that this figure was more radical than that, or more moderate or conservative – or at least that this figure was more radical *on this or that particular issue* than that one.[38] Categories and comparisons of this sort have great value within *limited* historical or normative language games. But we need to respect the contextual details that define those language games. Stripped of context, and transformed into a global classificatory schema applied to all thinkers of the Enlightenment, terms like "radical" and "moderate" turn into a jumble of criss-crossing and misleading connotations. It is surprising that a historian as erudite as Israel should have succumbed to the temptation to supply such a schema.

Once again, I want to stress that much of Israel's work has enriched, and fruitfully challenged, our thinking about the Enlightenment. He has brought to our attention many figures who were unjustly neglected in the past, made a strong, if perhaps overstated, case for the wide-reaching influence of Spinoza, and restored the idea, once widely held and surely more plausible than recent dismissals of it would suggest, that the revolutions at the end of the eighteenth century were informed at least as much by philosophical shifts as by economic and political factors. But his grand classificatory schema clouds, rather than enhances, these genuinely valuable contributions.

Notes

1   Jonathan Israel, *Radical Enlightenment* (Oxford: Oxford University Press, 2001), *Enlightenment Contested* (Oxford: Oxford University Press, 2006), *Democratic Enlightenment* (Oxford: Oxford University Press, 2011) and *A Revolution of the Mind* (Princeton, NJ: Princeton University Press, 2010). I shall abbreviate these books as follows: *RE, EC, DE,* and *RM.*

2   Israel tells us, for instance, that "anti-colonialism as a strand of modernity both actually derived from, and could only derive from, forms of radical thought based on materialist monism" (*EC* 594). "[I]n the cultural context of early modern empires," he says, "there was only one conceivable way in which a comprehensive anti-colonialism could evolve – and that was by means of a systematically monist philosophy embracing moral, social, and political concepts powerful enough comprehensively to challenge the tightly interlinked strands of justification of empire. For anti-colonialism to evolve into a comprehensively revolutionary political and moral thesis, it had to be anchored in forms of philosophy built on blanket denial of a prior transcendental order and affirming the fundamental equality and unity of Man. Only by negating all the religious, dynastic, and racial hierarchical components used to justify and organize empire . . . could such a rival system of thought emerge" (*EC*, 591).

3   See *RM,* ch. 7.

4   Israel explicitly criticizes multiculturalism as an example of how the unfortunate legacy of the moderate or conservative strand of Enlightenment thought lingers among us today. See *RM* xiii–xiv.

5   For Israel's use of moral rationalism as a criterion of radicalism, see *RM* 19–20. For his inclusion of Rush, Millar, and Jefferson among the radicals, see *DE* 229 (here he

also draws an exaggerated distinction between Smith and Millar) and 475–6, and *RM* 15 and 41–9. For Millar's sentimentalism, see John Craig's "Life of John Millar, Esq.," in Millar, *The Origin of the Distinction of Ranks*, ed. A. Garrett (Indianapolis, IN: Liberty Fund, 2006), pp. 20–4; and for Jefferson's, see his letter to Peter Carr, August 10, 1787. Most of what Rush says about our moral faculties evokes Hutcheson and Hume (and at one point draws explicitly on Kames) rather than their rationalist opponents. See Rush, *Lectures on the Mind* (Philadelphia, PA: American Philosophical Society, 1981), pp. 460–76, esp. p. 472: "the moral faculties distinguish and separate in an instant the objects of moral feeling, from those of intellectual perception; hence we find their *first* decision, like that of an external sense, is always just, whereas the first decisions of the intellectual faculties are frequently erroneous."

6   Israel claims that Rush "proposed stripping away practically all traditional theology" from Christianity (*RM* 43), but a glance at Rush's "Defence of the Bible as a School Book," in his *Essays, Literary, Moral and Philosophical* (Philadelphia, PA: Thos. and William Bradford, 1806) shows that this was not so. Rush insists there on the importance of the "doctrines" of the Gospels, not just their moral teachings (the latter, he says, rest on the former) – in particular the doctrine of "the vicarious life and death of the Son of God" (p. 105).

7   He was also not a metaphysical monist, insisting instead that human beings have an immaterial free will.

8   He says, for instance, that Hume thought it indispensable to morality to believe that the world has "an intelligent Creator and supervisor" who promises us "reward and punishment in the hereafter" (*DE* 211 and *EC* 684). Israel pulls this extraordinary claim out of an ambiguous passage in Hume's *Natural History of Religion* that most commentators (including those in Israel's own footnotes) take to be disingenuous, and that in any case says nothing about either morality or reward and punishment. In fact Hume argues throughout his writings that secular motivation is perfectly adequate for keeping people virtuous, and religious commitments are largely harmful to that motivation. Consider, for instance, his attack on "monkish virtues" in the second *Enquiry*, or Philo's response to Cleanthes' suggestion that religion (because of its promise of reward and punishment in an afterlife) is necessary as "a security to morals": "How happens it then . . . that all history abounds so much with accounts of its pernicious consequences on public affairs? Factions, civil wars, persecutions, subversions of government, oppression, slavery: these are the dismal consequences which always attend its prevalence over the minds of men. If the religious spirit be ever mentioned in any historical narration, we are sure to meet afterwards with a detail of the miseries which attend it. And no period of time can be happier or more prosperous than those in which it is never regarded or heard of" (*Dialogues Concerning Natural Religion*, ed. R. Popkin, second edition (Indianapolis, IN: Hackett, 1998), p. 82).

9   Emma Rothschild, *Economic Sentiments* (Cambridge, MA: Harvard University Press, 2001), p. 62.

10   Kent Willis, "Ideas of Smith in Parliament," *History of Political Economy* 11 (1979), 533–4, esp. n.106.

11   Willis, "Ideas of Smith," p. 516.

12   On Hume and Place, see E. P. Thompson, *The Making of the English Working Class* (Harmondsworth: Penguin, 1980), pp. 563–7. Thompson notes that Hume and Place had earlier voted against certain protections for workers "on Dr A. Smith's grounds of letting Trade alone." He also notes that Place believed that trade unions would naturally disappear once they were legalized.

13   Seymour Drescher, *The Mighty Experiment: Free Labor versus Slavery in British Emancipation* (Oxford: Oxford University Press, 2002), pp. 21–3.

14   See Rothschild, *Economic Sentiments*, pp. 29, 53–5, 269 n.10; Ian Ross, *The Life of Adam Smith* (Oxford: Clarendon Press, 1995), pp. 359–60, 408–9.

15 See my "Adam Smith's Reception among the American Founders, 1776–1790," *William and Mary Quarterly* 69(4) (2002), 897–924.

16 See Carl William Hasek, *The Introduction of Adam Smith's Doctrines into Germany* (New York: Columbia University Press, 1925).

17 *RM* 9, 14, 180–2; *DE* 237, 255, 260–1.

18 In addition, aside from the famous "invisible hand" passage in IV.i, the references to Providence in *TMS* rarely if ever do argumentative work. Even when he invokes God in connection with some phenomenon, Smith always gives a non-teleological, secular account of how that phenomenon works. Thus, Smith does not simply say that God gave us notions of justice so that society would survive (*TMS* 87); he also shows how systems of justice arise from our natural feelings of resentment, and are enforced in part because we realize that the fabric of society would disintegrate otherwise (*TMS* 86). Similarly, he provides an extended explanation of how our tendency to "respect the sentiments and judgments of others" serves our biological and social needs before ever suggesting that an "all-wise Author" may be at work behind these natural processes (*TMS* 13–23, 85, 104–5). And in *WN*, even the "invisible hand" passage is just a colorful way of describing naturalistic social processes. See further discussion in my *On Adam Smith's Wealth of Nations* (Princeton, NJ: Princeton University Press, 2004), §§ 9, 15. All references to Smith's works are to the US reprints of the Glasgow editions of *Lectures on Jurisprudence*, *An Inquiry into the Nature and Causes of the Wealth of Nations* and *The Theory of Moral Sentiments* (Indianapolis, IN: Liberty Fund, 1978, 1981, 1982).

19 Israel describes Joseph Priestley and Mary Wollstonecraft – two of the most radical of his radicals – as "convinced [that] God had a plan for the world's gradual improvement albeit not through direct divine action or miraculous happenings but through the ordinary processes of nature and society" (*RM* 3). I see no daylight between this view and Smith's.

20 For discussion of this issue, see my *On Adam Smith's Wealth of Nations*, §§ 9 and 15, and Ryan Hanley, "Skepticism and Naturalism in Adam Smith," in V. Brown and S. Fleischacker (eds.), *The Philosophy of Adam Smith* (London: Routledge, 2010).

21 This remark did not go unnoticed by Smith's readers. Arthur Lee, an American Southerner who opposed slavery but believed strongly in the inferiority of black people, wrote an angry rebuttal in 1764: see Christopher Brown, *Moral Capital: Foundations of British Abolitionism* (Raleigh: University of North Carolina Press, 2006); and Emma Rothschild, *The Inner Life of Empires* (Princeton, NJ: Princeton University Press, 2011), p. 212. Rothschild also notes that the passage from *TMS* was used by the lawyer for Joseph Knight, the slave whose successful suit for his freedom in 1775 essentially ended slavery in Britain.

22 *WN* 385. See also *TMS* 53–4, 62–4, 149–50, 181–5, *WN* 265, 385–6, and 418–19. Smith does think that an aristocracy of wealth and fortune helps maintain civil order (see especially *WN* 710–14), but this seems more a descriptive claim than a normative one. Given his moral disapproval of aristocrats, and of the effect of aristocracy on the moral sentiments of all of us, it is hard to imagine that he would fail to embrace a more democratic way of maintaining order, if he could be shown one that was effective.

23 *WN* 947; see also 448, 561–2, 582–90, 613–18, 626, 634–41, 752–4, and Sankar Muthu, "Adam Smith's Critique of International Trading Companies," *Political Theory*, 36 (2008), 185–212.

24 He cites *Economic Sentiments*, pp. 61–2, which has seven references to *WN* 157–8, 91–6 and 99, in addition to one to the unpublished "early draft" of *WN*.

25 See my *On Adam Smith's Wealth of Nations*, § 51.

26 Israel ends the paragraph I've been quoting with the claim that Smith thought "success in business, like aristocratic birth, should be regarded as a sign of divine favour" (*DE* 238–9). In support of this claim, he misreads a passage from *TMS* (166–7) that actually

argues just that the rewards proper to skill in business are different from those proper to moral virtue. In addition, he mis-*cites* this passage, attributing the phrases he quotes to two other sections of *TMS* (n.24 to 239), which, ironically, make precisely the opposite point from the one he tries to put in Smith's mouth. Indeed, they include Smith's famous claim that the admiration of riches is "the great and most universal cause of the corruption of our moral sentiments."

27 Samuel Fleischacker, *A Short History of Distributive Justice* (Cambridge, MA: Harvard University Press, 2004), pp. 62–8 and *On Adam Smith's Wealth of Nations*, pp. 206–8. Daniel Baugh argues that *WN* contributed more than any other eighteenth-century writing to a vast change in attitudes towards the poor. See his "Poverty, Protestantism and Political Economy: English Attitudes toward the Poor, 1660–1800," in S. Baxter (ed.), *England's Rise to Greatness* (Berkeley: University of California Press, 1983). Gertrude Himmelfarb suggests something similar in *The Idea of Poverty* (New York: Alfred A. Knopf, 1984), esp. pp. 46 and 62.

28 Walter Trattner, *From Poor Law to Welfare State*, fifth edition (New York: The Free Press, 1994), p. 18.

29 Included among the radicals by Israel (see esp. *EC* 232–8 and 577–80), without discussion of his contemptuous attitudes towards the poor.

30 Smith adds that "the vanity of the philosopher is willing to acknowledge scarce any resemblance" between the two, thus criticizing his own profession for its blindness to human equality.

31 The lower sort, said Mandeville, "have nothing to stir them up to be serviceable but their Wants, which it is Prudence to relieve but Folly to cure" (quoted in Baugh, "Poverty, Protestantism and Political Economy," n.53). Want is necessary to motivate the poor: "if nobody did Want no body would work." Mandeville here echoes William Petty, who thought the poor should be kept busy even if they merely moved "stones at Stonehenge to Tower-Hill, or the like; for at worst this would keep their mindes to discipline and obedience, and their bodies to a patience of more profitable labours when need shall require it" (quoted in Baugh, "Poverty, Protestantism and Political Economy," p. 77) and anticipating Arthur Young, who declared, in 1771, that "every one but an ideot knows, that the lower classes must be kept poor, or they will never be industrious." So wages must be capped, and leisure hours restricted. The poor should work long hours, for low wages, else they would lose the habit of working altogether. The common practice of "work[ing] for four days in order to drink for three, Saturday, Sunday and good St Monday being devoted to pleasure" was an evil one, and it illustrated well the addiction of the poor to idleness and to drink. See Neil McKendrick, "Home Demand and Economic Growth," in idem (ed.), *Historical Perspectives: Studies in English Thought and Society* (London: Europa Publications, 1974), p. 183.

32 Writings about the poor, in both Scotland and England, were permeated by the assumption that the poor tend to be people of inherent and ineradicable vices, prime among which is an addiction to alcohol. "The Scottish Poor Law," wrote T. M, Devine, "was underpinned by a set of values and attitudes which assumed that ... [t]he poor were poor because of defects of character, idleness and intemperance. In this view, only the combination of a rigorous poor law, expansion of schooling and the spread of evangelical Christianity could save urban society from moral catastrophe" ("The Urban Crisis," in T. M. Devine and Gordon Jackson (eds.), *Glasgow*, Vol. I: *Beginnings to 1830* (Manchester: Manchester University Press, 1995), pp. 412–13). Even the radical reformer John Bellers recommended his proposals to help the poor by saying that they may remove "the Profaneness of Swearing, Drunkenness, etc. with the Idleness and Penury of many in the Nation; which evil Qualities of the Poor, are an Objection with some against this Undertaking, though with others a great Reason for it" (George Clarke (ed.), *John Bellers: His Life, Times and Writings* (London: Routledge and Kegan Paul, 1988), p. 55; see also p. 52).

33   See also *LJ* 363. At *LJ* 540, Smith diagnoses the tendency of the poor to drunkenness as a product of poor education: a person "with no ideas with which he can amuse himself," he says, will "betake himself to drunkenness and riot." The conclusion he draws is that the poor should receive better education.

34   Henry Fielding was but one of many writers in the eighteenth and nineteenth centuries who worried about the blurring of ranks consequent on the lower order's consuming luxury goods: "the very Dregs of the People," he wrote in 1750, "aspire . . . to a degree beyond that which belongs to them." Sir Frederick Eden's famous report, in 1797, "constantly complained of the mis-spending of the poor on unnecessary luxuries and inessential fripperies." Even Elizabeth Gaskell, writing in the mid-nineteenth century, felt compelled "to offer some explanation of the extravagance of . . . working class wives" who indulged in ham, eggs, butter, and cream. See Neil McKendrick, "Home Demand and Economic Growth," in idem (ed.), *Historical Perspectives: Studies in English Thought and Society* (London: Europa Publications, 1974), pp. 167–8, 191–2. McKendrick writes that Smith's contemporaries "complained that those becoming marks of distinction between the classes were being obliterated by the extravagance of the lower ranks; that working girls wore inappropriate finery, even silk dresses" (p. 168).

35   On these points, see my *On Adam Smith's Wealth of Nations*, § 58.

36   Lynn Hunt has argued that sentimentalism was actually a major *source* for human rights doctrines in the eighteenth century, rather than an obstacle to them. See Lynn Hunt, *Inventing Human Rights* (New York: W. W. Norton, 2008).

37   See my *On Adam Smith's Wealth of Nations*, §§ 4, 11, 14.

38   We may say that Smith was more radical than Hume in his thinking on poverty, for instance, while Hume was more radical than Smith in his thinking on religion. Paine, undoubtedly, was more radical than either on both subjects. Rush and Price were more politically radical than either Smith or Hume, but religiously more conservative; while Jefferson was more radical in some respects than either Smith or Hume on politics, but far more conservative about slavery.

Adam Smith's dialogue with Rousseau and Hume

Yoshihiko Uchida and the birth of *The Wealth of Nations*[1]

Tatsuya Sakamoto

1. Introduction

Yoshihiko Uchida (1913–89) is generally known as one of the trio of leading post-war Smith scholars in Japan. The other two are Noboru Kobayashi (1916–2010) and Hiroshi Mizuta (b. 1919). Unlike the others, Uchida's highly influential works on Smith, Marx and others are little known outside of Japan. This is largely because he published almost nothing in English and also because he engaged in no substantial international academic activities. Mizuta is an internationally known Smith scholar and his *Adam Smith's Library* (Mizuta 2000) is a regular reference work for Smith scholars around the world (Sakamoto 2014). Kobayashi's German and English works on Friedrich List and James Steuart, though small in number, are recognized as indispensable contributions to List and Steuart scholarship (Kobayashi 1967, 1990; Hattori 2012). By contrast, Uchida's seminal work, *The Birth of Economic Science* (*Birth* hereafter), published in 1953, and its continuing influence on succeeding generations are totally unknown outside of Japan.

In what follows, I attempt to reinstate Uchida's work not only because of its special role in Japanese intellectual history, but, more importantly, because of its academic quality, which is outstanding, even by international standards. Uchida's final answer to his central question of 'Why did Smith become the father of modern economic science?' still deserves a serious reappraisal from various viewpoints. Particularly relevant in this context is to ask how Uchida managed to start his outstanding study of Smith during the years of Japan's militaristic oppression in the 1940s and how he accomplished it as a single monograph in the early 1950s, in the midst of the Korean War and the related intense national debate over the direction that should be taken in Japan's post-war democratic reconstruction.

2. Historical background of Adam Smith studies in Japan

Adam Smith was first introduced to Japan's intellectual world nearly a century after the publication of *The Wealth of Nations* (hereafter *WN*). The Meiji Restoration of 1868 put an end to 250 years of isolationism, and radically transformed the country's structure from a feudal aristocracy to a modern constitutional monarchy. The Imperial Constitution of Japan was promulgated in 1889 on the model of the Prussian Constitution under the strong leadership of Prime Minister Hirobumi Ito (1838–1909). For Japan, as a young but quickly growing and modernizing country, Germany presented a natural model to be followed in every respect. While British, French and American influences were certainly powerful and strong in the early stages of Japan's modernization, German influence became predominant once the new constitution was in place.

The overwhelming German influence in law, politics and culture naturally encouraged similar tendencies in higher education and learning. In the humanities and social sciences, for instance, Kant and Hegel rapidly replaced Locke and Hume in philosophy, and the German Historical School quickly overshadowed Smith and J. S. Mill in economics. It is fortunate for my present purpose, however, that the introduction of Western social and economic thought into Japan had started decades earlier. Among many other pioneers in this respect, the most representative was Yukichi Fukuzawa (1835–1901), the founder of Keio University. As the single greatest scholar, educator, social critic and reformer of his time, he was the first serious reader and interpreter of Western classics of social science, such as those of Smith, T. H. Buckle, F. Guizot and Mill.

Fukuzawa advised his Keio students to attempt a complete translation of *WN*. It was duly published in 1884–5 by Eisaku Ishikawa (1858–86) as the first Asian translation of Smith's work (it preceded Yan Fu's renowned Chinese translation (1902) by almost twenty years). Since then, as many as seven complete Japanese translations of *WN* have been published. In addition to Smith, the principal works of Mill and Rousseau were translated by Masanao Nakamura (1832–91) and Chomin Nakae (1847–1901), respectively (*On Liberty* in 1872 and *The Social Contract* in 1882), and continuing efforts were made by a number of pioneering scholars to introduce Western classics of modern thought in the early years of the Meiji era. They certainly prepared for the subsequent intellectual development by serving wider society rather than just the political and social elites of the time. Hence what Japanese historians commonly call the rise of the 'Meiji Enlightenment'.

What concerns us here in particular is the unique nature of Smith's place in Japan in this extensive historical context. Mill and Rousseau were widely read and appreciated as the founders of modern European liberalism and democracy during a time of vigorous political movements around the country after the restoration. The Constitution of 1889 was partly the government's response to bring these movements into relative stability and peaceful order. By contrast, Smith was seen first and foremost as the founder of modern economic science. His significance as the author of *The Theory of Moral Sentiments* (hereafter *TMS*) was entirely unknown until the 1920s. Fukuzawa (2007) recalls in his autobiography an interesting personal episode when briefing a government official on the recent trends of economics in the Western world. When attempting to explain the meaning of the word 'competition', as used by John Hill Burton in his small book on political economy (Burton 1852), Fukuzawa, finding no proper Japanese equivalent, coined the term '*kyoso*' (競争) – literally 'race-fight' in Japanese. The official complained that the word seemed to carry a sense of internal conflict or tension (Fukuzawa 2007: 190), but Fukuzawa refused to compromise and *kyoso* finally became an indispensable term in Japan's everyday vocabulary. Interestingly, the same translated word for 'competition' later became equally indispensable in the Chinese-speaking world.[2]

This episode shows Fukuzawa's far-sighted vision of the emerging market society in Japan, on the one hand, and the significant gap between the new social reality and the old conventional mindset of the country's ruling class, on the other. Fukuzawa died in 1901, three years before the start of the Russo-Japanese War, when Japan set off down the road to becoming one of the world's major imperialist countries. Japan fought the First World War (1914–18) as an Allied power, and her economy achieved remarkable growth through huge military expenditure. However, the end of the war caused serious economic difficulties throughout the country, such as a banking crisis, drastic deflation, soaring unemployment and considerable spread of poverty. This explains why the German Historical School quickly gained academic recognition and popularity as a more realistic system of economics by replacing Smithian and British idealistic and even utopian liberalism, which had dominated and divided the world under the guise of the imperialist ideology. The German Historical School, by contrast, was expected to endorse top-down management of the national economy and resolve the serious economic and social problems of the time. As such, it gained full and committed support among both academics and political leaders as a reliable guideline for their policy-making within an increasingly totalitarian and militaristic state.

Thus the Japanese Society for Social Policy (1897–1924) was established on the model of the German Verein für Sozialpolitik (founded 1872), and defined its political position as centre-left or democratic-socialist. The society's avowed enemies were both old fashioned free-market liberalism and, more urgently, the revolutionary Marxism and communism that were quickly gaining political influence in the aftermath of the Russian Revolution of 1917. The post-war crises were exacerbated by the Great Earthquake of 1923, which decimated the metropolis, and the Great Depression of 1929. These overlapping global and domestic crises devastated the country and left few means of national survival other than the military aggression that resulted in the fateful invasions of Manchuria (1931) and China (1937). A remarkable fact in this historical context is that in the tragic year of 1923 major universities in Japan held substantial academic events to celebrate Adam Smith's bicentenary. By that time, Smith had generally been recognized as a great thinker who was more than the author of *WN*. The iconic economist representing this period was Tokuzo Fukuda (1874–1930) from Tokyo University of Commerce (TUC, now Hitotsubashi University).

3. Smith, Marx, Weber and the birth of the theory of 'civil society'

Under the increasingly oppressive regime, Adam Smith studies in Japan came to acquire an interesting character. The field served as a hiding place for those who really wished to study Marx and Marxism but could not do so due to the authorities' growing repression of communism. Smith's name did not appear on the authorities' proscribed lists, so young scholars were free to read and discuss Smith-related subjects both privately and in public. Two outstanding young scholars appeared at this juncture to mark the true starting point of Smith scholarship in Japan. One was Zenya Takashima (1904–90) of TUC, a student of Fukuda and a specialist in German economic and social thought and, in particular, of Friedrich List. The other was Kazuo Okochi (1905–84) of the Imperial University of Tokyo (IUT, now the University of Tokyo), an expert in German economic thought from the New Historical School to Max Weber.

Takashima and Okochi read *WN*, like their predecessors, but they also studied *TMS*, in contrast to the majority of earlier Smith scholars in Japan. They not only recognized the importance of Smith as the author of *TMS*, but also launched a new intellectual project toward reading it as the moral and ethical foundation of *WN*. In so doing, as the titles of their works indicate (Takashima 1941; Okochi 1943), they approached the essential connection between *TMS* and *WN* from the post-Smithian and German point of view represented by List, Marx, the Historical School and Weber. Hence, they inevitably confronted the so-called 'Adam Smith problem' – that is, the possible contradiction or tension between the egoism of 'self-love' in *WN* and the altruism of 'sympathy' in *TMS*. German scholars had been the first to raise this issue, and Takashima and Okochi were already familiar with it. They firmly believed that the essential connection between *TMS* and *WN* could be grasped only by dissolving the Adam Smith problem by reading *WN* as a systematic extension of *TMS*.

Takashima argued that Smith's idea of 'civil society' comprised three funda-mental 'worlds' – morals, law and economy. He particularly highlighted the logical connection between 'sympathy' in *TMS* and 'justice' in the *Lectures on Jurisprudence* (hereafter *LJ*) as the two key concepts of Smith's theory of 'civil society' that he later developed in *WN*. Okochi, by contrast, under the strong influence of Max Weber's *Protestant Ethic and the Spirit of Capitalism* (1905), highlighted the virtue of 'prudence' as a secularized Protestant work ethic in *TMS* as providing the moral foundation for Smith's view of 'civil society' in *WN*. This slight difference of emphasis notwithstanding, the two scholars undoubtedly made highly original attempts to present unified accounts of the internal link between *WN* and *TMS* on the basis of the concept of 'civil society'.

Thus Takashima and Okochi presented far more profound views of Smith than those who viewed him as a stereotypical advocate of free-market economy and egoistic capitalism. They undoubtedly made ground-breaking steps toward a new generation of Smith studies in Japan. As is clear by now, their central idea was that of 'civil society' – *bürgerliche Gesellschaft* in German – and the younger generation of Smith scholars, including Uchida and Mizuta, would not only embrace this intellectual legacy but make even more original attempts to read into Smith's works their respective visions of 'civil society'. These attempts were not simply adaptations of the theories of Marx, Weber and other German thinkers, as in the older generation. In particular, Uchida's creative reinterpretation of Smith's works was conducted in a bold attempt to reconstruct Smith's intellectual growth from *TMS* to *WN* as an imaginary recreation of the kind of intellectual growth as lived and experienced by Uchida himself during and after the Second World War.

4. The birth of *The Birth of Economic Science*

Although Yoshihiko Uchida was less than ten years younger than Takashima and Okochi, the difference in their ages meant that he possessed a vastly different historical consciousness. The two pioneers of Smith studies in Japan had acquired their professional positions within academia in the critical mid-1930s. At that time, Uchida was working as a postgraduate researcher in the Faculty of Economics at IUT, where Okochi was a young professor. Though subsequently employed as a part-time researcher at several research institutes, his precarious social status during the war had paradoxical consequences. First, he was relatively free to immerse himself in the classical economic texts of Smith, Marx and others. But, second, for Uchida, as well as for Kobayashi and Mizuta, Marx's significance had already faded into something different from what it had been for the preceding generation. This was not simply because open academic debate of Marx and his ideas was forbidden in Japan during the war. More importantly, the ultra-militarism and nationalism of the time made it difficult for them to accept what the Marxist literature had to say about the imminent crisis of capitalism and the historical inevitability of a socialist or communist revolution in the foreseeable future.

Ironically, the oppressive reality of the time made it possible for Uchida, Kobayashi and Mizuta to formulate even more creative interpretations of Smith, List and Marx than the earlier generations had managed. Uchida had no choice but to immerse himself in the world of classical economic literature in a different way from his predecessors. He engaged in a solitary intellectual confrontation and dialogue with Smith's texts in complete isolation from Marxist interpretations of them. Meanwhile, Kobayashi published his first small book on List in 1943, and Mizuta was absorbed in Hobbes's *Leviathan* and Smith's *LJ* as Takashima's student at TUC. Mizuta also translated Franz Borkenau's *The Transition from the Feudal to the Bourgeois World View* (1934) while working for the civilian administration in occupied Java (Sakamoto 2014). It would be many more years before Uchida was able to give concrete shape to the new conception of Smith that he formed during those dark years.

Uchida's *The Birth of Economic Science* was published in 1953 to high acclaim in a number of academic reviews. It was also enthusiastically received by the wider reading public. The outline of the book is as follows:

- Introduction: The contemporary challenge and standard of the study of the economic classics
  - Two trends of studies of classical economics and their problems
  - Classical economics as a science of history

- o   The fundamental process and the theoretical structure
- o   Stages in classical economics
- Part One: The birth of economic science: *The Wealth of Nations* as a criticism of the old imperial system
  - o   A new age, a new science
  - o   The challenge Smith faced
  - o   The birth of economics and its foundation: *Homo economicus* and the invisible hand
  - o   *The Wealth of Nations* as a critique of the old imperial system
  - o   Appendix: The social foundation of *The Wealth of Nations*: English mercantilism and its dissolution
- Part Two: Analysis of the system of *The Wealth of Nations*
  - o   The concept of 'civil society' and the analytical viewpoint in *The Wealth of Nations*
  - o   The foundation of analysis: theory of the division of labour
  - o   Conceptualizing the commodity
  - o   Capital and labour: conceptualizing the surplus-value
  - o   The theory of capital accumulation and reproduction (1): from Quesnay to Smith
  - o   The theory of capital accumulation and reproduction (2): critique of Quesnay's category of the net-produce and the establishment of classical economics
- Postscript

The *Birth* therefore consists of three major components: a methodological argument of the right way to understand the history of economics in general (Introduction); a historical investigation into the nature and origins of *The Wealth of Nations* (Part One); and a theoretical analysis of *The Wealth of Nations* (Part Two).

In the methodological discussion, Uchida starts with the assertion that 'the fundamental conflict of the day lies not in the question of "Hayek or Keynes?", but in that of "Marx or Smith?" (Uchida 1953: 7). He believed that the history of economics after Marx, continuing through Keynes and Hayek, was an aberration from the right path that had been developed by Smith, Ricardo and Marx. The theoretical core of the development is the labour theory of value and the theory of surplus value that were brought to systematic perfection by Marx. This might sound as if Uchida was a dogmatic follower of Marx's economics. In fact, while clearly conscious of being a theoretical Marxist, Uchida was severely critical of the orthodox Marxists and communist economists who were reviving and strengthening their political forces in Japan's post-war democratization. At the core of Uchida's criticism was his belief that the mainstream Marxist interpretations of Smith's economics never understood the profoundly historical nature of the rise and progress of the labour theory of value since the time of William Petty. They understood the European history of economics as an autonomous history of the theory of surplus value while totally neglecting the historical process and context in which particular economic discourses were created as intellectual and political responses to certain historical problems and issues. Uchida discovered that, in the sense of developing an anachronistic understanding of the nature of the history of economics, not only Marxist but non-Marxist, neoclassical economists committed the same methodological error.

This is why Uchida writes of the 'two trends' in the history of classical economics. He highly rates the second trend of Smith studies in Japan, represented by Okochi and Takashima, which he says focuses on 'the historical formation of civil society'. However, this new trend does not escape his critical examination. Uchida says that the works of Okochi and Takashima, no matter how historically oriented, do not adequately clarify the precise sense in which Smith's view of 'civil society' provided a systematic foundation to his theoretical economics – that is, the theories of division of labour, exchange value and surplus value. In consequence, their views of Smith become either a sociological analysis (Takashima) or an ethical discourse (Okochi), and fall seriously short of the theoretical substance that is essential for a correct understanding of Smith's economics (Suzuki 2013).

Uchida further points out the essential link between the theoretical and historical aspects of Smith's system and places this at the centre of his question 'Why did Smith become the father of economic science?' In this problematic context, Uchida asked three questions that no other scholar had previously posed: 'What was the nature of the historical age in which Smith lived?' and, therefore, 'What was the nature of the fundamental question that Smith posed at the beginning of his career in *TMS*?'; and 'How did Smith formulate the same question in economic-theoretical terms and finally reach the solution in *WN*?' Part One of the *Birth* is devoted to addressing the first two questions and Part Two the third. Due to limitations of space, my argument hereafter will focus on Part One, which has generated a far more enthusiastic response in Japan's academia than the second; indeed, it is still widely recognized as the book's key element. By contrast, many regard the second part as a standard Marxian analysis of Smith's labour theory of value, notwithstanding the author's firm belief that he presented highly original arguments there, too. As I will argue, Uchida's insightful reconstruction of Smith's dialogue with Rousseau and Hume in Part One appeared almost twenty years before Western scholars covered similar ground (Colletti 1974[1969]; West 1971).

5. Smith's fundamental criticism of the mercantile system

While Uchida firmly believed that the nature of classical economics was a scientific anatomy of 'civil society', as Karl Marx had believed, he also argued that the stages of classical economics must be carefully designated. Classical economics was brought to a degree of systematic perfection prior to Marx by Ricardo's *Principles of Political Economy and Taxation* (1817). How was Ricardo able to complete the system in such a highly theoretical way? Simply because, as many scholars had argued, he lived in the age of the Industrial Revolution and could therefore develop his economic analysis by observing the established capitalist economy with his own eyes. This further resulted in their belief that Smith's economics was far from theoretically complete simply because he lived in the pre-industrial and largely agrarian society of the eighteenth century. If this mode of thinking applies, Uchida continues to ask, why did Smith become the father of economics in the way that he did? One answer might be that, notwithstanding his historical disadvantage and limitations, Smith's incredibly sharp insight allowed him to discover the secret of capitalist economy and, in particular, the mechanisms of the division of labour, distribution of income, and accumulation of capital.

However, Uchida was not satisfied with these opportunistic and teleological arguments. He admitted that Smith could not have become the father of economics without his unparalleled analytical power and insight, even considering the degree to which he was indebted to mercantilist writers and the French Physiocrats. But he further asked what aspects of Smith's way of tackling the problem enabled him to make all of these achievements. It was neither simply because he was a genius nor because he was lucky enough to live at the start of the Industrial Revolution. Countless other people lived at that time. Yet it was Smith who became the father of economics. Why? Uchida believed that the answer lay at the deeper level of Smith's intellectual development.

First, Uchida pointed out the profoundly anti-liberalist and even quasi-feudal nature of eighteenth-century Britain. Smith lived in a society in which the systematic encouragement of the British economy was energetically carried out from above by the Whig administration. At its heart was a system of governmental regulation, control and monopoly orchestrated by the British state. The intellectual and ideological wing of the system was a body of economic and political discourses that Smith called 'the system of commerce' and which is now generally called mercantilism. Uchida called the political ideology of the regime 'Whig totalitarianism' and characterized it as far from free and liberal. The mercantilist system as a whole oppressed the civil liberties of the people by regulation and control, on the one hand, and championed the principle of liberty as the hallmark of the system, on the other. The regime was brutally oppressive and unashamedly contradicted Britain's official profile as the freest country in Europe. Uchida cites Smith's passionate criticism of the mercantile laws 'which the clamour of our merchants and manufacturers has extorted from the legislature, for the support of their own absurd and oppressive monopolies' and his final verdict that 'these laws may be said to be all written in blood' (*WN* IV.viii.17).

Second, Uchida asks why Smith was able to identify the contradictory nature of the regime. Here he turns to Smith's early career. In short, Smith identified the issue not as an economist in the making but as the Professor of Moral Philosophy at the University of Glasgow. As John Millar reported, as reproduced in Dugald Stewart's *The Account of the Life and Writings of Adam Smith* (1811), *TMS* was a byproduct of the ethical part of his moral philosophy lecture, and *WN* was one of his jurisprudence lectures on 'police, revenue and arms'. The first part of his lecture on 'justice' was left unpublished but is now available as *LJ* (*LJA* from 1762–3 and *LJB* from 1763–4). *LJB* was available to Uchida only in Edwin

Cannan's edition (Smith 1896) and in the Japanese translation by Takashima and Mizuta, published in 1947. Against this background, Uchida started to launch an ambitious project to resolve how Smith was able to transform himself from moral philosopher into economist.

Smith as the author of *TMS* identified the profound contradiction in Whig totalitarianism between the principle of justice and liberty, on the one hand, and its practical application by mercantilist policy, on the other. He was able to do so only because he considered the issue with the searching eye of the author of *LJ*. Thus, Uchida understood Smith's economics as originating in the long tradition of natural jurisprudence since Hugo Grotius, and not in the tradition of mercantilist discourse. Indeed, theoretical criticism of mercantilist theory and policy had been developed by liberal economic authors such as Daniel Defoe, Jacob Vanderlint, Josiah Tucker and, more than anyone else, David Hume. Smith was clearly conscious of his profound debt to all of these authors and especially Hume. Nevertheless, Uchida emphasizes that Smith's criticism of the mercantile system originated not in the tradition of economic liberalism, but in his critical digestion of the tradition of natural jurisprudence. For Smith, the fundamental error of the mercantile system was not an error in economic theory. He identified the root cause of the problem as the misguided application of the theory of justice to the political and ideological justification of a mercantilist system that was commonly accepted in his time.

As will be discussed in greater detail, Uchida somewhat surprisingly argued that it was *Hume*'s theory of justice that provided Whig totalitarianism with its most sophisticated justification of the fundamental principle of justice. No matter how unaware of this Hume himself was, and how contradictory the claim sounds, given his widely accepted image as the most liberal economist before Smith, Whig totalitarianism was justified by Hume's theory of justice and, in particular, by its theoretical core – the principle of 'public utility'. To prove the point, Uchida cites a passage from *WN* in which Smith presented a resentful criticism of mercantile regulation as the violation of 'the ordinary laws of justice' ideologically justified by 'an idea of public utility':

> To hinder, besides, the farmer from sending his goods at all times to the best market, is evidently to sacrifice the ordinary laws of justice to an idea of public utility, to a sort of reasons of state; an act of legislative authority which ought to be exercised only, which can be pardoned only in cases of the most urgent necessity.
>
> (*WN* IV.v.39)

6. Smith's dialogue with Rousseau at the start of the path to *The Wealth of Nations*

Uchida's argument makes an even more surprising turn at this point by introducing Jean-Jacques Rousseau as the decisive figure who ignited Smith's awareness of the issue. Uchida argues first that Smith was struck by the problem by encountering

Rousseau's *Discourse on the Origin and the Foundation of the Inequality among Men* (1755) as he clearly indicated in his anonymous 'Letter to the *Edinburgh Review*' published in 1756.

Smithian scholars in Japan had known of this letter for a long time before Uchida published the *Birth*. But none of them had seriously considered why Smith might have embarked on such an extensive discussion of Rousseau's work and even included a substantial amount of translated text in his letter. Uchida's assessment of the document is highly original and even ground-breaking, not only among his contemporaries in Japan but among European and American scholars of the early 1950s. He uses it to establish a direct intellectual link between Rousseau and Smith by presenting a novel reinterpretation. Rousseau's discourse on inequality had been a devastating attack on the social and economic reality of modern European civilization. He identified the root of all evil in the system of private property as well as the consequent evils of economic inequality, moral corruption and political domination. Uchida argues that Rousseau's criticism devastated Smith's naive optimism about the nature and status quo of modern civilized society and awoke his new awareness of its critical reality. Smith read Rousseau's discourse as a full-scale attack on feudal landowners and the privileged and wealthy bourgeoisie. Uchida argues that Rousseau's true intention was not a simple rejection of civilization itself, but a fundamental reform or change of the French ancien régime. *The Social Contract*, published in 1762, would be his final statement on how to carry out the necessary revolutionary reform of the old system. Despite the obvious differences between Rousseau's and Smith's historical challenges, they certainly shared a critical awareness of the corrupt and oppressive nature of modern civilization.

> It is well known that the *Discourse*, the *Emile* and *The Social Contract* worked together to establish the foundation for the French Revolution as well as that *The Wealth of Nations* as the outgrowth of *The Theory of Moral Sentiments* justified American independence and the accompanying financial revolution in Britain. However, for a correct evaluation of these works, we need to view them in their global contexts. In other words, we see here the overlapping manifestations of two historically different challenges, i.e. the creation of bourgeois property right (Rousseau's French Revolution) and liberation from the state engaging in primitive accumulation of capital (Smith's attack on mercantilism). Rousseau's and Smith's works must be seen as the theories of French and British bourgeoisies confronting the Old Colonialism that was facing impending catastrophe under the pressure of these two issues.
>
> (Uchida 1953: 90)

How, then, did Smith respond to Rousseau's counter-Enlightenment project? As Uchida goes on to argue, Rousseau's development from *The Discourse on Inequality* to *The Social Contract* marked intellectual growth from simple criticism of modern natural lawyers as philosophical advocates of a corrupt society, to a positive proposal to create a just republic of free, equal and independent citizens under the sovereign leadership of the General Will. In contrast, although Smith was inspired by Rousseau's project to some extent, he did not accept it as a realistic strategy for reforming his own society. In Uchida's view, though Smith and Rousseau both started from an awareness of the crisis of jurisprudence in the midst of the 'crisis of civilization', they clearly diverged in their practical solutions. Rousseau pointed the revolutionary way toward the total reform of the corrupt political system through the creation of a new republic by the social contract. Smith chose the very different path of systematic reform of the established regime by exploring the possibility that mercantilist Britain could transform itself into a genuine system of natural liberty by dismantling the mercantile system. Rousseau identified the root cause of all social evil within civilized society in the system of private property itself, whereas Smith pointed to the corrupt and erroneous nature of mercantile regulation and control. Smith's utopia was not Rousseau's agrarian republic of equal independent producers, but a large-scale commercial and industrial civilization. In fact, Smith's system of natural liberty was envisioned as perfectly compatible with huge social and economic inequality among its members as a result of free, equal and unregulated competition in the market. *WN* was the final answer.

Smith clearly knew that his own challenge was very different from Rousseau's. Smith was fighting against the settlement of 1688 and Britain's system of regulation and control, not modern commercial civilization itself. Drawing on the works by H. Butterfield (1949) and others, Uchida gives detailed historical accounts of the political structure and social condition of Britain in the age of Lord North, when the nation was wrestling with the issue of American independence. Uchida also makes effective use of L. T. Hogben (1939) to suggest the strong historical connection between Smith's criticism of Britain's political regime and the rising democratic campaigns for parliamentary reform. For Smith, another bourgeois or quasi-republican revolution in Britain inspired by Rousseau's project was out of the question. At this point in Uchida's account, Rousseau's importance for Smith fades away significantly, to be replaced by David Hume.

7. Smith's dialogue with Hume, further along the path to *The Wealth of Nations*

As we saw in the previous section, Hume explained the artificial nature of justice through the idea of 'public utility'. While Uchida gives no detailed account of Hume's theory of justice itself, and seems unaware of the differences between Book III of *A Treatise of Human Nature* (1740) and *An Enquiry Concerning the Principles of Morals* (1751), in the latter work Hume does indeed emphasize the central importance of 'public utility' to explain the nature of justice:

> That public utility is the sole origin of justice, and that reflections on the beneficial consequences of this virtue are the sole foundation of its merit;

this proposition, being more curious and important, will better deserve our examination and enquiry.

(Hume 1998: 3. 1.1)

Notwithstanding what Hume intended to convey in the above extract, Uchida argues that Smith's consistent criticism of mercantilist regulation and control and of the British regime's systematic intention 'to sacrifice the ordinary laws of justice to an idea of public utility' probably drove him to interpret Hume's passage as playing an effective role in justifying the regime in philosophical terms. Uchida stresses that he is not talking about Hume's *intention*, but about the unintended ideological role that his theory of justice came to play. This interpretation caused a heated debate among scholars, some of whom pointed out that Smith never mentions Hume by name in any of his works. Uchida knew this and admitted that Hume's quasi-mercantilist theory of justice was inconsistent with the general tenor of his economic liberalism, and that he himself was unaware of the inconsistency.

In *Birth*, Uchida goes on to buttress his argument by citing a passage in *TMS* (II.ii.1), where Smith critically discusses the common distinction between the artificial virtue of justice and the other natural virtues, and mentions 'an author of very great and original genius'. Uchida takes this to mean Hume, and then cites another well-known passage on the distinction between the 'final' and 'efficient' causes of the world. Smith says:[3]

But though it commonly requires no great discernment to see the destructive tendency of all licentious practices to the welfare of society, it is seldom this consideration which first animates us against them. All men, even the most stupid and unthinking, abhor fraud, perfidy, and injustice, and delight to see them punished. But few men have reflected upon the necessity of justice to the existence of society, how obvious soever that necessity may appear to be.

(Smith 1982: II.ii.3)

Uchida summarizes Smith's intention in the following passage:

Here we can see Smith's fight against Hume's theory of law that founded the origin of justice on public utility for the whole (D. Hume, *Principles of Morals*, esp. chapter 3). Indeed, it was Smith's challenge to repudiate the doctrine which explained the foundation of justice from the tendency to the utility of the whole, and thereby to demonstrate that the sole law justifiably enforceable by the state is not to prevent injury against the utility of society as a whole, but to prevent only injury inflicted directly against an individual's life and property. Smith's accounts on this particular point are persistently detailed, although he does not mention Hume's name in either of them. In one sense, it is no exaggeration to say that it was his secret motive behind the logic pervasive through the whole of *TMS* to subvert Hume's theory in a constructive manner.

(Uchida 1953: 111)

The crucial point here is what made Uchida identify Hume as the principal target of Smith's criticism, despite his clear knowledge that Smith never mentioned Hume by name in either *TMS* or *WN*. Although Uchida explicitly mentions 'D. Hume, *Principles of Morals*, esp. chapter 3' as supporting evidence for his conjecture, there are circumstantial reasons for doubting that he reached his conclusion by personal examination of Hume's original text. One interesting fact in this context is that Uchida, when writing the *Birth*, almost certainly consulted the Japanese translation of *TMS*, published in 1948–9 by Tomio Yonebayashi, who based his translation on Dugald Stewart's popular edition, which has no editorial notes. However, probably feeling the need to strengthen the academic gravitas of his translation, Yonebayashi borrowed detailed editorial notes in their entirety from Walther Eckstein's well-respected German translation, published in 1926 (Smith 1926). The editors of the Glasgow edition of *TMS* point out that when Smith mentions 'an author of very great and original genius', 'Eckstein . . . thinks, with others, that the flattering description probably refers to Hume, but notes that Hume does not speak of a "stricter obligation" to justice than to other virtues, and therefore adds that the reference may be to Kames' (Smith 1982: 364). In fact, Eckstein refers to the relevant part of Hume's work in his note, and Uchida knew of the note through Yonebayashi's translation. As Uchida seemingly had very little knowledge of Kames, he was presumably encouraged by the note to think of Hume as Smith's main target in the problematic passage.

However, the technical question of whether Eckstein's note made Uchida think of Hume as Smith's principal target is of secondary importance when compared to Uchida's own conundrum and conclusion. Aside from the plausibility of his identification of Hume, and aside from how much he actually studied Hume's original texts, Uchida had a much more profound reason for reaching his conclusion:

Why was Smith so persistent in his opposition to Hume's legal theory? It was because the question of how to found justice involves not merely the theoretical point concerning the foundation of justice but also underlies the practical problem of 'what is the justifiable limit of the law that is enforceable by the state?' To put it more clearly, the view that 'public utility is the foundation of justice' provided a justification of the system of mercantilist policy by an unjustifiable expansion of the limit of the law enforceable by the state. Smith was probably convinced that the Whigs' positive laws, entrusted with enforcing power under the name of justice for the benefit of public welfare or public utility, were the very enforcing power which in turn was the idea of 'social utility' presupposing the mutually confronting states operated by mercantilist policies.

(Uchida 1953: 114)

Uchida concludes his argument on Smith's supposed dialogue with Hume with a forceful remark:

> The error of the past jurisprudence was its willingness to take the fact of competing states for granted and to attempt to found law on the principle of social utility. Even the great Hume, as far as he was not completely free from mercantilist predilections, could not liberate himself from this common sense.
>
> (Uchida 1953: 132)

Uchida thus concludes that Smith's criticism of Hume's theory of justice was directed – indirectly but most effectively – at the British regime which, in the name of public utility or the good of the whole, oppressed the fundamental rights and liberties of the people through the system of trade regulation and control that was imposed by politicians and legislators. This is exactly why Smith's *WN* was intended to create a system of economics to establish that modern commercial society could possibly transform itself into a system in which not only the working people would grow richer but the rules of natural justice to protect their rights and liberties would universally prevail. *WN* intended to clarify that the future capitalist society would ensure long-term growth of the market economy without any external regulation or intervention by any paternalistic government. It was written to show the path to the ideal 'civil society', which would be a just and fair society, not merely a rich and prosperous society.

8. Conclusion: Uchida's legacy in historical and international perspectives

Uchida argues that Smith was able to become the father of economics only through his critical dialogues with Hume's and Rousseau's versions of 'civil society'. His way of exploring the issue in relation to Hume, Rousseau and Smith in the tradition of natural jurisprudence deserves fruitful comparison with the well-known dichotomy between 'wealth and virtue' or 'needs and justice' in the major academic debate on the origins and nature of the Scottish Enlightenment. Istvan Hont and Michael Ignatieff's now classic article (Hont 2005: ch. 1) made the pioneering attempt to trace the historical origin of Smith's *WN* to a mid-eighteenth-century European moral and political debate over whether to prioritize the needs of the starving poor, on the one hand, or the strict execution of justice to protect the property of rich merchants, on the other. Indeed, Uchida, Hont and Ignatieff share the historical understanding that *WN* should be traced back to the tradition of natural jurisprudence, rather than mercantilist literature (Uchida) or the civic humanist or classical republican tradition (Hont and Ignatieff).

However, they differ sharply in detail, and most visibly in the relative importance that they attach to Smith, Hume and Rousseau. Hont and Ignatieff draw the critical dividing line between the natural jurisprudence tradition represented by Hume and Smith, on the one hand, and the civic humanist tradition exemplified by Rousseau, on the other. By contrast, Uchida presents a more complex and triangular structure, drawing *two* dividing lines between Rousseau, Hume and Smith. For Hont and Ignatieff, Hume was Smith's closest strategic ally to overcome the civic humanist Rousseau. For Uchida, Hume was indeed Smith's most reliable ally to overcome Rousseau's negative view of modern commercial society, but, at the same time, Smith attempted to overcome Hume's unintentional endorsement of the corrupt and oppressive mercantilist system. This latter aspect of Smith's criticism was initially inspired by his profound sympathy for Rousseau's criticism of civilized society as a fundamentally hypocritical system under the guise of free and equal society.

Notwithstanding Uchida's complex argumentative structure, this interpretive difference derives not from the three scholars' understandings of Smith's argument for the strict execution of justice and the complete protection of the civil rights and liberties of the people as the essential condition of civilized society. Rather, the major difference arises from the degree to which they appraise a democratic spirit in Smith's thought. For Uchida, Smith was a quasi-democratic thinker inspired by Rousseau and British democratic movements. Uchida's own political view of capitalism and the ideal 'civil society' was undoubtedly projected into his interpretation of Smith's personality. For Hont and Ignatieff, by contrast, Hume and Smith certainly shared the same political outlook as liberals, but they were not necessarily democratic thinkers. Uchida's ideal 'civil society', drawn from the legacy of Takashima and Okochi, embodied not only the core image of Smith's *Wealth of Nations* as envisioning a free, fair and prosperous society but his own optimistic vision of Japan's post-war reconstruction by democratic means.

Overlapping with Smith's way of criticizing Whig totalitarianism and its mercantilist theory and policies, Uchida revealed his own 'practical problem' behind his 'theoretical point' on the essential affinity between Hume's theory of justice, the principle of public utility and the inherent tendency of mercantile system constantly to expand 'the limit of the law' and thereby encroach on the rights and liberties of the people. Uchida reads into Smith's text his own vision of a future 'civil society' in Japan, and by so doing succeeds in presenting a highly original and imaginative rereading of Smith's work. Smith's 'Letter to the *Edinburgh Review*' was written immediately before the Seven Years War, at the climax of a series of wars between Britain and France, fought over their North American and Asian colonies. Uchida's *Birth* was written and published almost concurrently with the Korean War (1950–3). He wrote under increasing political and ideological pressure from nationalists who hoped for a political right-turn in Japan. Thus, it is easy to imagine the similarities he identified between eighteenth-century Whig totalitarianism and twentieth-century Japanese militaristic totalitarianism. For Uchida, Smith's solitary struggle against rising nationalism and militarism was not a matter of mere historical curiosity. It must have overlapped directly with his own historical and intellectual challenge in the mid-1950s, as the nightmare of a return to the mid-1940s started to seem ever more plausible. Smith's ideal of a just, peaceful and wealthy 'civil society' was surely what Uchida envisioned as a far better future for his own country.

Thus, Adam Smith was finally given a new life by Yoshihiko Uchida as the champion of economic liberalism and political democracy. Before Uchida, Japanese scholars (with the exception of Takashima and Okochi) regarded Smith first and foremost as a liberalist economic thinker, and no sort of democratic thinker. Instead, Japanese intellectuals credited Rousseau, Mill and others with the democratic role. Aside from whether modern Smithian scholars still view Uchida's Smith as essentially correct, his pioneering attempt to create a highly original view of this great Scottish thinker proves that classical texts can be infused with new life by scholars who endure their own struggles, no matter how distant they may be from the object of their study in space and time.

Notes

1   This article is dedicated to the memory of Istvan Hont.
2   Craig (2009) argues that the intellectual origin of Fukuzawa's thought in general is traceable to Scottish authors as instanced by Burton's book.
3   Uchida could have used another effective passage from the *Lectures on Jurisprudence* to prove his point that Hume's theory of justice afforded philosophical support to the mercantile system. Smith argued that the theory of justice founded upon the principle of public utility was wrong and the ultimate origin of justice should be sought in the impartial spectator's sympathy with the sufferer's resentment. Smith further links this philosophical criticism, though does not mention Hume by name, with his political criticism of harsh mercantile regulations in the name of public utility. This is exactly what Uchida tries to establish. Smith wrote, '[I]njury naturaly excites the resentment of the spectator, and the punishment of the offender is reasonable as far as the indifferent spectator can go along with it. This is the natural measure of punishment. It is to be observed that our first approbation of punishment is not founded upon the regard to public utility which is commonly taken to be the foundation of it. It is our sympathy with the resentment of the sufferer which is the real principle. That it cannot be utility is manifest from the following example. Wool in England was conceived to be the source of public opulence, and it was made a capital crime to export that commodity' (Smith 1978: 181–2).

Bibliography

Barry, N. (1995) 'Hume, Smith and Rousseau on Freedom', in R. Wokler (ed.), *Rousseau and Liberty*, Manchester: Manchester University Press.
Barshay, A. (2004) *The Social Sciences in Modern Japan*, Berkeley: University of California Press, ch. 6.
Burton, J. H. (1852) *Chambers's Educational Course: Political Economy for Use in Schools and Private Instruction*, London: William and Robert Chambers.
Butterfield, H. (1949) *George III, Lord North, and the People, 1779–80*, London: G. Bell and Sons.
Colletti, L. (1974) [1969] 'Mandeville, Rousseau and Smith', in idem, *From Rousseau to Lenin: Studies in Ideology and Society*, New York: Monthly Review Press.
Craig, A. M. (2009) *Civilization and Enlightenment: The Early Thought of Fukuzawa Yukichi*, Cambridge, MA: Harvard University Press.
Force, P. (2003) *Self-Interest before Adam Smith: A Genealogy of Economic Science*, Cambridge: Cambridge University Press.

Fukuzawa, Y. (2007) [1899] *The Autobiography of Yukichi Fukuzawa*, revised trans. Eiichi Kiyooka, with a foreword by A. Craig, New York: Columbia University Press.

Hanley, R. (2008a) 'Commerce and Corruption: Rousseau's Diagnosis and Adam Smith's Cure', *European Journal of Political Theory* 7: 137–58.

Hanley, R. (2008b) 'Enlightened Nation Building: The "Science of the Legislator" in Adam Smith and Rousseau', *American Journal of Political Science* 52: 219–34.

Hattori, Masaharu (2012) 'Noboru Kobayashi and his Study on the History of Economic Thought: National and Historical Characters in the Making of Economics', *History of Economic Thought* 54 (1): 1–21.

Hogben, L. T. (1939) 'The Theoretical Leadership of Scottish Science in the English Industrial Revolution', in idem, *Dangerous Thoughts*, London: George Allen & Unwin.

Hont, I. (2005) *Jealousy of Trade: International Competition and the Nation State in Historical Perspective*, Cambridge, MA: Harvard University Press.

Hume, David (1998) *An Enquiry concerning the Principles of Morals*, ed. Tom L. Beauchamp, Oxford: Clarendon Press.

Hurtado Prieto, J. (2004) 'Bernard Mandeville's Heir: Adam Smith or Jean-Jacques Rousseau on the Possibility of Economic Analysis', *European Journal of the History of Economic Thought* 11: 1–31.

Ignatieff, M. (1986) 'Smith, Rousseau and the Republic of Needs', in T. C. Smout (ed.), *Scotland and Europe, 1200–1850*, Edinburgh: John Donald.

Kobayashi, N. (1943) *An Introduction to Friedrich List*, Tokyo: Ito-shoten (in Japanese).

Kobayashi, N. (1967) *James Steuart, Adam Smith and Friedrich List*, Economic Series No. 40, Tokyo: Science Council of Japan, Division of Economics, Commerce and Business Administration.

Kobayashi, N. (1990) 'Friedrich Lists System der Sozialwissenschaft: von einem japanischen Forscher betrachtet', *Studien zur Entwicklung der ökonomischen Theorie* 10: 64–77.

Mizuta, H. (2000) *Adam Smith's Library: A Catalogue*, Oxford: Clarendon Press.

Mizuta, H. (2003) 'Adam Smith in Japan', in Tatsuya Sakamoto and Hideo Tanaka (eds), *The Rise of Political Economy in the Scottish Enlightenment*, London: Routledge.

Niimura, S.(1998) 'Modernization and the Studies of Adam Smith in Japan during and after World War II: Kazuo Okouchi, Zenya Takashima and Yoshihiko Uchida', in S. Sugihara and T. Tanaka (eds), *Economic Thought and Modernization in Japan*, Cheltenham: Edward Elgar.

Okochi, K. (1943) *Smith and List: Economic Morals and Economic Theory*, Tokyo: Nihon Hyoron Company (in Japanese).

Okochi, K. (2000) 'A Short History of Translations of the Wealth of Nations', trans. T. Sakamoto, in Cheng-Chung Lai (ed.), *Adam Smith Across Nations: Translations and Receptions of The Wealth of Nations*, Oxford: Clarendon Press.

Rasmussen, D. (2008) *The Problems and Promise of Commercial Society: Adam Smith's Response to Rousseau*, University Park: Pennsylvania State University Press.

Rasmussen, D. (2013) 'Adam Smith and Rousseau: Enlightenment and Counter-Enlightenment', in C. J. Berry, Maria Pia Paganelli, and Craig Smith (eds), *The Oxford Handbook of Adam Smith*, Oxford: Oxford University Press.

Sakamoto, T. (2000) 'Review Article of S. Sugihara and T. Tanaka eds., *Economic Thought and Modernization in Japan*', *History of Economic Ideas* 8: 159–67.

Sakamoto, T. (2014) 'Foreword', in Eriko Nakai (ed.), *The Mizuta Library of Rare Books in the History of European Social Thought: A Catalogue of the Collection Held at Nagoya University Library*, Tokyo: Edition Synapse; London: Routledge.

Smith, A. (1896) *Lectures on Justice, Police, Revenue and Arms delivered in the University of Glasgow by Adam Smith and Reported by a Student in 1763*, ed. E. Cannan, Oxford: Clarendon Press.

Smith, A. (1926) *Theorie der ethischen Gefühle; mit Einleitung, Anmerkungen und Registern herausgegeben von Walther Eckstein*, Leipzig: F. Meiner.

Smith, A. (1978) *Lectures on Jurisprudence*, ed. R. L. Meek, D. D. Raphael and P. G. Stein, Indianapolis, IN: Liberty Press.

Smith, A. (1980) 'Letter to *Edinburgh Review*', in *Essays on Philosophical Subjects*, ed. W. Wightman, J. Bryce and I. Ross, Indianapolis, IN: Liberty Press.

Smith, A. (1981) *An Inquiry into the Nature and Causes of the Wealth of Nations*, ed. R. Campbell and A. Skinner, Indianapolis, IN: Liberty Press.

Smith, A. (1982) *The Theory of Moral Sentiments*, ed. A. L. Macfie and D. D. Raphael, Indianapolis, IN: Liberty Press.

Sugiyama, C. and Mizuta H. (eds) (1988) *Enlightenment and Beyond: Political Economy Comes to Japan*, Tokyo: University of Tokyo Press.

Suzuki, N. (2013) 'Uchida Yoshihiko: A Japanese Civil Society Economist and Historian of Economic Thought of Postwar Japan', *History of Economic Thought* 55(1): 1–17.

Takashima, Z. (1941) *Fundamental Problems in Economic Sociology: Smith and List as Economic Sociologist*, Tokyo: Nihon Hyoron Company (in Japanese).

Uchida, Y. (1953) *The Birth of Economic Science*, Tokyo: Miraisha (in Japanese).

Uchida, Y. (1988–2002) *Collected Works of Yoshihiko Uchida*, 11 vols, Tokyo: Iwanami (in Japanese).

West, E. G. (1971) 'Adam Smith and Rousseau's *Discourse on Inequality*: Inspiration or Provocation?', *Journal of Economic Issues* 5: 56–70.

Yamada, T. (1982) 'Y. Uchida à la recherche d'une science sociale pour les hommes ordinaires', *Actuel Marx* 2: 88–91.

Yan Fu's *Wealth of Nations*
A Victorian Adam Smith in late Qing China

Jeng-Guo S. Chen

This essay has a twofold purpose. First and foremost, I shall describe how the translator Yan Fu (1854–1921) introduced to China the thought of Adam Smith, particularly his liberal thinking and political economy, paying close attention to historical context. Unlike other modern studies, which tend to dwell on how Yan "misunderstood," "mistranslated," and "misrepresented" *WN*, the present essay illustrates how Smith was reborn and transformed in China (Schwartz 1964: 113–29; Trescott 2007: 29–37; Lai 2000: 16–26).[1] To understand this process, one has to appreciate a number of contexts, both British and Chinese. This is transnational as well as inter-contextual history. My second purpose is to evaluate the complex legacy of Yan's translation, so that we can appreciate the trajectory between our own time and that of Yan.

The buoyant renaissance of Smithian scholarship may be due to a paradigmatic reinstatement of *TMS*. This critical revival of Smith's ethics is a worldwide phenomenon that can be traced back to the late 1970s, when publication of the Glasgow edition of Smith's collected works began. Many of the stereotypical and ahistorical interpretations of Smith that long dominated the general view, making him the champion of capitalism, of *laissez-faire*, of an early form of rational choice theory, of libertarianism, have been rebutted. As scholars have returned to *TMS*, many issues once hotly debated – the so-called "Adam Smith Problem," the invisible hand, agriculture versus commerce, the state versus individual liberty – have been reformulated or simply set aside as improperly formulated (Raphael and Macfie 1983; Otteson 2002).[2] Historians and economists alike are now much more conscious of the need to acknowledge Smith's many aspects, including his interests in virtue, love, justice, and cosmopolitanism, traits too often overlooked by imperialists and libertarians (Dwyer 1998; Phillipson 2010; Hanley 2009; Griswold 1999; Forman-Barzilai 2010; Hont and Ignatieff 1983; Frazer 2010; Raphael 2007; Evensky 2005; Rothschild 2001; Fleischacker 1999; Haakonssen 2006; Berry 2013).

The new paradigm of Smithian scholarship was first conceived over three decades ago by a group of scholars preoccupied with the historical problem of civic humanism. Led by J. G. A. Pocock, this group championed regional contextualism, in opposition to the methodological universalism that Ronald Meek and others ascribed to Smith's economic writings. According to Meek, Smith painted human social evolution in strictly materialist terms, foreshadowing Karl Marx's historical materialism (Meek 1976, 1977; Hont 2005; Berry 2013). The members of Pocock's contextualist group contended that Smith's economic and moral writings, viewed as a whole, offered a sophisticated and intriguing response to contemporaneous moral and political emergencies (Hont and Ignatieff 1983; Pocock 1974; Robertson 1983; Sher 1982). Other political theorists have paid special attention to Smith's statements about international politics, plucking out themes of sympathy, sensibility, and the impartial spectator (Forman-Barzilai 2010; Hanley 2009; Pitts 2005).

As this paper will show, however, this new *TMS* paradigm did not arrive in the Chinese world until the first decade of the twenty-first century. Until that time, whether in Taipei, Hong Kong, Shanghai, or Beijing, Adam Smith was simply the author of *WN*. The focus on *WN* resulted from many historical factors. Suffice to say for now that Yan Fu inherited Edward Rogers's rendering of the Gladstonite Smith; further, he saw Smith as anticipating the Darwinian notion of universal competition among individuals and nations, offering a recipe for China's self-strengthening. The liberal and libertarian legacy of Smith was taken up by a group of economists in republican Taiwan after 1950, through the intermediacy of, by and large, F. A. Hayek. Consequentially, Smithian political economy brought about the first wave of liberalism in China; it was, nevertheless, very much structured within the ideational parameters of Cobdenite *laissez-faire*, Darwinian competition and Hayekian individualism.

1. Western economic imperialism and social Darwinism in China

Before Yan Fu's translation of *WN* appeared in 1901, little was known of Smith in China (Zhu 2002: 211). Yan embarked on the project in the autumn of 1896, a precarious, chaotic, and uncertain moment after the shock of China's defeat in the Sino-Japanese War of 1894–5. Half a century earlier, the British "cannon of capitalism," as Marx described it, had thrown the Qing dynasty from its self-appointed throne of universal kingship. No longer could China lay claim to ruling *tianxia* (all under heaven). A new international political order appeared, based on state-to-state treaties; it was often referred to by the shorthand *wanguo* (literally, ten thousand states). Many Chinese intellectuals feared that China would be relegated to a peripheral place in the new world system.[3]

Yan responded to China's disastrous defeat with a series of essays in which he introduced Charles Darwin's theory of evolution and Smith's liberal view of trade (Yan 1998e: 35, 48, and 90). For him, the two ideas were connected through their reliance on competition as an explanatory force. Darwinism – or, more precisely, social Darwinism – not only provided the Chinese people with the most comprehensive and sweeping explanation of their country's dismal condition but illuminated some of the themes found in *WN*.

After these early articles, Yan took on a more ambitious project: explicitly in response to the Sino-Japanese War, he published a "translation" of Thomas

Huxley's *Evolution and Ethics* (1893) in 1896. Entitled *Tianyan lun* (On heavenly evolution), this publication offered Chinese readers an introduction to "the survival of the fittest" as racial and international competition. For the English word "nature," Yan used *tian* (heaven), a character that refers to an omnipresent and omnipotent god, to nature, and to the sky. The use of this character endorsed the struggles between individuals, between ethnic groups, and between nations – conflicts that Huxley, social Darwinists, and imperialists allegedly considered essential to human progress. In *Tianyan lun*, Yan told his readers that competition and struggle were as basic to human life as to the making of history:

> It is true that the world is changing. However, there is something unchange-able, called the "evolution of heaven." The evolution of heaven is a substance [*ti*] that has two applications [*yong*]: competition among species and the selec-tion by heaven (nature). The principles involved are applicable to all things, but they apply particularly well to living things. Competition among species is set into motion because all creatures struggle for survival. A creature competes against all of its fellows for survival; the upshot is determined by heavenly selection [natural selection]. Since struggle is perpetual, individual survivors must benefit from attributes bestowed on them by heaven and external circum-stances such as time and space. That is why we call it heavenly selection. Only by surviving can a creature become independent. From a pivotal point of view, this is, as it were, the result of heavenly selection. The hands of nature manage all of heavenly selection. Thus while it is a selection, no volition is involved. Likewise, the competition between individuals does not take place face to face. It is nonetheless a most vicious competition. Herbert Spencer said, "Heavenly selection means survival of the fittest." History comes into existence when all things compete for survival and heaven selects the winners.
>
> (Yan 1998c: 182–3)[4]

As long as struggle and natural selection were mandated by heaven, Yan agreed with Huxley that human beings would tend to present them in moral terms: "We must bravely persevere. When we are confronted by great and powerful men, we must stand fast and never retreat. We must fight, and though we may be conquered, we must never surrender" (Yan 1998c: 277).[5]

From the perspective of social Darwinism, the cause of China's predicament was crystal clear: the people did not appreciate the philosophical truth or the reality of natural selection, and they needed to acquire specific know-how if they were to thrive. Yan saw *WN* as the best way for the Chinese to equip themselves for survival. In the very last paragraph of his translator's note to *Yuan fu*, he characterized the importance of economics in the struggle for individual and national survival. For too long despotism had distracted people's attention from this truth. *WN* would change that.

> Alas! The rule "Species compete, nature selects" is applied everywhere at every single minute. The earth is finite; its offerings are limited. The clever

and the cunning take most of them and become rich, while the mute and the cowardly take little and become poor. Plenty and want are the principal reasons for the rise and fall [of nations] ... Learning can bear no fruit unless we follow the rules set down in the Western sciences. Two thousand years have elapsed since the First Emperor of Qin stupefied his people. No longer can stupidity and ignorance be tolerated, because advances in our understanding of nature have permitted communications to link the whole world. Millennia from now the peoples of East Asia [literally: the yellow nations] would surely disapprove if their ancestors had failed to act. Woe! Can we not be mindful?

(Simi 1998: 1.15)[6]

As China confronted a grave threat, with stronger nations intent on plundering her great wealth, it was clear to Yan Fu that things would not go well unless his fellow countrymen heeded the insights found in Adam Smith's masterpiece.

2. The British context: free trade and Darwinism

Modern historians have noticed that Yan was far more responsible than any other late Qing writer who took on the duty of introducing his readers to Western liberalism (Huang 2008: 181–2). I wish to argue that the economic liberalism Yan advocated was very much in keeping with the *laissez-faire* ideals developed from the followers of Gladstone and Darwin; it concentrated on individual liberty and competition, not on the interdependence of individuals and nations highlighted in Smith's works of moral philosophy.

Yan personally imbibed economic liberalism in England in the 1870s. This fact may have structured his perspective on international politics and his view of liberalism. At the age of fourteen, he enrolled in the Fuzhou Naval Academy, where he was taught Western arithmetic and English. Eleven years later, he was sent to England by the Qing government to study at the Britannia Royal Naval College. During his stay in Greenwich, which lasted from 1877 to 1879, his interest in naval studies faded. Instead, he read voraciously in the social sciences and became a close observer of English society. So well versed did he become that Guo Songtao (1818–91), China's first ambassador to the United Kingdom, frequently invited him to the embassy to discuss local issues (Guo 1982: 169).[7] The rise of Darwin's fame and the victory of his theory of evolution over all rivals occurred in the 1860s and 1870s, when the Liberal Party came to power in Britain.

Just as significantly, the edition of *WN* that Yan used for his translation was that produced by James Edwin Thorold Rogers (1823–90), a follower of Richard Cobden, whose ideas were encapsulated in the motto "Peace, free trade, and goodwill among nations." Yan eventually found himself subscribing to Rogers's free-trade tenets, which he deemed compatible with Spencerian Darwinism. It is a commonplace that *WN* has inspired writers of various schools and ideologies. Nationalists, such as Friedrich List, praised Smith's description of the division of labour because of their interest in national productivity. Marxists paid homage to Smith for his discovery of the value of labour, essential to their theory of alienation. For many Victorian Britons, Smith's ideas fed into the development of liberalism – a whole panoply of liberalisms (Tribe 2002: 27–49; Reinert 2009; Howe and Morgan 2006). After Smith's death in 1790, many turned their hand to editing new editions of *WN*, including William Playfair (1759–1823), David Buchanan (1779–1848), Edward Gibbon Wakefield (1796–1862), John R. McCulloch (1789–1864), and Joseph Shield Nicholson (1850–1927). With these successive editions, the book became a three-dimensional classroom in which younger economists contested with the author (Tribe 2002: 27–49; Chen 2010: 195–214). In Yan's time, two editions competed for readers' attention: the one edited by Rogers and the one by Nicholson, published in 1884. His decision to rely on the former implied a specific attitude both to the work and to Smith. Rogers first edited *WN* in 1867, when he was the Drummond Professor of Political Economy at Oxford. A revised edition was published in 1880, the year Rogers was elected to Parliament for Southwark (de Marchi 1976: 364–80). The editor's preface he wrote for the earlier edition stands as a Whiggish manifesto on the progress and triumph of the principle of free trade. Polemically, Rogers proclaimed that the ideal state Smith had imagined was being realized by the current generation. He confidently commented in the preface:

> How powerful the mercantile class was is to be discovered from their successful resistance of Walpole's excise scheme, and the hindrance which they put on the establishment of bonded ware-houses. It should be remembered, too, that the all but universal adoption of a guild or company system in chartered towns, the laws enforced against all combinations of labourers, and the excessive severity of the law of parochial settlement, made most kinds of labour cheap, and secured a somewhat beneficial monopoly to the employers of labour.
>
> With these facts before him, Smith concluded that the adoption of those principles which he argued for and upheld, was a mere Utopia. He believed that the trading and manufacturing classes would steadily and successfully oppose the emancipation of trade and labour, and that any radical alteration in the prejudices and laws which prevailed in his time was not to be expected. Thirty years after Smith's death the principles of Free Trade were adopted in the Merchants' Petition. Nearly sixty years after the same event, an energetic agitation for the utter repudiation of Protectionist principles, and for the general adoption the Free Trade policy, was crowned with success. The persecutors of one generation became preachers to the next.
>
> (Rogers in Smith 1880: xxix–xxx)

To be sure, in nineteenth-century Britain free trade and *laissez-faire* were commonly associated with social Darwinism (Taylor 1972; Keynes 1926).[8] For instance, in 1876 Leslie Stephen (1832–1904) observed, echoing Rogers on Smith, that the latter had been heralded as the great mouthpiece for libertarian doctrines: "Adam Smith's popular fame is that of the first prophet of Free Trade

– a doctrine which in the popular opinion is supposed to be the essence of all Political Economy" (Stephen 1991: 319) Stephen situated Smithian *laissez-faire* in opposition to the cultural triumphs that had permitted societies to rise above Darwin's struggle for existence: "The doctrines enunciated by Adam Smith refer chiefly to the superficial phenomena presented by a society in which it has hitherto been the greatest triumph to preserve a decent amount of fair-play between individuals and classes immersed in the blind struggle for existence" (Stephen 1991: 326).

I believe that Yan Fu may have been, on his return to Fujian, the only Chinese libertarian. He soon became the most powerful opponent of the protectionism advocated by those who described the rampant extension of trade privileges by belligerent Western powers as a trade war. Tan Sitong (1865–1898), a political martyr, argued that the commercial weapons in the hands of Western merchants were "capable of destroying an enemy country without a visible military manoeuvre. Their strategy is most sophisticated and their purpose malicious" (Tan 1954: 422). The most eloquent advocate of a trade war was Zheng Guanying (1842–1922), a successful businessman who began his career as an agent for a British company. The author of a piece on *WN* that appeared in 1892, nine years before Yan Fu's translation, Zheng reminded his readers that the traditional social hierarchy had always valued agriculture over commerce. He also published an essay simply entitled "Trade War," in which he argued that mercantile activity served as the basis for national power (Zheng 2008: 1.285–316).

When writers presented commerce as a war, they cast imports as intrusions or losses, exports as expansions or gains. Accordingly, protectionism was favoured by many officials and polemicists. In 1890 Xue Fucheng (1838–1894), who served as ambassador to the United Kingdom and to France, called for commercial strategies that would counteract the power of Western traders. Otherwise, he grimly predicted, all of the country's products and species would end up in foreign hands, ruining the people as foreigners became ever richer (Xue 1984: 297).[9] Elsewhere, Xue observed that European countries imposed heavy tariffs on imports but the lightest of duties on exports to promote the sale of their own products (Xue 1984: 542).[10] Zheng Guanying proposed that the Chinese government should do likewise (Zheng 2008: 1.327).

Zheng was one of the few Chinese writers to write about Smith before Yan Fu. For him, the kernel of *WN* was a lesson on the importance of industriousness and frugality (*qinjian*). His was very much a conventionally moralizing Confucian perspective, and he commented that many of the world's great empires had begun to decline because of selfishness, covetousness, and vanity. Smith's call for industry and thrift, remarked Zheng, had to be regarded as golden rules for great sovereign countries and small vassal states alike (Zheng 2008: 1.481).[11] Having been educated in the early Scottish Enlightenment that propagated ideas of sociability, manners, and other social virtues, and as an active member of the Edinburgh Society for Encouraging Arts, Sciences, Manufactures, and Agriculture in Scotland (1754–1764), Smith certainly appreciated industry and thrift (Sher 1985; Emerson 1973; Phillipson 1983). By emphasizing limits on the importation and consumption of foreign merchandise, however, Zheng made Smith look much like the seventeenth-century mercantilist Thomas Mun: "The ordinary means therefore to encreae our wealth and treasure is by Forraign Trade, wherein wee must ever observe this rule; to sell more to strangers yearly than wee consume of theirs in value" (Mun 1928: 5).

More important to Yan was Smith's idea of "enlightened self-interest," which came to oppose Confucian teachings diametrically. In translating Smith's well-known passage on "self-love" and the natural disposition towards barter, Yan added to the original a Darwinist tincture of the animal world. Here is my retranslation of Yan's effort:

> Since we are frequently in need of society, and cannot depend on other people's benevolence, how can we subsist ourselves? The answer is: it depends on everyone taking care of his own interest. Human beings are self-interested animals. It is impossible to ask self-interested animals to look after us. I buy meat from butchers, wine from tavern-keepers, and rice from rice dealers to prepare for my meals. To do this, however, I do not rely on the benevolence of butchers, tavern-keepers, and rice dealers but on their own self-interest.
>
> (Simi 1998: 1.38–9)

And here is Smith's own wording:

> In civilized society he [i.e., man] stands at all times in need of the cooperation and assistance of great multitudes, while his whole life is scarce sufficient to gain the friendship of a few persons. In almost every other race of animals each individual, when it is grown up to maturity, is intirely independent, and in its natural state has occasion for the assistance of no other living creature. But man has almost instant occasion for the help of his brethren, and it is in vain for him to expect it from their benevolence only . . . It is not from the benevolence of the butcher, the brewer, or the baker, that we expect our dinner, but from their regard to their own interest.
>
> (Smith 1981: I.ii.2)

While Smith, in his original text, endeavoured to distinguish human or civilized society from the animals or the state of nature, Yan Fu tended to *conflate* humanity with animal drive. And he implicitly criticized Confucianism, for it taught people to value compassion and benevolence over self-interest. Yan believed that self-interest was one of the pillars on which modern intellectual and material achievements in the West were founded. Accordingly, he attributed material backwardness and absence of modern political economy in China to the lack of it. He stated that only self-interest could save China:

> People believe that the benevolent are rewarded and others are corrupted because they imagine that there is a contradiction between righteousness and

interest, a belief that has been ruinous for both [our] government and [our] culture . . . Mengzi [a.k.a. Mencius] remarked: "As long as benevolence and compassion exist, why should we talk about interest?" Dong [Zhungshu] urged: "Calculate righteousness, not interest; pay attention to the method, not the result." Ancient teachings, both in the East and the West, always present righteousness and interest as incompatible. While the intentions behind those teachings are meritorious, their search for truth has not gone far enough, and by misleading the people they place both righteousness and benevolence in jeopardy. Since the rise of evolutionary theory, it is quite clear that interest is always inherent in righteousness, and that searching for the way is searching for a result. Economics is the progenitor of evolutionary theory in this regard.

(Simi 1998: 1.116–17)[12]

Probably because Yan contrasted Smithian enlightened self-interest with Confucian compassion, many Chinese intellectuals in the late Qing considered Smith as an archetype of materialism, standing in opposition to Confucian idealism. For instance, Chen Huan-Chang (1880–1933), the founder of the Society for the Confucian Religion and a friend of Yan Fu, remarked that Smith's moral philosophy accentuated material wealth or fortune, standing in opposition to Mengzi's idea of morality that attributed personal identity and dignity exclusively to virtue (Chen 2002: 212).[13] Like Chen, Yan saw little in common between Confucian and Smithian moral economies. But he would disagree with Zheng as the latter argued that, given the imperialist domination of trade by Western powers, a Confucianized mercantilism seemed a rational option.

Unlike those who adapted Smith to local conditions, Yan saw free trade as what Rogers had called an "incontestable" natural justice (Rogers 1880: xxxiii).[14] In contrast to the Confucian image of Smith that Zheng had carefully carved, Yan offered a social Darwinist–Daoist Smith. In a comment inserted into the text of his translation of *WN*, he told the story of Britain's mercantilist policy, explaining bullionism, tariff protectionism, and monopolism:

Did any other nation ever put more effort into protecting trade than the British? They relied on export bounties and re-export drawbacks, and they enacted the Navigation Acts. All of these regulations were meant to discourage imports. However, in the end rather than profit the British, these policies contributed to the loss of the North American colonies. Not long after Smith's work was published, merchants realized that the policies intended to protect their interests were in fact acting as a drag on trade. Even if one or two individuals benefited from these policies, the nation as a whole lost a great deal in the long term.

(Simi 1998: 1.11)

Furthermore, Yan's emphasis on free trade led him to argue that commerce could be developed separately from, if not in advance of, agriculture. After all, Smith's criticism of mercantilism was based on the presupposition of the predominance of agriculture. For him, capital had to be invested foremost in agriculture; the resulting surpluses enabled farmers and those who invested in farms to purchase commodities (Smith 1981: I.i.379–80).

In his response to this agriculture-first-trade-later creed, Rogers maintained that Smith had resorted to "exaggerated language" when he described the gains to be had from farming as a "splendid fortune." In fact, land was limited, and the profits of agriculture came exclusively from rents. On the other hand, capital in the manufacturing industry could "increase indefinitely." As long as the capitalists could command the markets, all capital was theirs (Smith 1880: 1.380 note).

Yan Fu followed Rogers's criticism and added his own comments on Smith's account of the British colonies in North America and their agrarian development. He argued that Poland, Russia, Spain, and Portugal all had long histories of farming, but they had not prospered (Simi 1998: 1.381). Although he agreed that agriculture had to be the basis of any thriving economy, he rejected the idea of a mechanical step-like movement from agriculture to commerce (Simi 1998: 1.381). In his view, the commercial and agricultural sectors of the economy were equally important and equally profitable. More important, in China it was easier to promote trade than to improve agriculture. Yan continued:

> The [Chinese] government cares little about its people, and the people give no thought to their own future. The country becomes daily more overpopulated. Nevertheless, the government has not initiated a sound financial policy, tolerating the status quo. This do-nothing policy results in poverty and weakness; it is the result of error, not bad luck. I believe that it would be easier to expand commerce than agriculture and manufacturing. Since we have sent ambassadors to countries lying east and west [of China], they ought to use their spare time to investigate the suitability of local markets for Chinese goods. Within a few years, we can begin trade using our own ships . . . But we will not be able to defeat the monopolies operated by other nations, which will continue to mine an inexhaustible financial mother lode. We have no choice but to leave this to the next generation.
>
> (Simi 1998: 1.372)[15]

To aid our understanding of Yan's choice of the Rogers revised edition, let us compare it with the edition Joseph Shield Nicholson published, recalling that the former was published in 1880 and the latter in 1884. In contrast to Rogers's encomium to liberalism, Nicholson set out to vindicate the moderation of Smith's "economic sentiments," to borrow Emma Rothschild's apt phrase (Rothschild 2001). Despite the polemical nature of his preface, Rogers was probably justified in emphasizing the idea of free trade in the last decades of the nineteenth century, a time when the rigour, breadth, and intensity of industrialization had far surpassed those of Smith's day. Even so, Nicholson, Professor of Political Economy at the University of Edinburgh, believed that Rogers's views undermined what Smith had written. He was determined, in his edition of *WN*, to undo that damage.

Nicholson emphatically insisted that Smith upheld the individual's inviolable right to bring his own "industry and capital" into competition with those of any other man, but this freedom could not violate "the laws of justice" (Nicholson 1884: 14).[16] Nicholson warned his readers, "Even on the question of Free Trade, with which the name of Adam Smith is always associated, the teaching of the 'Wealth of Nations' is not nearly so unqualified as is generally imagined" (Nicholson 1884: 17). More significantly, while Rogers consistently foregrounded trade, Nicholson maintained that Smith was much more interested in manufacturing and agriculture (Nicholson 1884: 15).

It would be idle to ask how Yan Fu would have understood Smith if he had consulted Nicholson's, instead of Rogers's, edition. But it is certainly crucial to remember that, in the late nineteenth century, there were many competing interpretations of Smith, including socialist, nationalist, and liberal versions. Among the liberals there were different approaches, methodologies, and emphases.[17] Yan's introduction of Smith into China was apparently very much structured and limited by the British context and personal experience (Nicholson 1909: x, xii and 153–74).[18] Some of those experiences can be attributed directly to historical currents in late Qing China. Yan apparently absorbed the trade war mentality, in spite of his disagreements with many of its Chinese proponents. He maintained that Edward Gibbon Wakefield was certainly right to comment that agriculture, manufacturing, and trade were mutually beneficial. The former had not necessarily been considered the condition of the later. For example, Yan argued that in many parts of North America cities were founded before nearby lands were cultivated. And the "natural" order of economic development described by Smith would not work for China, where railways would have to be built to unleash the productive potential of the heartland. British economists who witnessed the huge industrial surge of the nineteenth century discarded Smith's faith in the priority of agricultural development. To some extent, the predicament of China was a ramification of British industrialization. Yan and his fellow Chinese intellectuals were accordingly forced to respond to the "industrial" situation and found the picture of economic development presented in *WN* alien, from a Chinese perspective (Simi 1998: 1.386).[19]

Perhaps Yan Fu was attracted by the polemical and determined tone of Rogers's introduction, the sort of passion that would be crucial to a country seeking to bring about rapid and deep economic reforms. But beyond Wakefield and Rogers – and any other commenter – Yan's association of social Darwinist *laissez-faire* with Smithian free trade may be attributed to a specifically Chinese intellectual influence.

The idea of allowing things to take their course, of giving up any hope of bending events to one's will, is central to the works of Laozi (a.k.a. Lao Tzu, *c.* 571–471 BC) and Zhuangzi (a.k.a. Chuang Tzu, *c.* 369–286 BC). Yan did state that a thorough understanding of Western sciences, including economics, would be essential for China's rehabilitation, but he also found room for these two architects of Daoism (Yan 1998d). It would be ideal, he believed, if one could use Western methods to excavate the truth buried in such ancient Chinese texts.

Besides the massive translation projects Yan undertook, he devoted considerable energy to the study of Laozi and Zhuangzi, labouring to show that they had espoused ideas that were identical to Darwin's and Smith's key insights – evolution, natural selection, and *laissez-faire*. In a comment on a famous sentence in Laozi's *Dao de jing* (The classic of the way and virtue) – "Heaven and earth know no benevolence, treating every being as grains or dogs; the saints know no benevolence, treating people as grains or dogs" (5.1) – Yan drew a parallel to a passage in *On the Origin of Species* (Yan 1998a: 6).[20] Likewise, a passage from Zhuangzi – "Therefore, the superior man who feels himself constrained to engage in the administration of the world will find it his best way to do nothing" (Zhuangzi 1971: 130) – prompted Yan to remark, "This is exactly what was taught in the early days of the French Revolution: *laissez-faire et laissez-passer* was a principle proposed by naturalists [*ziran dangren*] such as [François] Quesnay and [Vincent de] Gournay, dubbed the Kongzi [a.k.a. Confucius] of Europe" (Yan 1998b: 125).[21] Such cases of intellectual serendipity may have made Yan's Darwinian reading of Smith seem all the more reasonable.[22]

Yan was well aware that competition and trade had to be viewed differently in a post-Malthusian age. Eight years after the death of Adam Smith, Thomas Malthus (1766–1834) published *An Essay on the Principle of Population* (1798), in which he maintained that a growing population would eventually outstrip its ability to feed itself. He also described the relationship between a growing labour pool and wages. Having seen that China, with its vast population, suffered not only low per capita income but successive military defeats by foreign powers, Yan appeared to have embraced Malthus's grim economics. Certainly, he translated the doctrine of demographic crisis into a rationale for competition. Adding a long commentary in *Tianyan lun*, Yan maintained that the "Principle of Population" – the inspiration that permitted both Darwin and his rival Alfred Wallace to grasp the essential mechanism driving evolution – unlocked the truths of the struggle for existence:

> It is most dangerous for those who want to learn the sciences that they habitually indulge in superficial knowledge but neglect to penetrate into the reality of things . . . The extraordinary degree of the struggle and competition found in the modern world often completely escape the attention of ordinary people unless they possess insight and uncluttered minds. The English economist Thomas Malthus said that the rate of a species' increase is geometric . . . Darwin spoke similarly of a species' struggle for survival . . . That is why those who foresee our impending predicament loudly advocate social protections and cultural progress. They know only too well that those who shamelessly natter on about the differences between Chinese and barbarians pay no attention to facts.
>
> (Yan 1998c: 189–91)

It is a commonplace that Darwin and his friends Spencer and Huxley were profoundly influenced by the Malthusian picture of population increase impinging on scarce resources (Weikart 1998: 21; Young 1985: 23–55). In the last decade of the nineteenth century, when he was translating *WN*, Yan infused Smith's texts with a distinctly late Victorian flavour. In a description of the extreme poverty he had witnessed along the Guangdong coastline, he pointed to Adam Smith as the progenitor of the theory of inevitable competition:

> On its publication Malthus's essay astounded Europe – many considered it unprecedented. His theory was accepted without reservations until Darwin and Spencer published their works. Even then, Malthus's theory was merely modified. When we read Smith, it is clear that Malthus followed him along the path he pioneered.
>
> (Simi 1998: 1.103)[23]

In *WN* competition is a crucial concept, and Smith believed that markets had to be free from any form of intervention. But the mechanism of exchange must not, he felt, override principles of propriety and justice. The goal of trade is not to gain a profit at the expense of the other party. Accordingly, in Smith's usage competition means little more than a natural way of producing the best price for consumers; he called it "the natural price," meaning the lowest price possible in a given condition of supply and demand.

Yan Fu reconfigured Smith's discussion of price in line with Malthus and Darwin, whose ideas about competition, struggle, natural selection, and *laissez-faire* shaped late Victorian society. Taking Yan's commentaries as a whole, readers will see that he conscientiously created for Chinese readers a genealogy of *Homo economicus* running from the patriarch, Smith, down to Malthus and other Victorian theorists. His Smith stands as an early champion of enlightened self-interest. It is certainly worth noting that in the same year he completed *Yuan fu*, Yan published his third edition of *Tianyan lun*, with a new commentary distinctively reflecting the image of the self-interested Smith he had previously carved out. Here was a figure who flouted the belief held by ancient writers in both the East and the West that self-interest and righteousness could not be reconciled (Yan 1998c: 273). Because Yan presented *Yuan fu* closely in line with some key precepts of struggle, self-interest, competition and others of *Tianyan lun*, Smith's moral and economic concepts are, accordingly, very much recontextualized in the Chinese intellectual environment as modulated and oriented by Huxley–Darwinian teachings. One can therefore state with little exaggeration that it was a Victorian –rather than a Georgian – Adam Smith whom Yan Fu introduced into Qing China.

3. The legacy of Adam Smith's economic liberalism

Yan's impact on the Chinese study of Adam Smith has been controversial. The historian Benjamin Schwartz wrote that "according to all accounts" *Yuan fu* was widely read (Schwartz 1964: 128). However, Liang Qichao (1873–1929), a very influential thinker, publicly criticized Yan's writing style as archaic and opaque, and predicted that the translation would be of limited influence (Liang 1902: 115).

Zhu Shaowen aptly commented in a recent study that other factors may have limited the book's popularity, including the sociopolitical conditions that prevailed during the late Qing, the Republican period, and the Communist era (Zhu 2002: 209–18).

Schwartz's assessment needs to be weighed against some significant considerations: literacy rates were low, and Yan's writing was a challenge even for those who had attained basic literacy. It is equally important to appreciate, however, that *Yuan fu* was the first comprehensive Chinese-language presentation of Smithian ideas on wealth and trade. Those ideas soon became an important intellectual resource for reformers. The book's discussions of free trade, agriculture, manufacture, and banknotes became part of elite discourse in the last decades of imperial China. A survey of newspaper articles reveals that soon after the publication of *Yuan fu* questions about Smith's economic principles appeared on the civil service examinations (*Shen bao* 9 June 1902, 6 October 1903, 4 May 1904). Because of this official endorsement, literati dubbed Smith a "Western Confucian" (*xi ru*) or "English Confucian" (*Ying ru*), implying that his teachings had already come to be regarded as classics (*Shen bao* 16 October 1904, 5 June 1906, 20 July 1906, 23 June 1909). In short, though Smith's ideas – as presented by Yan – did not have a pervasive influence on Chinese society at the turn of the twentieth century, they did become part of the lexicon of literati society.

Many writers and intellectuals proposed economic reforms based on Smith's teachings. Three suggestions came up repeatedly: encouraging commerce, supporting *laissez-faire*, and regarding self-interest as an ethical principle. All are in perfect accordance with, if not taken from, Yan's interpretation of Smith (*Shen bao* 21 February 1905, 25 April 1905, 31 July 1905, 25 September 1905, 16 November 1905, 5 June 1906, 1 November 1906, 9 November 1907).[24] But some went further, calling for new institutions, such as banks, schools, and local governments. For instance, in 1908 Zhu Fushen (1841–1919), an illustrious scholar–official and medical expert, urged the Qing court to establish a parliament. He condemned proposals that would have assigned those charged with engineering financial reforms the job of collecting taxes. He cited *WN* to support his view that government had to allow merchants the liberty to manage their own affairs. It followed that a parliament was indispensable: it would ensure that levying taxes took place with the consent of the people (*Shen bao* 5 July 1908).[25] Zhu's reference to Yan Fu's translation shows that it had started to take root in China's intellectual circles and was giving rise to some innovative ideas.

Smithian idiom, imbued with Yan's Victorian, social Darwinist image of Smith, may be found in all manner of early twentieth-century writings. Indeed, many authors combined Smithian political economy with Huxleyan–Darwinian natural selection to analyse the nation's predicament. In commenting on Manchuria, which was occupied first by Russia and then by Japan, one journalist namechecked many evolutionary and libertarian thinkers:

> Spencer, the English Confucian, comments that there are two kinds of people – military and commercial . . . When civilization advances, humans start to compete with one another for resources. So peace becomes uncommon, war

the norm . . . Since Huxley's natural selection has evolved into Adam Smithian economic wars, we are confronted with the perils constantly haunting the Far East. This occurs everywhere, without exception. I think again and again of the tragic sacks of Poland and India as if they were happening right in front of me. Can this be traced to any other cause apart from economic competition?

(*Shen bao* 12 May 1910)

The peculiarly Darwinian Adam Smith that Yan Fu presented to China could readily be enrolled in nationalistic – and even bellicose – ventures. But if he was to inspire a popular movement, such as resistance to foreign encroachment, Smith would have to be dressed in simpler language, as Yan's classical prose was a challenge for many readers. Hence, presses commissioned writers to produce lives of Smith based on the introduction to *Yuan fu*. Some of these were simply duplicate reproductions (Yan 1903: 21), but more were written in the vernacular to increase accessibility for ordinary or less literate readers (Xue Zhen 1903: 8; Anonymous 1904: 51–61).

For Chinese readers, Smith was primarily the author of *WN*. Almost no one paid attention to *TMS*. Because he had read Rogers's preface, Yan knew of the book; he commented on Smith's interest in sympathy and acknowledged his unconventional approach to moral philosophy. When he informed his readers that Smith had published more than ten works, he suggested that *WN* was the best and *TMS* second best (Simi 1998: 1.2–4). This evaluation justified his translation of *WN* and excused his silence on Smith's ethics. As Germany and the United Kingdom resounded with debates over the "Adam Smith Problem" and the supposed contradictions between the moral systems presented in *TMS* and *WN*, no one in China quibbled with the moral implications Yan had inferred from *WN* (Montes 2004: 15–56; Tribe 2008: 514–25; Cohen 1989: 50–72; Dickey 1986: 579–609; Teichgraeber 1981: 106–23). The focus was on self-interest because of its congruence with the tenets of social Darwinism. This legacy lasted for almost one hundred years.

After the Russian Revolution and the First World War, a wave of uncertainty about Western civilization fuelled socialism, Marxism, and Nazism, all of which assaulted the liberal economics with which Smith was preeminently associated. Concern for distribution overrode concern for production. Poverty was politicized. Gradually, peasants and workers came to see the concentration of agriculture and industry in the hands of a few as a threat to their existence. Zhu Shaowen has perceptively remarked in a recent essay that after the 1920s the situation in China did not allow people to dwell much on Smithian ideas. Following the founding of the People's Republic of China in 1949, Smith was lambasted as the framer of a bourgeois liberal economics, an irrelevant scholar who had been overtaken by socialist thinkers (Zhu 2009: 214).

In post-1949 Taiwan, Smithian ideas have fared better. But they have been constrained by two factors. First, until very recently the island's scholarly community had not delved deeply into Smith's major work on ethics. The popular reception of Smith remained, by and large, within the parameters Yan Fu had set for his readers. It was not until the beginning of this century that a single essay about Smith's ethics appeared in Chinese. More significantly, the most noticeable impact Smith has had on Taiwan has been through Friedrich Hayek's libertarianism, which has informed an agenda of liberal economic and, to a much less degree, political reform. Because of his public criticism of any form of socialism, Hayek was welcomed by Chiang Kai-shek's regime, which proclaimed the Chinese Communist Party a bunch of gangsters, and by his liberal opponents. *The Road to Serfdom*, Hayek's ringing attack on Marx, was translated into Chinese by a notable liberal critic of Chiang, Yin Haiguang, and published in Taiwan in 1955. When Hayek visited the island a decade later, he was a guest of Chiang – a totalitarian ruler, according to Yin.[26] Since then, in Taiwan, Smith's thinking has been entangled with Hayekian libertarian doctrine.

Hayek's reading of Smith emphasized the ideas of "spontaneous order" and the "invisible hand"; the idea that extra-human forces shaped society harmonized with social Darwinism (Petsoulas 2001; Birner and Zijp 1994).[27] To a considerable extent, Taiwan's intellectuals (and policy-makers) have seen Hayek's libertarianism through Yan Fu. As early as 1954, Wang Shifu, a professor of economics at National Taiwan University, had commented that Hayek revived Smith's *laissez-faire* thinking with his contention that individual enterprises had the capacity to regulate their own affairs (Wang 2003).[28] Zhou Dewei, one of Hayek's students at the London School of Economics and the Chinese translator of *The Constitution of Liberty*, remarked that the book could vie with *WN* in importance and influence. To Zhou, Hayekian liberty stood opposed to any egalitarian policies. He further commented that individual liberty had to be measured in the differentiation of personal achievements – survival of the fittest was the key (Zhou 1974). Hayek himself might not have approved of the tenets (by his day rather unpopular) of social Darwinism. But Zhou's corollary was identical to that which Yan Fu underlined. As I have shown, Yan used Darwinism and economic liberalism to understand the perils into which China was thrown in the nineteenth century. The thesis proved handy for the Republic of China as it confronted a huge foe across the Taiwan Straits.

4. Conclusion: a turn to Smith's ethics in the Chinese-speaking world

While *WN* was written during a quite peaceful stage of Smith's life in Kirkcaldy, the Chinese translation was created in the midst of the turbulence of war, as an ancient sociopolitical order collapsed.[29] As I have argued, Yan Fu believed that the superiority of European civilization was, by and large, a long-term effect of natural selection, free trade, *laissez-faire* policies, and the prevalence of individualism and self-interest. And he believed that Smith's book explained the basic forces underlying these mechanisms, and that this vein of liberalism would be an antidote for China's prolonged ailments in the long run. As Yan translated *WN*, Victorian and social Darwinist tenets crept into Smith's classic. Accordingly, Yan and other Chinese intellectuals downplayed Smith's discussions of the interdependence of human beings, polite culture, sociability, communal identity, theism, self-command, and other ethical concerns. Essential as such issues were to his philosophy of liberalism, they had to be sacrificed to permit a marriage between Smith's strictly economic thought and the social Darwinist doctrine of competition and struggle for survival.

Only at the turn of the new millennium have attempts been made to set Smithian scholarship on the new ground of his moral philosophy in general and *TMS* in particular. The new translations of *TMS* are particularly welcome. At least twenty-six were published in mainland China between 2003 and 2012 (Zhang 2013: 98–103). Such a phenomenal proliferation certainly deserves detailed study. In Taiwan, too, Smith's ethics has enjoyed a renaissance, driven I believe by the phenomenal development of Smithian scholarship in the West over the last few decades and the financial crisis of the 1990s (Xie 2007; Simisi 2011; Shi 2010; Chen 2012). Wu Huilin, a noted liberal economist in Taiwan, went so far as to claim that *TMS* is "the most important classic work by Adam Smith, the respected founding father of economics." This is a contrariwise statement against Yan's evaluation of *TMS* and *WN*. During an age of "moral dismay and corruption," Wu continued, the work is an antidote and panacea (Wu 2007).

Taiwan, along with mainland China, is now part of an international *TMS* revival. But it remains unclear how the new effort in exegesis and translation study of *TMS* will contribute to the tradition of enriching and elaborating liberalism in the Chinese world that stems from Yan Fu. One major advantage of the modern Smithian renaissance is that it relocates Smith's discussion of sympathy and sentiments to the core of his conceptualizations of justice and socio-political relations (Haakonssen 1981; Fleischacker 1999; Frazer 2010). Nevertheless, Taiwanese critics and economists alike have consistently linked Smith's liberalism to the idea of *wuwei*, a Daoist notion that parallels the idea of *laissez-faire* (Wu and Xie 1997: 136). This speaks to Yan's strong legacy on the one hand, and an uncertain fate facing Smithian studies in the Chinese-speaking world in this century on the other.

Acknowledgements

In the preparation for this publication I received many helpful and constructive suggestions from Professor Harry Dickinson, Mr Samuel Gilbert, Professor Emma Rothschild and Professor Peter Zarrow. I am greatly indebted to them. My thanks also extend to the two anonymous reviewers for this *Review* for their comments and useful suggestions.

Notes

1   Among these studies, Schwartz's deserves particular attention. He argued that Yan consistently and intentionally translated "nation" and "country" into the Chinese word *guo*, which corresponds more closely to the English word "state." By so doing, Yan misrecognized Smith's liberal agenda, ducking some of its implications in favour of ideas contributing to the strength and power of the (Chinese) state. Schwartz's

argument is much ado about nothing, since in Yan's time no terminology was available in Chinese to distinguish effectively among "nation," "country," "political community," "public sphere," and "state." Indeed, *guo* did not, at that time, exclusively or necessarily denote the state. To Yan and his contemporaries, the word also meant "nation" or "country," concepts to which Smith commonly referred. Nevertheless, like Schwartz, I find a great tension between Yan's embrace of *laissez-faire* politics and his advocacy of activism, but that is an issue beyond the concerns of the present essay.

2   I do not mean to claim that revisionist views are prevailing and hegemonic. For instance, D. D. Raphael and A. L. Macfie supposed that the "Adam Smith Problem" was "a pseudo problem based on ignorance and misunderstanding" of Smith's work as a whole. James Otteson and some others have argued that the question remained legitimate and revealing for modern critics (Raphael and Macfie 1983: 20; Otteson 2002: 157ff).

3   Dismayed by defeat at the hands of the Japanese, many Qing officials urged the Guangxu emperor to emulate their foes' Meiji Reformation. But a *coup d'état* by the empress dowager, though it nipped reform in the bud, added momentum to the Chinese (or Han) people's national movement. Sun Yat-sen began organizing the Nationalist Party, called the Guomindang. Within thirteen years of the empress's coup, the Manchurian regime was overthrown.

4   「雖然，天運變矣，而有不變者行乎其中。不變惟何？是名天演。以天演為體，而其用有二：曰物競，曰天擇。此萬物莫不然，而於有生之類為尤著。物競者，物爭自存也。此一物以與物物爭，或存或亡，而其效則歸於天擇。天擇者，物競焉而獨存。則其存也，必有其所以存，必其所得於天之分，自致一己之能，與其所遭值之時與地及凡周身以外之物力，有其相謀相劑者焉。夫而後獨免於亡，而足以自立也。而自其效觀之，若是物特為天之所厚而擇焉以存也者，夫是之謂天擇。天擇者，擇於自然，雖擇而莫之擇，猶物競之無所爭，而實天下之至爭也。斯賓塞爾曰：『天擇者，存其最宜者也。』夫物既爭存矣，而天又從其爭之後而擇之，一爭一擇，而變化之事出矣。」Unless indicated, all translations of Chinese texts in this paper are mine.

5   This paragraph is not found in Huxley's original text.

6   「夫計學者，切而言之，則關於中國之貧富；遠而論之，則係乎黃種之盛衰。故不佞每見斯密之言於時事有關合者，或於己意有所根觸，輒為案論。丁寧反覆，不自覺其言之長，而辭之激也。嗟乎！物競天擇之用，未嘗一息亡於人間；大地之輪廓，百昌之登成，止於有數。智佼者既多取之而豐，愚懦者自少分焉而嗇。豐嗇之際，盛衰係之矣！且人莫病於言非也，而相以為是，行禍也，而相以為福，禍福是非之際，盛衰係之矣！且人莫病於言非也，而相以為是，行禍也，而相以為福，禍福是非之際，微乎其微，明者猶熒之，而況其下者乎！殆其及之而後知，履之而後艱，其所以失亡者，已無藝矣！此予智者罟擭陷阱之所以多也。欲違其災，舍窮理盡性之學，其道無由。而學矣，非循西人格物科學之律令，亦無益也。自秦愚黔首，二千歲於茲矣。以天之道，舟車大通，通則雖欲自安於愚，無進於明，其勢不可。數十百年以往，吾知黃人之子孫，將必有太息痛恨於其高曾祖父之所為者。嗚呼！不可懼哉！」

7   Guo Songtao first learned of Adam Smith and *WN* when he met Inoue Kaoru (1836–1915) in 1878. A reformist statesman, Inoue had come to London to learn about modern financial policy. When Guo learned that Kaoru was reading Adam Smith and John Stuart Mill, he commented regretfully that China had failed to make a careful study of foreign learning. It is very likely that Guo talked about Kaoru's anecdote and Smith with Yan in London.

8   The extent to which nineteenth-century Britain subscribed to the *laissez-faire* mentality is debatable. But it is certain that Darwinism gave ammunition to those who championed *laissez-faire* (Taylor 1972: 53ff; Paul 1980: 53ff).

9   「居今日萬國相通也，雖聖人復生，必不置商務為緩圖。倘以其為西人所尚而忽之，則中國生財之極富，不數十年而漸輸海外，中國日貧日弱，西人日富日強，斯固西人所大願也。」

10 「夫西洋之國往往重稅外來之貨，而減免本國貨稅，以暢其銷路。」

11 Zheng's remarks appeared in a work entitled "Xu 'Fu guo tan yuan' lun" (Preface to *An Inquiry into the Nature and Causes of the Wealth of Nations*). This was a preface to Smith's book, possibly to a translation, but I am unable to identify the translation. See Zheng 2008: 1.481.

12 「民之所以為仁若登，為不仁若崩，而治化之所以難進者，分義利為二者之害也。孟子曰：『亦有仁義而已矣，何必曰利?』董生曰：『正誼不謀利，明道不計功。』泰東西之舊教，莫不分義利為二塗，此其用意至美，然而於化於道皆淺，幾率天下禍仁義矣。自天演學興，而後非誼不利非道無功之理，洞若觀火。而計學之論，為之先聲焉。」

13 "The classification of Mencius is essentially the same as that of Adam Smith. But their theories are entirely different. The theory of Smith is based on general facts, so that he thinks fortune is the most important of all the four causes in getting authority. The theory of Mencius is an ideal, though also based on facts, so that he puts virtue as the most honorable thing. Smith's theory may be true when he refers to the western world, but Mencius' theory also is true when he speaks of China' (Chen 2002: 212). Chen's book evolved from his doctoral dissertation, submitted to Columbia University.

14 This preface was not included in Yan Fu's translation.

15 This 'do-nothing' policy proposed by Yan seems to contradict his belief in the let-alone principle. Perhaps, there is an intrinsic paradox in the adoption of "let-alone" principle while asking for an effective and responsible government to initiate political reforms at the same time.

16 Many of Nicholson's recapitulations of Smith's work are quite cogent and revealing: for instance, "Adam Smith treats of actual societies, and considers normal conducts of average individuals" (Nicholson 1884: 14).

17 For a general view of heterogeneous or nuanced tenets within economic liberalism, see modern anthologies in *The Methodology of Economics: Nineteenth-Century British Contributions*, 7 vols. (London: Routledge, 1997), particularly, vols. 5 and 6.

18 In a work published in 1909, which Yan Fu would have been unable to consult before sending his translation of *WN* to press, Nicholson commented that although Smith had done more than any other figure to promote the idea of free trade, "in simplifying these ideas for popular consumption the setting was cast aside, and with the setting many of the ideas also. Free trade was converted into a kind of religious dogma far removed from the principles of the original author" (Nicholson 1909: xii). Cogent as Nicholson's interpretation may be, he went too far when he described Smith as "intensively nationalist" (Nicholson 1909: x).

19 "Wakefield says that division of labour and trading affairs are two sides of one coin. Therefore, agriculture, manufacture, and commerce are interdependent. There is no set order among them. In North America there are some cities founded before the lands nearby are cultivated. In sum, division of labour and trade are out of nature and cannot be done by artificial policy. Wakefield is certainly right. I would suppose that the key factor that will contribute to the sea-change of the Chinese situation is the railways. Once the routes of the railways are decided, agriculture, manufacture and commerce will sprout around the stations. In less than ten years, the constellation of cities in China will be completely different" (translator's commentary in Simi 1998: 1.386).

20 Yan wrote a commentary on this sentence in his own copy: "[It is like] an opening remark of heavenly evolution" (Yan 1998a: 6).

21 *Ziran dangren* means literally the partisans of nature. I suppose Tan was politicizing the Physiocrats school.

22 Interestingly, according to modern historians, the European idea of "spontaneous order," an idea closely related to *laissez-faire*, was derived from Zhuangzi (Ross 1987: ix)

23 「其論初出，大為歐洲所驚嘆，以為得未曾有。所不喜其說者，亦無以窮之。至達爾文、史賓塞爾諸家興，其說始稍變，然而未盡廢也。今觀斯密氏此所云云，則已為馬羅達導其先路矣。」

24 A few references to Smith that appeared in *Shen bao*: "Adam Smith considered labour the foundation of the economy. He emphasized the division of labour and the motive of self-interest, and he advocated *laissez-faire* in industry. This lent the precepts of free trade and natural rights a certain momentum. David Ricardo, Thomas Malthus, and John Stuart Mill all followed the principle until 1849 . . . Britain abandoned the Corn Laws and implemented a free-trade policy" (9 November 1907); "Due to the school of Adam Smith, the English have adopted *laissez-faire*, letting the people do whatever they like; the government does nothing to protect them. Consequently, production increases day by day; goods are more equitably distributed; and national strength increases" (1 November 1906). See also *Shen bao* 21 February, 25 April, 31 July, 25 September and 16 November 1905, and 5 June 1906.

25 *Shen bao*, 5 July 1908. Zhang Yuanji, the publisher of *Yuan fu*, was a student of Zhu Fushen.

26 Hayek visited Taiwan three times: 1965, 1966, and 1975.

27 In my opinion, the most crucial intellectual source for Hayek's view of spontaneous order is neither Hume nor Smith, but Bernard Mandeville. As far as Smith is concerned, if, as argued, Yan Fu read Smith into social Darwinism, Hayek, on the other hand, read him into Mandeville's radical demoralization, unsociability, and egoism (Petsoulas 2001; Birner and Zijp 1994)

28 The article, "Shi jingji ziyou" (On economic freedom), appeared in *Lianhebao* on 6 September 1965. Wang was born in Yan Fu's hometown, Hokuan, in Fujian province. His given name, Shifu, literally means emulating Fu. Could the Fu in question be Yan Fu? Wang named his eldest son Tianyun, presumably in homage to Yan's translation. See Wang 2003.

29 On 2 September 1900, Yan wrote – in English – the following words in the margin of p. 337 of his copy of *The Wealth of Nations*: "I commenced my translation again yesterday after a 5 1/2 month hiatus. The Boxer rebellion has delayed my completion of my work!" This book is now in the Department of Special Collections, Huadong Shifan University, Shanghai.

Bibliography

Anonymous (1904) "Jixuedajia yingru simiyadang zhuan" (A biography of the great economist and English Confucian scholar Adam Smith) (計學大家英儒斯密亞丹傳), *Shangwu bao* (商務報) 6.

Berry, C. (2013) *The Idea of Commercial Society in the Scottish Enlightenment*, Edinburgh: Edinburgh University Press.

Berry, C., Paganelli, M. P. and Smith, C. (eds.) (2013) *The Oxford Handbook of Adam Smith*, Oxford: Oxford University Press.

Birner, J. and Zijp, R. (eds.) (1994) *Hayek, Co-Ordination and Evolution: His Legacy in Philosophy, Politics, Economics and the History of Ideas*, London: Routledge.

Brown, J. A. and Forster, W. R. (2013) "CSR and Stakeholder: A Tale of Adam Smith," *Journal of Business Ethics* 112.2: 301–12.

Brown, V. (1994) *Adam Smith's Discourse: Canonicity, Commerce and Conscience*, London: Routledge.

Brown, V. (2007) "Commemorating Thirty Years of the Glasgow Edition of the Works and Correspondence of Adam Smith: Interview with D. D. Raphael by Vivienne Brown," *Adam Smith Review* 3: 1–12.

Chen Huan-Chang (2002) *The Economic Principles of Confucius and his School*, Bristol: Thoemmes Press (reprinted from the 1911 edition).

Chen Jeng-Guo (2010) "The Wealth of the Chinese Nation: British Economic Imaginings in the Long Eighteenth Century (1688–1832)," *Horizons* 1.2: 195–214.

Chen Zhengxiung (2012) "Preface," in Takuo Dome, *Simi Yadang: Daode qingchaolun yu guofulun de shijie* (Adam Smith: the world of *The Theory of Moral Sentiments* and *The Wealth of Nations*), Taipei: Zhiliangchubanshe.

Cohen, E. S. (1989) "Justice and Political Economy in Commercial Society: Adam Smith's 'Science of a Legislator,'" *Journal of Politics* 51.1: 50–72.

de Marchi, N. B. (1976) "On the Early Danger of Being too Political an Economist: Thorold Rogers and the 1868 Election to the Drummond Professorship," *Oxford Economic Papers*, new series, 26.3: 364–80.

Dickey, L. (1986) "Historicizing the 'Adam Smith Problem': Conceptual, Historiographical, and Textual Issues," *Journal of Modern History* 58.3: 579–609.

Dwyer, J. (1998) *The Age of the Passions An Interpretation of Adam Smith and Scottish Enlightenment Culture*, East Linton: Tuckwell.

Edwin, J. and Rogers, T. (1880) "Preface," in A. Smith, *The Wealth of Nations*, Oxford: The Clarendon Press.

Emerson, R. L. (1973) "The Social Composition of Enlightened Scotland: The Select Society of Edinburgh, 1754–1764," *Studies in Voltaire* 114: 291–329.

Evensky, J. (2005) *Adam Smith's Moral Philosophy*, Cambridge: Cambridge University Press.

Fleischacker, S. (1999) *A Third Concept of Liberty: Judgment and Freedom in Kant and Adam Smith*, Princeton, NJ: Princeton University Press.

Forman-Barzilai, F. (2010) *Adam Smith and the Circles of Sympathy*, Cambridge: Cambridge University Press.

Frazer, M. (2010) *The Enlightenment of Sympathy: Justice and the Moral Sentiments in the Eighteenth Century and Today*, Oxford: Oxford University Press.

Griswold, C. (1999) *Adam Smith and the Virtues of Enlightenment*, Cambridge: Cambridge University Press.

Guo Songtao (1982) *Guosongtao reji* (Diaries of Guo Songtao), vol. 2, Hunan: Hunan People's Publisher.

Haakonssen, K. (1981) *The Science of a Legislator: The Natural Jurisprudence of David Hume and Adam Smith*, Cambridge: Cambridge University Press.

Haakonssen, K. (ed.) (2006) *The Cambridge Companion to Adam Smith*, Cambridge: Cambridge University Press.

Hanley, R. P. (2009) *Adam Smith and the Character of Virtue*, Cambridge: Cambridge University Press.

Hayek, F. A. (2009) *Dao Nu Yi Zhi Lu* (The road to serfdom), trans. Yin Haiguang, Taipei: National Taiwan University Press.

Hont, I. (2005) *The Jealousy of Trade: International Competition and the Nation-State in Historical Perspective*, Cambridge, MA: Harvard University Press.

Hont, I. and Ignatieff, M. (eds.) (1983) *Wealth and Virtue: The Shaping of Political Economy in the Scottish Enlightenment*, Cambridge: Cambridge University Press.

Howe, A. and Morgan, S. (eds.) (2006) *Rethinking Nineteenth-Century Liberalism*, Burlington, VT: Ashgate.

Huang, Max Ko-Wu (2008) *The Meaning of Freedom: Yan Fu and the Origins of Chinese Liberalism*, Hong Kong: Chinese University Press.

Huxley, T. (2001) *"Evolution and Ethics" and Other Essays*, Bristol: Thoemmes Press.

Keynes, J. M. (1926) *The End of Laissez-faire*, London: Hogarth Press.

Lai Cheng-Chung (ed.) (2000) *Adam Smith across Nations: Translations and Receptions of "The Wealth of Nations"*, Oxford: Oxford University Press.

Liang Qichao (1902) "Shaojiexinzhu" (Introduction to new publications), *Xinmincongbao* (新民叢報) 1.

McLean, I. (2004) *Adam Smith Radical and Egalitarian: An Interpretation for the Twenty-first Century*, Edinburgh: Edinburgh University Press.

Meek, R. (1976) *Social Sciences and Ignoble Savages*, Cambridge: Cambridge University Press.

Meek, R. (1977) *Smith, Marx, and After: Ten Essays in the Development of Economic Thought*, London: Chapman and Hall.

Montes, L. (2004) *Adam Smith in Context: A Critical Reassessment of Some Central Components of His Thought*, New York: Palgrave.

Mun, T. (1928) *England's Treasure by Forraign Trade*, Oxford: Basil Blackwell.

Nicholson, J. S. (1884) "Introduction," in A. Smith, *The Wealth of Nations*, London: T. Nelson and Sons.

Nicholson, J. S. (1909) *A Project of Empire*, London: Macmillan.

Otteson, J. (2002) *Adam Smith's Marketplace of Life*, Cambridge: Cambridge University Press.

Paul, E. F. (1980) "Laissez Faire in Nineteenth-Century Britain: Fact or Myth?," *Literature of Liberty: A Review of Contemporary Liberal Thought* 3.4: 7–38.

Petsoulas, C. (2001) *Hayek's Liberalism and Its Origins: His Idea of Spontaneous Order and the Scottish Enlightenment*, London: Routledge.

Phillipson, N. (1983) *Universities, Society and the Future*, Edinburgh: Edinburgh University Press.

Phillipson, N. (2010) *Adam Smith: An Enlightened Life*, New Haven, CT: Yale University Press.

Pitts, J. (2005) *A Turn to Empire: The Rise of Liberal Imperialism in Britain and France*, Princeton, NJ: Princeton University Press.

Pocock, J. G. A. (1974) *The Machiavellian Moment*, Princeton, NJ: Princeton University Press.

Raphael, D. D. (2007) *The Impartial Spectator: Adam Smith's Moral Philosophy*, Oxford: Oxford University Press.

Raphael, D. D. and Macfie, A. L. (1983) "Introduction," in A. Smith, *The Theory of Moral Sentiments*, Indianapolis, IN: Liberty Fund.

Reinert, S. (2009) *Translating Empire*, Cambridge, MA: Harvard University Press.

Robertson, J. (1983) *The Militia Issues and the Scottish Enlightenment*, East Lothian: John Donald.

Ross, I. (1987) *The Scottish Enlightenment and the Theory of Spontaneous Order*, Carbondale: Southern Illinois University Press.

Rothschild, E. (2001) *Economic Sentiments: Adam Smith, Condorcet, and the Enlightenment*, Cambridge, MA: Harvard University Press.

Schwartz, B. (1964) *In Search of Wealth and Power: Yan Fu and the West*, Cambridge, MA: Belknap Press of Harvard University.

Shapiro, M. J. (1993). *Reading "Adam Smith": Desire, History, and Value*, Newbury Park, CA: Sage.

Sher, R. (1985) *Church and University in the Scottish Enlightenment*, Edinburgh: Edinburgh University Press.

Shi Jiansheng (2010) *Weida jingjixuejia Yadang simi* (The great economist Adam Smith), Taipei: Tianxiayuanjian.

Simi Yadang (1998) *Yuan fu* (The wealth of nations), trans. Yan Fu, in Yan Fu, *Yanfu heji* (Collected works of Yan Fu), vols. 8 and 9, ed. Wang Qingzheng *et al.*, Taipei: Chen-fu Koo Cultural and Educational Foundation.

Simi Yadang (2000) *Guofulun* (The wealth of nations), Books I–III, ed. Xie Z. L. and Li H. X., Taipei: Xianjiu.

Simisi Yadang (2011) *Daode qingchaolun* (The theory of moral sentiments), trans. Kang Ludao, Xinzhu: Henjiaoshe.

Smith, A. (1880) *An Inquiry into the Nature and Causes of the Wealth of Nations*, 2 vols., ed. Edward Thorold Rogers, Oxford: Oxford University Press.

Smith, A. (1981) *An Inquiry into the Nature and Causes of the Wealth of Nations*, 2 vols., ed. R. Campbell and A. Skinner, Indianapolis, IN: Liberty Fund.

Stephen, L. (1991) *History of English Thought in the Eighteenth Century*, Bristol: Thoemmes.

Tan Sitong (1954) "Bao bei yuanzheng shu" (A letter to Bei Yuanzheng), in *Tan Sitong chuanji* (Collected works of Tan Sitong), Beijing: Sanlian.

Taylor, A. J. P. (1972) *Laissez-faire and State Intervention in Nineteenth-Century Britain*, London: Macmillan Press.

Teichgraeber, R., III (1981) "Rethinking Das Adam Smith Problem," *Journal of British Studies* 20.2: 106–23.

Trescott, Paul B. (2007) *Jingji Xue: The History of the Introduction of Western Economic Ideas into China, 1850–1950*, Hong Kong: Chinese University Press.

Tribe, K. (1998) *Governing Economy: The Reformation of German Economic Discourse, 1750–1840*, Cambridge: Cambridge University Press.

Tribe, K. (2002) "Adam Smith in English: From Playfair to Cannon," in K. Tribe and H. Mizuta (eds.), *A Critical Bibliography of Adam Smith*, London: Pickering and Chatto.

Tribe, K. (2008) "'Das Adam Smith Problem' and the Origin of Modern Smith Scholarship," *History of European Ideas* 34: 514–25.

Wang Shifu (2003) *Jingji wenxuan* (Selected essays of economics), NP: Wang Tianyun.

Weikart, R. (1998) "Laissez-Faire Social Darwinism and Individualist Competition in Darwin and Huxley," *European Legacy* 3.1: 17–30.

Wu Huilin (2007) Blurb for A. Smith, *The Theory of Moral Sentiments*, trans. Xie Zonglin, Taipei: Wu-Nan Book Inc.

Wu Huilin and Xie Zonglin (1997) *Ziyoujingji de benzhi* (The essence of liberal economy), Taipei: Zhonghua zhengxinsuo Inc.

Xie Zunglin (2007) "Translator's Preface," in A. Smith, *The Theory of Moral Sentiments*, Taipei: Wu-Nan Book Inc.

Xue Fucheng (1984) *Xue Fucheng xuanji*, ed. Ding Fenglin and Wanf Xinzhi, Shanghai: Shanghai renmin chubanshe.

Xue Zhen (1903) "Simi yadan zhuan" (Biography of Adam Smith), *Shaoxing baihua bao* (紹興白話報) 14.

Yan Fu (1903) "Shizhuan: Simiyadanzhuan" (History: biography of Adam Smith), *Lujiang bao* (鷺江報) 27.

Yan Fu (1998a) *Hou guan Yanshi pingdian Laozi* (Yan of Houguan commenting on Laozi), in *Yanfu heji* (Collected works of Yan Fu), vol. 17, ed. Wang Qingzheng *et al.*, Taipei: Chen-fu Koo Cultural and Educational Foundation.

Yan Fu (1998b) *Hou guan Yanshi pingdian Zhuangzi* (Yan of Houguan commenting on Zhuangzi), in *Yanfu heji* (*Collected works of Yan Fu*), vol. 18, Wang Qingzheng *et al.*, Taipei: Chen-fu Koo Cultural and Educational Foundation.

Yan Fu (1998c) *Tianyan lun* (Evolution and ethics), in *Yanfu heji* (Collected works of Yan Fu), vol. 7, ed. Wang Qingzheng *et al.*, Taipei: Chen-fu Koo Cultural and Educational Foundation.

Yan Fu (1998d) *Yanfu heji* (Collected works of Yan Fu), vols. 15–16, ed. Wang Qingzheng *et al.*, Taipei: Chen-fu Koo Cultural and Educational Foundation.

Yan Fu (1998e) *Yanfu wenji biannian* (Essays in chronology), in *Yanfu heji* (Collected works of Yan Fu), vol. 1, ed. Wang Qingzheng *et al.*, Taipei: Chen-fu Koo Cultural and Educational Foundation.

Young, R. (1985) *Darwin's Metaphor: Nature's Place in Victorian Culture*, Cambridge: Cambridge University Press.

Zhang Zhengping (2013) "Daode Qingcao lun zai zhongguo: lue lun fanyi luanxiang yu 'genfeng chuban'" (*The Theory of Moral Sentiments* in China: a brief discussion of the chaotic state of translation and blind emulation of publication), *China Book Review*, 8: 98–103.

Zheng Guanying (2008) *Sheng shi wei yan* (Words of warning in a great regime), Shanghai: Shanghai guji chubanshe.

Zhou Dewei (1974) "Haiyeke lun soudefenpei yu keshueizhidu" (Hayek on the distribution of income and taxation), *Economic Daily News*, 15 December.

Zhuang Zi (1971) *Chuang Tzu: Genius of the Absurd*, trans. James Legge, ed. Clae Waltham, New York: Ace Books.

Zhu Shaowen (2002) "Adam Smith in China," in K. Tribe and H. Mizuta (eds.), *A Critical Bibliography of Adam Smith*, London: Pickering & Chatto.

Anonymous Shen bao *(*申報*) articles*

"Xuluyilingguanfongti" (Suggested questions of the imperial exams proposed by county government) (續錄邑令觀風題), 9 June 1902.

"Enke zhijiang xiangshierchang ti" (The questions of the second round in the secondary imperial exam) (恩科浙江鄉試二場題), 6 October 1903.

"Songjiang sueishi liuzhi" (Six notes on the second-level imperial exam in Songjiang province) (松江歲試六誌), 4 May 1904.

"Shuobanghoan zhuanlu nanyangguanbao" (Of exchange rate of monetary value: a record from Nanyang official gazette) (說磅後案轉錄南洋官報), 16 October 1904.

"Lun jinmichuko zhi wuyiyuminsheng" (On the ineffectiveness of banning rice exports on the people's welfare) (論禁米出口之無益於民生), 21 February 1905.

"Lun Zhongkongzhuyi" (On manufactures and industrialism) (論重工主義), 25 April 1905.

"Lun tongyuan" (On regulating copper coinage) (論銅元口宜限制), 31 July 1905.

"Zhidu chixuewuchu touyigetangxuesheng kongfeizifeizhangcheng zha" (Letter of the educational bureau of the province of Zhili on the regulation about public and private educational funds" (直督飭學務處妥議各堂學生公費自費章程札), 25 September 1905.

"Lun mijin" (On the banning of rice exports) (論米禁), 16 November 1905.

"Yuqing shutong migu zhe" (An appeal for the rice trade) (奏請疏通米穀摺), 5 June 1906.

"Xu liurixuesheng Yaomingder shang zhangdianzhuan tiaochen qingzhuzhongzixieyix-ingshiye" (Further thoughts on the request to pay attention to machines' role in industry written by a Chinese student in Japan) (續留日學生姚明德上張殿撰條陳請注重機械以興實業), 20 July 1906.

"Lun shangye yu gezhongxueke zhi guangxi" (Of the relation between commerce and knowledge) (論商業與各種學科之關係), 1 November 1906.

"Weiguoshangzheng zhi yange" (History of commercial policy in other countries) (外國商政之沿革), 9 November 1907.

"Jiangdu qinggei yanfu jinshichushen yuanzou" (The original appeal for conferring on Yan Fu the title of Jinshi) (江督請給嚴復進士出身原奏), 3 May 1908.

"Zhufushen zouqing kaisheyihuei zhe" (An appeal for opening a local parliament by Zhu Fushen) (朱福詵奏請開設議會摺), 5 July 1908.

"Jinggao sushengziyiju yiyuan kaijudiyicihueiyi dangyibenshengshiyie wei zongzhi" (A public appeal to the first parliament of Suzhou province that the main issue of the meeting has to be the industry of the province) (敬告蘇省諮議局議員開局第一次會議當以振興本省實業為宗旨), 23 June 1909.

"Lun dongsansheng jiyizhuyi zhi dianxuan" (On the most critical issues about the three eastern provinces) (論東三省亟宜注意之點選), 12 May 1910.

'Regarding the Pain of Others'

A Smith–Sontag dialogue on war photography and the production of sympathy

Eun Kyung Min

Taejon, 1950

> War is not a spectacle.
>
> (Susan Sontag, *Regarding the Pain of Others*)

In the morning of November 21, 2007, I opened up my home-delivered copy of the Seoul edition of the *International Herald Tribune* and saw for the first time a photograph that has not ceased to haunt me. The photograph was part of an article entitled 'Confronting Past, South Korea Digs up Killing Fields' by the journalist Choe Sang-Hun. Choe's article discusses the work of the South Korea Truth and Reconciliation Commission which was created in 2005 during the presidency of the late president Roh Moo-hyun in order to bring redress to the victims of war

Figure 1 Taejon, 1950

atrocities and other political crimes. Noting the commission's success in confirming stories of mass execution during the Korean War, Choe instances this photograph of prisoners before their execution by South Korean troops in Taejon in 1950.[1] When I first saw the photograph, I was deeply struck by the unreadable expression on the young boy's face – the boy who is lying on the ground, his feet held up by a blurred and faceless figure on the left, his arms locked around other young boys similarly immobilized before what is evidently the spectacle of their immediate future, a terribly shallow grave filled with dead civilian bodies. Why is he turning to look back, at whom, and why does his expression look so much like a smile?

At the time that I saw this photograph, I was working on a paper on Adam Smith that I was scheduled to deliver in about a week's time at a colloquium hosted by the department of philosophy at my university. I found myself continually straying from Smith, however, and obsessing over the photograph, until it struck me that the reasons I found it so troubling might connect in important ways with Smith's theory of sympathy. After all, Smith's theory is all about looking at others and the moral meaning of spectatorship. This thought, in turn, led me to query what relevance Smith's model of spectatorship has to our contemporary world, saturated as it is with visual representations that did not exist in Smith's time: photographic, cinematic, digital, infinitely reproducible, distributed in real time via the internet. Our vision of the world, today thoroughly mediated by television, digital cameras, cell phones, YouTube, and surveillance technology that evolves every minute, is not the same as Smith's. What would Smith have to say about my experience of looking at a photograph of a boy who was killed more than sixty years ago in a war that I never directly experienced? And how might he redefine the moral economy of seeing in today's media ecology of mass spectatorship? As I attempted to think through these questions, I found myself turning to Susan Sontag, whose passionate critique of the consumption of photographic images has repeatedly alerted us to the latent horror of becoming a modern spectator of war images.

In this essay, I build on the reflections that I hastily gathered for that colloquium many years ago, and bring Smith into dialogue with Sontag in order to throw into sharp relief the moral and theoretical perplexities that attend questions about looking at images, especially images of terror, in our digital age.[2] My focus, like Sontag's, will be on what Lilie Chouliaraki (2013) calls 'photojournalism of the battlefield'. For it is arguably in this 'battlefield' that some of the toughest questions about the connections between vision and violence, as well as aesthetics and ethics, arise. Bringing Smith into conversation with Sontag, I hope to show, is one way to test the ways in which Smith's ideas of sympathy and spectatorship may be related to, and updated for, our technological, global age. Recent efforts to place Smith's thought in international contexts and to think about ways in which he can serve as a resource for 'cultivating a twenty-first-century global ethics' have not sufficiently explored this dimension of his ethical thought (Forman-Barzilai 2010: 5). This essay is an attempt to follow up on Forman-Barzilai's passing remark in her recent book *Adam Smith and the Circles of Sympathy*, that

Smith would have had much to say were he reflecting today on the impact of the media on our moral sentiments, with its vivid narratives about ethnic cleansing, graphic depictions of starving infants, of young girls being genitally mutilated, of grinning soldiers torturing naked prisoners, and so on.

(Forman-Barzilai 2010: 145)

Making explicit what Smith might have had to say, of course, is necessarily a tentative and exploratory project. In this sense, this essay is an invitation to a conversation that I hope will be continued with others in the future.

The moral economy of spectatorship

> The very qualities that made the ancient Greek philosophers consider sight the most excellent, the noblest of the senses are now associated with a deficit.
>
> (Susan Sontag, *Regarding the Pain of Others*)

In order to ask with precision the question of how Smith's theory of the sympathetic spectator speaks to the photographic dilemma, it is helpful first to examine Sontag's formulation of the problem. In her 1977 book *On Photography*, Sontag (1977: 5, 11) declares that the evidentiary value of the photograph ('A photograph passes for incontrovertible proof that a given thing happened') is profoundly challenged by the fact that 'Photographing is essentially an act of non-intervention'. She writes:

> Part of the horror of such memorable coups of contemporary photojournalism as the pictures of a Vietnamese bonze reaching for the gasoline can, of a Bengali guerrilla in the act of bayoneting a trussed-up collaborator, comes from the awareness of how plausible it has become, in situations where the photographer has the choice between a photograph and a life, to choose the photograph. The person who intervenes cannot record; the person who is recording cannot intervene.
>
> (Sontag 1977: 11–12)

The photograph, then, is the record of a dilemma the photographer resolved by making one type of choice. What about the viewer or spectator of the photograph? When we gaze at photographs of 'the oppressed, the exploited, the starving, and the massacred', what happens to us (1977: 19)? Are we so different from the photographer who had the choice but did not intervene?

In *On Photography*, Sontag is sceptical. The spatial and temporal distance that separates us from the event recorded in the photograph does not grant us immunity. The shock, outrage, and grief the photograph may cause do not mean it will automatically 'strengthen conscience and the ability to be compassionate'. As she puts it, 'The knowledge gained through still photographs will always be some kind of sentimentalism, whether cynical or humanist'; 'while it can goad conscience, it can, finally, never be ethical or political knowledge' (1977: 23–24).

In the place of knowledge or action, what the photograph advocates is an aggressive passivity. For, in our age when the photographic image has become ubiquitous and habitual, when 'Photography has become one of the principal devices for experiencing something', we live in 'a chronic voyeuristic relation to the world which levels the meaning of all events' (1977: 10–11). In this way, Sontag indicts the modern culture of spectatorship that, in her view, corrupts individual conscience by creating aesthetic distance and sentimental pleasure out of the spectacle of other people's pain and suffering.

In her 2003 *Regarding the Pain of Others*, Sontag appears to rehearse some of these arguments again, as when she says, 'Being a spectator of calamities taking place in another country is a quintessential modern experience, the cumulative offering by more than a century and a half's worth of those professional, specialized tourists known as journalists', or 'The hunt for more dramatic images drives the photographic enterprise, and is part of the normality of a culture in which shock has become a leading stimulus of consumption and source of value' (2003: 18, 23). Noting that our 'knowledge of war' today is unavoidably 'camera-mediated' and that 'War was and still is the most irresistible – and picturesque – news' (2003: 24, 49), Sontag argues that as consumers of these 'camera-mediated' images, we become 'voyeurs, whether or not we mean to be', visually allured by the images, and politically apathetic to them (2003: 42). Sontag thus continues to accuse the modern culture of spectatorship of corrupting individual conscience by creating aesthetic distance and pleasure out of the spectacle of other people's pain. However, *Regarding the Pain of Others* is a more nuanced and hopeful book than *On Photography*. Writing almost thirty years after her manifesto against photography, Sontag (2003: 105) admits that she has become unsure about her former argument that we must inevitably grow 'callous' toward images merely because we live 'in a world saturated, no hyper-saturated with images'. Do photographs necessarily 'shrivel sympathy' (2003: 105)? Does the fact that sympathy feels like a passive, simple, even inappropriate response to the spectacle of other people's pain necessarily mean that sympathy produces a 'mystification of our real relations to power' and tricks us into a false sense of our 'innocence' (2003: 102)?

In her 2003 book, Sontag (2003: 115) says she is not so sure. War photography has its own 'vital function' of saying 'Don't forget', of reminding us that 'Remembering is an ethical act, has ethical value in and of itself'. She writes (2003: 117):

> It is not a defect that we are not seared, that we do not suffer enough, when we see these images. Neither is the photograph supposed to repair our ignorance about the history and causes of the suffering it picks out and frames. Such images cannot be more than an invitation to pay attention, to reflect, to learn, to examine the rationalizations for mass suffering offered by established powers.

It is up to us to accept that invitation and to do the psychological, mental, and historical work that it entails.

As Judith Butler points out in her essay on Sontag, the question that the latter continued to ask in both of her books on photography was 'whether photographs still had the power – or ever did have the power – to communicate the suffering of others in such a way that viewers might be prompted to alter their political assessment of the current war'. One problem in Sontag's work, according to Butler, is her underlying assumption that, as images, 'photographs can move us momentarily but that they do not have the power to build an interpretation' because they 'lack narrative coherence' (Butler 2005: 823). Photographs can memorialize the dead and they can 'haunt' us, but they cannot change our understanding or views, and they cannot spur us to action (Sontag 1977: 70; 2003: 115). For Butler, the main problem with this argument is that it assumes that seeing and understanding are essentially different kinds of activity, and that the visual image lacks the cognitive content that can be communicated only by language, especially narrative. In *On Photography*, this philosophical bias emerges very clearly in such statements as: 'Photography implies that we know about the world if we accept it as the camera records it. But this is the opposite of understanding, which starts from *not* accepting the world as it looks'; 'In contrast to the amorous relation, which is based on how something looks, understanding is based on how it functions. And functioning takes place in time, and must be explained in time. Only that which narrates can make us understand' (1977: 23). Sontag's suspicion of spectatorship, which she claims ends up affirming, accepting, and even desiring its visual objects, continues in her later book, where she argues that looking at something as a 'spectacle' implies that 'it cannot be stopped' (2003: 42). 'Narratives can make us understand. Photographs do something else: they haunt us' (2003: 89). In this way, we could say that Sontag participates in what Martin Jay (1993) has called the 'denigration of vision' in twentieth-century thought.[3]

Jacques Rancière has shown in his recent book *The Emancipated Spectator* that this divorce between looking and understanding is in fact rooted in an ancient Western critique of theatrical spectacle. According to this critique, 'being a spectator is bad for two reasons'. First, 'viewing is the opposite of knowing'; and second, viewing is 'the opposite of acting'. The 'immobile', 'passive' spectator in her seat watches a performance while being 'held in a state of ignorance about the process of production of this appearance and about the reality it conceals'. Thus, 'To be a spectator is to be separated from both the capacity to know and the power to act' (Rancière 2009: 2). Rancière's summary of this line of thought helps us see that Sontag's critique of photography is in alignment with this anti-theatrical tradition that construes theatre as 'the place where ignoramuses are invited to see people suffering'. Theatre subjects us to 'a machinery of ignorance, the optical machinery that prepares the gaze for illusion and passivity' (Rancière 2009: 3).

Critiquing this anti-theatrical line of thought, Rancière (2009: 12) asks us to consider these questions:

> What makes it possible to pronounce the spectator seated in her place inactive, if not the previously posited radical opposition between the active and the passive? Why identify gaze and passivity, unless on the presupposition that to

view means to take pleasure in images and appearances while ignoring the truth behind the image and the reality outside the theatre? Why assimilate listening to passivity, unless through the prejudice that speech is the opposite of action?

In contrast to these 'allegories of inequality', Rancière (2009: 12) proposes a new approach to the spectator that is fundamentally Smithian, although he does not make this connection. When Rancière argues that spectators are never merely passive, but are 'both distant spectators and active interpreters of the spectacle offered to them', I believe he is making a basic Smithian point. So, too, when he declares that the 'spectator also acts'; she 'observes, selects, compares, interprets' (2009: 13). The language of the following passage is likewise deeply Smithian:

> It is in this power of associating and dissociating that the emancipation of the spectator consists – that is to say, the emancipation of each of us as spectator. Being a spectator is not some passive condition that we should transform into activity. It is our normal condition. We also learn and teach, act and know, as spectators who all the time link what we see to what we have seen and said, done and dreamed. There is no more a privileged form than there is a privileged starting point . . . Every spectator is already an actor in her story; every actor, every man of action, is the spectator of the same story.
>
> (Rancière 2009: 17)

Rancière's point that spectatorship is 'our normal condition' rather than an abnormal one is also one that Smith makes in *The Theory of Moral Sentiments*. In that book, Smith defines spectatorship as an act of imaginative sympathy as well as self-reflective conscience that is admittedly never perfect but also never simply passive. By choosing a visual and theatrical language to analyse modern moral psychology, Smith was pointedly working against the anti-theatrical tradition. What, then, did Smith mean precisely by spectatorship? Can Smith's theory of the sympathetic spectator who lives an active ethical life in a social theatre in any way change the terms of the photographic dilemma as outlined by Sontag?

Cultures of visuality

New demands are made on reality in the era of cameras.
(Susan Sontag, *Regarding the Pain of Others*)

In *Adam Smith and the Circles of Sympathy: Cosmopolitanism and Moral Theory*, Forman-Barzilai (2010) argues that Smith's theory of spectatorship maps out a particular set of spatial parameters for the workings of sympathy. In other words, his theory of the sympathetic spectator is conditioned by his own historical and cultural moment. Describing Smith's world, Forman-Barzilai (2010: 149) draws attention to the slowness, the difficulty of travel and communication, the dearth of information about the condition of distant peoples, the comparative insularity of state and corporate activity, the impotence of international law, the absence of international and transnational dialogue, as well as international and non-governmental agencies that might assist distant spectators in their desire to act.

It is thus quite natural that Smith was 'primarily concerned with describing the effects of spectatorship on moral sentiment in relatively close quarters' (2010: 180). In other words, 'Spectatorship was primarily a local, visual affair for Smith' and his theory of sympathy depends on 'a basic physical proximity, a face-to-face transaction, between spectator and agent' (2010: 180, 143). Forman-Barzilai thus places *The Theory of Moral Sentiments* in historical perspective, reading it as both an analysis and description of a rapidly modernizing but still relatively parochial world. She balances this argument by pointing out that Smith envisioned his sympathetic observer as being physically near but also keeping sufficient affective distance in order to become successfully impartial.[4] None the less, her historical reading of Smith emphasizes the spatial limitations of Smithian sympathy.

If Forman-Barzilai is right, this might suggest that Smith's theory of sympathetic spectatorship will not have much to offer in response to Sontag's reflections on war photography. Looking at war photographs, Sontag (2003: 117) points out, is about 'watching suffering at a distance'. The 'camera's record . . . of a real person's unspeakably awful mutilation' may be taken 'from very near' and it may be brought very physically near us as a photograph, but the dead and dying people represented in the photograph more often than not lie at a great spatial as well as temporal distance from us and are in no position to engage with us in a face-to-face encounter (2003: 42). As Forman-Barzilai herself notes (2010: 137), however, the 'spatial texture' of Smith's thought does not mean that he believed sympathy worked only through vision. She writes, 'Although Smith's primary description of sympathetic activity rested on the faculty of sight, he acknowledged that a spectator might be moved by literature (he frequently drew on tragedy for his examples), or a vivid narrative of distant joy or suffering' (2010: 144). Smith's examples of reading sympathetically stories about 'heroes of tragedy or romance' (*TMS* I.i.1.4) or seafarers in a 'journal of a siege, or of a sea voyage' (*TMS* I.ii.1.4) show us that sympathetic spectatorship should not be interpreted always in a literal sense (Forman-Barzilai 2010: 144–145).

We are thus faced with two issues. One is that Smith's theory of spectatorship makes sense within a specific culture of visuality that is historically and cultural conditioned. Another is that Smith uses spectatorship as a 'primary and emblematic metaphor', as Vivienne Brown (1994: 24) puts it. In this sense, Smith's spectator is clearly distinguishable from Sontag's. As Brown explains, the key figure in Smith's *Theory of Moral Sentiments* is the impartial spectator who is 'an imagined spectator'; 'the impartial spectator stands as a metaphor for the mechanism of moral judgment, and that judgment is thus represented figuratively as observation' (1994: 24, 25). Smith's moral spectator is not simply someone who looks out at the world with her eyes, but one who is also always aware that she is the object of the gaze of others. Thus, Smith's spectatorship is moral, rather than literal. It is about always carefully looking at other people but also 'placing ourselves before a looking-glass' and endeavouring 'as much as possible, to view ourselves at the distance and with the eyes of other people' (*TMS* III.i.4). Unlike Sontag's theory of the spectator that is concerned with the seemingly insuperable gap between the seeing self and the seen other, Smith's theory is about the ways in which moral judgement necessarily requires us to perform simultaneously the 'character' of both the seeing 'spectator' (or the seeing self) and 'agent' (or the seen self) (*TMS* III.i.6).

> When I endeavor to examine my own conduct, when I endeavor to pass sentence upon it, and either to approve or condemn it, it is evident that, in all such cases, I divide myself, as it were, into two persons; and that I, the examiner and judge, represent a different character from that other I, the person whose conduct is examined into and judged of.
>
> (*TMS* III.i.6)

In this theatre of the mind, spectatorship is as much about self-observation as it is about examining others, and it is above all about developing the right perspective from which to view ourselves. That perspective, according to Smith, is that of someone who is detached and distanced from us: 'We can never survey our own sentiments and motives, we can never form any judgment concerning them; unless we remove ourselves, as it were from our natural station, and endeavor to view them as at a certain distance from us' (*TMS* III.i.2). What Smith means by distance here is not so much actual physical distance but moral distance. As Brown points out, the ultimate impartial spectator who can judge our actions is 'that divine Being'; from a divine perspective, we imagine, we are merely 'an atom, a particle, of an immense and infinite system, which must and ought to be disposed of, according to the conveniency of the whole' (*TMS* VII.ii.1.20; cited in Brown 1994: 60). Looking imaginatively at ourselves with the eyes of 'that divine Being' can put our moral lives in proper perspective.

Returning to the earlier point that Smith's philosophy should be understood in the context of a particular visual culture, we may ask why Smith prioritized visual experience in this way in his moral philosophy, and whether he was thinking of particular kinds of visual images or particular techniques of vision. Peter de Bolla's *The Education of the Eye*, which analyses a very particular 'culture of visuality' that itself became 'fully visible' in the mid-eighteenth century, helps us place Smith's emphasis on spectatorship and the visual dynamics of sympathy in historical context (de Bolla 2003: 5, 6). According to de Bolla (2003: 69, 76):

> Mid-eighteenth-century Britain was obsessed with visibility, spectacle, display. It constructed a culture of visuality in which seeing and being seen were crucial indices to one's social standing, to one's self-definition . . . This

was a culture in which one of the most notable publications was entitled the *Spectator* and in which all manner of public events, from hanging to masked balls, were deeply implicated within the conceptual folds of the spectacle.[5]

Vision began to take on a specific meaning in this mid-century culture of visuality as 'different practices of looking' at objects such as paintings, sculptures, landscapes, and architecture began to determine how individuals 'began to understand themselves as lookers, viewers, or spectators and, therefore, how they began to shape (and be shaped) and give coherence to themselves as subjects' (de Bolla 2003: 7). As eighteenth-century visual culture constructed the self as, first and foremost, a visible and visualizing (actively seeing) self, the activity of looking took on the meaning of a '*technique*, or technology, producing subjectivity' (2003: 8; original emphasis). In this sense, we could say that Smith still operates within what Jonathan Crary (1990) calls 'the classical regime of visuality' or what Martin Jay (1993) calls the 'ocularcentric bias', where vision is connected to objectivity, clarity, and subjectivity. Indeed, insofar as Smith's spectatorial ethics dramatically privileges the sense of sight over all others, he may be said to exemplify 'the Enlightenment trust in sight' (Jay 1993: 106).[6]

That said, we should note that the visual technique that Smith was interested in promoting crucially undermined the stability of the division between the seeing eye and the seen object. Smith's visual mode, as de Bolla puts it, is 'catoptric' (de Bolla 2003: 74). Smith's 'metaphorics of the eye' redirects 'attention from the anatomical ground of opticality, the eye, toward the social and cultural manifestation of a viewer, spectator, looker' (2003: 74, 75). Smith describes a public world of mutual gazes where seeing means, by the same token, being seen. As David Marshall (1984: 597) puts it, 'by compelling us to become spectators to our spectators and thereby spectators to ourselves', Smith places us in a 'kaleidoscope of reflections and representations'. De Bolla (2003: 78) glosses the subjectivity implied by this catoptric and kaleidoscopic vision as follows:

> In this sense subjectivity is precisely not positioned in the eye of the beholder but, rather, in the exchanges that occur in the phantasmic projection of what it might feel like to be constituted as a subject by looking on the onlookers of our selves.

What Smith might have to say to Sontag, I propose, is that her model of spectatorship is both too literal and too simple; that she renders her spectatorial subject too passive before the objects of vision; that her model of vision is one-sided and one-way rather than dialogic and socialized; and that she does not theorize the self-awareness that inevitably accompanies all our acts of looking. In Sontag, the seer and the seen cannot meet; for Smith, however, the seer is always also the seen. In turn, Sontag's retort, I suspect, might go something like this. Smith can have no real notion of modern photographic representation, as it was invented in the nineteenth century. Smith's spectator who engages in feats of catoptric, kaleidoscopic, and metaphoric visualization belongs to a world of camera obscuras, perspective glasses, landscape mirrors, and telescopes. These visual instruments, which were redefining the spatial parameters as well as the perspectival aspects of vision, still operate within what Crary (1990: 16) calls the confines of 'geometrical optics'. With modern photography, however, an entirely new set of aesthetic and moral dilemmas having to do with the temporality of vision was born.

Let us take the example of a photograph taken of a person who is now dead. In Smith's time, the only way to 'see' the dead was to look at paintings of them. What changes with photography? Suddenly we can *literally* see the dead. As Kendall Walton (1984: 251–252; original emphasis) explains, the invention of the camera 'gave us a new way of seeing':

> With the assistance of the camera, we can see not only around corners and what is distant or small; we can also see into the past . . . [Indeed,] we *see*, quite literally, our dead relatives themselves when we look at photographs of them.

With improvements in camera technology, the ability to see into the past has become more piercing. We can seize a fleeting moment in time and stop it for ever – a moment that we could not have isolated perceptually in real time. For this reason, Walter Benjamin believed that 'it is another nature which speaks to the camera rather than to the eye': the camera sees what the eye could never consciously see.

> Whereas it is a commonplace that, for example, we have some idea what is involved in the act of walking (if only in general terms), we have no idea at all what happens during the fraction of a second when a person actually takes a step. Photography, with its devices of slow motion and enlargement, reveals the secret. It is through photography that we first discover the existence of this optical unconscious, just as we discover the instinctual unconscious through psychoanalysis.
>
> (Benjamin 1999: 510–511)

Sontag (2003: 24) was also struck by the ability of photography to perform what she refers to as 'unprecedented feats of close observation', in particular its ability to stop and 'seize death in the making':

> Because an image produced with a camera is, literally, a trace of something brought before the lens, photographs were superior to any painting as a memento of the vanished past and the dear departed. To seize death in the making was another matter: the camera's reach remained limited as long as it had to be lugged about, set down, steadied. But once the camera was emancipated from the tripod, truly portable, and equipped with a range finder and a variety of lenses that permitted unprecedented feats of close observation from a distant vantage point, picture-taking acquired an immediacy

and authority greater than any verbal account in conveying the horror of mass-produced death.

According to Sontag (2003: 59), something changes drastically with this new photographic technology that can 'catch a death actually happening and embalm it for all time'. Indeed, our relationship to the dead forever changes with this new visual technology. To investigate this line of argument, let us briefly turn to Roland Barthes's discussion of the relationship photography bears to the dead.

Sympathy for the dead

> Photography has kept company with death.
>
> (Susan Sontag, *Regarding the Pain of Others*)

In *Camera Lucida*, Roland Barthes (1981: 9) identifies the uncanny 'return of the dead' as 'that rather terrible thing which is there in every photograph'. This 'terrible thing' is brought home to us most painfully in photographs where we cannot fail to be struck, stung, cut, and wounded by the realization that the photographic subject is moments away from death. In his well-known discussion of Alexander Gardner's 1865 portrait of Lewis Payne in his cell, where he was waiting to be hanged for his attempted assassination of Secretary of State W. H. Seward, Barthes uses the term *punctum* to distinguish what is most poignant about Gardner's photograph.

> The photograph is handsome, as is the boy: that is the *studium*. But the *punctum* is: *he is going to die*. I read at the same time: *This will be* and *this has been*; I observe with horror an anterior future of which death is the stake. By giving me the absolute past of the pose (aorist), the photograph tells me death in the future. What pricks me is the discovery of this equivalence.
>
> (Barthes 1981: 96; original emphasis)

As Nicholas Mirzoeff (1999: 74) comments, Barthes's *studium* refers to 'what can be named or described in a photograph', whereas the *punctum* denotes a subjective and affective response of the viewer of a photograph. Thus, the *studium* of the photograph invokes 'general knowledge that is available to every viewer'; it can be verbalized, discussed, and disseminated. In contrast, the *punctum* is a wound, 'something very powerful and unbidden', evoked in the viewer in response to the photographic object; as an affective response, it resists verbalization and explanation. Barthes (1981: 26) describes it as 'this wound, this prick, this mark', 'this element which rises from the scene, shoots out of it like an arrow, and pierces me'. In his gloss on Barthes, Mirzoeff (1999: 74) comments, 'Through the unknowable *punctum*, photography becomes sublime. The most important and yet most unknowable singularity of photography is this power to open a *punctum* to the realm of the dead.'[7]

What distinguishes photographic representation from other visual forms of representation, according to Barthes (1981: 76; original emphasis), is that the 'photographic referent' is not '*optionally* real' but '*necessarily* real'. The photographed person, we know, existed. However, the photographed person is not necessarily still existing. He may be a no-longer extant subject. None the less, through photography the dead person appears before us as if he were still living. For this reason, looking at photographs taken of people who are no longer alive is an uncanny psychological experience. In the case of photographs of subjects like Lewis Payne or the boy in the photograph of 'Taejon, 1950', we are dealing with a special class of photographed subjects who are going to die in the near future. According to Barthes, this class of photographs makes us experience a 'vertigo' of time: the present time of the photographed subject; the anterior future of the photographed subject ('death in the future'), and the 'absolute past' of his death. In addition, there is 'my time' (the present time of the spectator) as well as the time of the photographer to consider. These 'tenses dizzy my consciousness', says Barthes (1981: 97). The power of the photograph to refer to reality and to affect us, then, resides in this multiplicity of time signified by the photographic image. Barthes continues that the photograph of Lewis Payne deeply wounds him because what it signifies is ultimately the 'anterior future' of death, including his own. In short, every photograph is a document of the past as well as an allegory of the 'defeat of Time': 'It is because each photograph always contains this imperious sign of my future death that each one, however attached it seems to be to the excited world of the living, challenges each of us.'

Barthes's discussion has been criticized by Jacques Rancière (2009: 112, 110) for creating 'a short-circuit between historical knowledge of the subject represented and the material texture of the photograph' in order to turn 'photography into transport'. He points out that, in order for the *punctum* of time to affect us, we need more information than what is visually given to us. In order to feel the *punctum* of time Barthes describes in the photograph of Lewis Payne, for example, we need to know who the photographed subject is, and 'we also need to know that it was the first time a photographer – Alexander Gardner – had been allowed in to photograph an execution' (2009: 112). These facts condition our affective response to the photograph. The impact a photograph has on us, Sontag (2003: 29) agrees, 'depends on how the picture is identified or misidentified; that is, on words'. This is also true of the photograph of 'Taejon, 1950'. The boy in this photograph belongs to what Susie Linfield (2010: 66) calls 'the most morally vexing photographic genre: pictures of people about to be murdered'. Obviously it would not be a sufficient response simply to read this photograph as an allegory of death. To understand it, we need contextual and historical knowledge that cannot be obtained simply by studying the materiality of the photograph itself. Surely what we feel changes when we learn that the photograph was taken by a US Army major who had borrowed the camera of Lieutenant Colonel Bob E. Edwards, the US Army's attaché at the American Embassy, which failed to intervene successfully in the mass killings of political prisoners during the Korean War. None the less, it seems to me that Barthes's discussion of the affective and temporal dimensions of photography leads us in interesting ways to Smith's discussion of our sympathy for the dead.

'We sympathize even with the dead', Smith famously writes.

> It is miserable, we think, to be deprived of the light of the sun; to be shut out from life and conversation; to be laid in the cold grave, a prey to corruption and the reptiles of the earth; to be no more thought of in this world, but to be obliterated, in a little time, from the affections, and almost from the memory, of their dearest friends and relations. Surely, we imagine, we can never feel too much for those who have suffered so dreadful a calamity . . . That our sympathy can afford them no consolation seems to be an addition to their calamity.
>
> (*TMS* I.i.1.13)

A number of questions come to mind when we read this passage in conjunction with viewing the photographs discussed above. Is the reason why photographs wound us with the *punctum* of time because we sympathize with the dead in the manner Smith describes here? Does Smith's discussion of our sympathy with the dead sufficiently explain the power of photography?

To begin with, we should note that, in this passage from *The Theory of Moral Sentiments*, we are clearly not dealing with actual vision but with imaginary vision. What we imagine is precisely that which lies beyond 'the light of the sun'. What we imagine as we sympathize with the dead is not the spectacle of death so much as the progress of death – its future effects, as it were. We imagine that, 'in a little time', both the physical and psychical remains of the dead will be 'obliterated'. All too soon, it will be as if the dead had never existed. They will cease to matter. Imagining this, we also imagine how the dead would react to the knowledge of their future obliteration. How do we do this? We put 'ourselves in their situation'. To use Smith's rather gruesome image, we put 'our own living souls in their inanimated bodies' and try to conceive 'what would be our emotions in this case'. If we were dead and we had 'consciousness of that change', if we knew that every day we were decomposing and being more and more forgotten, we would suffer a 'dreary and endless melancholy', we think. So we try 'artificially to keep alive our melancholy remembrance of their misfortune'. We know, however, that 'our sympathy can afford them no consolation'. Nothing changes because we sympathize. Knowing this 'serves only to exasperate our sense of their misery' and to strengthen our 'dread of death' (*TMS* I.i.1.13).

There are a few things we can note about this very complex, as well as rather unusual, example of the operation of Smithian sympathy. As Charles Griswold (2010: 69) points out, the 'ocular metaphor' in Smith's thought 'tends to occlude the temporal dimension by suggesting a static, spatial model'. However, Smith's example here depends very little on visuality and instead emphasizes the temporal dimension of sympathy. In order for us to sympathize with the dead, in other words, we need to imagine what is happening to them over the course of time. We approach death, in this sense, not as the end of time but as a continued experience of time. Griswold suggests that Smith's version of what happens to the dead is 'actually quite selective, as it effectively dismisses the notion that the souls of the dead are happily off in some other-worldly place'. This is not quite accurate, since Smith says that when we sympathize with the dead we are 'overlooking what is of real importance in their situation, that awful future which awaits them' (*TMS* I.i.1.13). So it is not so much that Smith makes no reference to 'that awful future' of the religious other-world, but that our fear of death depends on something other than our religious belief. None the less, Griswold's point that our imagination of death depends crucially on cultural and narratives told about life after death is relevant here. So is his point that these diachronic and narrative aspects of the sympathetic imagination come into 'tension with the visual model of impartial spectatorship' (Griswold 2010: 69). This is a point that applies not just to our sympathy for the dead but to Smith's spectatorial sympathy in general.

Setting these problems aside for a moment, we can see that photography's *punctum*, as Barthes describes it, has much in common with Smithian sympathy, which makes 'the foresight of our own dissolution . . . terrible to us' (*TMS* I.i.1.13). When we look at a photograph of someone who is now dead, Barthes (1981: 96) says, 'the photograph tells me death in the future', and we 'shudder' because we are able to imagine this 'death in the future' at the same time as we see the person as a living reality. The photograph, surely, would not have this effect on us if we did not identify and sympathize in some way with the fate of the photographed subject. The multiple tenses conjured up by the photograph depend on the ability of the spectator to project the imagination into the future – both mine and the photographed subject's – and to see these futures as correlative. Both Barthes and Smith speak of our reaction to death as arising out of a complex act of the imagination in which multiple temporalities of multiple subjects are invoked. Clearly, in Smith's discussion we see the dead only in a figurative sense, whereas in Barthes's discussion we *physically* see photographs of the living-dead. However, this uncanny confusion between the living and the dead is also present in Smith's theory, where he says that, when we sympathize with the dead, 'we enter, as it were, into his body, and in our imaginations, in some measure, animate anew the deformed and mangled carcass of the slain' (*TMS* II.i.2.5).

The problem, I believe Sontag would say, is that although Smith's theory can explain how a photograph can produce the kind of *punctum* Barthes describes, it is far from clear that photographs of the dead either naturally or necessarily produce sympathy. Indeed, Sontag's chief quarrel with war photography is that the more we are able to see the dead, the less we are able to sympathize with them. Today, we are able to see not only people who are now dead, but people who were very much alive at the moment when they were photographed (the photographs in which Barthes is chiefly interested), and people who were photographed in the very moment of dying or just after death. For Sontag, a particular horror attaches to this latter category of photographs precisely because today it causes no *punctum* in us, no wound of any kind. Robbed of their ethical power through mass production and mass distribution, these photographs of the dead, especially the war dead, lead us instead to consume a particularly disturbing kind of sublime aesthetics. Smith's theory of the sympathetic spectator, she would say, is not only uninterested in this problem of sublime aesthetics but theoretically unable to respond to it. There is no place in Smith's theory for the allure of that terrible, 'challenging kind of beauty' we find in spectacles of the most terrifying events (Sontag 2003: 75). As to Barthes, I suspect she might say that photographs may once have had the ability to wound and hurt us into a consciousness of death, but this function of photography has dwindled drastically with the overuse of photographic images in modern media. 'Beautifying is one classic operation of the camera, and it tends to bleach out a moral response to what is shown,' she writes (2003: 81).

Sublime aesthetics

> But images of the repulsive can also allure.
>
> (Susan Sontag, *Regarding the Pain of Others*)

A dislike of emotional and physical violence runs through Smith's *Theory of Moral Sentiments*. In both cases, Smith asserts, our sympathy is apt to fail:

> There are some passions of which the expressions excite no sort of sympathy, but before we are acquainted with what gave occasion to them, serve rather to disgust and provoke us against them. The furious behavior of an angry man is more likely to exasperate us against himself than against his enemies.
>
> (*TMS* I.i.1.7)

If we do sympathize with this angry man, it is not because we are moved by the spectacle of his 'furious behavior'. If we are 'unacquainted with his provocation, we cannot bring his case home to ourselves' or sympathize with him. In fact, we are more likely to sympathize with 'the situation of those with whom he is angry', since 'we plainly see . . . to what violence they may be exposed from so enraged an adversary' (*TMS* I.i.1.7). Our feelings and our judgement, of course, may change once we learn *why* he is so angry. However, Smith believes that our sympathetic imagination naturally recoils from violent spectacles. This is why a person who is caught in the throes of 'the violent and disagreeable passions' and 'passionately desires a more complete sympathy' with her spectators will be able to achieve that sympathy only by controlling the violence of those passions. We need, in short, to 'flatten' the 'sharpness' of our 'violent and disagreeable passions' if we are to achieve 'harmony and concord with the emotions' of those around us (*TMS* I.i.4.7).

It is even more difficult to sympathize with bodily pain. Smith acknowledges that a basic bodily sympathy exists between human beings, such that

> When we see a stroke aimed and just ready to fall upon the leg or arm of another person, we naturally shrink and draw back our own leg or our own arm; and when it does fall, we feel it in some measure, and are hurt by it as well as the sufferer.
>
> (*TMS* I.i.1.3)

However, sympathy 'with bodily pain' is always very imperfect. My imaginary 'hurt' will never fail to be 'excessively slight' in comparison with that of the 'sufferer'. Therefore, Smith writes,

> if he makes any violent out-cry, as I cannot go along with him, I never fail to despise him . . . And this is the case of all the passions which take their origin from the body: they excite either no sympathy at all, or such a degree of it, as is altogether disproportioned to the violence of what is felt by the sufferer.
>
> (*TMS* I.ii.1.5)

There is, as Elaine Scarry (1987: 50) puts it in *The Body in Pain*, a 'radical subjectivity' in pain.

It is thus no accident that Smith concludes the section in which he discusses bodily pain with a discussion of tragedy. He argues that the attempt to arouse pity and compassion through the representation of bodily pain in Greek tragedy (his examples are Euripides' *Hippolytus* and Sophocles' *Trachiniae*) constitutes 'among the greatest breaches of decorum of which the Greek theatre has set the example'. Earlier in the same paragraph he writes, 'It is not the sore foot, but the solitude, of Philoctetes which affects us' (*TMS* I.ii.1.11). We do not sympathize readily with hunger, sexual desire, or bodily pain. We sympathize, rather, with what invisibly sustains our imagination; our sympathy feeds on the causal narrative behind pain rather than the punctuality of pain. 'The little sympathy which we feel with bodily pain is the foundation of the propriety of constancy and patience in enduring it' (*TMS* I.ii.1.12). This is why Smith believed that tragic theatre was a more effective school for sympathy than 'the sight of a chirurgical operation'. After the initial shock of the spectacle of bodily pain, Smith writes, when the 'novelty' wears off, we fail to find physical suffering interesting: 'One who has been witness to a dozen dissections, and as many amputations, sees, ever after, all operations of this kind with great indifference, and often with perfect insensibility.' In contrast, the theatre-goer who has 'read or seen represented more than five hundred tragedies' seldom feels so 'entire an abatement of . . . sensibility' (*TMS* I.ii.1.10).

Read in conjunction with Sontag's texts, these selections from Smith's *Theory of Moral Sentiments* suggest that he would agree with Sontag that the visual representation of the physical trauma of death is not likely to provoke much sympathy in the viewer. He would not agree, however, with Sontag's (2003: 95) statement that 'images of the repulsive can also allure'. Sontag argues that there is a long philosophical tradition behind the idea of sublime beauty. Plato provides the first acknowledgement of 'the attraction of mutilated bodies' in Book IV of *The Republic*, where Socrates retells a story about Leontius, the son of Aglaion:

> On his way up from the Piraeus outside the north wall, he noticed the bodies of some criminals lying on the ground, with the executioner standing by them. He wanted to go and look at them, but at the same time he was disgusted and tried to turn away. He struggled for some time and covered his eyes, but

at last the desire was too much for him. Opening his eyes wide, he ran up to the bodies and cried, 'There you are, curse you, feast yourselves on this lovely sight.'

(Sontag 2003: 96–97)

In this story of the conflict between reason and desire, reason is 'disgusted' and tries 'to turn away' from the horrific spectacle of executed bodies, but the eyes obey a different logic of 'desire'. In the end, desire overpowers reason, leading Leontius to curse his eyes even as he gazes at the dead bodies. Obviously, Plato believes that reason needs to control desire, but he also 'appears to take for granted that we also have an appetite for sights of degradation and pain and mutilation' (Sontag 2003: 97). Jonathan Friday (2000: 363) calls this particular appetite of the eye 'demonic curiosity', a 'morbid attraction to human suffering and what is most horrifying in human existence'.

Smith was not philosophically interested in this problem, but a contemporary of his was. A mere two years before Smith published *The Theory of Moral Sentiments*, Burke brought out his *Philosophical Enquiry into the Origin of our Ideas of the Sublime and Beautiful* (1757), in which he made a number of disturbing observations about the psychology behind our vision: 'we have a degree of delight, and that no small one, in the real misfortunes and pains of others'; 'there is no spectacle we so eagerly pursue, as that of some uncommon and grievous calamity' (Burke 1990: 42–43). In order to illustrate this point, Burke engaged in a thought-experiment. He asks what the effect of an earthquake in London might be.

This noble capital, the pride of England and of Europe, I believe no man is so strangely wicked as to desire to see destroyed by a conflagration or an earthquake, though he should be removed himself to the greatest distance from the danger. But suppose such a fatal accident to have happened, what numbers from all parts would croud to behold the ruins, and amongst them many who would have been content never to have seen London in its glory?

(Burke 1990: 44)

In Burke's theory we are naturally, irresistibly drawn to this spectacle 'antecedent to any reasoning, by an instinct that works us to its own purposes, without our concurrence' (1990: 43). Burke's logic goes as follows: the horror of the scene animates our terror; because 'terror is a passion which always produces delight when it does not press too close', we instinctively take a 'not ... unmixed delight' in the sublime object that causes our terror (1990: 42–43). In *Regarding the Pain of Others* Sontag returns repeatedly to the sublimity of war and the scopophilic eye that feeds on it with a secret relish. Smith, on the other hand, was never philosophically interested in the Burkean sublime. He does use the word 'sublime' in *The Theory of Moral Sentiments*, but only in conjunction with such other words as 'eloquence', 'contemplation', 'speculation', and 'doctrines'. Smith's sublime is about rhetorical elevation or supreme self-command, whereas

Burke's is about our strange avidity for terror. As Adam Phillips (1990: ix) notes, for Burke, as for Kant, 'the Sublime was a way of thinking about excess as the key to a deeper kind of subjectivity'. Burke was interested in the enthralling emotional experience of coercion, seduction, and submission. For this reason, his *Philosophical Enquiry* is a deeply erotic text.

Smith's *Theory of Moral Sentiments*, in comparison, seems almost strait-laced in its resolute propriety. If Burke was interested in self-abandon, Smith was interested in self-control. As we have seen, he believed that 'The little sympathy which we feel with bodily pain is the foundation of the propriety of constancy and patience in enduring it' (*TMS* I.ii.1.12). The fact that we are not attracted to spectacles of violence may strike us as a problem of sympathy insofar as we are unable to share the sufferings of others. However, Smith believes that this very aversion to violence has a crucial social use: it helps us to bear and endure our own suffering. Smith's preference for the masculine (in other words, 'the great, the awful and respectable') virtues of 'self-denial, of self-government, of that command of the passions' (*TMS* I.i.5.1) over the feminine virtues of 'exquisite fellow-feeling' and 'tenderness' is telling (*TMS* IV.ii.10). Declaring that 'Humanity is the virtue of a woman, generosity of a man' (*TMS* IV.ii.10), he attributes sublimity ('the great, the awful') to man. Beyond this gendering of the sublime as masculine, Smith's sublime has little to do with Burke's.[8] As David Marshall (1984) points out, Smith's *Theory of Moral Sentiments* is not oblivious of the problem of scopophilia. However, it locates its dangers not in the private thrill of looking at distress but in the public, collective fascination with wealth and rank, and in the 'disposition of mankind, to go along with all the passions of the rich and the powerful' (*TMS* I.iii.2.3). There is no space for the 'innate tropism toward the gruesome' (Sontag 2003: 97) in Smith's philosophy. The public eye turns rapidly away from the spectacle of the poor ('The poor man . . . in the midst of a crowd is in the same obscurity as if shut up in his own hovel'), while all eyes are on 'The man of rank and distinction' ('His actions are the objects of the public care'; 'In a great assembly he is the person upon whom all direct their eyes') (*TMS* I.iii.2.1). Smith's spectatorial ethics, in which he elaborates the ethical technique of imagining a distanced, impartial spectator who performs as an imaginative judge of our own actions, implies an aesthetics of decorum, propriety, control, and understatement befitting the world of public conversation in which Smith lived. For him, the possibility of a natural, socialized ethics had to be sought not in the radically subjective experience of pain but in the intersubjective, public realm where sympathy operates in a circular and self-reflexive manner. The real importance of sympathy for Smith lies in this self-reflexive, mirroring function of sympathy – the fact that we turn our sympathetic gazes back, reflectively, upon ourselves. As many critics have observed (e.g., Brissenden 1969; Bender 1987), the Smithian self is a profoundly social self, as well as a guilty and self-conscious self who constantly engages in self-regulation and self-surveillance in a public world.

Thus, even the examples that seemingly come closest to the Burkean sublime in Smith's theory serve a very different purpose. Smith seems to have been very struck by tales about the 'savages in North America' who were subjected to 'the most dreadful torments' when they were tortured by their enemies. He refers to these North American savages in several passages in *The Theory of Moral Sentiments*,[9] the most graphic of which runs as follows:

> While he is hung by the shoulders over a slow fire, he derides his tormentors, and tells them with how much more ingenuity he himself had tormented such of their countrymen as had fallen into his hands. After he has been scorched and burnt, and lacerated in all the most tender and sensible parts of his body for several hours together, he is often allowed, in order to prolong his misery, a short respite, and is taken down from the stake: he employs this interval in talking upon all indifferent subjects, inquires after the news of the country, and seems indifferent about nothing but his own situation. The spectators express the same insensibility; the sight of so horrible an object seems to make no impression upon them; they scarce look at the prisoner, except when they lend a hand to torment him. At other times they smoke tobacco, and amuse themselves with any common object, as if no such matter was going on. Every savage is said to prepare himself from his earliest youth for this dreadful end. He composes, for this purpose, what they call the song of death, a song which he is to sing when he has fallen into the hands of his enemies, and is expiring under the tortures which they inflict upon him. It consists of insults upon his tormentors, and expresses the highest contempt of death and pain.
>
> (*TMS* I.ii.9)

Smith's reference here to 'the sight of so horrible an object' and his painstaking description of this imaginary sight for his readers may suggest that he assumed that spectators would be overwhelmed and irresistibly drawn to this spectacle. However, it is clear that what fascinates him, and what he expects his readers to be fascinated by, is the insensibility of both the actor and the spectators toward pain in this scene of horror, rather than the visual details of the torture. This is a highly complex example because the tortured savage might seem to embody the Smithian virtues of 'self-denial, of self-government, of that control of the passions' (*TMS* I.i.5.1). This is not truly the case, however, because there is a complete absence of sympathy in this scene. The savage 'expects no sympathy from those about him' and his enemy spectators indeed show him none. On the one hand, Smith lauds the heroic 'contempt of death and torture' shown by the tortured 'savage' here and suggests that such 'magnanimity and self-command . . . are almost beyond the conception of Europeans'. On the other, he makes it clear that this example of the savage's 'heroic and unconquerable firmness' is also premodern and uncivilized: 'A humane and polished people . . . have more sensibility to the passions of others' and sympathize more readily with them. 'A polished people being accustomed to give way, in some measure, to the movements of nature, become frank, open and sincere', whereas 'Barbarians, on the contrary, being obliged to smother and conceal the appearance of every passion, necessarily acquire the habits of falsehood and dissimulation.' This is why the barbarian's 'vengeance' is 'always sanguinary and dreadful'. The savage, Smith implies, is more self-denying but also more violent. The civilized possess less hardiness but more sensibility and humanity. 'Before we can feel much for others,' he says, 'we must in some measure be at ease ourselves.' Sympathy does not operate when 'our own misery pinches us very severely' or when we are overwhelmed by our 'own wants and necessities', as in the case of the savages (*TMS* V.ii.9).

Sontag would probably agree with Smith's point that our modern sensibility is not comfortable with the kinds of violence and heroism exemplified by the example of the Native American death song. The view that extreme suffering is transcendent, heroic, and transfiguring, she says, is 'alien to a modern sensibility, which regards suffering as something that is a mistake or an accident or a crime' (Sontag 2003: 99). She might find Smith useful for analysing why it is difficult for us to sympathize with visual representations of bodily pain, mutilation, suffering, and death. However, she would not agree with his analysis that looking at such visual representations is solely a disagreeable and painful experience. In this respect, she is much closer to Burke than Smith. She points out that there are photographs of dreadful suffering that are nonetheless beautiful and move us. Photography, she points out, has 'dual powers': 'to generate documents and to create works of visual art'. 'Photographs tend to transform, whatever their subject; and as an image something may be beautiful – or terrifying, or unbearable, or quite bearable – as it is not in real life' (2003: 76). Burke (1990: 43) believed that our natural attraction to spectacles of horror had a social function: 'The delight we have in such things', he argues, 'hinders us from shunning scenes of misery.' Our delight in the sublime thus works in tandem with sympathy by bringing us close to precisely those spectacles where sympathy is most needed. Sontag (2003: 97), on the other hand, does not appear to believe that our 'innate tropism toward the gruesome' necessarily works in the service of moral sympathy. Our aesthetics and morals are not necessarily any more in sync than our aesthetics and politics. 'Recall the canonical example of the Auschwitz commandant returning home in the evening, embracing his wife and children, and sitting at the piano to play some Schubert before dinner,' she writes (2003: 102). For Sontag, our aesthetic responses can no longer serve as a guide for our ethics. The Smithian pact between aesthetics and ethics is broken.

The politics of sympathy

> Our sympathy proclaims our innocence as well as our impotence.
>
> (Susan Sontag, *Regarding the Pain of Others*)

Let us turn to a key passage in *Regarding the Pain of Others*, where Sontag (2003: 102) declares, 'if we consider what emotions would be desirable' in viewing war photography, 'it seems too simple to elect sympathy'. She continues:

The imaginary proximity to the suffering inflicted on others that is granted by images suggests a link between the faraway sufferers – seen close-up on the television screen – and the privileged viewer that is simply untrue, that is yet one more mystification of our relations to power. So far as we feel sympathy, we feel we are not accomplices to what caused the suffering. Our sympathy proclaims our innocence as well as our impotence. To that extent, it can be (for all our good intentions) an impertinent – if not an inappropriate response.

In this passage Sontag interprets sympathy as a passive response. When we sympathize, we are taking a particular moral and political stance. Sympathy creates an 'imaginary' but also an impotent 'proximity'. We absolve ourselves of responsibility when we sympathize. Sympathy is a substitute for acting. Sympathizers are either shameless liars or self-duping hypocrites. They are supposedly sympathizing, but ultimately they are distancing themselves from the scene of suffering. They are not implicated. They are not suffering. They are not responsible.

We should note that Sontag's suspicion of sympathy here harks back to arguments about the key role of self-love and self-preservation in theories about tragedy. As Arby Ted Siraki points out, through the seventeenth and early eighteenth centuries it was common for thinkers to explain the pleasure of tragedy as highly selfish in origin. Hobbes, for instance, followed Lucretius in theorizing that 'men usually are content . . . to be spectators of the misery of their friends' as long as they are assured of their 'own security' (cited in Siraki 2010: 215). Addison also proposed that 'the secret comparison which we make between our selves and the person who suffers' is the reason why we take pleasure in 'the description of what is terrible'. Pleasure does 'not arise so properly from the description of what is terrible, as from the reflection we make on our selves at the time of reading it' (cited in Siraki 2010: 215). Against Addison, Burke argues in the *Philosophical Enquiry* that we should not confuse 'a necessary condition' with 'the *cause*' of sympathy. Thus, 'it is absolutely necessary my life should be out of any imminent hazard before I can take a delight in the sufferings of others, real or imaginary', but 'it is a sophism to argue from thence, that this immunity is the cause of my delight' (Burke 1990: 44; original emphasis). Burke believed that safety was a condition rather than a cause of sympathetic delight in the distresses of others. The chief reason why the reflection of our safety cannot be a cause of sympathetic pleasure for Burke is that our feelings are not as influenced by our 'reasoning faculty' as we would like to think. 'I should imagine', he writes, 'that the influence of reason in producing our passions is nothing near so extensive as it is commonly believed' (1990: 41). In the attack Sontag mounts against sympathy, she appears to agree with Hobbes and Addison that a basic self-love or self-regard lies at the foundation of sympathy. Moreover, like Addison, but unlike Burke, she also appears to believe that tragic pleasure arises from 'reflection'. For Sontag, sympathy is not only a passive feeling that arises from the reflection of our comparative safety when we look at the suffering of others; it entails a more active form of negative political argument or judgement. Sympathy is thus doubly and triply distancing: when we sympathize, we absent ourselves from the scene of suffering in multiple senses; we are not there, we are not responsible, we cannot do anything.

Smith would have disagreed. To begin with, just as he objected to Hobbes, he would have objected to Sontag's assumption that our sympathetic feelings are ultimately self-regarding. 'That whole account of human nature . . . which deduces all sentiments and affections from self-love', he writes, 'seems to me to have arisen from some confused apprehension of the system of sympathy' (*TMS* VII. iii.1.4). It is not that Smith does not acknowledge the force of self-love. He notes that 'Every man . . . is much more deeply interested in whatever immediately concerns himself, than in what concerns any other man' (*TMS* II.ii.2.1). As we saw above, Smith acknowledges that a sense of security frees us up for the 'leisure' of sympathy: 'If our own misery pinches us very severely, we have no leisure to attend to that of our neighbor' (*TMS* V.ii.9). Smith also believes that the thought of our safety 'intrudes' upon sympathy: 'The thought of their own safety, the thought that they themselves are not really the sufferers, continually intrudes itself upon them; and . . . hinders them from conceiving any thing that approaches to the same degree of violence' (*TMS* I.i.4.7). However, he argues that we sympathize not *because* of self-love but *in spite* of it. In his discussion of tragedy, he writes, 'it is painful to go along with grief, and we always enter into it with reluctance' (*TMS* I.iii.1.9). When we sympathize with other people's grief, we do so naturally, but it is a struggle. We struggle against our constant awareness that we are different from the grieving sufferer and our knowledge that what we feel is a poor approximation of what the sufferer is feeling. For Smith, sympathy is what we actively achieve against all these odds.

Not all sympathy takes this much effort, of course. Sometimes the passions 'seem to be transfused from one man to another, instantaneously, and antecedent to any knowledge of what excited them in the person principally concerned' (*TMS* I.i.1.6). These cases of 'fellow-feeling' prove that we are innately social beings endowed with a 'natural disposition to accommodate and to assimilate, as much as we can, our own sentiments, principles, and feelings, to those which we see fixed and rooted in the persons whom we are obliged to live and converse a great deal with' (*TMS* VI.ii.1.17). However, Smith is less philosophically interested in these unreflecting, involuntary, and seemingly instantaneous forms of sympathy that occur with frequency between people who are closely related by blood or habit. The kind of sympathy Smith is most interested in is not the sympathy that obtains between friends, family, and acquaintances, already closely knitted together in a mutual web of obligations, debts, and gifts. Rather, as Allan Silver (1997) and Michael Ignatieff (1986) have pointed out, Smith's theory presupposes a commercial, civil society in which individuals are at bottom indifferent *strangers* to one another (see also Min 2002). This is why Smith speaks of the sympathizer as a spectator, someone who is not personally involved in the suffering that is being witnessed. As Luc Boltanski (1999: 36; original emphasis) points out, Smith is asking how the spectator and the sufferer can achieve a 'correspondence of sentiments' (*TMS* I.i.4.6) when they are in such radically different situations. And this is not simply a moral question but also 'a fundamental political question since it concerns the possibility of an agreement between unequally *affected* or unequally *concerned* persons which does not rely on force'.

Faced with the problem outlined by Sontag above, I believe Smith would say that sympathy is simply the wrong word to use in this context. What the spectator of the war photograph is feeling is not sympathy at all, but something closer to what others have called 'pity' – in Rousseau's definition, a kind of 'pure movement of Nature prior to all reflection'. According to Rousseau, our natural identification with, and pity for, the sufferer 'is obscure and lively in Savage man, developed but weak in Civil man'. As soon as we reflect on our self-interest, reason 'engenders vanity, and reflection . . . reinforces it', weakening our pity (Rousseau 1990: 162). Insofar as Sontag's spectator remains highly aware of the difference between herself and the sufferer in the photograph, however, we could say that what that spectator is feeling is only a very weak form of Rousseau's notion of pity.[10] What would happen if Sontag's spectator were instead engaged in Smithian sympathy? Sontag assumes that sympathy is disconnected to, and can be detrimental to, political action. Smith, on the other hand, interprets sympathy in such a way that it leads to judgement, action, and intervention. As he says,

> the sentiment or affection of the heart, from which any action proceeds, and upon which its whole virtue or vice depends, may be considered under two different aspects, or in two different relations: first, in relation to the cause or object which excites it; and, secondly, in relation to the end which it proposes, or to the effect which it tends to produce.
>
> (*TMS* I.i.3.5)

When Smithian sympathy operates properly, in other words, it activates and produces an effect. Thus, when 'we sympathize with the sorrow of our fellow-creature whenever we see his distress', our 'heart' not only 'beats time to his grief' but is also 'animated with that spirit by which he endeavours to drive away or destroy the cause of it' (*TMS* II.i.2.5).

> The indolent and passive fellow-feeling, by which we accompany him in his sufferings, readily gives way to that more vigorous and active sentiment by which we go along with him in the effort he makes, either to repel them, or to gratify his aversion to that what has given occasion to them. This is still more peculiarly the case, when it is man who has caused them. When we see one man oppressed or injured by another, the sympathy which we feel with the distress of the sufferer seems to serve only to animate our fellow-feeling with his resentment against the offender. We are rejoiced to see him attack his adversary in his turn, and are eager and ready to assist him whenever he exerts himself for defence, or even for vengeance within a certain degree.
>
> (*TMS* II.i.2.5)

Sympathy becomes morally and politically effective when it leads the spectator beyond 'indolent and passive fellow-feeling' to meaningful action. Smith would say that intervention in a fellow human being's suffering is conditional upon this ability to engage in fellow-feeling. Sympathy leads to moral judgement, which in turn paves the way for action. As Boltanski (1999: 48) puts it, Smith envisions a bipartite, split emotive response to the spectacle of suffering: on the one hand, tender-heartedness; on the other, indignation.

Unlike Sontag's spectator who draws a clear line between sympathetic feeling and social responsibility, diligently guarding the complacent innocence of the self, Smith's ideal spectator is thus a self-estranging, doubled, split, striving self. As R. F. Brissenden (1969: 958) has pointed out, Smith betrays a remarkable 'preoccupation with guilt and remorse' as well as with 'moral compulsion and obligation' in *The Theory of Moral Sentiments*. Smith's spectator worries not only about what she sees, but about how she is seen; she worries about the gap between her feelings and her action; she is self-judging and worries about how she is judged by others. In this sense, the rigorously self-scrutinizing Sontag might ironically be Smith's ideal spectator. Smith might continue Sontag's narrative in the following way. Realizing that our sympathy directed toward a dead victim of war is all too belated, and that no action of ours could possibly bring them back from death, we suffer a pang, a disquiet. Feeling the insufficiency of our sympathy, we feel less safe, less innocent. In *Regarding the Pain of Others*, Sontag (2003: 61) mentions the cache of six thousand photographs taken between 1975 and 1979 in a suburb of Phnom Penh, where the Khmer Rouge photographed their victims before executing them. The 'viewer', she notes, 'is in the same position as the lackey behind the camera; the experience is sickening'. Looking at the victims, we realize that we are mimicking the gaze of the camera that in turn mimics the aim of the gun that kills the victims. True sympathy would take us this far – to shame and guilt and, we might hope, also to change. This is not to say that Smith believes that sympathy will always produce meaningful social and political action. What he does believe is that in the best instances where such action takes place, it will be explained by the operation of sympathy.

Smith recognizes a political problem that is inherent in sympathy, but it is different from Sontag's. As mentioned earlier, Smith takes for granted a society of inequality with 'distinction of ranks'. Living in such a society, we are naturally led to show 'obsequiousness to our superiors' in rank and to 'go along with all the passions of the rich and the powerful' (*TMS* I.iii.2.3). Smith views 'This disposition to admire, and almost to worship, the rich and the powerful' as 'necessary both to establish and to maintain the distinction of ranks and the order of society', but recognizes that it is, 'at the same time, the great and most universal cause of the corruption of our moral sentiments' (*TMS* I.iii.3.1). Unfortunately, 'The great mob of mankind are the admirers and worshippers . . . of wealth and greatness'. In contrast, the admirers of 'wisdom and virtue' are 'but a small party' (*TMS* I.iii.3.2). Sympathy is apt to lead us to make peace with the status quo and 'to neglect persons of poor and mean condition' (*TMS* 1.iii.3.1). Smith's remedy for this tendency of sympathy to collude with existing social and political structures, however, is not less sympathy (Sontag's solution) but more sympathy – more extensive, more active, and more self-conscious.

Smith would also add that, in order for sympathy to operate properly and fully, certain political conditions need to be met. Sympathy works best in a stable and secure society where justice prevails. And in a just society sympathy serves to make possible the moral self-regulation of its members without the intrusion of external force. In a condition of war, which suspends and negates the rules of civil society and justice, sympathy and spectatorship cannot operate with the same ease or efficacy. As Smith pithily says,

> When two nations are at variance . . . the partial spectator is at hand: the impartial one at a great distance . . . The propriety of our moral sentiments is never so apt to be corrupted, as when the indulgent and partial spectator is at hand, while the indifferent and impartial one is at a great distance.
>
> (*TMS* III.iii.42)

It is difficult to find room for self-distancing and imaginative role-playing in war. War not only suspends the laws of justice but interferes with the operations of moral sympathy, since the 'real, revered, and impartial spectator' is 'upon no occasion, at a greater distance than amidst the violence and rage of contending parties' (*TMS* III.iii.43). Smith might say that politics needs sympathy, and sympathy needs politics.

The global spectator

> In Magnum's voice, photography declared itself a global enterprise.
> (Susan Sontag, *Regarding the Pain of Others*)

In *Distant Suffering*, Boltanski (1999: 12) argues that the problem of 'the spectacle of suffering . . . is not a technical consequence of modern means of communication, even if the power and expansion of the media have brought misery into the intimacy of fortunate households with unprecedented efficiency'. The 'problems posed to the spectator' are 'not . . . absolutely new'. While I am in basic agreement with Boltanski's point, I believe that we need to acknowledge that there is a large gap between Smith's idea of spectatorship and the new forms of spectatorship that advances in technology have made possible. In particular, today the spectator has access to a kind of globalized vision that did not exist in Smith's time. He lived in a world in which it was impossible to imagine that we would be able to see calamities occurring halfway around the globe. His famous example of an earthquake in China revolves around the question of how a European 'would be affected upon receiving intelligence of this dreadful calamity'. 'Let us suppose that the great empire of China, with all its myriads of inhabitants, was suddenly swallowed up by an earthquake.' How would a modern 'man of humanity in Europe . . . [with] no sort of connexion with that part of the world' react to this news? Smith's short answer is that he would probably express 'humane sentiments' of distress but then carry on with his life 'as if no such accident had happened' (*TMS* III.iii.4). In a passage brimming with irony, he asserts that this European 'man of humanity' would probably 'snore with the most profound security over the ruin of a hundred millions of his brethren', whereas, 'If he was to lose his little finger to-morrow, he would not sleep to-night.' Smith's irony cuts both ways. On the one hand, he pokes fun at the man of 'fine philosophy' who, for all his 'humane sentiments', can sleep peacefully after hearing of the death of 'a hundred millions' of Chinese (*TMS* III.iii.4). On the other, he is suspicious of 'affected and sentimental sadness' that stretches sympathy far beyond its natural boundaries: 'Whatever interest we take in the fortune of those with whom we have no acquaintance or connexion, and who are placed altogether out of the sphere of our activity, can produce only anxiety to ourselves, without any manner of advantage to them' (*TMS* III.iii.9).[11]

In a reading of this passage, John Durham Peters (1995: 665) suggests Smith's point is that China is simply too distant and too unreal for ordinary Europeans to be able to sympathize effectively with the Chinese people: Smith's 'social theory does not imagine that the inhabitants of China could ever be anything but an abstraction for Scotsmen'. I think this is put too strongly. Smith's remarkably even-toned discussion of distant cultures and peoples throughout *The Theory of Moral Sentiments* proves that he had not only the local but also the wider – indeed global – world in mind. He writes often of the French and the Italians, Native Americans, Africans, and the Chinese, reminding readers that they inhabit a larger world beyond their small circle of local relations. As Jennifer Pitts (2005: 43) points out in *A Turn to Empire*, Smith's moral philosophy 'encourages open-mindedness toward unfamiliar values and practices', and 'His moral theory both regards morality as developed necessarily within the context of a particular group or society, and also warns us against allowing moral judgments to rest complacently with the inevitably partial moral views of any given group.' None the less, Peters's (1995: 665) point that 'Smith's historical universe is able to contain the pathos of suffering at a distance in a way that ours is not' should be taken seriously. As he remarks, Smith can assume that his European man has 'no acquaintance or connexion' with China. However, 'Parochial containment for us, in contrast, has been shattered today, in our dispersed yet interconnected condition.' As 'dwellers within the fractured global flows of people, images, words, money, technology, and actions', we can no longer say with the same ease that we have no acquaintance or connection with those who live halfway around the globe, or that distant people 'are placed altogether out of the sphere of our activity' (*TMS* III.iii.9). If and when a Chinese earthquake occurs, images of the calamity circulate almost instantaneously via television and the internet. And it is possible to intervene by joining in humanitarian aid for disaster victims in distant parts of the world. For this reason, Susie Linfield (2010: 46) argues that the camera 'has done so much to globalize our consciences' by making it 'quite simply, impossible to say, "I did not know"'; 'photographs have robbed us of the alibi of ignorance'. Similarly, Sontag (2003: 114–115) writes that the reason why today 'No one after a certain age has the right to this kind of innocence, of superficiality, to this degree of ignorance, or amnesia' is that 'There now exists a vast repository of images that make it harder to maintain this kind of moral defectiveness.'

Given that Smith assumes that physical proximity generally aids sympathy, I believe that he would grant that photographs can bring distant scenes of human suffering closer to us. It is true that Smith criticizes the idea that 'Commiseration for those miseries which we never saw, which we never heard of, ought . . . to dampen the pleasures of the fortunate, and to render a certain melancholy dejection habitual to all men' (*TMS* III.iii.9). Smith made this point to underscore his assertion that our sympathies are not limitless and naturally centre on those who are proximate to us. But surely we are in a better position to sympathize with the victims if we see and hear of natural and man-made disasters occurring in distant parts of the world. I believe that Smith would acknowledge that photography, which can bring into our vision physically as well as temporally distant people, can serve a moral function by bringing their suffering visually – if not geographically – nearer to us. For this reason, I believe that Forman-Barzilai's (2010) argument that Smith is 'anti-cosmopolitan' needs to be historically qualified. I take her point that spatial nearness is no guarantee of sympathy and that close affective ties, as well as cultural homogeneity, also aid the workings of sympathy.[12] Photography, which bridges visual distance but not physical distance, cannot guarantee that spectators will enter into sympathetic relations with the people depicted. None the less, I believe Smith would agree that photography is one way in which we can become morally connected to global others.

The problem is that, while the development of visual technology has made a new kind of global spectatorship and global moral consciousness possible, it has also undermined it in multiple ways. As Sontag points out, the new digital and virtual technologies of vision do not necessarily have a greater power to refer to the global world. In particular, the digitization and virtualization of photography have undermined the power of photography to remember and document the past. As Mirzoeff (1999: 88–89) explains, 'After a century and a half of recording and memorializing death, photography met its own death some time in the 1980s at the hands of computer imaging'; today, 'the photograph is no longer an index of reality'. Sontag (2003: 58) adds, 'Technically, the possibilities for doctoring or electronically manipulating pictures are greater than ever – almost unlimited.'[13] A second challenge is that today's spectators, at least in countries with sophisticated visual technology, live 'in a world saturated, no, hyper-saturated with images'. According to Sontag, overexposure to 'such images just make[s] us a little less able to feel, to have our conscience pricked': 'Image-glut keeps attention light, mobile, relatively indifferent to content. Image-flow precludes a privileged image' (2003: 104, 106). Thirdly, increasing familiarity with digital image production and the wide circulation of photographic images via the internet have made possible a global culture of self-spectatorship that is arguably not so much about reaching out to others but rather about promoting, celebrating, and advertising the self. In our age of social network services and the cell-phone selfie, people are all too willing to record their daily, private, even erotic lives and make them available on social networks for public spectatorship. When Smith spoke of supposing 'ourselves the spectators of our behavior' and viewing 'ourselves at the distance and with the eyes of other people' (*TMS* III.i.5, III.i.4), he did not have in mind our celebratory culture of photographic, even cinematic, self-documentation and self-display.

Fourthly, global spectatorship has taken on an ominous new meaning as technologized vision has empowered the state to discipline the citizen by means of sophisticated surveillance technology and even to wage war against its enemies. As we have seen, Smith construed the moral imagination as a form of optical self-surveillance. He might have altered this optical metaphor, however, had he lived to see the degree to which surveillance technology would penetrate our political lives, turning us into visual objects for public surveillance and state discipline. As spectatorship increasingly turns into a state enterprise, it becomes a political rather than a moral affair. Indeed, with the development of visual technology, state spectatorship has become ever more powerful. As Sontag (2003: 67) remarks, today 'war itself is waged as much as possible at a distance, through bombing, whose targets can be chosen, on the basis of instantly relayed information and visualizing technology, from continents away'. At the same time, war is now perpetual and uncontainable. Allen Feldman points out that, post-9/11, wars are being fought as 'de-territorialized', spatially and temporally open-ended campaigns, 'not exclusively focused on territorial conquest, or on an easily locatable or identifiable enemy', but rather on 'imputed territorial contamination and transgression – "terrorist", demographic and biological infiltration'. Thus, the citizen today is more easily 'subjected to behavioral-optical appropriation by a variety of compulsory visibility regimes such as the homeland security apparatus' (Feldman 2004: 331, 341).[14] Meanwhile, war has become increasingly mediatized and spectacularized. War is increasingly conducted as a 'war of images' transmitted by 'the multiple media' of 'television, the internet and other networked information technology' (Der Derian 2005: 36, 26). This is true of both Western powers and their enemies, as the Islamic State's savvy use of YouTube and social media proves. In our global political culture, the dividing line between war and entertainment has become disturbingly thin. The Abu Ghraib photos and IS militants' beheading videos show how the visualization of terror has become 'a bizarre form of entertainment in the West as well as the East'. These travesties of Smithian self-surveilling spectatorship that aim at 'mutual loathing and mutual fear' serve as disquieting testimonies of the increasing challenges to global moral sympathy (Linfield 2010: 163, 152).

Given the historical and political differences between Smith's world and our own, then, what continuing relevance does his moral philosophy have for us? I believe that Smith's model of spectatorship, precisely because it is rooted in the very different world in which he lived, clarifies the ways in which the meaning of spectatorship has changed. We live in altered times in which the social, political, and technological conditions of spectatorship have been radically redefined. This does not mean that Smith's theory of spectatorship has become obsolete or that the moral meaning of spectatorship is no longer relevant. If anything, the technologization and militarization of vision have made Smith's discussion of moral spectatorship all the more pressing and important. We need not resign ourselves to being victims of modern spectacles. As Rancière (2009: 17) has said, we need to liberate ourselves from the idea that looking is necessarily a passive act; proper vision depends on 'the emancipation of each of us as spectator'.

I hope that this comparison of Smith and Sontag has shown that the former's philosophy helps us to interrogate the critical assumptions and arguments made in public discourse today about spectatorship and sympathy and to reimagine what it means to be a spectator in our age. Sontag, in turn, helps us to update Smith's concerns for our age. Smith rooted moral vision in our ordinary interactions with the world. For this reason, I believe his philosophy can speak in profound ways to our ordinary and daily experience of looking at the world in which we live. What are we looking at, why, and to what end? The verb 'regard' in Sontag's title, which is usually used in the sense of 'considering, taking into account, paying attention to', has a more basic etymological meaning of 'looking upon' and the correlative, obsolete meaning of 'looking after, taking care of'.[15] The question Sontag constantly asks in her book is: when we are looking at the suffering at others, are we caring for them? Smith understood spectatorship as a means of winning distance, detachment, and perspective from the self. Another way to put this is to say that, for Smith, spectatorship was a way of caring for the self as well as caring for the other. For all its limitations, that Smithian ideal is hard to give up.

Notes

1　This article is available on the *New York Times*' website under the title 'Unearthing War's Horrors Years Later in South Korea' (3 December 2007). Choe writes, 'South Korean troops executed tens of thousands of unarmed civilians and prisoners as they retreated in advance of the North Korean invaders during the war, according to historians. The victims were often accused of being Communist sympathizers or collaborators. The commission's investigators have discovered the remains of hundreds of people – including women and children – who were killed without trial. They have also identified 1,222 probable instances of mass killings during the war.' In this essay I will refer to this photograph as 'Taejon, 1950'.

2　That essay was published in Korean in the February 2008 issue of the journal *Chul Hak Sa Sang* 27: 67–88.

3　This is no doubt why Sontag's book *Regarding the Pain of Others* does not include any reproductions of the photographs mentioned.

4　Forman-Barzilai (2010: 159–160) concludes, 'In the end, it seems that the ideal Smithian perspective will be that of a spectator who is essentially Janus-faced: near enough to access the meanings and vicissitudes of a particular situation, but distant enough not to be entangled within them – both hot and cool. This tension is not entirely resolvable but Smith seemed to think that reflective moral agents could navigate it more or less successfully.'

5　De Bolla's examples of such public events include public hangings, theatrical performances, art exhibitions, masquerades, pleasure gardens, balls, dances, and scientific demonstrations.

6　Griswold suggests that the visual metaphor is useful for Smith for five reasons. First, 'ocular language is a natural way to talk about *perspective*'. Second, the visual metaphor 'suggests detachment from the object seen'. Third, 'sight suggests a model of knowing' that seems, 'in the ideal case, to leave the spectator's ego behind'. Fourth, we normally think of imagining as 'seeing'. Fifth, 'vision is correctable'. The metaphor thus helps construct sympathy as a perspectival, detached, non-egoistic, and correctable act (Griswold 2010: 68; original emphasis).

7   For Barthes, there are two different kinds of *punctum*. On the one hand, the *punctum* can simply refer to a detail or aspect of a photograph that for some irrational and illogical reason subjectively affects me. In this sense, the *punctum* 'shows no preference for morality or good taste: the *punctum* can be ill-bred' (Barthes 1981: 43). It is what my eye zeroes in on and obsesses over. It operates at the level of the unconscious. The other *punctum* does not have to do with visual detail but simply with the temporal aspect of photography that gives it its 'intensity' (Barthes 1981: 96).

8   Marshall's discussion on this point is very helpful: 'The moral of *The Theory of Moral Sentiments* is that one should not display one's sentiments unless one is sure of eliciting sympathy; indeed, it would be best not to display oneself at all, given the small likelihood of attaining fellow-feeling. This ethic of self-command (one might say self-concealment) helps explain the almost total absence of women from the world of *The Theory of Moral Sentiments*. One might expect Smith to have more to say about women in a treatise on moral sentiments written in an age that closely associated both sympathy and sentiment with "feminine" sensibilities; yet precisely these qualities appear to exclude women from the book' (Marshall 1984: 604). I would not go so far as to claim that Smith excludes women, but I do agree that the general ethos of Smith's book is masculine rather than feminine.

9   Other references to the stoic North American 'savage' appear in *TMS* I.ii.1.12 and VII.ii.1.28. On Smith's possible sources, especially Lafitau's *Moeurs des sauvages ameriquains*, see Ross (2010: 177–178).

10   For a more extensive discussion of Rousseau and Smith on pity, see Griswold (2010).

11   For interesting discussions of other examples of this Chinese hypothesis, see Ginzburg (2001) and Hayot (2009).

12   See Forman-Barzilai (2010: 137–195).

13   Michael Fried makes a similar point when he writes that the digitization of photographs, 'with its implication that the contents of the photograph have been significantly altered or even created out of whole cloth by its maker, threatens to dissolve the "adherence" of the referent to the photograph', without which Barthes's *punctum* would lose its power (Fried 2008: 107).

14   Dora Apel argues that such measures primarily serve a disciplinary rather than a protective purpose. She writes, 'The invidious practice of surveilling the body to contain and control the population promotes the illusion of safety through fear of the pervasive potential of terror without actually providing greater protection' (Apel 2008: 263).

15   'regard, v.', in OED Online, at: www.oed.com/view/Entry/161187?rskey=fXUDoo& result=2 (accessed 22 March 2015).

Bibliography

Apel, D. (2008) 'Technologies of war, media, and dissent in the post 9/11 work of Krzysztof Wodiczko', *Oxford Art Journal*, 31: 261–280.

Barthes, R. (1981) *Camera Lucida: Reflections on Photography*, trans. R. Howard, New York: Hill and Wang.

Bender, J. (1987) *Imagining the Penitentiary: Fiction and the Architecture of Mind in Eighteenth-Century England*, Chicago: University of Chicago Press.

Benjamin, W. (1999) 'Little history of photography', in *Selected Writings*, Volume 2: *1927–1934*, trans. Rodney Livingstone *et al.*, Cambridge, MA: Belknap Press, 507–530.

Boltanski, L. (1999) *Distant Suffering: Morality, Media and Politics*, trans. G. Burchell, Cambridge: Cambridge University Press.

Brissenden, R. F. (1969) 'Authority, guilt, and anxiety in *The Theory of Moral Sentiments*', *Texas Studies in Literature and Language*, 11: 945–962.

Brown, V. (1994) *Adam Smith's Discourse: Canonicity, Commerce and Conscience*, London: Routledge.

Burke, E. (1990) *A Philosophical Enquiry into the Origin of our Ideas of the Sublime and Beautiful*, ed. A. Phillips, Oxford: Oxford University Press.

Butler, J. (2005) 'Photography, war, outrage', *PMLA*, 120: 822–827.

Choe, S. (2007) 'Unearthing war's horrors years later in South Korea', *New York Times*, 3 December, at: www.nytimes.com/2007/12/03/world/asia/03korea.html (accessed 22 March 2015).

Chouliaraki, L. (2013) 'The humanity of war: iconic photojournalism of the battlefield, 1914–2012', *Visual Communication*, 12: 315–340.

Crary, J. (1990) *Techniques of the Observer: On Vision and Modernity in the Nineteenth Century*, Cambridge, MA: MIT Press.

De Bolla, P. (2003) *The Education of the Eye: Painting, Landscape, and Architecture in Eighteenth-Century Britain*, Stanford, CA: Stanford University Press.

Der Derian, J. (2005) 'Imaging terror: logos, pathos and ethos', *Third World Quarterly*, 26: 23–37.

Feldman, A. (2004) 'Securocratic wars of public safety: globalized policing as scopic regime', *Interventions*, 6: 330–350.

Forman-Barzilai, F. (2010) *Adam Smith and the Circles of Sympathy: Cosmopolitanism and Moral Theory*, Cambridge: Cambridge University Press.

Friday, J. (2000) 'Demonic curiosity and the aesthetics of documentary photography', *British Journal of Aesthetics*, 40: 356–375.

Fried, M. (2008) 'Barthes's *punctum*', in *Why Photography Matters as Art as Never Before*, New Haven, CT: Yale University Press, 95–114.

Ginzburg, C. (2001) 'To kill a Chinese mandarin: the moral implications of distance', in *Wooden Eyes: Nine Reflections on Distance*, trans. M. Ryle and K. Soper, New York: Columbia University Press, 157–172.

Griswold, C. L. Jr. (2010) 'Smith and Rousseau in dialogue: sympathy, *pitié*, spectatorship and narrative', *Adam Smith Review*, 5: 59–84.

Hayot, E. (2009) *The Hypothetical Mandarin: Sympathy, Modernity, and Chinese Pain*, New York: Oxford University Press.

Ignatieff, M. (1986) 'Smith, Rousseau and the republic of needs', in T. C. Smout (ed.), *Scotland and Europe, 1200–1850*, Edinburgh: J. Donald, 187–206.

Jay, M. (1993) *Downcast Eyes: The Denigration of Vision in Twentieth-Century French Thought*, Berkeley: University of California Press.

Linfield, S. (2010) *The Cruel Radiance: Photography and Political Violence*, Chicago: University of Chicago Press.

Marshall, D. (1984) 'Adam Smith and the theatricality of moral sentiments', *Critical Inquiry*, 10: 592–613.

Min, E. K. (2002) 'Adam Smith and the debt of gratitude', in M. Osteen (ed.), *The Question of the Gift: Essays across Disciplines*, London: Routledge, 132–146.

Mirzoeff, N. (1999) *An Introduction to Visual Culture*, London: Routledge.

Peters, J. D. (1995) 'Publicity and pain: self-abstraction in Adam Smith's *Theory of Moral Sentiments*', *Public Culture*, 7: 657–684.

Phillips, A. (1999) 'Introduction', in E. Burke, *A Philosophical Enquiry into the Origin of our Ideas of the Sublime and Beautiful*, Oxford: Oxford University Press, ix–xxiii.

Pitts, J. (2005) *A Turn to Empire: The Rise of Imperial Liberalism in Britain and France*, Princeton, NJ: Princeton University Press.

Rancière, J. (2009) *The Emancipated Spectator*, trans. G. Elliott, New York: Verso.

Ross, I. (2010) *The Life of Adam Smith*, 2nd edn, Oxford: Oxford University Press.

Rousseau, J.-J. (1990) *The First and Second Discourses*, trans. V. Gourevitch, New York: Harper & Row.

Scarry, E. (1987) *The Body in Pain: The Making and Unmaking of the World*, New York: Oxford University Press.

Silver, A. (1997) '"Two different sorts of commerce": friendship and strangership in civil society', in J. Weintraub and K. Kumar (eds), *Public and Private in Thought and Practice: Perspectives on a Grand Dichotomy*, Chicago: University of Chicago Press.

Siraki, A. T. (2010) 'Adam Smith's solution to the paradox of tragedy', *Adam Smith Review*, 5: 59–84.

Smith, A. (1976) *The Theory of Moral Sentiments*, ed. D. D. Raphael and A. L. Macfie, vol. 1 of *The Works and Correspondence of Adam Smith*, Oxford: Clarendon Press; Glasgow edition.

Sontag, S. (1977) *On Photography*, New York: Farrar, Straus and Giroux.

Sontag, S. (2003) *Regarding the Pain of Others*, New York: Farrar, Straus and Giroux.

Walton, K. (1984) 'Transparent pictures: on the nature of photographic realism', *Critical Inquiry*, 11: 246–277.

Adam Smith's early German readers

Reception, misreception, and critique

Fania Oz-Salzberger

Introduction

Adam Smith's earliest German reception came in several stages, which run roughly parallel to the profound historical and geopolitical changes associated with the demise of the Holy Roman Empire and the rise of Prussian supremacy. The late Enlightenment saw the early translations of *The Theory of Moral Sentiments* (by Christian Rautenberg, 1770) and *The Wealth of Nations* (by J. F. Schiller, 1776–8). The era of Napoleonic upheaval and war dovetailed with a second and highly effective translation of the latter (by Christian Garve, 1794–6) and the emergence of specialist German Smithians, especially from the University of Göttingen. The Stein–Hardenberg reforms in Prussia, signaling a recovery from defeat and launching Prussia's ascendancy in the early nineteenth century, ran parallel to a deeper reading in Smith, which partially impacted these reforms.

This story has often been told in overly simplistic terms. Some modern scholars still abide by Wilhelm Roscher's nineteenth-century saying that "the whole of political economy might be divided into two parts – before and since Adam Smith; the first part being a prelude, and the second a sequel" (quoted by Cliffe Leslie, 1875, p. 97). However, reception processes of paradigm-shifting works are never that simple. The early German reception of Smith's thought was a tortuous process, involving misunderstandings as well as deliberate shifts of meaning and context.

This paper offers an account of the earliest German receptions of Adam Smith's work, with a particular emphasis on misreception: the ways, often creative in themselves, in which his ideas, breakthroughs and emphases were misread, and at times deflected from the original contexts and set of intentions clearly traceable in the original works. I will also suggest that Smith's earliest German readers recognized his rootedness in the Scottish Enlightenment far more than his later readers, who removed him from that context and largely ignored his Scottish environs. Thus, the singling-out of Smith was also a process of decontextualization.

Adam Smith's German debut

The history of German political economy, as W. G. F. Roscher showed in his monumental *Geschichte der Nationalökonomie in Deutschland* (1874), grew from the university-proffered Cameralist "science," a far more academic origin than its English (or British) counterpart, where practical questions such as money, foreign trade and taxation were studied first, and grand theories followed later. From the late fifteenth century, when the Emperor Maximilian established his *Kammer* (deriving from the Latin *camera*), following the example of Burgundy, many German rulers kept a council or a small group of officials to manage the economic affairs of the regent, and oversee all aspects of societal economic behavior affecting his lawful rights and deserts. Gradually these councils acquired extensive executive powers. The rise of German universities met the need for theory to instruct economic practice, and, in an academizing process that was far earlier and more thorough than in any other European region, the science of Cameralism took root (Roscher, 1874; cf. Ingram, 1888, ch. 5). The University of Halle, followed by Göttingen, situated itself as a bastion of Cameralist teaching, mainly but not solely for the consumption of the growing Prussian administration. Students were taught practical and "natural" aspects of national economy, such as agriculture and forestry, and at the same time imbibed the mercantile doctrine that held sway during the seventeenth century and into the eighteenth. By the time of the arrival of Smith in Germany, institutionalized and time-honored Cameralist theory ruled the major universities. The formative works of J. H. G. Justi (1717–71) served as textbooks of Cameralism in its moderate Enlightenment form: he approved of relative economic liberalism and the inviolability of private property, but all within a carefully monitored, state-controlled structure that would allow frequent governmental intervention whenever good order was at risk of spinning out of control. By the last quarter of the eighteenth century, Physiocratic ideas were entering German intellectual circles with some success, albeit more in the learned journals than in the universities. But many thinkers were content with the Cameralism of a moderate, rational ruler, such as Frederick II ("the Great") of Prussia was deemed to be. The Scottish theorist James Steuart, Smith's nemesis, offered German readers a welcome mix of moderate mercantilism and what became known as "English liberty" on a small scale. Other thinkers, notably the Italian Genovesi and the Austrian Sonnenfels, belonged on the same shelf. But it was the Scottish Steuart – who became known in German about a decade before Smith – who arguably delayed the reception of Smith's "true meaning" – the understanding of his revolutionary economic proposals – in the German lands (cf. Ingram (1888) and, more recently and persuasively, Tribe (1988)).

From about the 1750s, a tide of German translations from the English marked a British–German cultural exchange that openly and defiantly circumnavigated France. To be sure, the surviving database of the Leipzig book fair proves that translations from French never lost their lead (Kiesel and Münch, 1997, p. 197), but in the fields of philosophy and art theory, as well as *belles lettres*, English works gained a qualitative advantage. The final decades of the eighteenth century were characterized by prompt, eagerly awaited and intensely discussed German publications of translated English poetry, drama and novels, as well as a broad range of theoretical texts in moral philosophy, aesthetics and political economy, notably those of the Scottish Enlightenment. Eagerness for Scottish works among

German readers was so great – and criticism of some translations so poignant – that several books were translated two or three times in the late eighteenth century. Although the average period between original publication and German translation is estimated – for such authors as Adam Ferguson, John Millar and Hugh Blair – at about nine and a half years, peak-period translations were often in press within a year of the first English editions. *The Wealth of Nations* is a case in point: the first volume of its first German translation appeared in 1776, the same year as the original English-language publication (Price and Price, 1934; Fabian, 1976; Oz-Salzberger, 1995).

While frequency and speed of translation can attest to the inner tensions of the German book market (such as tough competition and variable standards), other factors provide more solid evidence for the great and rising German interest in Scottish works: numerous reprints and new editions of translated works and, chiefly from the 1780s, even English-language reprints (Fabian, 1976, pp. 133–7).

Adam Smith was one of the Scottish authors who made a successful entry into the German Enlightenment, alongside Hume, Ferguson, Kames and Millar. His earliest reception in Germany, while generally positive, was neither unique nor outstanding in comparison with that of Hume or Ferguson. It is symptomatic of Smith-centered scholarship that a great deal is made of German praise for Smith during that earliest phase, without noting that other Scottish thinkers fared similarly well or better, and that very little of that praise was linked to any substantive discussion or interpretation of Smith's main ideas.

Thus, Smith's *Theory of Moral Sentiments* (1759) was rendered into German only in 1770, compared with Hume's *Enquiry Concerning the Principles of Morals* (1751), which appeared in German translation as early as 1756. Indeed, a translation of Hume's *Political Discourses* (1752) was published in Hamburg just two years after the original English-language edition (Price, 1934). When the speed of translation from British sources accelerated during the 1770s, Smith's *Wealth of Nations* benefited too, although, as we shall see, the quality of the first translation did not match its promptness.

Similarly, while *WN* was translated into German twice within a span of two decades – a better translation replacing the original one – this was by no means an exception, as other Scottish works were also translated twice, with Hume peaking at three German translations during the second half of the eighteenth century (Gawlick and Kreimendahl, 1987; Kuehn, 2005). And, although *WN* earned prominent and glowing reviews in major learned journals, including the *Göttingische Gelehrte Anzeigen* and the *Allgemeine Deutsche Bibliothek*, this was hardly an exception to the welcoming of other Scottish works, notably Hume's *Enquiry Concerning Human Understanding* and even his "stillborn" (but not in Germany!) *Treatise of Human Nature*, alongside Ferguson's *Essay on the History of Civil Society* and *Institutes of Moral Philosophy*, and works by Thomas Reid and James Beatty (Kuehn, 2005; Oz-Salzberger, 1995). *All* were glowingly reviewed; Smith was by no means singled out.

More importantly, while Hume's ideas were already part of a heated debate during the 1750s, especially amongst the anti-scepticist philosophers of Berlin and Halle, Smith's political economy gleaned very meager substantive responses (other than general praise) during the first two decades of its German reception. Thus, as Keith Tribe has shown, German readers were during that time far more open to James Steuart's political economy than to Smith's challenge. We shall return to this early reception in more detail later (Tribe 1988, ch. 7).

Likewise, much has been made of Kant's "favoring" of Smith. But Kant barely mentions Smith in his entire opus (save in passing) or in his letters. On 9 July 1771 Kant's close disciple and correspondent Marcus Herz wrote him a letter which made the following remark: "I have various comments to make about the Englishman Smith who, Herr Friedländer tells me, is your favorite" (Kant, 1999, p. 130). This statement is not corroborated, and, to be sure, Kant himself is notoriously ungenerous in acknowledging his intellectual sources or inspirations. So all of Smith's impact on Kant, or intellectual preferences that were common to both, must be traced via philosophical comparisons rather than documented readings and direct impact. Adam Smith did not share the privilege of David Hume, and was never acknowledged by Kant as a philosophical alarm clock or even a substantial scholarly source.

A Smithian vista opened up to German readers capable of deep-end analysis and reception (or rejection) of his ideas only in the mid-1790s, at the very end of the German Enlightenment and its ancien régime, predominantly "the Age of Frederick." In the following decade and a half of conquest, political turbulence and economic rethinking (at times bordering on revolution), Smith came into his own among German readers and leaders, notably the Prussian reformers Stein and Hardenberg.

It has long been acknowledged that the abandonment of mercantilism and temporary weakening of Cameralism, in the wake of Prussia's defeat at the hands of Napoleon, opened the floodgates to Smith-inspired reforms. French influence eased the way toward new free-market thinking, nurtured by the Physiocratic tradition, of which Smith was either mistaken for a full-fledged member or accepted as a worthy offshoot (Lai, 2000).

However, by the time Smith's ideas were ripe for serious German discussion and implementation, his Scottish context was already beginning to ebb away. His commitments to the Scottish Enlightenment's priorities, including a measure of civic engagement and civil equality, a strong emphasis on the "public sphere" and residual republican convictions were all wiped off the table. A new concept of "civil society" – the German (including the Hegelian) *bürgerliche Gesellschaft* – emerged, replacing the Lockeian and Scottish *societas civilis*, necessitating the constant attention of active citizens. Insofar as Smith inspired the political economy of early nineteenth-century German statehood, his ideas now belonged squarely in the *bürgerliche Gesellschaft* that paralleled the private sphere, its individuals pursuing their economic self-interest as subjects under the gaze of a benign ruler or the officialdom of the state (*Staat*). The residual republicanism of the Scottish Enlightenment, which the eighteenth-century Smith still carried, disappeared under this new reading lamp.

Earliest German readers of Smith: 1770–93

German readers of the Scottish Enlightenment, whether in the original English or in German translation, did not find all of its ideas easy to digest. Whereas Kames's and Millar's accounts of the progress of mankind and civilization appealed easily to historians (e.g. Isaak Iselin, Gotthold Ephraim Lessing and J. G. Herder, all of them avid readers of Scottish works), other aspects of the Scottish Enlightenment were far more disturbing for mainstream German sensibilities. For instance, Hume's attack on established religion was almost universally unacceptable to German readers, and it was often misread or deflected, especially in German translations, into a softer version that reintroduced theism and a philosophy of faith (Berlin, 1981). Similarly, Ferguson's republicanism, which shunned monarchy and embraced an active, arms-bearing, political-minded citizenry, was either attacked or ignored by most of his German admirers (Oz-Salzberger, 1995).

How did Smith fare during the late Enlightenment, in the era Kant dubbed "the Age of Frederick [the Great]"? On the one hand, *WN* broke away from the civic tradition – most ardently represented in the Scottish Enlightenment by his friend and rival Adam Ferguson – by abandoning the flag of politicized citizenry and civil militia. Instead, Smith followed Hume (and both were inspired by Bernard Mandeville) in developing a theory of political economy where individual, indeed selfish, pursuit of wealth could enhance everyone's welfare by fitting into the great natural course. Hume's and Smith's models of modernity envisaged a large private sphere pursuing the self-interests of a multitude of individuals, uninterrupted by governmental encroachment, but safeguarded by the British doctrine of parliamentary sovereignty and an effective judiciary (Robertson, 1983). The key figure in this philosophy is the polite, commercial individual, not the military-minded, politically vocal citizen. A good polity is governed by laws that are monitored by reason, upheld by subjects enjoying rights and observing duties, and vouchsafed by stable institutes.

One might expect this mild monarchism to appeal to mainstream German readers, or at least not to upset them. But Smith was not a typical defender of monarchy, and certainly not of the brand that was practiced in the Holy Roman Empire. Along with Hume (and Kant), he modernized, and at times revolutionized, the theory of the law-governed state. Smith's legalism dovetails with Hume's and Kant's, while working against the grain of Ferguson and Herder. His world is law-governed rather than led by the collective will of a nation or a republic. Natural laws are at work, and human laws must reinforce rather than hinder them, in strict adherence to the dictates of reason alone. Individual will is important, but it works best – Kant may have recognized their like-mindedness on this crucial point – when it adheres, undisturbed, to nature's basic laws of self-preservation and self-promotion. Governmental decrees should either underscore this basic natural dynamic or complement its deficiencies (providing such public services that the market alone will not sustain), or cease to exist.

Moreover, the Smithian model of economic liberty goes a long way beyond what Germany's (primarily Prussia's) prevailing Cameralist theory would allow.

Deeper still, his law-abiding government, gently overseeing the society of manufacturers and traders from a viable distance, is very far from the absolutist – or the hands-on, paternal – figure of the German prince and his tax-levying, customs-charging, market-intervening officialdom. At this deep end, Smith's ideas were poised to challenge not only Cameralism but also the uncontained monarchism of the ancien régime and indeed much of the stately authoritarianism of post-Napoleonic Germany.

This set of dissonances was not immediately recognized during the earliest phase of Smith's German reception. It is crucial to note that much of the immediate context was missing in translation. John Locke's political treatises were little trans-lated and little read in Germany throughout the eighteenth century. The reception for Montesquieu's *De l'esprit des lois* was highly selective, generally disregarding his thrust against unlimited monarchy. Thus, most German readers could not recognize either the suspicion of governmental encroachment (that Smith shared with Locke) or the abandoning of an aristocratic counterbalance to monarchy (replaced by courts and the middle class in both Montesquieu and Smith). Most crucially, very few German readers of Smith were able to acknowledge his point (inspired by and shared with Locke and Montesquieu) that the sovereign, the wielder of executive power, is no fairy godmother of liberty; indeed, that liberty must sometimes be defended *against* the sovereign (Oz-Salzberger, 1995).

Thus, when German reviewers and commentators incorporated his model of liberty into the far stronger paradigm of state-controlled national economy (Treue, 1951) their unfamiliarity with the philosophical build-up toward Smith's political economy facilitated this process of misreception.

Christian Rautenberg translated the third edition of *The Theory of Moral Sentiments*, "To which is added a Dissertation on the Origin of Languages" (London: A. Millar, 1767) into German as *Theorie der moralischen Empfindungen* (Braunschweig: Meyer, 1770). On 9 July 1771, as I have already mentioned, Marcus Herz wrote to Kant, "I have various comments to make about the Englishman Smith who, Herr Friedländer tells me, is your favorite [*Liebling*]" (quoted in Waszek, 2006, p. 56). It is important to note that neither Kant nor Herz elaborated on his reason for favoring Smith. Furthermore, Herz mentioned several other Scottish writers as favored by Kant. We are therefore left with no direct evidence of Smith–Kant influence, and must resort to the second-best strategy of comparative surmise and scholarly inference.

One interesting early explanation for Kant's affinity with Smith's *TMS* appears in Christian Garve's work on the history of moral philosophy of 1798:

> Smith assumes that a person has the rational ability to judge his own actions correctly when he does so at a certain distance. The greater the height from which reason surveys, and the more it includes not only the person's indi-vidual actions, but all the similar actions of other people; with so much the greater certainty can its decision be relied upon. But this is the height from which the legislator watches human behaviour. So Smith's sympathizing spectator is in fact Kant's legislator.
>
> (Trans. and quoted by Haakonssen, 1996, p. 148)

Modern scholars have built upon this and other common denominators, construing – to quote two notable studies – "Kantian themes in Smith" (Haakonssen, 1996, p. 148) or "Kant's Response to the *Wealth of Nations*" (Fleischacker, 1996). Much of this interesting work centers, like Garve's original pointer, on *TMS*. There is, however, at least one direct reference made by Kant to "Adam Smith," in *The Metaphysics of Morals* (1797), when he refers to money as "that material thing the alienation of which is the means and at the same time the measure of industry by which human beings and nations carry on trade with one another" (Kant, 1996, p. 71), which betrays acquaintance with at least one doctrine of *WN*. However, the paucity of Kant's direct dealings with Smith leaves this path of reception beyond the focus of this paper, which is on professed readers, conveyors and discussants.

We can nevertheless make use of Kant (never, of course, merely as a means to an end) to demonstrate the art of paraphrase. Numerous reviewers and writers in eighteenth-century Germany made allusions to Scottish ideas by way of paraphrase, a viable scholarly instrument in the era. Thus, Kant, in his introduction to his earlier work *Groundwork of the Metaphysics of Morals* (1785), wryly announces that he will be limiting himself only to the title discipline, rather than embarking on conventional moral theory with "empirical" as well as "rational" segments, because "All trades, crafts and arts have gained by the division of labor, namely when one person does not do everything but limits himself to a certain task that differs markedly from others in the way it is to be handled" (Kant, 1998, p. 2). This is obviously a (somewhat tongue in cheek) allusion to Smith's thesis. The choice of words suggests that Kant knowingly related to Smith's "division of labor" rather than Ferguson's "separation of arts and professions" or Millar's "separation of ranks" and other Scottish phrasings of the general theme that preceded Smith's specific twist.

By way of counter-example, when Friedrich Schiller writes of the debilitating effect of social and economic hierarchy, his lexicon points to Ferguson, and possibly Millar, rather than to Smith: "[O]nce the increasingly complex machinery of state necessitated a more rigorous separation of ranks and occupations, then the inner unity of human nature was severed too, and a disastrous conflict set its harmonious powers at variance" (Schiller, *Sixth Letter on the Aesthetic Education of Man*, quoted in Oz-Salzberger, 1995, pp. 306–7).

While paraphrases can be very informative, especially in conjunction with direct quotes and named engagements, when mapping eighteenth-century receptions, the present paper primarily concentrates on the latter two categories of primary sources. We therefore move to the earliest translations and reviews of Smith's *WN* in Germany.

The University of Göttingen was, from its establishment in 1737, a hub of British culture and a gateway in particular for Scottish philosophy and history into mainstream German scholarship. It was the most innovative German university in the eighteenth century, and had the strongest ties to Britain. Inaugurated by Gerlach Adolf von Münchhausen, the Hanoverian minister of King George II, it soon became the leading and most fashionable German university, with an outstanding group of professors and a select body of German (and British) students.

Its fame rested on its renowned scholars, fresh academic emphases and innovative teaching methods. Two advantages stemmed from its close connection with Britain: considerable academic freedom; and an excellent library. The four faculties – theology, law, medicine and philosophy – enjoyed almost equal status, and theology was restrained from censuring the others. Against the harsh competition and declining standards of Germany's all too numerous universities, this blend of moderation and innovation enabled Göttingen to survive and to prosper. Its *Anglophilie* – one facet of its fashionable image – meant that its positive reception for the Scottish writers was part of a general warm welcome for all things "English." The dynastic and administrative link between Hanover and Britain was readily echoed by cultural and intellectual tastes. Some of Göttingen's leading lights in the eighteenth century, notably Haller, Michaelis and Lichtenberg, traveled to England and became enthusiastic Anglophiles. Other professors were quick to buy, read and review new editions of English and Scottish works, sometimes in the original language but most often in German translations, as soon as they appeared. Among them were Feder, Meiners, Gatterer, Schlözer and Pütter (Hasek, 1925, p. 62; Bödeker, 1992; Oz-Salzberger, 1995, ch. 10).

Göttingen educated many future Prussian officials alongside members of the government apparatuses of numerous other German principalities. Among them were the great Prussian reformers Stein and Hardenberg. The prevailing economic theory was Cameralist, but at times tinged with a degree of liberalism. For many of the Göttingen professors, Anglophiles as they were, British economic thought (and practice), like British political thought (and practice), carried charming and alien uniquenesses, an "English liberty" (*englische Freiheit*) that Germans could not, and should not, emulate without careful reflection and/or long preparation. Educating administrators, closely linked to the Prussian regime and avowedly "practical" in its educational orientation, the University of Göttingen was self-consciously selective about the theories and practices it imported from Britain. Thus, even before Smith's *WN* arrived, the Hanoverian professors-cum-book reviewers had already developed a friendly yet cautious attitude to Scottish ideas (Hasek, 1925, pp. 60–3; Oz-Salzberger, 1995, ch. 3).

J. G. H. Feder, a prominent Göttingen philosopher and frequent reviewer of Scottish works in the *Göttingische Gelehrte Anzeigen*, reviewed *WN* promptly after the first volume of the German translation appeared in 1776. Feder taught Stein, and directly influenced both Kant (whom he attacked) and Hegel. But his engagement with Smith was far from substantial. His favorable review – he called the book "a classic" – did not delve deep into Smith's theories. Feder duly acknowledged that Smith presented serious opposition to James Steuart, Germany's favored political economist at that time. He also recognized Smith's proximity to the Physiocrats – an early example of a longer line of German scholars who conjoined Smith and Physiocracy without offering sharper distinctions (Lai, 2000).

While positively drawn to the idea of *laissez-faire*, Feder nevertheless critiqued, a little offhandedly, Smith's account of competition: "The inferior goods and deceptions which result from too great competition . . . the ruin of many . . . forced under through excessive competition, appear to be evils that outweigh any gains of such complete freedom" (*Göttingische Gelehrte Anzeigen*, 10 March 1777; quoted by Hasek, 1925, p. 64). Alongside several other specific rejoinders, Feder's main point about Smith's doctrine was that it was not a universal brand, and did not fit German economies as they stood: "many of his propositions dare not be incorporated in the universal principles of state, but are valid only at a certain stage of industry, wealth and enlightenment" (ibid.). This dovetails with his similar accusations against several "untenable principles" in Ferguson's *Institutes of Moral Philosophy*, which also point at excessive ideas of liberty, arguably applicable to Britons but not to contemporaneous Germans. In the case of Ferguson, Feder interestingly rejected any wholesale denouncement of slavery, as well as the claim that "a despot is always a usurper" (Oz-Salzberger, 1995, p. 242).

The Cameralist distaste is clearly voiced when Feder defends government regulation of consumption against Smith:

> [Smith] finds it quite vain and impertinent when kings and their ministers watch the economy of private persons, and seek to limit their expenditures by sumptuary laws and embargoes on foreign goods (a judgment, whose very expression betrays too much heat).
>
> (Feder is referring here to *WN* 346; quoted by Hasek, 1925, p. 64, fn. 3)

Clearly, then, Smith's political economy, to the degree it was understood and digested by Feder, was an attractive feat of scholarship marred by excessive enthusiasm for freedom of "private persons," a disrespect for ministers and kings, and a bid to curb what most Germans would consider the benign intervention of paternalistic crowned heads.

Feder's review places him, however, quite high on the scale of serious engagements with Smith during the first two decades of his German reception. Feder obviously read the book and grappled with some aspects of Smith's doctrine. Typically for a liberal-leaning German Enlightenment author, he was unwilling either to dismiss Smith's "English freedom" (as another reviewer dubbed it when critiquing Ferguson) or to cross swords with his "Physiocracy." Göttingen scholars could have it both ways, but they continued to teach Cameralist theory to their students, the future statesmen.

Two other major reviews from the same era, alongside many more marginal mentions and quotes, are on record. Both the anonymous reviewer of the two volumes of *WN*'s German translation in the *Allgemeine deutsche Bibliothek* (1777 and 1779) and the Swiss Isaak Iselin's review in his journal *Ephemeriden der Menschheit* (1777) treated Smith as a Physiocrat, and did little more than sum up, selectively, the more Physiocratic-tinged elements of his theses. Their impact was therefore small (Tribe, 2007, pp. 25–6).

It took a new translation, and a generation of repentant ex-Cameralists, to turn Smith into a household name among the economists and political thinkers of the Holy Roman Empire. But by then Smith's association with the Scottish Enlightenment's residual republicanism, with the "English freedom" of Ferguson and other Scottish thinkers, had declined.

The era of transition: 1794–1806

As mentioned earlier, the first German translation of *WN* was made by J. F. Schiller, of whom little is known, although according to some sources he lived in London, and according to others he was a cousin of the poet and philosopher Friedrich Schiller. There was general agreement that the translation was unsatisfactory and at times even incorrect, but also acknowledgment – as Sartorius put it – that "the original [English text] is extremely difficult," full of "technical and juridical expressions" (quoted by Hasek, 1925, p. 63, fn. 4).

Christian Garve's brilliant second translation of 1794/6 was therefore poised to open a new era in Smith's German reception, not least due to its timing, during the sensitive transition from the French Revolution to the Napoleonic wars and conquests, with many German readers already deeply troubled about the imminent fate of the Holy Roman Empire and the post-Frederician Prussian state.

Garve's rendering, with a preface and numerous notes, is seen as a key factor in Smith's somewhat belated German success. Earlier, but comparably, the same translator's excellent German version of Ferguson's *Institutes of Moral Philosophy* had overshadowed C. F. Jünger's unimpressive translation of the same author's much more original and important *Essay on the History of Civil Society*. Garve had known and admired *TMS* for a long time, calling its author "the true and profound Smith," but at the same time rejecting the major aspects of Smith's notion of sympathy. It is noteworthy that Garve made his most influential translations of British works into German during the 1770s, so Smith was a late addition in Garve's career: his time came in the mid-1790s, when most of the other Scottish Enlightenment authors were already slipping into obscurity (Zart, 1881, pp. 197–9; Oz-Salzberger, 1995, ch. 8).

But no less decisive than Garve's input was the unsettling impact of the French Revolution and the Prussian defeat by France, which gradually registered in academic and economic circles. Thus, a commonly echoed claim that "by the 1790s" Göttingen had become "a flourishing nucleus of Smithianism in the otherwise hostile German climate" (Rothbard, 2006, p. 494) is only partially true. In fact, by 1794 – when the first part of Garve's translation was published – Göttingen knew of Smith, but it had still not registered (and nor was it teaching) what he was about. This situation gradually started to change, but Smith had little real impact in the German lands before 1806.

Friedrich Georg Sartorius, Freiherr von Walterhausen (1765–1828), was a pioneering Smith specialist during the transitional phase. A student of several prominent Göttingen professors with English interests, notably Feder, he became a history teacher, and during the 1790s moved on to political and economic science. His *Handbuch der Staatswirthschaft* (Berlin, 1796) offered a pioneering compendium of Adam Smith's economic doctrines.

While most scholars (such as Roscher) have argued that Sartorius's *Handbuch* provides a reasonable short summary of the whole of *WN*, Keith Tribe has shown that it deviates significantly from the original text, especially in the latter sections:

The greatest and most significant divergence comes in the treatment of Smith's Book V, marked by a shift from précis to commentary, where the expenses and revenues of a state are assessed with respect to a specific objective of the state, "the security of all native persons and rightfully established law." This places the various institutions that appear in *Wealth of Nations* with respect to a *Staatszweck* [purpose of the state] which is proper to *Polizeiwissenschaft*, and is not clearly in evidence in Smith's text.

(Tribe, 2007, p. 27)

There is an element of understatement here, especially in light of Smith's later German followers, who adopted Sartorius's selective emphases. Tribe is more interested in the growing dissonance between Smithians who adhered to Cameralism and those who moved toward a philosophy of economic liberty. However, my alternative emphasis is that Smith was pushed into an extremist non-interventionism in order to leave space for Cameralist-size intervention in the public sphere. Sartorius and his generation obliterated Smith's civilian-oriented duties of government – the idea that even a minimalist administration in a self-regulating economy must use some of its revenues to promote the universal civil wellbeing that the market is unable to maintain. Note that for Sartorius, Book V of *WN* is only about the state's *security* expenses (and, briefly, its legal apparatus) as viable outlets for its legitimate revenues. Smith's discussion of public works, including the infrastructure of transportation and communication, and especially his treatment of education are not points of interest. However, these provisions are made by Smith in the context of a civil-minded, and even egalitarian, view of the basic deserts of society as a whole. Smith's non-paternalistic approach to the education of the poor, and to ensuring public standards of living for all, did not cross over to his German recipients.

The powerful emphasis on "security" as the state's only justifiable channel of public spending fell easily into place as part of the German academic tradition of *Polizeiwissenschaft*, which fed the Prussian administrative priorities of the late eighteenth century. Another Cameralist author of a Smithian compendium, F. B. Weber, who published his *Systematisches Handbuch der Staatswirthschaft* in Berlin in 1804, employed the Smithian vocabulary of "national wealth" to argue, wholly against the grain of Smith's original text, that the "goal of the internal administration of the state" is economic regulation and *Polizei* (Tribe, 2007, pp. 28–9). Once again, minimalistic public works give way to full-fledged paternalistic interventionism.

It was another ten years before Sartorius published three more Smith-oriented books. Both his approach and, more importantly, German geopolitics had significantly altered by then, and this forged his Smithian creed (Hasek, 1925, pp. 72–8; Rothbard, 2006, pp. 494–5).

1806: the tipping point of Smith reception in Germany

Two of Sartorius's 1806 volumes – *Von den Elementen des National-Reichthums* and *von der Staatswirthschaft, nach Adam Smith* (*Concerning the Elements of*

National Wealth and *State Economy According to Adam Smith*) – systematically covered all of the principal doctrines of *WN*. The third, which presented Sartorius's own ideas, was titled *Abhandlungen, die Elemente des Nationalreichthums und die Staatswirthschaft* (*Essays on National Wealth and State Economy*). This aired Sartorius's disagreements with Smith, including an attack on the latter's theory of value, "a strange and deceptive conclusion," in Sartorius's view, since labor, Smith's determinant of value, is a variable rather than a constant. More interesting, for our context, is that Sartorius now distanced himself from Smith's view of government's proper sphere and joined moderate Cameralism in advocating frequent intervention (Rothbard, 2006, p. 495). This move undermines Sartorius's fame as a pioneer of Göttingen's "flourishing nucleus of Smithianism." In effect, this early disseminator of *WN* stepped back and "de-Smithed" Adam Smith.

Was the impact of Austria's humiliation in the Battle of Austerlitz – which was preceded by the dissolution of the Holy Roman Empire at the hands of Napoleonic France and followed by Prussia's beating at Jena-Auerstadt – a resounding death knell to Cameralism? Not necessarily. Between 1803 and 1815, Smith's reception in the German-speaking lands, which ran in parallel to their military and political upheavals, occasionally yielded contradictory results. An opposite shift – into a radical embrace of Smith's idea of freedom – came from August Ferdinand Lueder (1760–1819), Sartorius's near contemporary, fellow-student and then fellow-professor at Göttingen. While Sartorius moved away from Smithian convictions, Lueder adopted a radicalized Smithian position.

Significantly, Lueder spent much of his professional life as a loyal servant of the Cameralist approach, both in practice and in theory: he was a court councilor to the Duke of Braunschweig and a proponent of the new academic field of *Statistik*, pioneered by August Ludwig von Schlözer (1735–1809). However, under the stress of historical events, as he himself confessed at length, he abandoned his faith in state-administered economy and embraced a radical liberalism informed (or, arguably, *misinformed*) by his reading of Smith.

Translating *Statistik* as "statistics" (as both Rothbard (2006) and Hasek (1925) do) clouds both its etymology and the new discipline's intended utility. Both linguistically and functionally, *Statistik* was conceived to serve the state. Lueder, a historian, collected and published several large compendia of historical and geographical data, which were intended to aid rulers and ministers in their economic planning and monitoring. He read *WN* during the 1790s, and then emerged as a repentant and extreme economic liberal. In *Über Nationalindustrie und Staatswirthschaft* (*On National Industry and State Economy*), and later writings, Lueder embraced Smith's views while also decrying government intervention more than Smith ever had. In an impassioned and self-deprecating confession, he denounced his own opus, claiming that *Statistik* was a useless discipline that taught pointless data to government officials whose intervention in the economy was, he now realized, unnecessary and even damaging.

Lueder's liberalism was now an all-embracing creed, personally as well as philosophically. "I hazarded everything for freedom, truth and justice; for freedom of industry as well as of opinions, of hand as of spirit, of person as well as of property," he wrote in the preface to *Kritische Geschichte der Statistik* (*Critical History of Statistics*) (quoted by Hasek, 1925, p. 81). As Rothbard (2006, p. 497) put it, "Statistics is not only misleading . . . it becomes a necessary condition for the very government intervention which must be repudiated." Even more dramatically, Lueder (quoted by Rothbard, 2006, p. 497) described his intellectual plight:

> As my insight grew and my viewpoint cleared, the fruits of statistics and policy appeared more and more frightful; all those hindrances which both threw in the path of industry, whereby not only welfare but culture and humanity were hindered; all those hindrances to the natural course of things; all those sacrifices brought to an unknown idol, called the welfare of the state or the commonweal, and bought with ridicule of all principles of philosophy, religion and sound common sense, at the cost of morality and virtue.

However, as this passage conveys, Lueder's critique of *Statistik* and embrace of Smith's "freedom of industry . . . of hand as of spirit" did not take on board Smith's balancing insistence, brought to focus in Book V of *WN*, that the state's interventional duties go beyond military protection and policing. For Lueder, "the purpose of the state [is] to furnish protection alone" (Hasek, 1925, p. 81). While deeply committed to individual liberty, and thus forcefully rejecting slavery of any type – unlike Feder a generation earlier – Lueder subscribed to Smith's universalist notion of human liberty, but he did not adhere to Smith's other commitment: to governmental duties that include education and caring – interventionist caring, to some extent – for the weakest members of society. Because some residues of the "welfare of the state" – which Lueder dismissed as an "unknown idol" – were still crucial props in Smith's envisaged political order. By throwing away *all* state-monitored actions, Lueder's new liberal enthusiasm overshot the Smithian mark.

Two other members of Sartorius's and Lueder's generation are also highly relevant to this narrative: the Prussians Christian Jakob Kraus (1753–1807) and Ludwig Heinrich von Jakob (1759–1827). They taught, respectively, at the universities of Königsberg and Halle, and both influenced Stein and Hardenberg in their attempted reform of the Prussian government and economy. Here I will focus on Kraus, the more important of the two for his decisive influence on the Stein–Hardenberg reforms.

Kraus, who spent one year studying at Göttingen, taught "practical philosophy and cameralia" at the University of Königsberg, alongside Greek classics, history, English literature and mathematics. His relatively early discovery of Smith's doctrines resulted in a total and somewhat hyperbolic embracing of "the only true, great, beautiful, just, and beneficial system." *WN*, he wrote, is "certainly one of the most important and beneficial books that have ever been written . . . certainly since the times of the New Testament no writing has had more beneficial results than this will have" (quoted by Rothbard, 2006, p. 495). Kraus's posthumously published manuscript, *Die Staatswirthschaft* (5 vols., Konigsberg, 1808–11), is described as "essentially a paraphrase of Smith's *Wealth of Nations*, substituting Prussian for British examples." But his Prussianization of Smith's text went beyond the new historical and geographical examples he generously sprinkled in his lectures and in the published compendium. As Hasek put it, Kraus was "to a large extent responsible for the economic changes which took place in Prussia after 1807, in so far as they can be ascribed to Smithian influence" (Hasek, 1925, p. 93). But Kraus's Smith, like Lueder's, was no longer the Scottish Enlightenment's Smith.

Murray N. Rothbard, himself a libertarian and free-market devotee, hailed the analytical part of Kraus's opus thus:

> Kraus addressed himself to Prussian economic policy, in lecture form. The volume was an incisive call for individualism, free markets, free trade, and a drastic reduction of government intervention . . . [I]f men wish to improve their own lot, then government coercion, requiring certain actions or forbidding others, must necessarily cripple and distort such effort at improvement. For otherwise, why don't individuals do what government wants of their own accord, and without coercion? And since they don't wish to do so, they will seek means of evading the government mandates and prohibitions. In all these cases, and in stark contrast to the cameralists, Kraus puts himself in the point of view of the individuals in society subject to government edicts, and not in the point of view of the officials issuing the decrees.
>
> (Rothbard, 2006, p. 496)

This endorsement of an early nineteenth-century economic liberal by a twentieth-century libertarian is a fitting place to end this paper. By accepting Lueder's, and especially Kraus's, understanding of Smith's doctrines as strictly individualistic, radically liberal and wholly anti-interventionist, scholars who adhere to the nineteenth-century scholarly tradition of Roscher (followed partially by Hasek and enthusiastically by Rothbard) place Smith on a libertarian pedestal.

Conclusion

The Stein–Hardenberg reforms, which fall beyond the scope of this paper, did not rest upon an extreme Smithianismus of the kind disseminated by either Lueder or Kraus. Pragmatically driven, these (largely unsuccessful) reforms were partially inspired not only by Smithian liberalism but also by the residual republicanism of the Scottish Enlightenment, including Adam Ferguson's call for active and participatory citizens. This inspiration may account for the abolition of serfdom, the civilian status granted to Jews, and the enlargement of Prussia's voting constituency. While short-lived, many of these reforms were effective in their symbolic weight, and staples for the future. The temporary liberation of the Jews, it has been argued elsewhere, enabled a generation to enter institutes of higher learning and white-collar professions, and facilitated the building of the educated families that nurtured Hess, Freud, Herzl and Einstein.

It can be argued that Stein (and possibly Hardenberg), whose own education included the Scottish thinkers who furnished Smith's original context, took up what I have dubbed his "residual republicanism" in a way that the contemporary Smith specialists, from Garve to Kraus, no longer did. Stein therefore believed in the "self-government" (*Selbstverwaltung*) of citizens, up to a point, no less than he urged "limited government" on a reformed Prussian administration. He may have been inspired directly by Ferguson (see Oz-Salzberger, 1995, pp. 254–5), or he may have read Smith against the grain of contemporary German interpretation. But he could not have found the component of civic participation – which entails a level of governmental presence in civil life, insofar as the government is directly informed by the citizens, or even elected by them – in the writings of the German Smithians.

The story told here is therefore one of misreception as much as one of reception. Smith's first twenty years in Germany were characterized by an under-representation of his uniqueness. To many readers, especially those of *TMS*, he was just "another Scotsman," albeit one of the greatest. By contrast, over the next two decades in the German lands he was singled out as a great economic theorist while most of his fellow-Scots disappeared into oblivion. At the same time, however, his political – and indeed civic – contexts were all but forgotten.

Bibliography

Backhouse, Roger E., *The Methodology of Economics: Nineteenth-Century British Contributions* (London: Routledge, 1997).

Berlin, Isaiah, "Hume and the Sources of German Anti-Rationalism", in *Against the Current: Essays in the History of Ideas* (Oxford: Oxford University Press, 1981), pp. 162–187.

Bödeker, Hans Erich, "Staatswissenschaften and Political Economy at the University of Göttingen: The Scottish Influence," *Transactions of the Eighth International Congress on the Enlightenment, Studies on Voltaire and the Eighteenth Century*, 305 (1992), pp. 1881–4.

Cliffe Leslie, Thomas Edward, "The History of German Political Economy," *Fortnightly Review*, 24 (1875), pp. 93–101.

Erämetsä, Erik, *Englische Lehnprägungen in der deutschen Empfindsamkeit des 18. Jahrhunderts* (Helsinki: Annales Academiae Scientiarum Fennicae, 1955).

Erämetsä, Erik, *Adam Smith als Mittler englisch-deutscher Spracheinflüusse: 'The Wealth of Nations'* (Helsinki: Suomalainen Tiedeakatemi, 1961).

Fabian, Bernhard, "English Books and their Eighteenth-Century German Readers," in Paul J. Korshin (ed.), *The Widening Circle: Essays on the Circulation of Literature in Eighteenth-Century Europe* (Philadelphia: University of Pennsylvania Press, 1976), pp. 119–95.

Fleischacker, Samuel, "Kant's Response to the Wealth of Nations", *History of Political Thought*, 17(3) (1996), pp. 379–407.

Garve, Christian, *Uebersicht der vornehmsten Principien der Sittenlehre* (Breslau: Wilhelm Gottlieb Korn, 1798).

Gawlick, Günter, and Lothar Kreimendahl, *Hume in der deutschen Aufklärung. Umrisse einer Rezeptionsgeschichte* (Stuttgart: Frommann Verlag, 1987).

Ingram, John Kells, *A History of Political Economy* (Cambridge: Cambridge University Press, 1888).

Haakonssen, Knud, "Kantian Themes in Smith," in Knud Haakonssen, *Natural Law and Moral Philosophy from Grotius to the Scottish Enlightenment* (Cambridge: Cambridge University Press, 1996), pp. 148–153.

Hasek, Carl William, *The Introduction of Adam Smith's Doctrine into Germany* (New York: Columbia University Press, 1925).

Kant, Immanuel, *The Metaphysics of Morals*, trans. and ed. Mary Gregor (Cambridge: Cambridge University Press, 1996).

Kant, Immanuel, *Groundwork of the Metaphysics of Morals*, trans. and ed. Mary Gregor (Cambridge: Cambridge University Press, 1998).

Kant, Immanuel, *Correspondence*, trans. and ed. Arnulf Zweig (Cambridge: Cambridge University Press, 1999).

Kiesel, Helmuth and Münch, Paul, *Gesellschaft und Literatur im 18. Jahrhundert: Voraussetzungen und Entstehung des literarischen Markts in Deutschland* (Munich: Beck, 1977).

Kuehn, Manfred, "The Reception of David Hume in Germany", in Peter Jones (ed.), *The Reception of David Hume in Europe* (London: Bloomsbury, 2005), pp. 98–138.

Lai Cheng-Chung, *Adam Smith across Nations: Translations and Receptions of* The Wealth of Nations (Oxford: Clarendon Press, 2000).

Oz-Salzberger, Fania, *Translating the Enlightenment: Scottish Civic Discourse in Eighteenth-Century Germany* (Oxford: Clarendon Press, 1995).

Oz-Salzberger, Fania, "The Enlightenment in Translation: Regional and European Aspects," *European Review of History—Revue européenne d'Histoire*, 13(3) (2006), pp. 385–409.

Price, Mary Bell and Price, Lawrence Marsden, *The Publication of English Humaniora in Germany in the Eighteenth Century* (Berkeley: University of California Press, 1934).

Robertson, John, "Scottish Political Economy beyond the Civic Tradition," *History of Political Thought*, 4 (1983), pp. 451–82.

Roscher, Wilhelm Georg Friedrich, *Geschichte der Nationalökonomie in Deutschland* (Munich: Oldenbourg, 1874).

Rothbard, Murray N., *Economic Thought before Adam Smith: An Austrian Perspective on the History of Economic Thought*, vol. 1 (Auburn, AL: Ludwig von Mises Institute, 2006).

Smith, Adam, *An Inquiry into the Nature and Causes of the Wealth of Nations*, ed. R. H. Campbell, A. S. Skinner and W. B. Todd, 2 vols. (Oxford: Oxford University Press, 1975).

Treue, Wilhelm, "Adam Smith in Deutschland: Zum Problem des 'Politischen Professors' zwischen 1776 und 1810," in W. Conze (ed.), *Deutschland und Europa: Festschrift für Hans Rothfels* (Düsseldorf: Droste, 1951), pp. 101–33.

Tribe, Keith, *Governing Economy: The Reformation of German Economic Discourse 1750– 1840* (Cambridge: Cambridge University Press, 1988).

Tribe, Keith, *Strategies of Economic Order: German Economic Discourse, 1750–1960* (Cambridge: Cambridge University Press, 2007).

Waszek, Norbert, "Adam Smith in Germany, 1776–1832," in Hiroshi Mizuta and Chuhei Sugiyama (eds.), *Adam Smith: International Perspectives* (London: Macmillan; New York: St. Martin's Press, 1993), pp. 163–80.

Waszek, Norbert, "The Scottish Enlightenment in Germany and its Translator Christian Garve," in Tom Hubbard and Ronald D. S. Jack (eds.), *Scotland in Theory: Reflections on Culture and Literature* (Amsterdam and New York: Rodopoi, 2006), pp. 55–72.

Zart, Gustav, *Einfluss der englischen Philosophie seit Bacon auf die deutsche Philosophie des 18. Jahrhunderts* (Berlin: Dümmler, 1881).

Adam Smith and the *Encyclopédie*[1]

Ryan Patrick Hanley

For several decades – and at least since the landmark publication of the important collection edited by Roy Porter and Mikuláš Teich – it was customary for intellectual historians of the Enlightenment to regard their subject from the perspective of "national context."[2] For students of Adam Smith, this has largely been beneficial insofar as it has called attention to the ways in which Smith's moral and political thought was deeply indebted to specifically Scottish political and philosophical contexts.[3] At the same time this perspective has its limits. For even if eighteenth-century British philosophy was, as has been recently argued, largely "insular,"[4] Smith's own intellectual debts were hardly confined to the contributions of his fellow Scots or even Britons more generally, and famously ranged across a wide canon of authors, both ancient and modern – as we now appreciate better than ever. But perhaps what especially remains to be appreciated is the degree of Smith's debts to the French Enlightenment.

The question of Smith's debts to French sources has been of interest at least since historians of economic thought began to debate the degree to which he owed his economic theory to his well-known engagement with the economic thought of the Physiocrats in the 1760s.[5] More recently, his engagement with the "citizen of Geneva," Rousseau, has given rise to a considerable literature.[6] Smith's debts to seventeenth-century French moralists and mid-eighteenth-century French sentimentalist novelists have likewise been examined in several important recent essays.[7] Further, Smith's reception in both revolutionary and post-revolutionary France has generated some excellent recent work.[8] Yet much still remains to be done. For instance, Smith's debts to Montesquieu are only now being explored in depth.[9] For all of his praise of Voltaire, we lack a sustained treatment of their relationship. And next to nothing has been written about some of the most important French sources in *The Theory of Moral Sentiments*, ranging from Smith's reliance on the aesthetics of Du Bos and Buffier, to his debts to the anthropological studies of Charlevoix and Lafitau for his views on the North American savages, to his explicit reliance on the memoirs of the Duc de Sully and Cardinal de Retz for their accounts of court life, to his references to the moral psychology and theology of La Placette and Pascal and Massillon – all explicitly cited in the *TMS*.[10] It is to be hoped that more work will be done soon on each of these fronts. In what follows, though, I will concentrate on Smith's sustained engagement with one particular French source that was evidently of great interest to him and has begun to interest Smith scholars in recent years, too: the famed *Encyclopédie* of Diderot and d'Alembert.[11]

That Smith was long interested in and engaged with the *Encyclopédie* is well known today and beyond dispute. He famously called prominent attention to the publication of its first five volumes in one of his own first publications, the 1756 "Letter to the *Edinburgh Review*."[12] By 1760, he had purchased seven volumes for the University of Glasgow's library in his capacity as quaestor.[13] In a letter of 1763, he praised its grammar articles as sources of considerable "entertainment."[14] Perhaps most intriguingly, his arrival in Paris in late 1765 or early 1766 for an approximately nine-month stay precisely coincided with the release of the final ten volumes of the *Encyclopédie*: a landmark intellectual event of which Smith would have been powerfully aware, given his frequent and intimate associations in Paris with such prominent *encyclopédistes* as Turgot, Quesnay, Diderot and d'Alembert.[15] Moreover, Smith's engagement with the *Encyclopédie* seems to have been appreciated even in his day; hence the suggestion made by the author of an anonymous (and indeed bitter) death notice that appeared in the *St. James Chronicle* of July 1790 that Smith's "illustrations are chiefly borrowed from the valuable French collection *sur les arts & métiers* . . . [though] his arrangement is his own."[16] All of this puts Smith's familiarity with the *Encyclopédie* beyond doubt. What remains to be demonstrated, however, is its substantive influence on his thought, and the significance of this influence. To this end, what follows offers first a brief survey of Smith's comments on the *Encyclopédie* in his 1756 review essay before turning to four specific entries or subject headings from the *Encyclopédie* – *Eclectisme, Economie, Grammaire,* and *Epingles* – for which the available textual evidence of Smith's corpus suggests a possibility – or likelihood – of direct influence.

The *Encyclopédie* and the "Letter to the *Edinburgh Review*"

The story of Smith's exposure to the *Encyclopédie* is notoriously complex.[17] His early access to the work certainly came in part in the form of the copies he purchased for the university library at Glasgow. He also likely would have had ready access to the copies available at the library of the Faculty of Advocates in Edinburgh, which from 1752 to 1757 was managed by his friend David Hume.[18] Further, the records of his library attest to his holding of several volumes that gathered together essays from the *Encyclopédie*.[19] Yet, lacking more specific information about the dates of his purchase of these volumes in his personal library and his accessing of the university and law library copies, we are forced to rely on what Smith himself tells us about his engagement with the work. His first recorded engagement with the *Encyclopédie* is the 1756 publication of his "Letter to the *Edinburgh Review*." This appeared in March 1756, by which time only the first five volumes of the *Encyclopédie* had been published.[20]

Smith's letter was itself a friendly challenge to the aims of the *Review*. Its stated aim was to call attention to new Scottish works. Yet Smith worried that such a project was impossible given the relative infancy of Scottish letters, and proposed that the editors "should enlarge [their] plan" in order to take into account new developments on the Continent (LER 2). As several excellent studies have demonstrated, Smith's aim was to encourage in his Scottish audience rivalry and emulation of other national literary cultures in order to promote the development and flourishing of Scottish letters.[21] In the letter he professes to limit himself to "France and England only" (LER 3), but in fact it is France that dominates his attention – as is evident in the fact that the letter names only two living English authors (the astronomers Robert Smith and James Bradley), as compared to nine living authors who were writing in French – Diderot, d'Alembert, Daubenton, Voltaire, Maurepas, Buffon, de Réaumur, Formey, and Rousseau (de Pouilly, also cited by Smith, had died in 1750). Indeed, perhaps the most striking aspect of the letter is Smith's celebration of the particular genius and talents of the French, and especially their "taste, judgment, propriety and order" (LER 4), and their capacity "to arrange every subject in that natural and simple order, which carries the attention, without any effort, along with it" (LER 5). Coming from Smith, this is no idle praise; in his own rhetoric lectures he was at this same moment recommending to his students writers like Swift, whose genius consisted in arranging their material in "the most proper order" so that even "one half asleep may carry the sense along with him" (*LRBL* 1.106, 1.10).[22] Smith's fascination with the French capacity for "arranging and methodizing" in any case leads him to praise the *Encyclopédie* in the letter in a manner that one prominent British scholar has called "undoubtedly the most eulogistic account of the *Encyclopédie* to be published in this country in the eighteenth century." But, as has been noted by others in response, eulogy is only part of Smith's aim in describing the *Encyclopédie* in the letter.[23] For he not only criticizes its style (occasionally too declamatory) and its article selection (occasionally too broad), but challenges its editors on specific grounds, including "the justness of their criticisms upon the celebrated authors of their own and of foreign nations," "how far they have observed or neglected the just proportion betwixt the length of each article and the importance of the matter contained in it," and, most intriguingly, "the candor or partiality with which they represent the different systems of philosophy or theology, ancient or modern" (LER 7). This last observation is particularly striking. Previous scholars have called attention to Smith's seemingly sympathetic attitude toward the *encyclopédistes*' approach to religion, citing his observation that their work "has several times been disagreeably interrupted by some jealousy of the civil or ecclesiastical government of France, to neither of which however the authors seem to have given any just occasion of suspicion" (LER 7).[24] Yet Smith's critique of the "candor or partiality" with which they have treated "the different systems of philosophy or theology" suggests some degree of unease with either the manner or the matter of their presentation of such.

Notwithstanding all these reservations, Smith clearly valued the *Encyclopédie*, especially for its commitment to order and arrangement. This commitment is especially evident in the famed *Discours préliminaire*, itself one of only two contributions to the *Encyclopédie* that Smith specifically mentions in the letter.

In his brief comment on the *Discours*, he calls attention to its "account of the connection of the different arts and sciences, their genealogy and filiation" (LER 6). Such a description has naturally and rightly led scholars to compare the enterprise of the *Discours* to Smith's own attempts to conceptualize philosophy as the science of nature's connecting principles in his *History of Astronomy*.[25] Others have identified in his criticism of the "spirit of system" in the *Discours* a precursor of his critique of "the man of system" in the sixth edition of *The Theory of Moral Sentiments*.[26] But it may well be that Smith was indebted to the *Discours* on two additional fronts, too.

The first of these concerns his views on the generation and arrangement of knowledge. In the *Discours* (1: xv)[27] d'Alembert notes that different minds are naturally disposed to follow different branches of the tree of knowledge:

> In the study of nature, men at first apply themselves altogether as if in concert, in order to satisfy their most pressing needs. But when they came to the study of that which is less absolutely necessary, they came to divide themselves, and each advanced in his own right at his own pace.

Smith, of course, was famously interested in the division of intellectual labor that he regarded as at once the consequence and the engine of social progress, explicitly noting that "philosophy or speculation, in the progress of society" naturally comes to be "subdivided into many different branches," with the consequence that "more work is done upon the whole and the quantity of science is considerably increased by it" (ED 20; cf. *LJA* vi.42–43; *LJB* 218). And as d'Alembert continues, he explains that while the generation of knowledge follows one pattern, its organization and proper presentation follow another. Here it is necessary for us to place philosophy

> at an elevated point of view above this vast labyrinth, from which it can take in all at once the principal sciences and arts, see at a glance the objects of its speculations and the operations it can make on these objects, distinguish the general branches of human knowledge and the points at which they overlap or diverge, and sometimes even anticipate the secret connections which bring them together. It is a sort of map of the world that serves to show the principal countries, their positions and their mutual dependence, and the paths that lead from one to another.
>
> (1: xv)

It seems reasonable to assume that d'Alembert's description resonated with Smith, given his own insistence on the importance of cultivating that philosophical perspective which can afford a glimpse of the "connexions and dependencies" that bind together the discrete parts of a given system (e.g., *TMS* 4.1.11; *WN* 1.1.11).[28]

Smith also likely would have been struck by a second claim in the *Discours*. Much has been made of the role of imagination in Smith's system. Studies of the imagination in Smith particularly tend to emphasize Hume as a source of his views of the imagination's role in system-building.[29] While it is clearly right to identify Hume as a source of influence, we should take care not to identify him as the *sole* source of influence, as the *Discours* itself presents a strikingly similar conception. Indeed, like Hume and Smith, d'Alembert's views on the imagination seem to point in the direction of a mitigated skeptical realism rather than a dogmatic skepticism or materialism. Thus, in describing our efforts to apprehend the nature of external bodies that we seem to perceive as extant, he writes that we are driven by

> an insurmountable desire to assure the existence of objects to which we bring these sensations, and which seem to us to be their cause – a desire that many philosophers have regarded as the work of a superior Being, and as the most convincing argument for the existence of these objects. Indeed, there being no relationship between each sensation and the object that gave rise to it, or at least to which we relate it, it does not appear that one can find by reason a possible passage from one to another: there is only a species of instinct, surer than reason itself, which can compel us to get across so great an interval, and this instinct is so strong in us, that even if we supposed for a moment that it subsists while the exterior objects are destroyed, these same objects reproduced all at once could not augment its forces. We thus judge without hesitating that our sensations in effect have the cause outside of us that we take them to have, because the effect that can result from the real existence of this cause would be different in no sense from the one that we feel.
>
> (1: ii–iii)

Such a conception not only closely mirrors Hume's conception of the productive capacities of imagination (see, e.g., *EHU* 5.21–22; *T* 1.1.3; *T* 1.4.2.31–37), but also anticipates the core of Smith's views on the productive capacities of the imagination in gap-filling (*HA* 2.7–8; cf. *TMS* 1.1.1.2 and 5.1.2). For students of Smith, the upshot of these similarities is that we need to take care not to ascribe his understanding of associationist epistemic principles solely or perhaps even principally to his reading of Hume, who in fact is only one among many sources to which Smith's understanding of associationism is likely indebted – sources that likely include, among others, the *Discours préliminaire*.

Eclectisme

Smith's interest in and engagement with the *Encyclopédie* was hardly limited to the *Discours préliminaire*. Yet it takes some legwork to uncover his debts. Smith himself hardly advertises them, and in fact the only other *Encyclopédie* entry directly referenced in Smith's corpus is the Abbé Yvon's entry for *Amour* – of which he is entirely dismissive (LER 7).[30] To appreciate his engagement with the *Encyclopédie* we thus need to work backwards from his published texts. One place we might begin is at his perplexing reference in *TMS* to the "Eclectics."

Smith's discussion of the "Eclectics" comes in *TMS* 7.2.3, dedicated to "those systems which make virtue consist in benevolence." The chapter's primary focus is Francis Hutcheson, here described by his former student as "undoubtedly, beyond all comparison, the most acute, the most distinct, the most philosophical, and what is of the greatest consequence of all, the soberest and most judicious" exponent of the view that virtue consists in benevolence (*TMS* 7.2.3.3). Yet, while Hutcheson is its main focus, the chapter itself – like others in Part 7 – begins with a review of the ancient foundations of the doctrine in question before turning to its modern exponents. It is here that we are told that the view that virtue consists in benevolence "seems to have been the doctrine of the greater part of those philosophers who, about and after the age of Augustus, called themselves Eclectics" (*TMS* 7.2.3.1). The question of who exactly Smith had in mind when referring to these "Eclectics" has generated some controversy. All he tells us is that they "pretended to follow chiefly the opinions of Plato and Pythagoras," and on such grounds are "commonly known by the name of the later Platonists" (*TMS* 7.2.3.1). This brief and opaque description has generated a good deal of scholarly confusion. The editors of the Glasgow edition suggest that "it is hard to say" who Smith has in mind here, and suggest that he may have been "reading back" certain Christian doctrines into Stoic or Neoplatonic thinkers.[31] Haakonssen's edition follows the suggestion put forth by the editors of the fine modern French translation that Smith is most likely referring to the middle Platonism of the fifth Academy that began with Antiochus of Ascalon.[32] Yet the little information that Smith provides itself seems to call into question such an identification; in locating Eclecticism "about and after the age of Augustus," he suggests a century's difference between Antiochus and the school that he has in mind. Who, then, might he mean when he speaks of the "Eclectics"?

For illumination we might turn to Diderot's entry for *Eclectisme* in the fifth volume of the *Encyclopédie*. Classified under the subheading "History of philosophy, ancient and modern," the article identifies the Eclectics as a school of "reformed Platonism" that was founded in Alexandria, beginning with Potamon (see 5: 273) and extending until the death of Hypatia in AD 415 (see 5: 283). That Diderot held these Eclectics in high regard is clear: he identifies a school of modern Eclectics and credits Bacon – the towering figure of the *Encyclopédie* – as its founder (5: 271), and distinguishes the entry on Eclecticism as the longest of all of the entries of the *Encyclopédie* under the "History of philosophy . . ." heading – including entries on Platonism, Aristotelianism, Stoicism, Epicureanism and skepticism. Even more striking are Diderot's bold opening claims in the essay that the true eclectic is one who "dares to think for himself," who desires "to see with his own eyes," and who will "admit nothing except on the testimony of his own experience and reason" (5: 270). The ancient Eclectics are thus clearly proper models for modern enlightened philosophers, given their capacities to pursue empiricism without skepticism, to transcend dogmatic sectarian divisions, and to appropriate and synthesize various positions in their efforts to transcend dogma and pursue the truth.

Diderot's striking entry on *Eclectisme* was hardly the only contemporary resource that gave careful attention to the ancient Eclectics; others well known to

Smith who also discussed Eclecticism and indeed identified it with the Alexandrine school include Mosheim and Brucker (from the latter of whom Diderot is sometimes said to have borrowed much of his material). Hume too briefly mentions the Eclectics in his *Essays*, and Smith's beloved Hutcheson dedicated the concluding paragraph of his "Dissertation on the Origin of Philosophy" to them.[33] Yet the substance of his account in *TMS* 7 suggests that Diderot's *Encyclopédie* article also contributed to shaping his conception of Eclecticism.[34] The key claims of the Eclectics that Smith highlights there are that in the deity "benevolence or love was the sole principle of action, and directed the exertion of all the other attributes," that "the whole perfection and virtue of the human mind consisted in some resemblance or participation of the divine perfections," and that the proper end of philosophy is to raise us to "immediate converse and communication with the Deity" (*TMS* 7.2.3.2). Diderot is not quite so insistent on the centrality of love or benevolence (although cf. 5: 279). Yet his descriptions of how the Eclectics understood their own proper ends – as in "we elevate ourselves to the knowledge of and to the participation in God" (5: 288; see also 5: 293) – is likely to have inspired or at least reinforced Smith's understanding of the place of transcendence in Eclecticism, even if Smith's conception of transcendence itself was surely shaped by multiple other sources as well.[35]

In any case, the significance of Smith's likely engagement with *Eclectisme* is twofold. First, it attests to another facet of Smith's engagement with the *Encyclopédie*, and specifically its treatment of the history of philosophy – an engagement that raises the question of the possible degree to which Smith's conceptions of other philosophical schools – ancient and modern – might have been shaped to a greater or lesser degree by his readings of the relevant entries in the *Encyclopédie*. Second, and more substantively, Smith's interest in the Eclectics and their emphasis on disinterested love points to his broader but equally underappreciated interest in the Christian charity that is a crucial if often neglected part of the larger story of *TMS*.[36]

Economie

A second article from the *Encyclopédie* likely to have been of considerable interest to Smith was *Economie*, also from the fifth volume of 1755. Given Smith's interests in this period, when he was lecturing on jurisprudence and laying the foundations for his defense of commercial society as presented in *The Wealth of Nations*, it is difficult to imagine that he would *not* have been interested in it. As others have noted, several of the entries under the heading of "*Economie politique*" seem to have attracted Smith's attention. The entry on *Fermier*, with its critique of sharecropping; that on *Foire*, with its critique of intervention in market orders; and that on *Grain*, with its prominent emphasis on the danger of confusing money with genuine wealth and the pernicious effects of national jealousy on reciprocally beneficial trade – all speak to quite prominent themes in Smith's work.[37] In a similar vein, it has been noted that Diderot's entry for *Art* develops views on the division of labor in ways that anticipate Smith's (although

Art, it should be noted, does not appear under the "*Economie politique*" heading).[38] Beyond these, however, the entry *Economie* itself is likely to have been of particular interest to Smith, if only for its byline: "*Article de M. Rousseau, citoyen de Genéve.*" As the "Letter to the *Edinburgh Review*" attests, Smith's engagement with Rousseau's *Discours sur l'inegalité* dated to the very year of its publication. And as we now know from recent scholarship, Smith's interest in Rousseau – not just his *Discours*, but also several other elements of his corpus dating from 1755 to 1762 – were key elements of his own synthesis in this same period, which itself witnessed the publication of *The Theory of Moral Sentiments* and *Considerations on Language*, as well as the likely composition of initial drafts of *The Wealth of Nations*.[39] Below, I will argue that there are two reasons for thinking that our study of Rousseau's influence on Smith should extend to his *Encyclopédie* article, which in time would be separately published as the *Discours sur l'économie politique*.

Two specific passages from the article demand attention. The first concerns the sentiment of humanity, and specifically its propensity to weaken as it widens in scope:

> It seems that the sentiment of humanity evaporates and weakens as it extends itself over all the earth, and that we would know not to be touched by the calamities of Tartary or Japan as by those of a European people. It is necessary in some fashion to limit or to compress interest and commiseration in order to render it active. Now, as this desire in us can only be useful to those with whom we live, it is good that humanity concentrated among fellow-citizens, takes in them a new force by habit of seeing one another, and by the common interest that unites them. It is certain that the greatest prodigies of virtue have been produced by love of the fatherland; this pleasant and lively sentiment, which joins the force of self-love to all the beauty of virtue, gives it an energy that, without disfiguring it, renders it the most heroic of all the passions.
>
> (5: 341/*OC* 3: 254–245)[40]

This same argument can be found in Smith, and in two particular instances he employs language that bears a decided resemblance to Rousseau's analysis. The first comes in his account of the earthquake in China in *TMS* 3.3.4. Smith explores this set piece in terms that closely parallel Rousseau's, introducing his problem as the way in which "a man of humanity in Europe" is likely to be moved (or remain unmoved) by such a "dreadful calamity." The disparity between distant disaster and European reaction had already been noted by several of Smith's contemporaries: Voltaire prominently mentions a Chinese earthquake of 1699 that claimed 400,000 lives in his *Essai sur les moeurs*; and Hume notoriously proclaimed in the *Treatise* that "'tis not contrary to reason for me to prefer the destruction of the whole world to the scratching of my finger."[41] Yet the substance of Smith's account is closer to Rousseau's than to either Hume's or Voltaire's. For Rousseau, the problem is that humanity evaporates and weakens as it spreads, and the question is how, in the face of this dissipation, it can be supported and animated. His answer is that the sentiment of humanity needs to be compressed or concentrated among fellow-citizens in such a way that their collective *amour-propre* might serve as an additional support for virtue. This is Smith's argument too. In what follows, Smith suggests it is not "fine philosophy" or "humane sentiments" that ensure "our active principles should often be so generous and so noble." Like Rousseau, he insists that "it is not the soft power of humanity . . . [but] a stronger love, a more powerful affection" alone that can lead us to such exertion (*TMS* 3.3.4). In this passage, Smith identifies this affection with "the love of what is honourable and noble." But elsewhere he employs a more identifiably Rousseauian trope. In his second critical analysis of humanity, Smith reiterates that it "consists merely in the exquisite fellow-feeling which the spectator entertains with the sentiments of the persons principally concerned" and that such sentimental fellow-feeling is shallow and requires "no self-denial, no self-command, no great exertion of the sense of propriety" (*TMS* 4.2.10). And again like Rousseau, Smith insists that this relatively shallow feeling needs a more forcible motive for its animation, in this case such "greater exertions of public spirit" as those of patriots (*TMS* 4.2.11).

A second passage in *Economie* suggests further convergence between Smith's views and Rousseau's. Here the context is more specifically economic, and concerns specifically the relationship between the poor and the rich. This relationship is the foundation of each thinker's views on government: just as Rousseau argues that government's origin lies in the efforts of the rich to protect their property from the poor (e.g., *OC* 3: 177–178, 248, 271, 273), Smith insists that "till there be property, there can be no government, the very end of which is to secure wealth, and to defend the rich from the poor" (*LJB* 20). Both thinkers are also interested in the way in which the tensions between rich and poor persist in civilized society. Rousseau's portrait of this relationship is famously bleak: "all the advantages of society – are they not on the side of the rich and powerful?" Rousseau answers his own question in the affirmative:

> The poor – what a different picture! The more humanity owes them, the more society refuses them: all doors are closed to them, even when it is right to open them, and if sometimes they obtain justice, it is with more pain than another would obtain favors; if there are duties to do, a militia to be raised, priority falls on him; he carries always, besides his own burden, that which his rich neighbor has the means to have himself exempted from.
>
> (5: 347/OC 3: 271–272)

This is classic Rousseau. Yet the same position is replicated in several of Smith's treatments of the relationship between the rich and poor. That the poor garner less sympathy and attention than the rich is one of his most familiar tropes (see, esp., *LRBL* 2.90–91 and *TMS* 1.3.2.1). But perhaps the most visible parallel in his corpus to Rousseau's treatment above may be found in his account of the relationship between the "opulent merchant" and the "poor laborer" in the Early Draft of *The Wealth of Nations*. Here Smith argues that "in a civilized society the

poor provide both for themselves and for the enormous luxury of their superiors"
– a provision that he, like Rousseau, equates to a burden. The poor laborer

> affords the materials for supplying the luxury of all the other members
> of the common wealth, and bears, as it were, upon his shoulders the whole
> fabric of human society, seems himself to be pressed down below ground by
> the weight.

> (ED 4–5)

Smith and Rousseau reach quite different conclusions regarding how this burden
is best alleviated, yet their conception of the fundamental economic problem
was much the same, and given Smith's engagement with both Rousseau's other
writings and the *Encyclopédie* more generally, there is reason to think that his
thoughts on this front may have been partly shaped by an engagement with the
Discours sur l'économie politique. At the very least, the parallels noted above
would seem to warrant further investigation of Smith's engagement with the
Discours, especially on several other points of both agreement and disagreement, including Smith's and Rousseau's respective conceptions of the role of the
statesman in economic intervention (*OC* 3: 246, 250–252; cf. *TMS* 2.2.1.8 and
6.2.2.14–18), on individual liberty and property rights (*OC* 3: 256–258, 262–263,
269–270; cf. *WN* 1.11.c.27), on luxury and sumptuary taxes (*OC* 3: 266–267,
275–278; cf. *WN* 5.1.d.1–13), on systems of public education (*OC* 3: 260–261;
cf. *WN* 5.1.f.48–61), on primogeniture and social mobility (*OC* 3: 263–264; cf.
WN 3.2), and on the relationship between the town and the countryside (*OC* 3:
268, 274–275; cf. *WN* 3.3). Such an analysis, I suspect, is likely to confirm that
Smith's engagement with the economic thought of the *encyclopédistes* extends
beyond engagement with the principal Physiocratic essays. Further, the question
of the degree to which Rousseau's political economy is founded on certain liberal
and individualistic commitments – which, superficially at least, seem difficult to
harmonize with his more notorious and familiar commitments – has increasingly
occupied recent scholars.[42] It is a side of Rousseau that is likely to have been of
interest to Smith in light of the latter's own commitments and his extended
engagement with much of Rousseau's other work. If so, this invites the question
of whether Smith might have been indebted to Rousseau not only for certain elements of his critique of commercial society but also for his conception of certain
of its foundational individualistic principles.

Grammaire

A third theme of the *Encyclopédie* with which Smith engaged concerned the
articles published under the subheading "*Grammaire*." In this case we have a
direct statement from Smith testifying to his interest. In a letter of 1763 he claims
to owe his understanding of language to the Abbé Girard's *Les vrais principes
de la langue françoise* (1747) and "the grammatical articles too in the French
Encyclopédie" – the latter of which, he notes, also afforded him "a good deal of

entertainment" (CAS 69).[43] Smith's declaration is significant. Only two years earlier he had published in the first and only volume of the *Philological Miscellany* (1761) his own extensive treatment of grammar and language in the form of his *Considerations Concerning the First Formation of Languages*, which would later be appended to the third (1767) and all future editions of *The Theory of Moral Sentiments*. His choice of venue for his initial publication of *Considerations* is itself significant for students of his relationship with the *Encyclopédie*. A principal aim of the *Philological Miscellany*, according to its editorial advertisement, was to reprint a "variety of articles from the French Encyclopedia, along with curious dissertations on Philological Subjects by foreign writers, with whose works the generality of readers in this country are little acquainted."[44] As others have noted, the *Philological Miscellany* in this respect seems to have been designed to carry the torch for the very project that Smith envisioned for the *Edinburgh Review* – a fact that has led to some speculation as to whether he might have been involved in some significant way with its conception or publication.[45] As it happens, the editors' envisioned project never came to fruition and the *Philological Miscellany* ran to only a single issue, which contained no articles from the *Encyclopédie*. However, it did include a host of pieces from various prominent French authors as well as its single original essay, Smith's *Considerations*.

In any event, it remains the case that, aside from his "Letter to the *Edinburgh Review*," Smith's only direct testament to his engagement with the *Encyclopédie* concerns its articles on grammar, and that his own publication specifically devoted to grammar appeared in a review that was dedicated to reprinting the articles on that subject from the *Encyclopédie*. In light of this, Smith's extensive drawing on the pre-1761 *Encyclopédie* articles on *grammaire* in the composition of the *Considerations* is perhaps less surprising.

These debts are evident in several places. For example, in describing the cases of various languages, Smith notes that "the number of cases is different in different languages. There are five in the Greek, six in the Latin, and there are said to be ten in the Armenian language" (*Cons* 18). The editors of the Glasgow edition are unable to trace a source for this assertion,[46] but it seems highly likely to have been Diderot's *Encyclopédie* article *Cas*, which also notes that the Greeks had five and the Romans six cases (2: 734), and, more importantly, that authorities "who have lived several years among the Armenians, say that there are ten cases in the Armenian language" (2: 734). This is perhaps the clearest point of contact between Diderot's essay and Smith's, but it is merely one of several. The others include their shared conceptions of word order and the effects of word transposition in modern languages (compare *Cons.* 21 and 45 to *Cas* at 2: 735 and to *Concordance* at 3: 822 and *Declinaison* at 4: 695), and the role of cases and prepositions in establishing relations between objects (compare *Cons.* 5 and 12 to *Cas* at 2: 736).

Smith's interest in the *grammaire* articles was likely not limited to their illumination of technical points of grammar. His well-known concern with literary style and the sound of spoken language probably led him to find much of interest in the *Encyclopédie*'s treatment of such topics in several places. Smith's concern on this front is evident in his discussions in *Considerations* of the role of the natural human predilection for sonority in the evolution of language. In this vein he explains that the endings of inflected languages are chiefly derived from "that love of similarity of sound, from that delight in the returns of the same syllables ... [which] is so naturally so very agreeable to the human ear" (*Cons.* 10–11); so too he will later call attention to "that love of analogy and similarity of sound, which is the foundation of by far the greater part of the rules of grammar" (*Cons.* 16). And in making his striking argument at the conclusion of *Considerations* for the superiority of ancient to modern languages, he insists on the capacity of the former to render themselves more "agreeable to the ear" (*Cons.* 44). These same concerns are central to the *grammaire* entries in the *Encyclopédie*. Several of them – especially *Breve, Cacophonie, Consonance* and *Euphonie* – conspicuously emphasize the significance of the way a language sounds. Euphony, we are thus reminded, comes from the Greek for "good voice" and strives for "easy and agreeable pronunciation" (6: 209), as opposed to cacophony, with its "disagreeable sound" (2: 510). So too in *Breve* we are reminded of the value of the arrangement of long syllables and short syllables for "the harmony of the period" (2: 414), while in the discussion of *Consonance*, which describes "the resemblance of sounds of words in the same phrase or period" (4: 49), we find a lesson that Smith not only transmitted in his own name but also one that he sought to internalize and then demonstrate in his writing.[47] Taken together, Smith's statement concerning his interest in the *Encyclopédie*'s articles on *grammaire*, his repetition of several of their lessons, and his internalization of some of their stylistic lessons in his own writing suggest the *Encyclopédie*'s likely influence on a number of elements of the *Considerations*.

Much work remains to be done on Smith's various debts in the *Considerations* (especially with regard to his debt to Rousseau's theory of the relationship of conceptual abstraction and metaphysics to the progress of language; see, esp., *Cons.* 6–7, 12, 19–20, 22–23, 28, 32, 34; cf. *OC* 3: 145–151), but it is to be hoped that future research into Smith's linguistics will include careful study of his debts to the *Encyclopédie*, too.

Epingle

I wish to close with a brief consideration of what is surely Smith's best-known debt to the *Encyclopédie*: his description of the pin factory. As scholars have long recognized, the account of the pin factory that opens his account of the division of labor in *The Wealth of Nations* seems to be drawn, in some of its details, from the *Encyclopédie* entry *Epingle*, with the chief point of similarity being the identification in each text of eighteen discrete steps in the manufacture of a pin.[48] However, in reconsidering this issue, excellent recent scholarship has raised the question of whether the *Epingle* entry was Smith's sole source or merely one among many.[49] In what follows, I ask a related but slightly different question: was the *Epingle* entry itself only one of two sources in the *Encyclopédie* on which Smith might have drawn when constructing his account of the pin factory?

Answering this question requires some analysis of the evolution of Smith's thoughts on pin-making. The famous account in *The Wealth of Nations* has a history that stretches back to approximately a decade and a half prior to its publication in 1776, encompassing the several accounts found in the Early Draft of *The Wealth of Nations* as well as both sets of jurisprudence lectures. Careful comparison of these accounts reveals several differences in detail concerning the various discrete tasks involved in the pin-making process. These have recently been helpfully traced and identified – labors I do not attempt to replicate here.[50] What I do wish to note is that, aside from the changes introduced in these different editions, which date from approximately 1760 to 1764, the final published account contains two specific additions that demand attention, because they seem to suggest a specific source.

The first of these changes concerns Smith's description of how a pin factory might be best conceptualized. In the paragraph directly before his introduction of the pin factory proper, Smith sets up his discussion with a comparison that did not appear in the previous accounts in ED, *LJA* and *LJB*:

> In those trifling manufactures which are destined to supply the small wants of but a small number of people, the whole number of workmen must necessarily be small; and those employed in every different branch of the work can often be collected into the same workhouse, and placed at once under the view of the spectator. In those great manufactures, on the contrary, which are destined to supply the great wants of the great body of the people, every different branch of the work employs so great a number of workmen, that it is impossible to collect them all into the same workhouse. We can seldom see more, at one time, than those employed in one single branch. Though in such manufactures, therefore, the work may really be divided into a much greater number of parts, than in those of a more trifling nature, the division is not near so obvious, and has accordingly been much less observed.
>
> (*WN* 1.1.2)

Smith's claim is that, to conceptualize the division of labor accurately, it is necessary to begin with instances of divided labor that we can see at a glance. Hence his use of the pin factory as an exemplar, as it is precisely the sort of "very trifling manufacture" (*WN* 1.1.3) that meets the criteria of "those trifling manufactures" mentioned in the paragraph quoted above. But the significance of this claim lies in Smith's explanation of why these trifling manufactures are so advantageous in our efforts to conceptualize this complicated process. The thrust of his claim on this front emerges in his repeated utilization of the visual metaphor throughout this paragraph: because the number is small, they can be collected under one roof, for the convenience of "the spectator," who can "see" or "view" or "observe" the process in action. This is the first element unique to the published account of the pin factory in *The Wealth of Nations*.

A second element not present in the manuscript drafts comes in the paragraph that follows. Here Smith rehearses his now-familiar account of the discrete operations of the making of the pin, but in concluding this account he ends with another addition:

> The important business of making a pin is, in this manner, divided into about eighteen distinct operations, which in some manufactories, are all performed by distinct hands, though in others the same man will sometimes perform two or three of them. I have seen a small manufactory of this kind where ten men only were employed, and where some of them consequently performed two or three distinct operations. But though they were very poor, and therefore but indifferently accommodated with the necessary machinery, they could, when they exerted themselves, make among them about twelve pounds of pins in a day.
>
> (*WN* 1.1.3)

While Smith's earlier accounts mentioned eighteen operations, he now also claims to have been a spectator and thus to have "seen a small manufactory" in which the tasks previously performed by eighteen men are accomplished by only ten.[51]

Taken together, these two additions to *The Wealth of Nations'* account of pin making compel us to wonder what may have happened between the drafting of the early versions and the drafting of the final published text. One possibility deserves particular mention as it points not away from but back to the *Encyclopédie*. In 1766, the fourth volume of the famous plates of the *Encyclopédie* was published – the twenty-first volume of the project as a whole. Included in this volume was a brief new entry under the title "*Epinglier*," which itself was accompanied by a new set of three annotated plates. Their relevance lies in the fact that the third plate clearly depicts a pin factory of *ten* workers assembled under one roof (21: 5: 7). Given that Smith himself owned a copy of these plates (the seven volumes of plates are the only volumes of the *Encyclopédie* that are recorded as part of his personal library), it seems possible that his inspection of this particular plate might explain both his new emphasis on the spectator's visualization of the factory and the shift from eighteen men to ten which are such prominent features of the final account but absent from both the ED and the *LJ* accounts that he drafted prior to 1766.[52]

Smith's claim in *WN* 1.1.3 that he has "seen" a "small manufactory" of ten men may thus refer to him seeing an etching of such a pin factory in the third plate of the twenty-first volume of the *Encyclopédie*. However, there is another possibility – namely, that Smith saw such a pin factory in person, and perhaps even the very pin factory that the plate in question depicted. This intriguing possibility is suggested by both the methods of the *encyclopédistes* and the dates of Smith's stay in Paris. The former we know from the *Discours préliminaire*, in which it is claimed that the authors of the various articles on the *métiers* owed their familiarity with their subjects to first-hand empirical research, which enabled them, as it were, to draw from life. Compelled "to seek out workers," we are told, they "spoke to the most skillful in Paris and beyond, taking the trouble to go to their workshops, to ask them questions, to transcribe their words, to develop

232   *Ryan Patrick Hanley*

their thoughts, to draw them in the terms proper to their professions" (1: xxxiv). This is particularly important for the entry for *Epingles*, given that the editors of the *Encyclopédie* included a note at the end of the piece attesting to the fact that they had explicitly sent the author of the piece to observe a pin factory first hand (5:807).[53] So, might Smith have made a similar visit?

One reason for asking this question lies in an interesting confluence of dates. Smith arrived in Paris at the very end of January or the beginning of February 1766.[54] The dates are significant, as two momentous events occurred in the philosophical world of Paris in January 1766: the departure of Hume and Rousseau for their ill-fated trip to England; and the controversial publication of the *Encyclopédie*'s final ten volumes of articles and the fourth volume of plates.[55] That Paris would have been alive with this latter event is beyond doubt, and surely it would have been an important time for Smith's most intimate contacts at the commencement of his stay. Smith arrived in Paris having already studied, written about and lectured on the details of the *Epingle* article, so it is easy to imagine that he read with great excitement the new account, fresh from the presses, and indeed persuaded one of his hosts to arrange a tour of the humble and "trifling" phenomenon that he was soon to turn into such a momentous example. There is no solid evidence for this conjecture, but one may hope that further research into Smith's visit to Paris may reveal more of what he did there and shed some light on how his engagement with both the *encyclopédistes* and the *Encyclopédie* shaped his thinking across the many subjects that his own encyclopedic scope encompassed. In the meantime, we can say that Smith's careful and evident synthesis of what he read and saw attests to his remarkable capacity to synthesize empirical evidence from a variety of sources as tests for his own theories, and marks perhaps his closest affinity with the ambitions of the *encyclopédistes* to balance broad theoretical scope with precise and discerning observation.

Notes

1   Earlier versions of this paper were presented at the "Journées d'études pour célébrer le 250e anniversaire de la publication de la TSM," PHARE, Université Paris 1 Panthéon–Sorbonne, October 2009; and at the "Adam Smith in International Contexts" seminar, Academia Sinica, Taipei City, December 2012. I am extremely indebted to both audiences, and to Robert Mankin and Henry Clark, for helpful comments and suggestions.
2   Roy Porter and Mikuláš Teich, eds., *The Enlightenment in National Context* (Cambridge, 1981); for students of Smith, this volume is especially important for its essay on "The Scottish Enlightenment" by Nicholas Phillipson.
3   Classic readings of Smith in the context of the Scottish Enlightenment include Donald Winch, *Adam Smith's Politics* (Cambridge, 1978); Michael Ignatieff and Istvan Hont, eds., *Wealth and Virtue* (Cambridge, 1983); and Christopher Berry, *The Social Theory of the Scottish Enlightenment* (Edinburgh, 1997).
4   James A. Harris, "Introduction," in James A. Harris, ed., *The Oxford Handbook of British Philosophy in the Eighteenth Century* (Oxford, 2013), 7.
5   For a helpful introduction to the history of the "French connection" thesis, see especially Leonidas Montes, *Adam Smith in Context* (London, 2004), 28–30. For a helpful review of Smith's relationship to certain of the central doctrines of Physiocracy, see

Andrew Skinner's "Introduction" in the Penguin Classics edition of Books IV–V of *The Wealth of Nations* (London, 1999), xv–xxix.

6   Pioneering contributions on this front include Lucio Colletti, *From Rousseau to Lenin* (New York, 1974); and Michael Ignatieff, *The Needs of Strangers* (London, 1984). More recently, see Pierre Force, *Self-Interest before Adam Smith* (Cambridge, 2003); Dennis Rasmussen, *The Problems and Promise of Commercial Society* (University Park, 2008); Ryan Patrick Hanley, "Commerce and Corruption: Rousseau's Diagnosis and Adam Smith's Cure," *European Journal of Political Theory* 7 (2008): 137–158; Ryan Patrick Hanley, *Adam Smith and the Character of Virtue* (Cambridge, 2009); and Charles Griswold, "Smith and Rousseau in Dialogue: Sympathy, *Pitié*, Spectatorship and Narrative," in Vivienne Brown and Samuel Fleischacker, eds., *The Philosophy of Adam Smith* (Routledge, 2009), 59–84.

7   See, especially, Deirdre Dawson, "Is Sympathy so Surprising? Adam Smith and the French Fictions of Sympathy," *Eighteenth-Century Life* 15 (1991): 147–162; and Neven Brady Leddy, "Adam Smith's Moral Philosophy in the Context of Eighteenth-Century French Fiction," *Adam Smith Review* 4 (2009): 158–180.

8   In this vein see especially Richard Whatmore, "Adam Smith's Contribution to the French Revolution," *Past and Present* 175 (2002): 65–89; Emma Rothschild, *Economic Sentiments: Adam Smith, Condorcet and the Enlightenment* (Cambridge, MA, 2001); Karin Brown, ed., *Sophie de Grouchy: Letters on Sympathy (1798): A Critical Edition* (Philadelphia, PA, 2008); and Eric Schliesser, "Sophie de Grouchy, Adam Smith, and the Politics of Sympathy," in Eileen O'Neill and Marcy P. Loscano, eds., *Feminist History of Philosophy* (New York, forthcoming).

9   See, e.g., Brian C. J. Singer, "Montesquieu, Adam Smith, and the Discovery of the Social," *Journal of Classical Sociology* 4 (2004): 31–57; and, especially, Henry C. Clark, "Montesquieu in Smith's Method of Theory and History," *Adam Smith Review* 4 (2008): 132–157.

10   An important exception which calls attention to the importance of Charlevoix and Lafitau for *TMS* is Maureen Harkin, "Adam Smith's Missing History: Primitives, Progress, and Problems of Genre," *English Literary History* 72 (2005): 429–451. Smith's heretofore largely underemphasized interest in French courtly life is helpfully treated in Spiros Tegos, "Adam Smith on the Addisonian and Courtly Origins of Politeness," *Revue internationale de philosophie* 68 (2014): 317–342. Also very helpful in this context is Michael Biziou's essay "Adam Smith and the History of Philosophy," Ryan Patrick Hanley, ed., *Adam Smith: His Life, Thought and Legacy* (Princeton, NJ, 2016), which likewise emphasizes the need for further inquiry into Smith's French sources.

11   Since my drafting of the initial version of this essay, three important studies that address in varying degrees Smith's engagement with the *Encyclopédie* have appeared: Robert Mankin, "Pins and Needles: Adam Smith and the Sources of the *Encyclopédie*," *Adam Smith Review* 4 (2008): 181–205; Neven Brady Leddy, "Adam Smith's Critique of Enlightenment Epicureanism," in Neven Brady Leddy and Avi S. Lifschitz, eds., *Epicurus and the Enlightenment* (Oxford, 2009), 183–205; and Frank A. Kafker and Jeff Loveland, "L'Admiration d'Adam Smith pour l'*Encyclopédie*," *Recherches sur Diderot et sur l'Encyclopédie* 48 (2013): 191–202. What follows aims to build on and extend these helpful studies without replicating them.

12   Hereafter "LER," as reprinted in *Essays on Philosophical Subjects*, ed. W. P. D. Wightman (Indianapolis, IN, 1982), 242–254. Subsequent citations of Smith's other works are also to the Glasgow edition, as published in Indianapolis by the Liberty Fund (1981–1984), and take the following abbreviations: *Cons.* = *Considerations Concerning the First Formation of Languages* in *LRBL*; ED = Early Draft of *The Wealth of Nations* in *LJ*; HA = *History of Astronomy* in *Essays on Philosophical Subjects*; *LJ* = *Lectures on Jurisprudence*; *LRBL* = *Lectures on Rhetoric and Belles-Lettres*; *TMS* = *The Theory of Moral Sentiments*; *WN* = *An Inquiry into the Nature and*

Causes of the Wealth of Nations. Numerical references are to the standard paragraph numbers of the Glasgow edition.

13   As described in W. R. Scott, *Adam Smith as Student and Professor* (Glasgow, 1937), 171 and 179n3.

14   Smith to George Baird, 7 February 1763, as reprinted in *The Correspondence of Adam Smith*, ed. E. C. Mossner and I. S. Ross (Indianapolis, IN, 1987), letter 69.

15   For accounts of his visit, see, especially, John Rae, *Life of Adam Smith* (1895; reprint New York, 1975), 194–231; and Ian S. Ross, *The Life of Adam Smith*, 2nd edn (Oxford, 2010), 209–233.

16   "Anecdotes of the Late Dr Smith," *St. James Chronicle*, July 1790, as noted in Ross, *Life of Smith*, 439.

17   See, e.g., Mankin, "Pins and Needles," 184.

18   As suggested in John Lough, *The Encyclopédie in Eighteenth-Century England and Other Studies* (Newcastle-upon-Tyne, 1970), 3.

19   Kafker and Loveland, "L'Admiration d'Adam Smith," 195–196.

20   Kafker and Loveland, "L'Admiration d'Adam Smith," 192. The fifth volume ends with the entry for *Esymnete*, and hence these first five volumes include the entries for *Eclectisme*, *Economie* and *Epingles*, as well as the grammar articles on *Cas* and *Consonance*, on which I focus below.

21   See, especially, Jeffrey Lomonaco, "Adam Smith's 'Letter to the Authors of the *Edinburgh Review*,'" *Journal of the History of Ideas* 63 (2002): esp. 659–666; on the specifically British and Scottish contexts of the letter, see also Mankin, "Pins and Needles," 184–189.

22   The particular author that Smith here discusses is Jonathan Swift. I develop this treatment further in "Style and Sentiment: Swift and Smith," *Adam Smith Review* 4 (2008): 88–105.

23   The quotation is from Lough, *The Encyclopédie in Eighteenth-Century England*, 14; for direct critical response to Lough's claim, see Mankin, "Pins and Needles," 184–186; and Kafker and Loveland, "L'Admiration d'Adam Smith," 192, 202.

24   See, e.g., Lough, *The Encyclopédie in Eighteenth-Century England*, 13; and Kafker and Loveland, "L'Admiration d'Adam Smith," 194.

25   See, especially, Mankin, "Pins and Needles," 183–184; and Kafker and Loveland, "L'Admiration d'Adam Smith," 197.

26   As noted by the editors of the Glasgow edition at *TMS*, 231n6.

27   References to the *Encyclopédie* are to volume number and page number. In preparation of this paper I have consulted the complete sets of the first editions of the articles (17 vols., Paris, 1751–1765), plates (11 vols., Paris, 1762–1772) and *supplément* (4 vols., "Amsterdam," 1776–1777), held by the Marquette University Library. I have also consulted the transcriptions published online by the University of Chicago's ARTFL Project (http://encyclopedie.uchicago.edu/). English translations are my own.

28   This same passage is also quoted by Mankin in a slightly different context; cf. Mankin, "Pins and Needles," 198, 203n33.

29   Particularly important accounts include Andrew Skinner, "Adam Smith: Science and the Role of the Imagination," in William B. Todd, ed., *Hume and the Enlightenment* (Edinburgh, 1974); D. D. Raphael, "'The True Old Humean Philosophy' and Its Influence on Adam Smith," in G. P. Morice, ed., *David Hume: Bicentenary Papers* (Edinburgh, 1977); and Charles Griswold, "Imagination: Morals, Science, and Arts," in Knud Haakonssen, ed., *Cambridge Companion to Adam Smith* (Cambridge, 2006). I offer a response to these in my "Skepticism and Naturalism in Adam Smith," in Brown and Fleischacker, eds., *The Philosophy of Adam Smith* and in "Hume and Adam Smith on Moral Philosophy," in Paul Russell, ed., *Oxford Handbook of David Hume* (Oxford, 2016).

30   For treatment, see, e.g., Kafker and Loveland, "L'Admiration d'Adam Smith," 197–198.

31 See the editorial note to the Glasgow edition of *TMS* at 300n1.
32 See the editorial notes to Haakonssen's edition of *TMS* (Cambridge, 2002) at 354n51; and to the impressive French translation of *TMS* prepared by Claude Gautier, Biziou, and Jean-François Pradeau (Paris, 1999) at 402n1; cf., again, Leddy, "Smith's Critique of Epicureanism," 184.
33 See, e.g., Johann Lorenz von Mosheim, *Ecclesiastical History* (1726), 2nd century AD, Part II, ch. 1; Johann Jakob Brucker, *The History of Philosophy, from the Earliest Times to the Beginning of this Century*, ed. and trans. William Enfield (London, 1791), vol. 2, 59–101; David Hume, "Of the Rise and Progress of the Arts and Sciences," in *Essays, Political, Moral, and Literary*, ed. Eugene F. Miller (Indianapolis, IN, 1987), 123; and Francis Hutcheson, "Dissertation on the Origin of Philosophy," in *Logic, Metaphysics, and the Natural Sociability of Mankind*, ed. James Moore and Michael Silverthorne (Indianapolis, IN, 2006), 7–8.
34 In his important study of Smith's relationship to Epicureanism, Leddy tantalizingly suggests that in voicing this last criticism Smith likely "had in mind Diderot's articles on eclecticism and Epicureanism from the most recent fifth volume of the *Encyclopédie*," which anticipates my claim here, though Leddy does not connect Smith's engagement with the *Encyclopédie* article to Smith's comments on the ancient Eclectics at *TMS* 7.2.3; see Leddy, "Adam Smith's Critique of Enlightenment Epicureanism," 184.
35 Cf. Kafker and Loveland, "L'Admiration d'Adam Smith," 199.
36 On Smith's treatment of Christian love in *TMS* and its relationship to his treatment of the Eclectics, see my "Adam Smith: From Love to Sympathy," *Revue internationale de philosophie* 68 (2014): 251–274.
37 These points are helpfully made in Ross, *Life of Smith*, 221, 476n2; and in Ian S. Ross, "The Physiocrats and Adam Smith," *Journal of Eighteenth-Century Studies* 7 (1984): 178–179; see also Kafker and Loveland, "L'Admiration d'Adam Smith," 201–202.
38 Kafker and Loveland, "L'Admiration d'Adam Smith," 198–199, following and extending the observation originally made by Edwin Cannan in the editorial apparatus of his 1937 Modern Library edition of *WN*.
39 In addition to the sources cited in n3 above, I further explore this relationship in "From Geneva to Glasgow: Rousseau and Adam Smith on the Theater and Commercial Society," *Studies in Eighteenth-Century Culture* 35 (2006): 177–202; and "Enlightened Nation-Building: The Science of the Legislator in Adam Smith and Rousseau," *American Journal of Political Science* 52 (2008): 219–234.
40 In citing Rousseau's essay, the first set of numbers refers to the volume and page of the passage as published in the *Encyclopédie* article *Economie*, and the second set to its publication as part of the *Discours sur l'économie politique* in vol. 3 of his *Oeuvres complètes*, ed. Bernard Gagnebin and Marcel Raymond (Paris, 1964).
41 See Voltaire, *Essai sur les moeurs*, sec. 195; and Hume, *Treatise*, 2.3.3.6.
42 For a recent attempt to provide a more liberal (or at least, non-anti-liberal) reading of Rousseau's political thought, see Joshua Cohen, *Rousseau: A Free Community of Equals* (Oxford, 2010). I seek to provide such a reading specifically of the *Discourse on Political Economy* in "Political Economy and Individual Liberty," in Eve Grace and Christopher Kelly, eds., *The Challenge of Rousseau* (Cambridge, 2013), 34–56.
43 Also quoted in Kafker and Loveland, "L'Admiration d'Adam Smith," 202.
44 *Philological Miscellany* 1 (1761): iii.
45 See Ross, *Life of Adam Smith*, 198–200.
46 See the Glasgow edition's republication of *Considerations* in *LRBL*, 211n5.
47 To take one example: compare Smith's efforts to balance the first line of the present paragraph (*Cons.* 16) with the first line of the previous paragraph (*Cons.* 15).
48 See, e.g., the editors' note to the Glasgow edition version of this passage at *WN*, 15n3; see also Ross, *Life of Adam Smith*, 292; and Kafker and Loveland, "L'Admiration d'Adam Smith," 199–200. For a review of the pre-history of the identification of this

resemblance, see Jean-Louis Peaucelle, "Adam Smith's Use of Multiple References for His Pin-Making Example," *European Journal of the History of Economic Thought* 13 (2006): 492.

49   This is the focus of Peaucelle's well-researched and entertaining "Smith's Use of Multiple References." See especially 494–501.

50   See, especially, Peaucelle, "Smith's Use of Multiple References," Tables 4–5, 506–510.

51   This shift from eighteen men to ten has been noted previously (see, e.g., Mankin, "Pins and Needles," 191), but still awaits explanation. Peaucelle offers one intriguing hypothesis – that Smith may have read in Macquer's 1766 *Dictionnaire portative des arts et métiers* (a text he owned) an account of a pin factory of ten discrete stages (see Peaucelle, "Smith's Use of Multiple References," 496–497, 504). But Macquer's account lacks illustrations; so, while it may well have contributed to Smith's familiarity with a ten-man factory, it seems unable, in itself, to explain what Smith might mean when he says that he has "seen" a small factory of this sort.

52   It should be noted, however, that the discrete activities depicted in the third plate do not perfectly comport with the discrete stages that Smith himself describes. Of the stages described in *WN* 1.1.3, the plate depicts the fashioning and fastening of the head, the packaging of pins in paper, and the coloring of the pins. Other stages mentioned by Smith – the drawing and cutting of the wire, and so forth – are depicted only in the first or second plate.

53   As noted by Mankin, who also provides a translation of the note; see "Pins and Needles," 190. The actual pin factory that served as a model for Deleyre's entry is taken to be that located at L'Aigle; see Robert C. Allen, *The British Industrial Revolution in Global Perspective* (Cambridge, 2009), 146–147, as cited in Fredrik Albritton Jonsson, "Adam Smith and Enlightenment Studies," in Hanley, ed., *Adam Smith*; see also Kafker and Loveland, "L'Admiration d'Adam Smith," 199.

54   For the relevant evidence, see Ross, *Life of Adam Smith*, 222–223. It should also be noted that Ross's volume itself reproduces the plate of ten men (Plate 9, 307; cf. 292) but does not connect it to the addition to the *WN* text (and seems to date it to 1764).

55   There is some doubt as to the exact date of the publication of the fourth volume of plates. Frank A. Kafker and Serena L. Kafker, *The Encyclopédistes as Individuals: A Biographical Dictionary of the Authors of the Encyclopédie* (Studies on Voltaire and the Eighteenth Century 257; Oxford, 1988), xxv, citing John Lough, *Essays on the Encyclopédie of Diderot and d'Alembert* (London, 1968), 2–12, 463, list the publication date as 1765. Others, however, give the date as January 1766. See, e.g., Jeanne Charpentier and Michel Charpentier, *L'Encyclopédie* (Paris, 1967), 3–10.

Scholarship on Adam Smith in China, 1949–2013

Luo Weidong

The dissemination of Adam Smith's thought and relevant scholarship in China can be traced back to 1901, when the first Chinese version of *WN*, translated by Yan Fu with the title 原富 *Yuan Fu* (The Origin of Wealth) was published. As is well known, Yan Fu emphasized the need for faithfulness (to ensure precision), expressiveness (to ensure fluency), and elegance (to ensure readability) during translation. Of these, the first is undoubtedly the most important, yet Yan Fu's translation of *WN* fails to meet this criterion, because there are numerous differences between the original English text and his Chinese version as far as content is concerned. It would be absurd to attribute such a lack of correspondence to the translator's poor grasp of English. A more reasonable explanation is that his version is based on his own interpretation of *WN*. To be more specific, *Yuan Fu* is not a translation of *WN*, but a *rereading* of *WN*.[1]

Although it would be interesting, both intellectually and ideologically, to explore Yan Fu's translation as symbolic of the initial mentality and motivation of the Chinese reception of Adam Smith's thoughts, that topic is not the focus of this paper. Rather, I treat Yan Fu's translation as a point of departure and intend to argue that the spread of Smith's thoughts in China is closely linked to the ups and downs of China's transformation as a country. My argument proceeds in four stages: 1949–1978 (the beginning of reform and opening up); 1979–1994 (the publication of the first Chinese version of *TMS*); 1995–present day; and the future.

1. 1949–1978

It is well-known that the foundation of People's Republic of China on 1 October 1949 ushered in a new regime which adopted Marxism as its political ideology. In fact, the country's ideology went far beyond pure Marxism, as it was a fascinating hybrid of refined Marxism (that of the former Soviet Union, with Leninism and Stalinism as its core) and the unique ideology of Chinese revolutionaries, which embraced Chinese traditional perception of the relationship between people and government, accumulated from thousands of years of history, as well as the unsophisticated outlook on life and social order of the rural population (the lowest level of Chinese society).

In the years following its foundation, the new regime largely followed the Soviet Union's example in everything from economic planning to government organization. A large number of Russian experts and consultants arrived from the Soviet Union to provide China with guidance and suggestions, until the breakdown in relations between the two countries in July 1960.

Against this background, Chinese intellectual circles were also greatly influenced by the Soviet Union. A great deal of Russian academic literature was translated into Chinese, and Soviet citizens were employed in educational institutions as both lecturers and advisers. This Soviet influence had a profound effect on the PRC's first generation scholars. First, Stalinized Marxism, which was regarded as the basic academic philosophy and methodology to observe and practice, came to dominate Chinese academia. Second, Chinese scholars started to use Russian when communicating within international intellectual circles, which led to an almost total breakdown of relations between Chinese and English-speaking academia. In the same vein, Chinese scholars who had been educated in English-speaking countries, and therefore had a good grasp of the language, found themselves marginalized; some were even forced to leave academia.

Although bilateral relations between China and the Soviet Union collapsed at the very start of the 1960s, and attempts to eliminate Soviet influence in China began almost immediately, there was no significant change in temperament until the end of the 1970s. Academic studies were still imbued with considerable political ideology, and political correctness remained the principal criterion that students and teachers had to observe. This ended only with the launch of the period of reform and opening up in 1978.

During the three decades from 1949 to 1978, how was Adam Smith received in mainland China? Owing to the influence of scholars from the Soviet Union, and especially D. I. Rosenberg, Chinese scholars learned about Smith's ideas only through Karl Marx's comments about his predecessor's theories in *A Theoretical History of Surplus Value*. Marx viewed Smith as the founder of the progressive bourgeois classical political economy, which provided direct inspiration for David Ricardo's labor theory of value. Marx then built his own "scientific" labor value theory on Ricardo's thesis. In this sense, Smith was regarded as the academic predecessor of both Ricardo and Marx, so he could be seen in a positive light. On the other hand, though, Smith's ideas were also regarded as the origin of the philistine bourgeois economics theory system, which Thomas Robert Malthus and Jean Baptiste Say then developed into a full-fledged theory to account for and defend the capitalist economic system in general and the economic activities and interests of the bourgeoisie in particular. From this perspective, Smith's thought was regarded as "incorrect," and he was painted as Marx's principal adversary. In a nutshell, Marx regarded Smith as the creator of a controversial economic theory system from which some "correct" elements should be accepted and developed, while other "incorrect" elements should be rejected and discarded. In *A Theoretical History of Surplus Value*, therefore, Marx attempted to interpret *WN* meticulously within the framework of what he regarded as the scientific economic system theory. For instance, in the chapter "Adam Smith and the Concept of Productive Labor," he spends hundreds of pages commenting on the relevant content of *WN*.

Rosenberg's *A Theoretical History of Political Economy* could be regarded as a further illustration of Marx's *A Theoretical History of Surplus Value*. Specifically written as a textbook, it failed to shed much new light on Smith's ideas, but it had a huge influence on Chinese scholarship. For instance, the principal textbook of my college years – *The Theoretical History of Economy*, edited by Lu Youzhang and Li Zongzheng – followed suit by introducing and commenting upon Smith's doctrine within Marx's framework. Predictably, then, in this period there was no significant breakthrough in the study of Adam Smith in China.

One Chinese scholar from the latter half of the twentieth century – Professor Chen Daisun – does, however, deserve special attention. He obtained his Ph.D. from Harvard University and then secured teaching posts at Tsing Hua University and Beijing University. In *From Classic Economic Theory System to Marx*, Chen systematically introduces and evaluates all of the main characteristics and contributions of Smith's theory of value. Although his analysis failed to shake off the influence of Marxism, it was the first work in a new era of Chinese scholarship in which reasoned criticism of Smith's theories on the basis of fact started to replace belligerent, blinkered criticism of his ideas. As a result, and despite its strong Marxist hue, his evaluation of Smith's thought was more fair and academic than anything that had preceded it in the PRC.[2]

As for the translation of Smith's works, young Chinese students found Yan Fu's version very difficult to read and understand, not least because it was more like the translator's own interpretation of Smith's ideas rather than a faithful reproduction of the original text, and because the language he used was quite archaic. Hence, as early as the 1930s, the young Marxist economist and translator Guo Dali and Wang Yanan collaborated to translate *WN* into modern, official Mandarin. The Chung Hwa Book Company published their effort with the shortened title 国富论 *Guo Fu Lun* (On the Wealth of Nations), and for many years this served as the only resource for Chinese readers who did not have sufficiently good English to read the original text. The Commercial Press reprinted *Guo Fu Lun* in 1972, whereupon it became an important work for Chinese economists who were conducting research into English classical political economy.[3]

2. 1979–1994

The year 1979 was crucial in the economic development of China. The central government announced that it planned to abandon Marxist fundamentalism (especially the economic and political model of Stalinism) and instead develop a specifically Chinese economic system to breathe new life and vitality into Chinese society. As a result, Chinese academic studies soon started to flourish to an unprecedented extent. Although Marxism was still regarded as the official guiding principle in academia, more reflections on and criticism of the old political institutions and economic system could be voiced. Marxist fundamentalism, at least, certainly seemed to be on the wane.

During this period, the reform of marketization and the decentralization of property rights quickly gathered pace, which demanded the support of new theoretical alternatives to Marxism. Chinese intellectual circles, especially in the field of economics, turned to the revolutionary theories of the Soviet Union and other socialist countries in Eastern Europe for new insights, owing to the political risk of borrowing directly from Western economic theories. As a result, the work of numerous Eastern European scholars – such as Ota Šik and János Kornai – was introduced into China. The Hungarian economist Kornai, having searched in vain for theoretical support within Marxism, created his own, distinctive economic concept in the hope of explaining the common phenomenon of the coexistence of massive surplus and extreme shortage. In the 1980s his theory became so prevalent in China that his book *Shortage Economics* was essential reading for the economists of the younger generation. However, his theory soon turned out to be a flash in the pan, possibly because it had been constructed under the strong influence of Marxist ideology. Hence it failed to provide any meaningful theoretical support for the deep reform that the Chinese government was implementing at the time.

The new generation of Chinese economists ultimately came to realize that they would never find a theoretical basis for a competition-oriented socialist economic system in the vein of Marxist tradition. Rather, the reform process demanded the support of a theory of price and market competition. As a consequence, a great deal of scholarship on economic libertarianism started to appear in China. For instance, *Free to Choose: A Personal Statement*, by Milton Friedman and Rose Friedman, and Ludwig Wilhelm Erhard's *Prosperity through Competition* were translated into Chinese in 1982 and 1983, respectively. Large print runs of both of these books were published by the Commercial Press, and both provoked heated debate within Chinese academia. The radical liberalist Benjamin Rogge's *Can Capitalism Survive?* was also translated into Chinese and published by Guangdong People's Press in 1982. Through these works, Chinese scholars came to understand Adam Smith's theoretical contributions to the free-market economic system at a time when China was in urgent need of such theoretical support. Smith, as the founder of economic liberalism, started to attract significant attention in the country for the first time.

What's more, Friedrich Hayek, as an important Western scholar, focused extra attention on Smith's views on *laissez-faire*. As early as the 1960s, long before the Chinese reform process got under way, his *The Road to Serfdom* (1944) was translated into Chinese. Then, in the 1980s, *The Constitution of Freedom* (1960), *Law, Legislation and Freedom* (1973, 1976, 1979) and *Individualism and Economic Order* (1948) were all translated and published in China in rapid succession. Hayek's thought-provoking assessment of Smith and other members of the Scottish Enlightenment stimulated Chinese academics to approach Smith's contribution to economics from a new perspective – that is, from an evolutionary and non-constructive liberalist point of view.

This marked a transitional point. Adam Smith began to be perceived as an advocate and champion of the market economy system in China, not merely as an inspiration for Marxist economics and the labor theory of value. This was a historical transformation, since Smith was no longer simply evaluated as a predecessor of Marxism, but admired as the standard-bearer of economic liberty. Consequently, the focus of Chinese Smithian scholarship gradually shifted from studying the relationship between Smith's classical political economy and Marxist economic theory to researching his contribution to the free-market economic system. Although Tang Zhengdong's *From Adam Smith to Marx* – which focuses on intellectual development from Smith to Hume and then to Ferguson – was published as late as 2002, it should be regarded as an extension of the earlier discussion, not as representative of mainstream Chinese Smithian scholarship at the turn of the century.

The fall of the Berlin Wall in 1989, as a symbolic moment, signified the end of the Cold War, and a wave of self-reflection swept through the world's socialist countries. China was no exception, and the political and economic reform process gathered pace in the early 1990s, prompted in part by the disintegration of the Soviet Union and drastic changes in some Eastern European countries, characterized by political democratization and economic liberalization. In the spring of 1992, Deng Xiaoping, the effective leader of China at the time, toured the southern part of the country and made a famous speech in which he called for a deepening of the reform process. He declared that China's goal should be to construct a market economic system, although – for the sake of ideological and political stability – he insisted that this would still be "socialist." This was the first time in history that a Chinese leader had explicitly stated that the ultimate aim of the country's economic reform was to construct a free-market economy.

China's ongoing development and reform generated several questions. What are the advantages and disadvantages of a free-market economic system? How should such a system be constructed in China? Is there any common ground between China's free-market system and similar ones in other countries? Is China's system unique in any way? In the first half of the 1990s, many Chinese scholars launched investigations into the working principles and institutional framework of the market economy and commercial society. A number of economics scholars were particularly drawn to Smith's notion of "the invisible hand" and explored whether it might coordinate the actions of self-interested people and, in effect, improve the public welfare of the whole of society. In the first few decades after the founding of the People's Republic such a proposal would have seemed totally alien to most Chinese scholars, who would have ridiculed and condemned such a notion. Now, though, several prominent academics started to advocate it. When doing so, they turned for inspiration not to the works of Adam Smith himself, but to a number of textbooks on neoclassical price theory that had recently been translated from English into Chinese.

During this period, most Chinese economists came to agree that the price theory of neoclassical economy was the systematic application of Smith's concept of the invisible hand, with the former concept entirely compatible with the latter. Only a handful of scholars noticed that there were actually substantial differences between the Austrian School (e.g., Hayek) and the Chicago School (e.g., Friedman and Becker), both of which were regarded as legitimate inheritors of Smith's liberalism doctrine. In the same vein, owing to inadequate understanding of the intellectual history of economics, the economists of the Lausanne School (e.g., Leon Walras, Vilfredo Pareto and Enrico Barone), who incline towards centrally planned economies, were also – ridiculously – mistaken as inheritors of Smith. As a result, neoclassical price theory, with its assumption of "rational economic man" and presupposition of a free competition market framework, was accepted as the default setting for Chinese economic education and research. Most universities started to offer courses in "Standard Neoclassical Microeconomics," while the study of Marxism lost ground. The course *"Das Kapital"* – which was still offered in many universities as late as the end of the 1980s – disappeared. "Marxist Political Economy" courses – which had been regarded as professional foundation courses for economics majors for decades – shrank, and in those that were left the tutors tended to concentrate on teaching theories of neoclassical economics. A few Chinese textbooks tried – but failed – to reconcile Marxism with neoclassical economics. Neoclassical economics is characterized by static comparative analysis, and its research focuses on resource allocation under given circumstances. The profound influences of history, institutions and technology on price fluctuation are often set aside as problems that are too difficult to study with economics' analytical tools. As a result of the increasing dominance of neoclassical political economy in Chinese academia, courses on political economy, economic history and the intellectual history of economics were gradually marginalized and then often cancelled altogether, with many tutors in those subjects losing their jobs. In consequence, the study of British classical economics declined in China. Adam Smith was cast simply as the founder of *laissez-faire* economics, and the richness of his social thoughts were not acknowledged at all.

Professor Zhu Shaowen, however, should be regarded as a lone-voice exception amid the chorus of *laissez-faire* economic thought. He studied in Japan under Kazuo Ōkouchi and adopted the research style of Japanese Smithian scholarship, but he also devised a new way to explore the complexity of Smith's thoughts and ideas. As early as 1987, Zhu published an article entitled "On the Attributes and Moral Qualities of 'Economic Man' in *WN*" in the most prestigious Chinese economics journal, *Economic Research*, which aroused considerable interest among his fellow Chinese intellectuals. Their attention was drawn to the focus of Zhu's research – namely, Adam Smith's exploration of the nature of human beings. Owing to the influence of this article, both academic and non-academic journals throughout China went on to publish numerous studies on the connotation, nature and function of the concept of "economic man." Almost a decade later, one of Zhu's best students, Fan Gang, who enjoyed significant influence in the initial period of Chinese reform, published an article – "Amoral Economics" – in which he denied that there was any relationship between economic theory and morality, and re-emphasized the traditional guiding principles of empirical economics. This article, which was published in the journal *Reading*, generated heated debate.

These two articles do not indicate that pupil and teacher adopted antagonistic positions to each other. In fact, Zhu and Fan were concerned with different problems. Zhu wished to explore the famous "Adam Smith Problem" – that is, how to reconcile Smith's elaboration of his economic thought based on self-interest in *WN* with his exploration of social order based on sympathy in *TMS*. Are there intrinsic contradictions between the two? Zhu focused on grasping the comprehensiveness of Smith's ethical philosophy and coming to a correct understanding of the humanistic foundations of the exchange system of economy. Fan, on the other hand, aimed to remove value judgments from the economic analysis system to maintain the purity of economics as a value-neutral analytical science. Anyway, all of these academic studies endeavored to find a satisfactory answer to the question: "What is the true connotation of the concept of economic man?"

Zhu is now considered the most outstanding, and certainly the most internationally well-known, expert on the study of Adam Smith in mainland China. His work is included in *Classical Economics and Modern Economics*, published by Beijing University Press in 2000. This book represents the highest achievements of Chinese scholarship on Adam Smith up to the end of the last century. Zhu has also attended many important international Adam Smith seminars as a representative of Chinese academia.

3. 1995–present day

Ever since China's political leaders first decided to encourage and develop a market economy, there has been ongoing doubt about the moral framework of that economic system. Any non-state traders who are found to be cheating in business incur fierce public criticism, which in turn leads to general accusations of immorality among the whole merchant class. In this way, the hostility towards commerce and the market economy increases.

In the mid-1990s, a number of professional bodies held symposia on the construction of a moral framework for the market economy. Economists were generally notable by their absence, although, of course, a few Chinese economists are interested in this topic, too. For instance, Professor Wang Dingding published an influential article entitled "On the Moral Basis of Market Economy," in which he argues that the successful operation of a market-orientated economic system demands that participants must behave in a self-interested, but not a selfish, manner. He discusses the Confucian notion of "virtue" and offers new insights on Adam Smith's concept of self-interested man in support of his argument. This article generated great enthusiasm among a number of Chinese intellectuals, most of whom were scholars from other social science disciplines or economists who had grave doubts about the doctrines of neoclassical economy.

The year after Wang published his article – 1997 – was a memorable one in the study of Adam Smith in mainland China because this was when Commercial Press published the first Chinese version of *TMS*. It was translated by Professor Jiang Ziqiang and his team at Zhejiang University. In his lengthy preface, Jiang discusses the relationship between *TMS* and *WN* in general, and the debate over the contradiction between egoism and the altruism of economic man in particular. It has been argued that Smith's two principal works are closely connected.

Although they have different focuses, they share a single essence. Three points have been emphasized in support of this claim:

- The two works were drafted and revised almost simultaneously, so the research questions and the development of the thoughts were closely related.
- Both works base their analysis of the motivation of human behavior on the human instinct of self-interest.
- Consistent references to the concept of the invisible hand indicate the organic connection between the two works.

In a word, the so-called "Adam Smith Problem" is merely a pseudo-problem that arose due to his successors' misunderstanding of his work.[4]

The publication of the Chinese version of *TMS* had a significant impact not only in Chinese intellectual circles but among the general public. Unprecedented numbers of people were now able to read and discuss Adam Smith's works. To some extent, the publication also ushered in a new era of Chinese Smithian scholarship, with the focus of study shifting from *WN* to *TMS*. Before the publication of the Chinese version of *TMS*, many Chinese economists had never even heard of the book, let alone read it, due to the language barrier and the unenlightened academic atmosphere that was prevalent in China at the time. Some sections of *TMS* had been translated into Chinese and included in Zhou Fucheng's *Selected Famous Works of Western Ethics* back in 1964, but this book's influence was limited to the field of philosophy, and few economists knew about it.

In the decade following the publication of the complete Chinese-language version of *TMS*, the relationship between it and *WN*, together with Smith's views on human nature and his moral philosophy, became hot topics in Chinese academia. The debate was fierce because there was a great deal of concern in Chinese intellectual circles about the developing market economy's impact on the moral and cultural foundations of society. On the one hand, this concern can be attributed to the traditional, family-centered system of social organization, which dates back millennia and emphasizes the importance of ethical order. The social status attached to the various professions in China decreases in the following sequence: scholars, farmers, artisans and, finally, merchants. So entrepreneurs and merchants are regarded as less morally reliable than scholars and farmers. This hostility towards entrepreneurs and merchants – that is, commercial society – continues to this day, even though the concept of market economy is now well established in China. On the other hand, many Chinese people still remember Marx's warnings about the moral decay that is unavoidable in a system that promotes private property and the pursuit of profit. They also recall that Marxism advocates the development of public ownership, planned economy and distribution according to labor to overcome the damage that market economies can do to human freedom. Both of these factors have contributed to a backlash against China's adoption of a market economy.

Between 1995 and 2005, Chinese scholars attempted to explore Smith's moral philosophy and the relationship between *TMS* and *WN*. Three works deserve special mention. Wang Ying and Jing Feng's *The Query on Morals from Economists: A Study on Adam Smith's Moral Philosophy* (2001) and Nie Wenjun's *On the Economic Ethics of Adam Smith* (2004) both summarized and reviewed Smith's thoughts and ideas from the perspective of moral philosophy, which helped to popularize Smith's role as a moral philosopher in Chinese academia. A couple of years later, Luo Weidong's *Sentiment, Order, Virtue: Adam Smith's Moral Philosophy* (2006) included references to the latest research into Adam Smith, especially the work of Japanese scholars like Tanaka and Mizuta, and made an in-depth textual study of the various versions of *TMS* to gain a profound understanding of the theme of the book and its gradual evolution over the last thirty years of Smith's life. Luo also explored the inherent conflicts in Smith's moral philosophy and his attempts to resolve them. The resemblances between Smith's moral philosophy and Chinese pre-Qin Confucianism have been pointed out, although no detailed discussion has been launched. In a recently published essay, Luo Weidong (2010) explored Smith's concept of enlightenment.

Other Chinese scholars have focused on the core concept of "sympathy" in Smith's moral philosophy. A number of articles have been published on this subject, with some exploring the exact connotation of "sympathy" and others comparing Hume's and Smith's thoughts on the matter. Two trends in these studies demand particular attention: the comparison between Smith's "sympathy" and the Confucian concept of "Ren" (仁), a field of research in which the Confucian philosopher Tu Weiming has been most notable; and the reductionist and naturalist exploration of the concept of "sympathy," in which Ye Hang's empirical fMRI research into the neurological basis of sympathy at Zhejiang University, Hangzhou, has been particularly illuminating.

In 2005, Zhejiang University held a symposium on "Adam Smith and China" during which the similarities and differences between "sympathy" and "Ren" were discussed at length. Several scholars at this symposium proposed that Smith may have had some knowledge of Confucianism, gleaned from the Physiocrats during his visit to France. Further research into this topic can be found in Ning Geng and Cheng Lisheng's essay "On the Concept of Sympathy and Consciousness of Mencius, Smith, and Husserl," published in the prestigious journal *World Philosophy*, and Zhou Guozheng's (2013) article which compares "sympathy" with Mencius's "doctrine of good human nature." Ever more Chinese scholars are reinterpreting the thoughts of Adam Smith with reference to traditional Chinese ideas (such as Confucianism), and Western scholars would be well advised to take notice of this trend.

In addition to Ye Hang, the likes of Wang Zhijian and Xu Bin of Zhejiang University have launched empirical studies into sympathy. They are exploring the behavioral foundations and the moral framework of economic action from the perspective of human nature through controlled behavioral experiments.

Chinese scholars are also studying Smith's moral philosophy by positioning it in a broader context – that is, the Scottish Enlightenment – within which Smith could be regarded as one of the most important representatives. These studies aim to reveal the intrinsic connections between historical background, cultural concepts and the development of a particular scholar's philosophy. Since 2006, Luo Weidong has organized an annual academic seminar on the Scottish Enlightenment, with each event exploring a specific theme. Thus far, topics have included Adam Smith and the law-of-nature tradition, Adam Smith and theology and Adam Smith and language. Many significant papers have been presented during these seminars, including: Wu Honglie's (2011) and Qu Jingdong's (2011) analysis of the specific connotation of the concept of "nature" in Smith's work and his consciousness of the law-of-nature; Zhang Yaping's exploration of the linguistic characteristics of Smith's texts and their relationship to his personality (Zhang Yaping and Luo Weidong 2012); the same scholar's discussion of the connections between Smith's thoughts and utilitarianism (Zhang Yaping and Luo Weidong 2011); Kang Zixing's (2014) interpretation of Adam Smith's views on justice; and Wang Nan's (2006) exploration of Smith's sociological thoughts.

Meanwhile, Zhejiang University Press has published a series of translations of books by the towering scholars of the Scottish Enlightenment, including Francis Hutcheson, David Hume, Thomas Reid and Adam Ferguson, whose work was unduly neglected in China for decades. Some important research into Adam Smith and the Scottish Enlightenment has also been translated into Chinese in recent years, such as Knud Haakonssen's *The Science of a Legislator: The Natural Jurisprudence in Scottish Enlightenment* and Istvan Hont and Michael Ignatieff's *Wealth and Virtue: The Shaping of Political Economy in the Scottish Enlightenment*, to name just two. The works of other famous Western scholars, such as Joseph Cropsey (2005), Patricia H. Werhane (2006), Donald Winch (2010) and Emma Rothschild (2013), have similarly been translated by various Chinese publishing houses in recent years.

Although this paper has mainly discussed Chinese scholarship relating to Adam Smith's moral philosophy, many other Chinese scholars have naturally focused on his economic doctrines, with topics ranging from the division of labor, capital, trade, distribution of income and national revenue to his status in the history of economic philosophy. The research into his theory of the division of labor and its application in China to achieve long-term economic growth has been especially noteworthy. Professor Yang Xiaokai developed the "Smith–Young Theorem" and founded the Ultra Marginal Economics Analysis School in order to develop a new economic growth theory that might take the place of the mainstream (neoclassical) theory. And Wei Sen (2009) of Fudan University has published several important articles on the driving forces behind the long-term Chinese economic growth and their limits.

In general, in the two decades since 1995, Adam Smith, as a Western scholar, has exerted unprecedented and unique influence on China, both in socio-economic studies and in the government's design of its economic policy. This may be partly attributed to the great impact that Milton Friedman, Friedrich Hayek and Ronald Coase have all had in China since the 1980s. It was only natural that Smith, as the predecessor that they all shared, was soon noticed and widely discussed. Moreover, some of Smith's most important works – principally *TMS* – were translated and published in China for the first time during this period. Nevertheless, Smith's preeminence in China is mainly due to the fact that his ideas provided urgently needed guidelines for the construction of the socialist market economy. Since the reform process was launched, the Chinese people have grappled with the concept of private economy, tried to establish the moral basis of the market system, and struggled with the design of the economic system and policy. These problems could not be solved simply by copying what the mature capitalist countries, such as the United States, did a hundred years earlier. The Chinese people had to develop *their own* understanding and insight by engaging in deep discussion and exploration, and both *WN* and *TMS* proved invaluable in these debates. Hence, Adam Smith earned a very high reputation and great respect in China in these years.

Since the publication of the first Chinese translation of *TMS* in 1997, and especially in the wake of Premier Wen Jiabao's recommendation of the book in 2005, a growing number of Chinese people have become interested in Adam Smith. Evidence is provided by the fact that twenty-four new Chinese versions of *TMS* have been published in recent years,[5] along with four simplified versions, with either Chinese notes or reading guidance. There are now at least thirty-seven Chinese versions of *WN*, too. Amazingly, this means that there are now more Chinese translations of these books than of either Marx's or Kant's classic texts. Some of Smith's other works, such as *Essays on Philosophical Subjects* (2012) and *Lectures on Rhetoric and Belles-Lettres* (2013), have also been translated and published in recent years, while *Lectures on Justice, Police, Revenue, and Arms* and *The Correspondence of Adam Smith* were both on their way to press at the time of writing.

As for biographies of Smith, as early as July 1983 Hu Qilin and Chen Yingnian translated John Rae's *Life of Adam Smith* into Chinese. A month later, the Chinese version of Dugald Stewart's *Account of the Life and Writings of Adam Smith* appeared, too. Over the next twenty years, these two biographies became important reference sources in the study of Adam Smith in China. Now, these have been complemented by Chinese versions of Buchan's (2007) and Kennedy's (2009) modern texts. Several Chinese scholars – such as Yan Zhijie (2011) – have also written their own biographies, in which they have explored Smith's life and academic achievements. Finally, in 2013, Zhejiang University Press published a Chinese version of Ian Simpson Ross's *The Life of Adam Smith* (originally published in 2010), which should be regarded as a significant moment for Smithian scholarship in China.

In November 2013, the 18th Chinese Communist Party Central Committee held its Third Plenary Session, during which a decision on "major issues concerning comprehensively deepening reforms" was approved. This signaled that China was determined to launch a new round of thorough social and economic reform that will allow the market to play a "decisive" role in the allocation of resources. This may well mean that economic liberalism is restored to the leading position it enjoyed in the 1980s. Most Chinese scholars regard Adam Smith as the founder of *laissez-faire* economics, so his influence will surely grow during this process, which could promote further study of his moral philosophy, too.

4. The future

It is never easy to forecast how Chinese scholarship on Adam Smith will develop. The question may be approached from at least two perspectives.

First, two contradictory forces may impact on Chinese academia in the near future. On the one hand, the study of Western philosophy may have had its day as ever more Chinese scholars turn their attention to reviving their own cultural traditions. Obviously, to some extent, this trend may stifle research into Adam Smith in China. On the other hand, as the country's economic development continues to accelerate, the relationship between China and the rest of the world is strengthening year by year. Moreover, the Chinese government wishes to press ahead with the development of its modern, market-oriented economic system. As a result, it is likely to promote the application of Smith's thought. Hence, the development of Smithian scholarship in China will depend on the interaction between these two antagonistic forces, and which one gains the upper hand.

Second, Chinese scholars are still grappling with the challenge of developing a comprehensive and precise understanding of Adam Smith's thought. Over the past century, the state, the particular ideology that was in place at the time, and the specific demands of the historical period have all had significant impacts on how Smith has been interpreted. Hence, his story has been told totally differently at different times and under different political conditions. It has been almost impossible to see the whole picture. Of course, this issue must be addressed.

Undoubtedly, Adam Smith will remain a significant figure in modern China. For example, his criticism of mercantilism, his classic defense of the free-market system, and his condemnation of private enterprise are as relevant today as they have ever been. In short, by relating his insights on human nature to social reality, Smith's ethical philosophical system and his concept of history will remain an important source of inspiration for China's future reform, transformation and development.

It seems likely that ever more Chinese scholars will start to compare Smith with traditional Chinese philosophy, such as Confucian humanism, Taoism and Buddhist transcendentalism. Such a perspective may well shed new light on the international study of Smith, too. Personally, I am interested in the theme of "Confucian humanism and Smithism," which could be regarded as a means to connect past and future, as well as West and East.

Acknowledgments

I wish to thank Professor Jeng-Guo S. Chen for his support and encouragement, without which this essay would not have been written. Thanks also to two anonymous reviewers of the *Adam Smith Review* for their constructive comments and suggestions. I am also grateful to Dr. Yaping Zhang and Ms. Chen Cheng, who assisted me with part of the data collection and the translation of the essay into English. I am responsible for any errors that remain, however.

Notes

1   For an extended discussion of Yan Fu's translation of *WN*, see Pi Houfeng (2000). It has been pointed out that Yan Fu's translation differs from the original *WN* in four chief respects: differences in organization; additions and deletions; difference in length; and the translator's notes relating to his interpretation of the text. Yan Fu's notes stretch to 80,000 words, and he omits or edits many of Smith's original passages. His version totals just 400,000 words, whereas a later Chinese translation (by Guo Dali and Wang Yanan) exceeds 600,000 words. Some errors concerning important terms have also been noticed. Hence, Yan Fu's translation should be seen as a commentary on and abridgment of the original *WN*. Another detailed study of Yan Fu's translation is Lai Jiancheng (2002).

2   Although the works of scholars from non-communist countries, such as the English economist Ronald Meek's work on the labor theory of value and Maurice Dobb's essays on capitalism and centrally planned economy, were translated into Chinese, they did not exert as great an influence in China as they might have done. Moreover, Dobb's seminal work *Theories of Value and Distribution since Adam Smith: Ideology and Economic Theory* (London: Cambridge University Press, 1973) is yet to be translated into Chinese.

3   This reprint used the Chinese translation of the full original English title *Guo Min Cai Fu De Xing Zhi Yu Yuan Yin de Yan Jiu*, divided into two volumes. Both of the translators (Guo Dali and Wang Yanan) were in their twenties when they embarked on the project, and unemployed after graduation. They treated this translation as a warm-up for their translation of Marx's *Das Kapital*. Over the next few years, they also translated David Ricardo's *Principles of Political Economy and Taxation*; Thomas Robert Malthus's *An Essay on the Principle of Population*; and John Stuart Mill's *Principles of Political Economy*.

4   Although *The Theory of Moral Sentiments*, ed. D. D. Raphael and A. L. Macfie (Oxford: Oxford University Press, 1976) was regarded as the most authoritative (and certainly the most up-to-date) version, Jiang Ziqiang based his translation on the edition published in London in 1833.

5   Surprisingly, not one of these new translations of *TMS* is based on Raphael and Macfie's 1976 edition.

Bibliography

Buchan, J. (2007) 真实的亚当.斯密 (*The Real Adam Smith*), translated by Jin Hui, Beijing: Zhongxin Press.

Cropsey, J. (2005) 国体与经体 (*Polity and Economy*), translated by Deng Wenzheng, Shanghai: Shanghai People's Press.

Daisun, C. (1996) *From Classic Economic Theory System to Marx* (in Chinese), Beijing: Beijing University Press.

Erhard, L. (1983) 来自竞争的繁荣 (*Prosperity through Competition*), translated by Zhu Shaking and Mu Jiaji, Beijing: Commercial Press.

Friedman, M. and Friedman, R. (1982) 自由选择 (*Free to Choose: A Personal Statement*), translated by Zhang Qi, Beijing: Commercial Press.

Haakonssen, K. (2010) 立法者的科学 (*The Science of a Legislator: The Natural Jurisprudence in Scottish Enlightenment*), Hangzhou: Zhejiang University Press.

Hayek, F. (1962) 通向奴役之路 (*The Road to Serfdom*), translated by Teng Weizao and Zhu Zongfeng, Beijing: Commercial Press.

Hayek, F. (1989) 个人主义与经济秩序 (*Individualism and Economic Order*), translated by Jia Zhan and Wen Yueran, Beijing: Beijing Economics College Press.

Hayek, F. (1999) 自由宪章 (*The Constitution of Freedom*), translated by Yang Yusheng, Beijing: Chinese Social Sciences Press.

Hayek, F. (2000) 法律、立法与自由 (*Law, Legislation and Freedom*), translated by Deng Zhenglai, Zhang Shoudong and Li Jingbing, Beijing: China Encyclopedia Press.

Hont, I. and M. Ignatieff (2013) 财富与德性 (*Wealth and Virtue: The Shaping of Political Economy in the Scottish Enlightenment*), translated by Li Dajun, Fan Liangcong and Zhuang Jiayue, Hangzhou: Zhejiang University Press.

Kang Zixing (2014) "Adam Smith's Insights on 'Wealth' and 'Justice' in Commercial Society" (in Chinese), *Journal of Zhejiang Social Sciences* 4: 4–12.

Kennedy, J. (2009) 亚当.斯密 (*Adam Smith*), translated by Su Jun, Beijing: HuaXia Press.

Kornai, J. (1986) 短缺经济学 (*Shortage Economics*), translated by Zhang Xiaoguang, Li Zhenning and Huang Weiping, Beijing: Economics and Science Press.

Lai Jiancheng (2002) 亚当.斯密与严复 (*Adam Smith and Yan Fu*) (in Chinese), Taibei: San Min Book Co.

Lu Youzhang and Li Zongzheng (1965) *The Theoretical History of Economy* (2 vols.) (in Chinese), Beijing: People's Press.

Luo Weidong (2006) *Sentiment, Order, Virtue: Adam Smith's Moral Philosophy* (in Chinese), Beijing: Chinese People's University Press.

Luo Weidong (2010) *Adam Smith's Concept of Enlightenment* (in Chinese), *Reading* 12: 25–31.

Marx, K. (2009) 剩余价值学说史 (*A Theoretical History of Surplus Value*), translated by Go Dali, Shanghai: Shanghai Sanlian Press.

Nie Wenjun (2004) *On the Economic Ethics of Adam Smith* (in Chinese), Beijing: Chinese Social Sciences Press.

Ning Geng and Cheng Lisheng (2011) "On the Concept of Sympathy and Consciousness of Mencius, Smith, and Husserl" (in Chinese), *World Philosophy* 1: 35–52.

Pi Houfeng (2000) "The Translation and Transmission of *WN*" (in Chinese), *Sinology Studies* 18(1): 309–330.

Qu Jingdong (2011) "The Three Conceptual Meanings of Nature in Adam Smith's Social Thought" (in Chinese), *Journal of Zhejiang University (Humanities and Social Sciences)* 5: 5–9.

Rae, J. (1983) 亚当.斯密传 (*Life of Adam Smith*), translated by Hu Qilin and Chen Yingnian, Beijing: Commercial Press.

Rogge, B. (1982) 资本主义能够生存下去吗? (*Can Capitalism Survive?*) translated by Huang Huixin, Guangdong: Guangdong People's Press.

Rosenberg, D. I. (1959) *A Theoretical History of Political Economy*, translated by Li Xiagong, Shanghai: Joint Publishing Co.

Ross, I. (2013) 亚当.斯密传 (*The Life of Adam Smith*), translated by Zhang Yaping, Hangzhou: Zhejiang University Press.

Rothschild, E. (2013) 经济情操论: 亚当.斯密 孔多赛与启蒙运动 (*Economic Sentiments: Adam Smith, Condorcet, and the Enlightenment*), Beijing: Social Sciences Literature Press.

Shaowen, Z. (2000) *Classical Economics and Modern Economics* (in Chinese), Beijing: Beijing University Press.

Smith, A. (1949) 国富论, *Guo Fu Lun* (*On the Wealth of Nations*), translated by Guo Dali and Wang Yanan, Beijing: Chung Hwa Book Co.

Smith, A. (1972) 国民财富的性质与原因的研究, *Guo Min Cai Fu De Xing Zhi Yu Yuan Yin De Yan Jiu* (*An Inquiry into the Nature and Causes of the Wealth of Nations*), Beijing: Commercial Press.

Smith, A. (1981) 原富, *Yuan Fu* (*The Origin of Wealth*), translated by Yan Fu, Beijing: Commercial Press.

Smith, A. (1997) 道德情操论 (*The Theory of Moral Sentiments*), translated by Jiang Ziqiang *et al.*, Beijing: Commercial Press.

Smith, A. (2012) 亚当.斯密哲学文集 *(Essays on Philosophical Subjects)*, translated by Shi Xiaozhu and Sun Mingle, Beijing: Commercial Press.

Smith, A. (2013) 修辞学与文学讲义 (*Lectures on Rhetoric and Belles-Lettres*), translated by Zhu Weihong, Shanghai: Shanghai San Lian Bookstore.

Stewart, D. (1983) 亚当.斯密的生平与著作 (*Account of the Life and Writings of Adam Smith*), translated by Su Jun, Beijing: Commercial Press.

Strauss, L. and J. Cropsey (2010) 政治哲学史 (*History of Political Philosophy*), Beijing: Law Press.

Wang Dingding (1996) "On the Moral Basis of Market Economy" (in Chinese), *Reform* 5: 89–96.

Wang Nan (2006) "Adam Smith's Philosophy of Society: The Natural Order Based on Human Nature" (in Chinese), *Sociology Studies* 6: 25–44.

Wang Ying and Jing Feng (2001) *The Query on Morals from Economists: A Study on Adam Smith's Moral Philosophy* (in Chinese), Beijing: People's Press.

Wei Sen (2009) *Economics Theories and Market Order: Exploration on the Ethnic Basis, Cultural Environment, and Institutional Conditions for the Healthy Operation of the Market Economic System* (in Chinese), Shanghai: Gezhi Press.

Werhane, P. (2006) 亚当.斯密及其留给现代资本主义的遗产 (*Adam Smith and his Legacy for Modern Capitalism*), translated by Xia Zheping, Shanghai: Shanghai Translation Press.

Winch, D. (2010) 亚当. 斯密的政治学 (*Adam Smith's Politics*), translated by Chu Ping, Nan Jing: YiLin Press.

Wu Honglie (2011) "Adam Smith's View on Nature: An Analysis on Nature in *The Theory of Moral Sentiments*," *Journal of Zhejiang University (Humanities and Social Sciences*) 5: 18–26.

Yan Zhijie (2011) *Illustration of Adam Smith* (in Chinese), Beijing: Beijing University Press.

Yang Xiaokai (2003) *Development Economics: Inframarginal versus Marginal Analysis*, translated by Zhang Dingsheng and Zhang Yongsheng, Beijing: Social Sciences Literature Press.

Yang Xiaokai (2003) *Economics: New Classical versus Neoclassical Frameworks*, translated by Zhang Dingsheng and Zhang Yongsheng, Beijing: Social Sciences Literature Press.

Ye Hang (2005) "On the Economic Explanation of Altruistic Behavior" (in Chinese), *Economist* 3: 22–29.

Zhang Yaping and Luo Weidong (2012) "Adam Smith's Philosophy of Rhetoric: The Communication of Passion and the Passion to Communicate" (in Chinese), *Zhejiang Social Sciences* 11: 106–113.

Zhang Zhengping and Luo Weidong (2011) "An Analysis on the Doctrine of Utility in Adam Smith's *Theory of Moral Sentiments*" (in Chinese), *Journal of Zhejiang University (Humanities and Social Sciences)* 5: 10–17.

Zhengdong Tang (2002) *From Adam Smith to Marx* (in Chinese), Nanjing: Nanjing University Press.

Zhou Fucheng (1964) *Selected Famous Works of Western Ethics* (2 vols.), Beijing: Commercial Press.

Zhou Guozheng (2013) "On the Doctrine of Benevolence in Adam Smith's *TMS*," *Journal of Shanghai University (Social Sciences)* 3: 15–26.

Articles

Empathy, concern, and understanding in *The Theory of Moral Sentiments*

Olivia Bailey

1. Introduction

When we observe and interact with other people, it seems to us utterly obvious that we have some acquaintance with the content and character of their experiences. I understand that the store clerk is bored, and that the children long for ice cream. I understand how the bitterly disappointed fourth-place finisher is feeling, and what the shame of the man who accidentally knocked over the Ming vase must be like. At the same time, it also seems obvious to us that we are interested in others' passions, thoughts, and attitudes, independent of their instrumental significance for us, and not only out of intellectual curiosity. That is, we are concerned about others' inner lives. What others think and feel matters to us in a way that can directly motivate us to act on their behalf.[1]

One of Adam Smith's aims in *The Theory of Moral Sentiments* is to vindicate these convictions about concern and understanding. Given that they are backed by the authority of common sense, we might ask: why does Smith think a further, more philosophical, defense is needed? At least part of the reason is that he endorses a particular picture of the difference between self-directed understanding and concern and other-directed understanding and concern. I will call this the 'picture of egocentric primacy'. This picture presents our self-concern and self-understanding as uniquely primitive and self-evident. Our own minds are immediately transparent to us, but 'we have no immediate experience of what other men feel' (*TMS* I.i.1.2; Smith 1976). Similarly, our self-concern is immediate, but our concern for others looks like the kind of thing that we can only come to through considerable mental maneuvering. Once one admits that our understanding and concern for others need to be explained, one had better follow up with an explanation. The skeptic can press the point: if the origin and nature of our understanding and concern for others are mysterious, and if we cannot dispel that impression of mystery with a plausible explanation of how and why we come to understand and be concerned for others, then our everyday impression that we do in fact understand and have concern for others may not be good enough reason to reject the skeptical alternatives.

One resource that has appealed to both early-modern and contemporary philosophers faced with this conundrum is the psychological phenomenon now generally known as 'empathy'. What exactly empathy consists in has been the subject of lively debate since the time of Hume and Smith's exchanges about the nature of what they called 'sympathy, or . . . fellow feeling' (*TMS* I.i.1.3; see also *TMS* VII.iii.3.17). For our purposes, though, the following loose but handily ecumenical definition of empathy should suffice: empathy consists in feeling what another person feels, or at least imagining feeling what another person feels, not because one is literally in the same situation as she is, but because one has in some other way come to engage imaginatively with something like the other person's experience. Empathy tends to interest philosophers operating with some version of the picture of egocentric primacy because it seems like it could provide the means of 'bootstrapping' up from our intimate understanding of and concern for ourselves to our understanding of and concern for others.

In this paper, I will consider Smith's attempts to fend off skeptical worries about understanding and concern by appealing to our capacity for empathy. My aim here is partly critical, and partly rehabilitative. Smith's explicit pronouncements about empathy's role in fostering understanding and concern generate a problem. He assigns a double duty to the series of mental operations that issue in empathy, treating it as the source of both our understanding of other people and our non-instrumental concern for them. However, if Smith's empathetic mechanism does generate an accurate understanding of the other, that understanding will simply not be the right kind of acquaintance to generate concern. Only a seriously confused grasp of the attitudes and passions of the other could give birth to a heretofore absent non-instrumental concern for others. As we will see, the fulfillment of either one of the empathetic mechanism's supposed functions requires conditions that will make it impossible for the other function to be fulfilled.

Smith's official account of empathy is seriously flawed. However, his theory of human sociability also contains within it the seeds of an important improvement upon the official account. Whether or not Smith recognizes it, one element of his account demands the conclusion that an important form of concern precedes empathy and empathetically derived understanding. Since Smith conceives of empathy as an effortful activity, he needs to explain why we are motivated to empathize. The explanation he gives is incomplete. Still, his scattered remarks about why we engage in imaginative projection entail (or at least come close to entailing) that some concern for the other's thoughts and feelings is often (if not always) a necessary condition of our being motivated to empathize. This would mean that concern for others is not just something we get to through empathetic 'bootstrapping up' from self-concern; it is prior to empathetic feeling. And if concern is prior to empathetic feeling, then the problem that emerges from his official account does not get off the ground: that problem arises only because Smith officially treats both concern and understanding as empathetically derived. I will aim to make it clear that, given Smith's conception of empathy, he should on pain of inconsistency be committed to a very different conception of concern's relation to empathy and understanding than the one he more explicitly endorses.

2. Smithian empathy: an overview, and a problem

Concern and understanding

Before entering into the details of Smith's account, I want to identify more precisely the nature of the concern and understanding that interest Smith. Let us first consider the range of attitudes we might classify under the heading of 'concern'. What does it mean to be concerned for or about someone? We tend to think of concern as an attitude of benevolence that is associated with a motivation to aid the object of our concern. However, we can also identify a broader sense of concern, one that encompasses *all* of our interest in others and their inner lives, benevolent or not. Of course, our interest in others may be more or less motivated by our own self-concern. The kind of concern that Smith regards as most in need of explanation is a concern for others' experiences, attitudes, emotions, and intentional actions that is not motivated by self-interest. I will refer to this particular kind of concern as *basic* concern. Significantly, this kind of concern includes distinctly non-altruistic attitudes. For instance, I might be concerned about my enemy's agony just because his unhappiness matters to me absolutely. Smith tends to focus on more positive versions of basic concern, but he does memorably mention a less palatable form of concern – namely, 'a malice in mankind' that renders minor episodes of others' suffering 'in some measure diverting' (*TMS* I.ii.5.3).

Understanding ranges along a scale of depth. At the shallow end, there is the understanding that consists in an acquaintance with another's behavioral patterns. This is mere predictive understanding. Then there are the varieties of understanding that are relevant only in those cases where we recognize the individual in question as having a mind. Classification of the various forms our understanding of other inner lives can take is inevitably contentious. One particularly difficult question is: if we are to understand another's inner life, how important is it that we appreciate that other's experience? By 'experience', I mean the felt character of inner life, that aspect of our mental existence that we tend to refer to as 'what it is like'. One might think that we can distinguish between two ways of understanding another as minded, as follows: on the one hand, some understanding of an individual's feelings and beliefs can be reproduced in propositional form without remainder; and, on the other hand, some understanding includes an ineffable sense of 'what it is like' for the other. But this way of carving up our understanding invites some difficult questions. Can I truly be said to understand that you are thinking of me if I do not know what thinking of me feels like for you? Can I truly be said to understand that you are sad if I do not have an idea of how your sadness feels 'from the inside'? Or, to take a more extreme case, can I truly be said to understand that you are sad even if I myself (through some happy stroke of luck) have never once experienced sadness myself?

I cannot begin to answer these questions here. I will say, though, that Smith generally takes understanding another's thoughts and feelings to involve either or both of drawing upon old knowledge about what it is like to be sad (or curious, or desirous of fame, and so forth) or producing a new and vivid idea of what the episodes of another person's life must be like for them.[2] For him, and also for those contemporary philosophers of mind who take inspiration from him, understanding another person's inner life critically involves acquaintance with that person's experience.[3] So, my discussion of the relation between concern and understanding will naturally focus on a conception of understanding that emphasizes the importance of experience.

Empathy as a 'bootstrapping' device: the official theory

On the very first page of *The Theory of Moral Sentiments*, Smith both gives us his version of the picture of egocentric primacy and identifies empathy (which he calls 'sympathy') as the means by which we get outside of ourselves and arrive at understanding of and concern for others. His identification of empathy as *the* means by which we come to understand others' inner lives is straightforward: 'As we have no immediate experience of what other men feel, we can form no idea of the manner in which they are affected, but by conceiving what we ourselves should feel in the like situation' (*TMS* I.i.1.1). Clearly, Smith thinks our apprehension of others' experience can come only through a mental operation that exploits our familiarity with the only inner life we directly apprehend, namely our own. His affirmation of the other half of the picture of egocentric primacy requires a little more work to see clearly, coming as it does in the first – rather garbled – sentences of the text. Smith writes:

> However selfish soever man may be supposed, there are evidently some principles in his nature, which interest him in the fortune of others, and render their happiness necessary to him, though he derives nothing from it except the pleasure of seeing it. Of this kind is pity and compassion, the emotion which we feel for the misery of others, when we either see it, or are made to conceive it in a very lively manner.
>
> (*TMS* I.i.1.2)

To see what is going on in these lines, we need to understand what Smith means by 'pity or compassion'. We tend to associate both 'pity' and 'compassion' with feeling bad about someone's unhappy situation, and feeling motivated to ameliorate it. These certainly seem to be phenomena that are distinct from what I have been calling empathy, which involves feeling (or imagining feeling) something akin to what someone else feels. However, Smith's later uses of 'compassion' suggest that he may not have in mind a notion of compassion that necessarily involves benevolence (see, for example, *TMS* I.i.1.10 and VI.iii.15). Rather, it is likely that he has in mind the more archaic (and now obscure) sense of compassion that merely denotes participation in someone else's suffering.[4] If that is correct, then we can understand Smith as holding the view that at least compassion (and possibly pity, too) is a subset of the feelings generated through the process of empathizing with another. This interpretation is supported by Smith's later statement:

> Pity and compassion are words appropriated to signify our fellow-feeling with the sorrow of others. Sympathy, though its meaning was, perhaps, originally the same, may now, however, without much impropriety, be made use of to denote our fellow-feeling with any passion whatever.
>
> (*TMS* I.i.3.5)

Smith writes that there are 'some principles in [man's] nature, which interest him in the fortunes of others, and render their happiness necessary to him', and that pity or compassion is 'of this kind'. I take him to be using the phrase 'of this kind' to signal that pity or compassion is one of the principles in human nature that has the effect of generating both interest in others' fortunes and concern for their happiness. Since Smith also describes pity or compassion as an emotion, and since an emotion does not seem to be the kind of thing that can be a principle, we can assume that what Smith really means is that our *tendency* to feel pity or compassion is one of these principles of our nature. At any rate, he seems to be endorsing the following general order of explanation: our tendency to feel pity or compassion (by which, I have argued, he means our tendency to empathize) is a principle of our nature that causes our basic concern for other people's feelings and fortunes, not the other way around.

So, according to the opening page of *The Theory of Moral Sentiments*, both understanding and basic concern are to come from empathy. This is what I will refer to as Smith's 'official theory' of empathy. In a moment, I will move on to the problem that this dual role generates, but first we need to look more closely at the details of Smith's conception of empathy.

Empathy as imaginative projection

Smith's description of this mental operation uses various spatial metaphors that help to give a sense of what he has in mind: frequently, we are told that empathy involves 'enter[ing] into' another's situation.[5] Smith also sometimes speaks of 'bringing the case home' to oneself (at *TMS* I.i.1.4, I.i.2.6, I.i.3.9, and II.i.3.2, among other points). Following the lead of these spatial descriptions, I will call the operation in question 'imaginative projection'.[6] Properly engaging in imaginative projection means mentally conjuring up as much of the detail of another's circumstances as possible, as though one were in the other's position: 'the spectator must, first of all, endeavor, as much as he can, to put himself in the situation of the other' (*TMS* I.i.4.6).

What, exactly, counts as another's situation is a difficult question. Should it include only a person's material circumstances? How about their previous experiences, or even their likes and dislikes? Smith wavers on this point. In relation to empathizing with the mother of a dead son, he writes:

> I do not consider what I, a person of such a character and profession, should suffer, if I had a son, and that son was unfortunately to die: but I consider what I should suffer if I was really you, and I not only change circumstances with you, but I change persons and characters.
>
> (*TMS* VII.iii.1.4)

Here, Smith is conceiving of agents' situations in what we can call a broad sense, one that encompasses facts about our inner life, as well as our material circumstances. However, he also writes:

> Sympathy . . . does not arise so much from the view of the passion, as it does from that of the situation which excites it. We sometimes feel for another, a passion of which he himself seems to altogether incapable, because, when we put ourselves in his case, that passion arises in our breast from the imagination, though it does not from his in reality.
>
> (*TMS* I.i.1.10)

This suggests that Smith is thinking of the situation with which we imaginatively engage as something more like the sum total of the other person's material circumstances, and less like the sum total of their material circumstances, *plus* their history, their preferences, their fears, and so on. Overall, though, it makes sense to think that, insofar as our goal is to understand someone, the more complete we can make our projection into her circumstances (broadly understood), the better. To illustrate: I will better understand how a lost child feels if I am able to imagine not just how I would feel if I – with my current education, size, emotional maturity, and so forth – were lost, but rather how I would feel if I could not read, did not know how to ask for help, and so forth.

When we imagine ourselves in another's situation, Smith thinks, we *experience* something like a weak version of the feelings we imagine the other to be having. Smith calls this kind of feeling a 'shadow':

> Every man feels his own pleasures and pains more sensibly than those of other people. The former are the original sensations, the latter the reflected or sympathetic images of those sensations. The former may be said to be the substance; the latter the shadow.
>
> (*TMS* VI.ii.1.2)

The comparison to a shadow helps to capture the quality of the feeling attained through projective imagination: just as a shadow mimics the outer form of an object exactly, but in a duller tone, an observer's empathetic feeling has the same object and the same phenomenal quality as the original emotion, except that it is less vivid. It is this less vivid feeling that is, according to the opening of *The Theory of Moral Sentiments*, supposed to be the source of our basic concern for others. The feeling is, apparently, enough to make us perceive others' fortunes as worth caring about for their own sake. In particular, it makes us see others' happiness as 'necessary to us' (*TMS* I.i.1.1).

For Smith, the imaginative transportation into the other's situation is typically effortful. It is true that we have a natural capacity for empathy, but we are all affected by various motivational and imaginative limitations that affect our ability to empathize, so we often 'find it … difficult to sympathize entirely, and keep perfect time' with other people's feelings (*TMS* I.iii.1.8). Especially when it comes to others' sorrows, we must battle against a 'dull sensibility to the afflictions of others' in order to see things from their points of view (*TMS* I.iii.1.13). The task of imaginatively abstracting from our own position is, Smith thinks, hard enough that we reserve some of our highest admiration for the person who is able to feel nearly as much for others as he does for himself (*TMS* VI.iii.1.1 ff.).

The problem with the official theory

The idea that a weak but actual feeling, rather than the mere conception of a feeling, is needed in order for us to have basic concern for others' feelings makes a certain sense given that Smith is, after all, a sentimentalist. Though his theory of empathy is ultimately quite different from Hume's, he has no quarrel with the latter's general insistence upon the idea that only sentiment, not reason, can ultimately motivate us. However, the idea that we need to feel a shadow of another's feeling in order to be concerned for him runs into a serious problem. In brief, the difficulty is this: it is hard to see how the experience of a feeling could be anything other than the experience of one's *own* feeling – and the experience of one's own feeling is not a suitable source of basic concern for others.

To bring out the problem more clearly, let us consider a case in which I am to empathize with another person's suffering. Suppose I have turned my attention to Morris, whose investments in the textiles market have collapsed spectacularly. Taking stock of Morris's circumstances and outward behavior, I attempt to enter into his position imaginatively. I imagine that I was once rich, but am now suddenly poor, and all because of some bad bets. Let us suppose (not, I think, implausibly) that part of Morris's inner state is a painful regret occasioned by the enduring presence of the thought: 'I have lost my fortune.' If I am to understand Morris's inner state successfully, I should, according to Smith, experience a shadow of this painful regret. What, precisely, will be the nature of that shadow? To answer that question, we need to think a little about what work the indexical 'I' and the indexical possessive pronoun 'my' are doing in the thought that is the focus of Morris's regret. What does Morris regret, exactly? In some sense, it would be correct to say that Morris regrets the loss of Morris's fortune. But unless he is highly unusual, it is not the loss of Morris's fortune *qua Morris's* fortune that matters to Morris. Rather, it is the loss of *his* fortune that concerns him. Morris's thought – 'I have lost my fortune' – is not really interchangeable with the thought 'Morris has lost his fortune' (or even 'I have lost Morris's fortune'). A counterfactual will clarify the point: if, by some fluke, Morris had forgotten that he was that person whom people call Morris, then the thought 'I have lost Morris's fortune' would have a very different resonance from that of the thought 'I have lost my fortune.'[7] It might prompt Morris to feel guilty for ruining another person's future, but it would not cause him to long for his own bygone salad days. Clearly, Morris's regret is not for the fortune of the man named Morris who happens to be him. Rather, it is essential to the nature of his regretful thought that the one who thinks it is the same person who has lost the fortune – and knows that he is that person.

The character of Morris's thought will not be accurately preserved if my shadow of Morris's regret includes the thought 'Morris has lost his fortune', or 'I have lost Morris's fortune.' Morris's thought 'I have lost my fortune' refers to the person who is thinking the thought as the one who has lost a fortune, so my recreation of Morris's regret must have this same structural feature. The thought's indexicals must be preserved 'as is' in my shadowy imaginative reconstruction of Morris's inner life. That means that when I come to understand Morris's regret through imaginative projection into his situation, I myself will be pained (if only a little) by the thought 'I have lost my fortune.' Otherwise, my experience of the putative shadow of his inner life will be inaccurate. But in that case, the only concern that painful thought should generate is concern for my own fortune, not concern for Morris or his fortune.

This conclusion needs a minor qualification: my regretful feeling could cause me to be concerned about Morris's regret, but only instrumentally. If empathy with painful sentiments will itself be somewhat painful, and if I am bound to empathize at least some of the time, it would be natural for me to prefer that others do not have such sentiments, so I might hope for the return of Morris's fortune. However, this is not basic concern, as I have defined it, and it is presumably not the kind of concern for other people that Smith has in mind. After all, my preference in this case would be just as well served by any circumstance that interrupts the empathetic mechanism, including my falling asleep or simply forgetting about Morris. Such purely instrumental concern for others' feelings is still fundamentally selfish.

Effectively, Smith is caught in a bind. According to his picture of how empathy works, we understand a person's feeling insofar as we are able to reproduce the other's passion accurately in ourselves through imaginative effort. When we succeed in understanding the other, only a variation in liveliness distinguishes their passion from the shadow of it that we experience. However, the development of understanding looks to be at odds with the generation of concern. My empathetic experience of someone else's regret about their situation can only result in my feeling regret about my own situation – a particularly strange result, given that I may well be in an enviable situation myself.

A confused grasp of Morris's regret does look like it could generate concern for Morris, of a sort. If my imaginative reconstruction of Morris's feelings included a bitter regret focused on the thought '*Morris* has lost his fortune,' then my empathetic feeling would involve a shadow of regret directed at Morris's loss of his fortune, rather than my loss of my fortune. If I come to regret Morris's loss of his fortune, then perhaps it makes sense that I would come to be concerned about Morris and his situation. But getting to concern in this way means sacrificing a real understanding of Morris's inner life. Morris's regret does *not* focus on the thought 'Morris has lost his fortune,' and if my reconstruction of Morris's regret includes this kind of focus, then I have misunderstood Morris's inner life in a significant way. Furthermore, there is something suspect about the kind of concern we could expect this kind of reconstruction to produce. Perhaps it would not seem so odd for me to be concerned about Morris's loss in the way that a regretful feeling would demand. But suppose that the feeling in question were Roy's unhealthy self-hatred. It would be utterly bizarre, and not at all consistent with our expectations of what basic concern should amount to, for my concern for Roy to arise from empathetic self-hatred (or, depending upon how we think of Roy's feelings, from hatred of Roy).[8]

Schopenhauer described the question of how our sharing others' feelings could lead us to be concerned for others as 'the great mystery of Ethics, its original phenomenon, and the boundary stone, past which only transcendental speculation may dare to take a step' (Schopenhauer 1915: 170). Smith's official attempt to dispel this mystery, whilst also accounting for our basic understanding of others' passions, does not succeed. His account draws on what strike us as familiar thoughts: it seems reasonable enough to think that I understand you at least in part by relying upon my ideas of my own experience, and that my feeling something like what you are feeling has something to do with my concern for you (witness the prevalence of injunctions to 'walk a mile in my/their shoes'). However, when we try to determine exactly how our empathy with others relates to our understanding and concern for them, difficulties like Smith's rapidly arise.

Later in *The Theory of Moral Sentiments*, Smith qualifies his 'substance is to shadow as original feeling is to empathetic feeling' analogy in a way that may indicate he sees a problem with his original take on the relations between empathy, concern, and understanding. Of those observed by another, Smith writes:

> What they feel will, indeed, always be, in some respects different from what he feels . . . because the secret consciousness that the change of situations, from which the sympathetic sentiment arises, is but imaginary, not only lowers it in degree, but, in some measure, varies it in kind, and gives it a quite different modification.
>
> (*TMS* I.i.4.7)

Smith does not say what this 'quite different modification' is supposed to be, and he does not mention anything like it again. Still, his appeal to it may signal a kind of recognition that an exact copy of another's emotion, taken by itself, is not a proper source of concern for the other. Perhaps without realizing it, Smith may be grasping for a way of having his cake and eating it too. That is, he may be trying to ensure that the empathetic emotion is different enough from the original that it can be a source of concern for the other, whilst also holding on to the idea that the one is enough like the other that it could be a source of true understanding of the other's inner life. The fact that Smith is willing to talk about the hypothetical modification only in the vaguest of terms does not bode well for this strategy, however.

In the next section, I shall suggest a more promising modification of Smith's theory. To resolve the problem concerning the apparent incompatibility of Smithian empathy's two tasks, I will turn to Smith's account of our motivation to empathize. Although Smith does not acknowledge the fact, his account of our motivation for empathizing with others practically entails that basic concern is at least sometimes a precondition of empathetic imagination. The mostly psychologically plausible way of filling out his motivational account will allow that concern is not a product generated via empathy, but rather a part of our psychology that needs to be in place if we are to be motivated to empathize (in a large and important set of cases). So, Smith should abandon his official commitment to the idea that empathy generates concern for others.

3. Concern and understanding: the implicit Smithian alternative

Sentimental harmony and the motivation to empathize

As I have mentioned, Smith describes imaginative projection primarily in terms that make it look like it involves deliberate work. For Smith, perfect fellow-feeling is a goal that we struggle to meet. He writes of the spectator's task:

> the spectator must, first of all, endeavor, as much as he can, to put himself in the situation of the other, and to bring home to himself every little circumstance of distress which can possibly occur to the sufferer. He must . . . strive to render as perfect as possible, that imaginary change of situation upon which his sympathy is founded.
>
> (*TMS* I.i.4.6)

Smith's talk of 'endeavoring' and 'striving' makes it clear that this is a difficult undertaking; it may be natural, but it is hardly automatic.[9] Because Smith rejects the conception of imaginative projection as automatic or effortless, he is faced with this question: why are we motivated to perform the imaginative exercises that generate fellow-feeling in the first place? In what follows, I will argue that Smith ought to treat basic concern as a precondition of a kind of imaginative projection that is central to human sociability, the only kind to which Smith pays any real attention. Were it not for the attitude of basic concern, we would not be driven to engage in imaginative projection in a large and important set of cases. As we have seen, for Smith, imaginative projection is the essential means by which we acquire experiential understanding of others. Taking the two previous points together, we will be able to conclude that in many cases, we would not come to understand the target agent if we were not already concerned about him.

We have no particular reason to assume that there is just one explanation for why we engage in imaginative projection. It seems obvious that imaginative projection could sometimes be helpful for securing benefits for, and avoiding harm to, ourselves. For instance, if I want to avoid losing my lunch money, it could be helpful to project myself into my bully's position, and imagine just what kind of groveling I would find most appealing if I were him. But Smith is quite clear that we do not only engage in imaginative projection when knowing a person's mind could be important to our fortunes. It is hard to see how fellow-feeling with another person could be useful to us in cases where the other is unlikely ever to interact with us, and yet Smith is adamant that our fellow-feeling can and does extend to such people: we are liable to 'bring home to ourselves' the misery of 'any innocent and sensible being', not just the misery of those in our own country (*TMS* VI.ii.3.1). So, in cases where knowing the other's mind does not seem useful to us, why do we nevertheless engage in imaginative projection?

Smith does have something to say about why we are motivated to engage in imaginative projection. And reflection upon the explicit reason he gives for our motivation will reveal that he should not endorse the claim that empathy produces concern. According to Smith, we 'passionately desire' to attain a 'harmony of hearts': we want our feelings to match those of others (*TMS* I.i.4.7). This desire is at work in our attempts to reconcile our opinions about things like art or philosophy with the opinions of others. As Smith points out, sharing others' opinions in these cases does not require 'sympathy, or that imaginary change of situations from which it arises, in order to produce, with regard to these, the most perfect harmony of sentiments and affections' (*TMS* I.i.4.2). But Smith argues that the desire for harmony is still stronger in cases where attaining a harmony of hearts means entering into another's position, and understanding things from that person's point of view. When we cannot harmonize our feelings with those that an agent feels about his surroundings, the result is 'shock' and 'pain' (*TMS* I.i.2.1).

Smith identifies the harmony of hearts as the source of great pleasure for us: '[N]othing pleases us more to than to observe in other men a fellow-feeling with all of the emotions of our own breast' (*TMS* I.i.2.1). When we fail in our efforts to bring our own feelings in line with those of another person, conversely, the result is a kind of pain: 'it hurts us to find we cannot share his uneasiness' (*TMS* I.i.2.6). Smith is careful to clarify, in response to an objection from Hume, that even when we feel another's pain, which is at least partly an unpleasant experience, the fact of our feelings' correspondence is itself an unfailing source of happiness. Of the silence and mirth of our companions, when we ourselves are mirthful, Smith writes: 'this correspondence of the sentiments of others with our own appears to be a cause of pleasure, and the want of it a cause of pain, which cannot be accounted for', except by the thought that the correspondence is an independent source of pleasure (*TMS* I.i.2.2). Note that Smith is not arguing that we find sentimental harmony pleasurable because it is good for us in some other way. We can, of course, imagine cases where this would be true: referring back to the case of the bully, feeling something like what the bully feels could be pleasurable, because I take pleasure in having the resources to avoid the bully's extortion. But on Smith's view there is something pleasurable about the sharing of sentiment *regardless of any consequences*. Sentimental harmony, it seems, is pleasurable in and of itself.

Smith does not pin down the relationship between the pleasurableness of sentimental harmony and its desirability as precisely as we might like. Pleasure makes its first appearance in the opening lines of *The Theory of Moral Sentiments*:

> How selfish soever man may be supposed, there are evidently some principles in his nature, which interest him in the fortune of others, and render their happiness necessary to him, though he derives nothing from it except the pleasure of seeing it.
>
> (*TMS* I.i.1)

We might wonder, here, what explanatory role (if any) pleasure is playing: should we think of the 'principles' as directly motivating our interest in and concern for others, whilst also making it the case that we take pleasure in sharing others' pleasures? Or should we instead think that the 'principles' are the facts of our nature that make it the case that sentimental harmony is pleasurable for us, and that the prospect of pleasure is in fact what directly motivates us to empathize? In other words, do we want sentimental harmony because it feels good, or is the fact that it feels good just an indication of its inherent desirability? Smith's attempts to characterize our desire for sentimental harmony do frequently invoke pleasure. Furthermore, he explicitly adopts the position that 'Pleasure and pain are the great objects of desire and aversion' (*TMS* VII.iii.2). These considerations encourage the thought that, for Smith, it is the *pleasurableness* of sentimental harmony that directly motivates us to pursue it.[10] However, there is simply not enough textual evidence to draw that conclusion with any real confidence, and one could argue that reading Smith in that way makes it look as though he accords pleasure an unrealistically prominent role in the explanation of empathy. For our purposes, however, this interpretive question is not critically important. The important point is that Smith regards sentimental harmony either as an end that is inherently desirable and thus capable of directly motivating us to empathize, or as an end that is desirable because it is pleasurable. I will refer to the pleasurableness of sentimental harmony, rather than its desirability, in the following section, but the distinction will not be critical to the success of my argument.

Before moving ahead, let us sum up what we have so far established. According to Smith, all experiential understanding is the product of (successful) imaginative projection. Smithian imaginative projection is typically effortful, so it makes sense to ask why we are motivated to engage in it. One reason to engage in it is that it provides an understanding of others that could be useful to ourselves. However, we have reason to think that not all imaginative projection is motivated by such benefits. Smith himself emphasizes the fact that we are motivated by a desire for sentimental harmony, which is itself pleasurable. He does not thereby supply a complete account of our motivation to project imaginatively, though. We are left with the question: why do people find sentimental harmony desirable and pleasurable, even in cases where there is no instrumental benefit to be accrued from the harmony? Smith does not give us an explicit answer, and I am not going to attempt to offer a full account of why we find sentimental harmony desirable and pleasurable on his behalf. Rather, I am going to argue that we can only make sense of the distinct pleasure that we take in sentimental harmony in and of itself, a pleasure that in turn appears to motivate our imaginative projection, if we conceive of ourselves as feeling basic care for others *prior to* imaginative projection.

Concern's role in the motivation to empathize

What would our attitude toward others have to be like in order for us to take pleasure in sharing their feelings, in cases where no instrumental benefits are at stake? At this point, I see two possibilities. The first is that there is nothing in particular that our attitude toward others would have to be like. On this view, the pleasure we take in the correspondence of sentiments would not in any way be contingent upon our regarding others' sentiments as independently valuable or worth knowing about. The other possibility is, of course, that the pleasure we take in the correspondence of sentiments *is* contingent upon our regarding others' sentiments as independently valuable or worth knowing about. How can we decide between these two possibilities? Smith is all for psychological realism. Therefore, I propose that we take a cue from him, and begin by considering whether the first view seems like a good fit with our pre-theoretical familiarity with human motivation.

One might argue that harmony *just is* a pleasing state to be in, regardless of whether we care about others' opinions, as such. It simply feels good to have the same feelings as someone else about the latest blockbuster, or the politician's behavior, or the German football team. It may not be immediately obvious that sharing sentiments could not feel pleasurable in itself in the absence of a pre-existing basic interest in others' feelings. Upon reflection, however, it seems hard to imagine how it would be psychologically possible to be motivated to seek sentimental harmony *just because* it is inherently pleasurable, without also being interested in or concerned with others' feelings.[11] It would be something like being motivated to keep a promise by the thought that breaking that promise would make one feel bad, even if one does not care about promises themselves. Why would one feel bad about breaking the promise if one did not care about promises, as such?

It is easy enough to think of cases in which we might value a correspondence of our attitudes with those of others without considering others' attitudes to be independently valuable or interesting. However, in every case I have been able to conjure up where we take pleasure in correspondence without considering others' attitudes to be independently valuable or interesting, the pleasurableness of the correspondence seems to be due to the instrumental benefits it affords. Take this example: I am pleased to share your positive feelings about the German football team. Now, it seems possible that I could be pleased by this without having any antecedent interest in your opinions. It could be that I just want the cheers for the German side to be loud, in order to increase their chances of winning. But suppose there are no instrumental benefits to our correspondence of sentiments in this case. Could I still desire that our sentiments correspond, without being interested in or concerned with your opinion, as such? Such a desire might be psychologically possible, but it strikes me as improbable and strange. It seems to me that the pleasure I take in our shared feelings about the German team must be either covertly instrumental or dependent upon my pre-existing interest in others' attitudes. And in some cases, even a pleasure in sentimental harmony that *is* instrumental will nevertheless be dependent upon a pre-existing care for others' sentiments, as such. For instance, I may take pleasure in our having the same sentiments about the German team at least in part because this means I will have someone with whom to cheer them along. But it could very well be that I would not enjoy cheering along with you unless I regarded your sentiments as independently interesting, something to care about.

I have argued that since Smith treats imaginative projection as effortful, it makes sense to ask why we are motivated to engage in it. On occasion, the instrumental benefits to be accrued from sentimental harmony, and the pleasure derived from those instrumental benefits, may motivate imaginative projection. However, Smith does not discuss such cases. He is interested in cases where we are motivated to project imaginatively just by the prospective pleasurableness of sentimental harmony itself. And when it comes to these cases, an attitude of interest or concern directed at the other seems to be a precondition of taking pleasure in sentimental harmony. Since we are talking about cases in which instrumental interests are not at play, we can further specify that the concern in question is basic concern. To be sure, this line of reasoning does not amount to a deduction that basic concern is sometimes a precondition of imaginative projection. There is no abstract, conceptual consideration that dictates this conclusion. Rather, the conclusion's warrant is based upon an observation about human psychology, one that is admittedly not drawn from a complete and thorough survey of our motivational profiles. Still, it seems to me that it hits on a true fact about the ways we take interest in other people's lives.

If Smith were to conceive of the relation between basic concern and imaginative projection (and, by extension, the relation between basic concern and understanding) in the way that I suggest he should, given his explanation of our motivation to empathize, then he would not end up in the bind in which his official theory is entangled. It may already be obvious why the alternative conception of the relation between concern and understanding avoids this problem, but let us make it explicit by employing one of Smith's own examples of an effort to achieve sentimental harmony.

An illustration of the amended theory

Late in *The Theory of Moral Sentiments*, Smith describes the operation of imaginative projection when one relates to a person who has lost a child:

When I sympathize with your sorrow or indignation, it may be pretended, indeed, that my emotion is founded in self-love, because it arises from bringing your case home to myself, from putting myself in your situation, and thence conceiving what I should feel in the like circumstances. But though sympathy is very properly said to arise from an imaginary change of situations with the person principally concerned, yet this imaginary change is not supposed to happen to me in my own person and character, but in that of the person with whom I sympathize. When I condole with you for the loss of your only son, in order to enter into your grief I do not consider what I, a person of such a character and profession, should suffer, if I had a son, and that son was unfortunately to die: but I consider what I should suffer if I was really you, and I not only change circumstances with you, but I change persons and characters. My grief, therefore, is entirely upon your account, and not the least upon my own.

(*TMS* VII.iii.1.4)

Now, let us consider the example of sympathetic grief in the light of what we have said about the relation between concern and understanding in Smith. In an effort to attain an understanding of your grief, to reach sentimental harmony with you, I put myself in your position by imagining that I am you. If the effort is successful, I will imagine feeling what you are feeling. I will feel devastated 'as' you. I will feel grief at having lost *my* child. This feeling could be described as selfish or self-directed, in the sense that it concerns me and what was in some sense mine. Smith's claim that I 'enter into your grief' by imagining being 'really you' suggests that this is what he has in mind. However, this feeling of mine can serve an informational function in the effort to arrive at a feeling that is *not* self-directed. As I have argued, it cannot spontaneously generate previously non-existent basic concern for you. But what if I am *already* concerned about you? What if I am already interested in your experiences? What if your feelings matter to me *before* I have experienced an echo of them? In that case, it makes sense that I would be motivated to put the feelings I derive from imaginative projection to use. In particular, I can infer that you are experiencing something like the grief that I am experiencing (faintly) in virtue of my imaginative engagement with your situation. And now that I have some idea of what your experience must be like, even though I cannot directly experience it myself, my general concern for you is better informed. This will help me to demonstrate my understanding of your plight and otherwise condole with you.

Importantly, the complaint I have lodged against Smith's official account of the relation between empathy, concern, and understanding does not hinge upon a denial that our understanding a person can make a difference to the extent or character of our concern for them. The picture I have just offered is entirely compatible with the notion that empathizing with a person can, say, intensify the benevolent interest I take in him, or cause me to see him as meriting my pity, or love, or resentment. Understanding can shape our concern in myriad ways, and giving a truly satisfactory account of them is not possible here. Since empathetic understanding is an effortful undertaking that is not always motivated by instrumental concerns, it stands to reason that it must (at least sometimes) be motivated by a basic concern for other people, but this basic concern need not be the robust, fully developed and well-informed concern that characterizes our relationship with those with whom we empathize. It need only be a quite general regard for other people as beings whose inner lives matter to us, and not only instrumentally. This relatively simple kind of concern is not all there is to our concern for other people, but Smith's theory would benefit from the acknowledgment that this concern often motivates our empathetic efforts – efforts that may in turn deepen and render more sophisticated our concern for other people.

I have argued that Smith should accept that basic concern is not the product of imaginative projection. Adopting this new position will allow Smith to avoid the problem his official theory encounters. Still, the new position leaves him (and us) with some unanswered questions. In particular, one might worry that by treating basic concern as prior to empathetic understanding, I will have left Smith without the resources to explain the fact that our basic concern is directed at persons, and not at boulders or rosebushes. I have said that basic concern is directed at beings whose inner lives we consider important, but if that concern precedes our understanding of others' inner lives, how are we to account for the fact that we are able to pick out those with inner lives, thus identifying the proper objects of our concern?

In response to this worry, I think it is important to emphasize that the picture of egocentric primacy I attributed to Smith at the beginning of this paper is a view about our acquaintance with the *content* of others' inner lives. Recall that Smith holds that 'we have no immediate experience of what other men feel', and that he is concerned to explain how we nevertheless manage to come by an understanding of their experiences. This is not the same project as explaining how we recognize that (and which) things other than ourselves have minds in the first place. Smith's account of how we come by our understanding of the content of others' inner lives was never intended to explain our conviction that others are minded, or our ability to distinguish minded from non-minded things. For that reason, this worry about the new position is misplaced as a worry *about the new position.*

Smith's official account also does not explain how we distinguish proper from improper targets of imaginative projection. Both the official account and my suggested emendation assume that some understanding of which things have minds precedes acts of imaginative projection. There are several possible explanations of such an understanding. For instance, Smith might hold that my recognition of others' mindedness is an inference made on the basis of my immediate grasp of my own mindedness, combined with my recognition of the many ways in which my own behavior and appearance resemble those of others. Alternatively, he might consider my recognition of others' mindedness to be non-inferential, perhaps even primitive. Smith is silent about this kind of recognition, and his one discussion of a case where the attribution of mindedness goes awry (our sympathy with human corpses, discussed at *TMS* I.i.I.13) does not provide enough material for us to extrapolate an account in which we can have any confidence. It is interesting that Smith never addresses the matter of how we come by our conviction that other minds exist, or our understanding of which things are minded, given his evident concern to account for our grasp of others' experiences. However, a proper exploration of the reasons behind the omission is beyond the scope of this paper.

4. Conclusion

From Smith's remarks about our desire for sentimental harmony, I have drawn out an implication that is in tension with some of Smith's more explicit pronouncements concerning the relation between concern, empathy, and understanding. Smith officially identifies the empathetic mechanism as the source of both our interest in others and our concern for them. However, he also maintains that we engage in imaginative projection because we desire sentimental harmony (either because it is inherently pleasurable or because it is a good in and of itself). And reflection upon our own psychological makeup supports the conclusion that an orientation of basic concern is in fact a condition of finding sentimental harmony non-instrumentally desirable. Therefore, if Smith wishes his theory to be coherent and does not want to give up his account of why we are motivated to empathize, he should treat basic concern not as the product of imaginative projection, but as something that often precedes it. In many cases, basic concern might even be regarded as the driving force behind the imaginative effort in question.

Treating basic concern as prior to empathy provides a means of addressing the problem discussed in the first half of this paper – namely, that the two tasks Smith assigns to the empathetic mechanism are at odds with each other. For Smith, the key to understanding another is to arrive at a conception of their passion that is as close as possible to the original, which is feasible thanks to the mind's imaginative capacity. This same mental process is also supposed to generate concern for the other. As the case of Morris's regret made clear, a truly accurate 'shadow' of another person's feeling is not the kind of thing that can generate the right kind of concern for the other. It might be misleading to say that the approach I have suggested on Smith's behalf would solve this problem. It would be more apt to say instead that it dissolves the problem. In effect, it prevents the problem of accounting for both concern and understanding through empathy from arising by scaling back on the explanatory ambitions for empathy.

In the first half of this paper, I suggested that Smith's response to threats of psychological egoism and skepticism about our understanding of others' inner lives is shaped by his commitment to the picture of egocentric primacy. This picture, which treats our own self-understanding and self-concern as uniquely primitive and not in need of explanation, has a prima facie plausibility that is reflected in its considerable philosophical staying power. Many of Smith's philosophical descendants endorse this picture to some degree. Indeed, the current wave of interest in empathy seems to be largely propelled by the thought that we somehow, as Nancy Sherman puts it, 'step beyond the egocentric point of view' (Sherman 1998: 83). Claims like Sherman's assume that we begin with self-understanding and self-concern, and must somehow turn outwards in order to relate to others as minded beings whose inner lives matter. If Smith were to adopt the view that basic concern precedes empathy, as I have suggested he should, would he need to rescind his commitment to the perennially popular picture of egocentric primacy?

Consider first his commitment to the epistemic component of the picture of egocentric primacy. The thought that we cannot feel others' feelings directly need not be affected. For better or for worse, the improvement upon Smith's explicit account that I have proposed retains the assumption that our acquaintance with others' inner lives must come through bootstrapping up from our primitive self-understanding. When it comes to the other half of the picture, the story is more complicated. I have argued that Smith should recognize basic concern as a necessary precondition for much of our empathetic engagement with others, and for the understanding that this engagement produces. Strictly speaking, this recognition would not undermine the claim that our concern for ourselves is primitive and needs no explanation, whereas our concern for others is not similarly primitive and does need to be explained. It does undermine Smith's official explanation of our basic concern for others, however. So we are left with two possibilities: Smith would either need to supply a new explanation of why we feel basic concern for others, one that does not rely on empathy to move from concern for ourselves to concern for others; or he would need to forgo the search for such an explanation and accept basic concern for others as a primitive psychological disposition on a par with our self-concern. With empathy eliminated as an explanation for basic concern, though, it is very difficult to see what realistic alternative explanations might be available to Smith if he were to pursue the former option. Therefore, although the claim that basic concern precedes empathy does not strictly require that we abandon the concern component of the picture of egocentric primacy, it does place would-be defenders of the concern component of the picture in a difficult position.

This paper has focused on the particular ways in which Smith appeals to empathetic mechanisms in his theory of mind and morals, but the problems that he encounters are not just the result of minor quirks in his descriptions of human psychology. They begin with the picture of egocentric primacy. When we posit such a dramatic gap between how we relate to ourselves and how we relate to others, it is entirely natural that we should attempt to bridge that gap by appealing to self-concern and self-understanding, phenomena with which we are so intimate that they seem to require no explanation. However, empathy-based solutions to the problem of accounting for concern for others run into the problem of appropriately acknowledging the distinction between self and other. Reproducing something like others' feelings 'in' ourselves cannot not generate basic concern for others. And, while I did not discuss the question in this paper, we might also ask whether this kind of reproduction actually gets us to a real grasp of others' passions, or if it only gets us to an idea of *our own* passions, which we mistake for others' passions.

Ultimately, I think that these and related problems give us a reason not just to look for alternative ways to bridge the gap between self and other but to look at the picture of egocentric primacy – which posits this gap in the first place – with a specially critical eye.

Notes

1   Or, indeed, *against* their interests – concern in the sense with which I am concerned is not always altruistically oriented.
2   Smith devotes most of his discussion of understanding to the latter mode (see especially *TMS* I.i.1–3); the former appears most prominently in his discussion of 'conditional sympathy' (*TMS* I.i.3.4).
3   Philosophers of mind who adopt this position, and also claim to draw upon Smith, include Gordon (1995) and Goldman (1992), along with authors who have a more pronounced cognitive-scientific orientation, such as Kiesling (2012).
4   This meaning of 'compassion', now deemed 'obscure' by the *Oxford English Dictionary*, first appeared in English in the 1340s ('compassion, n.', OED Online, accessed June 2012).
5   The phrase occurs a total of seventy-three times in *The Theory of Moral Sentiments*, including, for example, at: I.i.1.4, I.i.1.8, I.i.2.2, and I.i.2.6.
6   Here I am following Charles Griswold, who describes Smith's notion of imaginative engagement as 'projective imagination' (Griswold 1999: 90).
7   John Perry introduced the use of counterfactual analysis to show that indexicals are essential: substituting third-personal designators for first-personal designators inevitably alters the character of attitudes. See Perry (1993: 3–53).
8   The attitude I have described in these cases is a reflexive one; the intentional object is oneself and one's predicament. If one is inclined to think that reflexive attitudes are a relative rarity, then one might wonder whether the problem I have attempted to draw out will emerge only in a relatively small set of cases. It is worth bearing in mind, however, that Smith is particularly concerned with our capacity to share empathetically in this kind of attitude, a passion which 'is entirely occupied with what relates to you [the target agent]', because he thinks it is especially powerful evidence that psychological egoism is false (*TMS* VII.iii.1.4). This concern emerges with special force in *TMS* VII.iii.1.4, from which I quote at length below.
9   In the opening pages of *The Theory of Moral Sentiments*, Smith does discuss cases of sensation and passion that develop through 'instantaneous transfusion', rather than through imaginative projection (*TMS* I.i.1.6). For instance, he claims that the sight of a beggar's sores causes some delicate people to feel itchy. This kind of affective contagion is left behind at the end of the first chapter, though. The rest of the book focuses on empathy that is achieved through the deliberate work of imaginative projection.
10 Or, alternatively, we might say that it is the pain of disharmony that drives us to empathize with others.
11 Dick Moran has suggested (private correspondence) that a 'negative' version of this possibility might be more psychologically plausible. That is, it might be psychologically accurate to claim that we could find sentimental *dis*harmony *painful* even if we did not have pre-existing care for others. I am unsure what to say about this suggestion. Personally, this possibility does not strike me as any more realistic than did the corresponding claim about the pleasurableness of harmony, but I recognize that my intuition on this point may be idiosyncratic.

Bibliography

Goldman, A. (1992) 'In Defense of the Simulation Theory'. *Mind and Language* 7, 1–2: 104–119.

Gordon, R. (1995) 'Sympathy, Simulation, and the Impartial Spectator'. *Ethics* 105, 4: 727–742.

Griswold, C. (1999) *Adam Smith and the Virtues of Enlightenment.* Cambridge: Cambridge University Press.

Hume, D. (1975) *A Treatise of Human Nature*, ed. L. A. Selby-Bigge, 2nd edn, revised by P. H. Nidditch. Oxford: Clarendon Press.

Kiesling, L. (2012) 'Mirror Neuron Research and Adam Smith's Concept of Sympathy: Three Points of Correspondence'. *Review of Austrian Economics* 24, 4: 299–313.

Perry, J. (1993) 'The Problem of the Essential Indexical'. In *The Problem of the Essential Indexicals and Other Essays.* Oxford: Oxford University Press.

Schopenhauer, A. (1915) *The Basis of Morality.* New York: Macmillan.

Sherman, N. (1998) 'Empathy and Imagination'. *Midwest Studies in Philosophy* 22, 1: 82–119.

Smith, A. (1976) *The Theory of Moral Sentiments*, ed. D. D. Raphael and A. L Macfie, Oxford: Oxford University Press; Glasgow edition; reprint Indianapolis, IN: Liberty Press (1982).

Human development and social stratification in Adam Smith[1]

Paul Raekstad

1. Introduction

For Adam Smith, the key to human happiness is a society in which human beings are well developed as wise and virtuous beings. Numerous things influence a person's prospects for developing wisdom and virtue, inter alia one's profession, education, and the historical stage of one's society. One of these important factors is what Smith calls one's social 'rank' or 'order', by which I take him – as Wallech (1986) has shown – to mean what earlier and later thinkers have termed one's social 'class'. Commercial society, on Smith's view, is divided into three such orders or classes, each of which faces distinct conditions for the development of a wise and virtuous character. Only a handful of writers have discussed the importance of class in Smith's social and political thought in any detail, and most writers on Smith's moral theory have largely or completely avoided the topic.[2] None has so far been able to give a sufficiently detailed account of his views on social class and its effects on individuals' prospects for human development.[3] This paper seeks to fill that gap, and to correct occasional errors and oversights in the literature on the topic. I argue that Smith believes a person's class position strongly affects their prospects for developing a wise and virtuous character, and that he does so in sometimes surprising and innovative ways.

In order to address the connections between human development and social class in Smith's writings, I outline (in Section 2) Smith's conception of human development – his conception of wisdom and virtue – and (in Section 3) some general points on his revolutionary way of conceiving the relation between human endowments at birth and the material and social environment within which these endowments grow and develop. A brief exposition of these two themes is vital if we are to understand the differing conditions for the development of wisdom and virtue the members of different classes face on Smith's account. With these two matters addressed, I proceed (in Section 4) to detail Smith's more extensive accounts of how class position affects people's prospects for human development in commercial societies. Here I demonstrate, in particular, that he mounts a remarkably strong defence for the wisdom and virtue of labourers – a defence that must be compared with what he says about merchants and manufacturers.

Furthermore, I suggest that his views on the landlord class are considerably more scathing than is acknowledged in contemporary accounts.

2. Wisdom and virtue

The conception of wisdom and virtue, and that of wise and virtuous persons, appears in numerous places throughout *TMS* as a metric of human development. The phrase makes occasional appearances in *WN* and elsewhere, too, but does relatively little work there. I contend, though I cannot here demonstrate, that the concerns of *LJ* and *WN* are both derivative of this underlying commitment to human development. Some work on the connection does exist (see Fleischacker 1999; Hanley 2006, 2009), but more remains to be done. In this section I will briefly outline what we can reasonably say Smith's conception of wisdom and virtue comprises. Then, in later sections, I shall explore the effects a person's class position has on their prospects for such development.

Although *TMS* does offer 'an elaborate, systematic theory of moral judgement', it is well known that it contains 'nothing remotely resembling a theory of the nature of virtue' (Raphael 2007: 69). However, Smith does provide us with a number of virtues, and, in the new Part VI of *TMS*, some discussion of the overarching cardinal virtues he identifies. Of particular importance to Smith are humanity and self-command, upon which 'are founded two different sets of virtues' (Steuart *Account/EPS* II.16 in Smith 1980). 'Humanity' enjoins us as spectators to heighten our sympathy so as better to match the feelings of the person with whom we are sympathising, whilst self-command consists in the person who is the object of our sympathy lowering the pitch of his or her emotion so as better to match that which the sympathiser will be able to muster. Together, they are said to constitute the 'perfection of human nature' (*TMS* I.i.5.5).

The cardinal virtues in Smith – strikingly underdeveloped, with only the partial exception of justice, in the early editions of *TMS*; a fault that was somewhat remedied only after the new Part VI was added to the sixth edition – are prudence, justice, beneficence and self-command (cf. Raphael 2007: 73–80). Prudence covers one's care and concern for oneself – one's health, fortune, rank, reputation and so on. The prudent man is studious, industrious, skilled and frugal. His conversation is simple, honest and modest, and he takes care always to be inoffensive and to take upon himself only the cares and responsibilities imposed by duty and necessity. As a virtue, prudence commands a kind of cold esteem, and certainly approbation, but it is never as endearing or ennobling as the other virtues, even though it constitutes the noblest of characters when combined with those other virtues. Correspondingly, imprudence becomes the object of compassion, neglect or, at worst, contempt, but never of the hatred and indignation that other vices are prone to generate (*TMS* VI.i).

The cardinal virtues that primarily affect other people are justice and beneficence. For Smith, justice is the virtue of doing no harm to anyone unless to prevent or rectify harm done to others. Such harm rightly invokes the resentment of the impartial spectator, making it the proper object of forceful restraint and/or retribution, thus distinguishing it from the other social virtues falling under beneficence (*TMS* II.ii.I). Although justice is to be maintained by law whenever prudent and/or necessary, the virtue of justice rightly enjoins us to do no such harm even absent legal protections (*TMS* VI.ii.intro.2). Justice's absence from Part VI of *TMS* is not due to its excision from moral judgement proper, nor because it, like prudence, is given a lower-order status (cf. Brown 1994: 112). *Contra* any such claim, Smith highlights justice and beneficence together, in both *TMS* VI.ii.intro.2 and *TMS* II.ii, where justice receives detailed discussion. It is because the virtue of justice has already received specialised treatment in Part II that Smith, in the new Part VI, writes that this is 'a character sufficiently understood, and requires no further explanation' (*TMS* VI.ii.intro.2). The maintenance of justice is, for Smith as for Hume, a cornerstone of society, and as such the most important of the social virtues (*TMS* II.ii.III). The virtue of justice appears together with other virtues such as feeling for others, humanity and benevolence, and is always loved and admired for its own sake (*TMS* VI.ii. intro.2).

By contrast, beneficence is the cardinal virtue overarching the more positive virtues towards other people, such as kindness and generosity. These sentiments rightly apply differently as we are more or less acquainted with the persons in question (*TMS* VI.ii.2). Though easier and more common among those within closer circles, beneficence is technically unbounded and, where properly developed, finds those of wisdom and virtue ready and willing to sacrifice themselves for the greater good:

> The wise and virtuous man is at all times willing that his own private interest should be sacrificed to the public interest of his own particular order or society. He is at all times willing, too, that the interest of this order or society should be sacrificed to the greater interest of the state or sovereignty, of which it is only a subordinate part.
>
> (*TMS* VI.ii.3.3)

The final cardinal virtue, self-command (*TMS* VI.iii), is vital in Smith's account of virtue as a property or character trait of a moral agent. It is self-command that enables people to act according to the moral prescriptions laid down by the other virtues when these run contrary to other passions. Smith distinguishes between the command over sudden and strong passions like fear and anger, and that over weaker but more constant ones like the love of ease, applause and selfish gratifications. Self-command is always admirable for its own sake, even when in the service of base motives. It is from necessitating command over one's baser self in the service of higher ideals that the other virtues derive their benefits, placing self-command at the heart of the virtues:

> To act according to the dictates of prudence, of justice, and proper beneficence, seems to have no great merit where there is no temptation to do otherwise. But to act with cool deliberation in the midst of the greatest dangers and

difficulties; to observe religiously the sacred rules of justice in spite both of the greatest interests which might tempt, and the greatest injuries which might provoke us to violate them; never to suffer the benevolence of our temper to be damped or discouraged by the malignity and ingratitude of the individuals towards whom it may have been exercised; is the character of the most exalted wisdom and virtue. Self-command is not only itself a great virtue, but from it all the other virtues seem to derive their principal lustre.

(TMS VI.iii.11)

Lastly, the wise and virtuous person constructs in his mind two standards that help to guide his actions: an ideal of perfect wisdom and virtue; and another of the standard that is commonly obtainable in society. A wise and virtuous person holds himself strictly to accord with the latter, whilst constantly and consistently directing his efforts of self-improvement towards the former (*TMS* VI.iii.23–6).

We now have a workable outline of Smith's conception of virtue. A more difficult question concerns his notion of wisdom, a question which he leaves woefully underdeveloped. It seems probable, given the great influence of Aristotle on Smith's work, that the notion of wisdom is intended to replace Aristotle's notion of the intellectual virtues, on which, as Hanley (2006: 19) has noted, Smith remains notoriously silent. There are clear traces of Smith's concern with, and commitment to, wisdom throughout his works, inter alia *TMS* and *WN*, but what is it held to comprise?

I believe we may analyse wisdom, broadly speaking, as the cognitive skill or ability to handle and integrate both normative and empirical concerns: it is the ability properly to consider both general rules and the facts and details of particular cases, as well as the ability to mediate between these two moments in a productive manner, progressively refining one's perspective and adapting one's practical activity thereto. Where judgement is conceived as a complex skill or ability 'in sorting through empirical evidence, in making decisions in the common law, and in evaluating our ends for cogency and value' (Fleischacker 1999: 8), wisdom, as well-developed judgement, becomes 'the proper focus for a literal approach to the intellectual virtues' (ibid.: 17). Wisdom, then, is essential for, or extends over, a person's ability to form, critically reflect upon, evaluate and refine one's moral views, and one's abilities with regard to moral discussion and deliberation with others. It covers our ability to form – and to reflect upon, critique, deliberate upon and revise – an opinion of the interests of oneself, one's group, order or station, of one's society, and potentially of all of humanity. This conception seems to capture well Smith's usage of 'wisdom and virtue' in *TMS* I.iii.3, as well as many of the references throughout *TMS* and other works, where it seems closely connected to general intelligence or understanding, especially with regard to moral and (other) practical matters. The connection between wisdom and the intellectual virtues is vindicated by Smith's equivocation in *TMS* VI.i.15, where he writes that 'superior prudence' (unlike the virtue prudence already discussed) of the great statesman or legislator 'necessarily supposes the utmost perfection of all the intellectual and of all the moral virtues … It is the most perfect wisdom combined with the most perfect virtue.' Wisdom's further connection with conceiving and evaluating the general interest or the interest of one's society is further confirmed in *TMS* VI.ii.2.12 and 14. Wisdom's importance for moral reasoning is perhaps indicated by Smith's calling virtue 'real wisdom' early in *TMS* VII.ii.2.13, and in his emphasis on wisdom's importance for virtuous action later in the same paragraph. Lastly, wisdom's connection with critical thinking is made explicit in his discussion of wisdom as a tool against 'credulity' in *TMS* VII.iv.23.

By putting these admittedly sparse elements together, we can begin to form an image of the wise and virtuous person, and a society inhabited chiefly thereby: a society of wise and virtuous individuals is one where people work hard in a focused manner, both physically and mentally, in order to satisfy their moral, intellectual and material needs. They have a keen awareness of their own interests and affairs, and they ensure that these are well kept. Nevertheless, they are careful never to harm others, and to do the best they can to be fair and just to all. But beyond this, they reflect and deliberate on the right and best ways to lead a good life, and on what constitutes and promotes the general interest of their society – or even of humanity in general. People seek to do well not just by themselves, or even just by their friends, families, neighbours and associates, but also by their fellow countrymen and even all of their fellow human beings. Wise and virtuous people are careful to tend to their own affairs and well-being *and* to those of the people under their close care and supervision, whilst never losing sight of the lofty ideal – of the perfectly wise and virtuous person – to which they continuously aspire. All of this nurtures and secures that amiable sociality which constitutes Smith's conception of human perfection. He writes the following about the connection between his conception of wisdom and virtue and the goal of promoting human happiness and well-being by political means:

> The characters of men, as well as the contrivances of art, or the institutions of civil government, may be fitted either to promote or to disturb the happiness both of the individual and of the society. The prudent, the equitable, active, resolute, and sober character promises prosperity and satisfaction, both to the person himself and to everyone connected with him … What institution of government could tend so much to promote the happiness of mankind as the general prevalence of wisdom and virtue? All government is but an imperfect remedy for the deficiency of these. Whatever beauty, therefore, can belong to civil government upon account of its utility, must in a far superior degree belong to these.
>
> (*TMS* IV.2.1)

It goes without saying that I take this passage above all to stress that the development of wise and virtuous persons is the best means of promoting the general happiness and well-being of mankind. The perfection of human nature in this sense is, consequently, rightly a major concern; as is, derivatively, the prospects that different members of a society face for such perfection as a result of their differing circumstances. What these circumstances are, and how they generate and restrict people's prospects for the development of wisdom and virtue, can be understood only by first appreciating Smith's general picture of human nature, social structure and moral development.

3. Human nature, social structure and human development

According to Smith, human beings' characters are shaped by the day-to-day demands and activities of their ordinary lives, particularly those of their working lives. He famously writes that 'the understandings of the greater part of men are necessarily formed by their ordinary employments' (*WN* V.i.f.50). Smith grounds his views on the psychological plasticity of human nature in a conception of determinate human psychology (desires for social rank and status, to better one's condition, for communication and social interaction, and for mutual sympathy, capacities for language, basic abilities to reason critically, and so forth) on which environmental factors operate. These environmental factors thereby both affect the development of the person or organism (ontogenesis) and provide the resulting organism and its faculties with inputs. The question then immediately arises as to how much, and in which ways, different environments are able to generate persons with different character structures, and whether the differences observed among human beings are primarily the result of different environments or innate differences. Smith writes:

> The difference of natural talents in different men is, in reality, much less than we are aware of; and the very different genius which appears to distinguish men of different professions, when grown up to maturity, is not upon many occasions so much the cause, as the effect of the division of labour. The difference between . . . a philosopher and a common street porter, for example, seems to arise not so much from nature, as from habit, custom, and education.
>
> (*WN* I.ii.4)

Here Smith clearly affirms his belief that moral and cognitive capacities are at least largely equal at birth, such that all humans share the same set of basic cognitive capacities and that potentials for their growth and development are largely the same. A corollary to this is that it is the differential inputs – of, for example, different professions – which produce the resulting differences in, for example, manners and character structures in virtue of – and only in virtue of – their operation on these near-identical potentials. Smith's views on the equality of human potentials (psychic unity), coupled with his recognition that different environmental contexts produce a great deal of variety among human individuals and cultures, are today broadly accepted in the human sciences (see, e.g., Sperber and Hirschfeld 1999). This is in basic agreement with other key Scottish Enlightenment thinkers (cf. Berry 1997: ch. 4).

It follows that, for Smith, character is shaped not only by class, but also by other factors affecting one's everyday activities, such as one's particular line of employment, the effects of particular national cultures and the social-historical stage of one's society more generally (as discussed in detail in *TMS* V.ii). The manner in which people's class membership affects their prospects for human development is thus a special case of Smith's wider thesis that human beings' everyday lives and activities shape and determine their different characters and personalities. How, then, do the different class positions in commercial society mould the moral agents that inhabit them?

According to Smith's mechanistic conception of the economy of commercial society (Dobb 1973; Meek 1977: ch. 10), the joint social product is distributed among its members as three distinct sorts of income: the wages of labour (*WN* I.viii); the profits of stock (*WN* I.ix); and the rent of land (*WN* I.xi). These three distinct components of prices and sources of income correspond to the three principal kinds of structural functional role available to agents in the economic mechanism of commercial society: namely, the roles of worker, merchant or manufacturer, and landlord. These structural economic positions in turn entail differing positions within society's structural division of labour. These different positions in the structural division of labour affect the content of the daily life and work activities of the persons in question, which, in turn, leads them to develop differently as people, including in terms of wisdom and virtue. With this broader structure in place, let us now turn to the detailed discussion Smith provides of the links between class positions and their members' prospects for the development of wisdom and virtue.

4. Social stratification and moral development

Merchants and manufacturers

The class of merchants and manufacturers consists of those economically active agents in commercial societies who derive their incomes from the profits of stock (cf. *WN* I.xi). In order to earn profits on stock, merchants or manufacturers have to invest wisely in projects that will return the highest available yields – both to stay in the game and not be out-competed by their peers, and in order to distinguish themselves in the search for wealth, power and social rank or status. It is primarily the competitive drive among the class of merchants and manufacturers which, for Smith, drives the progressive economy of commercial societies. As he writes: '[T]he plans and projects of the employers of stock regulate and direct all the most important operations of labour, and profit is the end proposed by all those plans and projects' (*WN* I.xi.p.10).

Due to their functional roles in the economy of commercial societies, merchants and manufacturers are – indeed, must be – 'during their whole lives ... engaged in plans and projects' (*WN* I.xi.p.10). If they should ever cease to be so, they must either find an alternative source of income or forgo one altogether. More than this, however, their economic engagement is highly active. The merchant or manufacturer is constantly engaged in different plans and projects, many of which, such as long-distance trade,

> commit [his capital], not only to the winds and the waves, but to the more uncertain elements of human folly and injustice, by giving great credits in distant countries to men, with whose character and situation he can seldom be thoroughly acquainted.
>
> (*WN* III.i.3)

Moreover, merchants and manufacturers are required to supervise, evaluate and seek to improve their projects constantly throughout their duration, largely regardless of what those projects are. As a result of these demands, his functional role in the economy of commercial society and his structural position in the division of labour, a member of the class of merchants and manufacturers – if he is to distinguish himself relative to, say, other members of his own class or members of the landlord class – must, at least inter alia,

> acquire dependants to balance the dependants of the great, and he has no other fund to pay them from, but the labour of his body, and the activity of his mind. He must cultivate these therefore: he must acquire superior knowledge in his profession, and superior industry in the exercise of it. He must be patient in labour, resolute in danger, and firm in distress. These talents he must bring into public view, by the difficulty, importance, and, at the same time, good judgment of his undertakings, and by the severe and unrelenting application with which he pursues them. Probity and prudence, generosity and frankness, must characterize his behaviour upon all ordinary occasions; and he must, at the same time, be forward to engage in all those situations, in which it requires the greatest talents and virtues to act with propriety, but in which the greatest applause is to be acquired by those who can acquit themselves with honour.
>
> (*TMS* I.iii.2.5)

This functional role in the economy, and its corresponding position in the structural division of labour, demands considerable mental and physical exertion, keen attention to empirical detail, and the gathering of information and knowledge; it also offers frequent opportunities for creativity, invention and the use and development of one's problem-solving skills. These demands and opportunities produce a class whose mental faculties are, seemingly by leaps and bounds, by far the greatest in commercial societies.

However, these abilities are not without limitations. In particular, the limited scope of merchants' and manufacturers' everyday concerns restricts their knowledge of, and competence concerning, the general interest of society. Smith, when comparing the class of merchants and manufacturers to the landlord class, sums up the matter elegantly:

As during their whole lives they are engaged in plans and projects, they have frequently more acuteness of understanding than the greater part of country gentlemen. As their thoughts, however, are commonly exercised rather about the interest of their own particular branch of business, than about that of the society, their judgment, even when given with the greatest candour (which it has not been upon every occasion) is much more to be depended upon with regard to the former of those two objects, than with regard to the latter. Their superiority over the country gentleman is, not so much in their knowledge of the publick interest, as in their having a better knowledge of their own interest than he has of his.

(*WN* I.xi.p.10)

Thus, whereas they have keen knowledge of their own interests, and all the requisite abilities to evaluate the effects of public legislation and policy thereon, they are generally lacking both in interest and ability when it comes to judging the general interest of society (cf. *WN* IV.i.10 and the latter part of *TMS* I.iii.2.5).

Having examined this class's prospects for the development of wisdom and cognitive powers in general, I now turn to its paradigmatic moral virtues and vices. In general, Smith notes, 'great fortunes' are gathered by merchants and manufacturers not by luck or fortunate circumstances, but 'in consequence of a long life of industry, frugality, and attention' (*WN* I.x.b.38). Thus required to take good care of their affairs, the merchant or manufacturer must develop the virtues of prudence, self-command and perhaps also a sense of justice (*TMS* I.iii.3.5[4]). These are the paradigmatic virtues of the class of merchants and manufacturers in consequence of the facts that: they are the virtues the members of this class must seek to cultivate in themselves in order to achieve success in their economic lives; and their everyday work both affords opportunity and positively demands the exercise and development of these character traits.

On the other hand, the paradigmatic vices of merchants and manufacturers are also precisely those one would expect from a group of people whose sole focus of attention is on advancing their own plans and projects in order to further their own interests – often at others' expense. Consequently, they are often subject to 'mean rapacity' (*WN* IV.iii.a.9), to a spirit of monopoly (see, inter alia and especially, *WN* IV.ii.16 (cf. 21), IV.ii.38, IV.ii.43, IV.iii.c.9, IV.iii.c.10, IV.iv.1 and IV.vi.61–3) and to 'avarice and ambition' (*WN* V.i.a.2). Presumably, for Smith, this undermines and/or runs contrary to beneficence.

In light of the preceding discussion, it can be seen that I affirm Reisman's (1976: 95) summary of Smith's views on the characters of merchants and manufacturers:

[L]ike Weber, Smith identified the capitalist entrepreneur as being hardworking, rational, honest, ascetic in his preference of abstinence to ostentation, possessing business acumen and an ability to weight future against present utilities ... [T]o Smith [this constraint] was material: years of activity as a businessman cannot but breed habits of frugality, industry, and self-command, as without these no individual can survive and prosper in business.

Labourers

If Smith's views on the class of merchants and manufacturers have generally been well understood, the same cannot be said for his views on labourers and landlords. Only relatively recently, especially in the work of Himmelfarb (1984) and Fleischacker (2004 and 2005), have his revolutionising views on labourers received their proper due, while his views on landlords – and especially their moral development – remain unexplored in the literature (see the section on 'Landlords' below). Let us first turn to the class of labourers.

Labourers' sources of income are the wages that landlords or merchants and manufacturers advance to them for their labour. They work, manage and maintain the lands of the landlord class (where these have not been taken over by merchants or manufacturers), and they carry out the plans and projects of the merchant and manufacturer class. Smith construes this class broadly so as to include independent, self-employed and semi-self-employed workers of one sort or another. He holds these to be included under the rubric of the class of wage labourers even though he claims that they instantiate both roles – that of master manufacturer and labourer – and thus also includes both of the two distinct sources of revenue, profits and wages (*WN* I.viii.9). This being said, he insists that these cases are rare and exceptional to commercial society (*WN* I.viii.10), probably in an attempt to justify their assimilation to a strictly distinct category in a manoeuvre of simplifying abstraction.

The effects of labourers' structural positioning in the division of labour are, it seems, less uniform than those of being a landlord, a merchant or a manufacturer. Whilst the structural position in the division of labour enjoyed by landlords renders them all doing virtually identical tasks (and a uniform lack of productive work) over the course of their lives, wage labourers may do any of a range of different particular labours, all within the same structural position in the economy's structural division of labour. On a Smithian account of character structure and character development shaped chiefly by a person's everyday activities, it is natural to suppose that a greater convergence in actual everyday activities or work (including lack thereof) leads to stronger homogenising tendencies. In other words, it makes sense to suppose that the effect of position in the structural division of labour on the members of different classes roughly tracks the extent to which this structural position determines the content of their everyday life activities. As such, one would expect Smith's characterisations of labourers of different sorts to be more varied and sophisticated than those he gives of landlords, and also perhaps than those he gives of merchants and manufacturers. For example, Smith argues that the 'common ploughman', because he is less accustomed to social interaction as a result of his solitary working day, is 'more uncouth' and 'less accustomed to social intercourse' than an urban mechanic (*WN* I.x.c.24). On the other hand, 'though generally regarded as the pattern of stupidity and ignorance', the common farm worker is 'seldom defective' in his often highly complex judgements regarding his materials and instruments of labour (ibid.). In comparison to the urban mechanic, his overall level of understanding is 'generally much superior', because the mechanic's 'whole attention from morning to night is commonly occupied in performing one or two simple operations' (ibid.).

Before we move on, there is a feature of Smith's writings on labourers which is particularly interesting in the context of moral development. He marks a turning point in his complete rejection of the (then) widespread view that the poor were poor due to moral and/or cognitive deficiencies, and thus deserved to remain poor or even should be kept poor and deferent to their supposed betters (Himmelfarb 1984). He is able to do this, in large part, because he presents an alternative view as to what poverty and oppression are, what their causes in society and the division of labour are, and their subsequent effects upon the individual. I will show how Smith presents a view of ordinary labourers according to which they are innately equal to their 'betters', both cognitively and morally competent, and in fact virtuous beings.

To Smith, ordinary workmen are seen as remarkably intelligent and moral beings. For instance, by stressing that the machines in manufacturing are often invented by the workmen themselves, as well as by owners and overseers (*LJA* vi.41–2; *LJB* 217–18; ED/*WN* 16–20 and *WN* I.i.8–9), he emphasises the creativity and ingenuity of ordinary labourers (Fleischacker 2005: 76). Furthermore, as we have seen, he repeatedly stresses the inborn equality of all men, arguing, for example, that the philosopher and the street porter are initially almost exactly the same, and that the consequent differences they develop are the result of differential education and day-to-day activities. The key upshot of this is that individual inequality is largely the effect of the division of labour in society rather than vice versa (*WN* I.ii.5–6; cf. *LJA* vi.47–9; *LJB* 218–22; ED/*WN* 26–31). Third, far from being an isolated passage or the fragment of an argument, we find this point to be a common thread that runs throughout *WN*, especially Part I. He writes, for example, that 'species of labour' which require an 'uncommon degree of dexterity or ingenuity' are reasonably compensated higher than others precisely because they are not the result of lucky natural talents; rather, 'they can seldom be acquired but in consequence of long application' and thus deserve remuneration for time and labour so employed (*WN* I.iv.3). Fourth, whereas many in his day saw the poor as naturally indolent, Smith stresses that the converse is the case and that they are naturally apt to overwork themselves (*WN* I.viii.44). To the common view that the poor should be prevented from purchasing luxuries and improving their material station in life, Smith replies inter alia with the equity argument (*WN* I.viii.36) and by criticising kings and ministers – who 'are themselves, always, and without any exception, the greatest spendthrifts in the society' – for meddling in the affairs of private people of whom they have no knowledge (*WN* II.iii.36). Finally, Smith goes some way towards defending the poor in their tendencies towards high alcohol consumption and certain religious sects, arguing in the former case that man 'is an anxious animal, and must have his care swept off by something that can exhilarate the spirits' (LJB, 425; *WN* IV.iii.c.8) and in the latter case that, although 'disagreeably rigorous and unsocial', they at least provide community and moral guidance (*WN* V.i.g.10–12).

We should note, however, that in both cases he does not go so far as to defend the practices themselves.[5]

On top of this, Smith particularly emphasises the abilities of (more) independent workmen. He claims that these labourers work harder and are less liable to keep bad company, and that these characteristics increase with their level of independence (*WN* I.viii.48). Moreover, he holds that more free labour, such as that employed by active capital rather than rent surplus, is far more efficient and productive (*WN* II.iii.12). Consequently, the gradual shift from an economy dominated by the feudal nobility to an economy driven by merchants and manufacturers has significantly increased growth (*WN* III.iv.4–18) and thereby brought about – without anyone consciously intending it – a 'revolution of the greatest importance to the publick happiness' (*WN* II.iv.17). Furthermore, commercial society, by increasing the wealth of the class of labourers, and by increasingly replacing feudal relations of production with those between merchants and manufacturers, on the one hand, and labourers, on the other, itself leads to increases in the latter's freedom and independence (see, inter alia, *WN* III.iv.4–18). This is particularly important for their moral and intellectual development – that is, their cultivation of 'wisdom and virtue' – as there is nothing so likely 'to corrupt and enervate and debase the mind as dependency' (*LJA* vi.6; cf. *LJB* 205, 328).

To recapitulate: Smith sees ordinary labourers as hard-working, creative, productive and rightly concerned to improve their circumstances. Further, what he has to say about merchants and manufacturers, and the virtues and character structures they must cultivate in order to distinguish themselves, seems at least partly applicable to labourers, too. This goes especially for the more independent ones and those who are on their way up the continuum that Smith stresses between labourers and merchants and manufacturers. To the extent that these are significant virtues of men in commercial societies, labouring men seem fairly well developed as moral beings.

There is more to be said, too. First of all, members of the class of labourers, who undoubtedly belong to the 'middling and inferior ranks', face none of the systemic institutional biases to drive them towards a vicious mode of moral existence faced by the immensely rich and powerful (see 'Landlords', below). As with the class of merchants and manufacturers, ultimately labourers must distinguish themselves in society by developing industry, frugality and attention, and by cultivating the virtues of prudence, justice and self-command, which would seem to commit them to the wiser and more virtuous 'austere' system of personal morals (*WN* V.i.g.10; cf. *TMS* I.iii.3.5). Thus they have, at least prima facie, all the moral potential of merchants and manufacturers, and none of the strong, perverting influences that affect landlords. Furthermore, Smith believes that full moral development – at least with respect to the more social and humane virtues – can be achieved as long as quite straightforward conditions are met. Such conditions include a normal family life, being free from fear and deprivation, and being decently socialised when growing up. These are well within the reach of sufficiently prosperous members of the middling and inferior ranks. From the perspective of beneficence, it is interesting to note that labourers are unaffected by the spirits of monopoly or 'mean rapacity' that Smith identifies in merchants and manufacturers – a point that clearly counts in the former group's moral favour.

Given what we have just discussed, it seems true, as Himmelfarb (1984) writes, that perhaps even more important than the egalitarian policies that Smith was keen to promote, and his concern with the material bases of well-being and human development of the class of labourers, was the 'image of the poor' that is implicit in his writings. It is not surprising that Smith was concerned for the poor, as this was a common enough sentiment in his day. Rather, what

> is more interesting is his confident assumption that the overwhelming number of the poor were in fact sober and industrious . . . It was because the poor were presumed to have the same virtues and passions as everyone else, because there were no innate differences separating them from the other classes . . . These 'creditable' poor were capable and desirous of bettering themselves, capable and desirous of exercising the virtues inherent in human nature, capable and desirous of the liberty that was their right as responsible individuals.
>
> (Himmelfarb 1984: 62–3)

In fact, according to Smith, there seems to be only one significant structural obstacle to the moral and cognitive development of labouring people: namely, the problems posed by an extreme division of labour. It has been argued, in my view erroneously, that these discussions prefigure Marx's theory of alienation (e.g., Viner 1965; West 1969, 1974; Lamb 1973; Hill 2007, 2010) and that there is somehow a contradiction between these views and others he advances on the division of labour (West 1964; Rosenberg 1965). The scope of this article precludes detailed discussion of these issues (see Raekstad 2011: 54–9 for more). However, I should like to indicate briefly how my reading of Smith can illuminate the discussion in question.

According to Smith, an extreme division of labour, by precluding the exercise of deliberative, creative and problem-solving skills, by denying a broad range of activities, and by making no demands on focus or prolonged mental exertion, renders labourers' cognitive abilities vastly underdeveloped, leaving them mentally 'mutilated and deformed', just as they would be physically mutilated if they were to lose a limb (*WN* V.i.f.60). His discussion mentions lack of exercise of understanding, invention and problem-solving, labourers' resulting inability to engage in rational conversation, form proper moral judgements, develop a full understanding of their own and their country's interests, and even the underdevelopment of their martial abilities: 'The labourer's dexterity at his own particular trade seems, in this manner, to be acquired at the expence of his intellectual, social, and martial virtues' (*WN* V.i.f.50). By distinguishing technical innovation from the development of wisdom and virtue, we find that, for instance, West (1964) seems to conflate the two, while both he and Rosenberg (1965) are really concerned only with the former. However, it seems clear from Smith's writings that his concern is much broader than these commentators suggest. In this section of Book V he discusses the general cognitive and moral degeneration of workers under an extreme division of labour, regardless of its effects on technical innovation. This underscores the importance of Smith's enduring and consistent commitment to a conception of human development conceived as the development of wisdom and virtue.

Landlords

In terms of their structural function in the economy of commercial societies, the class of landlords governs and distributes the use of land; the form of income thus accruing to them is the rent of land. Living off the rent of land – property that they need not improve on their own[6] – landlords naturally lack any of the mental demands that come with having to plan and/or execute any projects of their own. Nor does their position provide any opportunity to exercise deliberating or problem-solving skills:

> They are the only one of the three orders whose revenue costs them neither labour nor care, but comes to them, as it were, of its own accord, and independent of any plan or project of their own. That indolence, which is the natural effect of the ease and security of their situation, renders them too often, not only ignorant, but incapable of that application of mind which is necessary in order to foresee and understand the consequences of any publick regulation.
>
> (*WN* I.xi.p.8)

Being in general content with the 'humble renown' the 'propriety of his ordinary behaviour' affords him – *qua* a man born into rank and status – the typical landlord, lacking any significant skill or indeed the ambition to acquire any, is furthermore 'unwilling to embarrass himself with what can be attended either with difficulty or distress' (*TMS* I.iii.2.5). Their resulting ignorance and stupidity has numerous unfortunate effects. For one, landlords, more often than others, settle for considerably less than the 'natural' rate of interest on their land (*WN* I.xi.a.1). For another, they are often misled by the brighter and better-organised merchants and manufacturers to support policies that are contrary to their own interests (see, inter alia, *WN* I.x.c.25, IV.ii.21 and IV.v.23).[7]

Members of the landlord class, unlike those of the other two, need do no form of proper labour. Indeed, as Smith writes, in some societies even trade and the lending of money is considered disgraceful to a nobleman (*WN* V.iii.1). Nor do they need to engage in, plan or carry out any plans or projects of their own. This leaves them with plenty of leisure time, which, coupled with the fact that riches, power, rank and status are theirs by birthright, means that they can indulge themselves in extravagant vanity (*WN* III.ii.7).

Now, if this were all there was to be said – that is, if landlords were faced with cognitive/intellectual deficiencies and the minor moral concern of childlike vanity and ostentation – then the vaguely patronising view of the landlord class as vain, childish and not too bright that other commentators have advanced would not be far off the mark. For instance, Cropsey (1957: 67) notes that landlords' concern with 'arts and appearances of rank must finally deprive them of the solid virtues of industry and application', and Hanley (2009: ch.1) points out that Smith complains about the moral failings of the rich. Both Berry (1997: 103) and Griswold (1999: 264) mention Smith's belief that moral judgements are perverted by our disposition to seek and admire wealth and ostentation over wisdom and virtue, and the former further notes Smith's view that landlords prefer superficial pastimes over the virtues of 'knowledge, industry, patience or self-denial', concluding that this constitutes a 'critique of aristocratic ethics'. Buchan (2006: 63) cites *TMS* (IV.1.11) on how the market enjoins landlords to aid the poor despite their 'selfishness and rapacity', points out that in commercial societies the rich are 'obliged by the very question of money and free commerce to share some of their riches with the poor', and mentions landlords' lack of industry. Finally, Rothschild and Sen (2006: 327) write that, on Smith's account, landlords are 'somewhat foolish', 'ignorant', 'indolent' and especially vain, and cite Smith's description of them as proud and unfeeling. However, attention to a greater range of Smith's writings, especially *TMS*, reveals a far more scathing view of the moral character of the landlord class.

According to *TMS* in particular, landlords face serious challenges to their development of a virtuous character. Our discussion must necessarily be brief, but a summary is essential. As Smith repeatedly points out, human beings wish to be both respectable and respected, praiseworthy and praised (*TMS* III.2), and the two are 'distinct and independent of one another' (*TMS* III.2.2). Now, since to 'deserve, acquire and enjoy' the respect of others is among 'the great objects of ambition and emulation' (*TMS* I.iii.3.2), by the search for social rank and status which Smith believes is a constant of human nature we are offered two very different 'images', 'roads' or ideals by which to attain this object (ibid.). On the one hand, there is the road of 'wisdom and virtue', with the corresponding character of 'humble modesty and equitable justice' (ibid.). While attracting the attention only of 'the most studious and careful observer', whenever it does so it appears both 'more correct and more exquisitely beautiful' (ibid.). On the other hand, there is the road of 'wealth and greatness', with the corresponding character of 'proud ambition and ostentatious avidity', which 'forc[es] itself upon the notice of every wandering eye' and appears 'more gaudy and glittering in its colouring' (ibid.).[8] The sentiments we feel for the two (wisdom and virtue versus wealth and greatness) are distinct, but usually very hard to distinguish, not, as Lamb (1974) believes, because they often come to the same results for the 'middling and inferior ranks', but because of their simple resemblance to each other (*TMS* I.iii.3.3). Because they are often hard to distinguish, and because wealth and greatness are more easily observed and thus better seen by more people, public esteem and admiration will often follow wealth and greatness rather than wisdom and virtue. Smith nevertheless insists that 'perhaps in all cases' the man of virtue is still better off than the wealthy man, for reasons we need not pursue further here (but see *TMS* VI.iii.31).

According to Smith, the tendency to confuse and conflate sympathies caused by wealth and greatness with sympathies caused by wisdom and virtue causes considerable complications for moral judgement and development in commercial societies. Fortunately, he says, this problem is negligible among the 'middling and inferior professions' because behaving virtuously will commonly be followed by due professional success. '[L]uckily for the good morals of society', Smith reflects, the conditions of the latter, and not the former, are the 'situations of by far the greater part of mankind' (*TMS* I.iii.3.5–8). Consequently, the difference between being motivated by the desire to be respected and praised, on the one hand, and the desire to be(come) respectable and praiseworthy, on the other, is of little practical consequence, and thus seems not to cause significant problems for the middling and inferior professions' moral development; there is no great temptation to follow one over and above, and at the cost of, the other.

By contrast, the situation is very different for the rich and powerful 'superior stations' – I think it is clear that he is referring to landlords here – because the requirements for achieving large(r) quantities of wealth, power and influence frequently encourage behaviour that is contrary to virtues such as justice and beneficence, with the result that others' sentiments are significantly skewed (cf., especially, *TMS* I.iii.2.5). Perhaps this is why landlords are described as 'proud and unfeeling' later in the text, and as seeing 'the oeconomy of greatness' as a matter of 'baubles and trinkets' (*TMS* IV.i.10). Furthermore, this perverting influence is doubtless the reason why they follow the vicious, 'loose' system of personal morals, accepting and forgiving breaches of chastity, intemperance and so on, only excepting severe falsehood or injustice (*WN* V.i.g.10).

The challenges produced by the attractions that the second 'road' to increased rank and status hold for the landlord class, coupled with the mental deficiencies that result from the consequences of their position in the structural division of labour, cause significant problems for their development of wisdom and virtue. Rather than engaging in demanding tasks, plans or projects, landlords devote themselves to court foppery and conspicuous consumption:

> To figure at a ball is his great triumph, and to succeed in an intrigue of gallantry, his highest exploit. He has an aversion to all public confusions, not from the love of mankind, for the great *never look upon their inferiors as their fellow-creatures*; nor yet from want of courage, for in that he is seldom defective; but from a consciousness that he possesses none of the virtues which are required in such situations, and that the public attention will certainly be drawn away from him by others. He may be willing to expose himself to some little danger, and to make a campaign when it happens to be the fashion. But he shudders with horror at the thought of any situation which demands the continual and long exertion of *patience, industry, fortitude, and application of thought. These virtues are hardly ever to be met with in men who are born to those high stations.*
>
> (*TMS* I.iii.2.5; emphasis added)

In short, then, members of the class of landlords will generally fail to develop virtues like industry, fortitude and so on, all of which fall under 'prudence'. Although they may well be courageous, this virtue is of little value in a peaceable commercial civilisation. However, it is unclear whether landlords have insurmountable problems with self-command (though see *WN* V.i.g.10). Importantly, the morally perverting effects of their unique position renders wealthy landlords severely defective in their love of mankind, as they see their social inferiors as less than fully human fellow-creatures. Perhaps this is why Smith writes of how 'the proud and unfeeling landlord views his extensive fields, and without a thought for the wants of his brethren', and is nevertheless driven by an 'invisible hand', as he must be, 'without intending it, without knowing it, [to] advance the interest of the society, and afford means to the multiplication of the species' (*TMS* IV.i.10). This being said, landlords are at least, 'of all people, the least subject to the wretched spirit of monopoly' (*WN* IV.ii.21). As a result of all this, and of their excessive self-admiration, coupled with their undue concern for wealth and greatness over wisdom and virtue, landlords are frequently accused of being prone to the vices of pride, meanness and vanity (*TMS* VI.iii.34–47).

This added dimension to Smith's treatment of the landlord class reveals a scathing view of the development of individual landlords as moral creatures that demands revision of the milder received view. On my amended account, Smith not only sees landlords as severely deficient both cognitively and motivationally, as well as susceptible to childish vanities, as the above-cited writers correctly acknowledge. Crucially, Smith also sees them as proud, mean and severely lacking in beneficence, especially towards their perceived inferiors. Some of this comes across in passages that the aforementioned authors cite, but the full conclusion is never drawn. Smithian landlords are not merely imprudent, vain and so on; they are also unjust and seemingly completely devoid of beneficence towards their perceived inferiors. Smith's overall views on the moral development of the landlord class are, therefore, far more damning than the contemporary literature has allowed.

5. Conclusion

This article has outlined Smith's conception of 'wisdom and virtue' and has discussed his views on the differential influence the social structure of a commercial society may have on the members of its three classes: merchants and manufacturers; labourers; and landlords. His analyses are characteristically complex, noting the advantages and drawbacks of each position. Nevertheless, he adopts some historically striking stances. Perhaps most well known are his highly laudatory views on the commercial virtues of the class of merchants and manufacturers – albeit with the distinctly moralistic criticism of their more moral characteristics. They are, it seems, wise within their own fields and in relation to their own interests, but rather less so when it comes to others and society at large. They are prudent, just and have excellent self-command, but they lack positive beneficence, presumably because of their constant preoccupation with advancing their own – and *only* their own – interests, often at others' expense. This moral short-coming is, however, worsened by the fact that merchants and manufacturers are the politically dominant class in commercial societies, according to Smith's analysis.

Of greater interest is Smith's overturning of the traditional valuation of the nobility vis-à-vis labourers. On Smith's account, the ordinary workman comes out as a remarkably wise and virtuous being, not just potentially but actually. By contrast, and to a surprising degree, the landlord class is cast as severely deficient both cognitively and morally. Labourers are identified as virtuous, intelligent, knowledgeable and creative within their individual domains, and are said to possess a capacity for much greater virtue and wisdom, both of which are stunted only by a lack of free time, difficulties of organisation, poor education and the ravages of an extreme division of labour (for those working in manufacturing). Landlords, on the other hand, are stupid, lazy and generally incompetent at any-thing apart from frivolity and warfare. They may possess self-command, but they lack all of the other cardinal virtues, such as prudence, justice and beneficence.

Notes

1   This article is based on my master's thesis (Raekstad 2011). I would like to thank Professor Christel Fricke, my supervisor, for all of her (very considerable) help, advice and support, Professor Carola von Villiez and Professor Donald Winch for their comments on the thesis, and Dr Paul Giladi for reading and commenting on drafts of this article. I must also thank an anonymous referee for the *Adam Smith Review*. Obviously, any remaining errors are entirely my own.
2   The most notable exceptions include Berry (1997), Buchan (2006), Cropsey (1957), Griswold (1999), Reisman (1976), Rima (1998), Rothschild and Sen (2006) and Song (2006). It would be long and fruitless to list the numerous commentators on Smith's ethics who fail to discuss this topic at all.
3   Since my concern here is with the contemporary literature, I leave aside, for instance, Wollstonecraft's (1995) excellent discussion, extension and application of Smith's thoughts on this matter.
4   I interpret merchants and manufacturers as at least generally falling under the 'middling' of the 'middling and inferior' stations.
5   This paragraph owes much to Fleischacker (2005: esp. 62–8).
6   In fact, improvements on such land are often due to the efforts of the workers themselves (*WN* I.xi.a.2, III.ii.7; cf. III.ii.7).
7   Smith also refers to the landlord class's cognitive and intellectual deficiencies – including, inter alia, their problems with concentration and abstract thought – in his earlier critical analysis of Shaftesbury (*LRBL* I.137–48), whom he describes, tellingly, as a 'nobleman' (138, 148; cf. Phillipson 2011: 101–2).
8   Smith returns to this subject, inter alia, in his criticism of Mandeville in *TMS* VII.ii.4.8–10.

Bibliography

Berry, C. J. (1997) *Social Theory of the Scottish Enlightenment*. Edinburgh: Edinburgh University Press.
Brown, V. (1994) *Adam Smith's Discourse: Canonicity, Commerce and Conscience*. London: Routledge.

Buchan, J. (2006) *Adam Smith and the Pursuit of Perfect Liberty*. London: Profile Books.

Cropsey, J. (1957) *Polity and Economy: An Interpretation of the Principles of Adam Smith*. The Hague: Martinus Nijhoff.

Dobb, M. (1973) *Theories of Value and Distribution since Adam Smith*. Cambridge: Cambridge University Press.

Fleischacker, S. (1999) *A Third Concept of Liberty: Judgment and Freedom in Kant and Adam Smith*. Princeton, NJ: Princeton University Press.

Fleischacker, S. (2004) *A Short History of Distributive Justice*. London: Harvard University Press.

Fleischacker, S. (2005) *Adam Smith's* Wealth of Nations: *A Philosophical Companion*. Princeton, NJ: Princeton University Press.

Griswold, C. L. (1999) *Adam Smith and the Virtues of the Enlightenment*. Cambridge: Cambridge University Press.

Haakonsen, K. (1981) *The Science of the Legislator: The Natural Jurisprudence of David Hume and Adam Smith*. London: Cambridge University Press.

Haakonsen, K. (ed.) (2006) *The Cambridge Companion to Adam Smith*. Cambridge: Cambridge University Press.

Hanley, R. H. (2006) 'Adam Smith, Aristotle and Virtue Ethics'. In L. Montes and E. Schliesser (eds), *New Voices on Adam Smith*. London: Routledge.

Hanley, R. (2009) *Adam Smith and the Character of Virtue*. Cambridge: Cambridge University Press.

Hill, C. (1991) *The World Turned upside down: Radical Ideas during the English Revolution*. London: Penguin.

Hill, L. (2007) 'Adam Smith, Adam Ferguson and Karl Marx on the Division of Labour'. *Journal of Classical Sociology* 7(3): 339–66.

Hill, L. (2010) 'Social Distance and the New Strangership in Adam Smith'. *Adam Smith Review* 6: 166–83.

Himmelfarb, G. (1984) *The Idea of Poverty: England in the Early Industrial Age*. London: Faber and Faber.

Israel, J. I. (2001) *Radical Enlightenment: Philosophy and the Making of Modernity 1650–1750*. Oxford: Oxford University Press.

Lamb, R. (1973) 'Adam Smith's Concept of Alienation'. *Oxford Economic Papers*, New Series, 25(2): 275–85.

Lamb, R. B. (1974) 'Adam Smith's System: Sympathy not Self-Interest'. *Journal of the History of Ideas* 35(4): 671–82.

Lindgren, J. R. (1973) *The Social Philosophy of Adam Smith*. The Hague: Martinus Nijhoff.

Meek, R. L. (1977) *Smith, Marx and after: Ten Essays in the Development of Economic Thought*. London: Chapman & Hall.

Montes, L. and Schliesser, E. (eds) (2006) *New Voices on Adam Smith*. London: Routledge.

Phillipson, N. (2011) *Adam Smith: An Enlightened Life*. London: Penguin.

Raekstad, P (2011) 'Class and State in the Political Theory of Adam Smith: A Chapter in the History of a Neglected Strand of Political Thought'. Master's thesis, University of Oslo. Available online at: www.duo.uio.no/publ/IFIKK/2011/123475/Raekstad.pdf, accessed 4 May 2016.

Raphael, D. D. (2007) *The Impartial Spectator: Adam Smith's Moral Philosophy*. Oxford: Clarendon Press.

Reisman, D. A. (1976) *Adam Smith's Sociological Economics*. London: Croom Helm.

Rima, I. H. (1998) 'Class Conflict and Adam Smith's "Stages of Social History"'. *Journal of the History of Economic Thought* 20: 103–13.

Rosenberg, N. (1965) 'Adam Smith on the Division of Labour: Two Views or One?' *Economica*, New Series, 32(126): 127–39.

Rothschild, E. (2002) *Economic Sentiments: Adam Smith, Condorcet and the Enlightenment.* London: Harvard University Press.

Rothschild, E. and Sen, A. (2006) 'Adam Smith's Economics'. In K. Haakonsen (ed.), *The Cambridge Companion to Adam Smith.* Cambridge: Cambridge University Press.

Smith, A. (1976) *An Inquiry into the Nature and Causes of the Wealth of Nations.* Ed. R. H. Campbell and A. S. Skinner. Oxford: Oxford University Press; Glasgow edition (reprint Indianapolis, IN: Liberty Press, 1982).

Smith, A. (1976) *The Theory of Moral Sentiments.* Ed. D. D. Raphael and A. L. Macfie. Oxford: Oxford University Press; Glasgow edition (reprint Indianapolis, IN: Liberty Press, 1982).

Smith, A. (1978) *Lectures on Jurisprudence.* Ed. R. L. Meek, D. D. Raphael and P. G. Stein. Oxford: Oxford University Press; Glasgow edition (reprint Indianapolis, IN: Liberty Press, 1982).

Smith, A. (1980) *Essays on Philosophical Subjects.* Ed. W. P. D. Wightman. Oxford: Oxford University Press; Glasgow edition (reprint Indianapolis, IN: Liberty Press, 1982).

Smith, A. (1983) *Lectures on Rhetoric and Belles Lettres.* Ed. J. C. Bryce. Oxford: Oxford University Press; Glasgow edition (reprint Indianapolis, IN: Liberty Press, 1982).

Smith, A. (1987) *Correspondence of Adam Smith.* Ed. E. C. Mossner and I. S. Ross. 2nd edn. Oxford: Oxford University Press; Glasgow edition (reprint Indianapolis, IN: Liberty Press, 1982).

Song, H. (2006) 'Adam Smith's Conception of the Social Relations of Production'. *European Journal of the History of Economic Thought* 4(1): 23–42.

Sperber, D. and Hirschfeld, L. (1999) 'Culture, Cognition and Evolution'. In R. Wilson and F. Keil (eds), *MIT Encyclopedia of the Cognitive Sciences.* Cambridge, MA: MIT Press.

Viner, J. (1965) 'Introduction'. In J. Rae, *The Life of Adam Smith.* New York: Kelly.

Wallech, S. (1986) '"Class versus Rank": The Transformation of Eighteenth-Century English Social Terms and Theories of Production'. *Journal for the History of Ideas* 47(3): 409–31.

West, E. G. (1964) 'Adam Smith's Two Views on the Division of Labour'. *Economica*, New Series, 3(121): 23–32.

West, E. G. (1969) 'The Political Economy of Alienation: Karl Marx and Adam Smith'. *Oxford Economic Papers*, New Series, 21(1): 1–23.

West, E. G. (1974) 'Adam Smith and Alienation: A Rejoinder'. *Oxford Economic Papers*, New Series, 27(2): 295–301.

Wollstonecraft, M. (1995) *A Vindication of the Rights of Men* and *A Vindication of the Rights of Woman.* Ed. S. Tomaseli. Cambridge: Cambridge University Press.

A revolutionary's evolution

The view over time of *The Wealth of Nations* in China

Evan Osborne[1]

1. Introduction

In the latter half of the nineteenth century the Qing dynasty found its authority under siege, and China's educated elite believed the country to be increasingly humiliated and endangered by the military and technological superiority of the nations of Western Europe and North America. By the end of the century, one response of young Chinese, as of young Japanese before them, was to travel to the West to acquire education, and on that foundation to read and translate the ideas encountered there that these young people thought were responsible for its power. One such translated book was *An Inquiry into the Nature and Causes of the Wealth of Nations* (*WN*). Throughout the century-plus since that first translation, China has undergone profound social upheaval and a series of literally revolutionary changes. But despite these transformations, Chinese intellectuals and, more recently, general readers have consistently attached great importance to this volume.

This paper traces the evolution of Chinese interpretations of *WN*. Translations from three eras are compared, to investigate what was important and what was unimportant at various stages in China's development. The translators' emphasis changes from a preoccupation with national power to issues in theoretical political economy to how to facilitate China's emergence as a modern market economy. This change over time to a great extent reflects changes in China itself. Section 2 looks at the original translation by one of the most important early translators of Western works in China; Section 3 discusses the 1930s translation by two Marxist analysts that was reissued at the height of Maoism; Section 4 explores two modern translations from the much more liberal publishing environment that has existed in China since 1979; and Section 5 reviews the particular changes over time in the Chinese translation of Smith's notion of "arbitrary" governance, which was a natural concept to Enlightenment British readers but whose meaning there and then did not always translate well into twentieth-century China.

2. Smith's arrival in China

China's relations with Western powers began to pose serious problems for the Qing dynasty and its administrators with the country's defeat in war first against

Britain (1840) and then against Britain and France (1856–1860). Prior to the outbreak of the first of these two so-called Opium Wars, China's ruling elite had perceived the Western presence in Canton (Guangdong) as merely one nuisance among many in a vast empire. But defeat in the first Opium War forced China to cede Hong Kong to Britain, and defeat in the second gave Westerners land concessions and exemption from Chinese legal jurisdiction. By the time China had lost a short war to a smaller but significantly modernized Japan in 1894–1895, there was widespread acceptance that China desperately needed to modernize.

At this time Chinese intellectuals and the educated young began to take a great interest in the Western knowledge that was thought to hold the key to how the West and its Japanese imitators had become so technologically advanced and militarily powerful. This knowledge was believed to be contained in the texts that Westerners in China themselves had imported since they had founded universities and pre-tertiary schools in the second half of the nineteenth century. In addition, after Chinese had traveled to the West, and especially England, to study, those who returned home began to translate these texts into Chinese. One of the most renowned members of this first generation of translators was Yan Fu (嚴復; 1854–1921). After receiving his education at a shipyard school in Fujian, a province long known for emigration, where many of the teachers were Westerners, and then serving at sea, he found himself in England, where he studied at the Royal Naval College from 1877 to 1879. After the Sino-Japanese War, he joined an organization that was opposed to the Treaty of Shimonoseki, which ended that conflict, and joined groups that supported modernizing the military and retaining the emperor as a constitutional monarch (as opposed to others, including Sun Yat-Sen, who favored a republic). As an activist intellectual he took it upon himself to begin translating classics of the Western humanities. He saw three important tasks in his translation work: to get Chinese to accept that Western ideas were independently generated rather than coming from China; to persuade them that Western power proved that it was imperative for Chinese to master these ideas; and to disabuse Chinese of the notion that Western philosophers had studied only superficial, utilitarian issues rather than the profound questions that had long preoccupied Chinese historians and philosophers (Cui and Forget, 2013). One of what were ultimately eight translations was *WN*, on which he began work in 1896 (Borokh, 2013).[2]

As the first translator of these works, it fell to Yan Fu to choose the Chinese titles with care. For his translation of *WN*, his second translation after Thomas Huxley's *Evolution and Ethics* (released in 1902), he chose *The Origin of Wealth* (原富, *Yuán Fù*). This suggests, first, that he saw Western wealth as a primary difference between China and the West, and, second, that Smith's book revealed the secrets of its accumulation. But many Western concepts, including some found in *WN*, were hard for him to translate into Chinese. In his translation of Mill's *On Liberty*, for instance, he struggled to explain why freedom was so important to the English, given that the Chinese translation, 自由 (*zì yóu*) – literally "emanating from the self" – denoted selfish behavior. Yan eventually decided that wisdom is neither culturally specific nor relevant only to a particular era, and that Western scholarship contained at least some profound, eternal truths that were none-theless unknown in China. Among all of Smith's ideas in *WN*, Yan most emphasized that enlightened pursuit of self-interest could work for the benefit of all – a claim he saw as core to Smith's analysis. Given China's traditional notions of the priority of duty to others, he felt this had to be made clear to the Chinese but introduced gradually, so as not to upset the traditional Chinese social order too rapidly.

After translating *Evolution and Ethics*, Yan turned to *WN*. He felt that its advocacy of free commerce and its explanation and rejection of Western mercantilist doctrines were also important for Chinese readers to understand, and for the Chinese state to master. He found an 1880 edition in the library of Shanghai's East China Normal University, edited by James E. Thorold Rogers for Oxford University Press (Smith, 1880). According to Yan's notes, he translated this text between 1896 and 1901, at the same time as he was translating other Western works.

His first challenge lay in translating it into the form of written Chinese that was most commonly used at the time. While over the previous five hundred years some novels had been written in the style of spoken Chinese – known as *bái huà* (白話) – the most widely used writing method by far for most historical, phil-osophical and other nonfiction (and many fiction) texts had long since been 古文 (*gǔ wén*; "ancient language"), known in English as "classical Chinese." Perhaps because the woodblock printing used in China had always been costly, all forms of classical Chinese (unlike *bái huà*) emphasized parsimony in the use of characters. That this style was difficult for someone to understand without extensive training limited the reach of Chinese literacy. While magazines began to be published in the vernacular in the 1890s (Huang, 2003), it was not until the May Fourth movement in 1919 that the campaign to use *bái huà* in written Chinese began in earnest. In the meantime, when Yan was translating *WN*, he felt obliged to use the ancient style. There were some unavoidable errors in the translation into classical Chinese, due to Smith's lengthy and – especially to a non-native speaker – occasionally dense English.

In addition, Yan has long been known to have altered the content of the original. For instance, he deleted some sections that he thought would be of little use to modern Chinese readers, such as those relating to British tax issues, some of the extensive charts and discussions of the same, the discussion of the English corn market, and certain elements of the history of English inheritance law. He also editorialized, adding or deleting content according to what he believed Chinese readers needed to know. For example, in I.3.7 Smith writes: "It is remarkable that neither the antient Egyptians, nor the Indians, nor the Chinese, encouraged foreign commerce, but seem all to have derived their great opulence from this inland navigation." Yan (1977: 20), after changing the failure to "encourage" foreign trade to a prohibition of it, added that "the three countries, while once flourishing, have since declined."[3] Finally, in sections marked 案 (*àn*; "note"), he added a great deal of commentary, explaining and interpreting what Smith may have meant. In addition, he directly translated and added many of Rogers's notes from the 1880 edition.

In his introduction to the text, Yan explained what he had learned from it, and why he had translated it. The term he chose for economics was *jì xué* (計學). The second character means "science" or "study," but the first has several meanings – numerical calculation, planning and strategizing, and the accounting information of a firm. (Such divergent meanings for the same character are fairly common in Chinese.) Yan noted that the Japanese term 經濟學 (*jīng jì xué*; the term in both modern Chinese and Japanese for "economics") had a connotation of control and management of every national matter, large or small, which went beyond what Smith was discussing, and was thus inappropriate. *Jì xué*, in contrast, while containing a meaning indicating the relations among different economic actors, also included the management of finances at the household or firm level, and was thus a better description of the changing pattern of production and distribution. And the fact that Chinese had no term for the *concept* of the structure of the economy forced Yan to choose. After discussing the Greek etymology of "economics," Yan (1977: 5) explained that he chose *jì xué* as the most appropriate translation. He also praised *WN* as a description of the laws of *jì xué* because, in his view, unlike later English texts written by and for specialists such as Mill, Walker and Marshall, it did not present the formal principles of the discipline. While acknowledging ideas that had been in the background earlier, Yan also credited Smith with using compelling reasoning to build on those scattered but persuasive observations and create a new science.

What was the essence of this new science? First, according to Yan, Smith saw gold not as a precious metal that was used to make treasures to be admired, but as simply one of many goods. Gold was money too, of course, in Chinese society, as in Smith's Britain, but to see it primarily as a means of accumulating capital rather than a luxury good could give scholars a language in which to speak of business that businesspeople could respect. Note that this argument was meant to bridge the gap between businessmen – who were politically influential in China (as everywhere else) but ranked very low in the Confucian social order – and the highly educated classes who comprised the civil service. Among the ideas that Smith postulated but were unknown in Chinese writing were the fundamental equality of all merchants with the rest of society and the costly privileges of the East India Company and similar firms, whose machinations had brought about the North American portion of the expensive Seven Years War, which damaged the rule of law in England and thus the interests of the overwhelming majority of its merchants (Yan, 1977: 9).

Yan also devoted substantial attention to how the public interest emerged from the individual pursuit of private interest. This was again contrary to traditional Chinese thinking. As noted above, merchants' activity was not seen in China as righteous, but Smith, according to Yan, painted the pursuit of profit and concern about loss as laudable, with the translator merely cautioning that this becomes a problematic view only if it is said that ethics *stops* at the pursuit of profit (Yan, 1977: 10). As long as it is recognized that there is ethical and unethical behavior both inside and outside of commerce, recognizing the intrinsic ethical worth of the pursuit of commercial gain is a stunning philosophical achievement, one that is seldom, if ever, attempted in Chinese thought. If the pursuit of profit is not done in an otherwise immoral way, the *public* interest can be defined simply as the aggregate of all private interests (積私以為公, *jī sī yǐ wéi gōng*; Yan, 1977: 10). And yet Yan noted that contamination of governance by private interest is fatal to Smith's system: again he stresses Smith's mentions of the East India Company, which, thanks to its manipulation of British policy (its monopoly privileges, presumably), amassed an empire in India equal in area to China that outshone those of Alexander and Genghis Khan. In so doing, it worked against the interest of the people of both India and Britain. Finally, Yan stressed the novelty of the Smithian worldview in Chinese thought, saying that the future of the Chinese nation depended on its acceptance of this way of thinking (Yan, 1977: 11–12).

With respect to Smith's concept of the "invisible hand," while in *WN* IV.2.9 it merely describes how an individual chooses to direct his capital, the metaphor as it is now understood is arguably developed throughout IV.2.2–10. But there is reason to think that Yan's translation of this phrase was not entirely accurate. As far as I can tell, there has never been any attempt to retranslate Yan's translation of IV.2.9 (Yan, 1977: 445) back into English – which is hardly surprising – but Liu (2013) *has* translated Yan's classical Chinese into *bái huà*. Translating this latter text into modern English reveals Yan's understanding. It reads:

> The annual revenue of a society depends on its annual production, on its exchange value. The merchants of today are willing to invest their funds inside the country, and unwilling to invest them abroad. When investing, they will strive to reap the greatest return. In so doing they will increase the national income. People will then say that these people invest in this way for the benefit of the country, that they must believe that is in the country's interest before they invest in this manner. But this is false. The reason investors invest near or far is that they hope to protect the value of their capital. They seek highly profitable investments in the pursuit of greater revenues. The interests to which they pay attention are their own, and in no way the country's. If they on this account reap large gains, does it follow that that pursuit of this profit damages the national interest? If people pursue their private interests and the public interest is thus served, the results are much better than those occurring because of the actions of people who act in the name of the public interest. While I have heard of people who speak of the public interest, this kind of talk actually is of no benefit to the country, and often works to its detriment.

This passage is different in several respects from Smith's original text, even noting the incongruity in translating from eighteenth-century English, into classical Chinese, into modern Chinese and finally into modern English. First, Yan's text is a rough summary rather than a word-for-word translation, which confirms that his goal was to educate his readers about important foreign ideas rather than to engage in a purely intellectual exercise. Smith's idea that the domestic merchant invests domestically only to the extent that is possible is replaced with a division in Yan between what the merchant is "willing" and "unwilling" to do. (And the concept of maximum feasible action certainly existed in classical Chinese.) The emphasis on the falsehood of the idea that investors specifically wish to do what is best for the country is also more pronounced in Yan; and the mildly sarcastic tone in Smith's original final two sentences is absent, suggesting that Yan felt a need to emphasize that public officials' declarations of what is in the public interest often have the opposite effect.[4] Moreover, the invisible hand metaphor itself is missing – it finds its way into none of Yan's sentences, including in his introduction. The enumeration of the investor's task, maximizing his revenue, and the link between that task and public gain are indeed preserved, but in a more direct way. Both Smith and Yan propose that the social interest is advanced through the individual pursuit of private interest. But whereas Smith is rhetorically playful and takes several sentences to spell out his argument, Yan seems to posit his claim against the default Chinese view that it is *bad* for the country if a private actor pursues his private interest.[5] On several occasions the latter states that the country benefits – if not by design – when investors do what is in their private interest. This suggests the novelty of the idea in China.

Yan was ultimately an advocate of Western economic liberalism and science (Chang, 1980), although, as noted above, he believed the reasons for the former's efficacy would occur to the reflexively non-individualist Chinese nation only gradually. In addition, he looked at liberalism and the harnessing of self-interest not as Smith usually did – as a way in which the "natural liberty" that Smith independently valued promoted the broad prosperity of individuals. Rather, he viewed liberalism as a way to build Chinese national power at a desperate time. Over the remainder of his career he advocated a number of new policies that were consistent with Smith's claims, including lowering the tax burden, anti-monopoly laws and modernizing the financial system, in addition to standardizing the system of weights and measures and improving the water-transportation system. Nonetheless he was not, as Smith was, a broad-spectrum liberal. He eventually came to believe that individual freedom should be limited, and viewed economic liberalism as simply a tool to increase national power (Zhang, 1999).

Overall, the difficult nature of Yan's translation limited the reach of the work. At a time when written Chinese was starting to change in ways that were thought to make it more accessible, Yan persevered with classical Chinese. Nevertheless, his translation's influence in China's intellectual circles was significant. The primary idea behind Yan's translation – that *WN* was a key text that laid out some of the reasons for Western power – persisted through the early post-Qing years. The largely accurately translated ideas in *WN* of self-improvement through schooling, as well as the extolling of natural liberty and the belief in free trade (at least as far as opposition to a prohibition on exports), all found their way into contemporary Chinese intellectual contention. Chinese advocates of liberal trade ultimately did not win these battles, as the influence of German political economy, from Friedrich List to Karl Marx, grew steadily over the next several decades as China fell into chaos.[6] And economic liberalism would, with the rise of Marxist thought, be relegated for several decades to a historically important but nonetheless ultimately erroneous role – a sort of museum piece of capitalist philosophy.

3. *WN* in the era of Mao and Marx

The chief criticism of Yan's translation in the new China after the end of the Qing dynasty in 1912 – in addition to his work's relative inaccessibility – was that he had taken liberties by omitting some text he thought of little use to Chinese readers and altering some of Smith's (European) examples to make his text more comprehensible to those readers. After the chaos of the immediate post-Qing period, two young scholars who were interested in political economy and disappointed with the failings of the Republic of China government met at Jinan University in 1928.[7] Guo Dali (郭大力) and Wang Yanan (王亞南) began to collaborate, and in 1931 their translation of *The Wealth of Nations*, the second in Chinese history, was published. They would soon become (if they were not already) devout Marxists, and they are now best known in China for publishing the first Chinese translation of Marx's *Capital* in 1938.

Although Zhu (1993) – who studied the two-volume 1972 (slightly updated) edition of Guo and Wang's translation – declared that they had nothing to say about *WN* itself (a claim that persisted in the literature for some time; see Lai, 2000), the translators did in fact discuss, and indeed praise, *WN* and its place in the history of economic thought in their introduction to the first edition (Guo and Wang, 1931). This introduction essentially presents Smith as the founder of modern economic thinking, although Guo and Wang suggest that the text reveals that he was influenced by the work of (unnamed) Physiocrats. They claim that Smith's thinking became so dominant among economists around the world that even his critics were forced to conduct their criticism entirely within Smith's framework, focusing on minor inconsistencies rather than fundamental errors while adopting many of his views as their own. Soon after *WN*'s publication, in their view, economic thinking became simply a matter of correcting Smith's comparatively minor errors. In China, though, whereas the book was seen as an essential text for aspiring mandarins in the late Qing, the ruling elite's understanding of the text was superficial.

To Guo and Wang (1931), Smith became the chief theorist for the rapidly developing capitalist economy of Britain in the eighteenth and nineteenth centuries. They note the frequency with which he criticizes commercial interests and businessmen, partly in relation to their ignorance of their own interests, and view Smith as someone who *taught* commercial actors where their interests truly lay – namely, in promoting the development of a capitalist economy. The belief that Smith should be seen as a very important but nonetheless transitional figure runs throughout their remarks. In their view, he draws on seemingly noble concepts that merely mask the inevitable class struggle. His concept of natural liberty, for example, is in fact "only freedom for a small number of people to invest," and his seeming optimism is merely an artifact of "the vitality characteristic of the early period of capitalist development" (Guo and Wang, 1931: 3).[8] In short, the Smith of Guo and Wang is a partisan of unfettered markets, precisely because it promotes the general social interest. This portrait is consistent with the view of Smith that is held by many of his Western admirers, of course, in contrast to more nuanced perspectives that see him as a sometime skeptic of commercial forces. But Guo and Wang believe that Smith's theorizing remained incomplete until Marx perfected it several decades later.

As has been mentioned, Guo and Wang's translation was reissued in two volumes in 1972, with a new introduction by Wang replacing the 1931 version.[9] By this time, the nature of publishing in China had changed completely, and the new introduction reveals Smith's place in Maoist political-economic orthodoxy. In 1931, despite Japanese rule over Manchuria and the suzerainty of the authoritarian Chiang Kai-Shek over much of the rest of China, book publishing was still substantially free. By 1972 all publishing was carried out under stringent Communist Party restrictions. Even though the Cultural Revolution is generally held to have begun in 1966, radicalism had been well entrenched in the corridors of power ever since the purges of the 1950s, and Wang's 1972 introduction could not but reflect an orthodox Marxist/Maoist spirit.[10] So, whereas the 1931 introduction acknowledges some of the problems of translating unfamiliar foreign ideas, the 1972 version focuses entirely on Smith in the history of political economy. The task was to put him where he belonged in the development of the ultimate economic truth – that of Marx. And because Smith was, in Marxist thinking, a significant element on the road to that truth, nineteenth-century political economists who were sympathetic to monopoly capitalism sought to disparage his thinking. Thus, Wang writes:

> At a time when vulgar capitalist economists seeking to counter Marxist economics are quite willing to strongly oppose the classical economics of Smith and Ricardo, while we must without fear fiercely attack this classical theory, in order to better understand it from a historical perspective and vigorously defend Marxist economics, it is important from a strictly scientific perspective to reintroduce their economic theories, an act with its own practical importance even now.
>
> (Wang, 2013: Vol. 1, 7)[11]

And yet, from the very first mention, Wang (2013: Vol. 1, 1) does depict Smith as a "capitalist economist" (自本階級經濟學者, *zì běn jiē jí jīng jì xúe zhě*). Eighteenth-century Britain is portrayed as a country making the transition from small- to large-scale industry, but fettered by the remnants of feudalism and mercantilist doctrines, which were obstacles to the growth of the capitalist classes. These classes needed a theory that would "pave the way for capitalist expansion" (為了清除〔資產階級〕前進道路上的障礙, *Wèi le qīng chú [zī chǎn jiē jí] qián jìn dào lù shàng de zhàng ài*), and Smith was the economist to provide it (Wang, 2013: Vol. 1, 1). There is no intimation that he supinely produced the theory that capitalists demanded of him, in the way Marx in *Capital* suggested that various bourgeois economists, such as Henry Dunning MacLeod and Frédéric Bastiat, did. Rather, Wang's suggestion is that Smith was the right economist at the right time, developing a theory to explain the early stages of the large-scale transition he was observing. Unlike Yan, who translated the text for its instructional value, Guo and Wang did so for historical purposes.

And their view of Smith's role is one with which Marx would have sympathized. In contrast to the other political economists shortly thereafter who supported liberalism, and whom Marx dismissed with great sarcasm, Smith (along with Ricardo) is frequently praised with faint damns, as in chapter 14 of *Capital*'s discussion of his defensible if incomplete comparison of the social and manufacturing divisions of labor and his real but limited advocacy of education for workmen spiritually crushed by the factory, or chapter 19's assessment of his earnest but mistaken attempt to get at the value of labor.[12] In 1972, Smith's mistakes were seen as more substantial, but his analysis was still progress, and appropriate for his era. However, Wang argues that it was then misappropriated by propagandists of a newer one.

In particular, according to Wang's introduction, Smith's era was now known to predate a stage that was not mentioned in the 1931 translation – "monopoly" (壟斷, *lóng duàn*) capitalism. The nineteenth-century rise of this form of capitalism, which Smith failed to foresee, made his analysis of competitive markets and of the beneficial role of the individual pursuit of self-interest of no use now. But, citing Lenin, Wang (2013: Vol. 1, 2) argues that scientists (and, to Marxists and eighteenth–nineteenth-century liberals alike, political economy was a *scientific* enterprise) should be judged by their contributions in light of what was known at the time, and by that standard Smith was truly great. Smith wrote during the age of mercantilism, when economists were asking fundamental questions about the definition and origin of wealth, whereas the mercantilists and Physiocrats were writing a few decades earlier, when there was insufficient capitalist development to answer such questions. Whereas the Physiocrats saw money (gold) as wealth, to Smith it was just a portion thereof, one asset among several. From this discovery it followed that the source of wealth was not really mines, colonies or trade surpluses. Indeed, it is striking that, to Wang, the importance of the directly translated first sentence in the introduction – "The annual labour of every nation is the fund which originally supplies it with all the necessaries and conveniencies of life which it annually consumes" – lies not in consumption as the ultimate end of economic activity, as many modern readers would sense, but in Smith's emphasis on the importance of labor generally and not merely agricultural labor (Wang, 2013: Vol. 1, 3). This analysis is what we would expect from an author analyzing Smith from a Marxist perspective. As Wang sees it, the Physiocrats' identification of agricultural labor as the only labor that ultimately mattered in terms of value creation was a mistake. (In the modern era of human-capital theory the idea that all labor is the same is dismissed, but this claim was also central to Marx's analysis in *Capital*, where the phrase "undifferentiated human labor" appears several times.)

Wang also suggests that while Smith's failure to foresee the monopoly stage of capitalism was a mistake, he does not merit the same condemnation as later work by "vulgar" (庸俗, *yōng sú*) economists who lived in the era of mono-poly capitalism and therefore should have known better. In this regard, Wang devotes special attention to the Austrian school, focusing on Böhm-Bawerk in particular, as a school of thought that, in the course of its apologetics for the new monopoly capitalism, violated the principles of classical political economy laid out by Smith and Ricardo in a vain attempt to counter the rapidly ascending theoretical framework of Marx. As Guo and Wang saw it, it was important to translate Smith into the Chinese vernacular in 1931 to enable a better understanding of Marx, and indeed Wang writes in 1972 that they translated Smith and Ricardo primarily to develop that understanding prior to tackling the translation of *Capital*. Nonetheless, in their view, *WN* in its proper time and place had its own revolutionary – albeit now purely academic – importance. In short, Guo and Wang, as committed Marxists, placed Smith in Chinese squarely where Marx had placed him in German – as an indispensable theorist, but with work left undone.

But Smith also argued that economic liberalism had an ethical aspect, too, which was problematic from a Marxist/Maoist perspective. Guo and Wang invari-ably translate the term "natural liberty" – which Smith vested with both moral and economic significance (and often British distinctiveness) in various places – conventionally. The terms they use for "natural" – 自然 (*zì rán*) and 天然 (*tiān rán*) – function in exactly the same way as the word "natural" does in English, in that they mean having a connection to the natural world *and* being an innate or appropriate characteristic of a thing. However, Smith's idea of natural liberty's role is somewhat misunderstood in one place in Guo and Wang's translation of *WN*, namely at IV.5.55, where Smith writes:

> The law which prohibited the manufacturer from exercising the trade of a shopkeeper endeavoured to force this division in the employment of stock to go on faster than it might otherwise have done. The law which obliged the farmer to exercise the trade of a corn merchant endeavoured to hinder it from going on so fast. Both laws were evident violations of natural liberty, and therefore unjust; and they were both, too, as impolitic as they were unjust.

In Guo and Wang's (2013: Vol. 2, 102) version, the last sentence is translated back into English as: "Both laws were evident violations of natural liberty, and therefore unjust; because they were unjust, they were thus miscalculations."[13] Therefore, to Guo and Wang, the error flows *from* the laws' injustice; it is not a simultaneous feature *of* it. Adding to the imprecision is that the word translated here as "unjust" (不正當, *bú zhèng dàng*) also means "unreasonable" or "inapt."[14] The idea that a violation of natural liberty is a matter of justice, in other words a separate matter from the lack of wisdom in the laws' design, is not carried through in this translation. The more recent Yang Jingnian (2014) translation (discussed below) is an improvement as it translates the sentence as: "Both laws were evident violations of natural liberty, and therefore unjust; and beyond this injustice, they were both, too, also impolitic."[15] Only Smith's rhetorical flourish of comparing the *level* of the laws' injustice with that of their unsuitability is missing.

With regard to the "invisible hand" metaphor (Guo and Wang, 2013: Vol. 2, 27), the translation is intended to be direct, as are all subsequent translations. The translation for "invisible hand" itself, in particular, is almost literal: "He is guided by a hand that cannot be seen" (他受著看不見的手的領導, *tā shòu zhě kàn bú jiàn de shǒu de lǐng dǎo*). The exact translations in the two modern versions discussed below both preserve the passive voice ("is guided by") and are overall inconsequentially different from Smith's original text. At this point the idea of doing the best for society by doing what is best for oneself was presumably no longer novel, so there was no need to explain it.

4. Smith in the China of competitive publishing

Following the 1980 trial of the Gang of Four, which closed the door on totalitarian, absolute control of thought and economic action, the Chinese publishing industry began to flourish.[16] Today there are many translations of *WN*, all of them similar in translation style to Guo and Wang's version. The difference lies in the way the significance of the work is framed, along with the presentation of the book itself. As before, the texts generally come with extensive introductions, but now there are often photographs of life in later periods, and diagrams of where Smith fits in the history of economic thought, along with images of social and economic life during Smith's time. Also common are extensive footnotes, some of which are designed to make Smith's sometimes lengthy discourses more congenial to modern readers, while others elaborate on his now-arcane historical references. Such translations are clearly designed for a much broader readership.

This article compares two modern versions of *WN*. The first is that of Yang Jingnian, which he completed – remarkably – in 1998, at the age of ninety. Yang received his Ph.D. from Oxford in 1948, and then worked at Nankai University. Purged in 1957, he endured labor reform, did his own translation work, and returned to a formal academic setting only after rehabilitation in 1978. He began his translation of *WN* in 1995 and finished most of the work within eleven months. The introductory remarks that are reproduced here are from the third version of his translation and commentary (Yang, 2014), which was first published in 2001. The second translation to feature here (by Tang Risong *et al.*) was first published three years later and includes a preface by Yang Zhaoyu (2012).

In Yang Jingnian's introduction, he writes as a Marxist of long standing, albeit one who suffered at the hands of the Communist Party for a number of years.

Similar to Guo and Wang, he emphasizes that Smith wrote at the dawn of modern capitalism, just as industry was beginning the turn toward large-scale production. At this time, capitalists were still subject to the restraints of the legacies of the feudal system and of the prevailing mercantilist ideology. He praises Smith for his presentation of their significant (if mistaken) economic theories, and his systematic narration of economic trends and events. He simultaneously recognizes Smith's argument that large firms can easily become special-interest lobbyists. He directly translates an excerpt from Max Lerner's introduction to *WN* (1937: vi) as noting that Smith vigorously opposed such special-interest politics.[17] Yang (2014: 6) contrasts Marx's and Smith's views of the dominant determinants of human progress, suggesting that the former viewed class struggle as the driving force of human society, while the pursuit of self-improvement (改善本身狀況, *gǎi shàn běn shēn zhuàng kuàng*) – rather than Smith's most famous postulated goal – "self-love" – was paramount for the latter. Competition, says Yang Jingnian, is Smith's key to channeling this desire to improve one's circumstances in a socially beneficial direction. It does this by ensuring that prices, and the distribution of the national product, are led to their "natural" (*zì rán*) level. Smith's growth is likened literally to a Newtonian machine, but only as long as politics is kept out of the control of special interests, which promote monopoly. Thus, the essence of "natural liberty" in Yang Jingnian's view is the absence of monopoly. This contrasts with the way Smith used this term – as a more general (and laudatory) description of a British subject's right to live and work wherever he pleased, provided he could secure the cooperation of others.[18] Overall, Yang Jingnian argues that Smith sympathizes with the poor and is generally contemptuous of business, whose critical role in promoting prosperity depends on sufficient competition.

Yang Zhaoyu (2012: 8), in partial contrast, describes *WN* not as a book that was relevant for the era of incipient industrialization, before the dominance of monopoly capital, but as one that is relevant for "today's China[, which] has returned to a market economy" (今日的中國已經回歸了市場經濟, *zhōng guó huí guī shì chǎng jīng jì*). He argues that among the key elements of Smith's worldview found in *WN* are the division of labor as the key to increased productivity, the labor theory of value, his opposition to "colonial policies" (殖民地政策, *zhí mín dì zhèng cè*), his advocacy of *laissez-faire*, and the importance of education (Yang, 2012: 7). Like Yang Jingnian (2014: 5), Yang Zhaoyu (2012: 4) invokes Newton (and Smith's familiarity with Newton's framework), but goes further and says Newtonian mechanics was the foundation on which the rest of economic science was built. He approvingly (Yang, 2012: 8) notes Smith's advocacy of reducing government interference (儘量減少政府干擾, *jǐn liàng jián shǎo zhèng fǔ gān rǎo*) and its relevance not only for contemporary China but for a world where the planned economy has been largely abandoned. Noting first that in a market economy the authority lies with the people rather than the government (市場經濟的權力在民, 而不在政府, *shì chǎng jīng jì de quán lì zài mín, ér bú zài zhèng fǔ*), he adds that in market economics "[t]he government that manages best manages least" (管理得最少的政府就是最好的政府, *guǎn lǐ dé zuì shǎo de zhèng fǔ jiù shì zuì hǎo de zhèng fǔ*.) Perhaps in a sign that Yang Zhaoyu is concerned that governance is drifting into the hands of big business in contemporary China – just as Smith was concerned that precisely the same thing was happening in eighteenth-century Britain – he repeatedly returns to this theme in his introduction.

Finally, both Yang Jingnian and Yang Zhaoyu emphasize that the text of *WN* alone – especially when oversimplified as "the freedom to pursue self-interest for all is sufficient to promote social welfare" – does not give a complete picture of Smith's beliefs about human nature and how it may be used to promote the good society. Both Yang Jingnian (2014: 4–5), who is sympathetic to the Marxist ideal, and Yang Zhaoyu (2014: 9), who is cognizant of the failures of Marxism in practice, suggest that *The Theory of Moral Sentiments* (*TMS*) must be considered alongside *WN* to achieve complete understanding of Smith's philosophy. In the two works combined, they both agree, Smith argues that human nature is forged from a combination of emotions, wisdom and sympathy, and the impartial spectator is invoked as the proper judge of the propriety of one's own or others' conduct given the overarching goal of self-preservation. Smith, in their view, builds a unified theory of society in which the combination of these three aspects of human nature need not put people in conflict but rather gives them ethical potential. Competition, in turn, is the way in which the aspect of human nature that reflects the fundamental desire for self-preservation can be channeled in the social interest. While this interpretation is fairly common in the West, in a modernizing China interested in the principles of how the market *does* operate it is a framework for thinking about the conditions under which it operates *well*. In particular, viewing Smith's description in *TMS* as the proper way to socialize the young from a base in which there is the potential for both altruistic and egotistical behavior is offered by Yang Zhaoyu as a *sufficient* condition for the market to promote the social good.

5. Translations of "arbitrary" in Chinese editions of *WN*

To some extent, all of the works cited above have struggled to translate concepts that are specific to the British Enlightenment. For instance, take their attempts to convey the importance Smith attaches to the need to avoid "arbitrary" rule. This suggests that contrasting cultural preconceptions can frustrate even translations that are superficially accurate.

The word "arbitrary" has two relevant definitions in Alexander Chalmers' update of Henry John Todd's amended version of Samuel Johnson's 1753 dictionary of the English language (Johnson, Todd and Chalmers, 1853: 33), as close to a definitive accounting as there is of what Smith might have meant by the word: "despotick; absolute" and "depending on no rule." The term "arbitrary" appears twenty times in *WN*, with all but one of them related in some way to the sovereign's conduct. (The exception, in V.1.138, relates to the governance of French universities.) All nineteen translations of the relevant passages are included in Table 1, although not all are discussed below. While common then in Britain, the idea that

Table 1 Chinese conceptions of "arbitrary" governance

Paragraph	Smith's English	Chinese characters	Hanyu pinyin
III.2.17	"These services, therefore, being almost entirely arbitrary"	1. 尚有無明之徭役。 2. 這種全無規定的勞役 3. 因此，這種幾乎完全是隨意決定的勞役	1. Shàng yǒu wú míng zhī yáo yì. 2. Zhè zhǒng quán wú guī dìng de láo yì 3. Yīn cǐ, zhè zhǒng jī hū wán quán shì suí yì jué dìng de láo yì
III.2.18	"The public services to which the yeomanry were bound were not less arbitrary than the private ones"	1. 田主一家之徭。其病農已如此。 2. 農民按照的公役又復同樣黃橐。 3. 自耕農應服的公共勞役，也和私人勞役一樣，是武斷隨意的。	1. Tián zhǔ yī jiā zhī yáo. Qí bìng yǐ rú cǐ. 2. nóng mín de sī yì, gong yì yòu fù tóng yang hèng bào. 3. Zì gēng nóng yìng fù de gōng gòng láo yì, yě hé sī rén láo yì yī yàng, shì wǔ duàn suí yì de.
IV.7.28	"violent and arbitrary government of Spain"	1. 西班牙之政之苛 2. 西班牙那樣強暴的政府 3. 強暴專制的西班牙政府	1. xī bān yá zhī zhèng zhī kē 2. xī bān yá nà yàng qiáng zhuān de zhèng fǔ 3. Qiáng bào zhuān zhì de xī bān yá zhèng fǔ
IV.7.74	"the nature of [the French] government, which though arbitrary and violent in comparison with that of Great Britain, is legal and free in comparison with those of Spain and Portugal"	1. 雖緣沿霸制。而法令纖悉。足以防奸。其治雖不逮吾英。而勝於波西二國者 2. 他們政府的性質，與英國相比。然與西班牙葡萄牙相比，則比較保法，比較自由。 3. 這些民族的正副的性質，雖然與大列顛政府相比較為專橫，但與西班牙和葡萄牙，卻是較為保法和自由	1. Suī yuán yán bà zhì. Ér fǎlìng xiān xī. Zú yǐ fáng jiān. Qí zhì suī búdài wú yīng. Ér shèng yú bō xī èr guó zhě. 2. Tā men zhèngfǔ de xìng zhì, yǔ yīngguó xiāng bǐ, suī jiào wèi zhuān hèng, rán yǔ xī bān yá pú táo yá xiāng bǐ, zé bǐ jiào bǎo fǎ, bǐ jiào zì yóu. 3. Zhè xiē mín zú de zhèng fǔ de xìng zhì, suīrán yǔ dà liè diān zhèngfǔ xiāng bǐ jiàowèi zhuān hèng, dàn yú xī bān yá hé pú táo yá, què shì jiào wèi bǎo fǎ hé zìyóu.
IV.7.76	"The law, so far as it gives some weak protection to the slave against the violence of the master, is likely to be better executed in a colony where the government is in a great measure arbitrary than in one where it is altogether free"	1. 民之自由。坐是以減。而黑奴之困。又緣此而蘇。民之其奴之不可唐用。最待之多寬。 2. 對奴隸給予些微保護，似乎在政治十分暴制殖民凌制之苦律，比在政治完全自由的殖民地上，可能施行得更有校益。	1. Zhèng shù zhī shàn fǒu mín shēng jìn ér yù kě zhī … Yǐ yīng zhī zhèng píng. Mín yǒu zì yóu zhī lè. Qí bù néng yuan guò fā zhǔ zhě. 2. Duì nú lì jǐ yǔ xiē wéi bǎo hù, shì bu dà shòu zhǔ rén qī líng de fǎ lǜ, sì hū zài zhèng zhì shí fēn zhuān zhì zhì mín dì shàng, bǐ zài zhèng zhì wán quán zì yóu de zhí mín dì shàng, kě néng shī xíng dé gèng yǒu xiào xiě.

		3. 法律,就其能給予奴隸一些微弱的保護始之不受主人侵待而言,在一個在很大程度上是專制政府的殖民地,比在一個完全自由的殖民地執行得更好一些。	3. *Fǎ lǜ, jiù qí néng jǐ yǔ nú lì yī xiē wēi ruò de bǎo hù shǐ zhī bù shòu zhǔ rén qīn dài ér yán, zài yī gè zài hěn dà chéng dù shàng shì zhuān zhì zhèng fǔ de zhí mín dì, bǐ zài yī gè wán quán zì yóu de zhí mín dì zhí xíng dé gèng hǎo yī xiē.*
IV.7.77	"[T]he condition of a slave is better under an arbitrary than a free government"	1. 君主之國。其民之待奴婢常恕。民主之國。其之待奴婢轉苛。 2. 奴隸在專制政治下,比在自由政治下,有更好的境遇。 3. 奴隸的處境再專制政府下比在自由政府下叫好 …	1. *Jūn zhǔ zhī guó. Qí mín dài nú bì cháng shù. Mín zhǔ zhī guó. Qí zhī dài nú bì zhuǎn kē.* 2. *Nú lì zài zhuān zhì zhèng zhì xià, bǐ zài zì yóu zhèng zhì xià, yǒu gèng hǎo de jìngyù.* 3. *Nú lì de chǔ jìng zài zhuān zhì zhèng fǔ xià bǐ zài zì yóu zhèng fǔ xià jiào hǎo. …*
IV.9.3	"arbitrary and degrading taxes" (levied on farmers)	1. 無術病民之賦 2. 橫征暴斂 3. 對耕種者的構徵暴斂	1. *Wú shù bìng mín zhī fù* 2. *Héng zhēng bào liǎn* 3. *Duì gēng zhòng zhě de gòu zhēng bào liǎn*
V.1.59	"arbitrary and uncertain nature of these presents" (given to ancient judges by litigants as compensation)	1. 高下任情。屈申視賄。 2. 由任意的不確定性的禮物 3. 由於這種送禮物的任意任含不確定性。	1. *Gāo xià rèn qíng. Qū shēn shì huì.* 2. *Yóu rèn yì de bù què dìng xìng de lǐ wù* 3. *Yóu yú zhè zhǒng lǐ wù de rèn yì xìng hé bù què dìng xìng ér zì rán zào chéng de sì fá fù bài.*
V.2.26	"The tax which each individual is bound to pay ought to be certain, and not arbitrary. The time of payment, the manner of payment, the quantity to be paid, ought all to be clear and plain to the contributor, and to every other person"	1. 賦必以信。信於時。信於歛數。 2. 各國民因當完納的賦稅,必須是確定的,完納的日期,完納的方法,完納的額變數,都應當讓者及其他的了解得十分清楚明白。 3. 每個國民的賦稅應當是確定的,不能是不定的。	1. *Fù bì yǐ xìn. Xìn yú shí. Xìn yú duō guǎ. Xìn yú shù shù.* 2. *Gè guó mín yīn dāng wán nà de fù shuì, bì xū shì què dìng de, bù dé suí yì biàn gēng. Wán nà de rì qí, wán nà de fāng fǎ, wán nà de é shù, dōu yìng dāng ràng yǐ qiè nà shuì zhě jí qí tā de liǎo jiě dé dào shí fēn qīng chǔ míng bái.* 3. *Yīng dāng shì què dìng de, bù néng shì bù dìng de.*

(Continued)

Table 1 (Continued)

Paragraph	Smith's English	Chinese characters	Hanyu pinyin
V.2.56	"The application is pretty much regulated according to the discretion of the intendant of the generality, and must, therefore, be in a great measure arbitrary" (referring to adjustments in the old 1666 *taille* assessment in Montauban)	1. 悉由省中長老董其事者之斷決。則果平與否。又不可得而知也。 2. 這種救濟方法的運用，大抵是惠稅區行政長官的裁奪，所以，在很大成度上是獨斷獨生的。 3. 不過這種辦法的運用完全由稅官行政長官自由裁奪，因而在很大程度上是獨斷專行的。	1. Xī yóu shěng zhōng cháng lǎo dǒng qí shì zhě zhī duàn jué. Zé guǒ píng yǔ fǒu. Yòu bùkě dé ér zhīyě. 2. Zhè zhǒng jiù jì fāng fǎ de yùn yòng, dà dǐ shì huì shuì qū xíng zhèng zhǎng guān de cái duó, suǒ yǐ, zài hěn dà chéng dù shàng shì dú duàn dú shēng de. 3. Bù guò zhè zhǒng bàn fǎ de yùn yòng wán quán yóu shuì qū xíng zhèng zhǎng guān zì yóu cái duó, yīn ér zài hěn dà chéng dù shàng shì dú duàn zhuān xíng de.
V.2.92	"The nations, accordingly, who have attempted to tax the revenue arising from stock, instead of any severe inquisition of the kind, have been obliged to content themselves with some very loose, and, therefore, more or less arbitrary estimation"	1. 國家終無術已賦之乎。曰有。國家不得已而賦及母財者。 2. 對資本收入課稅的國家，廣來都不採用嚴厲的調查方法，而任在不得已，以非常覺大的估算方法為滿足。 3. 因此，企圖對資本收入課稅的國家，不是採用這種非常嚴格的調查方法，爾是不得不滿足於採用某種非常寬鬆的，因而或多或少是武斷的估計方法。	1. Guó jiā zhōng wú shù yǐ fù zhī hū. Yuē yǒu. Guó bù dé yǐ ér fù jí mǔ cái zhě. 2. Duì zī běn shōu rù kè shuì de guó jiā, lì lái dōu bù cǎi yòng yán lì de diào chá fāng fǎ, ér wǎng wǎng bù dé yǐ, yǐ fēi cháng kuān dà de, yīn ér duō shào shì suí biàn de gū suàn fāng fǎ wéi mǎn zú. 3. Yīn cǐ, qǐ tú duì zī běn shōu rù kè shuì de guó jiā, bù shì cǎi yòng zhè zhǒng fēi cháng yán gé de diào chá fāng fǎ, ér shì bù dé bù mǎn zú yú cǎi yòng mǒu zhǒng fēi cháng kuān sōng de, yīn ér huò duō huò shǎo shì wǔ duàn de gū jì fāng fǎ.
V.2.105	"The real taille, as it is imposed only upon a part of the lands of the country, is necessarily an unequal tax, though it is so upon some occasions. The personal taille, as it is intended to be proportioned to the profits of a certain class of people which can only be guessed at, is necessarily both arbitrary and unequal"	1. 泰理真者不偏及。故其稅為不平。然皆有根據。則不平而且無據者矣。 2. 至於個人民的貢稅，則是打算對於某一階級人民的利潤，比例征收，而這種利潤究莫有多少，又只能推測，所以必然是專悉的，不公平的。 3. 個人的貢稅，用意是在和某類人民的利潤成比例，而這種利潤的大小只能猜測，所以必然即是武斷的。又是不平等的。	1. Tài lǐ zhēn zhě bù biān jí. Gù qí shuì wéi bùpíng. Rán jiē yǒu gēn jù. Zé bù píng ér qiě wú jù zhě yǐ. 2. Zhì yú gè rén de gòng shuì, zé shì dǎ suàn duì yú mǒu yī jiē jí rén mín de lì rùn, bǐ lì zhēng shōu, ér zhè zhǒng lì rùn jiù jìng yòu duō shǎo, yòu zhǐ néng tuī cè, suǒ yǐ bì rán shì zhuān zì de, bù gōng píng de. 3. Gè rén de gòng shuì, yòng yì shì zài hé mǒu lèi rén mín de lì rùn chéng bǐ lì, ér zhè zhǒng lì rùn de dà xiǎo zhǐ néng cāi cè, suǒ yǐ bì rán jí shì wǔ duàn de. Yòu shì bù píng děng de.

	English	Chinese		
V.2.110	"altogether arbitrary . . . altogether arbitrary"	多應定……。無應定者。	1. 多應定……。無應定者。 2. 不是任意抽征的。 3. 完全武斷的	1. *Duó yì dìng . . . Wú yì dìng zhě.* 2. *Bù shì rèn yì chōu zhēng de* 3. *Wán quán wǔ duàn de*
V.2.127	"They [taxes on property transfer] are in no respect arbitrary but are or may be in all cases perfectly clear and certain"	雖然不平矣。而無任情重輕。蓋其明著。欲救重輕不平等了。不過,此係在任何場合,都是明顯確定的,而不是任意決定的。它們在任何方面都不是武斷的,在所由的場合都是或可能是清楚明白的。	1. 雖然不平矣。而無任情重輕。蓋其明著。欲救重輕不平等了。不過,此係在任何場合,都是明顯確定的,而不是任意決定的。 2. 它們在任何方面都不是武斷的,在所由的場合都是或可能是清楚明白的。	1. *Suī rán bù pít. Er wú rèn qíng zhòng qīng zhī yí. Gài qí wù míng zhe. Yù rèn qíng zhòng qīng rèn qíng zhòng qīng. Shì bù kě yě.* 2. *Nà jiù gèng yào bù píng děng l. Bù guò, cǐ shuì zài rèn hé chǎng hé, dōu shì míngxiǎn quèdìng de, ér búshì rènyì juédìng de.* 3. *Tā men zài rèn hé fang miàn dōu búshì wǔ duàn de, zài suǒ yóu de chǎnghé dōu shì huò kě néng shì qīng chǔ míng bái de.*
V.2.128	"They give occasion, to much extortion in the officers of the farmers-general who collect the tax, which is in great measure arbitrary and uncertain . . . the abuse must arise, not so much from the nature of the tax as the want of precision and distinctness in the words of the edicts or laws which impose it"	蓋冊損吏錄為姦。而民之所出無藝嫌。無藝。必其詔令教條不為明晰。逐運賦賦寫。它使組稅包收人員有借口大事勒素的機會,而勒素又大抵是任意的,不定的。……那弊害倒竇可說是生於課稅教令或法規用語有欠精確合明了,而不是生於此稅的性質。據弊為,它們使 包稅總官的收稅人員友勒索的機會,這種稅在任很大程度上是武斷的和不確定的。	1. 蓋冊損吏錄為姦。而民之所出無藝嫌。無藝。必其詔令教條不為明晰。逐運賦賦寫。 2. 它使組稅包收人員有借口大事勒素的機會,而勒素又大抵是任意的,不定的。……那弊害倒竇可說是生於課稅教令或法規用語有欠精確合明了,而不是生於此稅的性質。 3. 據弊為,它們使 包稅總官的收稅人員友勒索的機會,這種稅在任很大程度上是武斷的和不確定的。	1. *Gài cè sǔn lì wéi jiān. Er mín zhī suǒ chū wú yì. Wú rèn qíng zhòng qīng zhī bì . . . Yòng cǐ fù ér zhì yú wú yì. Bì qí zhào lìng jiào tiáo bù wéi míng xī. Zhú shì zé fù xū lí.* 2. *Tā shì zǔ shuì bāo shōu rù shōu xià de rén yuán yǒu jiè kǒu dà shì lèi sù de jī huì, ér lèi sù yòu dà dǐ shì rèn yì de, bù dìng de . . . Nà bì hài dào níng kě shuō shì shēng yú kè shuì chì lìng huò fǎ guī yòng yǔ yǒu qiàn jīng què hé míng liǎo, ér bú shì shēng yú cǐ shuì dì xìng zhì.* 3. *Jù rèn wéi, tā men shǐ bāo shuì zǒng guān de shōu shuì rén yuán yǒu lè suǒ de jī huì, zhè zhòng shuì zài hěn dà chéng dù shàng shì wǔ duàn de hé bù què dìng de.*
V.2.139	"Capitation taxes, if it is attempted to proportion them to the fortune or revenue of each contributor, become altogether arbitrary"	雜賦首丁口之稅。使國家要欲民之財力比例而取之。則未有不任情為高下者。人頭稅,如企圖安照各納稅者的財富或收入比列到徵收,那就要完全成為任意的了。人頭稅,如果企圖使它和每一個納稅人的財富或收入成比列,那就會變得完全是武斷的	1. 雜賦首丁口之稅。使國家要欲民之財力比例而取之。則未有不任情為高下者。 2. 人頭稅,如企圖安照各納稅者的財富或收入比列到徵收,那就要完全成為任意的了。 3. 人頭稅,如果企圖使它和每一個納稅人的財富或收入成比列,那就會變得完全是武斷的	1. *Zá fù shǒu dīng kǒu zhī shuì. Shǐ guó jiā yào yù mín zhī cái lì bǐ lì ér qǔ zhī. Zé wèi yǒu bù rèn qíng wèi gāo xià zhě.* 2. *Rén tóu shuì, rú qǐtú ān zhào gè nàshuì zhě de cáifù huò shōurì bǐ liè zhēngshōu, nà jiù yào wánquán chéngwéi rènyì dele.* 3. *Rén tóu shuì, rú guǒ qǐ tú shǐ tā hé měi yī gè nà shuì rén de cái fù huò shōu rù chéng bǐ lì, nà jiù huì biàn dé wán quán shì wǔ duàn de.*

(Continued)

Table 1 (Continued)

Paragraph	Smith's English	Chinese characters	Hanyu pinyin
V.141	"Such taxes, therefore, if it is attempted to render them equal, become altogether arbitrary and uncertain, and if it is attempted to render them certain and not arbitrary, become altogether unequal"	1. 欲其平則無定。欲其有定，轉至不平。 2. 因此，這類稅，人企圖使其公平，就要完全成為任意的、不確定的；如企圖使其確定而不流於任意，就要完全成為不公平的。 3. 昔詞，這種稅如果企圖使它平等，它就要變得完全是武斷的和不確定的；如果企圖使它取定和不武斷，它就變得是不平等的。	1. Yù qí píng zé wú dìng. Yù qí yǒu dìng, Zhuǎn zhì bù píng. 2. Yīn cǐ, zhè lèi shuì, rén qǐ tú shǐ qí gōng píng, jiù yào wán quán chéng wéi rèn yì de, bù què dìng de; rú qǐ tú shǐ qí què dìng ér bù liú yú rèn yì, jiù yào wán quán chéng wéi bù gōng píng de. 3. Yīn cí, zhè zhǒng shuì rú guǒ qìtú shǐ tā píng děng, tā jiù yào biàn dé wán quán shì wǔ duàn de hé bù què dìng de; rú guǒ qǐ tú shǐ tā qǔ dìng hé bù wǔ duàn, tā jiù biàn dé shì wán quán bù píng děng de.
V.2.143	"In France the great easily submit to a considerable degree of inequality in a tax which, is not a very heavy one, but could not brook the arbitrary assessment of an intendant"	1. 法國之民，意亦調使其賦誠輕則雖不平可忍。而有司之意為重輕則難耐者。 2. 法國達官顯貴，對於對他們有影響的稅，如不過重，即使很不公平，一般也肯接受；但州長任意固定稅額的作風，他們則絲毫不能接受。 3. 在法國，大人物很容易接受稅收上的頗大的不平等，這種稅收收着其很重對他們的影響而言，並不是很重的；但他們不能忍受省長的任意評估。	1. Fǎ guó zhī mín. Yì yì wèi shì suǒ fù chéng qīng, Zěn àn bù píng kě rěn. Ér yǒu zhī yì wèi zhòng qīng. Zé nán nài zhě. 2. Fǎ guó dá guān xiǎn guì, duì yú duì tā men yǒu yǐng xiǎng de shuì, rú bù guò zhòng, jí shǐ hěn bù gōng píng, yì bān yě kěn jiē shòu; dàn zhōuzhǎng rèn yì gù dìng shuì é de zuò fēng, tā men zé sī háo bùnéng jiē shòu. 3. Zài fǎ guó, dà rén wù hěn róng yì jiē shòu shuì shōu shàng de pō dà de bù píng děng, zhè zhǒng shuì shōu shōu jiù qì duì tā men de yǐng xiǎng ér yán, bìng bù shì hěn zhòng de; dàn tā men bù néng rěn shòu shěng zhǎng de rèn yì píng gū.

the emperor and his mandarins who governed on his behalf might rule in an "arbitrary" (as opposed to an oppressive) manner received little, if any, attention in China.[19]

How has the translation of "arbitrary" changed over time? (For ease of reading, in this section, except for longer excerpts, only the original Smith English and the English retranslations of Chinese translations are included. Chinese versions and pinyin are included in Table 1. In addition, the only recent translation used is that of Yang Jingnian. While their introductions differ somewhat, there are no meaningful discrepancies between Yang Jingnian's (2014) and Yang Zhaoyu's (2012) translations of the text itself.)

"Arbitrary" obligations on the peasantry

As the translations evolve, the Chinese words chosen to translate "arbitrary" start to improve. Smith first uses the word at III.2.17: "[t]hese services [referring to the *corvée* obligations of peasants] therefore, being almost entirely arbitrary, subjected the tenant to many vexations." Yan (1977: 384) translates this as: "[tenants] still are subject to many unnamed faraway services." In combination, "unnamed" and "faraway" are an approximate rendition of "arbitrary," but perhaps 無定 ("lack of specification"), which is common enough in classical Chinese, would have been better. By the time of Guo and Wang (2013: Vol. 1, 359), the Chinese text offers "completely unfixed" (全無規定的, *quán wú guī dìng de*), which, while an improvement on Yan's version, does not quite contain the sense of despotism as dependence on just one man's will. In the next paragraph, III.2.18, Smith further argues that "[t]he public services to which the yeomanry were bound were not less arbitrary than the private ones," and goes on to note that when the king's troops came through any portion of the country "the yeomanry" had to provide them with animals and provisions. But Yan (1977: 384) does not invoke "arbitrary" per se, merely describing the tenants' service burden as "incomparable" (不言可喻, *bù yán kě yù*) in III.2.17, and then saying in the following paragraph that "what is difficult for the landlord is for the peasants equally difficult." Hence, the emphasis throughout is on *difficulty*, rather than *inconstancy*.

Smith also writes in III.2.17 of the many "vexations" the traveling king and his attendants imposed on local farmers, whom he recounts were "bound to provide them with horses, carriages, and provisions." Yan does not emphasize the unfixed nature of such obligations, but nonetheless indicates that the king's tours imposed a particular (unspecified) kind of "distress" (病, bìng) on farm workers. By the time of Guo and Wang (2013: Vol. 1, 359), the quality of the translation has not significantly improved, as they translate "arbitrary" as "brutal" or "pointlessly violent" (橫暴, *héng bào*), a rendition that does not capture the true meaning of Smith's term. But by the time of the Yang Jingnian (2014: 335) translation, "arbitrary" in III.2.17 has become "decided at will," while in III.2.18 it is "forcibly broken, at will," both of which imply a lack of concrete criteria. These are perhaps more consistent with Smith's original meaning. Similar errors in Yan and subsequent progress are found in the translations of IV.7.28 and IV.7.74.

The "arbitrary" treatment of slaves

In another usage (IV.7.76), Smith asserts that the laws protecting slaves, even if only weakly, are "likely to be better executed in a colony where the government is in a great measure arbitrary than in one where it is altogether free." (This is because, in Smith's classification, a "free" society protects property rights, including those relating to slaves.) As China lacks a commerce in slaves, Yan explains to his readers that only blacks and not Europeans endured slavery, and while he does not invoke the notion of arbitrariness per se, he does extensively discuss the idea that in England property rights are protected, and slaves are merely property. After drawing this distinction, he simply says: "As the people are freer, their morality declines, and the more the slaves suffer. Because of this it can be said, that if the people know their slaves cannot [legally] be abused, their treatment becomes more merciful." Despite the omission of the concept of "arbitrary," Smith's fundamental point about the British idea of liberties *worsening* the slaves' condition comes though. Strikingly, Yan discusses the cruel treatment of slaves in more detail than Smith does: "Mercilessly dominated by the scorching sun, with the suffering of burning backs and flowing sweat" (陽威酷烈。炙背流汗之苦, *Yáng wēi kù lìe. Zhì bēi liú hàn zhī kǔ*) (Yan, 1977: 570). All later translations lack such a horrendous description. As for "arbitrary," in Guo and Wang (2013: Vol. 2, 158) and Yang Jingnian (2014: 489), the word is translated as 專制 (*zhuān zhì*; "authoritarian").

In IV.7.77 the progression is similar. While Yan here compares only king-ruled and democratic countries (his term for "democratic," as in modern *bái huà*, is "ruled by the people"; 民主, *mín zhǔ*) in assessing the treatment of slaves, Guo and Wang (2013: Vol. 2, 159) make Smith's point that the treatment of slaves is better "under authoritarian governance" than "under free government." Although the word order is different, the wording is the same in Yang (2014: 554).

"Arbitrary" taxation

To Smith, the flaw of "arbitrary" taxation is somewhat different from the flaw of "arbitrary" rule. In IV.9.3, which describes Jean-Baptiste Colbert's commercial policy, "arbitrary and degrading taxes" is rendered in Yan (1977: 653) as "artless taxes that plague the people." In Guo and Wang (2013: Vol. 2, 230) this becomes "plundering taxation," which still does not have precisely the same meaning as Smith's use of "arbitrary and degrading." All three of the Guo and Wang (2013) translations are the same in Yang (2014).

All of chapter V.2 concerns taxation, and V.2.26 is about the importance of "certainty" of taxes. Smith uses "arbitrary" – the opposite of "certainty" and something to be avoided – once here. In Yan's (1977: 833) translation, "certainty" in every context is rendered as 信 (*xìn*), meaning "reliability" or "trust." The meaning is similar, with the only difference being that in Smith's phrasing, "the tax which each individual is bound to pay ought to be certain, and not arbitrary," it could be that taxes are uncertain merely because of systemic instability, rather than a lack of governmental credibility. But the meaning remains significantly intact: "The time of payment, the manner of payment, the quantity to be paid, ought all to be clear and plain to the contributor, and to every other person" in Smith becomes Yan's "Reliability as to time. Reliability as to amount. Reliability as to frequency." But throughout the paragraph, while the specific criteria that Smith insists must be non-arbitrary (time, manner and quantity of payment) are preserved, the overall theme of the importance of non-arbitrariness is lacking in the translation. In Guo and Wang (2013: Vol. 2, 385), Smith's original meaning is more or less restored: "With regard to taxes in every country, what is needed is certainty; taxes should not be changed at will. All taxes should be completely clear with regard to time, manner and amount."

In V.2.56, in the discussion of the French *taille* (a tax on all non-aristocrats), Yan's translation of "arbitrary" in the taxation context in V.2.56 as "unknowable" is arguably close to Smith's intended meaning. So too with translations later in *WN* of "arbitrary" as a feature of taxation, which are rendered in various places as "artlessly," "not universally applied," "not equal," and "based on emotion," all in ways that are adequate approximations of Smith's intended meaning. One translation, in V.2.141, is particularly elegant. Smith gives his readers: "Such taxes, therefore, if it is attempted to render them equal, become altogether arbitrary and uncertain, and if it is attempted to render them certain and not arbitrary, become altogether unequal." Yan's (1977: 878) translation here is: "If one desires equality, there is no certainty. If one desires certainty, then there can be no equality."

As for translations in the latter section of *WN* into modern Chinese, in V.2.92 Smith's "more or less arbitrary [tax] estimation" in Guo and Wang (2013: Vol. 2, 409) becomes "an as per-convenience estimation method" (多少是隨便的估算方法, *duō shǎo shì suí biān de gù suàn fang fǎi*), with "per-convenience" overlapping with, but not quite the same as, the "arbitrary" of Smith's era. In addition, Guo and Wang (2013) use 任意 (*rén yì*) or 隨意 (*suí yì*) at: V.2.110 (Vol. 2: 417), V.2.127 (Vol. 2: 423), V.2.128 (Vol. 2: 423), V.2.139 (Vol. 2: 428), V.2.141 (Vol. 2: 428) and V.2.143 (Vol. 2: 149). These terms correspond to "at will." In V.2.105 (Guo and Wang, 2013: Vol. 2, 414) 專恣 (*zhuān zì*) is a classical allusion, from *The Book of Han, the Biographies of Liu Xiang*, simply meaning "imperious." In Yang (2014) most of the translations in the later part of Book V are 武斷 (*wǔ duàn*), which is the closest meaning for "at the discretion or option" of one in power. In V.2.143 Yang (2014: 820) translates "arbitrary" as 任意, just as Guo and Wang (2013) do.

Overall, Yan used a number of different translations for "arbitrary." While subsequent translators did too, many of Yan's translations involve suffering or simple lack of certainty, especially in early chapters. The translations in earlier chapters especially fail to convey the traditional British idea of the threat of authoritarian government emanating in part from its seemingly random nature, which violates people's ideas of both wisdom and justice. This is a problem that appears to be only partially resolved later, even in the modern translations. The distinctiveness of the idea of arbitrary governance in Enlightenment thinking (in France as in England, judging by the importance Jacques Turgot attached in his short-lived Six Edicts, issued in March 1776 to the "arbitrary institutions" that stifled the rights of the poor to earn a living) may explain some of this gap.

6. Conclusion

In China, the changes in the understanding of *WN* reflect how Chinese intellectuals (and, increasingly, the Chinese people) think about their society. Interestingly, there appears never to have been any censorship of the content of *WN*; instead, even in the communist era, ideas that could have threatened the powers that be were retained. (This is a separate question from the extent of access to the work at this time; in today's China this is not an issue.) *WN* has gone from a mysterious tome full of scientific wisdom relating to what makes a nation strong and prosperous, to a profound – if incomplete – theory of political economy, to a combination of proper ethical and economic-policy instruction for a nation that is moving from an all-embracing, all-providing – but poor – society to a turbulent – but increasingly prosperous – one.

In the first translation, Yan Fu was substantially free to emphasize what he deemed important, omit what was less so, and repackage the text in a bid to make many alien ideas comprehensible to the limited circle of literate early twentieth-century Chinese. Subsequent translations focus on fidelity to the original, with varying degrees of success, and in the most recent versions any terms or references that are unlikely to be understood by contemporary Chinese readers are explained with supplementary text and/or graphics. But, irrespective of when the work was translated, *WN* has always been seen in China as the founding text of modern economics. While some modern translators attach some importance to Marxism as a contemporaneously important strain of economic thought, even they view *WN* as the original exposition of most of the principles of economics that are consistent with national flourishing. All of the interpretations share a belief in the book's revolutionary nature and permanent importance. In China, the Smithian foundation has remained solid. Only opinions of what ought to be built on it have changed.

Notes

1 I would like to thank, without implicating them in any errors herein, Chen Yinghua for invaluable assistance with classical Chinese, and Huang Ling for providing access to earlier Chinese-language editions of *The Wealth of Nations*.

2 Yan also translated Thomas Huxley's *Evolution and Ethics*, John Stuart Mill's *On Liberty* and *A System of Logic*, Herbert Spencer's *A Study of Sociology*, Edward Jenks's *A History of Politics*, William Stanley Jevons's *A Primer on Logic* and the Baron de Montesquieu's *The Spirit of the Laws*.

3 "埃及印度支那三古國。皆有海禁。以內地市場已廣。不願有外交以致窺伺。然而是三國者。皆古盛而今衰。" (Egypt, India and China had all prohibited overseas trade, had a substantial domestic market, and thus were not willing to pay attention to

the outside world. But these three countries, which once were prosperous, are now all impoverished.)

4   The English sentences are: "I have never known much good done by those who affected to trade for the public good. It is an affectation, indeed, not very common among merchants, and very few words need be employed in dissuading them from it."

5   The exact text in Yan's original translation is 知其有益國之效而後為之者。是又不然。 (*Zhī qí yǒu yì guó zhī xiào ér hòu wéi zhī zhě. Shì yòu bù rán.*) As noted in the text, Liu translates the second sentence as 其實並不然 (*qí shí bìng bù rán*), which emphasizes the state of contrast with the question asked in the prior sentence, which is whether investors know they behave in the country's interest.

6   For a dissenting view of Smith, which viewed him as seeking to enhance the strength of the government, see Schwartz (1964).

7   The first post-Qing government had failed, replaced by the dictatorship of Yuan Shikai. With his death in 1916, China fell into the chaos of the so-called "warlord years," which Chiang Kai-Shek's Kuomintang (the movement founded by Sun-Yat Sen) substantially, if temporarily, quelled in the late 1920s.

8   "Only freedom": 他所提議的自然的自由制度, 其實只是社會上一小不分人投資的自有制度 (*tā suǒ tí yì de zì rán de zì yóu zhì dù, qí shí zhī shì shè huì shàng yì xiǎo bù fēn tóu zī de zì yóu zhì dù*). "The vitality": 資本注意發達初期的特種的朝氣 (*zì běn zhù yì fā dá chū qī de tè zhǒng cháo qì*).

9   The two-volume edition that is used here, which is textually almost identical to the 1972 version, was published by Commercial Press in 2013.

10 While Mao was a harsh critic of Khrushchev, who had partly exposed Stalin's crimes, no Marxist state ever rejected Marx or Lenin as a source of truth about political economy and history's inevitable unfolding.

11 "當資本階級庸俗經濟學者為了反對馬克思主義經濟學, 不怕猛烈攻擊其先輩經濟者亞當‧斯密和李嘉圖的古典理論的時候, 我們為了捍衛馬克思主意經濟學, 為了從歷史發展上增進我們對於馬克思經濟學的理解, 對於斯密乃至斯密和李嘉圖的經濟學說, 應該科學地反待, 重新介紹他們的經濟學, 是有其現實意義的。" (*Dāng zī běn jiē jí yōng sú jīng jì xué zhě wéi le fǎn duì mǎ kè sī zhǔ yì jīng jì xué, bú pà měng liè gōng jí qí xiān bèi jīng jì zhě yà dāng‧sī mì hé lǐ jiā tú de gǔ diǎn lǐ lùn de shí hòu, wǒ men wèi le hàn wèi mǎ kè sī zhǔ yì jīng jì xué, wèi le cóng lì shǐ fā zhǎn shàng zēng jìn wǒ men duì yú mǎ kè sī jīng jì xué de lǐ jiě, duì yú sī mì nǎi zhì sī mì hé lǐ jiā tú de jīng jì xué shuō, yīng gāi kē xué dì fǎn dài, chóng xīn jiè shào tā men de jīng jì xué, shì yǒu qí xiàn shí yì yì de.*)

12 In chapter 24, Marx does term Smith's analysis of the disposition of product at the social level as "preposterous," but this is positively laudatory compared to his dismissal of Bastiat (one of the "bagmen of free trade"), Bentham (an "arch philistine") and Edmund Burke (a "sophist and sycophant").

13 "這兩種法律, 顯然都侵犯了天然的自由, 所以都是不正當的; 因為不正當, 所以都失策的。" (*Zhè liǎng zhòng fǎ lǜ, xiǎn rán dōu qīn fàn le tiān rán de zì yóu, suǒ yǐ dōu shì bù zhèng dàng de; yīn wéi bù zhèng dàng, suǒ yǐ dōu shì cè de.*)

14 The Guo/Wang version is:
"禁制造者兼營小賣業的法律, 企圖強使資本用途的這種劃分發展得比原來更快些。強迫依業家兼營谷物商業務的法律, 卻妨礙這種劃分的進行。這兩種法律, 顯然都侵犯了天然的自由, 所以都是不正當的；因為不正當, 所以都是失策的。" (*Jìnzhì zào zhě jiān yíng xiǎo mài yè de fǎ lǜ, qì tú qiǎng shǐ zī běn yòng tú de zhè zhǒng huà fēn fā zhǎn dé bǐ yuán lái gèng kuài xiē. Qiǎng pò yī yè jiā jiān yíng gǔ wù shāng yè wù de fǎ lǜ, què fáng'ài zhè zhǒng huà fēn de jìn xíng. Zhè liǎng zhòng fǎ lǜ, xiǎn rán dōu qīn fàn le tiān rán de zì yóu, suǒ yǐ dōu shì bù zhèng dàng de; yīn wéi bù zhèng dàng, suǒyǐ dōu shì shī cè de.*)

15 "兩種法律顯然都違反天然自由, 因而是不公平的; 兩者即是不公平的, 又都是失策的。" (*Liǎng zhòng fǎ lǜ xiǎn rán dōu wéi fǎn tiān rán zì yóu, yīn ér shì bù gōng píng de; liǎng zhě jí shì bù gōng píng de, yòu dōu shì shī cè de.*)

16 This is not to deny that the Chinese state is illiberal in some respects when it comes to property rights and freedom of expression. Rather, I wish to draw a contrast between the post-1979 era and 1949–1979, when the party exercised complete control over what could be published, and made certain from the mid-1950s to 1979 that all economic production took place under the direction of the state.

17 The quoted passage reads: "Here, then, is the thing itself: a strange mixture of a book, economics, philosophy, history, political theory, practical program; a book written by a man of vast learning and subtle insights, a man with a mind that was a powerful analytic machine for sifting out the stuff in his notebooks, and a powerful synthetic machine for putting it together again – in new and arresting combinations. Smith was sensitive to the various elements on the intellectual horizon of his day. Like Marx after him, he was no closet scholar, shut off from the world; he was all antennae, reaching out for and absorbing everything within reach. He wrote at the end of the break-up of feudal Europe, at the beginning of a modern world in which the old feudal institutions were still holding on with the tenacity that the vested interests have always shown. It was against these vested interests that he wrote. And the result is that his book has not been merely for library shelves. It has gone through many editions, and has been translated into almost every language. Those who read it were chiefly those who stood to profit from its view of the world – the rising class of businessmen, their political executive committees in the parliaments of the world, and their intellectual executive committees in the academies. Through them it has had an enormous influence upon the underlying populations of the world, although generally all unknown to them. And through them also it has had an enormous influence upon economic opinion and national policy. It has done as much perhaps as any modern book thus far to shape the whole landscape of life as we live it today."

18 See the criticism of the Poor Laws in I.10.118, of limitations on the right to enter a trade in IV.2.42 and IV.9.51, of legally mandated separation of commercial tasks in IV.5.55, and of British laws giving preferential access to trade with the colonies to the United Kingdom itself in IV.7.130. The only criticism of natural liberty is found in II.2.94, where limitations on bank issuance of "promissory notes" is granted to be a violation of natural liberty, but nonetheless necessary to lower the potential of financial panics, which is as justifiable as fire-safety codes.

19 For the extent to which one Chinese philosopher, Mozi, developed in parallel some tenets of liberalism, including Smithian liberalism, see Osborne (2012).

Bibliography

Borokh, Olga. "Adam Smith in Imperial China: Translation and Cultural Adaptation." *OEconomia* 2012(04) (2013): 411–441.

Chang Hao. "Intellectual Change and the Reform Movement, 1890–8." In John K. Fairbank and Kwang-Ching Liu (eds.), *Cambridge History of China*, Volume 11: *Late Ch'ing, 1800–1911, Part 2* (Cambridge: Cambridge University Press, 1980), 274–338.

Cui Yang and Evelyn Forget. "Yan Fu, Individualism, and Social Order." In Ying Ma and Hans-Michael Trautwein (eds.), *Thoughts on Economic Development in China* (New York: Routledge, 2013), 88–100.

Guo Dali and Wang Yanan. "Translator's Note." In Adam Smith, *An Inquiry into the Nature and Causes of the Wealth of Nations*, translated by Guo Dali and Wang Yanan (Shanghai: Shenzhou Light of the Nation Publishing, 1931), 1–4. (郭大力及王亞南。讀序。載於亞當斯密，國富論 (1–4頁。) 郭大力及王亞南 (譯者)。上海：神州國光社。1931 年。)

Huang Ko-Wu. "The Reception of Yan Fu in Twentieth-Century China." In Cindy Yik-yi Chu and Ricardo K. S. Mak (eds.), *China Reconstructs* (Lanham, MD: University Press of America, 2003), 25–44.

Johnson, Samuel, Henry John Todd and Alexander Chalmers. *A Dictionary of the English Language: In Which the Words Are Deduced from Their Originals, Explained in Their Different Meanings, and Authorized by the Names of the Writers in Whose Works They Are Found* (London: Longman, Brown, and Co., 1853).

Lai Cheng-chung. "Receptions of *The Wealth of Nations*." In Lai Cheng-chung (ed.), *Adam Smith across Nations: Translations and Receptions of* The Wealth of Nations (Oxford: Oxford University Press, 2000), xxi–xxxiii.

Lerner, Max. "Introduction." In Adam Smith, *An Inquiry Into the Nature and Causes of the Wealth of Nations* (New York: The Modern Library, 1937), v–x.

Liu Qunyi. "Efforts to 'Ethicize' and the Enlightenment of Modern Chinese Economic Thought: Yan Fu's Translation of 'The Wealth of Nations.'" *Guizhou Social Sciences Magazine* 2013(8) (2013). Available online at: www.gzsk.net/wqhg/201396105806.asp, accessed 4 May 2016. (劉群藝。去倫理化的努力與中國近代經濟學理念的啟蒙——以嚴復譯《原富》為中心, 貴州社會科學期刊, 2013 年8 期。)

Osborne, Evan. "China's First Liberal." *Independent Review* 16(4) (2012): 533–551.

Schwartz, Benjamin. *In Search of Wealth and Power: Yan Fu and the West* (Cambridge, MA: Belknap Press, 1964).

Smith, Adam. *An Inquiry Into the Nature and Causes of the Wealth of Nations* (Oxford: Clarendon Press, 1880).

Wang Yanan. "Introduction, Revised Translation." In Adam Smith, *An Inquiry into the Nature and Causes of the Wealth of Nations*, translated by Guo Dali and Wang Yanan (Beijing: Gao Wu Yin Shu Guan, 1972; reprint Beijing: Commercial Press, 2013), 1–8. (王亞南, 改訂議本序言。載於亞當斯密, 國民財富的性質和原因的研究 (1–8 頁)。郭大力及王亞南 (譯者)。北京: 高務印書館, 2013年。)

Yan Fu. "Procedural Introduction." In Adam Smith, *An Inquiry into the Nature and Causes of the Wealth of Nations*, translated by Yan Fu (Taipei: Taiwan Commercial Press, 1977), 5–15. (嚴復。議事例言。載於亞當斯密, 原富 (5–15 頁。)。臺北：臺灣商務印書館。1977 年。)

Yang Jingnian. "Translator's Introduction." In Adam Smith, *An Inquiry into the Nature and Causes of the Wealth of Nations* (Xian: Shanxi People's Publishing, 2014), 1–9. (楊敬年, 譯者導言。載於亞當斯密, 國富論 。楊敬年譯者 (1–9頁)。 西安: 陝西人民出版社, 2014 年。)

Yang Zhaoyu. "Preface to the Chinese Version." In Adam Smith, *An Inquiry into the Nature and Causes of the Wealth of Nations*, translated by Tang Risong, Yang Zhaoyu, Shao Jianbing, Zhao Kangying, Jiang Qian and Feng Li (Beijing: Huafu Press, 2012), 3–10. (楊兆宇。中譯本導論。載於亞當斯密, 國富論。唐日松, 楊兆宇, 邵劍兵, 趙康英, 姜倩及馮力譯者 (3–10 頁)。北京: 華復出版社, 2012 年。)

Zhang Yufa. *A History of the Development of Democratic Politics in Modern China* (Taipei: Eastern Book Company, 1999). (張玉法, 近代中國民主政治發展史。臺北: 東大圖書公司, 1999。)

Zhu Shaowen. "Adam Smith in China." In Hiroshi Mizuta and Chuhei Sugiyama (eds.), *Adam Smith: International Perspectives* (Chippenham: St. Martin's Press, 1993), 279–292.

Book reviews

Guest editor: Craig Smith

Christopher J. Berry, *The idea of commercial society in the Scottish Enlightenment*

Edinburgh: Edinburgh University Press, 2013, xii + 244pp.

ISBN-10: 0748645322; ISBN-13: 978-0-748-64532-9

Reviewed by Dennis C. Rasmussen

The Idea of Commercial Society in the Scottish Enlightenment is the latest offering of a distinguished scholar of the Scottish Enlightenment, and it does not disappoint. In one of his earlier works, *Social Theory of the Scottish Enlightenment* (Edinburgh University Press, 1997), Berry provided the first comprehensive account of the subject in more than a half century. The present book aims to narrow the scope somewhat – indeed to focus on a single 'idea' – but given the centrality of commercial society to the leading thinkers of eighteenth-century Scotland, it nonetheless constitutes a remarkably wide-ranging study of the period. Engaging with the work of Smith, Hume, Ferguson, Millar, Kames, Robertson, and others, Berry highlights both the similarities and the divergences among the Scots in their conceptualizations and assessments of commercial society.

After outlining the historical context and institutional setting of the Scottish Enlightenment in chapter 1, Berry turns to the Scots' views of the historical progress of society in chapter 2. He downplays somewhat the four-stages theory, which he rightly notes has been accorded 'undue prominence' in interpretations of the period (p. 38). More generally, Berry defends the Scots' use of 'natural' or 'conjectural' history – the use of inference and probabilistic evidence to fill in gaps in the historical record – in tracing the development of society (see especially pp. 49–50). As we might expect, he focuses principally on the emergence of commercial society out of the feudal/agricultural age that preceded it – 'one of the great themes in the writings of the Scots' (p. 50) – and explains how these Scottish thinkers saw foreign commerce and individual liberty as emerging together and reinforcing one another.

This leads to the heart of the book, where Berry expands on the many benefits that the Scots saw as attending commercial society: the alleviation of poverty (chapter 3), the development of the rule of law and the concomitant advancement in security (chapter 4), as well as the rise of modern/individual liberty and the encouragement of certain important virtues, such as industriousness, humanity, probity, and law-abidingness (chapter 5). In each of these chapters, Smith plays a central role. The division of labour, the extent of the market, the propensity to truck, barter, and exchange, the interdependence fostered by trade, the ills of mercantilism, and the proper duties of government all come in for sustained treatment. Berry is especially good on the Scots' insistence, *contra* many Stoics, Christians, and civic republicans, that there is nothing particularly 'noble' or 'redeeming' about poverty (pp. 78–84) and on how Smith's understanding of commercial society and its virtues meshes with his broader moral theory (pp. 134–7). As part of the latter discussion, Berry pointedly distances Smith from the Stoics, highlighting not only his praise of opulence over austerity but also his insistence that morality is an inextricably social phenomenon – a far cry from the detached sage that constituted the Stoic ideal.

For all of the undoubted advantages of commerce, Berry acknowledges that each of the Scots, including Smith, harboured certain misgivings about commercial society, and he devotes chapter 6 to this topic. It is with regard to the 'dangers' of commerce that Berry finds the greatest divergences among these thinkers, with some, such as Ferguson and Kames, voicing more worries than others, such as Hume and Smith. He takes issue with interpreters (including this reviewer) who would emphasize this side of Smith's thought, or 'saddle' Smith 'with the possession of some profound disquiet about the soul of modern man' (p. 175).

Much of Berry's discussion in this chapter revolves around three key elements of the civic republican critique of commerce:

1. the claim that liberty understood in terms of individual choice undermines liberty understood in terms of political participation;
2. the claim that luxury has corrupting effects; and
3. the claim that a standing army cannot provide the same moralizing effects as a citizen militia.

He is right to argue that Smith's worries did not run particularly deep on any of these scores (see pp. 158, 167, 170–2). Later in the chapter, Berry turns to the stultifying effects of the division of labour and the consequences of continually mounting public debt, offering nicely balanced interpretations of Smith on both counts.

However, the chapter overlooks some of the deepest misgivings that Smith voices about commerce. Above all, Berry scarcely alludes to Smith's acknowledgement that the pursuit of wealth frequently leads people to undergo nearly endless toil and anxiety in the accumulation of frivolous material goods that, in the end, provide only fleeting satisfaction. It is true, as he notes (pp. 137–8), that Smith *praises* the 'deception which rouses and keeps in continual motion the industry of mankind' – essentially, the illusion that money can buy happiness – because it helps to advance the process of civilization (*TMS* IV.1.10, 183–4). Yet it remains true that Smith calls this a *deception*. Happiness consists largely of tranquillity, for Smith (*TMS* III.3.30, 149), and there would seem to be little tranquillity to be found in 'the uniform, constant, and uninterrupted effort of every man to better his condition' (*WN* II.iii.31, 343) – which is, after all, the basic engine of commercial society and the ultimate source of the wealth of nations, in

Smith's view. Smith maintains that labour is 'toil and trouble' (*WN* I.v.2, 47), that it requires an individual to 'lay down [a] portion of his ease, his liberty, and his happiness' (*WN* I.v.7, 50). He speaks of

> all that toil, all that anxiety, all those mortifications which must be undergone in the pursuit of [wealth and greatness]; and what is of yet more consequence, all that leisure, all that ease, all that careless security, which are forfeited for ever by the acquisition.
>
> (*TMS* I.iii.2.1, 51)

This does not sound like a thinker who is breezily unconcerned about the effects of commerce on human well-being in the deepest or ultimate sense.

Further, given all that is covered in *The Idea of Commercial Society*, as well as the state of present-day political discourse, another omission is striking: there is no sustained discussion of the considerable economic inequalities that the Scots all agreed were a necessary attendant of commercial society. Berry is correct to note that these thinkers were more concerned with the alleviation of poverty than with inequality per se, but Smith, for one, discusses commercial inequality in tones that demonstrate his lingering unease. In both the Early Draft of *The Wealth of Nations* and the jurisprudence lectures, Smith admits that 'the labour and time of the poor is in civilized countries sacrificed to . . . maintaining the rich in ease and luxury' (*LJA* vi.26, 340; see also *LJB* 213, 490; *ED* 4, 563). He stresses how, in the midst of 'so much oppressive inequality', 'the poor labourer . . . bears, as it were, upon his shoulders the whole fabric of society, seems himself to be pressed down below the ground by the weight, and to be buried out of sight in the lowest foundations of the building' (*ED* 5, 564; see also *LJA* vi.28, 341). The analogous discussion in Book 1, chapter 1, of *The Wealth of Nations* drops the language of oppression, but later in that work Smith does claim that in established commercial societies (as opposed to new colonies) 'rent and profit eat up wages, and the two superior orders of people [i.e. landlords and employers] oppress the inferior one [i.e. workers]' (*WN* IV.vii.b.3, 565). Smith clearly believes that the productivity of commercial society is such that even the poor are ultimately better off, materially speaking, than they would be in a less affluent society, but the strong tone of these passages does seem to indicate some concern regarding the inequalities of this type of society. There should be no doubt that Smith was ultimately a staunch defender of commerce and commercial society – the present reviewer, at least, has always insisted as much – but we should not close our eyes to the full range of ills that he attributes to them.

These quibbles are not at all meant to detract from the great value of the book. It is difficult to say whether its overall 'argument' is convincing, for while Berry is generally approving of the Scots' outlook(s), there is no immediately apparent interpretive aim or target beyond the uncontroversial claim that the idea of commercial society was an important one for them. Instead, Berry provides a learned and even-handed overview on this theme, one that will serve Smith scholars particularly well as a resource for appreciating how his views compare to those of his lesser-known contemporaries.

Eamonn Butler, *Adam Smith – a primer*

London: Institute of Economic Affairs, 2007, 125pp.

ISBN: 978-0-255-36608-3

Reviewed by Bradley K. Hobbs

Eamonn Butler has provided readers with a smart, concise, and engaging introduction to the seminal works of Adam Smith: *The Theory of Moral Sentiments* (1759) and *An Inquiry into the Nature and Causes of the Wealth of Nations* (1776). Butler begins his primer with a discussion of Smith's contributions to the development of modern economics and, in particular, his emphasis on reconceptualizing wealth. Smith replaces the mere holding of gold and silver (*species*) by recognizing production as the fount for wealth. This provided a complete recasting of our understanding of economic value creation. Butler places Smith in the correct historical context by stressing his important contributions to our understanding of social order, competition and cooperation, social psychology, ethics, and other fundamental aspects of human nature.

The primer opens with a short chapter on Smith's role as a significant transitional figure in our understanding of value creation. This new view placed consumers, rather than producers, at the purposive forefront of commerce. Butler notes that this eventually undermined the existing mercantilist status quo. In addition, Smith recognized the benefits of providing a relatively wide range of latitude for people within a well-defined and stable framework. Freedom within a minimal framework of broadly conceived law is called for while the overly prescriptive and restrictive legislation, inherent to the existing mercantilist system, is eschewed. Butler notes Smith's call for "natural liberty [over] all systems of preference or of restraint" (p. 30).

The second chapter provides a short biography of Smith's life, education, experiences, and work. It is quite short, which seems appropriate. Chapter 3 provides a thematic overview of Smith's most famous work: *The Wealth of Nations*. Major themes covered include Smith's call for a limited government that would decouple mercantile interests from political power. Specialization, the division of labor, and individual freedom all feed innovation and economic development, according to Smith. Butler's focus is on free exchange and the encouragement of productive capacity through capital accumulation, all within a system of natural liberty and spontaneity.

Something that Butler keeps at the forefront is Smith's target focus, which is for the well-being of *all* of society. Smith's policy formulations point to the salutary effects for labor and the poor, rejecting the concerns of the political aristocracy and the crony class of the day: mercantilists. Cronyism and collusion are possible only with the aid of compliant and self-dealing political power. Butler provides an almost public-choice-like prism on Smith and mercantilism for the modern reader, noting Smith's extreme conservatism with respect to any laws and regulations that were designed to direct commercial activity.

Butler deftly points to the role that private capital accumulation plays in achieving wealth. He also points to the tendency for "kings and ministers" to be among the most profligate of spendthrifts. Butler then briefly addresses Smith's work on history, followed by a more extensive exploration of the thrust and content of his economic theory and policy. Absolute advantage, tariffs and subsidies, and economic policies aimed at the colonies, are all covered. Butler also does a good job of drawing clear distinctions between the views of Adam Smith and those of the French Physiocrats.

He accurately portrays Smith's common mis-characterization as wholly *laissez-faire*. Smith does focus on property, citing both defense and justice as vital for defending this penultimate foundation for both civil society and the encouragement of the commercial activities that produce wealth. His clear support for both basic public education and the public works that serve commerce are noted. Butler rightly takes umbrage with some of Smith's proposals in Book V, but notes that at the time when Smith was writing government seemed to be the only institutional mechanism capable of solving collective-action problems. Butler does point out Smith's relatively narrow guidelines for taxation and public debt.

Chapter 4 addresses *The Theory of Moral Sentiments* (TMS). This section is not quite as tight as Butler's analysis of *The Wealth of Nations*, though for good reason. As Butler aptly notes, Smith's contemporary, Edmund Burke, "described it (*TMS*) as 'rather painting than writing.'" Nevertheless, the major themes of *The Theory of Moral Sentiments* are covered in turn. Butler helps his readers' understanding of Smith's ideas. He informs them, for instance, that where Smith uses the word "sympathy," in modern parlance "empathy" might be a more accurate term. Also helpful is Butler's explanation of "the impartial spectator," whereby individuals judge their own actions with an eye open towards the broader judgment of society.

He rightly stresses Smith's contention that our natural empathies provide an important basis for social interaction and the development of shared norms of morality. I like Butler's emphasis on Smith's distinction between motives and results. It seems clear to me that this is one of Smith's lasting contributions and is especially pertinent for modern society. Smith's world is one in which individual responsibility is valued and important, and the approval or disapproval of others with respect to individual responsibility is also valuable and important. The impartial spectator helps to check passions and selfish manifestations of Smithian self-interest. Smith would have us reject hubris and embrace a reflective humility that is often missing from the policy proposals of the modern statesman, bureaucrat, or politician. This section also helps the reader to understand the framing of rights from the differing negative and positive rights perspectives.

We have always found Smith's discussion of wealth, and in particular of the proclivities of the "poor man's son," to provide deep insight into his understanding of human nature. Butler accurately points out that this seemingly critical perspective also provides a wellspring of positive benefits that accrue almost entirely to society. He closes this chapter with a discussion of the interplay between individual virtue and societal virtue.

Butler next addresses Smith's other works, including: *The Principles which Lead and Direct Philosophical Inquiries; Illustrated by the History of Astronomy*; *Lectures on Rhetoric and Belles Lettres*; and *Lectures on Jurisprudence*. The major contribution in this section is Butler's contention that while Smith's work was very wide-ranging, it is held together by a grand unifying theme: "Smith is not so much an economist, or moralist, or historian, or grammarian, as a social psychologist . . . [and his] explanations are what today we might call *evolutionary*" (pp. 87–88). In fact, throughout this section Butler notes how Smith's writings on science, justice, law, government, and social psychology, among other topics, are rightly classified as both "evolutionary" and "modern."

Butler's approach provides an introductory reader with a solid framework for Smith's significant contributions to thinking about the world. Smith stresses commerce but with a switch in emphasis from the production of goods primarily benefiting producers to an emphasis on consumers and the broader society. Butler also emphasizes themes that commonly pervade Smith's body of work, including: self-organizing or spontaneous orders; the role of self-interest for both individuals and society; the inevitable persistence of unintended consequences; and the self-dealing, hubris, and deep insensitivity to views not their own of nearly all "statesmen." In short, I very much like Butler's exposition and I can certainly envision using it to introduce a semester-long course on Adam Smith that I periodically teach. His primer admirably fulfills its promise as a brief, yet concise, introductory book on the life and work of Adam Smith.

David Casassas, *La ciudad en llamas. La vigencia del republicanismo comercial de Adam Smith*

Barcelona: Montesinos, 2010, 465pp.

ISBN Hardback: 978-84-92616-74-9

Reviewed by Maria A. Carrasco

La Ciudad en Llamas (The City in Flames) by David Casassas, who received his doctorate in sociology from the University of Barcelona, has a dual purpose: one academic and the other political. In the properly academic realm, the author works to identify Adam Smith as a paradigmatic exponent of the tradition he calls 'commercial republicanism'. His political motivation leads him to propose the theory of Smith – with appropriate adjustments to the times – as a political alternative for the contemporary world. While these two objectives could theoretically remain independent, in his efforts to defend the virtues of commercial republicanism the author runs the risk of developing an interpretation of Smith's texts that is somewhat unilateral, failing to recognize and discuss the abundant arguments of other scholars that situate Smith closer to liberalism or, at least, are nuanced in their presentation of his proposal.

Casassas, however, has opted for a different methodology – instead of debating his opponents he mounts a strident defence of both Adam Smith's adherence to commercial republicanism and commercial republicanism itself. His hermeneutical key is the famous passage in *The Wealth of Nations* (II.ii.94) where Smith, drawing an analogy with the necessity of building firebreaks in order to avoid the spread of fires, states that public authority has a duty to violate the natural freedom of a certain number of people when it threatens the security of society as a whole. On the basis of the metaphor of firebreaks – which is implicit in the title of the book and alludes, as Casassas makes clear, to the Great Fire that destroyed the City of London in 1666 due to a lack of preventive measures – the author explains the overall thesis of his book: one can assure the freedom of a society (the greatest extension of personal freedom) only when the material independence of its individuals is politically guaranteed, such that a community of peers (civically equal individuals) can arise, in which each person can define and develop his or her own life project. And this material independence, which is the condition for the existence of freedom, is achieved through a strong state intervention that eliminates at their roots those asymmetries of power (economic, class privilege, etc.) and relationships of domination that exist in every community.

The author develops his argument through a division of the book into four parts. The first two clarify the meaning of what he describes as the 'republican tradition' and then, in particular, what he calls 'commercial republicanism'. In the third part, he broadens the reach of his analysis to include the moral psychology of Adam Smith, and explains why only 'republican freedom' (which is guaranteed by material independence) can make possible personal self-realization and the development of virtues amongst the populace. Finally, in the fourth part, he shows that Smith had foreseen the threats to freedom that a commercial republic would suffer, threats which inspired him to develop a political-institutional design that – rather than correcting these abuses – would impede them from arising at all. These are the 'firebreaks' alluded to earlier. In addition to discussing the political solutions that Smith proposed for his time, taking into consideration the necessities of eighteenth-century Scotland, Casassas emphasizes Smith's political vision, in which the *sine qua non* for the flourishing of civil society is intervention and permanent vigilance on the part of the state in order to avoid asymmetries in power.

In order to understand the strain of republicanism into which the philosophy of Smith would fit, Casassas contrasts 'freedom in the republican sense' with the 'freedom of doctrinaire liberalism', using the definitions that were proposed by Quentin Skinner and Philip Pettit in the 1990s. He holds that in order to say that a person is free in the republican sense, it is insufficient for them not to be the object of arbitrary interference by third parties; rather, the political-institutional design of the society in which the person lives must prevent others from having even the *possibility* of interfering in arbitrary ways with an individual's decisions or the courses of action that they wish to undertake. By contrast, in the liberal tradition, it is sufficient that a person is not subjected to arbitrary interference in order for them to be called 'free', irrespective of whether there is the possibility that such interference might arise. That is to say, in the former case freedom is defined as 'absence of domination', whereas in the latter case it is simply 'absence of interference'. 'Absence of domination' does not merely imply the lack of arbitrary interference; it also guarantees it by means of society's political-institutional design. What the republican tradition would emphasize, therefore, is that there cannot be freedom where there is dependence; and ongoing political intervention is necessary if freedom is to continue.

> Smith aligns himself with those philosophers, from Aristotle to Marx, by way of Locke, Kant and Robespierre, among others, who make the civil law a central pillar for the design of an institutional reality where human nature can develop and express itself in a complete way.
>
> (p. 90)

On the other hand, this lack of domination requires the material or socio-economic independence of the individuals, which explains the centrality of *property* for the republican tradition in general (p. 161). Smith's republicanism has the peculiarity of being a 'commercial republicanism', which means that he – together with the entire Scottish School – sees the development of commerce and manufacture as facilitating the liberation of the creative energies of the people and the culmination of the process of civilization that the evolution of history aims towards. According to Casassas, one of the great contributions of the Scottish School – and of Smith in particular – to the modern age is their materialist conception of history: that is to say, an emphasis on the 'civilizing effects' of economic factors and their key role in marking the progress of the human species (p. 185). In this way, Smith would be a clear predecessor of the political socialism that developed in the nineteenth century, assuming that

> all study regarding the behaviour of individuals united in society should focus its attention principally on the manner of subsistence of these individuals. The set of laws and determining factors of the socio-political dimension in question would in turn vary as a function of changes in this manner of subsistence.
>
> (p. 185)

And, in a correlative manner, Smith would be situating himself at the very opposite pole from doctrinaire liberalism, which, precisely, 'de-politicizes' the economy.

For Smith, according to Casassas's interpretation, the normative ideal of the civilizing project is the 'free producer': an individual who is able to develop and carry out his or her own plan of life in an autonomous form. Here we find one of the great differences of Smith's republicanism from that of the Aristotelian tradition from which he proceeds (p. 89). For the Scottish philosopher, manufacturing work and commerce are also 'autotelic': that is, activities that contain their ends in themselves. In other words, in contrast to what Aristotle thought of them, they are activities that dignify. This is because, by permitting the material independence of the individual, they make their self-governance possible: the individual is able to carry out their own life plan according to their choices, developing all of their potentialities and realizing their talents.

> Republican virtue has nothing to do with moral perfectionism . . . the republican tradition holds that when individuals have a politically guaranteed material base that makes autonomous social existence possible, they can fully develop their capacity for self-governance in their private lives.
>
> (p. 297)

And, on that basis, in their public lives as well.

Thus, in contrast with earlier forms of republicanism, Smith sees commerce as having a freeing (civilizing) character: it is a path towards the social, economic and spiritual emancipation of the population (p. 309). This naturally demands free markets. But the market, for Smith, is an 'institutional technology', conformed by political decisions regarding the assignment of resources (p. 354): that is, it is a 'political achievement resulting from active institutional decisions and regulatory vigilance, in order that the distribution of resources may redound in benefit of the entire society and not merely of a few' (p. 371). Again, the condition of freedom is the political-institutional design that makes possible a meeting amongst *equals* – the encounter of a 'society of peers' or equally free (materially independent) individuals who can, through commerce, display their personalities in accordance with their own life plans. This is 'freedom of undertaking' understood as the freedom of each person to carry out their own project without suffering the arbitrary interference of others. The market is only free, it only permits the encounter and fosters the development of individuals, when 'firebreaks' are in place to avoid abuses and when a strict vigilance over its proper functioning is maintained. These 'firebreaks' are the political-institutional mechanisms that are able to guarantee a '*laissez-faire*' (let *do*) situation in which all participants can '*do*' – that is, in which all have real opportunities – and in which all of those asymmetries of power that threaten the independence of a group of participants have been eradicated.

From the perspective of the twenty-first century it is clear that Smith's dream failed. The 'great transformation' – the industrial capitalism that permitted the accumulation of wealth and the development of dependent labour – did not meet any 'firebreak' that would prevent the destruction of republican freedom. But Casassas calls for another look at the project of the Scottish thinker, in order to understand the hows and whys of the state intervention that he so fervently supported. And in this way, by re-examining the question of the material foundations of freedom, it may be possible to discover and construct appropriate 'firebreaks' for our time that will be able to extirpate – politically – the asymmetries of power and the links of social and economic dependence which, by impeding the civil liberty of individuals, end up blocking their potential for full development.

AUTHOR'S RESPONSE

David Casassas's response to review by Maria A. Carrasco

Liberalism before liberalism? One comment vis-à-vis
Maria A. Carrasco's review

I can only be thankful to Maria Carrasco for a loyal, comprehensive reconstruction of my presentation of what I call Adam Smith's 'commercial republicanism'. In this reply I shall only discuss what Carrasco sees as the 'risk' of the book: that of 'developing an interpretation of Smith's texts that is somewhat unilateral, failing to recognize and discuss the abundant arguments of other scholars that situate Smith closer to liberalism'. This will allow me to clarify the historical-methodological backdrop of my work.

The City in Flames is a book that tries to get rid of the misleading *liberal* appropriation of texts, authors, and political movements that emerged *before the rise of liberalism* and kept and reworked key features of the republican tradition. In effect, nineteenth- and twentieth-century liberal hermeneutics tries (and manages) to draw a picture of political and intellectual moments – those of Locke, Kant and Smith, for instance – that have little to do with the kind of theorization of freedom and citizenship that liberalism brings about. Without dwelling here on the intellectual and political historical reasons of its deployment, this great hermeneutic liberal turn blurred and keeps blurring the meaning of civilizing projects aimed at building non-atomizing societies where political institutions were called to act as key instances in the creation of a materially based undominated interdependence.

In sum, the aim of the book was not to (somewhat critically) 'discuss the abundant arguments' that support the liberal approach to Smith, but rather to situate the 'texts in context' and to do the exercise of reading Smith with the lenses that prevailed in his world. Then see what happened. Of course, the fact that such an exercise was anything but 'unilateral' helped a lot. In effect, authors as distinct as Sergio Cremaschi, Antoni Domènech, Ian McLean, Ronald Meek, Murray Milgate, Philip Pettit, Quentin Skinner, Shannon C. Stimson and Donald Winch, among many others, have been insisting, from very different viewpoints, on the need to grasp all of the non-liberal elements within pre-nineteenth-century radical political thought. But how to historicize liberalism as a strong rupture from what freedom and civilization had meant before?

As is sometimes forgotten, the term 'liberal(ism)' appears as it has been understood in contemporary Europe – that is, as something to be linked to *laissez-faire*, to untrammelled economic freedom (of the few) – only in 1812, on the occasion of the writing of the Spanish Cadiz Constitution. Of course, the geographical extension of Napoleonic Civil Codes helped consolidate this meaning. Before this moment, being 'liberal' meant, in many languages, merely being 'generous' or 'magnanimous.' The crux here is that this terminological mutation came along with a substantive mutation regarding the meaning of freedom. In effect, it had always been assumed, in keeping with the republican ideal, that what turns a person into a free actor is the enjoyment of a set of (im)material resources guaranteeing her social existence. In other words, being free had always meant not being arbitrarily interfered with and enjoying a social status guaranteeing the inexistence of the mere possibility of being arbitrarily interfered with. In this respect, property – or, more generally, resources – played a crucial role as the guarantor of freedom. But the liberal anomaly consisted in completely disregarding these material conditions of freedom and thus stating that we are all free insofar as we are equal before the law. The pairing of freedom and socioeconomic independence simply vanished.

It is important to note that this was a real novelty. Before the nineteenth century, the pairing of freedom and socioeconomic independence remained central. In fact, one can find it all along the republican tradition, from Aristotle to Cicero, 'Italian' republicanisms, seventeenth- and eighteenth-century revolutionary republicanism, and socialism, which can be seen as the nineteenth-century expression of the democratic republicanism that was finally defeated in revolutionary France and Europe. Within this long tradition, one can find oligarchic and democratic forms of republicanism. The former state that freedom (and hence property) is to be enjoyed by a portion of the population, while the latter establish that all members of a given society should access freedom (and hence property). But in both cases the connection between freedom and its material conditions is always present.

Liberal hermeneutics sometimes establishes that seventeenth- and eighteenth-century thinkers – including Locke, Kant and Smith – belong to the liberal tradition because they theorize and defend private property, individual freedom or freedom of undertaking, among other allegedly 'liberal' concepts and values. But two objections should be raised against this view. First, these concepts and values have been central to the republican tradition since the times of Pericles and Aristotle. Second, and more importantly, there is a need to note that the treatment of these concepts and values in the work of authors like Locke, Kant and Smith at no time obscures their concern about the material conditions of freedom within integrated societies; I leave aside here the question regarding the portion of the population these authors consider as full-fledged members of the community. When Locke discusses private appropriation of external resources, he states that it is legitimate insofar as it leaves 'still enough and as good' to others – otherwise, these 'others' lose their freedom. When Kant theorizes individual freedom, he picks up the Roman distinction between being a '*sui iuris*' – that is, someone who enjoys a set of resources that makes her civilly independent – and being an '*alieni iuris*' – that is, someone whose material dependence turns him subservient and incapable of living 'a life of his own', to put it in Harrington's terms. And when Smith presents his ideal of a society comprising 'free producers' he clearly draws a distinction between performing (materially) independent work and performing dependent work – the former being the only possible road to effective freedom, which should therefore be guaranteed by the polity. Interestingly, Marx receives this baton when he prompts the articulation of 'republican associations of free producers'.

In sum, Adam Smith cannot be part of a liberal project defining civilization as the simple ('isonomic') meeting of everyone's right to be free from any kind of social restraint.[1]

Note

1   For a more detailed discussion of these hermeneutic issues, see D. Casassas (2013) 'Adam Smith's Republican Moment: Lessons for Today's Emancipatory Thought', *Economic Thought* 2(2): 1–19.

Christel Fricke and Dagfinn Føllesdal (eds.), *Intersubjectivity and objectivity in Adam Smith and Edmund Husserl*

Philosophische Forschung, Volume 8; Frankfurt: Ontos Verlag, 2012, 315pp.

ISBN: 978-3-11-032594-2

Reviewed by Thomas Nenon

This collection of essays centers on the work of two figures who, as the editors acknowledge, are not normally considered together. Adam Smith, best known for his work in economic theory, and Edmund Husserl, whose contributions to moral theory have only recently become known, are not thought of primarily for their work in ethics; nor have they heretofore been studied together. The essays in this volume show not only that each has a significant contribution to make to moral theory, but also that it can indeed be helpful to study them together. The editors describe how the idea for this volume arose from a conference they convened that brought together scholars who are familiar with Husserl's philosophy generally and more specifically with his ethics and his work on intersubjectivity, with other scholars who are experts on Smith and Hume, with a particular emphasis on Smith's *Theory of Moral Sentiments*. The essays suggest that, for most of them, the work of one or other of these moral theorists was new for each of the participants prior to the conference (Fricke is clearly an exception here), but that there was nonetheless enough commonality in some basic themes to allow a genuine dialogue to emerge, and they show that the discussion of each of the two figures benefited from the exchange.

The common ground for the discussion is the way that both Smith and Husserl in their moral theories critically take up themes from Hume, allowing a comparison of similarities and differences in their responses to those themes. In particular, each agrees with Hume that feelings, including especially sympathy and the closely related phenomenon of empathy, play a key role in motivating moral action, so that much of the discussion turns on how each of the two understands those phenomena and what specific roles they play in their ethics. The guiding hypothesis of this volume is that

> Husserl provides a conceptual means for making Smith's methodology more explicit than Smith did himself. A phenomenological reconstruction of

> Smith's analysis of the intersubjective process by which people reach an agreement on impartial and thereby 'proper' concepts of feelings and actions will provide an opportunity to explore whether Husserl was right in his assumption: According to this assumption, his phenomenological method allows the philosopher to meet the challenges posed by the claims to Objectivity of our moral judgments of right and wrong along the lines of the challenges posed by the objectivity of our judgments of common and scientific knowledge.
>
> (p. 9)

The first essay, by Frode Kjosavik, addresses a specific problem in Husserl's later work: namely, the relationship between the life-world in general and specific *Sonderwelten* or 'sub-worlds' like the specialized world of some professions or that of modern natural science. At stake in particular are conflicting claims to objectivity of the beliefs in the everyday life-world and the sub-world of science. He concludes that there must be a process of negotiation that brings some sort of coherence into the belief system of anyone who participates in both so that a clear delineation between the life-world and the sub-world of science is impossible.

The essays by Henning Peucker, Ronald McIntyre, Christian Beyer, and John Drummond are all fine examples of contemporary Husserl scholarship at its best in that each is well informed about the recent developments following the publication of a much wider range of Husserl texts on intersubjectivity, the life-world, and ethics over the past few decades and each brings them to bear on systematic questions in moral theory. Peucker looks carefully at what seem to be two competing theories of the relationship between presentational and evaluative acts in Husserl. According to some readings of Husserl's static phenomenology, evaluative acts are founded on presentational acts in a problematic way that is overcome by his genetic account that traces them back to instincts and desires. Peucker correctly and importantly shows that the two accounts are not necessarily mutually exclusive if one understands what Husserl means by 'founding' correctly. If one recognizes that it means that there is always some presentational content involved in any evaluation, that it is always an evaluation of *something*, then it does not necessarily imply that the evaluation is *determined* by the content and it also would not rule out origins of evaluations in other, more basic evaluative stances. Nor does the emphasis on instincts and other drives in genetics mean that they themselves are not in some way directed to something that they are attracted to or repulsed by. Moreover, Peucker notes that the analysis simply of instincts and desires as such does not provide a sufficient account of the normative aspects that pertain to genuinely egoic activity in making moral judgments.

McIntyre presents a lucid and comprehensive overview of Husserl's account of the genesis of intersubjectivity and sociality. He shows how Husserl's transcendental subjectivity is also essentially a 'we-subjectivity' based on fundamental feelings like empathy and trust and on mutual understandings of each other's beliefs and ends. Beyer demonstrates how Husserl's moral theories are rooted in the notion of persons as developed in his *Ideas II*. He lays out how, for Husserl, understanding another means comprehending that person's motivation, and discusses how there nonetheless always remains a possible gap in that comprehension because, as Husserl and Smith both note, differences in character mean that not every person will be motivated in exactly the same ways.

Drummond undertakes a careful comparison of Hume, Smith, and Husserl on the role of imagination in understanding and evaluating other agents. His interest clearly goes beyond a simple historical comparison since he ends up drawing on elements from both Smith and Husserl in arguing for the essential role that empathic experience plays not only in understanding others but also in evincing moral action. He argues that culturally transmitted values can play an analogous role in the evaluation of morally relevant actions to the role that intersubjective agreement plays in the construction of objectivity for knowing:

> Our culture embodies a sense of how we ought to react affectively to various situations and actions, both our own actions and those of others . . . It is in this context of a common and public elucidation that the value-judgments we make – as well as our interests – must withstand critical appraisal by others and not merely sympathetic identification.
>
> (p. 131)

He argues that compassion is itself a social emotion, perhaps the primary emotion, and that justice is the fundamental social virtue. He also concludes that Husserl's analyses are more adequate to these insights because he escapes some of the empiristic assumptions about the self's motivation to which Smith remains tied: 'Intersubjectivity and objectivity, hard to seamlessly incorporate into Smith, are from the beginning co-implicated in Husserl' (p. 135).

Iso Kern's interest is also clearly directed to explicating what he sees as a valid insight, in this case from Mengzi or Mencius about the role of the feeling of spontaneous sympathy or compassion with the other as the source of the virtue of benevolence as the most basic human virtue. He compares Mengzi's account briefly to Husserl's and then in more detail to Smith's account of the role of sympathy in motivating concern for others and moral actions. He suggests that genuine moral feelings of compassion must go beyond the observations of the impartial moral spectator and come from an immediate sense of concern for the well-being of another person in need, more along the lines of the cases Mengzi and the Christian scriptures describe.

The most detailed side-by-side comparison of the moral theories of Husserl and Smith are provided by Fricke in her essay 'Overcoming Disagreement – Adam Smith and Edmund Husserl on Strategies of Justifying Descriptive and Evaluative Judgments'. She tries to show that, by reading the two together, one can gain a better understanding of the positions of each.

The issue is whether one can discover parallels between the justification of non-moral descriptive judgments and moral judgments. Using terminological distinctions and some basic positions from Husserl's phenomenological descriptions of intersubjectivity, she aims to elucidate better how Smith can be reasonably read as

making some progress in that direction. She argues that Husserl recognizes a role
for imagination and for empathy in establishing objective descriptive judgments
not just about how things look to me, but how they look to any other perceiver in
a similar situation. Objectivity means identifying a judgment with which any
competent observer would agree:

> Bringing forth such an agreement is, however, not a matter of a majority
> vote. Whether or not our judgments about the objects in the world are true
> depends on processes of respectful intra-subjective and inter-subjective com-
> munication, adaption and the constitution of coherent systems of belief, both
> descriptive and narrative.
>
> (p. 178)

She endorses Føllesdal's reading of Husserl, according to which the latter is not a
foundationalist about epistemic justification but rather an advocate of what
Føllesdal calls a process of 'reflective equilibrium': 'This method has a two-fold
function, namely that of building up consensus and justifying this consensus at
the same time' (p. 190). Another important concept from Husserl that she takes
as background for a better understanding of Smith is a notion of normalcy that
does not assume that each person is necessarily the same with regard to serving as
a competent judge, but does assume shared notions of optimality. Turning then
explicitly to Smith, she shows how 'Smithian *first-order sympathy* has to be distinguished from *second order sympathy*' and 'Smithian *second-order sympathy*
functionally resembles the faculty of *sympathy* as Husserl describes it' (p. 222).
Moreover, 'Smith's impartial spectator . . . is the moral counterpart to a normal
perceiver as conceived by Husserl' (p. 229). According to her reconstruction,
then, both thinkers end up pointing to a process of intersubjective communication
aimed at establishing the truth of justification of both descriptive and evaluative
claims that Fricke's analysis suggests is not only a philologically accurate way of
reading each of them but also seems to fit in well with how we actually engage in
the process of trying to develop and justify such claims.

   The remaining two essays – by Vivienne Brown and Sam Fleischacker – focus
exclusively on Smith. Brown argues that there is 'a consistent and intelligible
theory of mind in Smith's *Theory of Moral Sentiments*, one which receives some
support from recent research in psychology and neuroscience, and which also
helps unravel some interpretive puzzles concerning intersubjectivity and moral
judgment' (p. 243). She begins by distinguishing different senses of the notion
of sympathy in Smith. She argues that recently ascendant 'simulation theories' of
mind consistent with neurological research on mirroring phenomena make some
of Smith's claims about how we come to sympathize with others more plausible.
She argues that Smith's observations about how we can identify with others and
at the same time have the distance to make normative judgments about them can
be explained through recourse to these distinctions. They therefore also point to
interesting parallels in empirical research into how human beings do actually
come to understand and evaluate themselves and others.

Fleischacker undertakes a close reading of Smith and Hume on moral sentiments, presenting Smith's position as a conscious critical discussion of themes
from Hume, situating each of them in the context of the historical audiences they
were addressing. Both were seeking alternatives to the exclusively egoistic
accounts of human motivation advanced by Hobbes and Mandeville, but on
Fleischacker's reading Hume has a more spontaneous – almost biologistic –
account, whereas Smith's is a more intellectual and socialized account. Clearly
Fleischacker sides with Smith's version and his view that human beings not
only have a faculty for sympathy, but can also take pleasure in the ability to
sympathize with the (morally acceptable) feelings of others. At the end, though,
Fleischacker suggests that both of their approaches (and, although he does
not say so, perhaps Husserl's) are flawed in their assumption that one's feelings
are primarily private. He points instead to a Wittgensteinian approach according
to which the language of feelings is also a part of a public discourse into which
we are socialized and has not only descriptive but also normative dimensions
built into it from the outset.

The quality of scholarship and philosophical reflection in the essays in this
volume make it worthwhile not just for scholars who are interested in the points
of intersection between Smith and Husserl, but for informed readers who are
interested in the moral theories of either thinker. At the same time, though, the
volume as a whole does demonstrate that the experiment of reading them together
is successful in improving our understanding not only of the philosophical positions each of them holds, but also our understanding and critical evaluation of the
philosophical issues in moral theory that they both address in their own ways.

Ryan Hanley (editor), *Adam Smith's* The theory of moral sentiments, *with an introduction by Amartya Sen*

Harmondsworth: Penguin Books, 2010, 450pp.

ISBN: 0521598478

Reviewed by Neven Leddy

The two great developments in Smith studies during the twentieth century were the discovery of his lecture notes in 1958 and the realization, explained by Amartya Sen in this volume, that 'Smith's first book, the *Moral Sentiments*, was also his last, in the form of the much-expanded sixth edition, with *The Wealth of Nations* coming in between' (p. ix). Scholarship on Smith since the publication of his lectures on rhetoric in 1961 has made ample use of those lecture notes, for better or for worse, as Smith's 'unwritten books'.[1] The scholarship pertaining to the evolution of the *Moral Sentiments* through six editions was encouraged and enabled by D. D. Raphael's and A. L. Macfie's 1976 Glasgow edition of that text. The editor of this Penguin edition of the *Moral Sentiments*, Ryan Patrick Hanley, makes no claims that this volume is intended to replace the critical apparatus of the Glasgow edition. A Penguin Classics edition introduced through such an evolutionary framework nevertheless represents the institutionalization of that approach to Smith and relegates the 'Adam Smith Problem' to the place of a digression in twentieth-century Smith scholarship.

This volume might be seen as part of a Penguin Books 'Smith project' when coupled with Nicholas Phillipson's 2010 biography, suggesting a readership beyond the academy. Smith has likewise been well served by this very periodical, published not quite annually since 2004, along with the broad range of serious monographs discussed herein. We seem, in short, to be experiencing an unusually fecund period of Smith scholarship which is perhaps comparable to the work surrounding the Glasgow editorial project (1976–87). The introduction to the Penguin edition, penned by Nobel Prize-winning economist Amartya Sen, will be seen by many as the culmination of the rehabilitation of the *Moral Sentiments*.[2] Sen's introductory comments lend themselves to this kind of interpretation, as he describes the *Moral Sentiments* as 'one of the truly outstanding books in the intellectual history of the world' (p. vi).

Sen's presentation of Smith outlines how the *Moral Sentiments* might provide guidance in resolving the challenges of globalization, and how Smith's insightful critique of capitalism might illuminate the financial crisis of 2008. The introduction is a bold assertion of relevance which builds towards a cosmopolitan ethics of inclusion. Sen's introduction locates Smith's system in the broad sweep of the history of philosophy, rather than making an original exegetical contribution.[3] In contrast to Raphael's and Macfie's 1976 introduction, which was exegetical and interpretative, Sen offers a gentler and more accessible introduction to the less familiar of Smith's works.

At the same time, Sen seems intent on selling Smith to the uninitiated and to students of political theory in particular. In this endeavour, he makes Smith more salient than Rawls to global (and contemporary) challenges because Smith's model allows for a transnational ethics:

> Dealing with the global mess makes the Smithian engagement altogether necessary. In some ways the world is grappling with the Smithian route, and while the gradual shift from national thinking to the G-8 and now to the G-20 is a move in the right direction, we have to go much further, for Smithian reasons.
>
> (p. xix)

This amounts to what Sen calls 'the avoidance of parochialism' (p. xix), and while Sen is perhaps uniquely entitled to enlist Smith in a contemporary cosmopolitan political paradigm, it is possible that this introduction will not weather as well as Raphael and Macfie's. While Sen's Smith is easy to like, since he emerges as precociously colour-blind and egalitarian, one suspects that the living and breathing Smith was not quite so cuddly. The insistence on contemporary relevance and the tendency towards hagiography will make the more historically minded reader uncomfortable, and may ultimately erode the longevity of this accessible edition.

Hanley's biographical and textual notes achieve an excellent balance for readers coming to the *Moral Sentiments* for the first time. The biographical notes provide a useful glossary of names and dates, while the textual notes helpfully locate Smith and his work in the much-expanded scholarship on the Scottish Enlightenment. More than any other feature of this edition, the textual notes improve markedly on Raphael and Macfie's, which tend to point mostly at Hutcheson and Hume. By contrast, Hanley's reflect the broader and deeper work on Smith and his context since 1976, to which Hanley himself is a significant contributor.[4] The notes to Part VII: Of Systems of Moral Philosophy, in particular, demonstrate tremendous erudition which will prove especially useful to advanced students seeking to increase their understanding of Smith in this milieu, and the eighteenth-century intellectual context more generally.

Notes

1   For a history of which, see Bryce (1983).
2   Or, more precisely, the Bank of Sweden Prize in Economics Sciences, created in 1968.
3   Although Sen does make a novel case for Smith as a Hibernophile through an examination of his defence of the potato at pp. xxiii–xxiv.
4   This will come as no surprise to readers of this journal and members of this society. See especially Hanley (2006) and (2009).

Bibliography

Bryce, J. C. (1983) 'Introduction', in Adam Smith, *Lectures on Rhetoric and Belles Lettres*, Oxford: Oxford University Press; Glasgow edition.
Hanley, R. P. (2006) 'From Geneva to Glasgow: Rousseau and Adam Smith on the Theater and Commercial Society', *Studies in Eighteenth-Century Culture* 35: 177–202.
Hanley, R. P. (2009) *Adam Smith and the Character of Virtue*, Cambridge: Cambridge University Press.
Phillipson, N. (2010) *Adam Smith: An Enlightened Life*, New Haven, CT, and London: Yale University Press, 2010. (Also published by Penguin in the UK in the same year.)

Ian Simpson Ross, *The life of Adam Smith* (2nd edition)

Oxford: Oxford University Press, 2010, xxxii + 453pp.

ISBN: 978-0-19-955003-6

Reviewed by Maria Pia Paganelli

The Life of Adam Smith is a masterfully researched volume describing not just the life of Adam Smith, but also the life of the social and cultural environments around Adam Smith (1723–1790).

Ian Ross does the best possible with the limited information about Adam Smith himself and supplements it with a rigorous documentation of what seems to be all of the people we have record of interacting with Smith. In addition, the life of Smith is mounted in the historical events taking place while Smith was alive. This allows Ross to contextualize Smith's works, not just to offer a summary of them. For example, the relevance of *The Wealth of Nations* (*WN*) is highlighted through the description of the War of Independence of the American colonies. Ross seems to tell us that *WN* was a highly political book, meant to influence public opinion (or at least the opinion of the cultural and political elite) and meant to have an impact on political actions with respect to the American colonies (chapter 16). The relevance of the changes in the last edition of *The Theory of Moral Sentiments* (*TMS*) is highlighted through the presence of the French Revolution and the other revolutions and political instabilities of the time. The new additions, Ross implies, are meant as political advice for an enlightened leader in a tumultuous time (chapter 23). The historical details range from these macro views to the analysis of the rare representations of Smith, including the likely explanation of John Kay's print of Smith 'carrying in his left hand a bunch of flowers, perhaps to ward off the notorious Edinburgh effluvia' (p. 332).

The use of historical context to frame the life and the work of Smith draws, intentionally or unintentionally, a picture of Smith that does not necessarily fit the stereotype of the slightly antisocial, timid, absent-minded professor with a pleasant, warm personality. The descriptions of Smith walking deep in thought in his dressing-gown through the streets of Scotland (all the way to Dunfermline, fifteen miles from his home in Kirkcaldy (p. 254)) and dropping bread and butter in a teapot while engrossed in a conversation and then complaining about the poor quality of the tea are surely anecdotes that are in line with the absent-minded professor. Ross even reports the description of a woman who saw Smith walking in the streets of Edinburgh 'expressing surprise that an obviously well-to-do lunatic would be allowed to wander freely' (p. 332).

Yet, we are also left with the feeling Samuel Rogers expressed: 'Smith seemed to Rogers far more a man of the world' (p. 430). Indeed, we also read that Smith may have presented himself as 'a splendid figure: his personal effects at this time [during his tour of Europe as a private tutor of the Duke of Buccleuch] included black suits, gray and red silk ones, and a coat of crimson velvet to go with gold breeches and waistcoat' (p. 227). When he could not meet the top intellectuals in France, he complained of being bored. He belonged to several of the most important clubs in Britain (the Literary Society, the Poker Club, the Royal Society, the Club, the Philosophical Society, the Oyster Club, and the Royal Society of Edinburgh). When in Edinburgh, he had a large number of regular guests for supper on Sunday nights.

It seems that he was heavily, if indirectly, involved in politics. For instance, he seemed to have a role to play in the proposal for banking regulation in 1764 (p. 163) and with plans for the reform of state revenue (p. 237), among other things. When in Glasgow he was deeply involved in the administration of the university, and he had a loyal stream of student followers (chapters 8–11).

His 'warm' personality did not prevent him from getting close to fist-fights during faculty meetings – '[Samuel] Kenrick remembered Smith being "as fiery and choleric as [John] Anderson himself", and was told by Professor William Leechman that their "high words frequently brought them very near to blows"' (p. 155) – or to 'bang[ing] the table ... energetically' in a discussion about Voltaire (p. 429).

Ross tells us that Smith most likely gave away most of his money to help others. But he also tells us that his generosity did not include helping his dear friend David Hume. While Hume played a significant 'role in securing the opportunity for Smith to travel' as the tutor of the Duke of Buccleuch (p. 209), Smith played a significant role in *blocking* Hume's appointment to a university post: 'I should prefer David Hume to any man for a colleague; but I am afraid the public would not be of my opinion; and the interest of the society will oblige us to have some regard to the opinion of the public (*Corr.* No. 10)' (pp. 111 and 360). Moreover, despite writing about the importance of fulfilling someone's deathbed wishes, Smith refused to do so for his dearest friend Hume. On his deathbed, the latter asked Smith to publish his *Dialogues Concerning Natural Religion*. Hume was anxious and insistent about Smith's commitment to this publication. Yet, Smith never carried out Hume's wishes because he was too afraid of the 'clamour' that publication would generate. Eventually, Hume's nephew published the book – without clamour – in 1779 (p. 359).

And despite Smith's preaching about the importance of generosity, he was extremely jealous of his intellectual belongings and refused to share them with anybody. He quarrelled on more than one occasion because others (Robertson and Ferguson) appropriated his ideas, showing the 'little Jealousy in his Temper' (p. 245). He refused to lend books to friends (p. 343). He had his eighteen volumes of unpublished manuscripts burned in front of him just a few days before he died

(p. 435) because he was anxious about them and did not trust his executors to carry out his instructions. Smith was unforgiving toward Adam Ferguson, who had allegedly spread rumours about Smith plagiarizing Montesquieu (p. 107). Attempts to ease the tension occurred only once Smith was on his deathbed, when Ferguson went to visit him.

Ross explicitly points out another complex aspect of Smith's life: while he wrote generally in favour of free trade and against trade restrictions, he was a diligent Commissioner of the Customs. So much so that in one of his letters (*Corr.* No. 203) he says:

> about a week after I was made Commissioner of the Customs, upon looking over the list of prohibited goods . . . and upon examining my own wearing apparel, I found, to my great astonishment, that I had scarce a sock, a cravat, a pair of ruffles, or a pocket handkerchief which was not prohibited to be worn or used in Great Britain. I wish to set an example and burnt them all.
>
> (p. 339)

Ross also tells us that Smith's popularity was overshadowed by Thomas Reid's success at Glasgow, even while Smith garnered international fame (p. 206). And although much loved by his close friends and his future readers, reports of Smith's death were sober and cold, and possibly even slightly negative (chapter 25).

With the exception of a few odd comments – such as linking 1980s Reaganomics to Say's Law (p. 389), and a claim that 'Smith drew on the teaching of Hume about such matters as specie-flow adjustments' (p. 288) – and a sixty-six-page bibliography that is still somehow incomplete, Ross offers us a remarkably rounded portrait of Adam Smith as a multi-faceted individual, not just because of the variety of his interests, but also because of the complexity of his personality. Ross's strokes in painting Smith are light and unobtrusive, bringing to life his persona and his work. In short, this is a book that all Smith scholars and Scottish Enlightenment scholars should read.

Routledge Library Editions, *Adam Smith: 5-volume set*

Maurice Brown, *Adam Smith's economics: its place in the development of economic thought*

R. H. Campbell and A. S. Skinner, *Adam Smith*

D. A. Reisman, *Adam Smith's sociological economics*

T. D. Campbell, *Adam Smith's science of morals*

E. Royston Pike, *Human documents of Adam Smith's time*

Abingdon and New York: Routledge, 2009, 1222pp.

ISBN Hardback: 978-0-415-56194-5

Reviewed by Craig Smith

The *Adam Smith: 5-Volume Set*, part of Routledge's Library reprint series, sees the reissue of five Taylor and Francis stable books on Adam Smith that were originally published between 1971 and 1988. The aim of making these books available to libraries that did not purchase the original editions is laudable, but it is rather more questionable whether they constitute a coherent series in any real sense. Rather than attempt to connect these five very different volumes in an artificial manner or review books that will be familiar to the readers of this journal, I'll confine myself to a brief book note on each volume and how it might be considered to have stood the test of time set by the intervening three decades of Smith studies.

R. H. Campbell and A. S. Skinner's *Adam Smith* (1982) was intended as an accessible biography, a stopgap for the educated audience in anticipation of the eventual release of Ian Ross's full biography. The book is a competent survey of the events of Smith's life with a concise treatment of many of the familiar episodes. It was not intended as an intellectual biography, as the relatively brief discussion of Smith's ideas indicates. The formulaic nature of the chapters (they are all roughly the same length) means that major episodes (like *TMS* and *WN*) are afforded the same coverage as biographical sections such as 'Tutor to the Duke of Buccleuch'. Given the authors' experience as editors of *WN*, the chapter on that volume is slightly strange. It starts with the problems generated by Book V, moves on to Smith's reception, and only then discusses the general ideas in the book. The peculiarity of this approach may be explained by the overall purpose of the project, which the authors describe as clarifying Smith for those who wish to 'understand the nature of Smith's abiding influence in intellectual endeavour and in public policy' (p. 7). Given the emergence of Smith as a symbol in the early 1980s, this might well represent one of the first attempts to reclaim him from the popular misconceptions that often cloud his legacy. It is a pity, though, that this approach is adopted, as the chapter does not really do Smith or *WN* justice as part of a biographical introduction. That aside, this is an enjoyable and accessible short biography that does not pretend to challenge Ross's much more authoritative work.

E. Royston Pike's *Human Documents of Adam Smith's Time* (1974) is a strange book. It takes as its project the illustration of the lives of the sort of individuals who are described in Smith's books. Using Hogarth's sketches and John Ireland's prose descriptions, and extracts from the likes of Defoe, Royston Pike paints a picture of life in London and Scotland through descriptions of scenes from everyday life. He covers such characters as the shopkeeper and the labouring poor and offers descriptions of typical culinary habits and working conditions. The connection with Smith is tenuous, to say the least, and the author's characterisation of Smith's thought in the introduction and conclusion is brief and largely inaccurate. That said, the extracts are fun to read and they certainly bring eighteenth-century Britain amusingly to life (even when one takes into account the frequency of extracts that rail against the demon drink).

T. D. Campbell's *Adam Smith's Science of Morals* (1971) is an altogether more serious academic volume and will be very familiar to readers of this journal. Based on Campbell's doctoral thesis, it deserves the attention of Smith scholars for being the first serious, book-length study of *TMS* in the modern period of Smith studies. This becomes immediately apparent when one reads the targets of those passages where he disputes the interpretations of other studies of Smith (most of which are of Victorian or Edwardian vintage). Though *TMS* has become the focus of increasing attention, Campbell's volume still stands up as a clear study of the argument for Smith as socio-psychologist. The stress is on Smith's proto-sociological method and is contrasted to both more normative readings of *TMS* and to readings that see Smith as depending on an underlying religious argument. The evidence is marshalled in a straightforward fashion to demonstrate Smith's broad conception of the scope of the moral sphere. The careful exegesis of Smith's position remains as useful to the student of Smith today as it was in the early 1970s. The book is also remembered for the characterisation of Smith's 'meta-principle' (p. 219) as a form of utilitarianism that becomes particularly apparent in the policy recommendations that arise from the detached contemplation of the philosopher. The passages on the place of God as a final cause in Smith's system and the utilitarian consequences of this are perhaps the most controversial aspect of the argument, given the focus elsewhere on scientific explanation. While many have since disagreed with this reading of Smith as moral scientist and 'contemplative utilitarian', Campbell's case remains strong and his argument is something that those with opposing readings should feel that they have to address. Re-reading the book nearly twenty years after my first encounter with it has only strengthened the impression that it is among the strongest of the 'Science of Man' interpretations of Smith.

Maurice Brown's *Adam Smith's Economics: Its Place in the Development of Economic Thought* (1988) has much to recommend it as an attempt to understand what Smith understood as the proper subject matter and methodology of political economy. Firmly in the 'Science of Man' tradition, Brown provides chapters on key aspects of Smith's economic thought and conception of philosophy, with particular reference to the place of history in Smith's analyses. The approach is contextual in the sense that Brown rejects reading back of subsequent concerns into Smith's work and seeks to locate his views in the intellectual context of the late eighteenth century. That said, the opening methodological chapters – which seek to develop a theoretical approach to the history of ideas and Smith's notion of system through a consideration of twentieth-century philosophy of science in the form of Popper, Lakatos and Kuhn – seem more than a little at odds with the attempt to understand Smith within his own intellectual milieu. Indeed, if any aspect of the book now seems dated, it is this methodological discussion of research programmes rather than any of the specific analyses of Smith's writings. By the end of the volume, it remains unclear how the methodological approach helps to situate Smith in the history of economics. In terms of the specific themes examined, the chapters on 'Specialisation and Social Change' and 'Purposive Action and Unintended Consequences' are particularly interesting, as is the disagreement with Campbell's 'contemplative utilitarian' line (p. 139).

D. A. Reisman's *Adam Smith's Sociological Economics* (1976) sets out with the intention of avoiding reading Smith as a prototype for the modern economist and of providing a contextually sensitive reading that stresses the sociological elements that always frame Smith's economic arguments. What is slightly strange about this is that, as the book unfolds, it becomes clear that the argument largely depends on reading Smith as a prototype sociologist (rather than as an economist). Frequent comparisons with Weber, Wright Mills, Spencer and Durkheim are interesting, but seem curiously at odds with the initial commitment to context and correcting appropriations of Smith – which disappears only to re-emerge in the final chapter on Smith's policy advice. Reisman's Smith is an 'economic determinist' (p. 10) and materialist, and the interpretation that is offered is more 'Meekian' than Meek – reading Smith as a proto-Marxist. Attention is focused on the four-stages theory and labour theory, and the long chapters on the upper classes and lower classes are intended to persuade the reader that Smith was conducting an early and inchoate class analysis. That Marxist model becomes explicit when the chapters are described as studies 'in the relationship between economic basis and social superstructure' (p. 124). While there is probably still much of interest to say about the relationship between Smith and Marx, Reisman's approach – of reading Smith as working with a broadly Marxist conceptual toolkit – does not really seem to manage it. Indeed, this suspicion becomes more urgent when Reisman seems to assess Smith against the standards of a subsequently generated Marxist orthodoxy and finds him wanting: 'Smith's approach is teleological and partial, and seems at times to be more a philosophy of human development then [*sic*] a scientific investigation into the laws of history' (p. 137).

It is the Marxian terminology of the sociological thought that dates this volume. As Marxist analysis has passed from intellectual fashion, this book's reading of Smith now seems dated in its concerns and emphases. Many of the discrete points of interpretation are interesting, but the Smith-as-Marx line will appear strange to many contemporary readers. For example, it seems unlikely that one would find the following in a more recent volume on Smith: 'His dynamism did not extend from the negation to the negation of the negation's negation, and his guarded optimism about the future of civil society may not have been borne out by the events' (p. 16).

Notes for contributors

Submissions to *The Adam Smith Review* are invited from any theoretical, disciplinary or interdisciplinary approach (maximum 10,000 words, in English). Contributors are asked to make their arguments accessible to a wide, multidisciplinary readership without sacrificing high standards of argument and scholarship. Please include an abstract not exceeding 100 words.

Please send all submissions, suggestions and offers to edit symposia to the Editor, Fonna Forman, Department of Political Science, University of California, San Diego, 9500 Gilman Drive, La Jolla, California, USA; adamsmithreview@ucsd.edu. Email submissions are welcomed. Alternatively, please send three hard copies in double-spaced type.

Please prepare your manuscript for anonymous refereeing and provide a separate title page with your name. Interdisciplinary submissions will be sent to referees with different disciplinary expertise. Submitted articles will be double-blind refereed, and commissioned articles will be single-blind refereed. All contributions must be in English; it is the author's responsibility to ensure the quality of the English text. Where quotations in languages other than English are required, authors are asked to provide a translation into English.

Final versions of accepted papers will need to conform to the *ASR*'s Guidelines for Authors (Harvard reference system), but submitted papers are accepted in any format.

Submission to *The Adam Smith Review* will be taken to imply that the work is original and unpublished, and is not under consideration for publication elsewhere. By submitting a manuscript, authors agree that the exclusive rights to reproduce and distribute the article have been given to the publishers, including reprints, photographic reproductions, microfilm, or any other reproductions of a similar nature, and translations.

Book reviews

Books relating to Adam Smith or of more general relevance for Adam Smith scholarship will be reviewed in *The Adam Smith Review*. It is editorial policy to invite authors to respond to reviews of their work. Offers to review works published in languages other than English are welcomed. Please send books for review to the Book Review Editor: Dr. Craig Smith, Adam Smith Lecturer in the Scottish Enlightenment, School of Social and Political Sciences, University of Glasgow, G12 8RT, craig.smith@glasgow.ac.uk

Website

The website of *The Adam Smith Review* is: www.adamsmithreview.org/

The Adam Smith Review is the official publication of the International Adam Smith Society. The website for the International Adam Smith Society is: smithsociety.org/